Science and Philosophy in the Indian Buddhist Classics

Science and Philosophy

in the

Indian Buddhist Classics

Volume 4

Philosophical Topics

conceived and introduced by

His Holiness the Dalai Lama

Developed by the
Compendium Compilation Committee

Edited by Thupten Jinpa

Translated and introduced by
Dechen Rochard

Wisdom

Wisdom Publications
132 Perry Street
New York, NY 10014 USA
wisdomexperience.org

A translation of *Nang pa'i tshan rig dang lta grub kun btus, vol. 4*. Dharamsala, India: Ganden Phodrang Trust (Office of His Holiness the Dalai Lama), 2019.

Library of Congress Cataloging-in-Publication Data is available.
LCCN 2017018045

ISBN 978-1-61429-790-1 ebook ISBN 978-1-61429-814-4

27 26 25 24 23
5 4 3 2 1

Designed by Gopa and Ted2, Inc.
Cover art by Getty Images.

Printed on acid-free paper that meets the guidelines for permanence and durability of the Production Guidelines for Book Longevity of the Council on Library Resources.

Printed in the United States of America.

Contents

Part 4. Emptiness according to the Madhyamaka Tradition

Part 5. Buddhist Logic and Epistemology

Part 6. Denotation and the Exclusion Theory of Meaning

Preface

General Editor's Note

For centuries Tibetans have viewed their custodianship of the knowledge and wisdom of classical Buddhist India—especially from the great medieval monasteries like Nālandā, Vikramaśīla, and Odantapuri—to be a major part of their historic responsibility. It was in Tibet that, after the demise of Buddhism in its birthplace, India, the bright sun of "the threefold pursuit of exposition, composition, and debate" pertaining to classical Indian Buddhist thought and practice continued to shine on this planet. The first phase of Tibetan translation took place under imperial patronage in the eighth century, but it was in the thirteenth century that the vast body of texts the Tibetans had inherited from India and translated came to be compiled into two canonical collections—the Kangyur (translations of scripture) and the Tengyur (translations of treatises). These two collections are so revered that most every Tibetan monastery strives to house the sets, consisting of over three hundred large volumes. It is thanks to generations of Tibetan translators, scholars, and teachers that the thoughts and writings of great Indian Buddhist masters like Nāgārjuna, Asaṅga, Vasubandhu, Dharmakīrti, Candrakīrti, and Śāntideva thrive to this day as living traditions. The vision behind His Holiness the Dalai Lama's creation of this present four-volume *Science and Philosophy in Indian Buddhist Classics* is, as he states in his introduction, to make the key ideas, insights, and knowledge of India's great Nālandā tradition accessible to contemporary readers.

Briefly, the first two volumes in the series focus on conceptions of reality, with a volume each on "the physical world" and "the mind." Together, they present what could be characterized as "sciences" of the physical and mental world found in classical Indian Buddhist sources. The third and fourth volumes focus on philosophy in Indian Buddhist sources, with the former devoted to the presentation of the diverse systems of Indian philosophy, both Buddhist and non-Buddhist. In this final volume in the series, volume 4, we have chosen six major topics or questions representing important areas of philosophical inquiry and debate in ancient India as well as in Tibet.

Of these six topics, addressed in six parts, the first, "The Two Truths," explores the paradox at the heart any philosophical conception of reality, where, as we reflect on reality systematically, we "discover" that the way things appear to our naïve perception is not how things really are. Regardless of whether we use the explicit language of the two truths, this paradox reveals the central challenge for any coherent philosophical conception of reality. Part 2, "Analysis of Self and Selflessness," unpacks a hugely important debate in classical Indian philosophy on the nature of the subject—the person who experiences the world. Non-Buddhist Indian philosophies generally argue for the need to postulate a "self" (*ātman*) that is eternal, unitary, and indivisible, while Buddhist schools reject such a notion of self. The challenge for the Buddhists then is how to account for the way our everyday experience suggests the presence of such a unitary subject.

The next two parts, "The Yogācāra Explanation of Ultimate Reality" and "Emptiness According to the Madhyamaka Tradition," present two distinct visions of ultimate reality that developed early in in the history of Mahāyāna Buddhism in India. The first is according to the Yogācāra school of Asaṅga and Vasubandhu, while the second is according to Nāgārjuna and his philosophical heirs. In contemporary parlance, one could view these as two rival views on ontology, "what there is" in the ultimate sense. Part 5, "Buddhist Logic and Epistemology," presents key questions on the nature, criteria, and limits of knowledge. Referred to as *pramāṇa*, this epistemological tradition was a major discipline—one of the so-called five sciences alongside visual arts and construction, medicine, linguistics, and inner science—whose discourse transcended sectarian boundaries. The universal nature of this discourse was such that the history of epistemology in India can be justifiably described as a history of debates among key schools, with the Buddhist side dominated by two giants, Dignāga and Dharmakīrti.

The final part, "Denotation and the Exclusion Theory of Meaning," addresses the seemingly simple question "What does one refer to when one says the word 'cow'?" Does it relate to a "real cow" out there in the world, to an image of a cow in the speaker's mind, or to some kind of universal cow that is instantiated in all particular cows? In brief, this final part examines the challenging questions of what might be called the philosophy of language, such as the relationship between language, concepts, and the world; the ultimate unit of semantic meaning; the relationship between words and their referents; and how and where conventions fit in relation to semantic meaning.

It has been a profound honor to be part of the creation of this volume, as the general editor for both the original Tibetan version and this English translation. As someone schooled at Ganden Monastery, southern India, in the inquiries and debates curated here, I am truly thrilled to see this special volume published. Just as generations of students and scholars have sharpened their intellects, enriched their minds, and deepened their insights through intimate engagement with the philosophical inquiries presented in this volume, modern readers of English can now share in that opportunity.

First and foremost, I offer my deepest gratitude to His Holiness the Dalai Lama for his vision and leadership of this most valuable initiative of bringing the insights of ancient Indian tradition to our contemporary world. This volume is blessed to have an introduction from His Holiness himself. I thank the Tibetan editors who worked diligently over many years to create this compendium, especially for their patience with the substantive revisions I ended up bringing to the various stages of their manuscripts. I would like to thank the translator of this volume, my friend Dr. Dechen Rochard, for her monumental achievement. Dechen's training in philosophy at Cambridge and in Dharamsala combined with her mastery of the Tibetan language and her experience of having translated volume 2 of the series made her the perfect translator for this volume. Dechen's introductory essay, written in clear and engaging language, helps guide the reader through the rich and complex landscape of classical Indian Buddhist philosophy by way of comparison to Greek philosophy, a terrain more familiar to many contemporary readers, thus situating the inquiries in this special volume in a clear and cogent context. At Wisdom Publications, I must thank David Kittelstrom and Brianna Quick for their incisive and diligent editing of the English translation. Finally, I express my deep gratitude to the Ing Foundation for its generous support, which made it possible for me to devote the time necessary to edit both the original Tibetan volume and this translation.

Through this publication, may the insights and ideas of the great Indian

Buddhist philosophies serve as inspirations, sharpening the intellect and deepening the contemplations of today's readers across the boundaries of language, culture, and geography.

Thupten Jinpa

Translators' Note

This volume presents a selection of important philosophical topics addressed in the classical Indian Buddhist literature composed between 200 and 1200 CE. It cites a broad range of treatises on the nature of reality and on how to know such reality, as well as on logic, epistemology, and the philosophy of language. These texts were composed by masters whose breadth and depth of study is epitomized by the tradition of Nālandā University and similar monastic institutions of classical Indian civilization. This volume is the last in a series designed to convey the core teachings of these Nālandā masters. It contains treasures that may initially be hard to decipher. However, with research and reflection, one can unlock them and use them as medicine for one's mind and life. It is His Holiness the Dalai Lama's heartfelt wish that these treasures may be shared with the world.

As I found with volume 2, translating this work presented several challenges. First, not only is the material complex, it covers a wide spectrum of topics in technical detail. The specialized knowledge about Indian epistemology and philosophy of language conveyed here exceeds what is usually transmitted in traditional Tibetan scholastic training, and so it entailed my digesting a large selection of books and academic papers, which was certainly interesting but somewhat exhausting given the required timeline. Furthermore, each volume in this series, although technical, has been compiled with the intention of reaching a broad audience, including educated Tibetans and non-Tibetans in general as well as physicists, cognitive scientists, psychologists, philosophers, and Buddhist scholars in particular. The task of making such material accessible to a reader not already familiar with the subject matter has been a significant challenge, though I hope one that has been met with a measure of success.

Unlike with volume 2, I did not have the opportunity to work closely with the geshes who authored these texts when translating the present volume owing to the COVID-19 lockdowns of 2020–21. Fortunately, however, I had access to a great variety of books and papers that proved invaluable. These included certain Sanskrit sources, along with their English translations where available. This has been of great assistance as the Sanskrit versions are typically less ambiguous owing to the greater grammatical specificity of the Sanskrit language. Many texts, however, are preserved only in Tibetan, and some of these proved extremely challenging to translate, notably the long quotations from Dharmottara's *Investigation of Valid Cognition*.

I am honored to have been called to work on this magnificent project. I am profoundly grateful to His Holiness the Dalai Lama for his vast and compassionate vision in conceiving of this project and propelling it to completion. My gratitude extends to all the members of the Compendium Compilation Committee—Khen Thamthog Rinpoche, Thupten Jinpa, Yangteng Rinpoche, Geshe Thupten Palsang, and Gelong Thupten Yarphel—and especially to the four main editors of this text—Khen Rinpoche Geshe Jangchub Sangye of Ganden Shartse, Geshe Lobsang Khechok of Drepung Gomang, Geshe Chisa Drungchen Rinpoche of Ganden Jangtse, and Geshe Ngawang Sangye of Drepung Loseling—for their dedicated efforts. I would also like to express sincere appreciation to my old friend and fellow alumnus from Cambridge University Thupten Jinpa for his suggestions on terminology and edits to an early draft, as well as to Tenzin Tsepak, another old friend and a fellow alumnus from the Institute of Buddhist Dialectics, for kindly sharing his thoughts on certain points of scholarship. Tseten Samdup Chhoekyapa and Tenzin Sewo kindly took care of practical matters regarding the project. I also wish to thank senior editor at Wisdom Publications, David Kittelstrom, for his valued suggestions regarding style and clarity of content in preparing this text for publication, as well as publisher Daniel Aitken, copyeditor Brianna Quick, production editor Ben Gleason, and proofreader Megan Anderson for their helpful contributions. May this work bring the teachings of the Nālandā masters to the attention of the world, and may they be understood and used to develop both inner and outer peace.

Dechen Rochard

Introduction

The Dalai Lama

Nearly a decade ago, I suggested to a group of monastic scholars that it would be wonderful if a presentation could be developed in which the subject matter of the entire Tibetan canon, the Kangyur and Tengyur—the teachings attributed to Buddha Śākyamuni and the commentarial treatises—were differentiated in terms of three broad categories. If such a presentation could be developed, it would facilitate a comprehensive presentation of the essence of the entire collection of key Buddhist treatises. More importantly, this could help bring about a new educational resource for our human family of over seven billion, regardless of their religious beliefs or lack thereof. The three categories I proposed were (1) the nature of reality—the parallel of science in the classical Buddhist texts, (2) the philosophical views developed in Buddhist sources, and (3) based on these two, Buddhist spiritual or religious practice. My introduction to volume 1 of this series, *Science and Philosophy in the Indian Buddhist Texts: The Physical World*, explained the nature of each of these three categories and indicated their unique features. As volumes 3 and 4 on philosophy in the classical Indian sources are nearing publication, I offer this essay in the form of an introduction.[1]

There is a range of opinion on what exactly the term *science* means. I understand it to be a system of investigation with unique methods of inquiry and the body of knowledge derived from such investigation. When science explores a question, it does so with a hypothesis based on observations, experiments to test whether the hypothesis holds true, and verification of those results through replication. When results are replicated by other researchers, such findings are incorporated into the body of scientific knowledge, and they become part of what subsequent researchers must engage with in their own research. It is this system—a method of inquiry, a body of findings, and associated theories and explanatory principles—that is called *science*. Defined in this way, a scientist may hold a specific philosophical view, but this does not mean that that view has been proven scientifically.

Philosophy, on the other hand, is a system of views about the deeper or ultimate nature of reality developed by thinkers on the basis of rigorous observation, rational inquiry (often in the form of argument), and the authority of past thinkers. Thus philosophers are those whose minds, not content with immediate sensory data, probe deeper by asking the question "What hidden reality underlies the diverse everyday world we experience?" Thus we could say that it is philosophers who seek to open doors to the understanding of the world's more hidden dimensions. Historically, a great diversity of philosophical views has appeared, employing diverse methods of critical inquiry. These philosophical views continue to the present day, serving as resources to help human thinking evolve.

Knowing the numerous philosophical views that exist in the world, especially the essential points of the four Buddhist philosophical schools, can open our intellect and enrich our resources for critical reflection in other domains. In particular, the study of the profound philosophical topics presented in the Buddhist sources—such as the Cittamātra argument for constant dual cognition and its theory of emptiness, and the Madhyamaka understanding of emptiness in terms of dependent origination—can benefit us now in this life, regardless of whether we believe in future lives. It can broaden our perspective, dismantling the mental afflictions that blind us from seeing things in a comprehensive way, that keep us narrowly fixated; it can stop us from planting the seeds of unhappiness for ourselves and others. These are benefits I can attest to from personal experience.

In light of these points, I am happy that today, just as I had expressly wished, the two volumes on philosophy compiled from Indian Buddhist sources are now complete. Of these two philosophy volumes in the *Science and Philosophy in Indian Buddhist Classics* series, the first introduces the views of the main Indian philosophical schools. To that end, it presents their views on the nature of reality, including their logical arguments, using sources that the schools themselves consider authoritative. One important difference compared to the traditional Tibetan tenets genre is that this volume only presents views about the nature of reality; it does not include the schools' presentation of their path and results. The reason is that the purpose here is to help open the intellect of contemporary readers, especially their critical faculties; it is not to benefit exclusively the adherents of these Buddhist and non-Buddhist schools.

Volume 4, this second volume on philosophy, selects some major topics that have been the object of critical inquiry since ancient times. Part 1 of this volume presents the nature of reality within the framework of the two truths (conventional and ultimate). Part 2 presents the topic of self and no-self: the nature of the person that is the experiencer of pain and pleasure and is the agent of action. Parts 3 and 4 present ultimate truth from the perspectives of Cittamātra and Madhyamaka, respectively, as well as their key logical arguments. Part 5 presents the Indian approach to epistemology in general and, more specifically, the approach to logic and epistemology developed by Dignāga and refined by Dharmakīrti. Part 6 presents an important issue within epistemology and the philosophy of language: how words express their meaning. My objective and my hope for these two volumes on philosophy is that many discerning minds of our time will be able to gain an understanding of the deep philosophical insights of ancient India.

In conclusion, I pray that these two volumes on Indian philosophy, volumes 3 and 4 of the series, will benefit many interested readers.

The Buddhist monk Tenzin Gyatso, The Dalai Lama
Introduction translated into English by Thupten Jinpa

Translator's Introduction

THIS VOLUME IS the last in a series of four concerning the nature of reality as sourced in the classical Indian Buddhist literature of the first millennium. The first two volumes present topics broadly categorized as science, specifically those that concern the physical world (volume 1) and those that concern the domain of the mind (volume 2). The final two volumes present topics related to the realm of philosophy: one is a synopsis of Indian philosophical views (volume 3); the other is a selection of important philosophical topics (volume 4). The reader is recommended to browse Donald Lopez's introductory essay to volume 3, which contains useful information about the various Indian philosophical systems as well as a beautifully concise introduction to the Nālandā masters[2] whose teachings are presented in these volumes.

What Is Philosophy?

Philosophy is a notoriously difficult subject to define.[3] The ancient Greek term *philosophia* literally means "love of wisdom." While this goes some way toward indicating what the subject is about, philosophy in contemporary academia spans a vast terrain. A philosophy can be devised for almost any discipline, and it factors into every domain of experience and endeavor. It includes traditional topics such as metaphysics, epistemology, and ethics but also more recently developed variants such as environmental philosophy, feminist philosophy, and the philosophy of dance. It could be said that philosophy is more a *way of investigating* subject matter than it is the subject matter itself, though the latter is still relevant. For example, while science investigates what things exist in the world and how they operate, philosophy investigates what it means *to exist* or *to be a thing* (metaphysics), whether and how such a thing *can be known* (epistemology), how such a thing is *demonstrated correctly* (philosophy of science and philosophy of logic), and whether pursuing such a thing *has value* (moral and political philosophy). The many branches of philosophy are connected, and theories developed within each can yield implications for the other branches.

Western philosophy is generally considered to have originated with thinkers who lived in the diaspora of ancient Greece (sixth to fifth century BCE) beginning in Miletus and culminating in Athens.[4] Our knowledge of its origins is limited because the earliest written sources are fragmentary, often just scattered quotations found in the works of later philosophers and doxographers. In Ionia, where Miletus is located, the term *philosophia* meant "curiosity," and it seems to have begun with attempts to explain life and the cosmos in a manner perhaps more akin to what we would call *observational science* today. Topics under consideration included the flux, what might abide within it (some kind of primordial substance perhaps), the various physical elements and their interaction, and motion and rest. Prior to the development of philosophy in the Greek territories, there was the Olympian religion with its many gods[5] as well as more ancient nature cults, and later the cults that developed around the mythic poems of Orpheus.[6] All of these continued to be popular during the great flowering of philosophy, though the philosophers mostly ignored such accounts. Their investigations of topics such as the flux were not byproducts of religion or mythology. Practical considerations were paramount in their contributions to engineering, navigation, cosmology, biology, and medicine, and the underlying principles of these disciplines were studied in great depth. From inquiries into the origins of the cosmos arose the first philosophical questions about the fundamental principles, grounds, and reasoning behind what was observed, and whether diverse appearances might share a unifying principle.

Thales (fl. 585 BCE) is said to be the first person who engaged in such inquiry. Famous as an astronomer—a science imported from Mesopotamia—he is also said to have introduced geometry into Hellas from Egypt. Not much is known about his philosophy except that he posited water to be the primary substance or first cause. A follower of his, Anaximander, posited an undefined (*apeirōn*) nature to be the substratum—not any specific nature but something encompassing them all—from which opposites arose and into which they dissolved back again. His associate Anaximenes maintained that air was the fundamental principle—likened to the soul or the breath of life—whereby things were formed through a process of condensation and rarefaction.

Pythagoras (fl. 532 BCE) was both a scientific and a religious man, specializing in mathematics and Orphic theology, respectively. He used mathematics in his study of the acoustic ratios found in musical harmony, which he linked with the attunement of opposites: the Limit (fire) and the Boundless (darkness). The religious practices he espoused involved purification to release the soul from the wheel of birth (specifically reincarnation in animal or vegetable forms). The term *philosophia* in this context came to mean a "way of life," consonant with the notion of a perfectly tuned string.

Heraclitus (fl. 500 BCE) was very much influenced by the notion of *process*. Valuing the objects of the senses, he focused on the flux and is famous for having said, "You cannot step twice into the same rivers; for fresh waters are ever flowing in upon you."[7] While this expresses change and the many, Heraclitus does not do away with the one. In his opening fragment he declares, "It is wise to listen to my word and agree that everything is one." Here the term *logos* is introduced for the first time, though it is unclear what it means in this context. Some say it means "word," in reference to his own discourse,[8] while others say it means something like "system" or "principle," as in a law of nature that governs the cosmos.[9] Later it came to mean "reason," "ground," "measure," "account," "definition," and so on, which come to play a crucial role in philosophy. Now, when Heraclitus further declares that "all things come to pass in accordance with this word," the term seems to indicate an unchanging principle that manifests all the transformations in the cosmos. Since it is unchanging, it is one. Heraclitus likens it to fire, which he takes to be the primary substance that manifests all the objects of the senses. Just as a burning flame is one in form yet constantly changing in substance, so the world is simultaneously one and many.

Parmenides (fl. 504–500 BCE) employed the term *logos* to mean "argument" and offered a method for deriving a correct understanding of *what is*. He endeavored to derive the One, characterized elsewhere as a corporeal, spherical, continuous, eternal, and immoveable *plenum*. He argued that it is eternal because it cannot have been produced, which in turn is because it cannot have arisen from nothing (as there is no such thing as nothing) and because it cannot have arisen from something (as there is no room for anything but itself). This type of dialectic, introduced by Parmenides, is a style of argument that has become a cornerstone of philosophy. We see here too the beginnings of a distinction between what appears to the senses and what is true.

Empedocles (fl. 444–443 BCE) too was concerned with perception and understanding, though unlike Parmenides he was a pluralist and considered the four elements or *roots of all things* (fire, air, earth, and water) to be the ultimate reality—all of them continuously uniting and separating again through the forces of love and strife. Empedocles focused on ethics and the correct way of life, which mirrored his understanding of the cosmos. He is also said to have influenced the development of medicine in such a way that advanced the tendency toward scientific thinking, and to have regarded the heart, not the brain, as the seat of consciousness.

Zeno (fl. 464–460 BCE) is considered the originator of *dialectic*. A follower of Parmenides, he argued not from true premises but from premises admitted by the other side (specifically, the pluralist opponents of Parmenides). While the opponents argued that Parmenides's notion of reality as *one* led to conclusions that contradicted the evidence of the senses, Zeno demonstrated that the opponents' notion of reality as *many* led to contradictions of a similar nature. Although only a few fragments of Zeno's works survive today, his arguments can be found in the works of other philosophers, such as Plato's *Parmenides* and Aristotle's *Metaphysics*.

Socrates (469–399 BCE) considered notions of the soul, virtue, and knowledge to be central to philosophical reflection and debate. He wrote nothing himself, though many discourses and literary works in which he features prominently were written by others, including the comic-poet Aristophanes, the soldier-historian Xenophon, and most notably Socrates's student Plato (429–347 BCE). It is notoriously difficult to distinguish the historical Socrates from the characterizations of him found in such works, and this has come to be called the *Socratic problem*. Similarly, it might be difficult to distinguish between the views of Socrates and those of Plato in Plato's dialogues, though there is now a strong consensus that the early dialogues represent Socrates's own views and the later dialogues represent the views of Plato.

The dialogues of Plato are extensive and profound, and the points discussed in them far too numerous to mention here. Plato never appears in his own works but usually uses Socrates as a mouthpiece to instigate debate on doctrinal points, placing him at center stage among a number of interlocutors. Important topics in Plato's dialogues often begin with the question "What is it?" The method of inquiry and argument employed in his dialogues is known as *dialectic*, though this label actually encompasses several similar styles of argument. The most evolved of these is said to be an *a priori* method, which means it begins with presuppositions that are then subjected to analysis. Its core features can be reduced to two processes, similar to those employed by mathematicians at the time: first, identifying and drawing out the consequences of propositions, or hypotheses, to highlight any inconsistencies and answer the question at hand; second, confirming or justifying those hypotheses to arrive at a non-hypothetical first principle—a pure universal, the Form of the Good.

Famous for having described himself as a midwife, Socrates uses such a method for delivering *correct* or *incorrect* "offspring" (i.e., views or arguments), which he then either develops or disproves, respectively. He makes a clear distinction between *sophistry*, which he sees as a tool for manipulating others, and *philosophy*, which he sees as a tool for inner transformation. Socrates, enlisting another metaphor, sees his function in life as the doctor of the Athenians, helping them to become free from the greatest of misfortunes—to do wrong—a freedom that, he claims, is accomplished through philosophy. Philosophical inquiry of the right kind cultivates virtue within the mind of the philosopher primarily because it removes ignorance. The greatest evil is said to be ignorance about the truth or reality. Here, philosophy is taken to be a practice, a spiritual exercise, a "way of life."

Aristotle (384–322 BCE), the son of a doctor, was a student of Plato. He trained in Plato's academy for some twenty years and critically engaged with his theories. Aristotle developed a curriculum of study that encompassed practically every field of knowledge in his day, which he incorporated into three branches of learning, or science (*epistēmē*): theoretical, practical, and productive. *Theoretical* science seeks knowledge for its own sake; it includes metaphysics, epistemology, mathematics, and natural philosophy (*physics*). *Practical* science concerns conduct and action, which includes ethics and politics. *Productive* science deals with crafts such as shipbuilding and medicine, as well as music, dance, rhetoric, and so forth. Underlying these sciences are the tools, the methods of inquiry: deduction, induction, dialectic, and puzzles. These generally fall into what we now call *a system of logic*, which Aristotle is said to have invented.

Aristotle is especially famous for having introduced the syllogism as a form of deductive argument. A syllogism contains two premises and a conclusion, with one term (known as the *middle term*) appearing in both premises.[10] An example of a syllogism is the following: "All men are mortal; Socrates is a man; therefore Socrates is mortal."[11] Among different types of deductive argument, *dialectic* refers to that which proceeds from premises considered reputable or commonly agreed (*endoxa*). A topic of debate is identified, and the parties try to find some point of agreement as a basis for further argument.

In Aristotle's time at Plato's academy, debates took place between two people, a questioner and an answerer, often witnessed by an audience. The answerer upheld a thesis, and the questioner tried to elicit a contradiction by asking questions restricted to a "yes" or "no" answer, though the form of the argument could also be challenged.[12] Such an argument could disprove the opponent's thesis but could not prove any thesis of its own. This method of dialectic is contrasted with *demonstration*, not in terms of its deductive structure but in terms of the strength of its premises. A demonstration is "a syllogism productive of scientific knowledge."

Here, "the premises of demonstrated knowledge must be true, primary, immediate, better known than and prior to the conclusion, which is further related to them as effect to cause."[13] The first principles on which demonstrated knowledge relies are accessed via *induction*, where perception of a particular is persistently repeated so as to form memories that constitute *experience*, which is "the universal now stabilized in its entirety within the soul."[14] It is notable here that Aristotle's highest form of deductive knowledge, demonstration, is grounded in perception, which successfully allows it to avoid an infinite regress.[15] According to Aristotle, sense perception, though not infallible, is not systematically deceptive. He takes such appearances as a suitable starting point for his inquiry, shows what puzzles (*aporiai*) they reveal, considers how earlier philosophers dealt with them, disproves those that are inadequate, and posits his own solutions. This scientific approach is also employed by Buddhist philosophers, as we will see later in this volume.

Indian Philosophy

It is hard to say whether similarities between Greek and Indian philosophy occurred independently, as a result of having influenced one another, or owing to a common source. In any case, there is extensive archaeological evidence of significant interaction among the ancient civilizations of Greece, the Middle East, and India since at least 3000 BCE. This interaction included not only traders but also mercenaries, craftsmen, and scholars. People regularly visited neighboring territories, even creating settlements and mastering each other's languages, and in such circumstances the exchange of ideas seems not only likely but probable. The Persian empire, from the sixth century BCE, provided ideal conditions for this, as both Indian and Greek representatives were present in its royal courts. There was also the practice of deporting troublesome communities from one end of the empire to the other, such as when Greeks from Miletus, near the Mediterranean, were sent to Bactria, close to the Hindu Kush.[16]

As in Greece and its diaspora, the notion of philosophy in ancient India encompassed a range of meanings over time. Questions about the cosmos and human beings' place in it are found in the oldest Sanskrit sources, the Vedas.[17] The Vedic hymns are primarily poetic praises of the forces of nature in the guise of impersonal gods, along with injunctions to perform certain rituals and sacrifices.[18] Hymns containing accounts of origin, destination, and transformation were recorded. Those hymns considered by Vedic scholars to be of philosophical interest are mainly located in the tenth book of the *Ṛg Veda* and scattered throughout the first, perhaps added at a later stage.[19] In this context, the philosopher was a "poet" (*kavi*), philosophy was called "hymn" (*uktha*), and hymn chanting (*udgīta*) denoted the act of philosophizing.[20] Some early notions of philosophy they include are an inner search for the relation between existent things and primordial matter; an ascertainment of the original cause underlying plurality; and an inquiry (*sampraśnaṃ*) into the nature of things.

As for the Greeks, questions arose about the primordial ground of things in flux; and like for the first Greek philosopher, Thales, the initial answer was "water." The earliest known Indian philosopher, Agharmaṣaṇa, posits water as the origin of the world, activated by the "year" (or the "season," from which can be traced the doctrine of time), while his near contemporary Prajāpati Parameṣṭhin posits water as the origin, activated by "desire." When the question of origin arises in the Vedas, whatever the answer—water, air, fire, solar substance, regular order, or rhythmic progress—it is said to be unitary. Nonetheless, only the philosophical hymns indicate such a monism. Rather than monotheistic or polytheistic, the early Vedic religion is said to be henotheistic, where the deities are not yet fully distinguished from one another, and where each becomes a focus of worship in the relevant context then fades into the background. The notion of a supreme Lord of All Beings (Prajāpati) emerged gradually, only later becoming a distinct deity, with attributes similarly ascribed to the Creator of All (Viśvakarma).[21]

While such accounts of the origin of the world may be considered an early metaphysics, the vast majority of injunctions in the Vedas do not qualify as philosophy. Later discussions and debates about how to interpret them, however, which became very sophisticated, can be said to fall into this category. Discussion in its own right was considered a vital practice, and the *Ṛg Veda* (X.191.2) urges people to "meet one another, discuss and understand your minds."[22] It seems reasonable to suppose that such discussion eventually gave rise to more formal philosophical debate. B. K. Matilal tells us that "The art of conducting a philosophical debate was prevalent probably as early as the time of the Buddha," and it is out of such debate that "Logic, as the study of the form of correct arguments and inference-patterns, developed in India."[23]

It is not easy to date the origin of logic in India. The famous system presented in Akṣapāda Gautama's *Nyāya Sūtra* seems to have been relatively well formed by the time of Nāgārjuna.[24] The term *nyāya* itself means "logical argument," so it seems reasonable to suppose that the philosophical system bearing its name presents the earliest form of logic in India. However, the earliest surviving text in which logical debates are recorded appears to be *Points of Discussion* (*Kathāvatthu*), a Buddhist Abhidhamma text of the Pali canon attributed to Moggaliputta Tissa (third century BCE). Rupert Gethin acknowledges, "The *Points of Discussion* is a difficult text. There is no critical edition; the only available translation into a modern European language is a paraphrase (Aung and Rhys Davids 1915, li–lii). A full study remains a scholarly desideratum."[25] Following an early commentary, Gethin states that "this formalized system of debate and stereotyped analysis appear to mark a significant step in the development of Indian logic," and he notes the suggestion that "the basic form of argument reveals that the author of the *Points of Discussion* understood the 'definition of implication' . . . and the law of transposition."[26] Gethin helpfully sets out the structure of the argument in the form of a table. He also mentions that this text, although attributed to an individual author, is more likely to have been compiled over time; and philological evidence indicates that its core portions may have originated in Magadha, located in the Buddhist heartlands of the eastern Ganges Plain.

So the lineage of debate, and the logic that evolved out of it, seems to have a long history that predates written records. Yet the unique characteristics of Buddhist logic as we know them now did not manifest until several centuries later with the advent of Dignāga and his student Dharmakīrti. Matilal suggests that Dignāga "was perhaps the most creative logician in medieval (400–1100) India."[27] Here he is referring to Dignāga's definition of correct evidence as "that which is qualified by the three modes," with all that followed from it in the field of epistemology (see part 5), and to his exclusion (*apoha*) theory of meaning that yields stability of reference without committing to an ontology of real universals, with all that followed from it in the philosophy of language (see part 6).

Matthew Kapstein notes the importance of "the attention given to the analysis of language in ancient India, the early development there of linguistic science having been the direct outcome of the need to preserve the text of the sacred Veda intact after the Vedic language itself was no longer spoken."[28] It was indeed early and very significant. The most famous grammatical treatise that survives today is Pāṇini's *Aṣṭādhyāyī* (ca. fourth century BCE), which provides an astonishingly sophisticated derivation of all kinds of Sanskrit utterances from grammatical rules, employing an object-language and a meta-language that Pāṇini devised and set out over eight chapters. The derivation involved here is a grammatical one, not a logical one.

Regarding the notion of "Indian logic" in general, Kuppuswami Sastri informs us that "This phrase is usually rendered in Sanskrit equivalents—*ānvīkṣikī*, *nyāyavistara*, *nyāyadarśana*, *tarkaśāstra*, and *pramāṇaśāstra*."[29] The term *ānvīkṣikī* is initially found in Kauṭilya's *Treatise on Gains* (*Arthaśāstra*), a famous text on the practical goals of life, which was composed, expanded, and redacted from around the second century BCE. Kauṭilya outlines four main disciplines of learning: logic and philosophy (*ānvīkṣikī*), the three Vedas and the religious canon (*trayī*), the science of material acquisition (*vārtā*), and political administration and government (*daṇḍanīti*). These disciplines are all undertaken with the aim to live a more ethical and beneficial life. The notion of *ānvīkṣikī* seems to have acquired a range of interpretations over time. At a certain point, the first two disciplines of learning were considered inseparable: *ānvīkṣikī* was employed only for investigating the Vedas. At other times, *ānvīkṣikī* was considered inseparable from all the other three disciplines, since it was a tool for accomplishing them. Later it was taken to apply not just those three but to a great variety of disciplines. Then *ānvīkṣikī* took on a more secular meaning, since it was also used by the Lokāyata (Materialists) to accomplish their aims. There has been much discussion about what Kauṭilya meant when he stated that "*ānvīkṣikī* consists of Sāṃkhya, Yoga, and Lokāyata,"[30] but this is too complicated to go into here.[31] Suffice it to say that *ānvīkṣikī* came to be synonymous with *nyāya*, though perhaps before the Nyāya system itself took shape.

As a form of reasoning, *ānvīkṣikī* starts with a doubt—for example, "Is such and such a deed good or bad?" (Is *x* P or not-P?).[32] Then, similar to what is presented in the Nyāya system, it moves through the next six categories that follow doubt: purpose, example, tenet, components of inference, reasoning, and ascertainment.[33] It is significant that such a process of reasoning begins with an epistemological state—a doubt. This is an important feature that distinguishes Indian logic from Western formal logic. Although they share fundamental logical principles (the laws of excluded middle, noncontradiction, and identity), four main points differentiate them, as highlighted by B. K. Matilal: Indian logic contains epistemological notions since it concerns the development of inferential understanding; Indian logic also contains psychological notions since it concerns the arising of specific mental states; Indian logic was developed on the basis of grammar whereas Western formal logic was developed on the basis of mathematics; and the relationship between deduction and induction is treated differently by each system.[34] These points apply to Indian logic in general, both the Nyāya and the Buddhist systems, which share fundamental features.

A branch of "philosophy" well established in India but not documented in the West is *yoga*, which literally means "yoke" (presumably sharing an Indo-European linguistic root). This term evolved to connote a range of meanings. Dasgupta mentions that "In Pāṇini's time the word *yoga* had attained its technical meaning, and he distinguished this root *yuj samādhau* (*yuj* in the sense of concentration) from *yujir yoge* (root *yujir* in the sense of connecting)."[35] It seems that yoga started out as a spiritual exercise designed to harness the senses and *restrain* them from scattering toward external objects. The idea is that keeping the mind focused inward, by relying on the breath, leads to liberation from disturbing emotions.

Later the notion of *connection* became prominent, notably in the context of inferential argument (*yukti*), which relies on the relation between the reason and the predicate of the thesis. Such a connection applies in both Buddhist and non-Buddhist Indian logic. The notion of connection occurs in yet another way in the context of Buddhist practice—namely, the supreme yoga that unites the insight arisen from rational analysis with the meditative concentration of calm abiding. This will be discussed below. Dasgupta informs us, "The oldest Buddhist sūtras (e.g., the *Satipaṭṭhāna sutta*) are fully familiar with the stages of Yoga concentration. We may thus infer that self-concentration and Yoga had developed as a technical method of mystic absorption some time before the Buddha."[36]

What motivations drove the development of logic in India? The motivation to make one's own intellectual and religious heritage "more coherent and more resistant to critical questioning by outsiders"[37] is one commonly cited, and it is an important one, given that it is through dialogue and debate with each other that the various philosophical traditions have developed and grown over the centuries. However, it also happens to be the case that the authors of the founding scriptures, as well as the Indian philosophers promoting them, have explicitly stated that the motivation for their work is the attainment of liberation, *mokṣa.* This is because the intention to attain *mokṣa*—to remove the causes of suffering and gain freedom from saṃsāra—is considered the highest human aim.

Yet even this apparently pan-Indian notion developed over time. It is not found in the early Vedas but was introduced under the influence of the *śramaṇa* traditions: Sāṅkhya, Buddhism, and Jainism. Moreover, that each tradition embraces its own notion of *mokṣa* calls into question that this is a commonly shared goal. A skeptical Indian author remarks, "There seem to be a host of problems in Indian philosophy which do not appear to have any direct or indirect relation, even in the remotest way, to *moksa.*"[38] After highlighting a number of instances, he declares, "Except for the *sūtrakāras*' (author of the *sūtras*) own saying, it is difficult to believe that anyone could seriously believe that he or anyone else could achieve *mokṣa* through a knowledge of the types *of padārthas* (objects of experience) to be found in the world, or through a knowledge of the *pramāṇas* (means of valid knowledge), or the *hetvābhāsas* (logical fallacies) which are relevant in the field of reasoning and argumentation."[39] He may have a point, though I suspect his notion that *mokṣa* is attainable only through practical means (such as prayer, ritual, and meditation), and that philosophical or conceptual means can never be practical, creates this limited perspective. Contrary to that view, we will examine in the next two sections how specific philosophical analyses could become practical methods on the Buddhist path to liberation.

Buddhist Philosophy

Above, we noted that *philosophy*—both Eastern and Western—can encompass a variety of connotations and pursuits: inquiry, explanation, discourse, debate, dialectic, logic, argument, way of life, inner transformation, fulfillment of human aims (including *mokṣa*), love of wisdom, poetry, *ānvīkṣikī*, *nyāya*, *yoga*, and *darśana*.[40] One of the most popular in the West appears to be *explanation*. This is championed by Michael Loux, who suggests that the criterion of a "fruitful theory" in Western philosophy is: "one with the resources for explaining a wide range of phenomena."[41] Such a notion of philosophy has also been adopted by a number of Buddhist philosophers in Western academia, whereby "giving an account" of our intuitive notions or "providing explanatory value" is taken to be key.[42]

Nonetheless, while explanation may have a role to play, I suggest that its role is limited. I would argue that the primary *philosophical activity* engaged in by a Buddhist practitioner is rational analysis—specifically, an analytical search for "the way things are" in an ultimate sense. This rational activity using the tools of logic is motivated by the wish to free ourselves from the causes of suffering and to help others do likewise. To accomplish this task, both *debate about* and *analysis of* the way things are may be employed—the former as part of a preparatory stage in discourse with other practitioners, and the latter at a more advanced stage in combination with meditative concentration, which is a type of yoga.[43] Philosophy employed merely to provide an *explanation* of the way things are cannot be expected to accomplish such a goal, though it undoubtedly assists in preparing the ground for such an endeavor. This is crucial to understand, because if we take Buddhist philosophical teachings—such as Nāgārjuna's diamond slivers reasoning, or Candrakīrti's sevenfold analysis—to be an *explanation* of the way things are instead of an *instruction* on how to perceive the way things are, then the teachings can appear contradictory or nihilistic, and we would fail in our goal. To explain what this means, let us consider some examples from the present volume, particularly certain Prāsaṅgika Madhyamaka analyses in part 4.

First, however, we should clarify some assumptions about the nature of suffering (*duḥkha*) and its cause,[44] since these are what need to be removed. Each assumption may be defended with reasoning and established as a conclusion.[45] These assumptions include the notion that contaminated existence, or *saṃsāra*, which occurs owing to mental afflictions and contaminated action, is in the very nature of suffering; and the fundamental cause of this dire situation is ignorance of the way things are in terms of their ultimate nature. This is different from ignorance of the way things are in terms of their conventional nature, which can be rectified through ordinary perception, mundane reasoning, and scientific investigation, all of which are types of conventional analysis. The difference between *conventional reality*, arrived at through conventional analysis, and *ultimate reality*, arrived at through ultimate analysis, is discussed in part 1 of the present volume—though the various schools differ in their accounts.

Here, we are concerned with the ignorance of the way things are in terms of their ultimate nature as that is presented by the Prāsaṅgika Madhyamaka school. This ignorance is the root mental affliction known as the *identity view* (*satkāyadṛṣṭi*), which is equated with *self-grasping* (*ahaṃkāra*). It is the habitual misconceiving attitude that grasps objects of cognition as existing truly, from their own side. This generates inappropriate attention, from which the remaining psychopathologies such as attachment and aversion arise—leading to all kinds of social conflict, misery, and harmful behaviors. Buddhist philosophers articulate a sophisticated understanding of mind or consciousness and its qualities, and of how distinct moments of awareness flow from specific causes. A detailed account of the mental factors involved in such a process can be found in volume 2. Our present volume simply states, "Thus the final root of mental afflictions such as attachment is the delusion grasping at true existence. And the final antidote that removes the delusion grasping at true existence is the wisdom realizing emptiness, which directly counteracts it and its way of grasping."[46]

The path to understanding emptiness begins with receiving the relevant teachings. This is followed by a thought process that involves dialectical reasoning. Finally we engage in meditation on what has been understood so as to cultivate insight into the way things are as ultimate truth. This threefold scheme of learning, investigation, and meditation can be applied to any topic and is advocated by several Indian philosophical systems. Examples of appropriate dialectical reasoning can be found scattered throughout the present volume.

Debates can be directed toward someone with an opposing view, or it can be a debate with our own misconceptions. This stage of thinking, or contemplating, the second in the threefold scheme mentioned above,[47] starts with a verbalized form of argument. As the process gradually becomes more refined, it transforms into a subtle analysis searching for something bearing its own identity, or existing from its own side. Each stage of the analysis relies on a dialectical method that operates via logical principles, such as the law of noncontradiction (not (P and not-P)) and the law of excluded middle (P or not-P). The present volume quotes a stanza from Nāgārjuna's *Refutation of Objections* to show that he explicitly accepts these principles:

> If it negates *not inherently existent*,
> then it proves *inherently existent*.[48]

Here the commentary explains that "the two—inherently existent and not inherently existent—are directly contradictory, in the sense of being mutually excluding, since there is nothing that is neither of those two."[49] In other words, nothing has both properties, and nothing lacks both properties.

Now let us consider the two renowned logical refutations of inherent nature mentioned above: Nāgārjuna's diamond slivers reasoning and Candrakīrti's sevenfold reasoning. Regarding the first, after paying homage to the Buddha, the opening stanza of Nāgārjuna's *Fundamental Treatise on the Middle Way* declares:

> Not from self, not from others,
> not from both, not without a cause;
> any things, anywhere,
> do not arise at any time.[50]

At first glance, this verse seems to be saying that nothing ever arises. However, our commentary explains it as follows. "According to the systems of both Buddhist and non-Buddhist realists, who claim that phenomena exist from their own side, if a result arises inherently, then it must arise from one of the four alternatives; and if it doesn't arise from any of the four alternatives, then it cannot arise inherently. Since they accept this to be established by reasoning, they accept that things arise from one of the four alternatives. Therefore, if things are refuted to arise from any of the four alternatives, then it is easily established that they do not arise inherently."[51] This argument has the form of a consequence, where the pervasion between the reason ("arises inherently") and the predicate of the probandum ("arises from one of the four alternatives") can be expressed as follows: from the implication "if *a*, then *b*" we can infer *b* given *a*, or we can infer *not a* given *not b*. We may recognize this as a principle of reasoning known in Western classical logic as *modus tollendo tollens*. After having established the entailment (if *a* then *b*), Nāgārjuna shows that ultimate arising must occur in one of the four ways, and since it cannot occur in any of those ways, which establishes *not b*, this then entails that there is no inherent arising (*not a*).

If the opponent wants to defend inherent arising, he or she must locate it through engaging in ultimate analysis. Inherent arising must be able to withstand ultimate analysis—the search for something bearing its own identity, or existing from its own side. Since nothing can be found to exist in such a way at the culmination of ultimate analysis, nothing exists ultimately. This is the basic idea here. Our commentary then goes on to present the refutations of each of the four alternative ways of arising in turn. Thus inherent arising is refuted, which leaves mere arising intact. This may sound simplistic, but it requires a lot of deep analysis and contemplation to stop perceiving things as arising inherently.

Like Nāgārjuna, Candrakīrti also makes regular use of *modus tollendo tollens* in his analysis of the self, which he likens to the sevenfold analysis of a chariot.[52] And he evidently accepts other principles of reasoning such as the law of noncontradiction and the law of excluded middle. The chariot example is well established in Indian religious culture; it first appears in the Upaniṣads as an analogy of the person.[53] Buddhist texts use it differently, as an example of how the person is merely imputed on the basis of the aggregates. The venerable nun Arhantī Śailā declares:

> Just as a chariot is named
> in dependence upon the group of parts,

> so, in dependence upon the aggregates,
> we have the term *sentient being*.[54]

This verse is later cited by Nāgasena when debating with the Bactrian king Menander (ca. 155–130 BCE)—in Pali, Milinda—as described in the *Questions of King Milinda*.[55] Garfield discusses this debate and notes that neither party is responding to someone who espouses an independent self (*ātmavādin*); rather it presents "a careful refinement of the proper way to express a Buddhist position on the self."[56] What is shown is that the self is a dependent designation. To give an account of such a self is a perfectly acceptable approach for a Buddhist philosopher. But it is not the only acceptable approach. Indeed, based on Arhantī Śailā's verse, Candrakīrti offers something more profound. He shows how to use these teachings as a form of ultimate analysis of the self for the purpose of uprooting self-grasping. Candrakīrti's *Entering the Middle Way* says:

> How can what does not exist in the seven ways
> be said to exist? The yogin finds no such existence.
> By this means, he also enters into reality with ease;
> so its existence must be accepted as shown here.[57]

Like Nāgārjuna's diamond slivers, Candrakīrti's sevenfold analysis relies on logic, specifically on delineating, investigating, and eventually excluding all possible ways in which the object of scrutiny could inherently exist. At certain points (whether before, during, or after the process of analysis—and perhaps repeatedly at every stage) the meditator ascertains that the sevenfold analysis is exhaustive: there is no other way in which a self might possibly exist from its own side. The meditator needs to be totally sure of this, because if there is any room for doubt, then the held object of innate self-grasping (or identity view) will "leak through" the analysis, and innate self-grasping will remain, habitually arising in the mindstream.

In response to anyone who might think that the chariot can be conceptually reduced to its parts (e.g., the Ābhidharmika Buddhists), Candrakīrti adds:

> Just as when the chariot is completely burned by the fire of wisdom's incinerating activity of not perceiving [inherent identity],

> which is kindled by rubbing together the sticks of analysis, so its parts too, being the fuel of the fire of wisdom, no longer appear with the projection of inherent identity because they are completely burned up.[58]

Here Candrakīrti is emphasizing that the wisdom mind realizing selflessness negates inherent identity—it incinerates the object of self-grasping—and the projection of inherent identity cannot survive the flames of that wisdom, no matter what that projection may be based upon (a person, a *dharma*, a stream of *dharmas*). This gradual burning away of the grasped object is achieved by very subtle meditation practice. While ordinary notions of the self and the aggregates disappear during meditative equipoise, what is actually burned up is the habitual tendency to reify them. So when the yoginī arises from that meditation, she sees the self and the aggregates again, but she knows they do not exist as they appear to—that is, from their own side.

Candrakīrti's point is that *parts* and *wholes* have the same ontological status. Each is imputed on the basis of the other, and both dissolve in the light of the wisdom realizing the selflessness of the whole. Ultimate analysis yields the perception of a mere absence of the object. But the conventional nature of things is not denied in this process. After arising from this meditation, and for as long as its influence lasts, conventional things appear and are individuated in the same way, but their identity is understood as not coming from the side of the object.

Transition to Tibet

Buddhist teachings were transported to Tibet in two phases: the "early dissemination" of the Dharma from the seventh to the ninth century during the Tibetan empire, and the "later dissemination" of the Dharma beginning in the late tenth century with the arrival of Atiśa. These periods saw extensive translation projects under the auspices of Tibetan rulers and guided by great Buddhist masters who had traveled from India.

One of the first Tibetan emperors, Songtsen Gampo (r. ca. 618–49), who had become acquainted with paper and ink from China, took the crucial step of inaugurating literacy among the Tibetan people by sending his minister Thönmi Saṃbhota to India with the instruction to bring back a script for the Tibetan language. From this followed several centuries of collaboration between Indian and Tibetan scholars. The great translation projects of the earlier and later disseminations required a thorough knowledge of the languages involved, and there arose an extensive grammatical literature. In addition to the forty-seven translated works on Sanskrit grammar in the Tengyur, there are scores of texts on Sanskrit grammar written by Tibetans and indigenous works on Tibetan grammar.

Of special note is the *Two-Volume Lexicon* (*Sgra sbyor bam po gnyis pa*), a famous commentary on the *Mahāvyutpatti* (*Bye brag tu rtogs byed chen po, Great Detailed Scholastic Dictionary*), which is a hugely important Sanskrit-Tibetan lexicon dating from the late eighth to early ninth century. All of these genres of texts have played a crucial role in the transmission of Buddhist teachings in Tibet. Peter Verhagen remarks, "Certainly, not all Tibetan translations are equally good. There are good ones, there are *brilliant* ones, and there are also mediocre ones. But even the mediocre ones, I think, show great skill in analyzing and interpreting this foreign language, which of course, adding to the difficulty, was a language from a totally different language family."[59] Here he is referring to the fact that, despite sharing a similar alphabet and script, Tibetan and Sanskrit come from different families of languages, Tibetan from the Tibeto-Burman language family and Sanskrit from the Indo-European family.

In addition to this problem, Dasgupta explains that "Sanskrit is generally regarded as a difficult language. But no one from an acquaintance with Vedic or ordinary literary Sanskrit can have any idea of the difficulty of the logical and abstruse parts of Sanskrit philosophical literature."[60] This applies in the case of both Buddhist and non-Buddhist philosophical literature. One is left with the question, "How did the Tibetans, so few in number over the centuries, manage to translate so successfully such a huge body of extraordinarily complex literature?" In those days they didn't even have computers!

Three of the seventeen Nālandā masters traveled to Tibet, and each remained there until they died. The first two, Śāntarakṣita (725–88) and his disciple Kamalaśīla (ca. 740–95), were instrumental in propagating the first dissemination of the teachings, while the third, Atiśa Dīpaṃkara Śrījñāna (980–1054), was instrumental in propagating the second dissemination. Traditional sources claim that after Śāntarakṣita's death, Kamalaśīla was summoned from India to engage the Chan master Heshang Moheyan in a series of debates at Samyé Monastery on the topic of sudden versus gradual enlightenment and that Kamalaśīla won. Heshang Moheyan was assumed to have departed in shame. However, some more recently discovered Dunhuang documents indicate that he did not sink into oblivion but traveled to Dunhuang and became "one of the leading Buddhist teachers of the Tibetan administration."[61] The sudden enlightenment approach seems to have maintained some influence, which can even be seen today, notably in the Dzogchen lineage of the Nyingma tradition rooted in the first dissemination.

Prior to the arrival of Atiśa in Tibet, the king who ruled the western realm of Gugé, Yeshe Ö, sent twenty-one young Tibetans to study Buddhism in Kashmir. The most accomplished of these was Rinchen Sangpo, who stayed there for ten years, and upon his return to Tibet in 985 became a famous scholar and translator. Under his influence, many centers of learning and translation were established throughout the region, notably the monastery at Tholing, the capital of Gugé. Yeshe Ö and his successor, Jangchup Ö, then invited Atiśa and a number of other Buddhist masters from India and Kashmir, further nourishing the second great wave of translation and dissemination of the Dharma.

Soon after his arrival, Atiśa composed his short but influential *Lamp for the Path to Enlightenment* (*Bodhipathapradīpa*) as well as his autocommentary on it. These texts were written simultaneously in Sanskrit and Tibetan with the help of his translator Naktso Tsultrim Gyalwa, though now the Sanskrit version is lost. Atiśa's influence in Tibet was immense and enduring. He and his foremost disciple, Dromtönpa, founded the Kadam tradition, which no longer exists but whose influence continues to reverberate in all the remaining traditions of Tibetan Buddhism.

The tradition that it is said to have influenced most deeply is the Geluk tradition founded by Tsongkhapa and his immediate disciples, since this incorporates three lineages of the Kadam. Moreover, following the format of Atiśa's *Lamp*, Tsongkhapa wrote his famous and detailed *Great Treatise on the Stages of the Path to Enlightenment*, or *Lamrim Chenmo*. Like Atiśa, Tsongkhapa embraced the Prāsaṅgika Madhyamaka philosophy based on Buddhapālita's and Candrakīrti's commentaries on Nāgārjuna's *Fundamental Wisdom of the Middle Way*, which he expounded at length in his

Lamrim Chenmo and other major works. It is to Tsongkhapa's text that I would like to turn now briefly as an example of how Buddhist philosophy evolved in Tibet based on the treatises of the Nālandā masters.

In the previous section we noted that ultimate analysis is used not only in study and debate but also in meditation. Tsongkhapa advocates this approach, citing two distinct types of meditation: stabilizing meditation and analytical meditation. These culminate, respectively, in calm abiding (*śamatha*) and special insight (*vipaśyanā*). Both types of meditation are introduced in part 6 of volume 2 of the present series, where the description of how to develop calm abiding is quite detailed.

The same object can be used in either kind of practice. The difference comes in the way we meditate on the object. In calm abiding meditation we focus on a chosen object single-pointedly. We do not investigate the various aspects and qualities of the object; rather, having mentally gathered all its aspects together and synthesized them into a single thing, we focus on that single thing. In insight meditation we examine the same object but without focusing on it as a single thing. Instead we investigate the focal object by analyzing its aspects and qualities in progressively more detail.

To develop genuine insight into "the way things are" as ultimate reality, we must develop calm abiding. As explained in volume 2, there are nine stages of training to develop calm abiding, and the ninth of these stages is the most subtle and stable mental state of the desire realm.[62] But even this is not a ground of meditation. After the ninth stage we achieve calm abiding; and only at this point, upon entering the first *dhyāna* of the form realm, is our mind a ground of meditation. A mental state of the desire realm is never a ground of meditation—even if we are meditating. The sign of having achieved calm abiding is the experience of a special mental and physical pliancy, which induces a special physical and mental bliss, in that order. The development of calm abiding is vital because we cannot develop special insight without it. Both practices are necessary; the mind of calm abiding must be maintained together with analytical meditation.

When we finish a session of analytical meditation focusing on selflessness, we engage in stabilizing meditation on the meaning of that analysis for some time. By doing this we eventually accomplish the union of calm abiding and special insight—which is when the analytical meditation itself induces a special pliancy and bliss like that of calm abiding, but the result is very different. This now has become genuine special insight, one that has the ability to purify the mindstream of mental afflictions along with their seeds and eventually their imprints. At this point during meditation, only emptiness (*śūnyatā*) appears to the mind, without any dualistic mental image. This is what enables it to be so effective.

Tsongkhapa makes it clear in his *Lamrim Chenmo* that even once we have perceived emptiness directly, we must continue to engage in ultimate analysis during meditation sessions. He supports this with frequent reference to all three texts by Kamalaśīla called *Stages of Meditation*, which state that after establishing calm abiding, we continue to engage in analysis when we meditate. And he explains that when Candrakīrti says in *Entering the Middle Way* that "the yogi negates the self," he means that a yogi uses logical analysis when meditating.

It is a mistake to think that "nonconceptual meditation" involves only nonanalytical meditation. Without analytical meditation, we cannot eliminate distorted conceptions from our minds. So we must first engage repeatedly in analytical meditation, then focus the mind on what is perceived through that analysis. At a certain point, analytical meditation becomes very subtle indeed. Tsongkhapa further explains that having placed the mind single-pointedly on an object, we may not want to engage in analysis because it disturbs our concentration in the early stages. Nonetheless, when precise analytical meditation itself has the power to induce mental and physical pliancy, then it can also induce single-pointed concentration. This means that calm abiding and special insight, once they are sufficiently developed, need not interrupt each other.

This advanced level of analytical meditation is a prime example of how philosophy is used as spiritual practice in Buddhism. In Tsongkhapa's account we find a presentation that perfectly harmonizes the teachings brought over to Tibet during the first dissemination, as exemplified in Kamalaśīla's treatises, and the teachings popularized during the second dissemination, as exemplified in the treatises of Candrakīrti.

As Buddhism gradually disappeared from India, it was in Tibet that the vibrant philosophical traditions of India's famed monastic universities like Nālandā and Vikramaśīla were kept alive. Until the present day, even in exile, the practice of debate continued to form a core part of the monastic curriculum. Two particular Indian Buddhist philosophical heritages, Nāgārjuna's Middle Way (*madhyamaka*) philosophy and Dignāga and Dharmakīrti's epistemology (*pramāṇa*), became major focuses of philosophical inquiry, giving rise to a rich and diverse spectrum of views that still dominate the landscape of philosophy in the Tibetan tradition.

Categories and Views

An essential component of philosophy is the use of categories. These allow things to be identified as belonging to a certain kind; and inclusion or exclusion from specific classes provides a basis for deductive reasoning. A great deal of Buddhist philosophy is expressed in terms of classificatory lists, which include both the objects cognized and the subjects that cognize them. Most of these categories can be traced back to the earliest Buddhist teachings found in both the Northern tradition preserved in Buddhist Sanskrit and local Prakrit languages and the Southern tradition preserved mainly in Pali. Such classification has surely been useful for many reasons. Given that nothing was written down and everything had to be memorized, these lists (*mātṛkā*) facilitated recollection. As Gethin remarks, "The use of lists is an integral part of the literature and directly related to its oral nature. [They] provide a vehicle for the reciter and inform the literature with a structure, . . . what is almost a system of cross-referencing that prevents the reciter from losing his way."[63] He further notes, "Indeed, it is obvious that many Nikāya discourses can be readily resolved into an elaboration of one or more of these lists."[64] Such lists are useful also for a meditator, even today. Reflecting on these categories and subcategories may enable a practitioner to analyze his or her chosen topic in depth without omitting any crucial aspect, yielding an understanding of that thing's conventional or ultimate nature—depending on the style of analysis employed. The various ways of categorizing knowable objects are delineated in volume 1 of the present series.

In volume 2 we encounter the various ways of categorizing subjects, the agents of cognition.[65] Among the lists of *dharmas*, or units of reality, Johannes Bronkhorst identifies the earliest to be a list of seven lists—which he refers to as "List 1."[66] He draws our attention to the fact that the contents of the seven sub-lists are beneficial psychic characteristics, or mental factors, that are cultivated in meditation. These virtuous mental factors are known as the thirty-seven factors conducive to awakening, which include (1) the four foundations of mindfulness, (2) the four perfect endeavors, (3) the four bases of magical powers, (4) the five faculties, (5) the five powers,

(6) the seven aspects of enlightenment, and (7) the noble eightfold path. These lists are expressed in slightly different ways in different sources, but the commentarial explanations generally show that they agree in their fundamental meaning.

The final two volumes in the present series present the philosophical views (*darśana*) or tenets (*siddhānta*) of the various classical Indian traditions. Volume 3 sets out the tenets of each tradition in the context of its own distinct school, which has been admirably summarized in the introductory essay found there. Volume 4, the present volume, addresses specific philosophical views and examines how these are treated in selected traditions. It begins by examining the two truths—the two natures of reality, conventional and ultimate. In a traditional Tibetan text on tenets, this topic is included in the presentation of the basis in the threefold structure of basis, path, and result. As the basis, it encompasses every aspect of reality. Thus in the present volume too the two truths is the first topic. In the context of Buddhist philosophy, the term *conventional truth* is synonymous with "conventional reality" or "conventional nature," and *ultimate truth* is synonymous with "ultimate reality" or "ultimate nature." Here *truth* does not especially apply to phrases, sentences, or propositions. Moreover, the terms *conventional truth* and *conventionally existent* are often not synonymous, and likewise the terms *ultimate truth* and *ultimately existent.* According to the Prāsaṅgika system, nothing is ever ultimately existent; ultimate truth itself is only conventionally existent.

Part 2 of this volume discusses notions of the self and of selflessness in the various Buddhist and non-Buddhist schools. Much of the discussion centers around the relationship between the self, or person, and the psychophysical aggregates (form, feeling, discernment, conditioning factors, and consciousness). In general, non-Buddhist schools adjacent to the early Buddhist philosophers posit a self that, unlike the aggregates, is permanent, partless, and autonomous, while the Buddhist schools refute the existence of such a self. In some contexts the terms *self* (*ātman*) and *person* (*puruṣa*) are equivalent, and in other contexts they are not. The term *self* is sometimes interpreted to mean a "truly existent nature," where the absence of a truly existent nature is equivalent to ultimate truth or emptiness, as we saw above with Candrakīrti's understanding of selflessness.

Part 3 presents the explanation of ultimate reality according the Mahāyāna Buddhist tradition of Yogācāra, which is also called Cittamātra, or

Mind Only. To explain the meaning of the teaching in the Perfection of Wisdom sūtras that "all phenomena have no essential nature," the Yogācāra interpret the essencelessness of phenomena in terms of three natures: all phenomena have a dependent nature that lacks a self-produced nature; all phenomena have an imputed nature that lacks an intrinsically characterized nature; and all phenomena have a consummate nature that lacks an ultimately established dualistic nature. The dependent nature is the causally conditioned nature. The imputed nature is the conceptually constructed nature. The consummate nature is emptiness, which for the Yogācāra means an absence of substantial duality between subject and object. Here it is also represented as the nonexistence of the imputed nature, which is projected onto the dependent nature. The consummate is thus the absence of the imagined externality of the dependent nature. According to the Cittamātra system, nothing is external to the mind; everything is "cognition only" (*vijñaptimātra*). This includes the subject and the object of cognition (sometimes translated in this series as "cognizance"). The object of cognition here is an image that appears in the mind, and it appears owing to the activation of karmic propensities within the mindstream, not an external object.

Part 4 addresses the topic of emptiness in the Madhyamaka tradition. It focuses on how Nāgārjuna interprets the same teaching in the Perfection of Wisdom sūtras that "all phenomena have no essential nature," which he takes to mean that nothing exists by virtue of an essential nature. It explains how our grasping things as having an essential nature arises naturally and habitually, and is the root cause of all mental afflictions and suffering. Nāgārjuna's marshaling of manifold arguments for proving emptiness is meant to uproot this fundamental ignorance. The text then explores several of the most famous ones. The lengthy presentation of the various sets of reasoning refuting essential nature is followed by an examination of what they actually refute. Then there is the question of whether the Mādhyamika posit any assertions according to their own system. This is followed by an investigation into what type of reasoning should be employed—autonomous inferences (*svatantra*) or logical consequences (*prasaṅga*). Finally there is an examination of the meaning of dependent arising, which at its most subtle level is equivalent to emptiness.

Part 5 addresses epistemology, or valid cognition (*pramāṇa*). Although this cannot be separated from any other topic of Buddhist philosophy—all of which concern the development of understanding and perceiving the way things are—it can be studied on its own so as to examine the types of valid cognition, its definition, the object to be known, and the resultant understanding. Some aspects of this topic were presented in volume 2. The main focus in our present volume is inferential valid cognition, which ascertains its object through reasoning.

As we saw above, Dignāga pioneered the great flourishing of Buddhist logic, epistemology, and philosophy of language in the fifth century, and Dharmakīrti is the master who systematized and developed his teachings. Dignāga and Dharmakīrti posit two types of *pramāṇa*—direct perception and inferential cognition—which have, respectively, a particular and a universal as their appearing object. They consider perception to be nonconceptual, though some later Buddhist masters disagree with this. Dignāga and Dharmakīrti also accept four types of perception—sensory, mental, reflexive, and yogic—whereas some later Buddhist masters reject reflexive awareness. Dignāga differentiates between two types of inference: for one's own purpose and for the purpose of others. The former is an inferential cognition within one's own mindstream; the latter is a meaningful statement that induces such a valid cognition in others. Both give access to knowledge of something hidden from sensory perception.

Buddhist and non-Buddhist philosophers disagree about whether the result of *pramāṇa* is the same entity as the *pramāṇa* itself or a different entity. This rests on different ways of employing the term *pramāṇa*. Non-Buddhists use *pramāṇa* to mean the *instrument* of valid cognition, whereas Buddhists following Dignāga's tradition use it to mean the *act* of valid cognition. As for the notion of a correct reason, Dignāga defines this as "that which satisfies the three modes" and determines that there are just three types—effect, nature, and nonperception. He also emphasizes the logical relation that must obtain between the reason and the predicate of the thesis.

An account of epistemology as presented in the Prāsaṅgika Madhyamaka tradition of Candrakīrti is then offered.[67] The main point that distinguishes Candrakīrti's position from that of the Buddhist epistemologists is that he does not accept anything to exist by way of its intrinsic characteristics. Instead, he maintains that subjects that cognize and objects that are cognized exist only in mutual dependence, as merely imputed by thought and linguistic convention. This point also distinguishes Candrakīrti's Prāsaṅgika tradition from Bhāviveka's Svātantrika tradition, where the latter posits that objects exist by virtue of their own characteristics and a valid cognition must validly apprehend its object's intrinsic character. Moreover, according to this understanding of Candrakīrti's position, valid cognition is "cognition that is nondeceptive regarding its principal object."[68] This definition does not exclude subsequent cognitions from being valid, as they are in Dharmakīrti's definition, where valid cognitions must be new. Also according to Candrakīrti, direct perception need not be free of conceptuality. Finally, he does not accept that perception and inference must be differentiated in terms of their epistemic objects being, respectively, a unique particular and a universal.

Part 6 of this volume addresses issues raised in classical Indian philosophy of language. It opens by questioning whether a word indicates a particular individual or a universal, and whether the meaning of a sentence is primary, or that of the words it contains. After touching on the views of various Indian masters, it addresses the question of whether signifying terms engage their objects via affirmation or via exclusion. Dignāga argues that signifying terms engage their objects via exclusion (*apoha*). Here, a signifier denotes its object by excluding what is not it (its converse). So terms do not directly indicate unique particulars but engage them via a universal. The relationship between a term and its referent is merely imputed by thought; it is not established through any causal capacity of real things.

Dharmakīrti accepts Dignāga's theory, though with a subtle difference. Dignāga's presentation revolves around words and their referents, whereas Dharmakīrti examines both language and thought, particularly how a thought engages its object. Dharmakīrti's theory, outlined in chapter 29, is drawn from 143 verses of his *Exposition of Valid Cognition*. In this context, we distinguish between direct perception and conceptual cognition, where the latter, not the former, ascertains its object. Nonetheless, they are causally related because a conceptual cognition links back to the perception that induced it. Dharmakīrti explains that since different individuals produce the same result, a conceptual cognition qualified by excluding what is not it engages its object through combining those different phenomena into a single thing. This way of explaining the exclusion of other seems to have been adopted by most of the Buddhist logicians who came after Dharmakīrti.

This completes the four-volume *Science and Philosophy in the Indian Buddhist Classics*. Many topics contained in these volumes lend themselves to further investigation by Western philosophers. One that springs to mind is the nature of identity, which is a subject of philosophical importance within both Buddhist and Western systems. In the Buddhist context, however, an investigation into the nature of identity (*svabhāva*) provides a tool for uprooting selfishness, greed, and hatred; and given that the structure of human consciousness is a shared inheritance of humanity, such an investigation in the context of Western philosophy could well lead to a similar result. Appropriate attention to this topic could bring great benefit to the world.

Part 1

The Two Truths

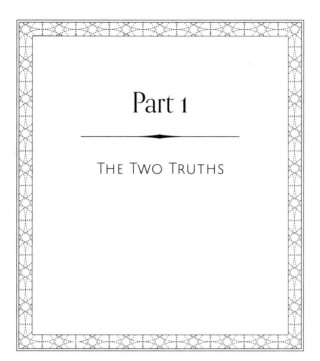

1

Appearance and Reality

IN THE THIRD VOLUME of this series we gave a brief explanation of the main tenets of both non-Buddhist and Buddhist philosophical systems as presented in the classical Indian texts. This fourth volume concerns the views themselves, focusing especially on six important themes. Here we begin by presenting the theory of the two truths—conventional truth and ultimate truth. After having presented the ultimate truth, we investigate the question of self and no-self, with the latter especially in the context of Madhyamaka and Cittamātra views. Then we offer a presentation on classical Indian epistemology, especially its views on knowledge or "valid cognition" (*pramāṇa*). This is followed by some crucially important additional topics pertaining to philosophy of language, especially the notion of word meaning[69] and the Buddhist theory of *apoha*, literally "the exclusion of other." The most important textual sources we have relied on concerning these topics are Nāgārjuna's Six Collections of Reasoning; Āryadeva's *Four Hundred Stanzas*; Buddhapālita's *Commentary on the Fundamental Treatise*; Bhāviveka's *Heart of the Middle Way* and *Lamp of Wisdom*; Candrakīrti's *Clear Words*, *Commentary on the Four Hundred Stanzas*, *Commentary on the Sixty Stanzas of Reasoning*, and *Entering the Middle Way* with its autocommentary; Śāntarakṣita's *Ornament for the Middle Way* with its autocommentary and his *Compendium of Reality*; Kamalaśīla's *Commentary on the Difficult Points in the Compendium of Reality* and *Illumination of the Middle Way*; Jñānagarbha's *Distinguishing the Two Truths* with its autocommentary; Maitreyanātha's *Teachings of Maitreya*; Asaṅga's [2] *Yogācāra Levels*; Vasubandhu's *Twenty Stanzas*, *Thirty Stanzas*, the *Treasury of Knowledge* with its autocommentary, and his commentaries on the *Teachings of Maitreya* and the *Compendium of the Mahāyāna*; the epistemological works of Dignāga and Dharmakīrti and their followers; then several philosophical texts of non-Buddhist masters, such as Īśvarakṛṣṇa's *Verses of Sāṅkhya*, and some texts of non-Buddhist masters on *pramāṇa*, such as Kumārila Bhaṭṭa's *Exposition of Verses on Mīmāṃsā*.

We begin with our presentation of the two truths. Most ancient Indian philosophers generally agree that the way things appear to the ordinary cognition of those whose minds are not inclined toward philosophy does not match the way things exist in reality. Regardless of whether they use the terminology of the two truths—*conventional truth* and *ultimate truth*—when explaining their views on how things exist, it is evident that this is the case. For example, the Sāṅkhya propose twenty-five categories of objects of knowledge. Among these, both the principal or primal nature (Skt. *prakṛti*) and the consciously aware self or person (Skt. *puruṣa*) are ultimate truth, while the remaining twenty-three are said to be mistaken conventional appearances. Moreover, they maintain that when one obtains the wisdom seeing the way things exist, all ordinary phenomena disappear. In a similar manner, the Vedānta state that only the great or pure self, a permanent nondual consciousness, is ultimate truth, while all phenomena that appear dualistically are mere conventional illusions.[70] The Vaiśeṣika and Naiyāyika consider the six categories (*padārtha*) of objects of knowledge—substance, quality, universal, particular, [3] activity, and inherence—to be truly established in reality.[71] These six categories, which encompass all existent phenomena, are posited in terms of their functions, according to which various ways of positing their illustrations occur. So the philosophical systems agree in stating that in the context of rationally ascertaining the mode of existence of something, a distinction is made between what appears or is merely seen temporarily and the ultimate state of existence of something in reality.

However, it is in Buddhist philosophy more generally, and especially among the followers of Nāgārjuna known as Mādhyamikas, that the language of the two truths and the use of the two truths as a foundational framework for establishing the nature of reality is emphasized. As a means to ascertain the way things exist based on the two truths, the Mādhyamikas set forth teachings that are found in the definitive sūtras such as the *Meeting of the Father and Son Sūtra*:

> Thus the Tathāgata comprehends both the conventional and the ultimate, and here the conventional and the ultimate are exhaus-

> tive of what is to be known. Moreover, since the Tathāgata perfectly perceives, perfectly knows, and fully actualizes [them in] emptiness, he is called "omniscient." Of these two, the Tathāgata perceives the conventional to be the purview of the world. That which is the ultimate is inexpressible: it is not an object of knowledge, it is not an object of detailed knowledge, it is not an object of thorough knowledge, [4] it is not shown.[72]

Also this same sūtra says:

> O master of the world, [you teach that] truth is twofold,
> which you perceived yourself without learning it from others—
> that is, conventional truth and ultimate truth—
> for there is no third truth whatsoever.[73]

The *Teachings of Akṣayamati Sūtra* also says:

> Moreover, there are two kinds of truth. What are they? Conventional truth and ultimate truth. Conventional truth, as when [Buddha] spoke of the truths, [includes] the truth of suffering, the truth of its cause, the truth of its cessation, the truth of the path, and the truth of customary classificatory conventions, the manifold indicated by letters, words, and labels. Ultimate truth is the inexpressible attribute: nirvāṇa. Why? Since it is always the suchness[74] of phenomena, it is classed as permanent. Bodhisattvas teach conventional truth, yet they are not at all disheartened; they directly perceive ultimate truth, yet they do not fall [into peace] but bring about the complete maturation of sentient beings. This is known as the bodhisattva's mastery of the truth.[75] [5]

Also, the *Questions Regarding Selflessness Sūtra* frequently makes such statements as the following:

> The conventional and the ultimate
> are correctly explained as two categories:
> mundane phenomena are conventional,
> and the supramundane is ultimate.[76]

On the basis of such definitive sūtras, Nāgārjuna's *Fundamental Treatise on the Middle Way* states:

> The Dharma teaching of the Buddha
> rests on the two truths:
> mundane conventional truth
> and the ultimate truth.
>
> Those who do not understand
> this distinction between the two truths
> do not understand reality in accordance with
> the profound teaching of the Buddha.
>
> The ultimate truth cannot be taught
> independently of customary conventions;
> and without realizing the ultimate,
> nirvāṇa will not be attained.[77]

This passage clearly states that any Dharma teachings spoken by the Buddha concern the two truths. His teachings begin with both the mundane conventional truth and the ultimate truth. Those who do not understand this differentiation of the two truths will not develop an understanding of the profound suchness taught by the Buddha. Furthermore, ultimate truth must be taught in dependence upon the conventional (*tha snyad*) or concealing (*kun rdzob*) truth; [6] and unless one realizes the mode of existence that is the ultimate truth, it is impossible to attain the state of liberation from suffering.

In accordance with this, Jñānagarbha's *Distinguishing the Two Truths* states:

> Those who understand the distinction between the two truths
> will not be confused regarding the Buddha's words.
> Having accumulated the collections[78] completely,
> they will pass beyond to the excellent state.[79]

Candrakīrti's *Entering the Middle Way* also says:

> Conventional truth is the means;
> ultimate truth is the end.
> One who does not understand the distinction between them
> enters an unwholesome path owing to distorted conceptions.[80]

Therefore, when the Madhyamaka texts of Nāgārjuna's disciples establish the way things are, they skillfully teach the distinction between the two truths, the definitions of each, the analyses of whether they are the same or different, the way to realize them, and so forth. Thus there arose a great tradition of establishing the two truths by means of reasoning, an explanation of which is presented below. [7]

2

The Two Truths in Buddhist Realist Schools

The Vaibhāṣika Tradition

First let us explain briefly how the two traditions of Buddhist realists—Vaibhāṣika and Sautrāntika—distinguish the two truths. In the case of the Vaibhāṣika, Vasubandhu's *Treasury of Knowledge* says:

> If something is no longer cognized
> when it is broken or mentally separated apart,
> like a pot or water, then it is conventionally existent.
> What is other than that is ultimately existent.[81]

The definition of conventional truth is: a phenomenon that, if broken or mentally split up, is no longer cognized as that by the mind that apprehended it. The example given here is a pot because when one smashes a pot with a hammer, the mind cognizing a pot is lost; also, when one mentally separates all the parts of a pot, the mind cognizing a pot is destroyed. Thus, once dissipated through mental analysis or destroyed with a hammer, such that the object of the mind apprehending it is lost and the mind cognizing it has ceased, they are considered to have become totally nonexistent. In this regard, *conventional truth* and *imputedly existent* are said to be synonymous.

To explain the etymology of *conventional truth*, since it is the object of a mind cognizing a conventional thing such as a pot, which is considered to be a "customary" or "classificatory convention," it is called "conventional truth." Yaśomitra's *Clarifying the Meaning of the Treasury of Knowledge* states: [8] "Just as it is apprehended by another mundane [cognition], so it is a conventional truth, in that it is apprehended by a conventional cognition or understanding that is either afflictive or nonafflictive. As such, it is a conventional truth."[82]

There are three ways of classifying conventional truth. The first way is in terms of whether it is dismantled physically or mentally, which is twofold. In the case of conventional truth that is dismantled *physically*, an example is a pot, for when a pot is smashed with a hammer, the mind cognizing it is lost. The second case, conventional truth that is dismantled *mentally*, concerns phenomena that cannot be broken by something like a hammer; instead the mind cognizing it is lost when it is mentally dismantled. An example is water, for a collection of water cannot be separated out by a hammer into taste, smell, and so on, but it can be mentally separated into individual constituents, like particles[83] and smell, whereupon the mind cognizing the water is lost. Pūrṇavardhana's *Investigating Characteristics* commentary on the *Treasury of Knowledge* says: "Those dismantled physically are such things as a pot. Those dismantled mentally are such things as water, because it cannot be separated into constituents such as taste by physical means."[84] Thus, if something is a conventional truth that is dismantled physically, then it must also be a conventional truth that is dismantled mentally, but if it is a conventional truth that is dismantled mentally then it need not be a conventional truth that is dismantled physically.

The second way of classifying conventional truth is twofold: a shape convention and a collection convention. The first—a shape convention—applies to things having shape, such as a pot. [9] The second—a collection convention—applies to a collection convention having many parts, such as the water inside a pot. Pūrṇavardhana's *Investigating Characteristics* says: "In one sense, convention is of two kinds: a shape convention, such as a pot, and a collection convention, such as water. Therefore it is spoken of as twofold."[85] The difference between these is as follows. If something is a shape convention then it must also be a collection convention, but if something is a collection convention, then it need not be a shape convention. For example, since water can be mentally separated into components, such as smell and taste, but cannot be physically broken or split into the eight substantial particles, it is not a shape convention.

The third way of classifying conventional truth is twofold: a convention based on other conventions and a convention based on other substances. In the first case—a convention based on other conventions—both those dismantled physically and those dismantled mentally are collection-endowed conventions, such as a pot. The second case—a convention based on other substances—is a convention that when analyzed into its eight constituent substances destroys the mind cognizing it but when physically broken up does not destroy it, such as the water inside a pot. Yaśomitra's *Clarifying the Meaning* says:

> In one sense, there are two kinds of convention: that based on other conventions and that based on other substances. What is a convention based on other conventions? [Losing cognition of it] occurs when it is physically broken up and also occurs when it is conceptually split up. What is a convention based on other substances? [Losing cognition of it] occurs not when it is physically broken up but only when it is conceptually split up [10] because that [cognition of it] cannot be maintained when it is separated into parts such as the eight substantial particles.[86]

So in the case of a pot or suchlike being called "that based on other conventions," the "other" refers to the basic constituents of a pot, such as clay, which differ from the pot itself. As for the water inside a pot being called "that based on other substances," the "other substances" refers to the different material substances present within the collection of water inside the pot, such as the eight substantial particles on which the pot's water is based. *Investigating Characteristics* says:

> Also, [Vasubandhu] posits the two examples, "Like a pot or water, then it is conventionally [existent]," in order to teach about two types of convention. Since pots and so on exist in dependence on their basic constituents such as clay, they are conventions based on other conventions. Since water and so on exist in dependence on physical form and suchlike, they are conventions based on other substances.[87]

The definition of ultimate truth is: a phenomenon that, if broken or mentally split up, continues to be cognized as that by the mind that apprehended it. Examples are directionally partless particles, temporally partless consciousness, and what is not causally compounded. Vasubandhu's *Treasury of Knowledge Autocommentary* says:

> What is other than that is ultimate truth. What is cognized even when it is broken, or is still cognized when mentally split up into other attributes, is ultimately existent. Consider, for example, a physical form. Even though it may be broken apart into subtle particles, [11] or mentally split up into attributes such as taste, the cognition of form's nature persists. Feeling and so on are to be seen likewise. Since it is ultimately[88] existent, it is called *ultimate truth*.[89]

Investigating Characteristics also says:

> As for the statement "Feeling and so on are to be seen likewise," although feeling, discernment, intention, and so on, when considered collectively are conventionally existent, they are seen to be just ultimately existent when considered individually. Why? In the case of feeling and so on, since even when mentally split up, the cognition of feeling's nature persists, feeling is substantially existent. The same also applies to intention and so on.[90]

In the case of form, feeling, and so on, although each has its continuity and parts, since the mind cognizing it is not lost when it is broken or mentally split up, it is said to be ultimate truth. A difference is posited between a physical form that is an ultimate truth and a physical form measuring one cubit that is a conventional truth; and between a feeling that is an ultimate truth and a feeling having three moments that is a conventional truth. *Ultimate truth* and *substantially existent* are said to be synonymous.

To explain the etymology, the wisdom that realizes the ultimate object—partless particles and so on—is called *ultimate*, and the object of this wisdom is called *ultimate truth*. [12] Yaśomitra's *Clarifying the Meaning of the Treasury of Knowledge* says: "Likewise, in the case of *ultimate truth*, since it is the object of ultimate wisdom, it is the ultimate object. While being the ultimate object, it is also true; thus it is the ultimate truth."[91]

There are two kinds of ultimate truth: that which is causal in nature and that which is not causal in nature. The first includes such things as directionally partless particles and temporally partless consciousness, while the second includes unconditioned space.

The Sautrāntika Tradition

Of the two types of Sautrāntika [those who primarily follow scripture and those who primarily follow reason], the Scripture-Following Sautrāntika posit the definitions and illustrations of the two truths in a manner similar to the Vaibhāṣika, though they differ in whether they accept physical form and so on and the three types of noncausal phenomena to be substantially existent. The Reason-Following Sautrāntika, unlike the Vaibhāṣika, posit the two truths based on whether they are ultimately able to perform a function [i.e., are included within a causal process], as defined in Dharmakīrti's *Exposition of Valid Cognition*:

> What is ultimately able to function
> is ultimately existent in this context;
> everything else is conventionally existent.
> These are respectively the particular and the universal.[92] [13]

As this explicitly states, the definition of ultimate truth is: ultimately able to perform a function. Conversely, the definition of conventional truth is: ultimately unable to perform a function. These are respectively explained to be: unique particulars, which are the observed objects of direct perception; and universals, which are the observed objects of conceptual cognition. The differences between unique particulars and universals have already been explained in chapter 12 on Sautrāntika tenets in volume 3 of the present work, *Science and Philosophy in the Indian Buddhist Classics*.

So according to this, the definition of ultimate truth is: that which is ultimately able to perform a function, such as a pot. Ultimate truth, real thing, unique particular, impermanent, causally compounded, and product are said to be synonymous. As for the etymology of *ultimate truth*, if something is true as it appears to an ultimate perceptual cognition, then it is said to be "ultimate truth." The definition of conventional truth is: that which is ultimately unable to perform a function, such as uncaused space. Conventional truth, unreal thing, universal, uncompounded phenomena, and permanent are said to be synonymous. So in the case of *conventional truth* according to this tradition, if something is true as it appears to a conventional conceptual cognition, then it is said to be "conventional truth," and if it is merely true as it appears to a conceptual cognition, then it is said to be "true for thought." Dharmakīrti's *Exposition of Valid Cognition* says:

> Owing to the capacity of thought,
> universals are declared to exist.[93]

The universal *tree* appears to a conceptual cognition apprehending a tree. It appears as a tree owing to the causal capacity of thought, so although it is not true in reality, it is said to fallaciously appear as if it were truly a tree. [14] Conceptual cognition is called "concealing cognition" because it obstructs seeing the appearing image of the unique particular object previously taken as the observed object [of a direct perception]. *Exposition of Valid Cognition* says:

> Real things that are distinct
> appear as one thing to [conceptual] cognition,
> which by its own appearing image
> conceals the appearing image of something else.[94]

In dependence on real individual trees that are different from non-trees, actual individual trees appear as a single kind, as in the case of a cognition apprehending the universal *tree*. So this is a cognition that obstructs seeing particular trees because it is based indirectly on the universal *tree*. Therefore it is said to be "concealing cognition."

In this tradition, particular individual things are considered ultimate truths, whereas uncompounded permanent phenomena are considered conventional truths. These are posited as such according to whether they can function to produce a result. *Exposition of Valid Cognition* says:

> If you say that everything lacks causal capacity,
> we see such capacity in seeds for [producing] sprouts and so on.
> If you accept this to be conventional,
> it would be whatever [you care to call it].[95]

In other words, if production did not exist ultimately, this would contradict a seed's capacity to produce a sprout that is directly perceived. If you accept that it has the capacity to produce a sprout, but only conventionally,

[15] then one might ask, "Is the sprout produced from the seed by way of its own uncommon mode of existence or not?" If not produced in that way, it would be like imputing a snake onto a patterned rope. If produced in that way, it would be incorrect to claim that this presentation is "conventional," as stated in the arguments of the Sautrāntika and Cittamātra schools against the Madhyamaka.

The Sautrāntika say that phenomena [like space] that are not causally compounded are not ultimately existent, which differs from the Vaibhāṣika system. Vasubandhu's *Treasury of Knowledge Autocommentary* says:

> According to the Sautrāntika, those that are not causally compounded are just not substantially existent; they are not substantially distinct, as are form, feeling, and so on. What are they? Space is the mere absence of anything tangible. Those in a dark place who encounter no obstruction call it "space." Analytical cessation is when, through the power of analytical wisdom, proclivities and rebirth cease to occur and further ones are not generated. Nonanalytical cessation is when they cease to occur, not through the power of analytical wisdom, but just because their conditions have not been met. An example is when premature death interrupts the continuity of existence.[96]

That is to say, space, analytical cessations, and nonanalytical cessations are mere negations that are not substantially existent.

Another point of difference between this and the Vaibhāṣika system is as follows. According to the Scripture-Following Sautrāntika, a shape—long, short, and so on—is merely imputed in dependence on the occurrence of different arrangements of color particles, [16] so it is not considered to be substantially existent but is asserted to be imputedly existent. *Treasury of Knowledge Autocommentary* says:

> The Sautrāntika say shape is not substantially existent. For an extended mass of color occurring in one area is designated as "long," a small mass in that area is called "short," one occurring mostly in four directions is called a "quadrangle," and one occurring equally in all directions is called "round." All the rest are like that too. For example, the appearance of a firebrand quickly

> moving laterally in one direction is considered to be "long," and the appearance of it quickly moving in all directions is considered to be "circular." Likewise, shape does not exist substantially as something separate. If it were substantially existent, then it would be apprehended by two [sense faculties]. For, when seen with the eye, it gives rise to the thought "long," and when touched with the body, it gives rise to the thought "long." Thus these two sense faculties would have one observed object. But it is said that "visible form is not apprehended by both of them."[97]

Thus the Vaibhāṣika accept *conventional truth* and *imputedly existent* to be synonymous, also *ultimate truth* and *substantially existent* to be synonymous. The Reason-Following Sautrāntika accept *conventional truth* and *permanent* to be synonymous, also *ultimate truth* and *causally compounded* to be synonymous. The Scripture-Following Sautrāntika posit the two truths in the same way as the Vaibhāṣika, but they do not accept the three phenomena that are not causally compounded to be substantially existent. [17]

3

The Two Truths in Yogācāra

The Yogācāra Tradition: The Three Natures within the Two Truths

The root texts of the Yogācāra or Cittamātra tradition in general are the treatises of Maitreya, such as *Ornament for the Mahāyāna Sūtras* and *Distinguishing the Middle from the Extremes*, as well as the treatises of Asaṅga and Vasubandhu (his later writings in particular). The explicit presentation of the framework of the two truths in these sources is in a manner common to the Mahāyāna tradition as a whole. However, when the Yogācāra tradition establishes their unique understanding of the way things exist, then as already described in the presentation of Cittamātra tenets in the third volume of this series, they do so by differentiating the nature of reality in terms of the theory of the three natures: the dependent nature, the imputed nature, and the consummate nature. To give a rough description of these, the dependent nature is that which arises in dependence on other causes and conditions; the imputed nature is the imputation of an entity and attributes onto them by a reifying cognition; and the consummate or ultimate nature is the emptiness that is the dependent nature (the basis of emptiness) being empty of the imputed nature (the object of negation). This consummate nature—the dependent nature empty of an imputed nature—is said to be the middle way. Thus the Yogācāra say that even a distorted dependent nature, such as a conceptualizing cognition, is truly existent. Based on that dependent nature, the imputed nature—which superimposes a dualistic subject and object as its entity and attributes—is not truly existent. [18] The emptiness that is the dependent nature empty of the imputed nature is truly existent. Maitreya's *Distinguishing the Middle from the Extremes* states:

> Distorted conceptualizing exists.
> It is devoid of duality.[98]

Likewise, when determining the nature of phenomena, Asaṅga's *Compendium of the Mahāyāna*, as well as Vasubandhu's *Thirty Stanzas*, his *Twenty Stanzas* with its autocommentary, and so on provide explanations mainly based on the three natures. What are considered the unique points of the Yogācāra interpretation of the suchness of phenomena based on the three natures will be presented below [in part 3].

The three natures are included within the two truths as follows. The dependent nature and the imputed nature are posited as conventional truth, while the consummate nature is posited as ultimate truth. Maitreya's *Distinguishing Phenomena from Ultimate Reality* says:

> When all these things are summarized,
> they are to be known as twofold,
> for everything is included within
> phenomena and its ultimate reality.[99]

Truth is divided into two kinds because it is posited from the perspective of two kinds of cognition, as Vasubandhu explains in *Principles of Exegesis*: "Thinking of the objects of a mundane consciousness and the objects of a supramundane consciousness, [the Buddha] posited two truths: conventional truth [19] and ultimate truth."[100]

The definition of conventional truth is: that which is found by valid conventional analysis—where this valid conventional analysis is established as valid conventional analysis regarding that object. Examples of this are shape and color. Vasubandhu's *Principles of Exegesis* says: "Actions and their ripened [effects] are substantially existent conventionally. They do not exist ultimately because they are objects of mundane consciousness."[101] The following are synonymous: conventional truth, falsity, deceptive phenomena, and phenomena that do not exist as they appear.

To explain the etymology, what is true, or what exists from the perspective of or by means of any of the three—an imputation convention, a cognition convention, and an expression convention—is a conventional truth. Vasubandhu's *Principles of Exegesis* says: "An expression is a convention, so the truth known by means of it is a conventional truth—in other words, that which it signifies. For example, a ford to be crossed by foot is called a *foot-ford*."[102] In an etymological explanation of conventional truth, the three types—an imputation convention and so on—are posited respectively as the three: a conceptual cognition that projects an imputation, a mistaken cognition that has a dualistic appearance, and a signifying term. [20]

Also, since an imputed nature is not truly existent, when it is imputed by thought it is called an *imputation convention*. Although external objects do not exist, when a dependent nature thinks of an object, since it is a cognition, it is called a *cognition convention*. As for the consummate nature, although it cannot be taken as an object just as it is by a signifying term or thought, since it can be expressed by certain synonyms—suchness and so on—it is called an *expression convention*.

Conventional truth is of two kinds: imputed phenomena and dependent phenomena. This tradition asserts conventional truth to be phenomena that are not the final focal object of a pure path,[103] so it follows that all dependent and imputed phenomena are conventional truths. But since they posit *conventionally existent* to mean existing through the capacity of a convention, it follows that only the imputed nature is conventionally existent. The dependent nature and the consummate nature are ultimately existent, so they do not exist conventionally. Therefore one must distinguish between how this tradition posits *conventional truth* and *conventionally existent*.

The definition of ultimate truth is: that which is found by a reasoning consciousness analyzing the final nature, where this reasoning consciousness is established as a reasoning consciousness analyzing the final nature of that object. An example of this is the emptiness of substantial duality between subject and object. As it says in the *Unraveling the Intention Sūtra*: "Subhūti, that which is the pure focal object in relation to the aggregates is proclaimed to be the ultimate truth."[104] The following are synonymous: consummate, emptiness [21], suchness, the perfect culmination, signlessness, ultimate truth, the dharma expanse, and so on. Maitreya's *Distinguishing the Middle from the Extremes* states:

> When emptiness is summarized,
> it is synonymous with suchness,
> the perfect culmination, signlessness,

> the ultimate, and the dharma expanse.[105]

The meaning of suchness and so on is explained in Vasubandhu's *Commentary on Distinguishing the Middle from the Extremes*:

> It is *suchness* since it is not otherwise, for it is always just so. It is the *perfect culmination* since it is not distorted, for it is not a basis of distortion. It is the *signless* since it is the cessation of signs, for it is the total absence of all signs. It is the *ultimate* since it is the object of experience of an ārya's exalted wisdom, for it is the object of ultimate wisdom. It is the *dharma expanse* since it is the cause of the ārya dharmas, for the ārya dharmas arise due to perceiving it. Here the meaning of *expanse* is "cause."[106]

To explain the etymology [given here for] ultimate truth, an ārya's exalted wisdom of meditative equipoise is ultimate, and in being the object of that [wisdom, ultimate truth] is the ultimate object.[107] And since the object of that wisdom is true, it is called *truth*. *Principles of Exegesis* says: "The supramundane is the ultimate exalted wisdom; and since it is the object (*don*) of that [wisdom], the ultimate [22] is that which is its object (*yul*)."[108]

When it comes to categorizing ultimate truth, Vasubandhu's *Commentary on Distinguishing the Middle from the Extremes* lists sixteen types in terms of the subject or basis of emptiness. However, we need not discuss this here because—apart from some dissimilarity regarding the different objects of negation, and substituting the emptiness of things for the emptiness of the imperceptible in the fifteenth place—it is the same as the presentation given in Candrakīrti's *Entering the Middle Way Autocommentary*.[109] In terms of how the object of negation appears to cognition, there are two ways: the emptiness that is the emptiness of existing by virtue of its own characteristics as the basis of conception of a thought apprehending it, which applies to all phenomena; and the emptiness that is the emptiness of substantial difference between cognizer and cognized, which only applies to phenomena that are causally compounded. Thus they differ in scope.

Ornament for the Mahāyāna Sūtras says that ultimate truth is endowed with five characteristics:

> Neither existent nor nonexistent, neither the same nor different,
> neither arising nor disintegrating, neither diminishing
> nor increasing, and devoid of purification yet purified:
> these are the characteristics of the ultimate.[110] [23]

The five characteristics are the characteristic of neither existing nor not existing, the characteristic of being neither the same nor different, the characteristic of neither arising nor disintegrating, the characteristic of neither increasing nor diminishing, and the characteristic of being devoid of purification yet being purified. The meaning of these five is stated respectively as follows: (1) Ultimate truth is not existent as an imputed nature nor as a dependent nature, but it is not nonexistent as the consummate nature, which is characterized as the mere absence of the object of negation. (2) It is not the same conceptual identity (*ldog pa*) as the dependent nature, its basis of emptiness, yet it is not a different individual entity (*ngo bo*). (3) It does not arise or disintegrate. (4) It is not exhausted by the exhaustion of the thoroughly afflictive, and it is not increased by the increase of the perfectly pure. (5) It is forever free from the natural stain [of true existence] so it is not made pure again, yet it is not that it is not purified of the temporary stains.[111] Since these five characterize the ultimate truth as an object of cognition, it is said that the ultimate truth is endowed with these five characteristics. In his commentary explaining the meaning of Maitreya's *Ornament for the Mahāyāna Sūtras*, Vasubandhu states:

> The nondual object is the ultimate; also the nondual object is correctly indicated by way of five features. With the characteristics of the imputed nature and the dependent nature it is nonexistent, but with the characteristics of the consummate nature it is not nonexistent. The imputed nature and the dependent nature are not identical with the consummate nature, so they are not the same, yet they are not other than it, so they are not different. The dharma expanse is not causally compounded, so it does not arise or disintegrate. It remains the same in the case of the cessation and the production of the thoroughly afflictive and the perfectly pure [respectively]; [24] thus it does not diminish or increase. It is not afflictive by nature, so it does not become

> pure, yet it is freed from the temporary afflictions, so it is also not unpurified. These five characteristics of nonduality should be understood to be the characteristics of the ultimate.[112]

Asaṅga's *Compendium of Ascertainments* states: "The ultimate has five characteristics: the characteristic of inexpressibility, the characteristic of nonduality, the characteristic of being beyond objects of logical analysis, the characteristic of being beyond difference and non-difference, and the characteristic of being the single taste of everything."[113] This account of how the ultimate possesses five characteristics is a little different from that given in Maitreya's *Ornament for the Mahāyāna Sūtras*.

The Yogācāra school considers the nondual consummate nature—which is the emptiness of the imputed nature (a superimposed substantial difference between cognizer and cognized) on the basis of the dependent nature—to be truly established. However, Bhāviveka's *Blaze of Reasoning* says:

> A nondual real thing
> is untenable because it is contradictory.
> Is a nonexistent sky flower real?
> Do not imagine it to be real!
>
> If it is a nondual real thing, how could it be nonexistent? [25] If it is nonexistent, then it is not a real thing. Therefore a nondual real thing is untenable because it contradicts your own assertions. If you maintain that since it is always ascertained only in a nondual manner, such nonexistence itself is a real thing. In that case, there will be the consequence that the nonexistence of a sky flower could also be a real thing. If you do not accept the nonexistence of a sky flower to be a real thing, you cannot conceive nonduality to be a real thing either.[114]

Thus he says that the dependent nature being empty of the imputed nature is an instance of nonexistence, and nonexistence is not admissible as truly existent. For if it were admissible then this would incur the fallacy that although a sky flower does not exist, it is nevertheless real and therefore truly existent.

Vasubandhu's *Thirty Stanzas* says:

> The consummate [nature], based on that [dependent nature],
> is the eternal nonexistence of the above [imputed nature].[115]

As already noted, the consummate nature is the nonexistence of an imputed nature, such as a substantial difference between cognizer and cognized, projected onto a dependent nature. It is an unreal thing in relation to the imputed nature and the dependent nature, though it is a truly existent real thing in relation to the consummate nature. There is no contradiction between the two. Therefore, even though we accept the consummate nature to be both an absence as well as truly existent, there is no problem here. However, to point out that for those who think in this way, the same above-mentioned fault remains, the *Blaze of Reasoning* states:

> If they think that the ultimate is not different
> from the nonexistence of the imputed, then [26]
> since it is like the presentation of a definition
> and the thing defined, this is not the answer.

> [An opponent says] there is no difference between the nonexistence of the imputed nature and of the dependent nature within the consummate nature. However, when the thing defined and its definition are presented, the defined thing itself and its definition are said to be a "nondual real thing," so if something is a nondual real thing, how can it be nonexistent? If it does not exist, it is contradictory to call it a "real thing," because it is similar to the case already demonstrated. The answer presented by the opponent remains unsatisfactory.[116]

In the case of the object of negation, one might allow that the consummate nature is the nonexistence of an imputed nature such as a superimposed self of phenomena,[117] or indeed the nonexistence of a dependent nature where cognized and cognizer are substantially different [both of which are objects of negation in this system]. However, in the context of giving a presentation of a thing defined and the definition based on it, the thing defined is considered to be a dependent nature that is nondual and has the characteristic of being truly existent. As stated earlier, if something is nondual and truly existent, then it cannot be an unreal thing. Being an unreal thing contradicts being truly existent. Since it succumbs to this fault of entailing a contradiction, the answer given by the opponent to refute this fault is not correct. That is the main point here.

In brief, although the Yogācāra masters offer a presentation of the two truths that accords with the Mahāyāna in general, their main approach remains that of presenting the nature of reality in terms of the theory of the three natures. Furthermore, they do not seem to offer a comprehensive account of how to relate this to the framework of the two truths. [27] It is for these reasons that Madhyamaka masters such as Bhāviveka, Candrakīrti, and Jñānagarbha took their theory of the three natures as a special object of critique and engaged in its refutation.

4

The Two Truths in Madhyamaka

The Definition and Enumeration of the Two Truths

As mentioned, the Buddhist philosophers who prioritize the framework of the two truths for establishing the way things exist are the Mādhyamika: Nāgārjuna and his disciples. Among Nāgārjuna's disciples are the Svātantrika Mādhyamika, who follow masters such as Bhāviveka, and the Prāsaṅgika Mādhyamika, who follow masters such as Buddhapālita and Candrakīrti. Although there are several minor differences between their explanations of the two truths, their ways of positing the definition or essential nature of each of the two truths, and of establishing their number, are the same.

First, the definition of ultimate truth for a Mādhyamika is: the object found by valid cognition analyzing the final nature, with regard to which that valid cognition becomes a valid cognition analyzing the final nature. Alternatively, the definition of ultimate truth is: the object realized by a mind that realizes it directly without any dualistic appearance.[118] The *Meeting of the Father and Son Sūtra* gives a lengthy explanation using numerous statements of negation, which begins with the extract quoted above: "That which is the ultimate [28] is inexpressible, for it is not to be cognized,"[119] up to "Thus whatsoever phenomenon and whatsoever kind of expression, that expressed phenomenon is not expressed by that kind of expression."[120] Likewise, *Teachings of Akṣayamati Sūtra* says: "Regarding the ultimate there is no movement of mind, let alone speech."[121] This clearly states that in the case of ultimate truth, language and thought cannot get to the object as it is in reality, and phenomena simply do not have an inherently established essential nature. The meaning of these points is presented in Nāgārjuna's *Fundamental Treatise on the Middle Way*:

> Not known by means of another, calm,
> not elaborated by elaborating tendencies,
> devoid of conceptualization, without differentiation:
> these are the characteristics of ultimate reality.[122]

Here, ultimate reality is described as endowed with five characteristics: (1) It cannot be known from teachings given by someone else but must be cognized directly for oneself. (2) It is calm in that it is empty by nature. (3) It is not elaborated by the elaborating conceptualizations, so it is free from elaboration.[123] (4) It is devoid of conceptualization in that it is free of discursive thought investigating *this or that*. (5) It is without differentiation in that the ultimate nature of phenomena is of one taste, so ultimately things are not discrete. [29]

In accordance with how it is stated above in *Fundamental Treatise on the Middle Way*, Bhāviveka in *Blaze of Reasoning*, his *Heart of the Middle Way* autocommentary, identifies the essential nature of ultimate truth:

> It establishes the negation of
> all the nets of conceptualization;
> calm, [known through] one's own cognition,
> without thought, without words,
> beyond sameness and difference,
> and stainless like the sky.
> It is wisdom that engages
> with non-engagement that knows the ultimate.
>
> To explain these words, that which "establishes the negation of all the nets of conceptualization" is the ultimate nature of phenomena because it is a state in which all the nets of conceptualizations have been cleared away, such as permanent and impermanent, existent and nonexistent, eternal and annihilated. "Calm" means it is completely beyond all elaborations. "One's own cognition" means it is not known from someone else. "Without thought" means it is without discursive thought such as investigation. "Without words" means it is not something that can be expressed. "Beyond sameness and difference" means it cannot be expressed as the same, or different, or both,

> or neither. "Stainless like the sky" means that just as the sky is free of layers of clouds, it is stainless. With regard to the ultimate nature of phenomena, there is "engaging with non-engagement" in the factors mentioned above, because [a mind of wisdom] is engaging with that non-appearance and non-engagement itself. This is "wisdom that knows the ultimate." As it has been taught, [30] "Not-seeing is seeing suchness."[124]

Furthermore, all authoritative Madhyamaka treatises, such as Āryadeva's *Four Hundred Stanzas*, Candrakīrti's *Entering the Middle Way* with its autocommentary, Śāntideva's *Engaging in the Bodhisattva's Deeds*, Jñānagarbha's *Distinguishing the Two Truths*, and Śāntarakṣita's *Ornament for the Middle Way*, agree in how they establish the ultimate truth to be beyond linguistic and conceptual elaborations. In addition, from among these texts, the meaning of the words of Śāntideva's *Engaging in the Bodhisattva's Deeds*, "The ultimate is not an object of intellect,"[125] has been examined extensively in a great many commentaries by Tibetan masters.

To explain the etymology of *ultimate truth*, or literally *ultimate object truth*, since it is the "object" found by the "ultimate" wisdom of nonconceptual meditative equipoise, it is the "ultimate object." Since it is not deceptive—in that how it appears to exist is not different from how it actually exists—it is called "truth." As for a general interpretation of the term *ultimate*, Bhāviveka's *Blaze of Reasoning* states:

> As for *ultimate object*, it is called "object" because this indicates that which is to be known, that which is to be investigated, that which is to be understood; and "ultimate" because this means "supreme." So the compound *ultimate object* indicates both the object and the ultimate. Or, it indicates the object of the ultimate, because it is the object of ultimate nonconceptual wisdom. Alternatively, [31] it indicates the approximate ultimate: since both a direct realization of the ultimate and a conceptual wisdom that approximates it have the ultimate [as their object], the latter is called the *approximate ultimate*.[126]

In accordance with this passage, there are three ways of explaining the etymology of *ultimate object*: (1) Where the two terms [*ultimate* and *object*] refer to one and the same thing, it is called "object" since it is that to be realized, and it is called "ultimate" since it is the supreme object. (2) Where the two terms mean "object of the ultimate" in reference to a subject and object, the term *ultimate* indicates the experiencing subject, in this case the ultimate nonconceptual wisdom, while *object* indicates what is obtained by such wisdom. (3) Something that exists from the perspective of inferential analytical wisdom realizing emptiness via a mental image of it, which approximates the nonconceptual wisdom realizing the ultimate, is also called "ultimate" since it accords with the ultimate [i.e., the object of the nonconceptual wisdom that it approximates]. Candrakīrti's *Clear Words* says, "Since it is the object as well as the ultimate, it is the 'ultimate object.' And since it is the truth, it is the ultimate truth."[127] This seems to accord with the first of the three etymological meanings given in *Blaze of Reasoning*.

In general, a crucial difference needs to be drawn between "ultimate" as it occurs in the context of discussing ultimate truth and "ultimate" as it occurs in the context of analyzing whether things exist ultimately. In the former context, "ultimate" is the suchness of phenomena, which is the ultimate truth. This "ultimate" in the first sense is something that the Mādhyamika themselves accept. "Ultimate" in the second sense is something that cannot be posited even on the conventional level, and as such its existence remains untenable.

Second, the definition of conventional (*kun rdzob*) truth is: the object found by valid cognition analyzing the conventional (*tha snyad*), [32] with regard to which that valid cognition becomes a valid cognition analyzing the conventional.[128] Alternatively, the definition of conventional truth is: the object realized by a mind that realizes it directly along with a dualistic appearance. In the context of identifying the essential nature of conventional truth, the *Meeting of the Father and Son Sūtra* says, "The Tathāgata perceives the conventional to be the purview of the world."[129] Likewise, the *Teachings of Akṣayamati Sūtra* states, "What is conventional truth? It is the manifold indicated by customary classificatory conventions, letters, words, and labels."[130] So customary classificatory conventions and the various mundane appearances that are objects of language and thought are said to be true merely conventionally (*tha snyad*) or for the concealer (*kun rdzob*). This point is put forward concisely and clearly in Jñānagarbha's *Distinguishing the Two Truths*:

> Only what corresponds to appearances is the conventional.[131]

Accordingly, the Madhyamaka treatises state that the ultimate truth, being of one taste, is reality as it is (*ji lta ba*), while truth for a concealing mind is the manifold (*ji snyed pa*), or the conventional (*tha snyad*).

The etymology of *conventional truth* (Skt. *saṃvṛtisatya*, literally "truth for the concealer") is: That which, although true from the perspective of ignorance (a concealing mind that obscures the seeing of suchness), is in reality not true; hence it is called "truth for the concealer." Jñānagarbha's *Distinguishing the Two Truths* says:

> That by which something is
> obstructed is called a concealer. [33]
> Thus everything that is true for this [concealer]
> is not true as an object of the ultimate.[132]

The meaning of "conventional" in the context of *conventional truth* is expressed in the *Descent into Laṅkā Sūtra*:

> Conventionally, real things exist;
> ultimately, they do not inherently exist.
> What is mistaken regarding the lack of inherent existence
> is asserted to be conventional truth.[133]

Here, the word "conventional" in the context of conventional truth refers to the ignorance grasping at true existence. Additionally, it is very important to understand what Candrakīrti explains as three senses of the term *conventional* based on the meaning of *saṃvṛti* (the Sanskrit word for "conventional") as stated in his *Clear Words*:

> The term *saṃvṛti* means "to completely block," and since ignorance completely obstructs the suchness of things, it is called a "concealer" (*saṃvṛti*). Alternatively, *saṃvṛti* means "reciprocity"; it is a convention meaning "mutually dependent." Alternatively, *saṃvṛti* means "linguistic convention" or "customary classificatory convention," having the characteristics of the signifier and the signified, the knower and the known, and suchlike.[134]

On the first interpretation, the term *saṃvṛti* in the context of *conventional truth* refers to the delusion of ignorance grasping at true existence—which blocks or obstructs the perception of the ultimate mode of existence; [34] from this perspective, conventional phenomena appear true and are therefore called "conventional truth." On the second interpretation, the way in which phenomena conventionally exist is to exist as dependently related; thus they are said to exist conventionally or relatively. On the third interpretation, "conventional" refers to linguistic conventions (initially applied) and classificatory conventions (later employed), so this teaches that inner and outer phenomena are conventional in that they are merely posited by linguistic labels and classificatory conventions.[135]

As for establishing the definitive enumeration of truth into two only, it is explained as follows. The nature of phenomena is twofold in terms of the *way it appears* and the *way it exists* in the final analysis. Alternatively, objects of knowledge are divided into the two truths because they are found by two different types of cognition.[136] Moreover, as cited above, the *Meeting of the Father and Son Sūtra* says, "And here the conventional and the ultimate are exhaustive of what is to be known," which presents a twofold enumeration in relation to objects of knowledge. In general there are three types of definitive enumeration: definitive enumeration as mutually excluding; definitive enumeration eliminating distorted conceiving;[137] and definitive enumeration with a purpose. The definitive enumeration in this context is definitive enumeration as mutually excluding, meaning no third alternative is available. Also, from the teachings given in the *Meeting of the Father and Son Sūtra* it can be understood that there is no third truth. Candrakīrti's *Entering the Middle Way Autocommentary* says, "Likewise, one should understand that any truth that exists at all can only be included within the two truths."[138] So, everything having the name "truth" that is taught in the *Ten Levels Sūtra*, [35] the *Teachings of Akṣayamati Sūtra*, and so on—such as genuine truth, differentiated truth, and definitely realized truth—is clearly established to be included within the two truths.

Now let us consider the reasoning that establishes the definitive enumeration of the two truths. Truth is enumerated as two on the basis of objects of knowledge because, given that there are two kinds of objects of knowledge, there is no need for more and no possibility of fitting into less. In the case of the pair—the deceptive (i.e., the conventional) and the nondeceptive (i.e., the ultimate)—when one side is denied the other side is necessarily affirmed, and when one side is affirmed the other side is necessarily denied, because the two truths are directly contradictory in the sense of being mutually excluding, just as physical and nonphysical. This accords with what Kamalaśīla says in his *Illumination of the Middle Way*:

> The defining characteristics of any pair of factors that are mutually excluding are as follows: if one is not established via positive determination when its opposite is eliminated via negative determination, then neither exists. These characteristics of mutual exclusion are all-pervasive; and in being all-pervasive, they eliminate any other possibilities. Consider, for example, *embodied* and *non-embodied*.[139] [36]

THE RELATIONSHIP BETWEEN THE TWO TRUTHS

Although all Buddhist philosophical systems agree that there is a definitive enumeration of truth as twofold with respect to objects of knowledge, they do not agree about whether the two truths are the same entity or different entities. The Vaibhāṣika—in taking *ultimate truth* and *substantially existent* to be synonymous, and *conventional truth* and *imputedly existent* to be synonymous—posit the two truths to be two different substantial types; thus they consider them to be different entities. Likewise, the Reason-Following Sautrāntika posit *ultimate truth* to be that which is able to perform a function, or which has the capacity to produce its own effect; and they posit *conventional truth* to be that which is a universally characterized, uncompounded phenomenon that lacks the capacity to produce its own effect, and so on; thus they appear to consider the two truths to be different entities. As for the Mahāyāna schools, both Yogācāra and Madhyamaka understand the two truths to apply to a single thing as a *basis of attributes* and its *attribute*; thus they skillfully present the two truths to be the same entity. In the case of the Mādhyamika in particular, in reliance on statements such as "Form is empty, emptiness is form, form is not other than emptiness, emptiness is not other than form," from the *Heart Sūtra*,[140] and "Kāśyapa, according to the Middle Way that finely investigates phenomena, their emptiness [37] does not make phenomena empty because phenomena themselves are [already] empty," from the *Kāśyapa Chapter Sūtra*,[141] they define the ultimate truth to be the final nature of the thing, which is the basis of emptiness, and firmly establish it to be not a different entity from that [thing]. Nāgārjuna's *Commentary on Bodhicitta* presents the same point, with an example:

> The ultimate is not observed to be a
> different [entity] from the conventional,
> because the conventional is explained in terms of emptiness
> and emptiness only in terms of the conventional;
> thus one does not occur without the other,
> just like the produced and the impermanent.[142]

Ultimate truth or suchness does not exist as a different entity from the conventional phenomena upon which it is based. Conventional phenomena, as the basis of emptiness, are empty of existing by their own nature. Therefore those two—conventional truth that is the basis of emptiness and ultimate truth that is its emptiness—are not different entities, just like the produced and the impermanent.

The two truths do not apply to different objects. Instead, in relation to a single object, they apply to that which is found by either of two types of mind: a mind that sees the false [mode of existence] or a mind that sees the actual mode of existence. This is stated in Candrakīrti's *Entering the Middle Way*:

> Everything is found to have two natures
> as apprehended by correct or mistaken seeing.
> What is seen by perfect vision is the ultimate truth [38]
> and what is seen by mistaken vision is conventional truth, it is
> taught.[143]

A single sprout, for example, has two natures: that which is found by a conventional mind is its conventional nature and that which is found by a mind cognizing ultimate reality is its ultimate nature. The way the two truths are posited on the basis of one thing is clearly expressed in the *Entering the Middle Way Autocommentary*:

> The ultimate is the *own nature* (*bdag gi ngo bo*) that is found
> because it is the special object of the exalted wisdom of those

> who see correctly, though it is not established by its own nature. So that is one nature. The other is the *own being* (*bdag gi yod pa*) that is found by means of the mistaken seeing of ordinary beings whose wisdom-eye is completely covered by the cataract of ignorance, yet such a nature as that which is the object of ordinary seeing is not established by its own nature. Therefore all things are apprehended as having two natures.[144]

When examining whether the two truths are the same entity or different entities, there is an important point one must understand. The *Unraveling the Intention Sūtra* says that if one accepts the two truths to be different entities (*ngo bo tha dad*), then four unacceptable consequences would ensue; and if one accepts them to be the same conceptual identity (*ldog pa gcig*), then four unacceptable consequences would ensue.

Regarding the former (the four objections against the two truths being different entities) [39] the first is as follows. The "Questions of Suviśuddhamati" chapter in the *Unraveling the Intention Sūtra* says:

> If the defining characteristics of conditioning factors and the defining characteristics of the ultimate were different, then those who see the truth would not become free from the signs of conditioning factors. Because they do not become free from the signs of conditioning factors, those who see the truth would not become liberated from the fetters of the signs. If they do not become liberated from the fetters of signs, they would not become liberated from the fetters of the sorrowful states of existence.[145]

So if the two truths were different entities, then, as stated above, the following fault would ensue: even when seeing the ultimate truth—emptiness—based on a conventional thing such as a pot, one would not be able to abandon one's conceptual grasping at that conventional thing; it would become impossible to abandon conceptual grasping at conventional phenomena; it would be impossible to become liberated from the fetters at any time whatsoever; and so on.

As for the second objection, the "Questions of Suviśuddhamati" chapter in the *Unraveling the Intention Sūtra* says: "If the defining characteristics of conditioning factors and the defining characteristics of the ultimate were different, then among all the characteristics of conditioning factors, the characteristics of the ultimate would not be one of their general characteristics."[146] This states that if the two truths were different entities, then the emptiness of the self of phenomena based on a pot and so forth would not exist as a general characteristic of conventional things such as a pot; so pots and so on would not be empty of the self of phenomena. [40]

As for the third objection, the same chapter in the *Unraveling the Intention Sūtra* says: "If the characteristics of conditioning factors and the characteristics of the ultimate were different, then conditioning factors' mere selflessness or mere lack of essential nature would not be characteristics of the ultimate."[147] In other words, the following fault would ensue: if the two truths were different entities, then the emptiness based on conventional things such as a pot would not be the ultimate mode of existence of a pot and so on.

As for the fourth objection, the sūtra continues: "It would follow that the characteristics of the thoroughly afflictive and the characteristics of the completely purified would at the same time be established as different characteristics."[148] In other words, the following fault would ensue: if the two truths were different entities, then even buddhas would see conventional phenomena and ultimate phenomena as different entities at the same time.

Now let us make these objections a little easier to understand. If forms and so on were different entities from the ultimate truth, which is the suchness of those forms and so on, then the following four faults would ensue. (1) The mind realizing the emptiness of form would not harm the thought grasping at the true existence of form, just as, for example, a valid cognition of the presence of fire on a mountain pass would not harm the reifying apprehension of the presence of fire on a lake. (2) The emptiness of true existence of a form would not be the mode of existence of that form, just as, for example, a pot is not the mode of existence of a woolen shawl. (3) The mere negation of the conceptual elaboration of true existence based on a form would not be the suchness of that form, just as, for example, [41] a pot is not the suchness of a woolen shawl. (4) Buddhas who see suchness would see forms as truly existent and would see their emptiness of true existence separately, just as, for example, a form is seen as causally compounded and that which is not causally compounded is seen separately.

Regarding the latter (the four objections against the two truths being conceptually identical) the first is as follows. The "Questions of Suviśuddhamati" chapter in the *Unraveling the Intention Sūtra* says: "Suviśuddhamati, if the characteristics of conditioning factors and the characteristics of the ultimate were not different, then even all ordinary beings would see the truth; and merely having become just an ordinary being, one would attain the unsurpassable bliss of nirvāṇa."[149] In other words, the following fault would ensue: if the two truths were not different conceptual identities, then even ordinary beings would directly see the ultimate truth just as they directly see conventional things, and in seeing that, ordinary beings would become liberated without effort.[150]

As for the second objection, the same chapter in the *Unraveling the Intention Sūtra* says: "Suviśuddhamati, if the characteristics of conditioning factors and the characteristics of the ultimate were not different, then just as the characteristics of conditioning factors are included among the characteristics of the totally afflictive [class of phenomena], so the characteristics of the ultimate [42] would also be included among the characteristics of the totally afflictive."[151] In other words, the following fault would ensue: if the two truths were not different conceptual identities, then just as seeing conventional things such as a pot gives rise to attachment and so on, likewise seeing the ultimate—the emptiness based on it—would also give rise to attachment and so on.

As for the third objection, the sūtra says: "Yogins would not strive for the ultimate in any way beyond how to see, how to hear, how to discriminate, and how to understand conditioning factors."[152] In other words, the following fault would ensue: just as there is no need for yogins to make effort to directly see conventional things such as pots, likewise it would be purposeless for them to make effort to directly see the ultimate attribute, emptiness.

As for the fourth objection, the *Unraveling the Intention Sūtra* continues: "Suviśuddhamati, if the characteristics of conditioning factors and the characteristics of the ultimate were not different, then just as the characteristics of the ultimate do not have the diversity of the characteristics of conditioning factors, so likewise all the characteristics of conditioning factors would not have diversity."[153] In other words, the following fault would ensue: if the two truths were one conceptual identity, then just as the ultimate truth does not have various different aspects such as shape or color, blue or yellow, [43] likewise conditioned things also would not have these kinds of diversity.

Now let us make these objections a little easier to understand. If forms and so on were the same conceptual identity as the ultimate truth that is the suchness of those forms and so on, then the following four faults would ensue. (1) Ordinary beings who directly see a form would also directly see that form's mode of existence, because form and form's emptiness are one conceptual identity. This is like, for example, a pot and that pot's form [which ordinary beings always perceive simultaneously]. (2) Just as seeing a form gives rise to mental afflictions such as attachment, likewise, seeing a form's emptiness would also give rise to mental afflictions such as attachment. This is like, for example, attachment to an attractive form [which arises within the mindstream of an ordinary being when seeing something attractive]. (3) A yogin would not need to make any effort to realize a form's mode of existence, because a form and that form's mode of existence are one conceptual identity. This is like, for example, an ordinary being seeing a form quite naturally without needing to make any effort. (4) Just as a form's mode of existence does not have various different aspects, form also would not have various different aspects, because a form and that form's mode of existence would be one conceptual identity. This is like, for example, the emptiness of a pot and of a pillar, which, in being the mere negation of the object to be negated, are of one taste.

In brief, according to the followers of Nāgārjuna, the difference between the two truths consists in the difference between the object found by a mind analyzing a single thing in terms of the conventional and in terms of the ultimate. [44] The object found in each context is not established as a different entity. Nāgārjuna's *Seventy Stanzas on Emptiness* says:

> The ultimate truth consists in just that.[154]

External and internal phenomena are empty of true existence, and that emptiness itself is posited to be their ultimate nature or suchness. Also, Nāgārjuna's *Sixty Stanzas of Reasoning* says:

> Nirvāṇa is the only truth.[155]

In other words, the emptiness of inherent nature, which is the natural nirvāṇa, alone is the truth.

Distinction between the Expressible and the Inexpressible Ultimate

As mentioned earlier, those proponents of Buddhist philosophy who focus on the presentation of the two truths (i.e., the Mādhyamika) explain *conventional truth* to be the manifold appearances of phenomena, and *ultimate truth* to be the suchness of phenomena, or reality as it is, whose mode of existence is of one taste. In terms of its entity in general, the ultimate truth seems not to have any internal subdivisions. Nevertheless, three great Svātantrika Madhyamaka masters—Bhāviveka, Jñānagarbha, and Śāntarakṣita—propose in their texts that the ultimate can be differentiated in terms of the *expressible* and the *inexpressible* ultimate, or the *approximate* and the *actual* ultimate. Since [45] Tibetan commentators on Madhyamaka give different explanations as to what exactly is meant by this differentiation and how each of the two are defined, first let us cite the actual texts in which these three Indian masters explicitly present this twofold division of the ultimate.

First, Bhāviveka's *Blaze of Reasoning: Heart of the Middle Way Autocommentary* says:

> *Qualm*: The ultimate is beyond all thought whatsoever; however, the negation of the essential nature of things is an object of language, so would not that negation be nonexistent?
>
> *Response*: There are two kinds of ultimate. The first operates without conceptual activity; it is supramundane, stainless, and free from mistaken elaborations. The second operates with conceptual activity; it accords with the collections of merit and wisdom, it is known as *pure mundane wisdom*, and it involves conceptual elaborations.[156]

Similarly, Bhāviveka's *Summary of the Meaning of the Middle Way* says:

> The ultimate is free from elaborations.
> Of this there are two types:
> the expressible ultimate and
> the inexpressible ultimate.
> The first also has two types:

> the ultimate that is rationally expressible
> and the ultimate negation of arising.
> The four inferential reasonings that refute
> arising from the four alternatives and so on
> are the ultimate negation of arising
> although everything appears as real.
> The emptiness of all elaborations [46]
> should be known as the ultimate
> that is inexpressible.[157]

This text states that in general the ultimate truth is free from elaborations. However, it has two subdivisions: the inexpressible ultimate, which is empty of all the elaborations, and the expressible ultimate, which also is of two types—the ultimate that is rationally expressible and the ultimate negation of arising.

Second, Jñānagarbha's *Distinguishing the Two Truths* says:

> Since the negation of arising and so on
> accords with reality, it is accepted [as ultimate].
> Since the object of negation does not exist,
> clearly its negation does not exist in reality.
> As for an imputed essential nature,
> how could its negation be non-imputed?
> So here, the conventional is
> reality-as-object but not reality [in a real sense].
> That which is nondual in reality
> is free from conceptual elaborations.
> When Mañjuśrī asks about this reality,
> the bodhisattva remained without saying anything.[158]

What the above states is understood as follows. Since the negation of ultimate arising and so on conforms with the wisdom cognizing reality, it is said to be ultimate. Also, since the object of negation—true existence—does not exist at all, clearly its negation does not really exist and is not ultimately established. For how could the negation of an imputed essential nature not be the non-imputed ultimate? It exists conventionally but does not exist ultimately or in reality. [47] Although this kind of non-arising is the ultimate truth or reality, it is beyond all elaborations of arising or not arising ultimately, and therefore it does not exist ultimately.

Third, Śāntarakṣita's *Ornament for the Middle Way* says:

> Therefore in reality
> nothing whatsoever is established.
> So the tathāgatas taught
> the non-arising of all phenomena.
> Since this approximates the ultimate,
> it is called the "ultimate."
> In reality [the ultimate] is free
> from all collections of elaborations.[159]

Śāntarakṣita's autocommentary on these verses says, "Non-arising and so on have been included within veridical conventionalities." Also, "In the case of the ultimate, all the nets of elaborations are abandoned, such as real or unreal, arising or non-arising, empty or not empty. Since non-arising and so on approximate an engagement with that, the term *ultimate* is applied to it."[160] When we examine the intention of the Madhyamaka texts just cited, we find the Madhyamaka tradition [48] considers it crucial to distinguish between *ultimate truth* and *ultimately established*. Although the emptiness or suchness of phenomena and so on is the ultimate truth, it does not ultimately exist; and although it is not a conventional truth, it exists conventionally. A fine distinction between these cases needs to be made.

Also, based on the Madhyamaka texts cited above, some Tibetan Madhyamaka commentators say that the ultimate is divided into two in terms of its essential nature: the emptiness of ultimate arising, ceasing, and so on is the *imputed* ultimate but not the actual ultimate; the *actual* ultimate is beyond all elaborations and cannot be expressed or even cognized as either existent or nonexistent and so on. It is said to be the object directly experienced by an ārya being's exalted wisdom of meditative equipoise, which is a mind of wisdom reflexively aware of itself alone.[161]

According to Jé Tsongkhapa's explanation, this division of the ultimate is from the perspective of the subject, not from the perspective of the ultimate truth itself. He explains the *inexpressible subjective ultimate* to be: an ārya being's exalted wisdom that is free of all elaborations and directly sees emptiness. He posits the *expressible subjective ultimate* (so called since it approximates the ārya's exalted wisdom even though it is not free from all the elaborations) to be either of the two: an ārya being's exalted wisdom of subsequent attainment that realizes ultimate reality by means of an object universal, or the analytical wisdom arisen from thinking that realizes emptiness in reliance on reasoning that refutes arising from the four alternatives and so on. Accordingly, he explains that one must posit the *inexpressible objective ultimate* to be: ultimate reality, or emptiness, as it is seen [49] by an ārya being's exalted wisdom. And one must posit the *expressible objective ultimate* to be: ultimate reality, or emptiness, as it is realized by inferential analytical wisdom arisen from thinking and so on.[162]

Moreover, to understand the meaning of the texts of the three Svātantrika Madhyamaka masters mentioned above, it is crucial to examine the meaning of each point in its context. For example, Bhāviveka's statement from the *Blaze of Reasoning* about this differentiation emerges in the context of responding to the following qualm, anticipating a doubt raised by an opponent regarding the Madhyamaka position: "The sūtras speak of the ultimate as free from all verbal and conceptual elaborations; so is it not contradictory to claim that emptiness—the absence of arising ultimately—can be realized in dependence on reasoning?" In response, he differentiates between two types of ultimate in relation to which the ultimate truth is posited. It is clear that the ultimate that is free from all elaborations specifically refers to the stainless exalted wisdom of an ārya,[163] and it is easy to understand that what is presented in the *Summary of the Meaning of the Middle Way* also accords with the *Blaze of Reasoning*.

As for Jñānagarbha's explanation in *Distinguishing the Two Truths* concerning this issue, it seems primarily aimed at refuting the Yogācāra assertion that the consummate nature is ultimately existent. He states that the absence of ultimate arising is accepted to be the ultimate because it accords with perfect wisdom; however, it is not ultimately established but exists conventionally. The Yogācāra assertion—that the consummate nature (which is the dependent nature [50] empty of the imputed nature) is ultimately established—is not correct. For if the imputed nature that is the object of negation is not truly existent, then it cannot be correct for the consummate nature, which negates it, to be ultimately existent—because it is free from all elaborations such as ultimately arising or not arising. For example, if one examines the sources Jñānagarbha cites, such as the *Instructions of Vimalakīrti Sūtra*, where the bodhisattva Vimalakīrti does not reply when Mañjuśrī asks what the nondual nature is,[164] this master seems to be saying that although the emptiness that negates ultimate arising is the ultimate truth, it is not like the Cittamātra assertion about the consummate nature being ultimately existent. Rather, it exists conventionally or on the conventional level.

Śāntarakṣita states above in his *Ornament for the Middle Way* that nothing at all is established truly or ultimately. The Buddha taught that all phenomena are unborn. This kind of non-arising, since it approximates the object of the ultimate, is accepted to be the ultimate truth. Ultimately it is free from the collection of elaborations such as arising, non-arising, and so on. Thus the meaning of all three texts—Bhāviveka's *Blaze of Reasoning*, Jñānagarbha's *Distinguishing the Two Truths*, and Śāntarakṣita's *Ornament for the Middle Way*—appear to be in agreement.

Now, if the distinction between the expressible and the inexpressible ultimate is to be made in terms of a differentiation regarding the ultimate nature itself, this seems to entail making a differentiation within ultimate truth, which is said to be of one taste and the singular mode of being of all phenomena—the way things truly are. This, however, would be utterly unsuitable. [51] Consider the earlier quotation from Nāgārjuna's *Sixty Stanzas of Reasoning*:

> Nirvāṇa is the only truth;
> thus the buddhas have taught.[165]

The Buddha taught that natural nirvāṇa—the emptiness of inherent nature—is the only truth. So how would the above-stated distinction not contradict this teaching? If, however, one asserts that the emptiness that is the lack of ultimate arising is the imputed ultimate, but not the ultimate truth, then it would have to be a conventional truth. In that case, it would be found by valid conventional analysis, and the reasoning that refutes arising from the four alternatives and so forth would not be ultimate analysis. Furthermore, there would be three truths: conventional truth, the expressible ultimate, and the inexpressible ultimate. The second of these three—the expressible ultimate—would not be subsumed into either of the two truths. In that case, this would contradict the meaning of what is taught in the *Meeting of the Father and Son Sūtra* cited above, that objects of knowledge have a definitive enumeration as two truths [i.e., the two truths are mutually excluding]. Thus it seems many objections would ensue for this suggested position. From this we may conclude that a differentiation of the ultimate is not to be made in terms of an essential difference within the ultimate truth.

In general, all Madhyamaka proponents are in agreement that ultimate truth is beyond any object of language and thought as it is. However, it is important to note that in the texts of Nāgārjuna, the great trailblazer of the Madhyamaka system, and of Prāsaṅgika Madhyamaka masters such as [52] Buddhapālita, Candrakīrti, Śāntideva, and so on, there is no differentiation of the ultimate in terms of the actual and the imputed, or in terms of the expressible and the inexpressible. As to why these masters did not speak of such a differentiation while the three Svātantrika Madhyamaka masters, such as Bhāviveka, did so—and what exactly is the underlying significance of that—is one of the more difficult points with regard to understanding the Madhyamaka presentation of the two truths.

Since the instances of ultimate truth based on various subjects are of one taste—the mere absence of the object of negation—they cannot be differentiated in terms of different aspects, as in the case of phenomena included within conventional truth. As for the subjects that are the bases of emptiness—the various conventional phenomena—different ways of enumerating [ultimate truth] are found in relation to existence and purpose; apart from some divergence with respect to the subtlety and coarseness of what is being negated, the masters of the Madhyamaka and the Cittamātra traditions agree on these different enumerations. A selection of Madhyamaka and Perfection of Wisdom texts illustrate some of these enumerations. First, there is the enumeration of eighteen emptinesses, as presented in the *Kauśika Perfection of Wisdom*:

> What is called the *perfection of wisdom* consists of the eighteen emptinesses. These are as follows: emptiness of the inner, emptiness of the outer, emptiness of the outer and inner, emptiness of emptiness, emptiness of great immensity, emptiness of the ultimate, emptiness of the conditioned, emptiness of the unconditioned, emptiness of that beyond extremes, emptiness of that without beginning or end, [53] emptiness of that not to be discarded, emptiness of the final nature, emptiness of all phenomena, emptiness of defining characteristics, emptiness of the

> unobservable, emptiness of non-things, emptiness of essence, and emptiness of essence of non-things. In brief, these emptinesses are called the *perfection of wisdom*.[166]

Then there is the categorization of the twenty emptinesses, as presented in Haribhadra's *Short Commentary on the Ornament for Clear Knowledge*:

> The collection of wisdom consists of twenty aspects of emptiness that are its instances—namely, the emptiness of: the inner, the outer, both of those, emptiness, great immensity, the ultimate, the conditioned, the unconditioned, that beyond extremes, that without beginning or end, that not to be discarded, the final nature, all phenomena, defining characteristics, the unobservable, essence of non-things, things, non-things, self-entity, and other-entity.[167]

Candrakīrti's *Entering the Middle Way* and its autocommentary outline three ways of categorizing emptiness: brief, extended, and intermediate. First, the brief categorization consists in the selflessness of persons and the selflessness of phenomena. Candrakīrti's *Entering the Middle Way* says:

> In order to liberate sentient beings, the Buddha taught this
> selflessness [54]
> in terms of two aspects, that of phenomena and that of
> persons.[168]

The extended categorization is as follows. (1) *Emptiness of the inner* is the emptiness based on the six internal phenomena, such as the eye sense faculty and so on. (2) *Emptiness of the outer* is the emptiness of the external phenomena that are their six types of objects, such as forms and so on. (3) *Emptiness of the outer and inner* is the emptiness of the inner supports of the sense faculties that are posited as *outer* in terms of not being included among the sense faculties and as *inner* in terms of being pervaded by the continuum of consciousness.[169] (4) *Emptiness of emptiness* is emptiness's emptiness [of inherent nature]. (5) *Emptiness of great immensity* is the emptiness of the ten directions, such as the east, that pervade the entire world and its inhabitants. (6) *Emptiness of the ultimate* is the emptiness of nirvāṇa that is the supreme purpose or goal. (7) *Emptiness of the conditioned* is the emptiness of compounded phenomena that arise in dependence on causes and conditions. (8) *Emptiness of the unconditioned* is the emptiness of uncompounded phenomena that do not rely on causes and conditions. (9) *Emptiness of that beyond extremes* is the emptiness based on that which is free from the two extremes of permanence and annihilation. (10) *Emptiness of that without beginning or end* is the emptiness based on saṃsāra, which is without beginning or end. (11) *Emptiness of that not to be discarded* is the emptiness based on the Mahāyāna that should not be discarded anywhere or anytime. (12) *Emptiness of the final nature* is the emptiness of the suchness or final nature of causally compounded things and so on. (13) *Emptiness of all phenomena* is the emptiness based on the eighteen elements (Skt. *dhātu*). (14) *Emptiness of defining characteristics* is the emptiness based on the definition that encapsulates the general and particular characteristics of phenomena, such as forms and so on. (15) *Emptiness of the unobservable* is the emptiness based on the three times—present things at the time of their occurrence are not perceived, [55] past things having occurred and disappeared are not perceived, and future things about to occur but not yet arisen are not perceived. (16) *Emptiness of essence of non-things* is the emptiness based on non-things, because the essence of the arising of things from a gathering of causes and conditions does not exist inherently.[170] Candrakīrti's *Entering the Middle Way Autocommentary* says:

> And again for the sake of diverse trainees, he expounded
> these two
> in other diverse terms through further enumerations.
>
> This selflessness divided into two aspects was again taught by the Buddha as divided into many, owing to his disciples' various ways of thinking.
>
> After teaching in an elaborate way
> sixteen kinds of emptiness,
> the Buddha summarized these into four,
> and he held these to be the great way as well.
>
> As it says in the *Perfection of Wisdom Sūtra in Eight Thousand Stanzas*: "Subhūti, the great vehicle of the bodhisattvas is as follows: emptiness of the inner, emptiness of the outer, empti-

> ness of the outer and inner, emptiness of emptiness, emptiness of great immensity, emptiness of the ultimate, emptiness of the conditioned, emptiness of the unconditioned, emptiness of that beyond extremes, emptiness of that without beginning or end, emptiness of that not to be discarded, emptiness of the final nature, emptiness of all phenomena, emptiness of defining characteristics, emptiness of the unobservable, and emptiness of essence of non-things."[171]

Although emptiness is posited as the basis in two of these sixteen subdivisions of emptiness—the emptiness of emptiness and [56] the emptiness of the final nature—there is no fault of repetition because they have different purposes. The first is presented to eliminate the idea that the emptiness of outer and inner phenomena is truly established because it is established by an analytical wisdom determining the ultimate. The second is presented to eliminate the idea that this emptiness is truly established because it is the final nature that is established naturally and not created by anyone.

The intermediate categorization is as follows. When the sixteen divisions of emptiness are abbreviated, they are included in four types of emptiness. (1) *Emptiness of things* is the emptiness of the five aggregates that are real things. (2) *Emptiness of non-things* is the emptiness of unconditioned phenomena that are unreal things. (3) *Emptiness of the final nature* is the emptiness based on the final nature or mode of existence of phenomena that is not newly created by a mind realizing emptiness. (4) *Emptiness of other-entity* is the emptiness based on the supreme suchness of phenomena or the other nature.[172] Candrakīrti's *Entering the Middle Way Autocommentary* says:

> As it says [in the same sūtra], having taught emptiness as the sixteen, he again taught emptiness as the four: "Subhūti, moreover, a thing is empty of thing, a non-thing is empty of non-thing, the final nature is empty of final nature, and the other-entity is empty of other-entity." These emptinesses are called the Mahāyāna.[173]

Where Candrakīrti lists the *emptiness of other-entity*, [57] the "emptiness of self-entity" refers to the emptiness of the final nature. Although emptiness is posited as the basis in two of the four divisions of emptiness—the emptiness of self-entity, or final nature, and the emptiness of other-entity—there is no fault of repetition because they have different purposes. The first is presented to dispel the idea that this suchness is truly established as its own nature because it is the final mode of being of things. The second is presented to dispel the idea that this suchness, in being accepted to exist as permanent and as an object of impermanent wisdom, is truly established.

Distinction between Veridical and Distorted Conventionality

An important point in the presentation of the two truths concerns the distinction between two types of conventional truth: veridical conventionality and distorted conventionality. Nāgārjuna's treatises do not appear to distinguish between veridical and distorted conventionality, nor does Bhāviveka's *Heart of the Middle Way* and its autocommentary, where it is explained how conventional truth is like a ladder without which one cannot climb up to the mansion of suchness.[174] When identifying the conventional Bhāviveka states the following: "The term *conventional* refers to all things, forms and the rest, which are undistorted worldly conventions. It is 'truth' because everything is posited according to the valid cognition of sentient beings."[175] So here too, other than positing as conventional truth a thing that is established by conventional valid cognition, [58] there is no mention of any differentiation in terms of veridical and distorted conventional truths. The earliest division of the conventional into veridical and distorted in a Madhyamaka treatise appears to be Jñānagarbha's *Distinguishing the Two Truths*. As cited above, the text says:

> Only what corresponds to appearances is the conventional.[176]

This identifies the essential nature of conventional truth. Then, when presenting the divisions of conventional truth, it says the following:

> Although similar in appearance, it is according to
> whether or not they can perform a function
> that a differentiation is made within the conventional
> between what is veridical and what is nonveridical.[177]

So the conventional is divided into two types—a veridical conventionality and a nonveridical or distorted conventionality—depending on whether it is able to function as it appears to the mind perceiving it. The autocommentary on this says:

> Although cognitions of such things as water or a mirage are similar in how they appear, ordinary people know that they are veridical or nonveridical [respectively] by determining whether they are deceptive or nondeceptive with regard to being able to function according to how they appear. In terms of reality, these two are the same in being empty of essential nature. In terms of corresponding to how they appear, they are distinguished. As for being deceptive or nondeceptive with regard to being able to perform a function, this simply corresponds to popular convention, because [in reality] this too is empty of essential nature.[178] [59]

Illustrations of veridical and distorted conventionalities are respectively posited as the appearance of water as water to an eye consciousness apprehending water and the appearance of a mirage as water to an eye consciousness apprehending a mirage as water. In the first case, what appears as water to the mind is able to function as water, just as it appears to. In the second case, even though the mirage appears as water, it is not able to function as water in the way it appears to, so it must be posited as a distorted conventionality. However, ultimately, both are empty of essential nature, so they are the same in this regard. Accordingly, such things as water are veridical conventional truths, for they are true in being able to function just as they appear to a mind directly perceiving them. Yet when analyzed by means of ultimate analysis, they cannot withstand scrutiny. Jñānagarbha's *Distinguishing the Two Truths* says:

> Since its nature is as it appears,
> it is not suitable to be analyzed.[179]

Based on how the essential nature of each of the two types of conventionality is posited in Jñānagarbha's *Distinguishing the Two Truths*, the definition of a veridical conventionality is: that which is commonly accepted to be a veridical object just as it appears to the conventional cognition clearly perceiving it. Examples of this are water and fire. The definition of a distorted conventionality is: that which is commonly accepted to be a distorted object just as it appears to the conventional cognition clearly perceiving it. Examples of this are reflections, mirages, and echoes. If something is a veridical conventionality, then it is necessarily a conventional truth. If something is a distorted conventionality, however, it is not necessarily a conventional truth. For example, a sky flower is a distorted conventionality but not a conventional truth. [60] Therefore Jñānagarbha's *Distinguishing the Two Truths Autocommentary* says that veridical conventional truth is free from distorted superimpositions:

> Unlike imputed things—such as ultimate arising, an image in consciousness, primal nature, an evolute of elements, and so on—whatever is a mere thing is able to function as it appears. That which arises in dependence on causes and conditions is known as *veridical conventional truth*. The various things that are caused to appear in the cognitions of ordinary beings are accepted to be veridical conventionalities because they exist in reality just as they appear to cognition.[180]

The superimpositions of distorted tenets—such as ultimate arising, the Cittamātra assertion that consciousness is truly existent, the Sāṅkhya notion of primal nature, the Cārvāka assertion that consciousness is an evolute of the elements, and so forth—are said to be distorted conventionalities.

Śāntarakṣita and his disciple Kamalaśīla agree with Jñānagarbha's categorization of the conventional into the two—veridical and distorted. But in their tradition, conventionalities are presented in a way that accords with the Yogācāra system, since they do not accept external reality. Consider the example of water. The water that appears to a mind directly perceiving it does not exist as an external object even though it appears to exist in that way. So, since these masters do not assert that it is able to function as it appears to that mind, they define veridical and distorted conventionalities [61] a little differently. According to the Yogācāra-Svātantrika Madhyamaka tradition, the definition of a veridical conventionality is: that which appears to a conventional consciousness clearly perceiving it and is commonly accepted to be a veridical object. Also, the definition of a distorted conventionality is: that which appears to a conventional consciousness clearly perceiving it and is commonly accepted to be a distorted object.

In brief, the texts of the three Madhyamaka masters mentioned above [Bhāviveka, Jñānagarbha, and Śāntarakṣita] take the main meaning of conventionality to be *veridical conventionality*, such being endowed with three attributes: (1) they dependently arise, or they have arising and disintegration; (2) they are able to perform a causal function; and (3) they are not able to withstand ultimate analysis. This is stated clearly in Śāntarakṣita's *Ornament for the Middle Way*:

> Those that are acceptable only when not analyzed,
> have the attributes of arising and disintegrating,
> and are endowed with the ability to function
> are known to be of conventional nature.[181]

They are unable to withstand analysis by a reasoning consciousness analyzing the ultimate, and they are acceptable in the sense that what is to be adopted or abandoned is posited only from the perspective of conventional nonanalytical consciousness. Consider, for example, something that newly arises within one's own continuum without having existed before and that disintegrates without remaining a second moment. Although it does not exist ultimately, it is not nonexistent because it can function to produce its own result. [62] Therefore it is said to be a conventional object of knowledge.

Candrakīrti and his Prāsaṅgika Madhyamaka followers explain that all cognitions within the mindstreams of ordinary beings are mistaken cognitions,[182] thus they do not accept that conventional phenomena are established or able to function as they appear. For this reason, they do not differentiate between veridical and distorted in terms of the definition of conventionality. However, they do differentiate between true and false from the perspective of mundane consciousness, in that water is veridical and a mirage is distorted. This way of distinguishing is clearly presented in Candrakīrti's *Entering the Middle Way*:

> Mistaken seeing is also said to be of two kinds:
> that with clear senses and that with impaired senses.

> Cognitions operating with impaired sense faculties are
> held to be distorted compared with those that are
> unimpaired.[183]

In view of this, the definition of what is veridical in relation to the mundane perspective is: that which cannot be posited as distorted by a mundane cognition not directed toward suchness. This includes both subject and object—namely, the six sense faculties that are unaffected by temporary causes of error as well as their objects. For example, an eye consciousness apprehending a visual form is a veridical *subject* from the perspective of a mundane cognition, while form itself is posited as a veridical *object* from the perspective of a mundane cognition. Candrakīrti's *Entering the Middle Way Autocommentary* says: "In this context, clear sense faculties are free of cataracts [63] and not impaired by jaundice and so on; they hold their respective external objects undistortedly."[184] It goes on to say: "Therefore the objects held by the six sense faculties, free from the conditions that impair the sense faculties described earlier, are realized by these kinds of mundane [cognitions]. They are true from the mundane perspective but not from the ārya's perspective."[185]

The definition of what is distorted in relation to the mundane perspective is: that which can be posited as distorted by a mundane cognition not directed toward suchness. This includes both subject and object—namely, the six sense faculties that are affected by temporary causes of error and their objects. For example, a sense consciousness to which a snow mountain appears to be blue is a distorted *subject*, while the reflection of a face appearing as a face is posited as a distorted *object*. Candrakīrti's *Entering the Middle Way Autocommentary* says: "In comparison to cognitions based on good sense faculties, any cognition based on an impaired sense faculty is said to be a distorted cognition."[186] It goes on to say: "Something such as a reflection and so on, which appears to be the thing itself if the sense faculties are impaired, is distorted from the mundane perspective."[187]

To make this distinction between veridical and distorted conventionality from the perspective of mundane cognition, [64] there is no need for conventional phenomena to be rationally analyzed in terms of whether it exists by virtue of essential nature. The criterion of valid cognition, or the grounds for distinguishing between veridical or distorted, true or false, depends only on mundane conventional cognition. Since it is only a case of being veridical or true from the perspective of a mind that is a mistaken cognition, or a mind seeing a false [appearance], there is no need for it to be veridical [in an ultimate sense]. Buddhapālita explains this clearly using an example, as stated in *Buddhapālita's Commentary on the Fundamental Treatise*:

> Once upon a time, two men from a village went to the city to do some sightseeing. They entered a temple and began looking at the paintings. The first villager said: "The one holding a trident in his hand is Nārāyaṇa, and the one holding a wheel in his hand is Maheśvara."
>
> The second villager said: "You have it wrong. The one holding a trident is Maheśvara, and the one holding a wheel is Nārāyaṇa."
>
> While the two were disputing this, they approached a mendicant sitting nearby. Having paid homage, each expressed his own opinion. In response, the mendicant said to one villager, "What you say is true," and to the other, "What you say is false." Then he said to them, "However, in any case, Maheśvara is not there at all, and Nārāyaṇa is not there either, for they are pictures painted on a wall." They all knew this, but it was nevertheless true or not true from the perspective of worldly convention.[188] [65]

Although the image drawn on the wall holding a trident in his hand is a painting of an individual deity, in a discussion about whether the deity is Īśvara or Viṣṇu, a distinction is made between what is true and false from the perspective of worldly convention, and such speech would not be false. Likewise, although the Mādhyamika differentiate between water and a mirage in terms of being veridical and distorted, respectively, the Mādhyamika are able to understand that this does not imply an acceptance of water to exist ultimately or in reality.

In brief, since Prāsaṅgika Madhyamaka does not consider phenomena to be inherently existent even conventionally, both an illusory horse and a genuine horse are equally untrue in relation to the reasoning consciousness analyzing the ultimate, so the Mādhyamika do not differentiate between true and false in this context. However, they explain that one must be able to apply the conventions of true and false in relation to worldly convention. If not, this would incur the fault that all presentations of the conventional are erroneous. According to Candrakīrti, since the distinction between veridical and distorted conventionalities applies only in relation to the mundane perspective, this way of differentiating between veridical and distorted from the mundane perspective is applicable to both object and subject. In contrast, given that Svātantrika Mādhyamika such as Bhāviveka accept intrinsic characteristics[189] on the conventional level, they seem to confine distorted conventionality only to objects and accept the subject, cognition, to be necessarily a veridical conventionality. [66]

Realizing the Two Truths

Now, if the mode of being of phenomena consists of two truths—the conventional truth and the ultimate truth—one might ask, what then is the sequence in which the mind of a person searching for the nature of reality engages with them? In general, this is expressed in a verse cited earlier from Nāgārjuna's *Fundamental Treatise on the Middle Way*:

> The ultimate truth cannot be taught
> independently of customary conventions;
> and without realizing the ultimate,
> nirvāṇa will not be attained.[190]

A similar approach is taught in a verse mentioned in the preceding section from Bhāviveka's *Heart of the Middle Way*:

> Without the ladder of veridical conventionality,
> it would be impossible for the wise
> to climb up to the top
> of the house of ultimate reality.
>
> The fact that it is impossible
> to climb up to the roof of the house of ultimate reality
> without the ladder of veridical conventionality
> is so for that reason.[191]

Candrakīrti's *Entering the Middle Way* says:

> Conventional truth is the means,
> while the ultimate truth is the end.[192]

There are many such passages in the Madhyamaka texts. Unless one relies on a conventional or relative truth, [67] there is no means of engaging with the ultimate truth. In particular, when initially developing an understanding of suchness—the absence of true arising and so on—through Madhyamaka reasoning, such as the neither-one-nor-many argument or the refutation of arising from the four alternatives, first one's mind must take something as the subject or the basis upon which emptiness is being established. This can be either an internal phenomenon, such as the "I" that is the focal object of the identity view,[193] or an external phenomenon, such as a sprout. On the basis of this, one must employ inferential reasoning to prove such things as that it is neither one nor many. Similarly, having ascertained the pervasion—that if it is neither truly one nor truly many, then it cannot be truly existent—one eventually needs to ascertain that this subject does not truly arise. So without taking to mind a conventional thing, one has no method for ascertaining the ultimate truth.

Thus to establish that some phenomenon, such as a sprout, is a conventional truth, one must first negate that it is truly existent. Then one must ascertain the ultimate truth based on the sprout. When establishing any given thing as a conventional truth, one must ascertain such a basis to be deceptive and an object of a mistaken consciousness. If one cannot rationally refute such a thing to be truly existent, then one will not be able to establish it to be false.

In conclusion, the extensive presentations of the two truths found in the Madhyamaka treatises skillfully explain the definitions of each of the two truths, especially that the ultimate truth is not an object of the intellect (*blo*), language, or thought. They also explain that without realizing the ultimate truth, it is impossible to attain liberation, and that realizing the ultimate truth must depend on realizing conventional or concealing truth. [68] Such teachings are found in a variety of scriptures. Furthermore, they explain that the truth is natural nirvāṇa, for it is the very emptiness that is the emptiness of true existence only. In contrast, they explain conventional truth to be distorted in that it is the object found by a mind that perceives something false. They also state that, even within the purview of worldly convention, there is the need to differentiate between an illusory horse and a genuine horse in terms of one being false and the other being true. Thus there are various statements connected with the presentation of the two truths that appear, at least on the surface, to be somewhat contradictory. Seeing that there is a need to engage with these questions using a refined analysis free of conflation, we have addressed some of these difficult issues by way of a broad introduction. For further detail, one must study the treatises of the great Madhyamaka masters of India. [69]

Part 2

Analysis of Self and Selflessness

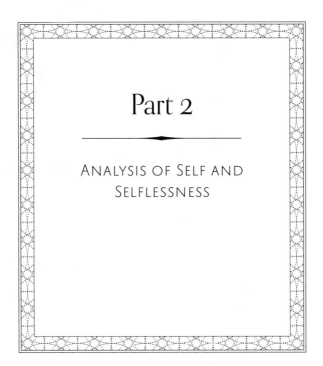

5

Notions of the Self

Ancient Indian philosophers generally agree on the need to posit a person who is an agent and who undergoes pleasant and unpleasant experiences. But as for whether such a person is something different from the mental and physical aggregates or, indeed, identical with them—or whether a person should be identified as something entirely other than those two alternatives—there is a divergence of views among the Buddhist and non-Buddhist thinkers. The eternalist non-Buddhist schools declare the self to be endowed with three attributes: (1) it is permanent, since it does not arise or perish; (2) it is unitary, since it does not have parts; and (3) it is autonomous, since it does not depend on anything else. In contrast, they maintain that the aggregates are impermanent, multiple, and reliant on others. Hence they assert the self to be something separate from the aggregates. Buddhists, however, employ many avenues of reasoning to refute the existence of such a permanent, unitary, and autonomous self. Nevertheless, even though such a self does not exist, they posit a person that is imputed in dependence on the aggregates. Therefore, since ancient times in India, Buddhist philosophical schools came to be known for following the theory of selflessness (*anātmavāda*), and tīrthika schools for following the theory of the self (*ātmavāda*). Thus the custom emerged in India of considering this differentiation between notions of self and selflessness to be the most important feature distinguishing Buddhist from non-Buddhist philosophy. [70]

Each non-Buddhist school, such as Sāṅkhya and Vaiśeṣika, has its own unique way of positing the nature of the self, which will be presented below. First we explain the notion of a self endowed with the three attributes mentioned above, which is generally common to the non-Buddhist systems. The main proof they present of the existence of such a permanent self seems to be the argument that it exists from recollection. Candrakīrti's *Commentary on the Four Hundred Stanzas* presents this position as follows:

> The self is permanent because there is memory of former births. Recollection of other lives is not feasible for composite things, whose nature is to disintegrate as soon as they arise. Given that the composite phenomena of a former life have disintegrated in that which will arise, it is only new ones that arise [in the next life]. Therefore it would be impossible to posit "The self of the previous life became so-and-so in this life" as expressing a memory of the former life. But if a permanent self existed, then because it would go to the next life, one would remember it.[194]

This is to say that since the aggregates of the previous life have disintegrated and the aggregates of this life are newly arisen, if one does not posit a permanent self that is separate from them, then it would not be possible to remember one's former birth.

This kind of permanent self is asserted to be partless and unitary, as explained in Bhāviveka's *Lamp of Wisdom* in the context of critiquing the opponent's theory of *puruṣa* ("person") as the cause [of the universe]. Presenting the opponent's position,[195] this text states: "Some say that according to us the self is only singular. [71] Just as the space inside pots and so on is posited on the basis of different things, so this [self] is imputed on many individuals. Since there is no counter-example, there is no inferential reason that refutes it. Without that, there will be no faulty thesis."[196] They assert that just as the space in a pot and the space in a room and so on do not exist separately but are merely imputed as "this space" or "that space" owing to different bases, likewise the self of Devadatta and the self of Yajñadatta[197] are the same partless entity. Since a counter-example cannot be found, there is no evidence that refutes it. Thus, the opponent claims, the fault of contradicting his own thesis does not arise.

The opponent posits this kind of permanent, partless, and autonomous self to be something separate from the aggregates. He argues that if we do not accept an essentially existent self that is different from the aggregates, then we must explain what could be the agent that functions to make the body move, such as bending and stretching the arms and legs. It would be like a chariot that cannot be made to move without a driver. So, he claims, we must definitely accept an inner being separate from the aggregates to be the agent that makes the body move, just as a driver is the agent that makes the chariot move. In presenting such a view, Candrakīrti's *Commentary on the Four Hundred Stanzas* says: "If the self is not essentially existent, then who is the operator making the body move, as in the case of bending and stretching? A chariot without a driver also will not move. Therefore one must undoubtedly [72] accept some kind of inner being as an agent that, like a chariot driver named Devadatta, causes the body to move."[198]

Critically, ancient non-Buddhist Indian schools argued that if there exists no accruer of virtuous and nonvirtuous actions and no experiencer of their results, then the results of actions would be wasted. The aggregates of body and mind have the nature of arising and disintegrating so they cannot be the self. Based on many such reasons as this, they assert the existence of a self that is separate from the aggregates.

Now, does such a self, which is the basis of karmic actions and their results, have a beginning? Those who accept the universe to have been made by a divine creator believe that the self has a beginning. Then there are those who, like the Buddhists, do not accept a creator of the universe but instead accept that animate and inanimate worlds have arisen in dependence on their own causes and conditions. They must posit the existence or nonexistence of the beginning of the self in dependence on whether the aggregates have a beginning, because the self is imputed on the basis of aggregates. From among the five aggregates that are the basis of imputation of the person, let us consider the consciousness aggregate as an illustration. What is referred to as "consciousness" is something in the nature of mere experience or subjectivity, which has no physical form, such as color or shape.[199] The substantial cause of consciousness, which is in the nature of mere experience, must be something of a similar kind. Thus one cannot posit subtle physical particles to be the substantial cause of consciousness, since they are not in the nature of awareness. Moreover, if one were to trace the earlier moments within a continuum of consciousness in general, and the subtle moments within a stream of mental consciousness in particular, [73] one would find no beginning. Since it is not possible to posit a beginning to consciousness, it is also not possible to posit a beginning to the self that is imputed on the basis of consciousness. This is the argument proposed by most Buddhists.

As for whether there is a final end to the self, ancient Indian philosophers give different accounts. The non-Buddhist Cārvāka school and the Buddhist Vaibhāṣika school, for example, consider that the self has an end, whereas most of the Mahāyāna Buddhist philosophers say that since consciousness has no beginning or end, the self too, which is imputed in relation to it, does not have a beginning or an end.

6

Non-Buddhist Assertions of Self

The Sāṅkhya Assertion of the Consciously Aware Self or Person

The ancient philosophers known as the Sāṅkhya, followers of the ancient rishi Kapila, give a presentation of twenty-five objects of knowledge.[200] Among these categories, the consciously aware self or person (Skt. *puruṣa*) is described as that which is not endowed with the characteristics of passion (*rajas*), darkness (*tamas*), and purity (*sattva*).[201] It is not an agent, and it is not the primal nature (*prakṛti*) nor its transformations, thus it is neither a cause nor an effect; it is permanent in the sense of being eternally unchanging; it is an experiencer that enjoys the transformations created by the primal nature; and it is clear and cognizing in nature. So it is said to be a permanent entity endowed with these attributes. Thus the following are considered to be synonymous: self, person, consciousness, and knower.

In describing the characteristics of such a self, which is consciousness and the knower, Bhāviveka's [74] *Blaze of Reasoning* says:

> The self is never other than consciousness; it is not produced; it is permanent; it is not created; it is an experiencer; it is primordial; it pervades; it is without activity; and it is not a quality, because it is not endowed with characteristics such as purity. Since it is not like purity, which, though by itself is characterized by non-arising, produces cognition through the finding of conditions, the self is not a quality. It is characterized by non-arising for it is devoid of creation; it is a subject because it experiences; it is permanent because it neither arises nor diminishes; it is signless because it is other than the primal nature and the transformations; it is partless because it is unitary; and it is limitless

> because it has no beginning or end. These are the defining characteristics of the person.[202]

Here Bhāviveka explains that the self, according to Sāṅkhya, is never other than consciousness. It is not produced, it is permanent, it is not created, it is an experiencer, it is primordial, it pervades, it is not created, it is not a quality, it is in the nature of non-arising, it is a subject, it is signless for it has no dissolution, it is partless, and it is limitless. These are its attributes. Similarly, Bhāviveka's *Lamp of Wisdom* states: "The Sāṅkhya speak of the self as something other than cause and effect; [they say] it is not a creator, it is an experiencer, it is pure, it is omnipresent, it does not change, and it is sentient."[203] This passage explains that the self is neither a cause nor an effect. It is not a creator of resultant transformations. It is an experiencer because it can enjoy resultant transformations. [75] It is pure because it is clear, which is the nature of consciousness and knowing. It is omnipresent because it pervades every living being and every past and future life. It does not change because, by its nature, it remains without disintegrating. It is sentient because it is of the nature of consciousness and knowing.

Candrakīrti's *Entering the Middle Way* identifies the nature of the self according to Sāṅkhya through the following summary:

> A self that is an experiencer, a permanent entity, a non-creator,
> without qualities or activity, is conceived by the tīrthikas.[204]

The text thus lists the following five attributes of the Sāṅkhya notion of "self." (1) It is an experiencer of pleasure, pain, and so on. (2) It is a permanent entity. (3) It is not a creator of resultant transformations. (4) It does not have qualities that are the nature of passion, darkness, and purity. (5) It is devoid of activity since it is present in every agent.

Proof of the existence of such a self is offered as follows in the *Verses of Sāṅkhya*:

> Because all composite products are for the sake of another's use;
> because of the subordination of the three qualities and other
> properties;
> because there must be some controlling agency; because there
> must be an experiencer;

> and because there is the striving for the goal of isolation—the person exists.[205] [76]

This verse lists five inferential arguments to prove, either directly or indirectly, the existence of the consciously aware self or person. (1) Things that are composite and an aggregation, such as the eyes and so on, function for another's use because they are composite and an aggregation, such as a bed. This argument proves that the twenty-three objects, such as the eyes and so on, function for another's use, just as a bed functions for another's benefit. The beneficiary is the consciously aware self or person. Therefore, by relying on this argument, the existence of the person and the functioning for the person's benefit are proved. Also, by relying on this reason, it is proved that the eyes and so on are objects employed by the self, which in turn proves the existence of the self that employs them. (2) The person is existent because it is devoid of the three qualities of passion, darkness, and purity. Moreover, real things that are produced, such as physical forms and so on, are endowed with these three qualities, and they are objects, manifestations, and resultant phenomena, because a viewer that is different from them exists. (3) The body, or group of aggregates, has a controller that is separate from it because it engages in action, just as a chariot engages in action by the command of a charioteer. (4) Taste—sweet, sour, and so on—must have a consumer or enjoyer that is separate from it, because it is the object enjoyed. (5) The form aggregate must have a so-called person separate from it because it strives for the goal of perfect isolation (*kevala*). It also strives for the goal of liberation from suffering because it engages in such activities as listening to the treatises that show one how to become liberated, just as a farmer who engages in cultivation seeks varieties of grain. [77]

Likewise, Kamalaśīla's *Commentary on the Difficult Points in the Compendium of Reality* says:

> [They say:] "That which is composite in nature and thus a real thing is seen to function for another's use—for example, beds and seats, as in the case of limbs. The eyes and so on are composite in nature." These proofs are inferred by nature-inference. What is implied by the term "another" is the self, which it is said to prove. This is the line of thinking of the other party.[206]

So it is by reason of being composite and an aggregation that the eyes and so on, like beds and seats, are proved to function for the purpose of a self that is different from them.

As for the consciously aware self or person, it is also accepted that there is variety, as stated in the *Verses of Sāṅkhya*:

> Because birth, death, and faculties
> are specific for each individual, they operate successively,
> and the three qualities are subordinated;
> so the plurality of persons is proved.[207]

The five reasons for asserting that there are many persons are as follows. (1) Just as all these [phenomena] are directly perceived in this world, the existence of many living beings is proved by the reason that there are different manners of birth—such as plants and trees from the ground, bugs and worms from warmth and moisture, birds from eggs, and people from the womb. (2) The existence of many persons is proved by the reason that the time of death and so on of sentient beings is diverse. [78] (3) The existence of many persons is proved by the reason that different kinds of beings, humans and so on, have different aggregates, and the causes and conditions for each are specific. (4) The existence of many persons is proved by the reason that individual beings have different desires and when they engage in the objects of their own desires they engage in them successively. (5) The existence of many persons is proved by the reason that there are different ways in which the qualities are subordinated: in a god, the quality of purity predominates and the other two qualities are subordinated; in a human, the quality of passion predominates and the other two qualities are subordinated; in an animal, the quality of darkness predominates and the other two qualities are subordinated.

This system explains bondage and liberation on the basis of ignorance or lack of ignorance pertaining to the true nature of the twenty-five objects of knowledge. Elucidating this, Āryadeva's *Compendium of the Essence of Wisdom* quotes a Sāṅkhya text:

> When this [yogin] knows the twenty-five,
> whether he has matted hair or a crown on his head,

in whatever situation he wishes,
he becomes liberated, there is no doubt![208]

When upon hearing and contemplating the guru's teachings there arises the wisdom ascertaining that the resultant transformations are emanated from the primal nature, then the divine eye arises through the power of concentration and perceives the primal nature, while the consciously aware self or person remains inactive. Freed from the mistaken perception of the self and the primal nature as one, [79] it directly sees the ultimate reality of the principal or primal nature as it is, which is the true nature of those various manifestations. At that time the primal nature withdraws its manifestations, as if embarrassed. When all the conventional appearances displayed to the yogin's mind have dissolved, the consciously aware self or person dwells without doing anything and without experiencing anything, at which point, they maintain, liberation or freedom is attained.

THE VAIŚEṢIKA AND NYĀYA ASSERTIONS OF THE SELF

The Vaiśeṣika and Nyāya schools posit the nature of the self as follows. The self is distinct from the body, sense faculties, and intellect (*blo*; Skt. *buddhi*). It is an all-pervading and self-sufficient substance, the substrate of nine qualities: intellect, pleasure, pain, desire, aversion, effort, merit, demerit, and activity. It is the cause of these qualities assembling in itself, it has the nature of insentient matter, it is omnipresent, it is the agent of various virtuous and nonvirtuous actions, and it is the enjoyer experiencing the results of virtue and nonvirtue. The *Vaiśeṣika Sūtra* says: "The self's substance and permanence must be explained in the same way as that of the extremely subtle wind."[209] Bhāviveka's *Lamp of Wisdom* describes their position as follows: "The self is different from the body, sense faculties, and intellect. It is posited as the basis of happiness and so on. It is an agent, without sentience, [80] permanent, and present in everything."[210] And in Bhāviveka's *Blaze of Reasoning*, in the context of presenting the view of self according to Vaiśeṣika and Nyāya, it says: "The self exists, for it is unproduced, eternal, an agent, an enjoyer, pervasive, and without activity."[211] This is to say the self is unproduced because it does not function; it is permanent because it does not change; it is an agent because it accomplishes virtuous and nonvirtuous actions; it is an enjoyer because it experiences their ripened results; it is pervasive because it is present in all beings; it is passive because it is present in all agents. Thus it is said to be endowed with six attributes.

This point about such a self being endowed with nine qualities is made clear in Candrakīrti's *Entering the Middle Way Autocommentary*:

> The Vaiśeṣika speak of nine qualities of the self: intellect, pleasure, pain, desire, aversion, effort, merit, demerit, and activity. Here, *intellect* apprehends objects. *Pleasure* is the experience of desirable objects. *Pain* is the opposite of that. *Desire* is the hope for desirable things. *Aversion* is the resistance toward undesirable objects. *Effort* is the mental skill that helps one to complete a task in fulfilling one's goal. *Merit* is that from which definite goodness and high status is established.[212] [81] *Demerit* is the opposite of that. The force of *activity* arises from consciousness and is a cause of consciousness itself. For as long as those nine qualities are assembled and present within the self, saṃsāra will occur, because there will be virtuous and nonvirtuous actions created by those qualities. The self is liberated when the roots of those qualities are cut off by means of correct understanding, at which time the self abides alone with its own essential nature. Such a self is asserted to be permanent, an agent, an experiencer, endowed with attributes, and without activity since it is pervasive. Some say that the self has activity since it reaches out and withdraws.[213]

Śāntarakṣita's *Compendium of Reality* summarizes how the self is asserted by the Vaiśeṣika and Nyāya schools:

> Again others assert the self
> to be a substrate that is
> permanent, omnipresent,
> and insentient in its own nature.
>
> Of virtuous and nonvirtuous actions
> it is the agent, while of their results
> it is the experiencer, thus conjoined with mind. [82]
> But it is not mind by its own nature.

> Conjoined with consciousness, effort, and so on,
> it is said to be an agent.
> Conjoined with cognition of pleasure,
> pain, and so on, it is an experiencer.
>
> Conjoined with previously nonexistent
> intellect, feeling, and so on,
> as well as a specific kind of body,
> it is said to be born.
>
> Separated from those taken up before,
> it is considered dead; for life consists in
> being conjoined with body and mind
> under the influence of merit or non-merit.
>
> When the body, eyes, and so on are harmed,
> this self is said to be hurt.
> Though the person is permanent,
> this convention is said to be faultless.[214]

These six verses clearly identify the nature of the self asserted by Vaiśeṣika and Nyāya. The first verse indicates that the self is the basis of qualities such as desire [83] and that its own nature is permanent, omnipresent, and without a mind. The second verse says that although the self is by nature not mind, since it is the agent of virtuous and nonvirtuous actions and the experiencer or enjoyer of the results of those actions, it is connected with mind. The third verse explains that such a self is permanent and unitary, and owing to qualities such as consciousness of objects, effort, wish to act, and so on being included in and conjoined with the self, that very self is an agent; also, because the feeling that cognizes pleasure, pain, and so on is spontaneously conjoined with it, that very self is an enjoyer or experiencer. The fourth verse explains that this very self takes birth because previously nonexistent bodies, sense faculties, and so on of specific kinds of beings, such as humans and gods, become conjoined with this self. The fifth verse says that when the self is separated from the body, sense faculties, and so on that it had previously taken up, this is posited to be death; and while that self remains endowed with a body, sense faculties, intellect, feelings, and so on, the self is alive. The sixth verse explains that they consider it perfectly acceptable to say the self is hurt when the body is harmed and so on and to label the self an agent even though it is permanent.

One might ask, "On what grounds does one know that a self endowed with such attributes exists?" To this, the *Vaiśeṣika Sūtra* says: "These are the signs indicating the self: (1) ascending and descending of the subtle wind, (2) opening and closing of the eyelids, (3) life, (4) fluctuation of the mind, (5) modification of the sense faculties, (6) pleasure and pain, [84] and (7) desire, aversion, and effort."[215] Thus seven proofs of the self appear to be presented, each of which may be explained as follows. (1) Because one's body moves up and down when the subtle wind also moves up and down, indicating there is something particular that moves the wind, this proves that there is a self that moves the wind. (2) Because the activity of opening and closing one's mouth, eyes, and so on has a specific time and measure at which it is done, this proves the existence of a self that controls this action in a specific way. (3) Because one naturally wants to eat and drink when one is tormented by hunger and thirst, this proves that there is a self that impels one to take nourishment. (4) Because one's mind undergoes changes causing the sense faculties to meet with their respective objects, this proves that there is a self that causes the mind to fluctuate. (5) Because the eye sense faculty, for example, is modified while looking at an apple, the tongue consciousness experiences the taste of sweet, sour, and so on, and the mental consciousness remembers the delicious taste of such an apple, this proves that there is a self that is the agent affecting the sense faculties. (6) Pleasure and pain arising within oneself proves that there is a self who is the experiencer of pleasure and pain. (7) Because one experiences a desire to obtain good qualities as yet unobtained, aversion that turns away from pain, and the wish to obtain pleasure and dispel pain, this proves that there is a self that is the agent of happiness, suffering, and effort. [85]

Among the principal proofs for the existence of the self proposed by the Vaiśeṣika and Nyāya masters listed in Śāntarakṣita's *Compendium of Reality* is the tīrthika Aviddhakarṇa's argument:

> Because it cognizes the body and so on
> that are different from it,
> it is consciousness, like those of others.[216]

In other words, direct perception, inferential cognition, and so on, which are the cognizers, are different from the body, sense faculties, and intellect, which are the cognized. This is so because direct perception and so on: (1) are generated in reliance on their own causes, (2) are endowed with the universal and the particular, (3) are of the nature of conceptual cognition, (4) disintegrate very quickly, (5) give rise to conditioning factors, and (6) are consciousness alone. In brief, what is being proven here is that such a cognizer is the self. Then, when presenting the Nyāya master Śaṅkarasvāmin's argument, Śāntarakṣita's *Compendium of Reality* states:

> All such things as desire and so on
> must be based on something because,
> as real things, they are effects, [86]
> like physical form.[217]

Here it says that qualities such as desire and so on must subsist in something because, given that they are real things, they are effects, like physical form and so on. In brief, desire, aversion, and so on must have a substrate that is none of the eight other substances [or *qualities*, as listed above]. And such a substrate, he argues, is the self. As for the Nyāya master Uddyotakara's argument, Śāntarakṣita's *Compendium of Reality* states:

> All cognitions of physical form and so on,
> characterized as one and many,
> are connected by the notion
> of being "cognized *by me*,"
> just as the dancer's eyebrow gesture
> is recognized by many onlookers.
> Otherwise, without a cause,
> there would be no connection.[218]

One and many cognitions apprehending forms, sounds, and so on within the continuum of Devadatta must have a single cause because they are connected by a single notion: "I saw it, I knew it." For example, when a dancer makes a unique eyebrow gesture [87] in a performance, this acts as a single cause of different cognitions for various audience members [as each person draws conclusions about its significance]. So the consciousnesses apprehending forms and so on have a single cause in common, which proves that this cause cannot be other than the self. To summarize the Nyāya-Vaiśeṣika master Aviddhakarṇa's argument, Śāntarakṣita's *Compendium of Reality* states:

> All my subsequent consciousnesses
> must be cognized by the cognizer
> of my first consciousness immediately upon birth,
> because they are my own cognitions.
> Objects located far away
> are yet correlated with my own self
> because they have bodies and so on, like my own body.[219]

In other words, my cognitions at any time must be cognized by the cognizer of the first cognition I had immediately upon leaving my mother's womb because they are my own cognitions, just like my first. Kamalaśīla's *Commentary on the Difficult Points in the Compendium of Reality* explains the meaning of these verses as follows:

> "All my subsequent consciousnesses" and so on are like the first. Here, the "first" of those is the first of my cognitions arising at a later time. In order to prove the omnipresence [of the self], this same author [Uddyotakara] presents the following argument: "Earth, water, fire, and mind, which are the objects of dispute and located far away, are yet correlated with my own self because they have physical bodies, strength, otherness, sameness, mutual connection, and disconnection, just like my own body." [88] This is indicated with the words "objects located far away" and so on.[220]

The Vaiśeṣika master Praśastapāda explains that the self is endowed with fourteen qualities: (1) intellect apprehending its object, (2) pleasure experiencing a desirable object, (3) pain experiencing an undesirable object, (4) desire hoping for desirable things, (5) aversion turning away from undesirable things, (6) effort bringing to completion accomplishment of the goal, (7) merit establishing high status and definite goodness, (8) demerit preventing high status and definite goodness, (9) force of activity or conditioning that are causes of consciousness and that arise from consciousness, (10) enumeration such as one or ten, (11) measure such as large or small, (12) separate individuality, (13) conjunction that is mutual connection, and (14) disjunction that is mutual disconnection. Praśastapāda's *Compendium of the Attributes of the Categories* states: "Its qualities are: intellect, pleasure, pain, desire, aversion, effort, merit, demerit, conditioning activity, number, dimension, individuality, conjunction, and disjunction."[221] Among these, the first nine are unique qualities of the self, while the last five are shared qualities of the self. Of these, the first six qualities, intellect and so on, [89] are said to be established by valid direct perception within one's own experience, while merit, demerit, and effort are established by valid inferential cognition based on correct reasoning.

The Vaiśeṣika say that the self may be categorized in terms of *one's own* and *others'*. It is *one's own self* that establishes within one's own experience whether one is being benefited or harmed. Based on one's own experience of being benefited and harmed, one can infer the existence of *others' selves* that establish within their own experience whether they are being benefited or harmed. The *Vaiśeṣika Sūtra* says: "From having directly experienced activity and inactivity within one's own self, one can infer it in others' selves."[222] The self that dwells within the body and activates the sense faculties, such as the eye sense faculty, is the inner self that causes the apprehension of "me" and experiences pleasure and pain resulting from virtuous and nonvirtuous actions. Furthermore, two kinds of self are said to exist: The *inner self* that has the nature of a combination of body and sense faculties and the *outer self* that assists it. Candrakīrti's *Commentary on the Four Hundred Stanzas* says:

> The tīrthikas posit two kinds of self: an inner self and an outer self. The inner self is that which dwells within the body and activates the sense faculties in specific ways. The inner agent or person, who is the cause of the apprehension of "me," [90] experiences the results of virtuous, nonvirtuous, and neutral actions, and is subdivided into many individual streams and thought processes. The outer self, which is characterized by the combination of body and sense faculties, assists the inner self.[223]

In brief, the basic views of Vaiśeṣika and Nyāya assertions on the existence of self can be summed up in the following verse found in Śāntarakṣita's *Compendium of Reality*:

> Thus having ascertained that the self exists,
> is permanent, and is pervasive,
> it is unfeasible to claim that
> all phenomena are selfless.[224]

The Mīmāṃsā Assertions of the Self

The Mīmāṃsā view of the self is as follows. In contrast to individual states of pleasure and pain that interrupt each other, the self, which in its very nature has sentience, is present at all times; is intellect in essence, as it is sentient; is permanent by nature though its states are impermanent; is a unitary substance by nature; is the agent of virtuous and harmful actions; and is the experiencer of pleasant and painful results. For example, when a snake changes from coiled to straight, [91] although each alternating state ceases, the nature of the snake is not interrupted but continues to be the same in all those states. So it is with the self; when various states of pleasure, pain, and so on cease, the self continues to have the same nature—sentient, permanent, and unitary. Śāntarakṣita's *Compendium of Reality* puts forth this view as follows:

> Others assert the self to be interrupted
> [in its states] and continuous in character:
> it is sentient in nature, where to be sentient
> is characterized by the intellect.
> Just as when a snake whose coiled state
> upon ceasing is immediately followed
> by the occurrence of a straightened state,
> so likewise the self permanently
> has the nature of sentience,
> where its nature is never entirely lost
> nor yet continued completely intact.[225]

The Mīmāṃsaka do not agree with the Sāṅkhya that the intellect is material and therefore different from consciousness. According to their own tradition, they consider *intellect* and *sentience* to be the same, and they posit the self to have the nature of sentience. They also disagree with the Buddhists, for they argue that if the self has the nature of disintegrating without continuity, then this incurs the fault that karmic actions would be wasted. And they disagree with the Naiyāyika, for they argue that if the self were continuous for every being and its individual states never interrupted, then the experience of pleasure and pain would be unchanging; and like space, there would be no difference between the state of being or not being an experiencer of the result of karmic action. [92] According to the Mīmāṃsā tradition, in terms of continuity, the self remains the same nature, while its states of pleasure and so on are interrupted. Thus the agent or experiencer is the same person that has these different states but is not identical with those states. The Mīmāṃsā master Kumārila states:

> Therefore, having discarded the two extremes,
> a single person should be accepted to have
> an interrupted and a continuous nature,
> like a snake that is coiled and so on.[226]

They also proffer a proof for the existence of such a self, which is presented as follows in Śāntarakṣita's *Compendium of Reality*:

> A person of such description
> is proved to exist by reason
> of recognition, and by means of that,
> selflessness is disproved.[227]

They argue that since a single agent can recognize the cognizer and knower by thinking "I am cognizing this" and "I am seeing this," this establishes that a person—as described above, having an interrupted and a continuous nature, sentient, permanent, a doer, and an experiencer—in fact exists. They also maintain that this same argument [93] greatly undermines the Buddhist assertion of selflessness as well.

The Mīmāṃsaka now ask, "Given that such a knower who cognizes by way of thinking 'I know' is something incontrovertibly established for both parties in the debate, then would the cognizer, the object of the thought 'I know,' be the *self*, or would it be *consciousness*, which the Buddhists explain as having the nature of disintegration?" If it is the first, this would mean that both parties would be in agreement. If, however, it is the second, then since this would be unreasonable, it would lead to utterly inexplicable problems. Śāntarakṣita's *Compendium of Reality* presents this qualm as follows:

> Given that the notion of "I" in the thought "I know"
> is the cognizer that does the realizing,
> then is it an individual [self],
> or is it the utterly impermanent
> disintegrating consciousness?
> If such an object is the self,
> then everyone would be in agreement.
> If the other, momentary consciousness,
> then everything would become inexplicable.[228]

Here, a question arises: "If [the cognizer] were this intellect of sentient nature or the permanent and unitary person, then how could it realize its objects, such as physical forms, consecutively?" Given that the intellect or self is permanent and unitary, this would mean it would realize everything simultaneously. The Mīmāṃsā response to this question is stated in Śāntarakṣita's *Compendium of Reality*:

> For example, fire, by nature,
> always has the function of burning.
> But it burns only what is in its vicinity
> and capable of being burned—
> not any other thing nor at any other time—
> just as a clean mirror
> or a rock crystal [94]
> can only reflect the image
> of something in its vicinity.
> Likewise, when the permanent sentient person
> dwells within a body that has sense faculties,
> it can apprehend forms and so on.
> This we call *intellect*.[229]

Here fire is posited as an example [of how perception operates]. Although fire always has the nature of burning, it burns combustible things that are in its vicinity—it does not burn every combustible thing in general. Another example is a mirror, which reflects physical forms that are in its vicinity, not every form. Likewise, although the self is permanent consciousness, its objects are forms and so on that are in the vicinity of the sense faculties, not any other objects. This distinction is considered to be correct without succumbing to the fault of contradiction. In brief, this tradition posits the self to be a permanent and unitary consciousness that is different from the aggregates and so on.

Thus, based on their arguments as described above, the Mīmāṃsaka posit the self to be in the nature of the intellect or sentience. Furthermore, given that they implicitly accept attachment and other mental afflictions to belong to the nature of the mind, they maintain that it would be impossible for the mind to be free from those faults of the mind. So they do not accept the possibility of a person being completely free from all faults or the possibility of the state of omniscience. However, they do accept that, through engaging in such activities as the performance of rites prescribed in the Vedas, through the ritual of sacrifice and so on, one could attain the state of peaceful liberation from the sufferings of lower rebirth and so on. [95]

The Self according to the Vedānta

Proponents of the Vedānta school, following the Upaniṣads, posit the self as follows. The essential nature of the self, or Brahman, is posited to be eternal, unitary, consciousness, the source of the elements such as earth, the basis of the first arising and of the final dissolution of the world and its inhabitants, omnipresent, and nondual. This view is presented in Śāntarakṣita's *Compendium of Reality* as follows:

> Moreover, others assert:
> "Earth, fire, water, and so on
> are the manifestations of permanent consciousness;
> that which has such a nature is called the *self*."[230]

Concerning this, Kamalaśīla's *Commentary on the Difficult Points in the Compendium of Reality* says:

> Others who follow the Upaniṣads and who uphold the nondual (Skt. *advaita*) view consider the earth and so on to be transformations whose nature is eternal unitary consciousness. To cite their treatise, the text says "earth" and so on and [speaks of] their "nature," which means that the earth and so on are transformations whose nature is eternal unitary consciousness. "Others" here refers to the proponents of the Upaniṣads.[231]

The proponents of the Upaniṣads assert the following: If consciousness exists, then the appearances of earth and so on can be posited, and if not, then the appearances of earth and so on cannot be posited at all. [96] Furthermore, they say there is no earth and so on apart from their appearances to consciousness, and since they do not speak of appearances in terms of a differentiation between unique particulars and general characteristics, they speak of the elements—earth and so on—to be consciousness.

As for how they view this self to pervade the world and its inhabitants, Bhāviveka's *Blaze of Reasoning* says: "Any human beings and so on that there were in the past, that there are in the present in a visible form, or that there will be in the future exist through having been controlled by the puruṣa, and the entirety of the three realms is pervaded by it."[232] For example, just as the letter *a* permeates every signifying sound and is the first among them all,[233] so likewise the self, or *puruṣa*, permeates everything and is the first among them all. Again, just as the letter *a* is not different in meaning or nature from signifying sounds, so the all-pervading puruṣa and the dualistic world are not different in nature from the ultimate reality that is Brahman.

They maintain that such a self, though not having qualities endowed with conceptual elaboration, does possess qualities free of conceptual elaboration. This is explained in Bhāviveka's *Blaze of Reasoning*:

> Just so, this is taught in the following sequence:
>
> It is single, omnipresent, eternal,
> Brahman, supreme, deathless, and the state;
> when the yogin meditates upon it
> he will not be reborn again.
>
> It is single because it is the Lord of all bodies. It is omnipresent because it pervades every migrating being. It is permanent

> because it never deteriorates. It is Brahman because it is the nature of nirvāṇa. [97] It is supreme because it is the most perfect. It is deathless because it has no beginning or end. It is the state because it is the object. When the yogin focuses with concentrated absorption and meditates definitively in this way, he fully realizes such Brahman, at which point his rebirths cease.[234]

Blaze of Reasoning also states: "Because it exists having perished previously or is another having awoken from sleep, it is the puruṣa; because it protects or fulfills, it is the puruṣa. It is 'great' because it is beyond all."[235] It is these qualities, devoid of elaboration, that the self is said to possess.

There are many synonyms for the word *self* according to the Vedānta, and these are listed in the *Blaze of Reasoning*: "They use the word Brahman to refer to it, as well as the self, the person, the Lord, omnipresent, eternal."[236] That is to say, they take Brahman, self, person, Lord, omnipresent, and eternal to be synonymous.

When the self is categorized in terms of its basis, there are said to be two types: the self bound by karma and afflictions and the supreme self that is liberated from that bondage. Bhāviveka's *Heart of the Middle Way* states: [98]

> The self, the Vedānta say,
> is categorized as two kinds:
> a bound self that is embodied
> and a supreme self that is liberated.[237]

The self is categorized as two different kinds in terms of its basis, but it is not differentiated in terms of its nature, because the self is accepted to be eternal, single, and autonomous. *Heart of the Middle Way* says:

> Although pots and so on are different,
> the clay is not different at all.
> Likewise, although the bodies are different,
> the self is not different at all.[238]

This is to say, just as a pot and a cup both made from clay have different shapes and so on yet there is no difference between them in having the nature of clay, likewise the self bound by karma and afflictions and the self liberated from those are different in terms of having diverse limbs and so on yet are not different in terms of having the nature of the self.

In brief, the Vedānta school, following the Upaniṣads, teaches that the self is the ultimate truth, like space, and the appearances of beings' different selves is like the space inside different clay pots. The space inside the pots is the same, but the mind conceiving them to be different is like the mind mistaking a coiled rope for a snake. Likewise, in relation to the main basis of error—the nondual ultimate consciousness—illusion [99] occurs due to apprehending it in dualistic terms under the power of ignorance. Thus the eternal self is like a seed of both the world and its inhabitants. Moreover, just as the mistaken apprehension of a snake is overturned once one knows that the rope is not a snake, so the mistaken appearances apprehended dualistically are overturned once one realizes that outer and inner phenomena are created by ignorance from the luminously clear self that is the locus of error. At this point, one abides in a state of pure nonconceptuality beyond the extremes of subject-object duality. Thus this philosophical school's unique views regarding the ground, path, and result are based on their uncommon assertions concerning the self. To summarize, the Vedānta master Gauḍapāda says:

> Just as children consider the sky
> to become defiled with dust,
> so the unwise consider the self
> to become defiled with distortions.
>
> Just as in the dark, not fully cognized,
> a rope is imagined to be various things
> such as a snake, a stream, and so on,
> so the self is likewise imagined in various ways.
>
> Just as when the rope is ascertained,
> these imaginings are overturned and
> the rope alone remains nondual,
> so too is the self ascertained.[239] [100]

The Jaina View of the Self

The Jaina tradition, like Mīmāṃsā, considers the self to be eternal and unitary in nature. In the form of a substance, it does not differ as a state-possessor in relation to its various states. In presenting this view, Śānta-rakṣita's *Compendium of Reality* says:

> The followers of Mahāvīra, like the Mīmāṃsaka,
> maintain that the person is defined as sentient,
> with a nature that is continuous or interrupted [respectively]
> in the form of a substance or of successive factors.[240]

Commenting on this, Kamalaśīla's *Commentary on the Difficult Points in the Compendium of Reality* says:

> The "followers of Mahāvīra" refers to the Digambara Jaina (literally, "sky clad" or "naked" Jaina). They say that the self is characterized only as sentient. Moreover, in the form of substance, as a state-possessor, it does not differ in relation to its different states, and thus it has a continuous nature; in the form of successive factors, its individual states are different, and thus it has an interrupted nature. These two aspects of the self are established by direct perception, thus they are not established by other types of valid cognition. The sentient being that exists in all states, whatever nature they may be—including different states such as pleasure and so on—is a substance. The successive factors are the different states, such as pleasure and so on, that occur one after another. [101] These are also established by direct perception. Such is the view of the other party.[241]

Jaina maintain the self to be coextensive with a person's body. Since its essence is permanent, it continues throughout infinite time. Since its states are impermanent, it has the character of interrupting other states and the nature of sentience. The self of this or that state where there is no mutual continuity is said to be interrupted.

The Jaina tradition considers the self (*bdag*, Skt. *ātman*) and the life force (*srog*, Skt. *jīva*) to be synonymous. They say that in essence the self is permanent; however, since life force pervades all bodies, in the case of a large body the self is correspondingly large, and in the case of a small body the self is correspondingly small. Prajñāvarman's *Commentary on Praise of the Exalted* says:

> The words "coextensive with the body" refer to the dimensions of the body or physical form. [The self] corresponds to the dimensions of the body because it occupies that. In a [body] that is subtle, it is subtle. In one that is large, it is large. The "living being" pervades all bodies. The body is like its casket. So if that [body] reduces, then it reduces. If that [body] increases, then it increases. In a reduced one, it contracts and fills it completely. In an increased one, it expands. It is called *life force*, *sustaining force*, and *self*.[242] [102]

This tradition considers the self to be a life force where there is the convergence of cognition, vision, bliss, and power.

A later twelfth-century Jaina master, Nemicandra, wrote in *Compendium of Substances*:

> [The living substance has vitality and] is sentient, formless,
> a doer, coextensive with the body, an enjoyer,
> and a worldly existent, with the power to attain and to rise upward.[243]

Here we have the source for how this tradition posits the self: [vital,] sentient, formless, a doer, coextensive with the body, an enjoyer, and a worldly existent, endowed with the power to attain liberation and the power to rise upward. *Compendium of Substances* states that the self and the person are synonymous. In general, according to the Jaina tradition, when enumerating the six types of substance, the self and the person are listed separately. The self has the essence of knowing and cognizing, whereas the person is said to be a material substance endowed with form, smell, taste, and touch but without mind or life. The Jaina text, *Clear Realization of the Nature of Reality Sūtra*, states:

> Those endowed with touch, taste, smell,
> and color are called "persons."[244] [103]

Synonyms of the person are explicitly stated in *Clear Realization of the Nature of Reality Sūtra*: "Sound, binding, subtlety, coarseness, assemblage, division, shadow, darkness, light, illumination."[245] Here, sound and so on are presented as synonyms of the person, but it does not mention the self as a synonym of the person. However, Prajñāvarman's *Great Commentary on Praise of Excellent Distinction* says: "It is called life force, sustaining force, and self, because life force, born, nourished, person, and being are synonymous. 'So they say' means that the Jaina teacher states it thus."[246] Here, self and person are listed as being synonymous.

As for ways of categorizing the self, *A Source-Book in Jaina Philosophy* informs us that the *Bhagavatīsūtra* and the *Sthānāṅga* have mentioned eight divisions of self or soul: "(1) *dravyātmā* (soul as substance), (2) *kaṣāyātmā* (soul in the affective state), (3) *yogātmā* (soul as active), (4) *upayogātmā* (hermetic energy of the soul), (5) *jñānātmā* (soul as knowledge), (6) *darśanātmā* (intuitive experience of the soul), (7) *cāritrātmā* (soul as an ethical being), (8) *vīryātmā* (the inherent energy of the soul)."[247] So when enumerated in terms of its categories, the self is said to have eight divisions. However, the first among these is the self as substance, and the rest are its modifications. [104]

7

Buddhist Proofs of Selflessness

Refuting a Permanent, Unitary, Autonomous Self

The Indian Buddhist philosophical schools, as mentioned above, have been known since ancient times as *anātmavāda*, "proponents of no-self." Selflessness is one of the four axioms presented in the Buddhist scriptures: "All products are impermanent, all contaminated things are suffering, all phenomena are empty and selfless, and nirvāṇa itself is peace."[248] In general, Buddhist philosophers are united in not accepting a self that is a permanent real thing, so this needs no further comment here. But the Vātsīputrīya, according to their own Buddhist system, accept a substantially existent person that cannot be expressed as either permanent or impermanent, which has on occasion, as will be explained below, been the object of critique of other Buddhist schools on the grounds that this would be tantamount to accepting the notion of a [real] self. Now, although Buddhist thinkers speak of no-self in a united voice, there are differences of subtlety regarding the self refuted. So here, in establishing selflessness, we will analyze what is being negated on the basis of differentiating three levels, from coarse to subtle: (1) refutation of a permanent, unitary, autonomous self, (2) refutation of a substantially existent, self-sufficient self, and (3) refutation of an inherently existent self. [105] Of these, the arguments for refuting the first two appear in the vast majority of Indian Buddhist scriptures, the most well-known of which are Vasubandhu's *Treasury of Knowledge* and its autocommentary; Bhāviveka's *Heart of the Middle Way* and its autocommentary, *Blaze of Reasoning*; Dharmakīrti's *Exposition of Valid Cognition*; and Śāntarakṣita's *Compendium of Reality* with the commentary on it by Kamalaśīla. The third level—the refutation of an inherently existent self—is presented extensively in Nāgārjuna's *Fundamental Treatise on the Middle*

Way and Candrakīrti's *Entering the Middle Way* with its autocommentary. So this topic of no-self, and what is being refuted, will be investigated on the basis of these texts.

As for the first—the refutation of a permanent, unitary, and autonomous self—such a self is refuted in the Buddhist treatises as follows. Since what is permanent is not dependent on conditions, it cannot have two contradictory functions—to produce results and not produce them. Also, if the self were permanent, then the one who creates a karmic action and the one who experiences the result of that karma would be identical. Also, since it is established that the self cannot be apprehended in isolation without depending on the apprehension of its parts such as the aggregates, the concept of a self as a unitary entity is untenable. For example, if Devadatta were to exist without depending on causes and conditions, then he would either exist permanently or be totally nonexistent. Arguments such as these are illustrations of those employed to refute the notion of a permanent, unitary, and autonomous self. Buddhist philosophers have a variety of arguments in common to refute what the non-Buddhist schools seek to establish—namely, a permanent self that is separate from the aggregates. [106] Dharmakīrti's *Exposition of Valid Cognition* says:

> Since what is permanent is not dependent [on a causal chain]
> it is incompatible for such a self to function
> and to cause arising in succession,
> where producing and not producing would be alike
> and cause and effect would become identical.[249]

Since a permanent thing does not depend on anything else, it is incompatible with the function of making successive results arise or not arise. Thus positing such [a self] is incorrect. Indeed, if it were to operate like that, then everything would necessarily occur simultaneously and cause and effect would be identical. Such faults as these would be entailed.

Certain tīrthikas assert that, like beds and seats, the body and so on are for the use of the permanent unitary self to accomplish its purposes. However, if it is permanent, then no cause whatsoever could bring about the production of specific attributes within it. If there is no cause that can bring about the production of specific attributes within it, then that self cannot be benefited. Therefore it is incorrect to claim that the body and the rest benefit the permanent, partless, unitary self.

The Buddhists explain this fault by means of the example of the Himalayan mountains and the Vindhya hills: neither is the cause of the other. Kamalaśīla's *Commentary on the Difficult Points in the Compendium of Reality* explains: "That which does not bring about the production of specific attributes in another thing is unable to benefit it. This is like, for example, the Himalaya and the Vindhya ranges. The body and the rest do not bring about the production of different attributes in a self that is permanent and unitary in nature. [107] This is an argument from the nonobservation of the pervader."[250] The same text goes on to say: "In that case, there is nothing that can benefit what is permanent, because nothing can be done for it at all."[251]

Some non-Buddhist tīrthikas argue that if there is no permanent self, then the results of karmic actions would be wasted. The Buddhists reply that even without a permanent self, an external thing such as a seed will gives rise to a sprout, as is directly perceived; likewise, even without a permanent self, the relationship between karma and its effect would not be wasted. Suppose someone claims that external seeds and so on are, like the body, controlled by a permanent self that experiences them. In response to this the Buddhists would contend that such an argument—to say that "If the body of a living being has no self, then it would be lifeless"—is presented with the premise that its negative pervasion—to say that "external things such as pots are lifeless, since they have no self"—would involve an internal contradiction. This is how it is refuted, for example, in Kamalaśīla's *Commentary on the Difficult Points in the Compendium of Reality*:

> Just as the potency of seeds and so on is specific to sprouts and so on even in the absence of a self as controller, this would be the case with internal things. Seeds and so on are not controlled by a self that is the receptacle of experience, like the body. Otherwise, the argument "This living body [108] does not lack a self because that would imply it does not have life and so forth," would be unfeasible. For to say, "In the case of things like pots, if they lack a self, they would be seen to be lifeless and so forth," would not be a negating inferential proof. For even if pots and so on had

> a self, how could this be a form of inference where its negative entailment holds?[252]

The Mīmāṃsaka say that just as the identification of a snake is not lost even though its coiled state and its extended state are different, likewise the self is permanent in nature even though its states are impermanent. The Buddhists respond: "To take your example, if that snake is permanent and unitary in nature, it would be unfeasible for different states to occur. Likewise, if you accept the self to be permanent and unitary in nature, it cannot occur in different states. If something occurs in different states, then it must definitely arise and perish moment by moment." This form of argument is presented in Kamalaśīla's *Commentary on the Difficult Points in the Compendium of Reality*:

> As for the example of the snake and so on cited above,[253] the following verse demonstrates that such things are not established as permanent and unitary in nature:
>
> > The snake also, [because it is momentary,
> > is liable to become coiled and so on.
> > If it were a real basis, like the person,
> > it would never be joined with another state].
>
> Just as if a person is a single unchanging entity, it is impossible for another state to occur, the same is true in the case of the snake. If it were disintegrating moment by moment, then another state could occur, [109] because the definition of "the occurrence of another state" is the arising of another nature.[254]

If one accepts such a self, then within the continuum of a single person there would be two different selves: a permanent self and an impermanent self. If one accepts a permanent nature along with its impermanent states, this would facilitate illogical consequences, such as asserting that a particular embodied being is a horse in nature but a sheep in terms of its present state!

In the context of disproving the Sāṅkhya view that inside each sentient being's body there dwells a self—and furthermore, since all of them are partless, they are all mutually pervasive Bhāviveka's *Blaze of Reasoning* presents the following objections to the concept of a partless unitary self. If this were the case, when one being is liberated, all would be liberated; similarly, when one being is bound, all would be bound; when one being hears a sound through the ear faculty, all would hear such a sound; when one being accomplishes a virtuous deed, all would accomplish such a deed; and when one being accomplishes a nonvirtuous deed, all would accomplish a nonvirtuous deed. In light of this argument, just as a certain part of the sky that is dark cannot be the same part that is endowed with light, and just as an area that is moist with rain cannot be the same area that is dry from heat, the self too cannot be said to be partless, unitary, and omnipresent. This would entail such incompatible attributes as those listed above. Bhāviveka's *Blaze of Reasoning* gives a detailed explanation: [110]

> Here is the Sāṅkhya tenet: within every individual body of all the migrating beings—gods, demigods, humans, animals, and so on—there dwells a person, and every one of these persons pervades all the others. Now, if these persons become liberated, then how can it be on one side only? In the case of one person becoming free from mental hindrances through enhanced purity, there would be the consequence that all beings would become free. If all the other persons remain in bondage, then how can only one become free? Their status remains the same. Thus not only does the liberation of beings become impossible, but there would also be the following problems:
>
> The same faults will ensue
> with respect to perceiving a sound,
> and so too with respect to virtue and nonvirtue.
> The unseen too would be indeterminate.
>
> Thus, upon apprehending a sound with the ear and so on, all persons would obtain exactly the same experience. Similarly, when one engages in virtuous deeds, all beings too would engage in virtue. Also, when one person engages in nonvirtue, every person would become endowed with nonvirtue. So too liberation, which is unseen, would be indeterminate. Why? Because the states have no differentiation. Similarly, it is impossible for one area of sky to be both dark and light or both wet and dry.[255]

Furthermore, if such a self were a partless unitary entity, [111] then, like space, there would be no difference at all between its states of experiencing and of not experiencing pleasure or pain, so it would not be one that experiences pleasure or pain. Kamalaśīla's *Commentary on the Difficult Points in the Compendium of Reality* explains this fault as follows: "If the self remained the same in nature, it would not experience pleasure, pain, and so on, because as in the case of space, there would be no difference between its state of experiencing and its state of not experiencing."[256]

With regard to refuting an autonomous self, the Buddhists argue that there cannot be such an autonomous self that is not dependent on the aggregates or their parts because there is no apprehension of a self in isolation, without relying on apprehending the aggregates or their parts. Also, if the self were utterly separate from the aggregates, then since they would have neither a causal nor an intrinsic relationship, they would be totally unrelated. Just as a pillar can be apprehended on its own without apprehending a pot, [such a self would be seen without the aggregates], but it is never seen in this way. Such an autonomous self is thus refuted. Nāgārjuna's *Fundamental Treatise on the Middle Way* says:

> It is impossible for the self to be separate
> from the appropriated [aggregates]; for if it were separate,
> then it would be apprehended without the appropriated,
> but there is no such apprehension.[257]

Non-Buddhist philosophers commonly accept the self to have three attributes: permanent, partless, and autonomous. In Candrakīrti's *Entering the Middle Way* and its autocommentary, one finds a way to refute all three attributes in one fell swoop, which we will present here. [112] The autocommentary says:

> With respect to the self that is asserted in each of these treatises of the tīrthikas, I say:
>
> > Because it is not arisen, like a barren woman's child,
> > such a self simply does not exist
> > and cannot be the basis for grasping at an "I."
> > It cannot be claimed to exist even on the conventional level.

This is because it contradicts their own inferences. The self asserted in this way is just nonexistent because it is not arisen, like the child of a barren woman. Also, it cannot be the object of self-grasping because it is simply not arisen. Not only is it impossible for it to exist ultimately, or to be the object of self-grasping ultimately, but also it cannot exist as these two even conventionally. This must be understood. Not only is it impossible for it to exist, or to be the basis of self-grasping, but also:

> Because all the various attributes of such a self as proposed
> in one treatise after another by the tīrthikas are undone
> by this logical proof that "It is not arisen," which they accept,
> none of the attributes of their self remain tenable.

In the Sāṅkhya texts the self's attributes are asserted to be: permanent, a non-creator, an enjoyer, without qualities, and without activity. In that case, [a counter-argument is proposed that] the self is not permanent, not a non-creator, and so on up to not without activity, because it is not produced by itself, like the child of a barren woman. Likewise, we could say also in relation to the Vaiśeṣika texts that the self is not permanent and is not a creator and so on because it is not produced by itself, like the child of a barren woman. One must understand that through this, [113] using the reason "It is not arisen" and the example "like the child of a barren woman" against all those proponents of self, the self and its attributes are refuted.[258]

[Thus Candrakīrti refutes these non-Buddhist notions of the self and its attributes using a reason that the opponents themselves accept: "It is not produced."]

Refuting the Vātsīputrīya Assertion of a Substantially Existent Inexpressible Person

Some Buddhists, such as the Vātsīputrīya, assert the existence of a substantially existent person that is inexpressible—as either permanent or impermanent, as either identical with the aggregates or different from them, and so forth—yet is self-sufficient and substantially established. The main point here, according to this school, is that if one accepts a "self" or "person" that is separate from the aggregates, then it would have to be a permanent real thing, as posited in the non-Buddhist traditions, and the self would be apprehended separately without any apprehension of the aggregates. Conversely, if one accepts such a self to be the aggregates themselves, then like the aggregates the self would be many, and when the aggregates disintegrated the self would also disintegrate—so at the time of death its continuum would be severed like that of the aggregates and actions done would be wasted. Unacceptable consequences such as these would be incurred in either case. Moreover, according to the scriptures, the Buddha did not reply when asked whether the body and the living being are the same substance or different. Having considered many such reasons, the Vātsīputrīya accept a self that is the basis of karmic action and result and that is not only inexpressible as identical with or different from the aggregates but also inexpressible as permanent or impermanent. [114] They accept such a self to be known by means of the six types of consciousness and to be the focal object of self-grasping. Since it is the agent of virtuous and nonvirtuous actions and the experiencer of the results of such actions, they say it is substantially existent. This is explained in Candrakīrti's *Entering the Middle Way Autocommentary*:

> In order to refute the assertions of the ārya Sāṃmitīya [that is, the Vātsīputrīya], who imagine the person to be substantially existent, their assertions are explained as follows:
>
> Some assert a substantially existent person that is inexpressible
> as identical or different, as permanent or impermanent, and so on.
> They say it is an object of knowledge of the six consciousnesses.
> They also say it is the basis of self-grasping.
>
> In brief, since the person is not apprehended apart from the aggregates, it is not different from the aggregates. Also it does not have the nature of the aggregates, for then it would arise and disintegrate [moment by moment]. In that case, it is not expressed as either identical with or different from the aggre-

> gates. Just as it is neither identical nor different, similarly the person is not expressed as permanent or impermanent. Moreover, it is known by the six consciousnesses. These proponents say that the person must be substantially existent because it is expressed to be an agent and an experiencer and is intimately related with bondage and liberation, saṃsāra and nirvāṇa. Also it is the very object of self-grasping.[259]

Similarly, Śāntarakṣita's *Compendium of Reality* states:

> Because it would constitute the tīrthika's view, [115]
> the person is not separate from the aggregates;
> and since it would become many and so on, it is not identical
> to them.
> Therefore it is best considered to be inexpressible.[260]

Now, what is this "self-sufficient substantially existent self" that is being refuted here? This refers to an autonomous person that is not imputed on any of the aggregates—whether taken individually, as a collection, or as a continuum—and this is called "the self-sufficient substantially existent self of the person." The arguments refuting this are presented in the ninth chapter of Vasubandhu's *Treasury of Knowledge Autocommentary*. To summarize, Vasubandhu asks: Do you Vātsīputrīya assert the person itself to exist as a self-sufficient substance? Or do you assert it to exist as a designation imputed on the basis of the aggregates? If you assert the first, then since the self would be separate from the aggregates, you would be accepting the tīrthika view, and furthermore, this would contradict your own standpoint of it being inexpressible as either identical to or different from the aggregates. If you assert the second—namely, that it is imputedly existent—then you are in agreement with our own position. Now if you say that the self is neither substantially real nor imputedly existent, but is designated as "self" with the aggregates as its causal basis, then does this mean that "self" is conceived on the basis of viewing the aggregates? Or does it mean that "self" is designated in dependence on the aggregates? If it is the first, then this is similar to the imputation of milk that occurs upon having perceived the assembled constituents of the milk. Just as there is no milk apart from those constituents, so there is no self apart from the aggregates. If it is the second, [116] then since the aggregates are the causal basis of imputation of the person, without those there would be no self.[261] In this way, the above view is refuted.

Wishing to avoid these objections, the Vātsīputrīya might respond by saying that the imputation of a self that occurs upon taking the aggregates as a causal basis is like the imputation of fire that occurs upon taking fuel as its cause, since the imputation of fire would be impossible without its fuel. Vasubandhu replies: In that case, just as both fire and fuel have no existence without being merely imputed upon the eight substantial particles, the person too would be imputedly existent in that it is imputed on the aggregates. And if you accept that the self arises in dependence on the aggregates in the same way that fire arises in dependence on fuel, then you would have to accept that the self is separate from the aggregates and is impermanent. Just as fuel and fire are separate in occurring at earlier and later moments respectively, you would have to accept that the aggregates and the self are also separate in the same way. Moreover, if you say that the statement "having taken the aggregates as a cause" means that the aggregates coexist with the self, having been taken as its basis, then the self would have to be separate from the aggregates. And just as when the fuel is finished there is no fire, so too when the aggregates are annihilated the self would be annihilated. In this way, the Vātsīputrīya rejoinders are rebutted by pointing out their faults.[262]

Now with respect to the Vātsīputrīya assertion that such a self is known by the six primary consciousnesses—from the visual to the mental consciousness[263]—Vasubandhu asks: Are you saying that although the eye consciousness knows the self in dependence on visual form, it cannot be said that "The self is form" nor that "The self is other than form," [117] and the same is true of all remaining classes of consciousnesses? In response, Vasubandhu argues: In that case, not only with respect to the self but also to something else like milk, you could say that milk is known by means of visual consciousness in dependence on visual form, yet milk cannot be said to be form nor separate from form. If so, this would contradict your own tenet wherein when differentiating objects of knowledge into five types—that which existed in the past, that which will exist in the future, that which exists in the present, the unconditioned, and the inexpressible—you posit the self alone as an inexpressible object of knowledge. Furthermore, when you say that the self is an object known by the six primary consciousnesses, if you accept it to be an object known by the ear consciousness, then the self would be something other than a visual form, in this case a sound. In that case, it would be contradictory to say that it is inexpressible as other than a visual form. The same applies to the other sense consciousnesses. Since the five sense consciousnesses each have their own kind of object, your position is undermined by this, too.[264]

Vasubandhu continues with his argument as follows: If you accept such a self, then this is tantamount to saying that the sūtra passage that states all dharmas[265] are selfless is incorrect. The Vātsīputrīya might respond by saying, "The self cannot be said to be a dharma nor said to be a non-dharma, so we do not contradict that sūtra passage." In that case, Vasubandhu argues, they would be contradicting their own claim that the self is an object known by the mental consciousness.[266] [118]

Now, in response to the objection that their position would contradict the statement in the sūtra that all manners of viewing as a self are distorted, the Vātsīputrīya might say that such a statement is pointing out that viewing the aggregates and so on as the self, where there is none, is distorted. Thus their position is not open to such a fault. In response, Vasubandhu states that this reply would contradict what they have said earlier—namely, that they neither assert the self to be the aggregates nor that it is not the aggregates.[267]

The Vātsīputrīya further object: "If the person is accepted to be just the aggregates, then surely this contradicts the sūtra passage that states that the five aggregates are the burden and the person is the bearer of the burden?" Vasubandhu responds that since this sūtra passage states that the former moments of the aggregates' continuum are the burden and the later moments of the aggregates' continuum are the burden bearer, there is no problem.[268]

Having thus extensively refuted the assertions of the Vātsīputrīya, as illustrated above, Vasubandhu establishes the so-called self (or person) to exist as an imputation, merely imputed upon the continuum of the aggregates. All of these analyses are found in Vasubandhu's *Treasury of Knowledge Autocommentary* in the section of chapter 9 that begins with the lines "So in what way do the Vātsīputrīya accept the person to exist? This is something that needs to be analyzed carefully. Do they assert it to exist as a substance? Or do they assert it to exist as an imputation?"[269]

A passage from Candrakīrti's *Entering the Middle Way* and its autocommentary—beginning from the line "Just as mind's distinctness from body is not considered to be inexpressible" up to the line "and because the self lacks those attributes of a real thing, [119] it does not exist"[270]—makes the following argument. It states that if the self were substantially existent, then since it would have to be established definitively either as the same substance as the aggregates or as a different substance from them, it is incorrect to say that it is inexpressible. For example, the Vātsīputrīya themselves do not accept the mind to be inexpressible as either the same substance or a different substance from visual form. Moreover, if the self existed as neither the same substance nor a different substance from the aggregates, then it would have to be imputedly existent. For the Vātsīputrīya themselves consider a pot to be imputedly existent, in that it does exist as a different substance from its own components, such as visual form. Also, if the self were not established as either the same substance or a different substance from the aggregates, then it could not exist as a real thing. For the Vātsīputrīya consider consciousness to be a real thing, not different from itself but different from visual form and so on. Real things must certainly be seen in those two ways, as the same or different. But if the self, as asserted by the Vātsīputrīya, does not have those attributes, then it would not be a real thing. Many such refutations as these are presented that negate their position.

In brief, through these statements it clearly says that if the self is substantially existent then it cannot be inexpressible, and if it is inexpressible then it must be imputedly existent. Also, an inexpressible self does not have the attributes of a real thing, so it cannot be a real thing.

Similarly extensive refutations of this view are presented in Śāntarakṣita's *Compendium of Reality* and Kamalaśīla's commentary on it. [120] Accordingly, *Commentary on the Difficult Points in the Compendium of Reality* says: "A real thing is not beyond being either the same as or different from another thing, because there is no third alternative. If that were not so, then form and the rest would also be mutually inexpressible [as identical or different from one another]."[271] It is incorrect to claim that the person is inexpressible as either the same as or different from the aggregates, because if it is a real thing, then necessarily it must be either the same as that very thing or different from it, since there is no third alternative. Otherwise, form could not be expressed as mutually identical to or different from any of the other aggregates. This explains how faults such as these would be incurred.

With regard to the third notion of self to be negated—namely, the refutation of an inherently existent person—this is negated by means of ultimate analysis, such as Nāgārjuna's fivefold reasoning set forth in his *Fundamental Treatise on the Middle Way* and Candrakīrti's sevenfold reasoning based on the example of the chariot. These arguments will be explained later in the presentation of the Madhyamaka view of emptiness.

A Brief Presentation of the Reasoning That Refutes the Self in the Sense of a Self-Sufficient Person

To present some examples of arguments establishing selflessness found in Buddhist texts in general, consider the following argument (let us call it "argument A"): "The *subject*, an autonomous self, does not exist by its own nature—as imagined by some philosophers—because it is not established either as the same nature or as a different nature from the aggregates—like, for example, a rabbit's horn."[272] [121] This is a typical argument aimed at establishing the absence of a self-sufficient self of person. It is similar to the neither-one-nor-many argument presented in Śāntarakṣita's *Ornament for the Middle Way*, which begins with the words "These things posited by our own and others' systems" and so on, which will be examined later in the presentation of suchness according to the Madhyamaka system.

To establish the reason to be an *attribute of the subject* in relation to this argument establishing selflessness (i.e., argument A), the first part—that such a self is not the same in nature as the aggregates—must be established. This is done through the following argument (argument B): "One's own aggregates are not the same nature as—that is, inseparably coexistent with—a self-sufficient person because they are impermanent, changing moment by moment, and are dependent on other causes and conditions." Now, to establish the reason to be an attribute of the subject (in argument B), the following argument is posited: "One's own aggregates are dependent on other causes and conditions because they have arisen from contaminated actions and mental afflictions." The pervasion[273] is established as follows: "If something were a self-sufficient person, it would necessarily be permanent and independent." This is explained by Devendrabuddhi in his *Commentary on Difficult Points in the Exposition of Valid Cognition*:

> This is a method that gives rise to seeing selflessness itself: by ascertaining through the reasoning that anything that disintegrates each moment is necessarily impermanent, one establishes that whatever is impermanent is necessarily at the mercy of other causal factors and disintegrates each moment without there being any [additional] agent causing such disintegration.[274]

The second part of the logical reasoning that an autonomous self and the aggregates are not different in nature is established by the following argument (argument C): "An autonomous self does not exist as different in nature from the aggregates, because if it did, then this would be perceived by valid cognition, but it is not perceived." For example, Candrakīrti's *Clear Words* says: "If you say that the self [122] is different from the aggregates, just as consciousness is different from the physical body, then it would have characteristics different from theirs. If its characteristics were different from theirs, like those of body and mind, then it would be apprehended as such [as something different], but it is not apprehended. Therefore it is not different from the aggregates."[275] That is to say, if someone claims that the self and the aggregates have different characteristics, as do body and mind, then just as body and mind are apprehended separately, the characteristics of the self and those of the aggregates would have to be perceived as different, but it is impossible to perceive them in this way.

Although the explicitly stated subject of the basic argument (argument A) does not exist, the logical evidence could still be said to be established in the subject. This is because the opponent of the argument, the non-Buddhist, conflates the two—the notion of a self-sufficient person and its appearance—and yet harbors the desire to know what such a self is. So the logical reason is established on the basis of the concept, the linguistic referent,[276] that appears to the opponent's conceptual cognition. For if the self-sufficient self were not taken to be the subject, then such a self of person could not be refuted. Moreover, given that the opponent has conflated such a self with the linguistic referent or conceptual image that is perceived, there is no fault incurred by that linguistic referent not being the subject of that argument. Therefore it is important to understand the difference between the following two things: If it is a correct form of reasoning, then the subject of such an argument, about which the opponent wants to know, must be existent. This does not mean, however, that if something is the subject of such a correct logical argument, then it must necessarily be existent.[277]

Again one could argue that the subject, the person, does not exist in an autonomous manner—in the sense of not being merely imputed on the aggregates—because [123] if it existed in that way then it could be perceived by valid cognition, but it is not. This form of argument is presented in Asvabhāva's *Commentary on the Ornament for the Mahāyāna Sūtras*:

> Existent things, whatever they may be, are known by valid perception or by inference. Visual forms and so on are known by direct perception. The visual sense faculty and the rest are known by means of inference. The self is not known by direct perception or by inference, hence the self does not exist. So this means that it is in relation to the mind alone that the self is imputed. That which is viewed as self has arisen in error, just like when a rope has been mistaken for a snake; this is merely a case of error in relation to a rope. Therefore, by being free from the illusion of the rope as a snake, one's body and mind become freed from fear. The term "merely" is stated here because in reality there is no self, and what exists is only an error [where what is perceived] is not the self.[278]

This is to say, in general, anything that exists in the manner of a real thing must be realized by one of the two types of valid cognition. In particular, if a self-sufficient, substantially real self or person were to exist, then it must be known either by valid direct perception, such as visual consciousness, or by valid inferential cognition based on reasoning. If it is not known in such a manner, then the mind apprehending a self-sufficient self would be a mind that is erroneous with respect to its conceived object[279] engaging it in a mistaken way, just like the mind apprehending a coiled rope to be a snake. [124]

Another argument is posited as follows. "The *subject*, the contaminated appropriated aggregates, are empty of a self-sufficient self because they arise due to causes and conditions and they perish due to changing every moment." This is a syllogism (*sbyor ba*)[280] refuting such a self. The pervasion [between the reason and the predicate of the thesis] is established because if it is a self-sufficient self, then it must exist without depending on anything else, while the aggregates are the converse of this [i.e., they are dependent on others]. This way of establishing the pervasion is presented in Haribhadra's *Short Commentary on the Ornament for Clear Knowledge*, where he writes: "By meditating with the thought 'Because it is empty of arising and perishing, the self does not exist,' the manifest conceiving [of something] as a self is completely abandoned."[281]

Furthermore, in his *Compendium of Abhidharma* Asaṅga explains how the external aggregates of form and so forth do not exist as the self's objects of experience. He also underscores how the internal aggregates not only do not exist as a self-sufficient self, they do not exist as belonging to such a self. As the *Compendium of Abhidharma* states:

> The Buddha said, "All these things are not mine, not me, not my own self. Thus it is so." What is the meaning of the words "Thus one should really understand that through right wisdom"? The words "All these things are not mine" are spoken with this intention: external things are not mine; internal things are not me; and this is not my own self. In this way, with respect to external things he negates the notion of "mine," [125] and with respect to internal things he negates the notion of "me" and of "my own self."[282]

Although in a general sense one will realize selflessness through refuting the dharmas to be established as the self in terms of their own nature, the sūtra passage cited above in *Compendium of Abhidharma* speaks of no-self in three ways. External things are "not mine" because they are not established to be under the control of an autonomous self. The internal aggregate of consciousness is not an autonomous self—in other words, "not me"—because it is not the essential nature of a self of person. The remaining internal aggregates are "not my own self" because they are not established to be under the control of an autonomous self. External things are never apprehended as "me" so they are negated only as "mine" here. Internal things can be apprehended as either "me" or "mine" so they are negated both as "me" and as "mine" here.

Furthermore, one may prove that an autonomous or self-sufficient self does not exist based on the reason that it arises in dependence on causes and conditions. For example, Asaṅga's *Śrāvaka Levels* says:

> "Whatsoever conditioning factors endowed with the characteristic of suffering do not exist autonomously because they are dependently arisen. Whatever does not exist autonomously is selfless." Contemplating thus, one engages in the notion of selflessness by means of the notion of not existing autonomously.[283]

Similarly, Vinītadeva's *Commentary on the Thirty Stanzas* [126] says:

> If persons are asserted to arise dependently, then they would be impermanent. But the notion of an impermanent self is pointless because then it would be just like the body. If persons are asserted to not arise dependently, then they would be permanent. But a permanent entity cannot create virtuous and nonvirtuous actions nor experience their results because it would be devoid of change.[284]

In other words, if the person arises in dependence on causes and conditions, then it must be impermanent. If so, then like the body, to accept it to be an autonomous self would be pointless. But if the person is asserted to be permanent, then since its nature would be unchanging, it could not be the creator of actions nor the experiencer of pleasant and unpleasant results.

8

Repelling Objections to No-Self

How Karma and Its Effects Remain Tenable in the Absence of Self

In response to the refutation of self presented with extensive reasoning by the Buddhists, the tīrthikas raise objections—such as how, if there is no self, recognition could not occur, cognition of an object by an awareness would be impossible, the thought "I" could not arise, to posit an agent of karmic actions and an experiencer of their resultant pleasure or pain would become impossible, the presentation of cause and effect would be obliterated, and many presentations included within ordinary mundane conventions would become untenable. Such objections and the Buddhist's responses to these [127] are explained in the ninth chapter of Vasubandhu's *Treasury of Knowledge Autocommentary*.[285] These objections are as summed up in Madhyamakasiṃha's *Compendium of Distinctions among Different Views*, where he writes: "Brahmin Uttamagotra declared: If the self did not exist, your generosity and so on would be meaningless, just as a dead body has no feeling of pleasure and so forth. If the self did not exist, how could there be any results of generosity and so on?"[286] According to the tīrthikas, without a self, there would be no person at all who accumulates karma and experiences pleasure and pain resulting from those actions, just as a dead body does not experience pleasure and so on. This would incur the fault that actions and their results would be wasted. Thus the tīrthikas dispute the Buddhist view and argue that their standpoint will be undermined, providing reasonings they presented earlier to prove that the self exists.

In general, the object to which the term *self* refers may be either of the two: the self that conventionally exists or the self that is the object of negation. When one says such things as "I am going," "I am sitting," "I am experiencing pleasure or pain," and so on, this "I" being referred to is the conventionally existent self. Conversely, if one speaks of an autonomously established "I" that is not dependent on other things such as the aggregates, the referent of such a "self" is the object of negation. In particular, Candrakīrti's *Commentary on the Four Hundred Stanzas* says: "Here the term *self* refers to an essential nature of things that does not depend on others."[287] [128] That is to say, the term *self* refers to an essence of things that does not depend on a linguistic or conceptual convention in that it is not posited through the force of that. This inherent nature itself is the self to be refuted. Therefore what is being referred to as the *self* in the context of "selflessness" presented in the Buddhist texts is either a self-sufficient self that is conceived to be separate from the aggregates or an inherently existent self.[288] It is not the case that the Buddhists do not accept a self that is the basis of conventions as the experiencer of pain and pleasure, going and coming, and so on. Thus it is extremely important to differentiate between the self that conventionally exists and the self that is the object of negation. When making this differentiation, Buddhist realists say that even though a permanent, unitary, autonomous person that is a different entity from the aggregates does not exist, a person is found among the aggregates that are its basis of imputation. Hence, they maintain, there is no danger of there being no accumulator of karmic actions or experiencer of their results.

However, according to the Prāsaṅgika Madhyamaka master Candrakīrti, the way in which the person is posited in all the other tenet systems—from the non-Buddhist tīrthikas up to the Svātantrika Mādhyamika—falls into the extreme of permanence. Thus he maintains that self is neither separate from the aggregates, its basis of imputation—as proposed by the tīrthikas—nor is it identical with the aggregates—as asserted by Buddhist tenet systems [from Vaibhāṣika] up to Svātantrika.[289] Instead, Candrakīrti posits the person to be merely an imputation constructed by thought in dependence on the aggregates. Since he accepts this alone to be the accumulator of karmic actions and the experiencer of their results, he maintains his standpoint to be free from all the faults. These points are spelled out in Candrakīrti's *Entering the Middle Way Autocommentary*: [129]

> Just as one simply accepts "This arises in dependence upon that" and does not arise from a noncause and so on—so as not to annihilate the presentation of conventional truth—likewise, here, given that [the self] is totally dependent in being imputed upon

> a basis, having disproved the presentations with the aforementioned faults one must then accept it to be merely "imputed in dependence upon the aggregates." In this way, one fully abides within worldly conventions, because one does observe the convention of self as imputed [in the world].[290]

In other words, although there is no arising without a cause, one accepts things as mere dependent arising so as not to lose the presentation of conventional reality. Similarly, in the case of a convention that agrees with what is accepted in the world, such as "I did this deed," once we have rationally refuted various faults—such as a self being either utterly separate from or identical with the aggregates that are the basis of imputation, and so forth—then we must accept it to be *merely imputed* upon the aggregates that are its basis of imputation.

Furthermore, just as a chariot, though not established as permanent, unitary, and autonomous, is not totally nonexistent but exists as a mere imputation in dependence on its parts, such as the wheels, likewise the self, though not established as permanent, unitary, and autonomous, merely exists as something posited by linguistic convention and accepted in the world. It is the appropriator of the appropriated, which are the five aggregates, six elements, and six sense bases. [130] The appropriated five aggregates are what is acted upon, and the self is the agent, as explained in Candrakīrti's *Entering the Middle Way Autocommentary*:

> Just as a chariot is imputed in dependence upon its wheels and so on, in that the chariot is the appropriator and its wheels and so on are the appropriated, likewise, to not annihilate worldly conventions as conventional truth, the self is considered the appropriator, like the chariot. The five aggregates, six elements, and six sources are the appropriated objects of the self, because the self is imputed in dependence upon the aggregates and so on. Just as the wheels and so on are the appropriated objects of the chariot, so the aggregates and so on are called the "appropriated objects" of the self. Just as this presentation of the appropriated and the appropriator is given according to worldly convention, so too the presentation of the object acted upon and the agent is to be accepted in the same way, like the chariot.[291]

Also, Nāgārjuna's *Fundamental Treatise on the Middle Way* says:

> Afflictions, karmic actions, bodies,
> agents, and results are
> like a city of gandharvas and
> like a mirage or a dream.[292]

Thus, as stated above, although the self is not inherently established, it is accepted to exist conventionally, [131] and owing to this an agent and object of action can be posited. Mental afflictions such as attachment, actions accumulated under their influence, the body endowed with sense faculties, the self that is the agent, the results of actions, and so on, although not inherently existent, are not totally nonexistent either but exist merely conventionally. Prāsaṅgika Madhyamaka considers them to be like a city of gandharvas, mirages, dreams, and so on, which appear but are not true.

In brief, most Buddhist and non-Buddhist philosophers accept that there is karmic action and an experiencer of its resultant pleasure and pain. Thus, in relation to the fear that if there is no self there would be no accumulator of karmic actions and no experiencer of its resultant pleasure and pain, Buddhists allay this objection by distinguishing between the self that is the object of negation and the self that is the experiencer of pleasure and pain. In general, "karmic action" refers to the creation of a new causal condition in the form of an action done with intention by an agent. The Sanskrit term *karma* refers to something that has the nature of an action, as is stated in Saṅghabhadra's *Commentary on the Treasury of Knowledge*, where it says: "Since it is in the nature of something done, it is called *karma*."[293] The view here is this: whatever activity of body, speech, and mind one engages in, it leaves a variety of imprints—good and bad—upon one's mental continuum; in turn, these give rise to results in the form of happiness and suffering in the future. [132]

Positing the Conventional Nature of Persons

Upon hearing such views, one might ask, "What do the Buddhists who propound selflessness posit to be the person—the one who engages in karmic action and experiences its result?" In general, the *person* is defined as a living being imputed in dependence upon any of the five aggregates. Several terms synonymous with "person" are listed in the texts. For example, the *Teachings of Akṣayamati Sūtra* states the following: "Some sūtras use terms such as self, sentient being, living being, nourished being, creature, person, vital being, able being, agent, and experiencer."[294]

Within the continuum of a single person, although there is only one "me," several facets of "me" can be posited. For example, in Bhikṣu Devadatta's continuum there is the facet that is a human, the facet that is a male person, the facet that is a monk, and so on; and viewing each one of these different facets, the thought "me" arises in his mindstream. Indeed, just as in one's own case there are many facets of "me," so in the case of other people many facets of "me" must be posited. Moreover, each one's identity is posited primarily in relation to a specific collection of aggregates that are the basis of such identification. For example, on a collection of aggregates that are specific to the bodily basis of a human, there is a *human being*; on a collection of aggregates that are specific to the bodily basis of an animal, there is an *animal*; and so on. Regarding a human being too, there is male or female, large or small, wise or foolish—all posited on the basis of the different attributes of the corresponding collection of aggregates. [133]

Buddhist schools recognize that if one posits the person in too affirmative a manner, this leads to the extreme of eternalism; yet if one posits it in too negative a manner, this leads to the extreme of nihilism, where it becomes impossible to accept the notion of an agent of karma and an experiencer of its resultant pleasure or pain. Seeing this, each school of Buddhist philosophy posits its position according to its own understanding of how to avoid falling to either of the two extremes, presenting arguments based on scripture. An example of a scriptural source taken as authoritative by each Buddhist school is a stanza from an early Buddhist sūtra that Candrakīrti quotes in his *Entering the Middle Way Autocommentary*:

> Just as we refer to a chariot
> based on the group of parts,
> so, based on the aggregates,
> we have the convention "sentient being."[295]

Although they do not differ in accepting this sūtra verse to be authoritative, various tenet systems have differences between how they posit the person can be discerned based on how they flesh out the implications of the words of this verse. For example, most Buddhist realist schools read "the aggregates" in the above verse to mean each of the five aggregates individually. Since, in general, a collection is posited in dependence upon individuals, [134] they read the sūtra passage to mean that the collection of aggregates itself is posited as the person, which they understand to be indicated by the lines "based on the aggregates, we have the convention 'sentient being.'"

The Scripture-Following Yogācāra maintain that when one searches for the referent of the term *person*, there must be something that is found to be the person. Since nothing separate from the aggregates is found, it must be located among the aggregates, which they understand to be the meaning of the phrase "based on the aggregates." Furthermore, upon searching for the person among the aggregates, only the foundation consciousness can be posited as the basis of identity of the person since nothing else is suitable as its basis of identity. This is what they claim to be the meaning of the above scripture.

According to Svātantrika Madhyamaka masters such as Bhāviveka, since the sūtra states that the person is posited in dependence upon the aggregates, this implies that there must be something else that posits it. Since it cannot be posited merely by thought, it must be posited through the force of appearing to a nonerroneous cognition[296] that is unmistaken with regard to the intrinsic character of its object. Moreover, it is not enough for it to be posited merely by appearing to a nonerroneous cognition. It must be something that is established as the basis of imputation from the side of the aggregates. If it were not dependent on being established, or non-established, from the side of the aggregates as its basis of imputation, then this would entail the fault that human aggregates and so on could be the basis of imputation for another kind of living being. Therefore they say that the phrase "based on the aggregates" has two meanings. On the negative side, the person is not established without depending on something else that posits it. On the positive side, there must be something established as its basis of imputation from the side of the aggregates and so on that are its basis. [135]

According to Prāsaṅgika Madhyamaka, although the shape and parts of a chariot, whether individually or taken together, cannot be posited as the chariot, the mere name *chariot* imputed in dependence upon them as its basis of imputation allows one to posit such conventional expressions as "The chariot goes out and comes back." Similarly, in the case of the term *person*, although there is nothing found to be the person among the aggregates that are its basis of imputation, and nothing found to be the person that is a separate entity from these aggregates, there is the mere "I"—merely imputed by language and thought in dependence on the causes and conditions and on the aggregates that are its basis of imputation—that is posited as the person. This is stated concisely in Candrakīrti's *Entering the Middle Way*:

> [Self] is not something different from the aggregates,
> nor is it the aggregates themselves;
> the aggregates are not its support, nor does the self possess them;
> this proves that the self exists in dependence on the aggregates.
>
> A chariot cannot be said to be different from its parts;
> it is not identical with the parts, nor does it possess the parts;
> it is not in the parts, nor do the parts exist in it;
> it is not the mere collection, nor is it the shape.[297]

In general, all Buddhist philosophical schools [from Vaibhāṣika] up to Svātantrika Madhyamaka consider the person to be imputedly existent, yet they accept there is something substantially real, such as mental consciousness, that is the basis of identity of the person. [136] Thus when they posit the basis of identity of the person, some Sāṃmitīya (a subschool of Vaibhāṣika that includes the Vātsīputrīya) say that the person is the mere aggregates, while others say it is all five aggregates, or it is just the mind, or it is the inexpressible self. The Kashmiri Vaibhāṣika and the Scripture-Following Sautrāntika say it is the continuum of aggregates. The Reason-Following Sautrāntika, the Reason-Following Cittamātra, and the Svātantrika Mādhyamika say it is the mental consciousness. The Scripture-Following Cittamātra say it is the foundation consciousness, while Reason-Following Yogācāra say it is the mental consciousness.

Those who say that the basis of identity of the person is all five aggregates do not accept it to be the aggregates individually but rather consider the collection of five aggregates to be the person. Those who say that the basis of identity of the person is consciousness posit the mental consciousness—

the accumulator of actions and experiencer of their results, which circles in saṃsāra continuously without interruption through past and future lives—to be the person. The Avantaka (another subschool of the Sāṃmitīya) accept the mind alone to be the basis of identity of the self. In presenting their view, Candrakīrti's *Entering the Middle Way Autocommentary* says:

> Others say, "The mind is the self," for it is stated in the following scripture:
>
> > Oneself is one's own protector;
> > what other protector could there be?
> > With self well tamed,
> > a master attains the supreme state.
>
> Here, the mind itself is referred to by the term "self." If you ask, "How do we know this?" it is because there is no self apart from the aggregates, and another scriptural passage teaches that it is the mind that is to be tamed:
>
> > Taming the mind is excellent; [137]
> > a tamed mind leads to bliss.
>
> Therefore "self" refers to the mind, which is the basis of grasping at "I."[298]

The Kaurukullaka (also a subschool of the Sāṃmitīya) accept all five aggregates to be the self. Candrakīrti's *Entering the Middle Way Autocommentary* says:

> This is the position of some of those among the ārya Sāṃmitīya Buddhists. The root text says:
>
> > Some say the basis of self-viewing is all five aggregates;
> > some say it is just the mind.
>
> Some consider all five aggregates—form, feeling, discernment, conditioning factors, and consciousness—to be the focal object of the identity view, which is also the grasping at the self to be real. For it says in a sūtra:

> O monks, be it a renunciant or a brahmin, whosoever views with the thought of "I" views so only in terms of these five aggregates of appropriation.

They base their interpretation on this passage.[299]

The Kashmiri Vaibhāṣika and some Sautrāntika assert the continuum of aggregates to be the basis of identity of the self, which is the basis of actions and their results. This is explained in Vasubandhu's *Treasury of Knowledge Autocommentary* as follows: "This expression 'self' refers only to the continuum of aggregates, not to any other expressed object."[300] [138] Both Reason-Following Sautrāntika and Reason-Following Cittamātra say that the mental consciousness is the self, which accords with Dharmakīrti's *Exposition of Valid Cognition*:

> As for the terminal mind, it is in no way contradictory
> for it to connect up with another mind.[301]

The above passage, which appears in a context presenting positions common to both Sautrāntika and Cittamātra, states how among the five aggregates it is the mental consciousness that connects up with another life [at the time of death]. Thus clearly they accept mental consciousness to be the basis of identity of the self or person.

The Svātantrika Mādhyamika accept the mental consciousness to be the self based on the following argument. They posit the term *self* as that which takes up the aggregates, and since the aggregates of each rebirth are taken up by the mental consciousness, the mental consciousness is posited as the self. They consider this to be proof that the mental consciousness is the self. Bhāviveka's *Blaze of Reasoning* states: "In this way, we too consider that the term *self* explicitly designates the mental consciousness conventionally."[302] Also, Haribhadra's *Commentary on the Perfection of Wisdom in Eight Thousand Stanzas* says:

> As for what is called *person*—whose nature is characterized in terms of cause and effect, propensities, and that which imprints such propensities—it would be incorrect for it to be

> a permanent entity. So it is something replete with propensities of virtuous and nonvirtuous karma and is impermanent. So, in accordance with those [propensities], one appropriates and takes up corresponding rebirth as beings. [139] Thus, to be more exact in meaning, the term refers to the continuum itself—namely, a person.[303]

The Scripture-Following Cittamātra similarly present as their proof the reasoning that "because the foundation consciousness takes rebirth, it is the self." And as for how the foundation consciousness is asserted to be the self, the Scripture-Following Cittamātra say that the foundation consciousness is the person because a consciousness must be posited as the basis for death and rebirth, but the six collections of consciousness[304] are coarse and are not present when one connects with a new life so they cannot be the appropriator of rebirth nor a basis for carrying karmic imprints. However, there remains no other basis for the imprints, so if one does not accept the foundation consciousness, then all virtuous and nonvirtuous karmic seeds would be wasted. Thinking in this way, they assert the foundation consciousness, separately from the six types of engaging consciousness, to be the mind that maintains a connection between lives and is the basis of virtue, nonvirtue, and so on. The *Descent into Laṅkā Sūtra* states:

> For the [afflictive] mind, the foundation consciousness is the self and the other consciousnesses are what belong to the self.[305]

That is to say, with regard to the thought "I," the foundation consciousness is the basis conceived as "self" by the afflictive mental consciousness, while the collection of six consciousnesses is the basis conceived as "mine." The *Unraveling the Intention Sūtra* says: "Vipulamati, this consciousness is to be known as the 'appropriating consciousness' because it takes hold of this body and appropriates it."[306] That is to say, the foundation consciousness is the consciousness that takes up a body [140] and is posited as the self or person. Many rational proofs for the foundation consciousness and the afflictive mental consciousness are put forward by this tradition. One can learn about these from the explanation of Cittamātra tenets presented in volume 3 of *Science and Philosophy in the Indian Buddhist Classics*.

The Prāsaṅgika Mādhyamika posit the mere "I" to be the self as follows.

The mere "I," which is the object that upon being perceived gives rise to the thought apprehending "I," is posited to be the self conventionally. Thus what is called a "person" exists neither as an entity that is different from the aggregates, as asserted by the tīrthikas, nor as the aggregates, as explained by the lower Buddhist schools. This point is clearly stated in the *Great Final Nirvāṇa Sūtra*:

> O monks, in the case of all sentient beings, physical form is not the self; physical form does not exist within the self; the self does not exist within physical form and so on up to and including consciousness. O monks, what the tīrthikas and so on claim to exist as the self, this too is not separate from the aggregates, because statements such as "The self exists on the other shore following the discarding of the aggregates" are baseless.[307]

Moreover, that same sūtra says: "Śāriputra, countless monks will, through realizing the absence of 'me' and 'mine' in these five aggregates, attain the state of an arhat."[308]

"What then is the nature of the person?" one might ask. Whether individually or as a collection, the parts of a chariot, for example, cannot be posited as the chariot; however, [141] in dependence upon these bases of designation, the *chariot* as a mere name can be imputed. Owing to this, one can use conventions such as "The chariot is departing" and "The chariot is arriving." Similarly, when the thought "I" arises in dependence upon the aggregates, there is nothing on the part of the aggregates—whether based on a collection of the aggregates in a continuum of earlier and later moments, a collection of them at one time, or any of their parts—that could even to the slightest degree be posited as the basis of identity of the self. Yet there is nothing that is a different entity from the whole or parts of the aggregates that could even to the slightest degree be posited as its basis of identity either. Therefore the self is merely posited by conceptual cognition in dependence upon the aggregates, but it does not exist by way of its own nature even in the slightest.

Nevertheless, since one can undeniably posit agents and actions such as "I am going" or "I am staying" on the level of mere convention, the person conventionally exists. Also, when the thought "I" arises, since it arises in dependence upon taking the aggregates of one's own continuum as a basis, the mere "I" imputed in dependence upon the aggregates is asserted to be the person. Nāgārjuna's *Precious Garland* says:

> The "person" is not earth, not water,
> not fire, not wind, not space,
> not consciousness. If it is not all these,
> then what else could the "person" be?
>
> Because it is composed of the six constituents,
> the "person" is not truly real.
> Likewise for the "constituents," because each
> is also a composite, they are not truly real.[309]

Here it is explained very clearly that the living being or person is merely imputed in dependence upon a composite of the six constituents, but that the person cannot be the constituents individually or collectively, nor anything that is a different entity from them. [142]

The Reasoning That Establishes Former and Future Lives

In general, except for Cārvāka, ancient Indian philosophical schools are united in their agreement that sentient beings take birth in this life after a previous one and that after the bodily basis of their life ceases they will depart to the next life, thus creating an uninterrupted continuum of former and future lives. The Cārvāka, on the other hand, do not accept that consciousness travels from a former life to this one or from this life to the next. They say that immediately upon being born, the mind arises only from the natural elements of this life. Now, although most of the other religious and philosophical systems apart from the Cārvāka school accept past and future lives, they give many different explanations concerning the person that takes birth, the way they take birth, how past and future lives are connected, and so on. Some do not accept that humans and gods can be born interchangeably; instead they say that a human can be born only if they had been a human previously, and a god can only be born if they had been a god previously. Also, some assert that there are no former lives, only an afterlife.[310]

All Buddhist schools accept both former and future lives, and they soundly refute views that suggest the mind at birth arises without a cause, from a permanent creator god or a permanent consciousness, from the material elements, or from someone else's stream of consciousness. They consider that the aggregate of physical form, which is the locus, exists separately from the consciousness located in it, and that after death the continuum of consciousness without interruption again takes on a new bodily locus in reliance on various dependently related causes and conditions that are conducive to it. [143] From the Buddhist perspective, the presentation of former and future lives is very important, and many explanations of Buddhist practice are based on the assumption of past and future lives.

In general, rejecting that sentient beings arise from no cause at all or arise from an incongruent cause, the Buddhist sūtras extensively present the manner in which consciousness continues without interruption after leaving this bodily support and connects with the next bodily support by way of eight analogies. We present these with a brief introduction here.

(1) When a student has understood the teacher's oral instruction regarding reading words aloud and is able to utter them in the same way, the teacher's utterance is not transferred to the student's speech; if it were, this would entail the fault that the teacher would never utter those words again. Additionally, the words spoken by the student are not established as independent of the teacher's utterance; if they were, this would entail the fault that they would be without cause. Similarly, when a former life connects with the subsequent one, the consciousness at the time of death is not unalterably transferred to the next consciousness; if it were, the consciousness at death would be permanent, which would entail the fault that it would not go to the next rebirth. Additionally, the consciousness of the subsequent rebirth does not arise without depending on the consciousness at death; if it did, this would entail the fault that the next consciousness would lack a cause. Moreover, just as the student's reading of the words is dependent on the teacher's oral instruction in how to utter them, so the subsequent life's consciousness arises in dependence on the previous life's consciousness at the time of death as its cause.

The remaining seven analogies are as follows: (2) the flame of a subsequent oil lamp lit from a previous oil lamp, [144] (3) a reflection of a form appearing in a mirror, (4) the imprint on paper from a stamp, (5) fire arising from a flint stone, (6) a sprout arising from a seed, (7) the occurrence of saliva from someone mentioning the word "sour," and (8) an echo from resonant sound. The linking of the consciousness at death with the subsequent consciousness should be understood in accordance with each of these examples by applying them to the referent in turn. This is stated in the *Questions Regarding Transference of Life Sūtra*:

> Great King [Śuddhodana] asked: "Blessed One, when sentient beings pass on from life they take rebirth; they do not do so as something permanent, nor as something annihilated, nor without a cause, nor due to the act of a creator. So, it is difficult to understand how rebirth takes place in the world beyond. Are there any suitable analogies?"
>
> The Blessed One replied: "O Great King, regarding this there are eight suitable analogies: the analogy of a student's understanding arising from the guru's verbal instructions, an oil lamp arising from a previous oil lamp, a reflection arising from a mirror, the design and imprint of a seal arising from the seal, fire arising from a flint stone, a sprout arising from a seed, saliva arising from mention of the word 'sour,' and the sound of an echo. It can be understood by means of these analogies. O Great King, these eight analogies, with the former giving rise to the latter, illustrate that passing on is not permanent; and with the latter arising from the former, they illustrate that it does not arise causelessly, and they illustrate that it is not annihilated or ceased."[311] [145]

The reasoning that establishes the existence of former and future lives is twofold: the reasoning to prove former lives and the reasoning to prove future lives. In the first case, there are a great many logical arguments to prove the existence of former lives, of which some of the main ones are: (1) the precedence of a prior substantial cause, (2) the precedence of a prior congruent cause, (3) the precedence of prior habituation, and (4) the precedence of prior experience.

1) The reasoning that former lives exist from the precedence of a prior substantial cause is the principal argument for former lives. Buddhists categorize causes into two types: substantial causes and cooperative conditions. Any caused thing must have both a substantial cause and cooperative con-

ditions. In the case of a clay pot, for example, a lump of clay suitable to be fashioned into a clay pot is its substantial cause, while the potter and the implements he uses to fashion it are the clay pot's cooperative conditions. Likewise, the aggregate of physical form of an ordinary newborn has both a substantial cause and cooperative conditions. Its substantial cause is the parents' egg and sperm and so on, from which it has evolved. The bodies of both parents also arose from the bodies of others, specifically from the egg and sperm of each of their respective parents. When one investigates how one's body arises from a previous one in a constant stream, there is no beginning to its substantial continuum. Āryadeva's *Four Hundred Stanzas* says:

> In the case of even a single effect
> its first cause cannot be seen, [146]
> but seeing the extent of such an effect
> who then would not be afraid?[312]

In a similar manner, the consciousness aggregate of a newborn has both a substantial cause and cooperative conditions. If consciousness did not have a previous moment of consciousness as its substantial cause, then it would have no substantial cause at all, because physical form and so on, which are not included in the continuum of consciousness, cannot be the substantial cause of consciousness—just as a rice seed cannot be the substantial cause of a barley sprout. [Stating the reason for this] Dharmakīrti's *Exposition of Valid Cognition* says:

> Because what is not consciousness
> is not the substantial cause of consciousness.[313]

That is to say, if something is not the *substantial continuum* of consciousness, then it cannot be the *substantial cause* of consciousness. But it does not say in general that if something is the substantial cause of consciousness then it must be consciousness, because its seed must also be posited as its substantial cause. The subtle particles of the four internal elements are utterly incongruent with the nature of consciousness and thus cannot be the substantial cause of consciousness, as is stated in Bhāviveka's *Heart of the Middle Way*:

> The characteristics of cognition are not congruent
> with the elements, so how can it arise from them?[314]

Since things arise with a nature similar to their causes, the great elements, endowed with tangible resistance and without mind, [147] cannot give rise to cognition, whose characteristics are utterly incongruent with them.

In brief, the substantial cause of external physical things that are derived from the elements is the elements, the substantial cause of the elements is earlier instances of the elements, and so on, prior to which again there must be something physical. Likewise, the substantial cause of consciousness is an earlier instance of consciousness, the substantial cause of that is yet again an earlier instance of consciousness, and so on, prior to which there must be a continuum leading back to something that is consciousness. Here then is the actual reasoning:

> *Subject*: A newborn's cognition.
> *Predicate*: It must have a precedence of a prior instance of cognition that was its substantial cause.
> *Reason*: Because it is a cognition.
> *Example*: Like the cognition of the present moment.

Śāntarakṣita's *Compendium of Reality* says:

> Therefore the initial consciousness
> arises from the capacity of its substantial cause
> by reason of merely being consciousness and so on,
> like the present moment of consciousness.[315]

2) The argument to prove the existence of former lives from the precedence of a prior congruent cause is as follows. A causally conditioned thing cannot arise from no cause at all nor from an incongruent cause, but must arise from a congruent cause. For example, from a piquant seed comes a piquant fruit and from a sweet seed comes a sweet fruit. Also, from a barley seed comes a barley sprout and from a rice seed comes a rice sprout, [148] not the other way around. The *Questions of Surata Sūtra* says:

> Piquant seeds
> produce piquant fruits.

Sweet seeds
produce sweet fruits.[316]

Here then is the reasoning. In the case of a newborn's cognition, when it actually takes birth it is not born from just the body without relying on a prior instance of similar type as itself, because it is a cognition, like the present moment of cognition. This applies likewise to the inhalation and exhalation of the breath, clear visual sense faculties, and so on. Dharmakīrti's *Exposition of Valid Cognition* says:

When [one] actually takes birth,
the breathing, sense faculties, and mind
do not arise from the just body itself
without relying on its own type.[317]

Also, if consciousness were to arise from the elements alone, then a thing that is materially composed would have to be of the nature of mere experience or cognition, not of something material. In that case, from among particles of similar type, it would be impossible to differentiate between those that are and those that are not of the nature of consciousness. This would entail the fault that all physical things must be of the nature of clear and cognizing consciousness. Dharmakīrti's *Exposition of Valid Cognition* says:

Therefore, if the sense faculties were to arise
without relying on their own type, [149]
then just as one would occur so would all,
because there would be no differentiation.[318]

3) The argument for the existence of former lives from the precedence of prior habituation is as follows. In the case of ordinary beings, it is through the force of prior habituation that, innately from the time they are small, some have clearer wisdom and greater compassion, while others have greater attachment and hatred. The actual argument can be formulated as follows. Attachment, hatred, and so on were preceded by similar earlier types because they are seen to arise naturally and with increasing intensity through habituation to them. Dharmakīrti's *Exposition of Valid Cognition* says:

> Through habituation, attachment and so on manifest
> because this is seen.[319]

As proved by one's own experience, ordinary beings strive earnestly to give rise to virtuous mental states, yet these only arise weakly for a short time, and though they try to prevent attachment and so on from arising, those arise intensely in a more continuous fashion. This is said to occur through the force of greater habituation to attachment and so on in former lives along with less habituation to virtuous states of mind.

4) The argument for former lives from the precedence of prior experience pertains to the act of recollection of former lives that involves being able to unmistakenly recognize one's previous home, companions, relatives, and so on. [150] This has been recorded not only in ancient times but even in the present day, as many similar accounts are found in various countries around the world. While some people might declare these to be such things as "false claims" or "blind faith," this response does not represent genuine investigation but rather discredits direct experience. In any case, if there were no transference of consciousness from a previous life to a subsequent life, such unmistaken recollections could not occur. Indeed, the proof of former lives based on the evidence of recollection or experience is an extremely compelling one.

As for how this remembering occurs, some people have recollection right from the beginning, while others have no recollection at first but when they see the place or belongings of their former life they suddenly remember it. Most ordinary people, once they pass the age of five or six, gradually forget their former life. Remembering one's own former life is not similar to clairvoyance, for in the latter case one knows another person's situation and is able to recall such knowledge. When recollection occurs, however, it takes the form of a first-person account where one identifies with what is being remembered. So this is very different from remembering what one may have seen or heard about another person's experience that one then later recalls. Āryaśūra's *Garland of Birth Stories* says:

> With recollection that is clear, through being habituated to
> concentration,
> former lives are remembered having this or that detail.
> Owing to this situation, other lives in the world are inferred.[320]

Bhāviveka's *Blaze of Reasoning* says:

> Among those who in this life remember their former lives, there are some who recall their past lives in numerous ways, and then there are some who, through their practice of morality and so on, conduct themselves quite differently from their parents and have different ethical discipline. [151] In this way so many varieties can be observed. Therefore their behavior and so on must be understood to come only from habituation in former lifetimes.[321]

Let us now briefly turn to Dharmottara's treatise, *Proof of the Afterlife*, where he presents the views of those philosophers who do not accept past and future lives and responds to them in the format of a dialectical debate. The text states:

> Some speak of the continuum of consciousness that remains uninterrupted prior to birth and subsequent to death as the afterlife. Such a statement is not a correct assertion. Consciousness that is different from the great elements of the body, which are not observed separate from the body, cannot be perceived even in the slightest. If the mind were *not different* from those bodily elements perceived to have a beginning and an end, how could it remain as a continuum of unending experience and not be severed? Even if it were *different*, the consciousness arises initially from the four great elements, then continues in the nature of the earlier consciousness for a short time, after which it perishes. Alternatively, even if on all occasions it is accepted that what gives rise to consciousness is cognition, [152] it is not established to be another life because the child's consciousness is born from the mother's mind.[322]

This text presents how some people do not accept past and future lives because they say that consciousness that is a different entity from the great elements of the body is not directly perceived, yet consciousness that is not a different entity from the bodily elements, due to having a beginning and end, cannot remain continuously without limit. And if one says that consciousness is a different entity from the body, one must still accept that it arises initially from the four great elements then remains constant for a short while, after which it perishes. Alternatively, even if one claims that consciousness is necessarily based on an earlier stream of consciousness, it is acceptable to say that the child's consciousness is born from the mother's consciousness. In this way, the position of the opponent is presented.

To refute these assertions, we need to understand Dharmottara's extensive statements in *Proof of the Afterlife*, where he begins with the following: "To these we present our response. First, out of their attachment to rejecting an afterlife, it is incorrect to say that there is no consciousness that is distinct from the body whose nature is the collection of the four great elements."[323] At this point, however, let us offer some further explanation to make the meaning of the debates in this text a little easier to understand.

When a visual consciousness perceives a physical form, a pleasant or unpleasant feeling that is experienced contemporaneously must be posited as something other than the perceived form. It is the mind induced by an experience—thinking "This is pleasant" or "This is unpleasant"—that ascertains what is being experienced, indicating that the consciousness (the subject) must be posited to be different from the form being perceived (the object). [153] This would mean that such a consciousness must be posited as distinct from the body as well.[324] The materialists may claim that just as the first moment of smoke arises from fire as its substantial cause but later moments arise only from a continuum that is of similar type as itself (i.e., earlier instances of smoke), likewise, consciousness initially arises from the bodily elements as its substantial cause but continues to remain afterward only from what is of similar type as itself. Yet such a statement is not correct, for just as the first moment of an oil lamp arises from the wick, flame, and so on, the second and subsequent moments must also arise from proximity to the wick, flame, and so on. Likewise, in each moment a visual consciousness relies on proximity to the eye sense faculty, space, and its immediately preceding condition, which is an attentive desire to look at a visual form. This is quite unlike how smoke arises.[325]

Similarly, it is in dependence on the latent propensities of having seen a blue color previously that the thought of a blue appearance arises in the mind, which occurs through the causal capacity of the ripening of such propensities [and not through the causal capacity of something outside the mental continuum]. It does not arise from the four elements, which is a cause that is dissimilar to itself. Moreover, it is incorrect to say that even if another mind precedes it, the child's mind is born from the mother's mind, because the child's mind is born with greater or lesser intelligence through the propensity of prior habituation. If it were born from the mother's mind, then the attributes of the child's mind would necessarily depend on the attributes of the mother's mind. That this too is incorrect is stated at length [in Dharmottara's text].[326] [154]

Now we come to the second case—the reasoning that proves the existence of future lives. Just as the mind of one's former life has connected with the mind of this life, so too the mind at the point of death will definitely connect to a later instance of mind. Thus it is said that future lives are proved. Dharmakīrti's *Exposition of Valid Cognition* states:

> It is not the case that all minds at the point of death
> cannot connect [with subsequent minds].[327]

The actual argument is posited as follows: The final cognition at the moment of death will connect with a subsequent cognition that is its own effect because it is a cognition having attachment, such as the present moment of cognition. As Kamalaśīla's *Commentary on the Difficult Points in the Compendium of Reality* says: "Any mind that is furnished with attachment is able to give rise to another mind that is its own substantial effect because it has attachment, like the mind on an earlier occasion; the mind at the moment of death is also furnished with attachment. This is a nature-inference."[328] [155]

Part 3

The Yogācāra Explanation of Ultimate Reality

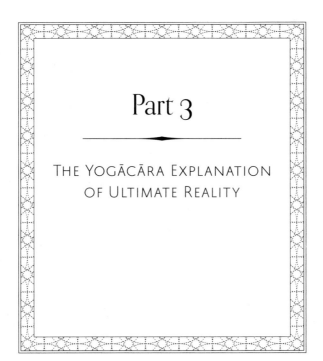

9

The Absence of Essential Nature according to Asaṅga

EARLIER WE EXPLAINED how the Indian Buddhist philosophical schools in general and the two Mahāyāna traditions, Madhyamaka and Cittamātra, in particular present the mode of existence of all phenomena on the basis of the theory of the two truths. Stemming from that discussion we will now explain first, of the two Mahāyāna traditions, how the Yogācāra, or Cittamātra, school presents the nature of ultimate reality.

The two brothers and key philosophers for this school, Asaṅga and Vasubandhu, considered the Madhyamaka system to be incorrect in their interpretation of the meaning of the Perfection of Wisdom sūtras, that all phenomena ultimately have no essential nature, to be equally applicable to everything [i.e., that everything is essenceless]. According to their system, the essencelessness of phenomena is interpreted in three distinct ways: the imputed nature lacks an intrinsically characterized essential nature; the dependent nature lacks a self-produced essential nature; and the consummate nature lacks an ultimately established essential nature. In this way, they initiated a new philosophical system, which has been explained in chapter 13 of the third volume of this series when presenting the tenets of the Indian philosophical systems. Asaṅga clearly states in his treatises that this system of delineating three ways of lacking essential nature as a means to elucidate the meaning of the Perfection of Wisdom sūtras' teaching that "all phenomena have no essential nature" is based mainly on the *Unraveling the Intention Sūtra*. In order to expound this unique philosophical system, Asaṅga [156] authored treatises such as the *Levels of Yogācāra*[329] and the *Compendium of the Mahāyāna*.

The *Compendium of the Mahāyāna* begins with a summary:

> The support of the knowable, its nature, entry into that,
> its causes and results, their divisions,
> the three higher trainings, the resultant abandonment,
> and wisdom: [these are] the superior qualities of the supreme vehicle.[330]

This passage identifies ten topics of great importance taught in the Mahāyāna sūtras that are not taught in the sūtras of the Śrāvakayāna and Pratyekabuddhayāna,[331] which is followed by an explanation of each in consecutive order. As presented by Asaṅga, these topics can be understood roughly in terms of: the *basis* that is the mode of existence of things; in dependence on that, the *path* that leads to liberation; and the *result* that is the final liberation. The ten topics are as follows. (1) The *support of the knowable* refers to the foundation consciousness. Since it is like the root or basis of all phenomena, it is called the "support of the knowable." Also it is said that the *fruitional foundation consciousness*, which is the support, serves as the basis of the *seed foundation consciousness*, which is the supported; and through the capacity of the seeds' awakening, causally compounded phenomena are produced and uncompounded phenomena are established. (2) The *nature*[332] *of the knowable* refers to the three natures—the imputed nature, the dependent nature, and the consummate nature. (3) *Entry into the nature of the knowable* means to enter into cognition only (*rnam rig tsam*, Skt. *vijñaptimātra*),[333] without external objects, by means of knowing the character of the three natures exactly as they are. The dependent nature, which is the basis, is itself the basis of emptiness. [157] Its existence as an external object, or its existence as substantially different subject and object, or suchlike, is the imputed nature that is the object of negation. The consummate nature is the basis of emptiness' mere emptiness of the imputed nature that is the object of negation. By knowing this one realizes all phenomena to be merely an internal appearance in the mind. This is called "entry into that nature." (4) The cause and result of this entry into the nature of the knowable are the *ordinary practices* of generosity, ethical conduct, and so on (which constitute the cause), as well as their *exalted practices* (which constitute the result). (5) Their *divisions* refers to the various ways of cultivating the six perfections on the ten bodhisattva grounds. (6)–(8) The *three trainings* are: ethical conduct, concentration, and wisdom. (9) The resultant fulfilled cultivation is the final *abandonment*. (10) The *wisdom* of the resultant fulfilled cultivation is the final realization.

As for the significance of the sequence in which these unique topics of the Mahāyāna are presented, Asaṅga's *Compendium of the Mahāyāna* states:

> Suppose someone asks: "Why are these ten topics taught in this sequence?" It is thus: In the beginning, based on their expertise in the causes of phenomena, bodhisattvas must develop expertise in dependent arising. Then, so as to gain expertise in abandoning the extremes—the faults of reification and denial—they must develop expertise in the nature of dependently arising phenomena. Bodhisattvas who train well in this must realize the nature in which they have developed expertise, which will liberate their minds from obscurations. Next, [158] after having realized the nature of the knowable, on the basis of pure superior intention they must actualize the realization of the six perfections introduced previously. Then, for three countless eons, they must cultivate the six perfections held with pure superior intention and apportioned among the ten grounds. After that, they must perfectly complete the three bodhisattva trainings. When perfectly completed, they must bring to fulfillment the resultant nirvāṇa and the unsurpassable perfectly complete enlightenment. So this is the order in which these ten topics are taught.[334]

Among the ten topics set forth in *Compendium of the Mahāyāna* above, those that are most closely connected with philosophical tenets are the first three: (1) the foundation consciousness, which is the *support* of the knowable; (2) the three natures, which are the *nature* of the knowable; and (3) cognition only, which is the *entry into the nature* of the knowable. The first of these—the foundation consciousness, which is the support of the knowable—has already been explained, along with logical proofs for its existence, in chapter 13, presenting Cittamātra tenets, in volume 3 of *Science and Philosophy in the Indian Buddhist Classics*. Here we would like to investigate the next two topics in particular: the three natures, which are the nature of the knowable, and cognition only, which is the entry into the nature of the knowable. [159]

10

The Three Natures

Defining the Three Natures Individually

The theory of the three natures is presented not only in the *Unraveling the Intention Sūtra* but also in other sūtras such as the *Descent into Laṅkā Sūtra*. However, Asaṅga relies primarily on the *Unraveling the Intention Sūtra* for his clear presentation of the three natures in the *Compendium of Ascertainments*, one of his treatises included within the *Levels of Yogācāra*. Given that knowing how this theory is presented in the *Compendium of Ascertainments* facilitates a good overview of the topic, let us cite from this treatise. The text says:

> The nature of phenomena must be viewed as taught in the *Unraveling the Intention Sūtra*. There it states, "The bodhisattva Guṇākara posed a question to the Tathāgata: 'O Blessed One, a bodhisattva who is expert in the nature of phenomena is called *a bodhisattva expert in the nature of phenomena*. O Blessed One, how should a bodhisattva be expert in the nature of phenomena?'" and so on....
>
> [The sūtra] then reads, "I will explain to you about being expert in the nature of phenomena. Guṇākara, the nature of phenomena is threefold. What are the three? They are the imputed nature, the dependent nature, and the consummate nature. Guṇākara, what is the imputed nature of phenomena? [160] It is the essential nature of phenomena owing to terms and conventions, or more specifically, the entity and attributes of phenomena as posited nominally or conventionally. Guṇākara, what is the dependent nature of phenomena? It is the dependent

> arising of phenomena, or that which can be expressed as follows: since this exists, that arises; because this is produced, that is produced; and from 'conditioned by ignorance, conditioning factors arise,' up to 'in this way precisely, the aggregates of suffering arise.' Guṇākara, what is the consummate nature of phenomena? It is that which is the suchness of phenomena. . . .
>
> "Guṇākara, it is thus: in the case of a person who has an eye disease, for example, the problem of this eye disease—like attachment—should be viewed as the *imputed nature*. Guṇākara, it is thus: in that very same case, the appearances that are the signs of this eye disease—like falling hairs, flies, or sesame seeds, or blue marks, yellow marks, red marks, white marks, and so forth—should be viewed as the *dependent nature*. Guṇākara, it is thus: in the case of that same person's eyes having become completely purified and freed from the problem of this eye disease, the nature of those eyes is unmistaken regarding their perceived object, [161] and such a perceived object should be viewed as the *consummate nature*."[335]

Thus the three natures are presented in a clear way along with some analogies. To explain them in the format of a concluding summation, the *Compendium of Ascertainments* says: "The nature of phenomena, in a nutshell, has three aspects: the imputed nature, the dependent nature, and the consummate nature."[336] This gives the basic presentation of the nature of all phenomena as definitively three in number: the imputed nature, the dependent nature, and the consummate nature. To posit the definitions of each of these three natures, the *Compendium of Ascertainments* says:

> What is the definition of the *imputed nature*? It is the nature that comes from applying a name or label, because it is the aspect that is imputed by convention. What is the definition of the *dependent nature*? It is the nature that is dependently arisen. What is the definition of the *consummate nature*? It is just as it is, because it is the perfectly pure object and because it is that which leads to complete liberation from the bindings of unwholesome states and from signs [of true existence].[337]

In other words, the definition of the *imputed nature* is that which is merely posited or imputed by name or label designated upon a dependent nature, which is the basis of designation or the basis of attributes.[338] The definition of the *dependent nature* is that which is a conditioned thing that arises in dependence on something else—its causes and conditions—and does not arise through its own capacity. [162] The definition of the *consummate nature* is: that which is the object of experience of perfectly pure wisdom or the final focal object of that wisdom.

In the section identifying the definition of the imputed nature, Asaṅga's *Compendium of the Mahāyāna* explains (1) the conceptualizing that designates the imputed nature, (2) the basis of designation [imagined] as the imputed nature, and (3) the entity of such imputation itself, as follows:

> What is the conceptualizing that imputes? What is the imputed? What is the entity of such imputation? A mental consciousness [does] the conceptualizing because it is furnished with conceptualization. It arises from seeds that are latent propensities for expressing itself and from seeds that are latent propensities for expressing every notion. Thus it arises with limitless possibilities for conceptualizing. Since it conceptually constructs [imputations] by conceptualizing in every way, it is called "conceptualizing." The dependent nature is the object imputed upon. The manner in which imputation is constructed in relation to the dependent nature constitutes the entity of imputation.[339]

So how does conceptualizing impute onto the dependent nature? *Compendium of the Mahāyāna* says:

> How does conceptualizing engage in imputation? What is the focal object, the apprehension of signs, the adherence, the motivation to speak, the classificatory convention, and the superimposition by means of which it imputes? It arrives at the object by way of a name; it apprehends signs based on the dependent nature; [163] it adheres to them by means of viewing; it motivates speech by way of inquiry; it designates by means of the four classificatory conventions, such as seeing; and it imputes by superimposing existence onto the nonexistent.[340]

By way of its name, conceptualizing arrives at the object that is the focal object. By way of discernment, it apprehends its signs. By way of viewing, it adheres to the thing whose signs are apprehended by discernment. By way of inquiry and analysis, it motivates speech, such as wishing to express to others what is adhered to. The terms "viewing," "seeing," and so on refer to applying a classificatory convention by means of one the four classificatory conventions—seeing, hearing, differentiating, and understanding. To superimpose is to consider that certain nonexistent imputed natures actually exist. This is the most important point here. For example, having perceived in the past what is called a "snake," one apprehends the signs of a snake, such as a coiled form, to be the signs of a rope; and having conceived that non-snake to be a snake, so as to communicate it to others one declares, "I see a snake!"[341]

To further illustrate the three natures, consider a visual form. In the case of a conceptual cognition apprehending a visual form, the visual form that is the basis upon which the superimposition is made, or in other words the visual form that is its support, is the dependent nature. The basis that appears to be something external to the mind apprehending it, or that is conceived to be something external by a conceptual cognition—whereby such a superimposition is imputed onto the form itself, or in the case of form's production, onto its attributes—is the imputed nature of form. [164] The *nonexistence* of the basis, form, established by its own characteristics as the basis of term and concept just as it appears to the mind—or the *nonexistence* of it being an external object just as it is conceived by the thought apprehending it—is the consummate nature of form. Asaṅga's *Compendium of the Mahāyāna* says:

> These cognizances that are cognition only are included within unreal conceptualizations that do not exist, and that which is the support of the appearance of an erroneous thing is a dependent nature. What is an imputed nature? It is that which appears as an object when there is no object but cognition only. What is the consummate nature? It is the complete absence of any objective nature in the dependent nature.[342]

This passage clearly explains that the basis of superimpositions is the dependent nature, whatever is superimposed on that basis is the imputed nature, and the emptiness of any superimpositions imputed on the dependent nature is the consummate nature. Regarding whether they exist by way of their own characteristics or ultimately, the difference between these three natures of the knowable is stated in Maitreya's *Distinguishing the Middle from the Extremes*:

> That which is incorrectly conceptualized exists.
> It does not exist as a duality.
> Emptiness exists as this [absence of duality].
> It exists based on that [dependent nature].[343]

The basis, such as a form, that is a dependent nature, though incorrectly conceptualized, is ultimately existent. The basis, form, does not exist in the manner in which a duality of subject and object as different substances [165] is superimposed [by distorted conceptualizing]. The emptiness of subject and object as different substances, which is the consummate nature, is inherently established. It exists on the basis of the dependent nature that is incorrectly conceptualized. Someone might wonder, "If, on the basis of a dependent nature such as a visual form, its inherently established consummate nature exists, then just as sentient beings realize the visual form directly, wouldn't they realize its consummate nature directly too?" Since within the continuum of those sentient beings there is a mistaken dualistic appearance—a distorted conceptualization of the dependent nature—that causes an obstruction regarding emptiness, they cannot realize it directly as they can with forms and so on.

Now, if there is such a difference between the three natures regarding whether they exist ultimately, then how does one posit the middle way that is free from the two extremes [of reified existence and absolute nonexistence] on their basis? Maitreya's *Distinguishing the Middle from the Extremes* says:

> Not empty and not nonempty—
> in this way all is explained.
> By existing and by not existing, it exists.
> That is the middle way.[344]

The basis, the dependent nature, is not empty of the consummate nature that exists ultimately or by virtue of its own characteristics. The dependent nature itself is not nonempty of the duality of subject and object as different substances. In this way everything is explained—all phenomena compounded by causes and conditions and all uncompounded phenomena. The dependent nature, such as form, exists by way of its own characteristics. On the basis of the dependent nature, the imputed nature—that is, the substantial difference between subject and object—does not exist by way of its own characteristics, however the inherently established consummate nature does exist. Not only that, but in the case of the consummate nature, [166] its basis—an intrinsically established dependent nature—also exists. These natures of the knowable exist as the nature of all phenomena. This is the final middle way free from both extremes.

These three natures of the knowable can each be illustrated by way of analogies, as shown in Asaṅga's *Compendium of the Mahāyāna*:

> Phenomena do not exist, yet are perceived.
> Afflictions do not exist, yet are purified.
> Like illusions and so on, they do not exist.
> They should be known to be like space.[345]

The imputed nature is likened to when a magician creates illusory horses and elephants out of pebbles and sticks. Although pebbles and sticks do not exist as actual horses and elephants, they exist as mere appearances of horses and elephants during the magician's show that affects the eyes of audience. Similarly, although the dependent nature's entity and attributes do not exist through their own characteristics as the basis of terms and concepts, they appear to do so, and although they do not exist as something external, they do exist as mere appearances. The dependent nature is likened to when pebbles and sticks appear as horses and elephants through the power of the magician's substances yet do not actually exist as horses and elephants. Similarly, although the dependent nature appears to be something that exists through its own characteristics as the basis of terms and concepts, or as an external thing, it does not exist in that way. So the way it appears and the way it exists are discordant. The consummate nature is likened to the nature of the sky in general that, although by nature completely clear and not obscured by clouds and so on, when those are absent it is said to be completely clear and pervading all directions.[346] Similarly, the consummate nature is stainless by nature and pervades all [apparently] outer and inner phenomena. [167] So the three natures are said to be like these examples.

The dependent nature in particular is likened to eight analogies, such as a magical illusion, that illustrate the disparity between how it appears to a consciousness apprehending it and how it actually exists. More specifically, to dispel any doubts about how the dependent nature is an object of cognition that appears to be an external object even though there are no external objects, we will explain each analogy briefly. (1) Just as a magical illusion appears as horses and elephants even though there are no horses and elephants in that place, likewise, although the six sense bases—forms and so on—do not exist as external objects, they are objects of consciousness and thus appear as things to that consciousness. (2) Just as there is no water at the site of a shimmering mirage and yet a mind apprehending it as water arises, likewise, although there is no externally established worldly environment and so on, a mind apprehending it arises. (3) Just as in a dream, feelings of pleasure and pain arise in the mind and its concomitant factors while sleeping, likewise, pleasure and pain arise in dependence on requisites such as food and clothing, even though they do not exist as external objects. (4) Just as the reflection of a face in a mirror does not exist as an actual face and yet pleasant and unpleasant attributes of the face appear there, likewise, although virtuous and nonvirtuous actions do not exist as external objects, from both arise the pleasure and pain that are their karmic results. (5) Just as the object of an optical distortion does not really exist and yet the consciousness to which it appears arises, likewise, though there is nothing external, the consciousnesses to which various forms and so on appear do arise. (6) Just as an echo does not exist as an actual sound and yet it appears as an object of the ear faculty, likewise, although speech acts do not exist as external objects, they are the support of various classificatory conventions. (7) Just as the moon does not exist in a clear and limpid body of water and yet its reflection appears, likewise, although the object of the mind of meditative equipoise does not exist as an external object, it is nonetheless perceived. (8) Just as an emanation does not exist in reality and yet fulfills various purposes, likewise, [168] although the bodies of holy beings do not exist externally, they accomplish the goals of sentient beings.

As for how these analogies correlate with their referents, Asaṅga's *Compendium of the Mahāyāna* says:

> Why is the dependent nature likened to a magical illusion and so forth? It is in order to dispel other people's erroneous doubts

> about the dependent nature. How do such erroneous doubts about the dependent nature arise in some people? (1) Some people wonder how a nonexistent thing can be experienced, so in order to dispel this erroneous doubt it is likened to a magical illusion. (2) They wonder how the mind and mental factors that have no object can arise, so in order to dispel this erroneous doubt it is likened to a mirage. (3) They wonder how the experience of pleasure and displeasure can occur if there is no object, so in order to dispel this erroneous doubt it is likened to a dream. (4) They wonder how pleasure and pain—the results of virtuous and nonvirtuous karma—can manifest if there is no object, so in order to dispel this erroneous doubt it is likened to a reflection. (5) They wonder how various cognitions can arise if there is no object, so in order to dispel this erroneous doubt it is likened to an optical distortion. (6) They wonder how various classificatory conventions can occur if there is no object, so in order to dispel this erroneous doubt it is likened to an echo. (7) They wonder how the experiential images apprehended correctly in meditative concentration can arise if there is no object, so in order to dispel this erroneous doubt it is likened to [a reflection of] the moon in water. (8) They wonder how the bodhisattvas' nonerroneous minds can arise in accordance with their intention to accomplish the goal of sentient beings if there is no object, so in order to dispel this erroneous doubt [169] it is likened to an emanation.[347]

Asaṅga's *Compendium of Ascertainments* and *Compendium of the Mahāyāna* offer extensive presentations of the three natures, their definitions, and explanations of how they relate to each other. Vasubandhu's *Thirty Stanzas* is an important synopsis of those, and since his student Sthiramati's *Commentary on the Thirty Stanzas* presents the root text along with a commentary that is easy to understand, we quote it here. *Commentary on the Thirty Stanzas* says:

> *Qualm*: If these [natures] are cognition only, then how does it not contradict the sūtras, for the sūtras speak of three natures—the dependent nature, the imputed nature, and the consummate nature?

Response: There is no contradiction in positing three natures on the basis of cognition only.

Qualm: How so?

Response: Because the root text says:

> Any real thing conceptualized
> by whatever conceptualization
> is itself the imputed nature,
> and that does not exist. (v. 20)

So as to indicate the limitless conceptualizing of particular conceptualizations of internal and external things, the root text says, "by whatever conceptualization." The phrase "any real thing conceptualized" refers to everything from internal and external things up to the Buddhadharma, indicating it "is itself the imputed nature" for the reason "that does not exist." Any real thing that is an object of imputation, since it has no inherent nature, [170] does not exist. In that case, that real thing is only an imputed nature, which is not the nature that is dependent on causes and conditions. A thing of this kind and its nonexistence are not perceived without entering into mutually incompatible conceptualizations. But a real thing and its nonexistence cannot be several different incompatible natures. Therefore all these are only conceptualizations because that is the meaning of the imputed nature. Thus it says in the sūtras: "Subhūti, phenomena do not exist in the way that ordinary beings conceive them."

Then after the imputed nature, the dependent nature is explained. The root text says:

> The dependent nature is a conceptualization
> in that it arises from conditions. (v. 21ab)

The term "conceptualization" here indicates the dependent nature. The phrase "arises from conditions" indicates the cause of arising, expressed as the other-powered or "dependent" nature. With regard to that there is conceptualizing, which consists in the various different virtuous, nonvirtuous, and neutral minds and mental factors of the three realms, as stated in Maitreya's *Distinguishing the Middle from the Extremes*:

> Conceptualizing that pertains to the unreal
> consists of minds and mental factors of the three realms.
> (1.9)

Being created through the capacity of other causes and conditions, they are said to be "dependent"—that is to say, they are "produced" in that they are produced in dependence on causes and conditions other than the self. With this, the dependent nature has been now explained.

Regarding the consummate nature, the root text states:

> The consummate [nature], based on that [dependent nature],
> is the permanent nonexistence of the above [imputed nature]. (v. 21cd)

Since it is unchanging, it is the consummate nature. [171] The phrase "based on that" indicates the dependent nature. The phrase "the above" indicates the imputed nature. In that conceptualization, the cognizer and the cognized are imputed as real things. Accordingly, on that basis, the cognizer and cognized are imputed in a way that they do not exist, which is called the "imputed nature." The fact that the cognizer and cognized are always completely absent in the dependent nature is the consummate nature.

> Therefore this [consummate nature] itself is neither separate from
> nor nonseparate from the dependent nature. (v. 22ab)

The phrase "therefore this itself" refers to the consummate nature, which is the complete absence of the imputed nature in the dependent nature. That complete absence is suchness: the ultimate reality of phenomena. The ultimate reality of phenomena and phenomena themselves cannot be either separate or nonseparate. The consummate nature is the ultimate reality of the dependent nature. Therefore it should be understood that the dependent nature and the consummate nature cannot be either separate or nonseparate. Indeed, if the consummate nature were separate from the dependent nature, then, understood accordingly, the dependent nature would not be empty of the imputed nature. If they were not separate, then the consummate nature would not be the pure focal object, because like the dependent nature it would be afflictive in nature. Accordingly, if the dependent nature were not afflictive in nature, then since it would not be separate from the consummate nature, it would be just like the consummate nature. The root text says:

> Just as impermanence and so on are to be expressed.
> (v. 22cd)

The phrase "as not different" is to be appended to the above line. For example, impermanence, suffering, and selflessness are not separate from impermanence and so on but also are not nonseparate from them. [172] Indeed, if conditioned things were separate from impermanence, then, understood accordingly, conditioned things would not be impermanent. If they were not separate from it, then upon disintegration conditioned things would be utterly nonexistent. As in the case of impermanence, the same applies to suffering and so on.[348]

Examining Whether the Three Natures Are Identical or Different

So are the three natures, which are the nature of the knowable, the same or different from each other? While the passage cited above from Vasubandhu's *Thirty Stanzas* does give a rough explanation, a more explicit analysis is found in Asaṅga's *Compendium of the Mahāyāna*. The text says:

> As for these three natures, are they different [from each other] or not different? We say they are neither different nor nondifferent. The dependent nature is dependent in one sense, imputed in another sense, and consummate in a third sense. In what sense is the dependent nature "dependent"? Because it arises in dependence on something else—from seeds that are propensities—it is dependent. In what sense is it "imputed"? Because it is the basis of conceptualizing and is imputed by that [conceptualizing

> consciousness], it is imputed. [173] In what sense is it consummate? Because it does not exist at all in the way it is imputed.[349]

This passage takes the dependent nature as a basis for explaining the manner in which the three natures are not different from each other. It explains how in one sense the dependent nature is dependent: it arises in dependence upon some other causal capacity—specifically seeds that are latent propensities deposited in the foundation consciousness. In another sense it is imputed: the dependent nature is the basis or rationale of conceptualizing, where forms and so on are imputed by such a mind. And in a third sense it is consummate: the dependent nature does not exist in the way in which it is imputed by conceptualizing. That is how the meaning of the above passage is explained in Asvabhāva's *Explanation of the Compendium of the Mahāyāna*.[350]

Now, someone might ask, "Are the three natures not different but the same?" Asaṅga's *Compendium of the Mahāyāna* says:

> If in certain senses the dependent nature is the three natures, then how are these three natures not indistinguishable? In the sense in which it is the dependent nature, it is not the imputed nature, and it is not the consummate nature. In the sense in which it is the imputed nature, [174] it is not the dependent nature, and it is not the consummate nature. In the sense in which it is the consummate nature, it is not the dependent nature, and it is not the imputed nature.[351]

The three natures are not identical because whichever sense is posited in each case, in that sense it remains distinct. For example, in the sense in which the dependent nature is posited [i.e., as dependent on seeds and propensities], it is established as not imputed and so forth. The three natures are also posited as different for another reason in Asvabhāva's *Explanation of the Compendium of the Mahāyāna*: "As for saying they are also not nondifferent, since it is incorrect for the existent and nonexistent to be the same, likewise it is so in the case of the two—the dependent nature and the consummate nature—because they are defined from the point of view of being naturally pure and impure."[352] Consider the dependent nature and the imputed nature superimposed onto it as an external object: since the dependent nature is ultimately existent and the imputed nature is not ultimately existent, they cannot be identical. Then consider the dependent nature and the consummate nature based on it: since they are differentiated in terms of whether they are posited or not posited as naturally pure of any stain, they cannot be identical.

Moreover, in the context of discussing the relationship and mutual differences among the three natures, Asaṅga's *Compendium of the Mahāyāna* applies the criterion of whether they are thoroughly afflictive or perfectly pure.[353] The imputed nature superimposed by conceptualizing onto the dependent nature is a thoroughly afflictive phenomenon. [175] The emptiness of the imputed nature as projected onto the dependent nature is a perfectly pure phenomenon. Since the dependent nature itself appears as an external object and is conceived as such when perceived by impure conceptualizing, in terms of that factor it is included within the thoroughly afflictive class. Since on the basis of having perceived the dependent nature, the wisdom directly realizing its mode of existence—the consummate nature—manifests, in terms of that factor it is included within the perfectly pure class of phenomena. The dependent nature thus includes both classes: the thoroughly afflictive and the perfectly pure. This is explained by means of a very clear analogy in Asaṅga's *Compendium of the Mahāyāna*:

> What did the Bhagavan mean when he said in the *Questions of Brahma Sūtra*: "The Tathāgata does not see saṃsāra and does not see nirvāṇa"? He made this statement with the understanding that, since the dependent nature is the imputed nature and is also the consummate nature, there is no difference between saṃsāra and nirvāṇa. For the dependent nature itself is saṃsāra in terms of the factor that is the imputed nature, and it is nirvāṇa in terms of the factor that is the consummate nature.
>
> The *Abhidharmasūtra* states: "Phenomena are of three kinds: that which is included in the thoroughly afflictive, that which is included in the perfectly pure, and that which is included in both classes." What did the Bhagavan mean when he said this? The dependent nature, having the imputed nature based on it, is included in the thoroughly afflictive class, and having the consummate nature based on it, is included in the perfectly pure class; so the dependent nature itself is included in both classes.

> [176] This is what he meant when he spoke thus. Is there an analogy that illustrates this point? The analogy is a dirt-encrusted lump of gold, which has three aspects: the earth element, the dirt, and the gold. As the earth element, the dirt that does not exist [as a solid lump] is seen, whereas the gold that does exist [as a solid lump] is not seen. If the dirt is burned away by fire, the dirt does not appear but the gold does appear. The earth element appears deceptively when appearing as dirt, but when it appears as gold it appears exactly as it is. Thus the earth element is included in both classes. Similarly, when conceptual consciousness is not burned away by nonconceptual wisdom, that conceptual consciousness appears as the unreal imputed nature and does not appear as the real consummate nature. However, when conceptual consciousness is burned away by nonconceptual wisdom, that conceptual consciousness appears as the real consummate nature and does not appear as the unreal imputed nature. Accordingly, the dependent nature that is the unreal conceptual consciousness of conceptualizing is included in both classes, just like the earth element in the analogy of dirt-encrusted gold.[354]

The presentation of the three natures in the Yogācāra tradition given here is mainly based on Asaṅga's treatises. Given the seminal importance of this presentation of the three natures for this tradition in general, there are of course other authoritative sources on the topic, such as Maitreya's *Ornament for the Mahāyāna Sūtras* and *Distinguishing the Middle from the Extremes* and Vasubandhu's *Thirty Stanzas*. [177] These Yogācāra treatises exhibit some minor variations in their presentations, but fundamentally they accord with what is found in Asaṅga's texts, as presented above.

This tradition's assertion of truly existent consciousness that is free from the duality of a substantially different subject and object could give rise to qualms. For example, is such a consciousness the same as the Vedānta assertion of an eternal, truly existent nondual consciousness? And could such a truly existent consciousness be the self asserted by the tīrthikas? In view of this, the Madhyamaka masters do not distinguish matter from consciousness in terms of whether they are truly existent. Instead, they hold that all phenomena are not ultimately established. Nevertheless, one does read the following in Maitreya's *Distinguishing the Middle from the Extremes*:

In dependence on perception,
nonperception arises.
In dependence on nonperception,
nonperception arises.[355]

Commenting on this verse, Vasubandhu's *Commentary on Distinguishing the Middle from the Extremes* says:

> In dependence on the perception of cognition only, the nonperception of an object arises. Likewise, in dependence on the nonperception of an object, the nonperception of cognition only arises. Thus one enters into what is characterized as the absence of subject and object. Therefore perception is not perceived, and this is the essential nature. For when there is no perceived object, perception is impossible. Thus perception [178] and nonperception are to be known as equal, since perception is not established as perception itself. Although it is the essential nature that is nonperception, since it appears as an unreal object, it is called *perception*.[356]

Now, on the surface, the above passage appears to suggest that from the perspective of cognition only, after negating the external object, cognition only itself needs to be negated too. This suggests that both matter and consciousness are stated equally to be devoid of true existence. However, the assertion that consciousness is truly existent is widely known to be a fundamental tenet of the Yogācāra tradition. If that is correct, these texts, *Distinguishing the Middle from the Extremes* and its *Commentary*, must be explained to mean that both the apprehending subject and the apprehended object are equally nonexistent from the perspective of nonconceptual meditative equipoise.

11

The Consummate Nature

How the Dependent Nature Is Empty of the Imputed Nature

HAVING DEFINED each of the three natures above and examined whether they are the same or different, let us now consider the final mode of existence of phenomena according to the Yogācāra tradition—the consummate nature, which is the dependent nature's emptiness of imputed nature. Maitreya's *Distinguishing the Middle from the Extremes* says that the consummate nature in this tradition is the ultimate truth, the dharma expanse (Skt. *dharmadhātu*), the perfect culmination, and suchness.[357] So to fully understand this tradition's way of positing suchness, [179] it is crucial to know how it determines the dependent nature. Therefore let us offer a somewhat extensive explanation here of the presentation of the dependent nature in the Yogācāra tradition.

Distinguishing the Middle from the Extremes states:

> Emptiness, in brief,
> must be understood in terms of
> defining characteristics, synonyms,
> meanings, divisions, and proof.[358]

This says that the consummate nature must be known in terms of its definition or defining characteristics, its synonyms, their meanings, its divisions, and corresponding proofs. To explain these, we begin with the definition of emptiness in *Distinguishing the Middle from the Extremes*:

> The unreality of duality and the reality of that unreality
> are the defining characteristics of emptiness.[359]

This defines emptiness as: the dependent nature's emptiness of a real duality of subject and object as substantially different, which is imputed by conceptualizing. As for its synonyms and their meanings, *Distinguishing the Middle from the Extremes* states that these are:

> Suchness and the perfect culmination.[360]

As for its divisions and corresponding proofs, the same text states that these are: [180]

> The afflictive and the pure.
> The stained and the stainless.[361]

Two types of the consummate nature—the stained and the stainless—are posited in terms of whether the dependent nature that is the basis of emptiness contains afflictions or is purified of them, respectively. Similarly, sixteen types of the consummate nature, or the selflessness of phenomena, are posited in terms of the sixteen different objects superimposed onto internal and external phenomena as their basis. These types and bases of emptiness need to be purified of the stains of superimposition in perception, as explained above in the context of the two truths.[362]

As a summary of these points, Vasubandhu's *Commentary on Distinguishing the Middle from the Extremes* states the following:

> The definition of that [consummate nature] is: that which is in the nature of a negation with regard to the real and the unreal, because all categories are pervaded by emptiness. A synonym is: another name for something. The meaning of a synonym is: the cause of using a synonym in a context that accords with that synonym. That [consummate nature] is like space because it is undifferentiated in character. Although it is nonconceptual, it is nevertheless categorized into two temporal states: being associated with adventitious afflictions and being freed from them. Furthermore, owing to different superimpositions as persons and phenomena, [the consummate nature] is categorized into sixteen aspects. The proof is: the argument that demonstrates those classifications.[363]

Similar to points found in the texts of Maitreya, [181] Asaṅga also offers presentations of the Yogācāra tenets in general and of the consummate nature in particular, such as the following from his *Compendium of the Mahāyāna*:

> The consummate nature is shown
> in dependence on the four purities.
> These purities are: natural,
> stainless, path, and object.[364]

Here he teaches the consummate nature in terms of four purities: the natural purity, the stainless purity, the pure path, and the pure object. (1) The consummate nature that is the *natural* purity is understood as follows. It is *suchness* because all phenomena are changeless in their shared characteristic of being of one taste. It is *emptiness* because it is empty of the imputed nature based on the dependent nature. It is the *perfect culmination* because it is the final truth. It is *signlessness* because it is free from all signs of forms and so on. It is the *ultimate* because it is the cognized object of a mind directly realizing the mode of existence. It is the *dharma expanse* because the act of perceiving and then meditating on it is the cause of purifying all the ignorance within one's own continuum. (2) The consummate nature that is the *stainless* purity refers to the consummate nature itself, which is perfectly pure and free of the stains such as the two obstructions and so on. (3) The consummate nature that is the pure *path* is known as such because it is the path gained in dependence on realizing the consummate nature. (4) The consummate nature that is the pure *object* is known as such because it is the object that is known on the basis of the teachings that cause those pure paths to be generated through hearing and so on. Among these, Vasubandhu's *Commentary on the Compendium of the Mahāyāna* states that the first two are the changeless consummate nature and the last two are the undistorted [182] consummate nature.[365] This means the first two are the actual consummate nature and the last two are not the actual consummate nature.

This Yogācāra presentation of the consummate nature in terms of the four purifications or purities is also stated by Dignāga in his *Stanzas Summarizing the Perfection of Wisdom*:

> In the Perfection of Wisdom
> the teaching depends on the three:

> the imputed, the dependent,
> and the ultimate natures only.
> By words such as "do not have" and so on,
> all imputed natures are negated.
> By examples such as an illusion and so on,
> dependent natures are properly taught.
> By means of the four purities
> the consummate nature is correctly known.[366]

Thus he explains how a statement in the Perfection of Wisdom sūtras that says that all phenomena have no essential nature cannot be taken literally; is to be taken only in terms of the three natures. Words such as "have no essential nature," "are not produced," and so on negate an intrinsically characterized essential nature in the imputed nature. Examples such as illusions, dreams, and so on negate a produced essential nature in the dependent nature. The texts' statement about the four purities negates an ultimately established essential nature in the consummate nature. The term *purifications* means "purities," because it explains the factor of the object that, when perceived, purifies the obstructions.

In the context of establishing the consummate nature that is the dependent nature's emptiness of the imputed nature, the following statement is made in Asaṅga's *Compendium of the Mahāyāna*: [183]

> In the dependent nature, the imputed nature does not exist;
> there the consummate nature does exist.
> Therefore, in that [nature], both of these are
> not perceived and perceived at the same time.[367]

In other words, based on the dependent nature, the imputed nature does not exist although the consummate nature does exist. For this reason, one who does not see with valid cognition the dependent nature's suchness thereby perceives the imputed nature and does not perceive the consummate nature, while at the same time one who does see its suchness does not perceive the imputed nature but perceives the consummate nature.

Many texts of the Yogācāra tradition explain grasping at a self of phenomena in terms of grasping at the duality of subject and object as substantially different; they do not give much explanation of other accounts of grasping at a self phenomena. However, as has been stated numerous times above, the *Unraveling the Intention Sūtra* teaches how the dependent nature is not established through its own characteristics as the entity or attribute imputed in relation to it, and that this absence of essential nature is the selflessness of phenomena. Thus it indicates that grasping at the dependent nature, imputed as entity or attribute, to be established through its own characteristics is grasping at a self of phenomena. Similarly, as will be explained below, Asaṅga's *Bodhisattva Levels*, *Compendium of Ascertainments*, and *Compendium of the Mahāyāna* set forth many reasons to prove that emptiness—which is the dependent nature being empty of how it is grasped as the imputed nature—is the perfect culmination, the meaning of the middle way, and the consummate nature that is the selflessness of phenomena.

In this tradition, when delineating the fundamental view that differs from other Mahāyāna systems [184] and negating the object of negation in terms of how [phenomena] appear to conceptual cognition, the criterion of what constitutes the self of phenomena, from the perspective of conceptual mental cognition, is defined as: an object established by way of its own mode of being, independently of applying a name or label, which is taken to be the basis of engagement of a term or concept that applies a label to that phenomenon as an entity or an attribute. Consider the example blue. Here, blue is the object of the mind positing it or the term signifying it. However, if the object blue, without depending on the application of a name or linguistic convention, is the object of the mind or the term from its own side, then it is necessarily the object of negation, the self of phenomena. This selfhood of phenomena has two forms: that which is established by its own mode of being as the basis of the term or concept applying a label as an *entity* and that which is established by its own mode of being as the basis of the term or concept applying a label as an *attribute*.

The criterion of what constitutes the self of phenomena, from the perspective of nonconceptual sensory cognition, is defined as: a phenomenon such as a visual form that is not a mere appearance or the nature of the sense consciousness apprehending it but is established as a different entity from such a consciousness or is established as external and separate from it. Consider again the example of the color blue. If the visual consciousness apprehending blue and the blue that is its observed object are not the same nature, and blue is established by its own capacity as a composite of many external particles, then this would be the object of negation. [185]

Identifying the Superimposition That Is the Object of Negation

Asaṅga addresses how this tradition identifies the superimposition that is to be negated. His *Bodhisattva Levels* states:

> If it does not exist in that way and yet is not completely and utterly nonexistent, then how does it exist? It exists on the basis of not existing by way of its own characteristics, whereby inappropriate superimposition is abandoned, and on the basis of being real, whereby inappropriate denial is abandoned.[368]

In this way we can understand that *superimposition* is where the dependent nature itself does not exist through its own characteristics as the basis of application of a term or concept but is apprehended to exist through its own characteristics as such. *Denial* is where the dependent nature itself exists through its own characteristics but is apprehended not to exist through its own characteristics.

What are the superimposition and the denial that must be abandoned? The *superimposition* to be negated is: the conceptualizing mind that grasps the dependent nature to exist through its own characteristics as the basis of conception[369] of a term or concept that expresses it. The extreme of superimposition is: the conceived object of such a mind. This is the object of negation of the reasoning that proves the dependent nature to be empty of the imputed nature. The *denial* to be negated is: the conceptual cognition that grasps the dependent nature to not exist through its own characteristics. The extreme of denial is: the conceived object of such a mind. This is the object of negation of the reasoning that proves the dependent nature to exist through its own characteristics. Asaṅga's *Bodhisattva Levels* states:

> [The superimposition is thus:] phenomena such as forms do not exist by virtue of an intrinsically characterized essential nature as the referent of terms denoting forms and so on, but this is superimposed onto them and they are overtly conceived as such. [186]

> [The denial is thus:] real things, which exist ultimately with an inexpressible nature as the *basis* of illustration of denoting terms or as the *support* of illustration of denoting terms, are declared to be completely and utterly nonexistent.[370]

Here Asaṅga explains that the dependent nature, which does not exist by virtue of its own characteristics as the basis of application of terms or concepts, is overtly conceived to do so by proponents of fellow Buddhist schools as well as non-Buddhist schools, and this constitutes the superimposition. The ultimately existent dependent nature, which is the basis of illustration of denoting terms, is viewed by the Madhyamaka schools to lack ultimate existence, and this constitutes the denial.

Just as viewing the dependent nature in these ways constitutes the denial and the superimposition, the same is also true of the consummate nature. For example, Asaṅga's *Compendium of Ascertainments* says: "To overtly conceive the dependent nature and the consummate nature to be the imputed nature should be known as the extreme of superimposition." It goes on to say, "The extreme of denial refers to the denial of their own characteristics, in terms of saying that the dependent nature and the consummate nature, which do exist [ultimately], are devoid of such existence."[371] So here, to view the dependent nature and the consummate nature as lacking ultimate existence constitutes the denial, not simply holding or stating that they do not exist conventionally. Likewise, among the various views and assertions, to view the imputed nature as existent, or to say it exists ultimately or by its own characteristics, [187] is not to view or claim it to be conventionally existent. The *Compendium of Ascertainments* says:

> Are those clear realizations, posited by whatsoever name and whatsoever expression, essentially the expressed object [of those names and expressions] or not essentially their expressed object? From a *conventional* perspective, they are essentially their expressed object, but in an *ultimate* sense, they are not essentially their expressed object.[372]

As explained above, holding on to the *denial* is present only within those who propound philosophical tenets—therefore it is a cognition that is *acquired*. However, holding on to the *superimposition*—that the dependent nature is established by its own characteristics as the basis of terms and concepts as an entity or an attribute—is present even within people who have no notion of philosophy; therefore it is a cognition that is included among those that are *innate* or naturally arisen. According to Asaṅga, the presence of these is clearly identified by analyzing how the appearance and the conceiving [which is a type of grasping] occur in the minds of ordinary beings. The *Compendium of Ascertainments* says: "Here it should be known that, owing to five reasons, ordinary beings overtly conceive of things that are the referents of expressions to be essentially just as they are named and just as they are expressed."[373] The manner in which ordinary beings have innate cognitions conceiving of a thing, such as a form, to exist by its own characteristics as the basis of conception [188] of the signifying term or referential thought "form" is distilled into five reasons, which we will explain in detail.

First there is the reason inferring through *questions and answers* the presence of such an overtly construing awareness.[374] When the label "form" is first applied, if those people who have no notion of philosophy ask, "What is a form?" they do not answer saying, "A form is that which appears as a form through the capacity of the ripening of internal propensities." Instead they answer, "A form is that which appears as such to one's visual consciousness." The fact that they answer in this manner is the reason that proves that people have innate cognitions conceiving form, or such like, to be established by its own characteristics as the basis of the term or concept just as it appears. Here is an analogy. Suppose you ask a person whose eyes are affected by a magician's recitations and substances and who experiences both the appearance and the conception of pebbles and sticks as horses and elephants, "What are these things that you refer to as 'horses and elephants'?" They do not answer saying, "They are appearances arising through the power of recitation and substances affecting my eyes." Rather they say something like, "Those things in front of me are horses and elephants." Thus the *Compendium of Ascertainments* states: "So if someone asks, 'What is the nature of this thing?' they would answer, 'Its nature is something physical.' They would not say, 'What is referred to as a physical form is just a name.'"[375]

Second, there is the reason inferring through *the search for defining characteristics* the presence of such an overtly construing awareness. Those people who have no notion of philosophy have innate cognitions conceiving form, or such like, to be established by its own characteristics as the basis of application of a term or concept. This is so because [189] when they look for the unique and the universally shared characteristics of form and so on, they look for the basis of the term and concept having held it to be established by its own characteristics as the basis, but they do not look for it having held it to be merely imputed by term and concept as the basis. Here is an analogy. When a person who is affected by a magician's recitations and substances experiences both the appearance and the conception of pebbles and sticks as horses and elephants and then looks for the illusory horse and elephant, they look for it anticipating, "That is a horse and elephant." They do not look for it anticipating, "That is a horse and elephant conjured up by a magician." The *Compendium of Ascertainments* says: "Moreover, when alone and in solitude one enters into a thorough investigation of the particular and general characteristics of phenomena, one searches thoroughly, considering, 'This thing's defining characteristic is a form, but its name is not a form.'"[376]

Third, there is the reason inferring through *the inducement of happiness and unhappiness* the presence of such an overtly construing awareness. People who have no notion of philosophy have innate cognitions conceiving form and so on to be established by its own characteristics as the basis of conception of a term or concept. This is evident because when they investigate form and so on, as described above, they are unhappy if they do not find the entity imputed as "form" to be a form, but they are not unhappy if they do not find the mere nominal imputation to be a form. Here is an analogy. A person who experiences both the appearance and the conception of an illusory horse and elephant is unhappy if he doesn't find a horse and elephant within the illusion that he sees, but he is not unhappy if doesn't find a mere hallucination of a horse and elephant. The *Compendium of Ascertainments* says: "Moreover, when he looks for the defining characteristics of a real form to be a form, he is unhappy if he doesn't find it, but when he looks for the name to be a form, [190] he is not unhappy if he doesn't find it."[377]

Fourth, there is the reason inferring through *ordinary beings' conceiving* the presence of such an overtly construing awareness. Ordinary beings have innate reifying cognitions that apprehend a referent to be established by its own characteristics as the basis of application of its name or linguistic convention. This is evident because when a name individuates one of its unique or diverse characteristics and so on, it cannot individuate another; thus it involves different referents. Those names that are initially applied as linguistic labels are applied by ordinary beings to a referent insofar as it appears to them, but although it does not exist as it appears, it is reified and conceived in such a way. Here is an analogy. In the case of a person who experiences both the appearance and the conception of illusory horses and elephants to be horses and elephants, even though pebbles and sticks do not exist as horses and elephants, they nevertheless appear and are conceived to be horses and elephants by this person. The *Compendium of Ascertainments* says: "Here, any name that individuates the referent of a unique characteristic does not also individuate the referent of diverse characteristics."[378]

Fifth, there is the reason inferring through *being bound by propensities* the presence of such an overtly construing awareness. People who have no notion of philosophy have innate cognitions conceiving form, or such like, to be established through its own characteristics as the basis of terms and concepts. This is because through the force of habituation to propensities for grasping at signs since time without beginning, they conceive of them just as they appear. Here is an analogy. In a person whose eyes are affected by a magician's recitations and substances and who experiences both the appearance and the conception of pebbles and sticks as horses and elephants, [191] both the appearance and the conception as those [horses and elephants] arise. The *Compendium of Ascertainments* says: "Moreover, because all ordinary beings are bound by grasping at signs, those [people] must be viewed to be conceiving things essentially just as they are named or expressed."[379]

Thus for reasons such as these five, ordinary beings conceive an imputed nature established through its own characteristics to be superimposed onto the dependent nature as an entity or attribute. Then, through this kind of confusion about the reality of things, the conceptualizations that view [their object] in terms of a self and "mine" arise. And because of this, the conceptualization of inappropriate attention increases, which gives rise to mental afflictions such as attachment and so on. This is how the resultant suffering is brought about, as is clearly taught in Asaṅga's *Bodhisattva Levels*.[380]

Proving the Dependent Nature to Be Empty of the Imputed Nature

How does one refute the superimposition and denial described above? To refute the superimposition, first we disprove the notion that terms and concepts apply to objects through the force of objective reality. Then we disprove the notion that not only the basis of application of a term or concept itself, which is a conceptual imputation, but also its instantiations, which are unique particulars, are established through their own characteristics as the basis of application of the term or concept. This is explained through a wide variety of reasonings in Asaṅga's *Compendium of the Mahāyāna*, *Bodhisattva Levels*, and *Compendium of Ascertainments*. [192]

With respect to a visual consciousness apprehending blue, for example, there are three aspects to the single perception: (1) the perception of blue as blue, (2) the perception of blue as the basis of application of the convention "blue," and (3) the perception of it existing by virtue of its own characteristics as such a basis. Of those three aspects of perception, blue apprehended by a conceptual mental cognition within the continuum of an ordinary being in the third way—namely, to exist by virtue of its own characteristics as the basis of the term *blue*—constitutes the superimposed reification as a self of phenomena here. This should be understood as follows. When one investigates the way in which a form, or such like, is established as the basis of application of a name or label by such a conceptual cognition, if it appears to exist as the basis of application of the name or label from the side of the form itself—without depending on being verbally expressed or conceptually imputed—then such a reification is taking place. The *Bodhisattva Levels* says: "Phenomena such as forms do not exist by virtue of an intrinsically characterized essential nature as the referent of terms denoting things such as forms, but this is superimposed onto them, and they are overtly conceived as such."[381]

Now, if the existence of a form, for example, through its own characteristics as the basis of application of the name or label is posited to constitute the self of phenomena that is the object of negation, and its negation is posited to constitute the subtle selflessness of phenomena, then one might ask the following. Is such a negation of the existence of a form through its own characteristics as the object of the name or label meant to be understood in terms of a negation of it existing through its own characteristics as the *direct object of the term*[382] or the *conceived object of the term*?[383] If it is the first, [193] then there would no need to prove to the Vaibhāṣika and Sautrāntika schools that the dependent nature is empty of existing through its own characteristics as the direct object of the term, and the emptiness of that would not be viable as the subtle selflessness of phenomena. If it is the second, then the question remains as to whether this negation of existing through its own characteristics pertains to the conceived object's instantiation (*gzhi ldog*) or to the conceived object's status as a general category (*rang ldog*). So which one is it? If it is the first, then this would negate the dependent nature to exist through its own characteristics. If it is the second, then since even the Sautrāntika establish general characteristics to be unreal things, this is not a feasible option. Furthermore, this type of emptiness—the emptiness of a form existing through its own characteristics as the basis of the name or label—does not satisfy the meaning of cognition only, which negates a substantial difference between the apprehending subject and the apprehended object. So how could it qualify as the subtle selflessness of phenomena in this tradition?

To respond to these questions in a comprehensive manner it is vital to understand the following six crucial points. (1) There are many different ways of appearing, owing to the causal capacity of diverse latent propensities, even in the case of a single sense consciousness. (2) In the case of a sense consciousness apprehending blue, for example, there is the appearance of blue as blue, the appearance of blue as an external object, and the appearance of blue as existing through its own characteristics as the basis of application of the name or label. (3) There is a difference between blue merely existing as the basis of the name or label and blue existing through its own characteristics as that color. (4) There is a difference between a form, for example, being the conceived object of thought and it being the basis of conception of thought in the context of the object of negation, as stated repeatedly. (5) There is a vast difference between a form being a conceptual cognition's *conceived object* that is not established through its own characteristics and a form not being established through its own characteristics as a conceptual cognition's *basis of conception*. (6) There is a difference between the Sautrāntika and Cittamātra systems as to whether things exist or do not exist as they appear and as they are conceived. Let us explain these one by one now. [194]

1) There are many different ways of appearing, owing to the causal capacity of diverse latent propensities, even in the case of a single sense consciousness. For example, to a sense consciousness apprehending blue, blue appears through the causal capacity of *propensities for concordant types*; also blue appears as the basis of application of the name or label "blue" through the causal capacity of *propensities for verbalization*; and blue appears to be established from the side of the object as the basis of the name or label with-

out relying on the name or label through the causal capacity of *propensities for the view grasping at a self.* Thus even in the case of an appearance within a single sense consciousness that has arisen in dependence on latent propensities, there are many facets, such as: an aspect that pertains to the dependent nature established by its own characteristics; an aspect that pertains to the imputed nature merely posited by a name or label; and an aspect that pertains to pure conceptual imputation that cannot be posited to exist by way of a name or label. As for how the Yogācāra tradition understands the way an appearance of a form, for example, arises through the ripening of latent propensities based on the foundation consciousness, and how there are various types of propensities—propensities of concordant type, propensities of verbalization, propensities of the view grasping at a self, and so on—these have already been presented in the section on the Cittamātra school's tenets found in volume 3 of *Science and Philosophy in the Indian Buddhist Classics.*

2) To a visual consciousness apprehending blue, not only does blue appear as blue, but when blue appears it appears as something separate at a distance, so blue appears to the visual consciousness to be established as something external. In particular, to a visual consciousness apprehending blue, blue appears to be established from the side of the object's own mode of existence as the basis of the label without depending on language or thought. The reason for this is as follows. Suppose someone asks: "What is the essential nature of the referent of the expression 'blue'?" Because one apprehends with the mind how blue appears to visual consciousness as something existing from its own side as the basis of the name and label, one answers, "The nature of that [which I perceive] is a visual form." [195] Even the thought that motivates this kind of suitable response is induced through the operation of that visual consciousness itself. This indicates that form does not appear to our innate perception as something merely nominally or conceptually imputed as the basis of the name or label; instead, it appears as if it is indeed the basis of such a term from the side of its own mode of existence, without depending on being established by language or thought.

3) There is a difference between blue merely existing as the basis of a name or label and blue existing as that through its own characteristics. The meaning of "merely existing as the basis of a name or label" refers to, for example, blue existing as the object of the term or thought "blue" in

dependence on applying a name or label. The meaning of "existing by its own characteristics as the basis of a name or label" refers to, for example, blue existing as the basis of application of the signifying term *blue*, or as the basis of conception conceived by the thought *blue*, through the capacity of its actual mode of existence, without depending on applying a name or label.

4) There is a difference between a form being a *conceived object* of thought and it being the *basis of conception* of thought in the context of the object of negation. In the former case, the form that is conceived by the conceptual cognition apprehending a form is taken to be the object as cognized. In the latter case, the form that has appeared to a sense consciousness to be the basis of the name or label from its own side without depending on the application of a convention by language or thought, and subsequently conceived by conceptual cognition just as it appears, is taken to be the basis of conception of the statement "This is a form."

5) There is a vast difference between a form being a conceptual cognition's *conceived object* that is not established through its own characteristics [196] and a form not being established through its own characteristics as a conceptual cognition's *basis of conception*. In the first case, since a form is its conceptual cognition's conceived object, its being this conceptual cognition's conceived object exists; and since its being this conceptual cognition's conceived object is merely posited by thought, it is acknowledged to be not established by its own characteristics. However, in the second case, what it means for a form not to be established by its own characteristics as a conceptual cognition's basis of conception is that the form is its conceptual cognition's basis of conception in dependence upon having applied a convention by language or thought, not through the force of reality.

6) There is a difference between the Sautrāntika and Cittamātra systems as to whether things exist or do not exist as they appear and as they are conceived. The Sautrāntika tradition asserts that blue appears to the visual consciousness to be established by its own characteristics as the basis of application of the name or label, and it is established in the way it is conceived as such by the conceptual cognition induced by that visual consciousness. The Cittamātra tradition asserts that it is not established in that way. The Sautrāntika tradition maintains that although the referent of a signifying term is not a real thing, a pot, for example, is established by way of its own mode of existence as the basis of the signifying term. The Citta-

mātra tradition says that if it were established by its own mode of existence, then it would necessarily be established as the self of phenomena.

As for the actual reasoning that refutes that form and so on exist through their own characteristics as the basis of a name or label, there are three found in each of three texts by Asaṅga: *Compendium of the Mahāyāna*, *Bodhisattva Levels*, and *Compendium of Ascertainments*. First, the *Compendium of the Mahāyāna* says:

> Because something is not cognized as such prior to being named, this contradicts its being [intrinsically] that very nature; because something can have many names, this contradicts its being [intrinsically] many natures; because something does not have a definitive name [i.e., the same name can be applied to different individuals], this contradicts its being [intrinsically] a combined nature.[384] [197]

The reasonings given here are: (1) the reasoning that contradicts something being intrinsically that very nature, (2) the reasoning that contradicts something being intrinsically many natures, and (3) the reasoning that contradicts something being intrinsically a combined nature.

The first reasoning can be presented as follows: "The *subject*, a bulbous thing, is not established by its own characteristics as the basis of application of the name 'pot' because a mind thinking 'pot' does not arise merely upon seeing the bulbous thing prior to the name 'pot' being applied." Also, if a bulbous thing were established by its own characteristics as the basis of application of the name *pot*, then it would necessarily be established as that basis from the side of the bulbous thing's unique mode of existence. If it were so established, then the bulbous thing, having merely been established, would necessarily exist in its own right as the basis of application of the name *pot*. If it did so exist, then a mind thinking "pot" would arise without depending on the label, which would entail the fault that even without having applied the label *pot*, a mind thinking "pot" would arise. In this way one should understand how the second and third reasons mentioned above—many names and a single name—contradict something being established through its own characteristics as the basis of application of a name.

The second reasoning takes into account a single person having two different names, such as a boy who prior to ordination as a monk was called Tsering and after ordination is called Tenzin. This reasoning can be presented as: "The *subject*, such a boy named Tenzin, is not established by way of his own characteristics as the basis of application of many names—Tsering, Tenzin, and so on—because he is not established as many different continua."

The third reasoning can be presented as follows: "The *subject*, both Upagupta of the princely caste and Upagupta of the brahmin caste, [198] are not established by way of their own characteristics as the basis of application of a single name, Upagupta, because these two people are not a single continuum."

Asaṅga's *Bodhisattva Levels* similarly presents three reasons as follows. (1) The reason that proves the dependent nature to be empty of the imputed nature is that [if it were not so] one thing would be many entities. *Bodhisattva Levels* says: "If any phenomena or any thing at all were by nature those phenomena or that thing in the way they are linguistically expressed, then a single phenomenon or a single thing would be many diverse entities."[385] [This is obviously an absurd outcome.] The gist of this refutation can be presented in the form of a consequence as follows: "The *subject* Devendra, for example, would exist as many different entities because he is established by virtue of his own characteristics as the basis of application of many names, such as Devendra and Puraṇdara." What is implied by the above consequence is presented in the form of a syllogism as follows: "The *subject* Devendra is not established by way of his own characteristics as the basis of application of many names because he is not established as many different entities."

(2) The reason that proves the dependent nature—whether an entity or an attribute—to be empty of the imputed nature is that the object would not exist at a time when its name had not been applied. *Bodhisattva Levels* says: "Moreover, if you consider, as previously described, phenomena such as forms to be the essential nature [i.e., referent] of denoting terms, and [199] you later apply a denoting term as you wish to a previously existent thing, then prior to that denoting term having been applied—when that denoting term does not designate anything—the essential nature of that phenomenon or that thing would simply be nonexistent."[386] The gist of this refutation can be presented in the form of a consequence as follows: "If the *subject*, a thing with branches and foliage, for example, were to exist before

being given its name, it would not be established as a tree during the time it was not labeled a 'tree,' because when established by its own characteristics as the basis of application of the term or concept 'tree,' that name does not exist on that occasion." What is implied by the above consequence may be presented in the form of a syllogism as follows: "The *subject*, a thing having branches and foliage, is not established by its own characteristics as the basis of a name or label, because it exists even at a time when the name 'tree' does not designate anything."

(3) The reason that proves the dependent nature—whether an entity or an attribute—to be empty of the imputed nature is that the object's entity would not exist. Asaṅga's *Bodhisattva Levels* says:

> Suppose a form is in the nature of form prior to a denoting term being applied, since a denoting term based on the nature of form may be applied subsequently even to an assembly of forms. In that case, just as without the denoting term *form* being applied, it would still be a phenomenon called *form*, so based on a real thing called *form* a cognition of form would rightly occur. But it does not occur. Therefore, due to this inference and through this reasoning, all phenomena must be understood to be inexpressible in essential nature.[387] [200]

The gist of this refutation can be presented in the form of a consequence: "The *subject*, that which is suitable as a form, would engender the thought 'it is a form' in any person at all even before the label *form* is applied, because it would be established by virtue of its own characteristics as the basis of application of the term *form*." What is implied by the above consequence may be presented in the form of a syllogism as follows: "The *subject*, that which is suitable as a form, is not established through its own characteristics as the basis of application of the label *form*, because it does not engender a cognition thinking 'it is a form' in any suitable person without the label *form* being applied."

In brief, these above-stated reasons establishing that forms and so on are empty of the imputed nature that is the object of negation should be understood as illustrative of all phenomena as described in Sāgaramegha's *Commentary on Bodhisattva Levels*: "Because three faults would be incurred if that were so, it is said that 'one must understand all phenomena to be inexpressible in essential nature.' Likewise, one must know that everything, from feeling up to nirvāṇa, is encompassed by the application of terms."[388]

Asaṅga's *Compendium of Ascertainments* also presents three reasons proving that the dependent nature is empty of the imputed nature; two of these reasons are similar to those found in both the *Compendium of the Mahāyāna* and *Bodhisattva Levels*. The first reason in the *Compendium of Ascertainments*, [201] the first reason in the *Compendium of the Mahāyāna*, and the third reason in *Bodhisattva Levels* are the same. In addition, the second reason in the *Compendium of Ascertainments*, the second reason in the *Compendium of the Mahāyāna*, and the first reason in *Bodhisattva Levels* are the same, so there is no need to present them separately here. The third reason in the *Compendium of Ascertainments* differs slightly from the reasons found in the *Compendium of the Mahāyāna* and *Bodhisattva Levels*, so to present this here separately, it states: "The *subject*, a bulbous thing, is not established through its own characteristics as the basis of application of the name 'pot' because it is dependent on language and thought designating the name 'pot.'" This is presented in the *Compendium of Ascertainments* where it begins with the following sentence: "Therefore, in dependence on the reason of being designated, it is not suitable [to be established through its own characteristics]."[389]

Thus, when subject-object duality in relation to the conceptual mental consciousness is rationally refuted through the above-stated reasons, the apprehension of blue where blue appears to be the basis of conception of the thought "blue" is established to be mistaken regarding its appearing object. When this is established, then that blue is proved not to exist as a separate substance from the consciousness in which it appears. This emptiness of existing through its own characteristics as the basis of application of the term and concept—as taught in Asaṅga's *Compendium of the Mahāyāna*, *Compendium of Ascertainments*, and *Bodhisattva Levels*—fulfills the meaning of cognition only in the sense of negating a substantial difference between subject and object according to the general tradition of the Yogācāra school. [202]

12

Emptiness of Subject-Object Duality

The Reasoning that Refutes Substantially Different Subject and Object

Earlier it was noted that there are two ways in which Yogācāra texts establish the suchness of phenomena. One is from the perspective of how things appear to a conceptual mental consciousness, where the consummate nature—namely, the dependent nature being empty of the imputed nature—is presented by way of proving that form, for example, is not established through its own characteristics as the basis of application of the thought apprehending it. The second is from the perspective of how things appear to a nonconceptual sense consciousness, where the consummate nature is presented by way of proving that form, for example, is not established as external to, or substantially different from, the sense consciousness apprehending it. Having explained the former based primarily on how it is presented in the texts of Asaṅga, we now present how the latter—suchness in terms of the negation of a substantially different subject and object, from the perspective of how things appear to nonconceptual cognition—is established together with its reasoning.

According to this tradition, the criterion for being established as an external thing, or as the self of phenomena, in relation to a nonconceptual sense consciousness is: phenomena—form and so on—not existing as the very nature of the sense consciousness apprehending them or as mere experience but existing as external to, or as a different entity from, that consciousness. Vasubandhu's *Twenty Stanzas* says:

> These are all cognition only
> because nonexistent things appear. [203]

> For example, those with impaired vision
> see nonexistent hairs, a double moon, and so on.[390]

The above states that the three realms[391] are merely established as the nature of the mind or cognition. They do not exist as established through the causal capacity of an aggregation of external particles, even though they appear to exist as an external thing. Just as in an objective sense there are no falling hairs nor double moon, yet from the perspective of those with visual impairment, an appearance of falling hairs or a double moon arises even though they do not exist.

According to the two Buddhist realist systems[392] that accept external objects, *blue* is not the mere appearance as blue in the mind, but it arises from something taken as a basis composed of partless subtle particles, which is separate from the mind and asserted to be an external form. Moreover, the existence of external phenomena such as forms is established by experience, and their mode of existence is rationally investigated as follows. It is like when, for example, a coarse form such as earth or stone is separated into fragments or continuously divided into parts so that there cannot be anything smaller, it must reach the ultimate particle; yet if such a particle itself has parts, it must be yet further divisible into parts, which would incur the fault that it is not the smallest. Therefore one cannot avoid accepting either that it is partless or that its parts are limitlessly divisible. Indeed, if one says that parts are limitlessly divisible, then even the task of dividing a tiny drop of water into all its parts could never be completed. So they say one cannot avoid accepting them to be partless.

According to the Cittamātra, a so-called subtle particle is not something that exists in the sense of an external thing that does not depend upon the consciousness apprehending it. [204] Rather, the state of existing as subtle particles divisible into parts is projected by the mind as an appearance within consciousness. Although it seems to be a physical phenomenon, in the final analysis it is not established through an aggregation of partless subtle particles as an external composite entity; it is established as merely an appearance within the mind.

Now, with respect to the phrase "the emptiness of substantially different subject and object," one might ask the following. Does this refer to the emptiness of a substantial difference between cognition and its object in general? Or does it refer to the emptiness of a substantial difference between *conceptual* cognition and its *observed* object? Or does it refer to the emptiness of a substantial difference between *sensory* cognition and its *observed* object? The first is incorrect because, in itself, an object of cognition is not a causally conditioned phenomenon, and its not being established as a different substance from consciousness can be known by a valid conventional cognition. The second is incorrect for the very same reason. The third is also incorrect because even an elderly person uneducated in philosophy knows through direct perception that a sense consciousness to which a double moon appears is not established as substantially different from its observed object. Therefore this should be defined in terms of the emptiness of a substantial difference between (1) the direct perception that arises on the basis of latent propensities and (2) its object—a form, sound, and so on. Dharmakīrti's *Ascertainment of Valid Cognition* says: "Blue and the cognition of it are not different. For although they appear utterly different, blue is not something different in nature from the experience of it because these are necessarily simultaneously perceived,[393] as in the case of a double moon."[394]

As for what is referred to by the phrase "consciousness that arises based on latent propensities," [205] *Ascertainment of Valid Cognition* says: "In the other case, because it depends on latent propensities, it is continuous and uninterrupted as long as saṃsāra pertains; and being nondeceptive with regard to the conventional, it is valid cognition."[395] Thus it refers to a cognition that is produced by latent propensities within a stable and inexhaustible continuum and that is also not undermined by temporary causes of error.

Based on understanding the above points, let us now present the actual reasonings refuting the object of negation—a substantial difference between subject and object—which are cited as follows: (1) the reasoning that divergent cognitions can arise in relation to a single thing and (2) the reasoning concerning dreams, reflections, and so on—both as presented in Asaṅga's *Compendium of the Mahāyāna*; (3) the reasoning that refutes subtle particles or a composite of particles to be the observed object—as found in Dignāga's *Investigation of the Object*; (4) the reasoning that refutes partless particles—as presented in Vasubandhu's *Twenty Stanzas*; and (5) the reasoning that refutes the definition of the object of apprehension to be "that which it resembles and from which it has arisen" and (6) the reasoning of the necessary simultaneity of perception and the perceived—both as presented in Dharmakīrti's *Exposition of Valid Cognition*.

First is the reasoning that divergent cognitions can arise in relation to a single thing, presented in Asaṅga's *Compendium of the Mahāyāna* as follows:

> How does one view things as nonexistent while they keep appearing [to the mind]? Here, the Buddha said: "O bodhisattva, when one is endowed with the four qualities, one will understand that the objects of all cognitions do not exist. One will understand this through knowing how a single object is the cause of divergent cognitions, such as how, for example, hungry ghosts, animals, humans, and gods [206] perceive a single thing in different ways."[396]

Thus, if phenomena were not the mere appearance within consciousness but were established as external things, this would entail the fault that just as when different kinds of beings, such humans and animals, view a bowl full of liquid they see different things, in reality, too, the bowl of liquid would exist differently as it is perceived by them. For example, in the case of a river, animals such as fish perceive it as their home while humans see it as a drink; therefore the river would have to be both a home and a drink.

Moreover, if objects were to exist as external realities, then when they appear to directly perceiving sensory cognitions, those forms and so on should appear in such a manner by projecting their image onto the sensory cognitions—and the sensory cognitions too should arise as if assuming the image of the object. This would mean that things must exist just as they appear [to sensory cognition]. Consequently, when two people—an enemy and a friend—look at a certain person, even though the person they are looking at is the same individual, they perceive the person differently—as attractive or unattractive. Thus the person would have to be both attractive and unattractive. Likewise, if food considered appetizing and unappetizing were fixed in that way as an external object from its own side, then what is appetizing food for one person would have to be appetizing food for everyone else, and what is unappetizing for one person would have to be unappetizing for others. So no matter what is seen by whatsoever perception, any basis would be seen in the same way by every person. [207]

Also, just as food has two dissimilar ways of appearing to individuals, as appetizing and as unappetizing, so the food itself that is the basis of the appearance would have to be both appetizing and unappetizing. Therefore it is asserted that not only is the food posited on the basis of the mere appearance factor in the mind of each person who considers it to be appetizing or unappetizing, but it does not exist as something established from the side of an external object unconnected with the way it appears in cognition.

Second, the reasoning concerning dreams, reflections, and so on is presented in Asaṅga's *Compendium of the Mahāyāna* as follows:

> This is because, like the past and so on,
> in dreams and the two types of reflection,
> the perceived object does not exist,
> yet perception can arise regarding them.[397]

Although blue, for example, does not exist as an external object, a consciousness perceiving it can arise. This is similar to how past and future appear in the present moment to cognition. Also, although a tiny room able to contain a crowded herd of elephants does not exist, such a thing can appear to a dream consciousness. Although the reflection of a face in a mirror does not exist as a face, it appears as a face. Although the surrounding ground is not filled with skeletons, in the meditative concentration on foulness there can arise a consciousness to which the surrounding ground appears filled with skeletons. The "two types of reflection" in this verse refers to the reflection of a face in a mirror and to the reflection in the sense of an image experienced in the meditative concentration on foulness. There are also other reasonings similar to this. [208]

Third, the reasoning that refutes subtle particles or a composite of particles to be the observed object is presented in Dignāga's *Investigation of the Object* as follows. Sautrāntika assert external forms and so on to be external reality on the grounds that they are the objective conditions of the sensory cognitions apprehending them, as explained in Vinītadeva's *Commentary on Investigation of the Object*: "Among those who propound external objects too, some such as Bāgvaṭa assert the form of a composite of subtle particles to be the cause of sensory cognition. They say that in the case of subtle particles, too, there does exist a form of their composition."[398] Thus the text explains how Sautrāntika assert an aggregation of partless particles to be the external objective condition.

To refute that, Cittamātra challenges Sautrāntika and the rest with an argument that can be presented as follows. "The *subject*, an external form, is not the objective condition of the sensory cognition apprehending it because its observed object is neither an external subtle particle nor a coarse external thing." The first [outcome] is entailed because even if one allows subtle particles to be the cause of a sensory perception, they do not appear to it. For example, even though the visual sense faculty is a direct cause of a visual consciousness, it is not its objective condition. As for the second [outcome], a coarse or composite particle is not suitable to be the observed object of a sense perception because a composite particle is not substantially existent, just as a double moon does not exist substantially. This is how the refutation is formulated. According to the Sautrāntika tradition, in the case of a sensory cognition, the objective condition and the observed object are synonymous. [209] These reasonings are presented in the following stanza from Dignāga's *Investigation of the Object*:

> Even if one allows subtle particles to be
> the cause of sensory consciousness,
> since they do not appear to it, its object
> is not the subtle particles, like the sense faculty.
> It does not come from that which it appears to resemble
> because it does not exist substantially, like a double moon.[399]

Fourth, the reasoning that refutes partless particles is presented in Vasubandhu's *Twenty Stanzas*, summarized as follows. "A pot, for example, is not established as an external object because it is impossible for there to be any partless subtle particles to compose them, since even the smallest particle in the final analysis must be accepted to have parts." Furthermore, "The *subject*, a subtle particle in the center surrounded by six particles having six directional parts—the four cardinal directions as well as above and below—must have parts because the side of the central particle facing east is not the facet facing south or north." If that were not so, then the subtle particle in the eastern position would also be the subtle particles in the other five directions, which would incur the fault that the position of the six subtle particles would converge. If their positions converged, then this would incur the fault that a composite aggregation of such particles would merge into a single particle and remain the same size. Vasubandhu's *Twenty Stanzas* says:

> If six converge at the same time,
> a subtle particle would have six parts.
> If these six occupied a single location,
> a composite mass would be merely a particle.[400] [210]

Among the rational arguments disproving external objects, this reasoning that refutes partless particles is especially important. Realists of both Buddhist and non-Buddhist traditions who accept external objects consider that in the case of external physical phenomena, coarse forms are established from an aggregation of much smaller ones. The final basic constituents of coarse forms—the partless particles that are the smallest limit of form—along with how they come into contact and so on are explained in part 3 in volume 1 of *Science and Philosophy in the Indian Buddhist Classics*. Many arguments are given in Vasubandhu's *Twenty Stanzas* and its autocommentary to refute partless particles. Since it is so important to understand how the Yogācāra tradition denies external objects, this being their main philosophical tenet, we quote at length here a passage from Vasubandhu's *Twenty Stanzas Autocommentary*, which is self-explanatory:

> The root text says:
>
> > The [sensory] object is not unitary
> > nor a plurality of subtle particles,
> > not even when they are aggregated,
> > because particles are not established. (v. 11)
>
> What does this mean? If a sense base such as form and so on is taken to be the object of each cognition of form and so on, then either it must be unitary, like a composite whole imputed by the Vaiśeṣika school, or it must be a plurality of subtle particles, or it must be a composite of those subtle particles. The sensory object cannot be unitary because a whole cannot be

apprehended separately from its parts. The object cannot be a plurality because individual subtle particles cannot be apprehended. The object cannot be a composite of those because subtle particles of this kind are not established as one substance. [211] Why not? Because:

> If six converge at the same time,
> a subtle particle would have six parts. (v. 12ab)

If six subtle particles were conjoined on six sides at the same time, then a subtle particle would have six parts because the place where one is located cannot be occupied by others.

> If these six occupied a single location,
> a composite mass would be merely one particle. (v. 12cd)

If the location of one subtle particle were also the location of the others, then since it would be the location of all of them, every composite mass would be just one subtle particle; and since they would be no different from each other, a composite mass would not appear.

The Kashmiri Vaibhāṣika, thinking that such a fault would not arise, say: "Since subtle particles do not have parts, they are not conjoined; however, composites are conjoined with each other." In response, we say: "That which is a composite of subtle particles is not something separate from them." The root text says:

> If there is no conjunction of particles,
> then this composite would be
> a conjunction of what?
> Their conjunction is not established
> since they do not have parts. (v. 13)

If they say that even composites are not conjoined, we reply: "In that case do not say that subtle particles are not conjoined because they do not have parts, for you also do not accept composites endowed with parts to be conjoined. Therefore subtle particles are not established to be unitary substances." Regardless of whether they can accept subtle particles to be conjoined or not, the root text says:

> Anything having diverse directional parts
> cannot be unitary. (v. 14ab)

How can something in the nature of having diverse directional parts—from a distinct south-facing part to a distinct downward-facing part—be [212] a unitary subtle particle? The root text says:

> How could they have shadows or be shaded? (v. 14c)

If each subtle particle had no distinct spatial parts, then when the sun shone, how could a shadow fall on its other side? This would mean there would be no other spatial parts where the sun's rays would not fall. If you do not accept that there are different spatial parts, how could some subtle particles be shaded by other subtle particles? If a subtle particle did not have different parts, then a place where light comes through would be the same as one that is obstructed. If there were no obstruction, then since all sides would merge at the same place, all composites would be just a single subtle particle. This has been explained.

Qualm: Why do you not accept that, although shadows and shaded areas are not subtle particles, they are composites?

Response: So is there a composite over and above the subtle particles? The root text says:

> A composite is not something separate, so those are not
> [attributes] of it. (v. 14d)

This shows that if a composite is not other than the subtle particles, then those shadows are not attributes of it. This is the main point to be fully understood. Now, as long as the defining characteristic of forms, for example, is not contradicted, then why bother to wonder whether they might be subtle particles or a composite? So what then is their defining characteristic? It is that they are the object of eye consciousness and so on or blue and so on. In saying that they are the object of eye consciousness, such as blue, yellow, and so on, it is crucial to analyze whether such an object is a unitary substance or a plurality. Why? Conceiving it to be a plurality has already been explained. The root text says:

> If unitary, then there would be no gradual movement,
> nor perception and nonperception simultaneously, [213]
> nor separate parts in different places,
> nor the invisibility of very small beings. (v. 15)

If the object of visual consciousness, such as blue or yellow, is understood to be a unitary substance without any distinct parts, then there would be no way to gradually walk across the ground because in a single step the entire ground would be traversed. Also it would be impossible to simultaneously perceive the nearer part [of the ground] and not perceive the further part, because to perceive and not perceive the same thing at the same time would be impossible.

If elephants, horses, and so on, which are diverse and distinct, were one [thing], then they could not be situated [in their own places] because where one is situated in that very same spot the other would also be situated—so how could they possibly be distinct? Or, since empty space between them is apprehended, how could the places occupied and not occupied by them be the same? Indeed, if it is only in terms of having different defining characteristics that a different substance is recognized, not anything else, then very small aquatic beings would not be invisible because in terms of being forms they are the same as large ones. Therefore they must definitely be conceived in terms of being different subtle particles, for they are not established as unitary. And since they are not established as unitary, forms and so on are also not established as the objects of visual consciousness. Thus they are established as cognition only.[401]

Fifth, the reasoning that refutes the definition of the object of apprehension to be "that which it resembles and from which it has arisen" is presented in Dharmakīrti's *Exposition of Valid Cognition*, as follows. When the Cittamātra ask the proponents of the two Buddhist realist schools,

"What cognition knows the existence of an external object?" they reply, "It is known by the very one that directly perceives and knows individually blue, yellow, and so on." [214] The Cittamātra again inquire, "By virtue of what reason do you say that the cognition perceiving blue, yellow, and so on knows an external object?" The Buddhist realists reply, "The reason by virtue of which we say that such cognition knows an external object is because it resembles the external object." The Cittamātra respond, "In that case, this is not a flawless reasoning. For, in the case of a sensory cognition to which one moon appears as two, that sensory cognition would realize two moons since it arises bearing a resemblance to two moons." In this way, the assertion that cognition and its object of apprehension arise endowed with a resemblance of form is refuted.[402] Dharmakīrti's *Exposition of Valid Cognition* says:

> What [mind] knows the object? That which knows
>   individually;
> it is the very one that directly perceives.
> By virtue of what does it know the object?
> It is by virtue of a resemblance. But this is erroneous.[403]

The Cittamātra would hence declare, "Even if it were allowed that cognition bears a likeness to an external object, the proof that this external object is in the nature of that which is experienced, where that is taken to be the apprehended object, is an erroneous proof, so it would not be able to prove that." To this the two Buddhist realist schools would reply, "The definition of that which is experienced is 'the object that it resembles and from which it has arisen,' where that resemblance is taken to be the apprehended object, so this proof is not erroneous." The Cittamātra respond, "In the case of a consciousness apprehending blue, since it resembles and has arisen from an earlier apprehension of blue that is its immediately preceding condition similar to it, [215] there would be the consequence that it would experience the preceding moment of cognition by way of taking it as its apprehended object!" This refutation is stated in *Exposition of Valid Cognition*:

> Even if it were so, since it is erroneous,
> it would not be able to prove that this [external object] is
> in the nature of that which is experienced.

> The definition [they provide] of "that which is experienced" is
> "that which it resembles and from which it has arisen."
>
> But since they are similar in cognizing the same object,
> its immediately preceding condition would be that which is
> experienced.[404]

Sixth, the reasoning of the necessary simultaneity of perception and the perceived, which refutes external objects, is as follows. Those who accept external objects claim that it is incorrect to assert the necessary simultaneity of perception and the perceived, as stated in Prajñākaragupta's *Necessary Simultaneity of Perception and the Perceived*:

> Having refuted that such [an object] is in the nature of consciousness, first there is the perception of the appearance of individual aspects of the object, such as white, yellow, and so on. Although this is seen in the ten directions, since there is no perception of the aspect of consciousness, the necessary simultaneity of perception and the perceived is not established. In that case, it is proven that it is not established.[405]

According to those who accept external objects, there is the appearance of individual aspects of the object, such as white and yellow, which are not in the nature of consciousness; [216] however, although such appearances are seen in the ten directions, there is no appearance of an aspect of consciousness. So in the case of the consciousness and its object, if there is no necessary simultaneity of perception and the perceived, then how could something that lacks necessity be proven to have necessity? Thus the reasoning of the necessary simultaneity of perception and the perceived is refuted.

In the context of this argument to refute external objects by means of the necessary simultaneity of perception and the perceived, the term *simultaneity* means "at the same time," *perception and the perceived* means to be "perceived by valid cognition," and *necessary* means "pervasion" (i.e., entailment). In brief, the *necessary simultaneity of perception and the perceived* means "the necessity of cognizing together at the same time." This means that there is a mutual pervasion: when one is validly perceived the other must also be validly perceived, and vice versa. For example, in the case of blue and a valid perception of blue, the image and the object occur at the same time. The perception of blue is necessarily perceived by reflexive awareness, and when reflexive awareness perceives a valid perception of blue, it is said that blue too is necessarily perceived by the valid cognition apprehending blue. In contrast, if two things are different in terms of substance they cannot be necessarily simultaneously perceived. For example, although blue and yellow may exist simultaneously, since they are different substances they are not necessarily simultaneously perceived. This also indicates that if there is no cognizing subject then there is necessarily no object, so the establishment of the object must depend on the subject.

This argument of the necessary simultaneity of perception and the perceived is presented in Dharmakīrti's *Exposition of Valid Cognition* as follows:

> The object that is experienced necessarily
> occurs simultaneously with the cognition of it.
> By what would its separateness
> from that be established then?[406]

Blue and the sensory direct perception of a blue appearance are empty of substantial difference because of [217] the necessary simultaneity of perception and the perceived. The modes[407] of that reason are established because the pervasion is established and the attribute of the subject is established.

With regard to the first, the pervasion, Dharmakīrti's *Exposition of Valid Cognition* says:

> A difference is seen owing to a distorted cognition,
> just as a double moon [appears but] does not exist.[408]

The above states that [the case of a direct perception and its object] is likened to when a distorted cognition clearly sees two moons, even though two different moons do not exist. *Exposition of Valid Cognition* also says:

> In the case of different [things like] blue and yellow,
> there is no necessary [simultaneity] of being experienced.[409]

If those two phenomena were necessarily simultaneously perceived, then those two phenomena could not be substantially different because substantially different things, such as blue and yellow, may exist simultaneously but are not necessarily simultaneously experienced. The pervasion of the main reason is established by means of positing the homologous example and the heterogeneous example.

With regard to the second, the attribute of the subject, Dharmakīrti's *Exposition of Valid Cognition* says:

> An object that lacks an experience,
> or an experience that lacks an object,
> is not seen to be experienced.[410]

This states that blue and the visual consciousness of a blue appearance are necessarily simultaneously perceived because when a visual consciousness apprehending blue *lacks an experience of itself by reflexive awareness*, then the visual consciousness apprehending blue has no experience of the object, blue, at all. When a visual consciousness apprehending blue [218] *lacks an experience of the object*, blue, then the experiential visual consciousness apprehending blue is necessarily not seen to be experienced by reflexive awareness [which is a type of mental direct perception].

The point proved by that reasoning is summed up in Dharmakīrti's *Exposition of Valid Cognition* as follows:

> Thus an object appearing at the time of cognition
> is not separate from that cognition,
> and that this is so is impossible to refute.[411]

To conclude, then, since blue and the visual consciousness apprehending blue are not substantially different, the object, such as the blue appearance at the time of cognizing it, is not substantially different from that consciousness; and since this cannot be refuted by valid cognition, external objects are not established.

Of these six types of argument presented above, there are two—one that refutes particles to be the perceived object of perception and the other that refutes partless particles—that refute partless particles as an aid toward refuting external objects; thus the refutation of external objects remains intact. In contrast, the remaining arguments—the reasoning that divergent cognitions can arise in relation to a single thing; the reasoning concerning dreams, reflections, and so on; the reasoning that refutes the definition of the object of apprehension to be "that which it resembles and from which it has arisen"; and the reasoning of the necessary simultaneity of perception and the perceived—are all arguments that refute external reality in a direct manner.

Having refuted the existence of external objects by means of several arguments in this way, the tradition also provides other arguments to prove that there are no external objects and that consciousness is truly established. These include the following: "The *subject*, consciousness during the waking state, is empty of external objects, because it is consciousness, just like consciousness during the dream state." [219] Also, "The *subject*, the object perceived by consciousness during the waking state, appears as an external object but does not exist in such a way and thus is deceptive, because it is an object, just like an object of consciousness during the dream state." And, "If the *subject*, the dependent nature that is the basis of the thoroughly afflictive and the perfectly pure, does not exist through its own characteristics, then all thoroughly afflictive and perfectly pure phenomena based on it would be nonexistent, because without it whatever is based on it would not exist, just like a cloth made of tortoise hairs." These three arguments are put forward to prove that external objects do not exist and that consciousness exists through its own characteristics.

In this way, by presenting many arguments that undermine the assertion of external reality and that support the denial of external reality, one establishes all external and internal phenomena to be in the nature of the internal—the mind only—which is the foundational tenet of this philosophical school.

The Conclusion: There Is No External Reality

Now let us explain the conclusion of the rational arguments refuting the substantial difference between subject and object—namely that *there is no external reality*. Here, the key arguments include those presented above, such as the reasoning that divergent cognitions can arise in relation to a single thing, as found in Asaṅga's *Compendium of the Mahāyāna,* and the reasoning concerning dreams, reflections, and so on. They also include those not mentioned earlier, such as the argument that if external reality were to exist then sentient beings would become liberated without making any effort, or conversely would not become liberated even if they made effort, and the reasoning that proves, by means of evidence concordant with the three ways of knowing, that external objects such as the earth do not exist. [220] Based on such arguments as these, Asaṅga, the great trailblazer of the Cittamātra tradition, maintains that the nonexistence of external reality is easily established. For example, the *Compendium of the Mahāyāna* says:

> Here, the Buddha said: "O bodhisattva, when one is endowed with the four qualities, one will understand that the objects of all cognitions do not exist. One will understand this by way of: (a) knowing how a single object is the cause of divergent cognitions, such as how hungry ghosts, animals, humans, and gods perceive a single thing in different ways; (b) perceiving cognitions that are devoid of objects, such as when perceiving the past, the future, a dream, a reflection, and so on; (c) knowing it effortlessly and without error, for if the external object were to exist then cognizing this object would be effortless and without error, since it would be a cognition of reality; and (d) knowing in conformity with the three ways of knowing, as follows: (1) for bodhisattvas and those in meditative absorption who have gained mastery of mind, objects appear to them in conformity with their power of aspiration; (2) for yogins who have attained calm abiding and who strive for insight into phenomena, objects appear only as attended to; and (3) for those who have attained and remain in a state of nonconceptual wisdom, no objects at all appear." Thus, based on conformity with these three ways of knowing the object and the reasonings stated above, it is established that external objects do not exist.[412] [221]

In relation to the above, where it says, "O bodhisattva, when one is endowed with the four qualities," the four qualities are those clearly stated in the quotation: (1) knowing the cause of divergent cognitions; (2) perceiving cognitions devoid of objects; (3) knowing that if there were external objects, then there would be neither effort nor distortion; and (4) knowing in conformity with the three ways of knowing. The phrase "in conformity with the three ways of knowing" refers to the following: (1) in the case of bodhisattvas and those who have gained mastery of mind, having attained the mundane paths and so on, colors, shapes, and the rest are emanated; (2) in the case of yogins who have attained calm abiding (Skt. *śamatha*),[413] earth, water, and so on appear in conformity with their aspirations; (3) in the case of superior meditative equipoise, no appearances of external objects occur. Therefore forms and so on are established to be only in the nature of the mind and to be truly existent also.

Furthermore, as mentioned earlier, through the reasoning that refutes subtle particles or a composite of particles being the observed object, it was shown how the subtle particles—which are asserted by Sautrāntika and so on to be the basic constituents of external objects—do not appear [to perception], hence a key condition for the resultant cognition to arise bearing its aspects is lacking. Also it was shown how the composites that they assert to constitute the external object appear, but because they do not exist substantially, another key condition for the resultant cognition to arise bearing its aspects is not satisfied. Thus it was demonstrated how neither the subtle particles, as the basic constituents of external objects, nor the composite of subtle particles, as the basic constituents of external objects, can be established as the objective condition, or the external object. These points are summed up by Dignāga, the great pioneer of Cittamātra, in his *Investigation of the Object Autocommentary*:

> Thus in both cases the external object
> cannot be the object of cognition.
>
> Since the condition is not satisfied, [222] an external thing, whether taken to be *subtle particles* or *a composite of them*, is not the objective support.[414]

Similarly, through the reasoning that refutes the definition of the object of apprehension to be "that which it resembles and from which it has arisen," which was presented earlier, it has been demonstrated that the blue that is the experienced object of a sense consciousness apprehending blue is in the nature of a sensory cognition apprehending blue, thus this sensory cognition apprehending blue does not experience something substantially different from itself. Also, forms, sounds, and the rest, which are the objects known individually by direct perception, are established as in the nature of their respective directly perceiving cognitions and not as external objects. To sum up the above point, Dharmakīrti, the great upholder of the Cittamātra system, states the following in his *Exposition of Valid Cognition*:

> An experience of that [object] is in the nature of that
>   [cognition],
> it is not something separate from that at all.
> It is the object known individually by perception.
> That [object] is in the nature of that [cognition].[415]

In brief, these great masters of the Cittamātra system rationally refute the establishment of substantially different subject and object, whether directly or indirectly, thereby maintaining that there exists no external reality. And since other masters of the Cittamātra system offer much the same explanations, a key conclusion of the Cittamātra school is that there is no external reality. [223]

13

Being Established as Cognition Only

What It Means to Be Established as Cognition Only

As we have seen, the Yogācāra tradition utilizes many reasons to refute external objects and states with emphasis how all phenomena are established as cognition only. They explain how it is in terms of this truth of cognition only that one can engage with the characteristics of phenomena—namely, the three natures. According to this tradition, it is maintained that just as falling hairs and a double moon do not exist in reality yet may appear to those with an eye disease, likewise all internal phenomena, such as minds and mental factors of the three realms, and external objective phenomena, such as forms, sounds, and so on, are nothing but appearances of one's own mind. Hence there are no appearances projected to the mind from outside, and no such external reality exists at all. This is explained as follows in Vasubandhu's *Twenty Stanzas Autocommentary*:

> In the Mahāyāna tradition, the three realms are posited to be *cognition only* because it says in the [*Ten Levels*] sūtra: "O heirs of the Victorious One, the three realms are *mind only*." The terms mind, mentality, consciousness, and cognition are understood to be synonymous. Here, "mind" is taken to include its concomitant mental factors, while "only" is a restricting term because it excludes external reality. Just as those with an eye disease [224] see nonexistent hairs and a double moon, consciousness itself arises appearing as the object, for the object does not exist at all.[416]

This passage indicates that visual form and the sense consciousness apprehending it are one substance. To analyze the Cittamātra assertion that form and the consciousness apprehending it are the same nature, consider the following question: "When two people—Devadatta and Yajñadatta—look at one thing in common, such as a pot, is the object looked at the same substance as *both* of those visual consciousnesses looking at it, or is it the same substance as *each* of those visual consciousnesses? If it is the first, then the two visual consciousnesses would be the same substance as each other. If it is the second, then the pot that is the same substance as Devadatta's visual consciousness would be a different substance from Yajñadatta's visual consciousness—in which case, that pot would not be seen by Yajñadatta, so this would contradict the original assumption that the pot is an object seen in common." Now, when both Devadatta and Yajñadatta look at a single pot, although the image that appears to one does not appear to the other, it does not contradict the claim that the mere pot is the object that is seen. For example, when both Devadatta and Yajñadatta declare, "Sound is impermanent," the utterance spoken by Devadatta is not the utterance spoken by Yajñadatta, yet it does not contradict the fact that the mere words "Sound is impermanent" are spoken by both of them in common. While the words uttered by each person are a different substance from them, the words "Sound is impermanent" that they speak in common are not. Therefore, one may say that although the pot that appears to the visual consciousness of each of the two—Devadatta and Yajñadatta—is the same substance as each one's own visual consciousness, [225] the two visual consciousnesses need not be the same substance.

When a visual consciousness apprehending a pot views the pot, the pot's appearance that manifests as if from an external source is not a real pot but an appearance that is a mere imputation manifesting through the causal capacity of habitual latent propensities without beginning. It is not in any way a real pot that manifests as an object separate from the pot-apprehending consciousness, and it is also not the pot-apprehending consciousness itself. Rather it is posited as an appearance that has arisen from latent propensities of a similar type as that pot-apprehending consciousness. For example, a dream-elephant is not an elephant that exists objectively in the place it may appear, nor is it the dream consciousness itself; rather it is posited as an appearance of that consciousness.

Proponents of external reality present the following argument. "If Yajñadatta's mind, which is the observed object of a valid cognition knowing Yajñadatta's mind within Devadatta's mental continuum, were the same substance as that valid cognition, then those two would be one and the same continuum. For example, since the bodily and speech acts of a person are included within the speaker's own continuum, they cannot be in the nature of the hearer's consciousness. This would entail the fault that from the hearer experiencing the speaker's bodily and speech acts, the speaker's motivation would be included within the hearer's continuum, which is unacceptable." Cittamātra respond to these criticisms as follows. "The hearer does not directly perceive the speaker's bodily and speech acts, but from the appearance of an aspect similar to that, which is in the nature of the hearer's own consciousness, he understands the speaker's motivation. Therefore the implied faults, such as both oneself and the other person to be sharing one and the same continuum or not to be people of different continua, do not occur." [226]

To explain this more precisely, proponents of external reality believe that the bodily and speech acts of the other person, the speaker, directly appear through the force of being projected toward the hearer. Proponents of the Mind Only system argue that the bodily and speech acts within the speaker's continuum are established through the latent propensities within that person's continuum, thus they cannot appear to the hearer exactly as they are. However, bodily and speech acts arise from the movement of the mind of motivation when one wishes to speak. So given that one can know one's own mind, one can use the evidence of how such speech acts arise in one's own case and apply it similarly to the case of other people. When convinced of the need to ascertain another's motivation to speak, an aspect similar to the other person's speech act arises in the hearer's own consciousness and this is conventionally imputed to be the other person's speech act. Such evidence for knowing another person's mind is described in Dharmakīrti's *Proof of Other Mindstreams* as follows:

> Having seen that in oneself an act of mind
> precedes a bodily action, one apprehends this
> in others too, and thus knows their minds.
> This accords with the Cittamātra approach also.[417]

In view of all the above, the meaning of the statement "All phenomena such as forms, sounds, and so on are established as cognition only" can be understood as follows. (1) There is no external reality except for cognition only. [227] (2) A single cognition appears as a cause or observed object and as a viewing or apprehending subject. (3) When a cognition of a painting with various aspects arises, there arise simultaneously one aspect of that cognition as the variegated object and one aspect of it as the apprehending subject. Thus, owing to these three reasons, with respect to the *cognizance* of the body, the embodied, the experiencer, the things experienced, the experiences themselves and so on, even though such phenomena are not *actually* the cognitions perceiving them, they do not exist as something separate from their appearances; that is to say, they do not exist as a different substance from that cognition. This is the meaning of "All phenomena are established as cognition only" in the context of a passage from Asaṅga's *Compendium of the Mahāyāna*, which states:

> How are these cognizances established as cognition only? In brief, this is by virtue of three factors: by being merely *that alone*, for there exists no external reality; because the cognizances have the twofold aspect of causal sign and viewing; and because of the simultaneous arising of the manifold they appear in diverse aspects.[418]

Since it is challenging to make sense of the statement that all phenomena are established as cognition only, let us explain this by way of analogy. For example, although the appearance of a person in a dream is not the mind itself, this [person] exists as a mere appearance of that dream consciousness and does not exist as a different substance from the mind. Similarly, for example, when a reflection of a face appears in a mirror, such a reflection is not the mirror yet it has no reality apart from that mirror; it is merely a likeness of the face appearing in the mirror. [228] Therefore, to understand the term *cognition only* in this context, one should discern it to mean "cognizance only" or "appearance only," where the term *cognition* refers not to "the mind that cognizes" but instead refers to "the image that appears to cognition."[419]

There are fifteen ways that this kind of cognizance may be categorized, such as the cognizance of the body. Also, since both unassociated conditioning factors and permanent phenomena are included in the cognizance of the things experienced, there are no phenomena that are not included in the fifteen types of cognizance. As for their enumerations and illustrations and the explanations of how any cognizance is established through the activation of its respective latent propensities, together with their authoritative sources, these topics have already been presented in the context of the Cittamātra tenets set forth in volume 3 of *Science and Philosophy in the Indian Buddhist Classics*. In view of the above account, the term *mind only* does not mean that the mind can just fabricate external objects according to whatever it wishes, or that one does not accept the inner and outer world beyond the mind. Rather it means that from the perspective of each sentient being's own cognition, the various appearances as pleasant or painful, good or bad, and so on are established to be in the nature of one's own mind or as mere appearances within the mind. It means that they are not accepted to be established from the side of the object beyond being mere cognitive appearances. Asaṅga's *Compendium of the Mahāyāna* says:

> For the statement that posits, with respect to these cognizances, "There is no external reality, they are cognition only," what analogy do you have for this? Here, consider dreams and so forth to be the analogy. For example, although in a dream there are no objects but only cognition itself, various objects appear, such as forms, sounds, smells, tastes, and tangibles, as well as houses, forests, plains, mountains, and so on, [229] even though no object is there at all. By means of these analogies it is to be understood that everything is just cognition only.[420]

In Vinītadeva's *Commentary on the Twenty Stanzas* it similarly says: "With seeds and appearances in mind, it is taught that the sense bases such as forms exist, but it is not taught that they exist separately from consciousness."[421]

If a pot, for example, were established as an external object, then it must link back to a partless particle. But since there is no possibility for a solid mass to exist by means of an aggregation of partless particles, such a method for establishing a pot remains untenable. Therefore, when a visual consciousness apprehending a pot is generated, the appearance of a pot that arises within it is itself what is referred to as the *pot*. That appearance as a pot is not projected by an external object [to the perception] but arises through the force of internal latent propensities, and since it is the same nature as that visual consciousness, the pot is stated to be established through the force of internal latent propensities and established in the nature of mind or consciousness only. For example, when looking at tiny written letters through a magnifying glass, those letters that are seen as larger than before do not appear to exist from the side of the magnifying glass, but appear to be cast as an image from the side of the paper. If those images of larger letters were cast from the side of the paper, then such images of larger letters would also have to be seen whether there is a magnifying glass or not, but they are not seen in that way. Therefore, [230] given that such images of larger letters do not exist separately from the magnifying glass, they can be understood to be established in the nature of the magnifying glass.

With respect to "consciousness" in the context of the phrase "Form and so on are established in the nature of consciousness," this does not need to be a consciousness that necessarily realizes what is being perceived. For example, if a pot is established through the activation of latent propensities, its attributes, such as impermanent and produced, are established simultaneously. In that case, they must be posited to *appear to* the direct perception apprehending the pot and to be established through the activation of latent propensities. However, they are not necessarily *realized by* the direct perception apprehending the pot.[422]

Someone might ask, "If Cittamātra do accept forms, sounds, and so on, then wouldn't their refutation of them as external reality be just a matter of debating about mere semantics, because they posit the very things that appear as external, such as forms and so on, to be external?" According to this tradition, if forms, sounds, and so on did not exist, then the presentation of the five aggregates, the eighteen elements, and the twelve sense bases would be incorrect. For example, Asaṅga's *Compendium of the Mahāyāna* says: "Why is it called the appropriating consciousness? Because it is the cause of all the physical sense faculties and because it the basis that appropriates an embodied existence. Upon entering into this life and for as longs as it lasts, it holds on to the five physical sense faculties up to the point of death."[423] Asaṅga makes similar statements in his *Compendium of Ascertainments* as well.

Vasubandhu too, in his *Explanation of the First Dependent Origination and Its Divisions*,[424] [231] when describing how *name and form* are established having the foundation consciousness as a condition, explains that *name* refers to the last four aggregates, while *form* refers to the elements and element derivatives that are physical forms. He also speaks of how, although the form aggregate does not exist in the formless realm, it exists in the other two realms. Thus there seem to be numerous sources in the Cittamātra tradition where form is accepted to have existence. The appellation of the tradition's followers as Proponents of Knowable Objects as Internal also refers to the fact that they do not accept knowable objects, such as forms, sounds, and so on, to constitute external reality but to be in the same nature as internal consciousness.

How Ordinary Conventions Remain Tenable on the Basis of Cognition Only

We will now explain how, on the basis of cognition only, all the presentations of conventional reality remain tenable.[425] The Sautrāntika generally define *existence* and *nonexistence* in terms of being perceived or not perceived by valid cognition, and they consider valid direct perception to be foremost among all the types of valid cognition. So they say to the Cittamātra: "If you maintain that there is external reality at all, then how can the thought 'I directly see forms, sounds, and so on' ever arise?" The Cittamātra respond: "Although there is no external reality, a mind directly seeing a form, for example, arises—just as in a dream where there are no external objects yet a consciousness to which horses and elephants appear nevertheless arises. If you Sautrāntika believe that when the thought 'I directly see this object, form, and so on' arises, the object does not appear at that time because it has already ceased,[426] then it is irrational for you to maintain that the object is seen directly." Vasubandhu's *Twenty Stanzas Autocommentary* presents these exchanges as follows: [232]

> *Qualm*: Existence and nonexistence are differentiated in terms of being perceived by means of valid [cognition]. Among all the types of valid cognition, the principal one is valid direct perception. If there is no external reality, then how can the thought "I see this" arise?
>
> *Response*:
>
> Just as perceptual minds [arise] in dreams. (v. 16a)
>
> That is to say, [they arise] even without external objects, as indicated earlier.

> When such a mind arises, if at that time,
> according to you, the object does not appear,
> then how can you say it is direct perception? (v. 16bd)

> When a perceptual cognition arises, as with the thought "I directly see this object," you claim that the object does not appear at that time, in that it is discerned by a mental consciousness because the visual consciousness has ceased. More specifically, since you claim it is momentary, how can you assert it to be direct perception? If it is [momentary], then at that time those forms, tastes, and so on will have already ceased.[427]

Now, with respect to the Cittamātra standpoint that a direct perception seeing a form, for example, does not see an external object but sees the mere appearance of a form, the two Śrāvakayāna schools [Vaibhāṣika and Sautrāntika] challenge them as follows: "If an appearance of form, for example, to the direct perception apprehending it does not arise through the causal capacity of an external object, then it cannot be the case that this appearance is restricted with regard to place—where it arises in some places but not in all—or restricted with regard to time—where it arises on certain occasions but not always. Such specificity with regard to place and time would not be possible; rather it could arise in all places and at all times. For example, hairs, flies, and so on appear without restriction to those affected by an eye disease, but not to others without eye disease. [233] Likewise, since this appearance of form arises without restriction in all beings who are present in certain places at certain times, but not in other places and times, it is not unrestricted with regard to minds. Thus the appearances should be experienced by all beings without relying contingently on specific conditions. Similarly, hairs, flies, and so on perceived by those affected with eye disease cannot perform the functions of tying, stinging, excreting, and so on, whereas when perceived by those without eye disease, the appearance of hairs, flies, and so on do perform their respective functions. Likewise, the food, drink, clothing, poison, weapons, and so on that appear in a dream cannot function for the purpose of eating, drinking, keeping warm, killing, and slaughtering, whereas the food, drink, and so on that appear while awake do function for such purposes. Similarly, a city of gandharvas[428] cannot function as a city, whereas a real city does function as a city." Such differentiations cannot be explained, so the opponents of the Cittamātra argue and raise these objections. To present these points, Vasubandhu's *Twenty Stanzas Autocommentary* says:

> Here, they dispute [Cittamātra claims] by stating the following objection:
>
> > If a cognition [arises] without an object,
> > then for it to be restricted with regard to place and time
> > and unrestricted with regard to minds
> > and to functionality would be unreasonable. (v. 2)
>
> What does this indicate? If a cognition of a form, for example, arises not from the object but without an object, then why does it arise in some places but not everywhere? And even in those places, why does it arise sometimes but not at all times? And why does it arise in the minds of all those present at those places and times without restriction [234] and not just for a few people? In fact, falling hairs and so on appear to the minds of those with an eye disease but not to others. Furthermore, why is it that the hairs, flies, and so on seen by those with an eye disease are unable to perform the function of hairs and so on, whereas those seen by others do perform such functions? Food, drink, clothing, poison, weapons, and so on seen in a dream do not perform the function of food, drink, and so on, whereas those seen by others do. A city of gandharvas does not exist, so it does not perform the function of a city, but others [that are real] do. If by being similarly nonexistent these [cognitions] have no object, then for them to be restricted with regard to time and place and unrestricted with regard to mindstream and to functionality would also be unfeasible.[429]

In response, Cittamātra would argue: "Although the appearances of forms, sounds, and so on, to the direct perceptions apprehending them, do not come from the causal capacity of external objects, they are established by valid cognition as being restricted to certain places and to certain times and so forth. For example, although there are no external objects in a dream, in some places in the dream there appear cities and pleasure groves, men and women, but because they do not appear everywhere they are restricted with regard to place; and since they appear only sometimes and not at all times, they are restricted with regard to time. However, the minds to which forms, sounds, and so on appear are established without restriction. This is like the experience of hungry ghosts, where some hungry ghosts who have the corresponding ripening karma see a river filled with pus while others who have the corresponding ripening karma see a river filled with urine, [235] because there is no restriction with regard to the mindstreams of hungry ghosts. So although there are no external objects, the hairs, flies, and so on that appear to those without an eye disease are able to function for tying and so forth; the food and so on that appears to those who are awake are able to function for eating and so forth; and real cities are able to function as cities. For example, in a dream, even without having intercourse with an actual woman, an appearance of having intercourse may arise within the man and cause him to ejaculate; or even without encountering beasts of prey, such as tigers, leopards, and bears, an appearance of encountering them may arise within him and cause him to fear being harmed." Vasubandhu's *Twenty Stanzas Autocommentary* puts these points as follows:

> *Response*: It is not unfeasible. As it says:
>
> > Restriction as to place and so on is established
> > like in a dream. (v. 3a)
>
> Concomitant with what is experienced in a dream, it is "like a dream." How so? In a dream, although there are no external objects, things such as cities and pleasure groves, men and women, appear in some places but not everywhere, and in those very places they appear only sometimes and not always. So even without external objects, places, and so on, they are established as restricted.
>
> > Minds, however, are not restricted,
> > as in the case of hungry ghosts . . . (v. 3bc)
>
> This is established in the lines that follow. Concomitant with the experience of hungry ghosts, it is "as in the case of hungry ghosts."

> ... since all of them
> see a river of pus and so on. (v. 3d)

"A river of pus" is a river filled with pus, like a pot filled with butter. Hungry ghosts who have the corresponding ripening karma—as is the case with all of them, not just some—see a river filled with pus. As in the case of those who see a river filled with pus, those who have the corresponding ripening karma see a river filled with urine, [236] feces, burning lava, saliva, or snot, or a river being guarded by men armed with clubs and swords, which is indicated by the phrase "and so on." Thus even in the absence of external objects, these cognitions are established without restriction with regard to mindstreams.

> They function like emission in a dream. (v. 4a)

One must know this to be the case. For example, owing to intercourse in a dream, even though there is no intercourse, the dreamer ejaculates. This characteristic is referred to by the phrase "emission in a dream." Likewise, the four restrictions—regarding place, time, [mindstream, and functionality]—are established by other examples also.[430]

With respect to the Cittamātra assertion that these four restrictions regarding place and so on remain feasible purely on the basis of the appearances of direct perception, and that forms and so on do not exist externally as if at a distance but are in fact mere appearances of the direct perception apprehending them, the two Śrāvakayāna schools raise the following objection: "If these phenomena such as forms are only appearances to the direct perception apprehending them, then are other minds known or not known by a cognition knowing other minds? If they are not known, then it cannot be called a 'cognition knowing other minds.' If they are known, then since at that time an image of subject and object as substantially different appears, how can the cognition knowing other minds know other minds as they are in reality without subject-object duality? If you cite as an example of not knowing others' minds just as they are in reality the case of not knowing one's own mind just as it is in reality, then why is it that one's cognition knowing one's own mind does not know it as it is in reality?" In response to this argument, [237] Cittamātra reply: "For example, just as in a mundane sense when a pot is covered by a cloth of a similar hue it is said that when one sees the outer cloth one sees the pot, so too it is said that when the cognition knowing one's own or others' minds respectively knows the appearance-image of one's own or others' minds, it knows one's own or others' minds. However it does not know one's own or others' minds as they are in reality, because one's own and others' minds as free of subject-object duality and inexpressible in nature is the experienced object of a Buddha's perception. This is because people endowed with those attributes have not abandoned the conceptualization that apprehends subject and object to be substantially different—while subject and object are not substantially different, they distortedly appear to be substantially different." In these ways, the objections raised are repelled, as presented in Vasubandhu's *Twenty Stanzas Autocommentary*:

> *Qualm*: If all these are just cognition only, then are others' minds known or not known by cognition knowing others' minds?
>
> *Response*: What is the point of this?
>
> *Qualm*: If they are not known, then how can it be called "cognition knowing others' minds"?
>
> *Response*: Indeed they are known:
>
> They are known by a cognition knowing others' minds,
> but not as they are in reality. So how? For example,
> as in the case of knowing one's own mind. (v. 21ab)
>
> *Qualm*: So why are they not [known] as they are in reality?
>
> *Response*:
>
> Because the experienced object of a Buddha
> is not known in that way [by that cognition]. (v. 21cd)
>
> Because a Buddha's experienced object is in nature inexpressible, it is not known in that way by that cognition. So neither of them are known as they are in reality because they appear in a distorted manner given the subject-object conceptualization has not been abandoned.[431] [238]

Again, the two Śrāvakayāna schools lay down a further challenge: "In a dream, for example, where there are no external objects, a consciousness arises to which there appears a tiny room containing a crowded herd of elephants. If likewise even while awake a consciousness arises to which something such as a form appears without an external object, then ordinary people would have to know that this consciousness has arisen to which a form appears without any external object, but they do not know it. Thus this [scenario] is not like a dream consciousness, where every consciousness to which forms and so on appear have no external focal objects at all." To this Cittamātra respond: "The inference that ordinary people must know that a cognition can arise to which a form appears without any external object is not established—just as, for example, ordinary people cannot know until they wake up that the elephants seen in a dream do not exist. Ordinary people have fallen into an intoxicating sleep caused by the latent propensities of habituation to distorted conceiving that apprehends subject and object as different substances, where even though there are no external objects they appear to exist, like a dreamer and the dream. They cannot realize anything that appears in a mistaken way as it is in reality until they have woken up from the intoxicating sleep caused by those pernicious latent propensities. Once they have attained the wisdom realizing that subject and object are not different substances, which is the antidote to those pernicious latent propensities, they wake up from the sleep caused by them. At this point they realize the absence of external objects, as it is in reality, and that they are like a dream." These points are presented in Vasubandhu's *Twenty Stanzas Autocommentary* as follows: [239]

> *Response*: For example, they are like the objects of a dream consciousness, which do not exist.
>
> *Qualm*: If they were like that, then ordinary people would understand that they do not exist in reality while awake, but they do not [understand]. Therefore it cannot be the case that all perceptions of external objects are objectless, like a dream.
>
> *Response*: That argument is not suitable.
>
> The objects seen in a dream do not exist,
> but this is not realized until one awakens. (v. 17cd)

> Ordinary beings overpowered by the sleep of habitual latent propensities based on distorted conceiving see unreal objects, like in a dream. Until they awaken they do not realize them to be nonexistent, as they are in reality. When they attain the transcendent nonconceptual wisdom that is its antidote, they awaken. Then, when the subsequent attainment of pure mundane wisdom manifests, they understand the nonexistence of objects, as it is in reality, which is similar [to awakening from a dream].[432]

Again the two Śrāvakayāna schools argue: "For example, just as on a mundane level, the objects of a dream have no external reality, if the objects of cognitions of the waking state too lack external reality, then why are the results of good actions in both states—awake and asleep—not to the same degree pleasant? And why are the results of bad actions in both states—awake and asleep—not to the same degree unpleasant?" To this, Cittamātra respond: "Although these are similar with regard to the absence of external reality, in the sleep state [240] both good and bad actions do not accord with how things are in reality and that state of mind remains overcome by the drowsiness of sleep, while in the waking state both good and bad actions accord with how things are in reality and the state of mind is not overcome by the drowsiness of sleep. Therefore the results of both good and bad actions in the sleep state and the results of both good and bad actions in the waking state are not to the same degree pleasant or unpleasant, respectively." Vasubandhu's *Twenty Stanzas Autocommentary* presents the exchange as follows:

> *Qualm*: If the waking state were similar to the dream state, where the objects of cognition do not exist as external, then why would the results of virtuous and nonvirtuous actions later experienced in the waking state and the sleep state not be to the same degree pleasant and unpleasant?
>
> *Response*:
>
> Since the mind is overcome by drowsiness
> in the dream state, the results are not similar. (v. 18cd)
>
> This is the cause here, for it is not the absence of objects.[433]

How Liberation Is Attained through Seeing This Ultimate Reality of Cognition Only

With this understanding, we now turn to an explanation of how liberation is attained through seeing the suchness of cognition only [for the Yogācāra tradition]. Suppose someone asks, "If animate and inanimate phenomena lack subject-object duality, are cognition only, and are inexpressible in nature, then why do other people use expressions to explain this inexpressible nature of cognition only?" If the suchness of cognition only is inexpressible as it is in reality, [241] then the ultimate nature, which is inexpressible as it is, could not be explained to others as it is in reality, nor heard by others as it is in reality. If words cannot express it nor ears hear it as it is in reality, it would be impossible to know the inexpressible nature of cognition only as it is in reality. Nevertheless, to assist in hearing it and knowing it as it is in reality, someone [who is a teacher] needs to connect other trainees to this subject matter through verbal expression. Even so, owing to their complete ignorance of this inexpressible nature of cognition only as it is in reality, ordinary beings engage in a conceptualization of things and project an objective support or locus, in terms of a conceptualizing subject and conceptualized object. In this way, they conceptualize about three factors—forms and so on; view and pride thinking "I"; and attachment, hatred, and delusion. Thus the eight conceptualizations arise that constitute the cause that creates sentient beings and their environments. Asaṅga's *Bodhisattva Levels* states:

> If all phenomena are inexpressible in nature, then why are words used in connection with them? Without words, the inexpressible ultimate nature cannot be stated to others nor heard by them. If there is neither statement nor hearing of words, then the inexpressible nature cannot be known. Thus, for the purpose of making it heard and known, words are used to express it. Even so, owing to complete ignorance about the ultimate nature as it is in reality, untrained beings engage in conceptualization about the three factors, and consequently the eight conceptualizations, which create all sentient beings and their environments, arise.[434] [242]

The eight conceptualizations referred to above are said to arise owing to one's complete ignorance about the inexpressible nature of cognition only. The first three are: (1) the conceptualization of entities, (2) the conceptualization of attributes, and (3) the conceptualization that apprehends wholes. From these three arise the conceptualization that projects an objective support or locus, the conceptualization that projects real things perceived such as forms, and the various conceptualizations of distinct names based on such things. The next two are: (4) the conceptualization that thinks "I" and (5) the conceptualization that thinks "mine." These respectively give rise to all the other views, except for the identity view, and to all the other kinds of pride, except for the pride thinking "I."[435] Then there are the remaining three: (6) the conceptualization as attractive, (7) the conceptualization as unattractive, and (8) the conceptualization as neither of those two. These three respectively give rise to attachment, hatred, and delusion. In brief, these eight conceptualizations constitute the causes that produce the three factors: (1) the objective support or locus, such as forms and so on; (2) view and pride thinking "I" and so on; and (3) attachment, hatred, and delusion. Furthermore, the conceptualization that projects real things functions as the basis of the identity view and the pride thinking "I." The identity view and the pride thinking "I" in turn function as the basis of attachment, hatred, and delusion. [243] These three, attachment and so on, function as the basis of one's own later continuum and all one's suffering in saṃsāra, characterized by birth, aging, sickness, and death. So in dependence on these three bases,[436] according to the Cittamātra tradition, one can understand all the ways in which sentient beings are bound by various kinds of suffering. Asaṅga's *Bodhisattva Levels* says:

> What are the eight conceptualizations that give rise to the three factors? The first three are: the conceptualization of entities, the conceptualization of attributes, and the conceptualization that apprehends wholes. These three give rise to the conceptualization that projects a support and the conceptualization that projects things that are perceived, such as forms, which are named. If, in dependence on those things, a projection is made, then expressions of distinct names are observed. So from a real thing arise many kinds of conceptualizations that are understood through the expressions of those distinct names. Based

> on these, there arise the two—the conceptualization that thinks "I" and the conceptualization that thinks "mine"—that constitute the identity view, which is the root that gives rise to all the other types of view, and the pride thinking "I," which is the root that gives rise to all the other types of pride. On the basis of these arise the conceptualization [of something] as attractive, the conceptualization as unattractive, and the conceptualization as neither of those two, which respectively give rise to attachment, hatred, and delusion. So this is how the eight conceptualizations operate. [244] The conceptualization that projects real things, the [identity] view, the pride thinking "I," and attachment, hatred, and delusion all function to give rise to the three factors. In dependence on the conceptualization that projects real things, there arise the identity view and the pride thinking "I." In dependence on the identity view and the pride thinking "I," there arise attachment, hatred, and delusion. So it is said that owing to these three bases, one continually enters into all kinds of saṃsāric existence without exception.[437]

To further illuminate the conceptualizations that project real things and so forth, which give rise to the three bases, we present the following definitions. (1) The "conceptualization of entities" refers to the grasping at form and so forth to be established through its own characteristics as the basis of application of the term *form* and so on. (2) The "conceptualization of attributes" refers to the grasping at the material and the nonmaterial, at the demonstrable and the indemonstrable, at the obstructive and the nonobstructive, at the contaminated and the uncontaminated, at the causally compounded and the uncompounded, at the virtuous and the nonvirtuous, at the scripturally specified and the scripturally unspecified, at the past and the non-past, at the future and the non-future, at the present and the non-present, and so on, taken to be established through its own characteristics as the basis of application of the term *material* or *nonmaterial* and so forth. (3) The "conceptualization that apprehends wholes" [245] is explained in Sāgaramegha's *Commentary on the Bodhisattva Levels* as follows: "The conceptualization that apprehends wholes is the conceptualization that apprehends the manifold as unitary."[438] It is the grasping at things labeled with different names—such as self, sentient being, living being, creature, household, army, forest, food, drink, steed, clothing, and so on—gathered into a single unit, to be established through its own characteristics as the basis of application of a term such as "phenomenon." (4) The "conceptualization that thinks 'I'" and (5) the "conceptualization that thinks 'mine'" are explained in Sāgaramegha's *Commentary on the Bodhisattva Levels* as follows: "The conceptualization that thinks 'I' or that thinks 'mine' is the conceptualization that grasps at conditioning factors within one's own continuum as 'I' or as 'mine.'"[439] It is the beginningless grasping at "I" or at "mine" based on the contaminated aggregates, in terms of the appropriator and the appropriated, belonging to one's own continuum of contaminated aggregates. (6) The "conceptualization as attractive" refers to the superimposition of excessive attractiveness upon something seen as desirable. (7) The "conceptualization as unattractive" refers to the superimposition of excessive repulsiveness upon something seen as undesirable. (8) The "conceptualization as neither of those two" refers to the superimposition of excessive mediocrity, without the superimposition of either attractiveness or repulsiveness upon something seen as neither desirable nor undesirable. [246] Asaṅga's *Bodhisattva Levels* says:

> What is the conceptualization of entities? The conceptualization apprehending the thing named "form" to be a form, for example, is called "the conceptualization of entities." What is the conceptualization of attributes? The conceptualization apprehending the thing named "form," for example, to be material or nonmaterial; demonstrable or indemonstrable; obstructive or nonobstructive; contaminated or uncontaminated; causally compounded or uncompounded; virtuous, nonvirtuous, or scripturally unspecified; past, future, or present; and so on—thereby making innumerable such differentiations based on the conceptualization of entities—is called "the conceptualization of attributes." What is the conceptualization that apprehends wholes? That [conceptualization] apprehending a thing named "form," for example, to be the bearer of [various] names or labels—such as self, sentient being, living being, creature, household, army, forest, food, drink, steed, clothing, and so on—through apprehending as a whole many phenomena gathered into a single unit, is called "the conceptualization that

> apprehends wholes." What is the conceptualization that thinks "I" and that thinks "mine"? Things associated with persons and associated with appropriation [247] are introduced and conceived as a self or as belonging to self, and having become habituated to that since time beyond beginning, they are distortedly grasped as such. From that introduction, in dependence on things concordant with one's own perspective, a distorted conceptualization arises that is called the conceptualization that thinks "I" or that thinks "mine." What is the conceptualization as attractive? It is the conceptualization that perceives something desirable to be attractive in reality. What is the conceptualization as unattractive? It is the conceptualization that perceives something undesirable to be repulsive in reality. What is the conceptualization as neither of those two? It is the conceptualization that perceives something neither desirable nor undesirable without labeling it as either attractive or repulsive in reality.[440]

The above passage from *Bodhisattva Levels* states that the first three—the conceptualization of entities, the conceptualization of attributes, and the conceptualization that apprehends wholes—are the grasping at a self of phenomena. The next two—the conceptualization that thinks "I" and the conceptualization that thinks "mine"—are the grasping at a self of persons. Then, the remaining three—the conceptualization as attractive, the conceptualization as unattractive, and the conceptualization as neither of those two—are the conceptualizations that constitute inappropriate attention. Thus, according to the Cittamātra tradition, it seems that the grasping at a self of phenomena is the basis of the grasping at a self of persons, while the grasping at a self of persons is the basis of inappropriate attention. Thus the grasping at a self of phenomena, which is differentiated in terms of three aspects, is presented first; [248] grasping at a self of person, which is differentiated in terms of two aspects, is presented in the middle; and what arises from this—namely, the conceptualization of inappropriate attention, which is differentiated in terms of three aspects—is presented last.

To understand how these eight conceptualizations, whether directly or indirectly, are distorted cognitions whose object as conceived (*'dzin stangs don*) does not exist in that way, they must be understood on the basis of four kinds of thorough searching and four kinds of thorough understanding. The four kinds of thorough searching are as follows. (1) The thorough search for the name is: to analyze how the name does not apply by way of essential nature to that referent—independently of the name, the referent, and the relation between name and referent. (2) The thorough search for the referent is: to analyze how a bulbous thing, for example, is not established by way of essential nature as the basis of application of the name *pot*—independently of the name, the referent, and the relation between name and referent. (3) The thorough search for imputation as an entity is: to analyze how the mere entity of something such as a pot is not established by way of essential nature as the basis of application of the name expressing the mere entity *pot*—independently of the name, the referent, and the relation between name and referent. (4) The thorough search for imputation as an attribute is: to analyze how an attribute, such as form's arising, is not established by way of essential nature as the basis of application of the name expressing the attribute, "form's arising" or so forth—independently of the name, the referent, and the relation between name and referent.

The four kinds of thorough understanding are as follows. (1) The thorough understanding of the name is: to understand, at the culmination of analyzing whether the name applies by way of essential nature to that referent—independently of the name, the referent, and the relation between name and referent—that it does not apply in that way. However, [249] in a general, ordinary sense, there is a need to discern what is seen or heard where names are applied appropriately to things—such as "carrying milk," for example—for if there were no application of names to referents, then a thought such as "This is milk" regarding the appropriate object would not be understood by anyone. If this were not understood, then there would be no conceiving or reifying that object to be established by way of essential nature as the basis of application of the name—independently of the name, the referent, and the relation between name and referent. If there were no conceiving or reification, then there would be no antidote or nonconceiving. If there were no reification and its antidote, or no conceiving and nonconceiving, then there would not even be the conventions of cognition, expressions, and their application that are motivated by them.[441]

(2) The thorough understanding of the referent is: to understand, at the culmination of analyzing whether a bulbous thing, for example, is estab-

lished by way of essential nature as the basis of application of the name *pot*—independently of the name, the referent, and the relation between name and referent—that it is not established in that way. (3) The thorough understanding of imputation as an entity is: to understand—at the culmination of analyzing whether the mere entity of something such as a form is established by way of essential nature as the basis of application of the name expressing the mere entity, such as *form*—independently of the name, the referent, and the relation between name and referent—that it is not established in that way. Also, this thorough understanding of imputation as an entity, which knows that the mere entity of a form, for example, is not established by way of essential nature as the basis of application of the name expressing the mere entity, such as *form*—independently of the name, the referent, and the relation between name and referent—sees it to be in nature like an apparition, a reflection, an echo, a mirage, a moon in water, a dream, and an illusion. [250]

(4) The thorough understanding of imputation as an attribute is: to understand, at the culmination of analyzing whether an attribute, such as form's arising, is established by way of essential nature as the basis of application of the name expressing the attribute "form's arising"—independently of the name, the referent, and the relation between name and referent—that it is not established in that way. Also, it is to know that an attribute such as "form's arising" does not exist by way of essential nature as the basis of application of the name expressing the attribute "form's arising"—independently of the name, the referent, and the relation between name and referent—yet that it is not utterly nonexistent but exists as the inexpressible nature of cognition only. The above points are explained in Asaṅga's *Bodhisattva Levels* as follows:

> How is that conceptualization known? By means of the four kinds of thorough searching and the four kinds of thorough understanding of ultimate truth as it is in reality. What are the four kinds of thorough searching? They are the thorough search for the name, the thorough search for the referent, the thorough search for imputation as an entity, and the thorough search for imputation as an attribute. The thorough search for the name is a bodhisattva's viewing of that which is the name to be a mere name. Likewise, the thorough search for the referent is their

viewing of that which is the referent to be a mere referent. The thorough search for imputation as an entity is their viewing of that which is an imputation as an entity to be a mere imputation as an entity. The thorough search for imputation as an attribute is their viewing of that which is an imputation as an attribute to be a mere imputation as an attribute. Thus in seeing the name, the different defining characteristics of the referent, and their relationship, they also understand the imputation as an entity and the imputation as an attribute to be dependent on the relation between the name and the referent. [251]

What are the four kinds of thorough understanding ultimate truth as it is in reality? They are the thorough understanding of ultimate truth as it is in reality upon searching for the name, the thorough understanding of ultimate truth as it is in reality upon searching for the referent, upon searching for the imputation as an entity, and upon searching for the imputation as a attribute. What is the thorough understanding of ultimate truth as it is in reality upon searching for the name? That bodhisattva, after having thoroughly searched for the name as a mere name, thoroughly understands this name as it is in reality—that is, that such a name is posited on a real thing as the referent, as the conditioned referent, as the viewed referent, and as the designated referent. Indeed, if the name *form* were not posited on the thing the name designates, such as a form, then nobody would know that the thing is called *form*. If nobody knows that, then there would be no manifest conceiving or reification. If there were no manifest conceiving, there would be no expression. So any such thorough understanding of ultimate truth as it is in reality is called "the thorough understanding of ultimate truth as it is in reality upon searching for the name."

What is the thorough understanding of ultimate truth as it is in reality upon searching for the referent? Similarly, that bodhisattva, after having thoroughly searched for the referent as a mere thing, sees that the thing the name designates, such as a form, is not associated with any expression at all and is inexpressible. This is "the thorough understanding of ultimate truth as it is in reality upon searching for the thing." [252] What is the

> thorough understanding of ultimate truth as it is in reality upon searching for the imputation as an entity? Similarly, that bodhisattva, regarding the thing the name designates, such as a form, after having thoroughly searched for it as a mere imputation as an entity, comes to know that the imputation as an entity, even though it appears to be the entity itself, is not a real entity, and thoroughly understands this ultimate truth as it is in reality—seeing it to be in nature like an apparition, a reflection, an echo, a mirage, a moon in water, a dream, and an illusion. When that appearance is seen as not being its nature, the very profound meaning [i.e., the ultimate nature] will be the object experienced, which is "the thorough understanding of ultimate truth as it is in reality upon searching for the imputation as an entity." What is the thorough understanding of ultimate truth as it is in reality upon searching for the imputation as an attribute? Similarly, that bodhisattva, after having thoroughly searched for the imputation as an attribute as a mere imputation, sees those imputations as attributes based on the thing the name designates, such as a form, to be nondual objects, and the thing to be neither existent nor nonexistent. For since it is not established to be expressible by nature, it is not existent, and since it is not established to be inexpressible in nature, it also is not nonexistent.[442]

When those endowed with intelligence, in reliance on the four kinds of thorough understanding, know that the eight conceptualizations, [253] whether directly or indirectly, are distorted cognitions whose object as conceived does not exist in that way, then the delusion that is complete ignorance of the inexpressible nature of "cognition-only" as it is in reality—which is the basis of the eight conceptualizations as well as the conceptual projections of real things that are the focal objects congruent with those conceptualizations—will not arise even slightly in the future. Since the basis or cause and the congruent focal objects do not arise, their resultant eight conceptualizations also will not arise. It is crucial to understand that the cessation of any opportunity for the conceptualizations and their causes to arise also entails the cessation of any opportunity for all projected elaborations—such as the causes of ordinary beings (the mental afflictions) and their results (the sufferings of birth, aging, sickness, death, and the rest)—to arise. Asaṅga's *Bodhisattva Levels* explains that one must understand that the complete cessation of any opportunity for all such elaborations to arise constitutes the liberation from mental afflictions and saṃsāra, respectively the cause and the result, as follows:

> When bodhisattvas, in dependence on the four kinds of thorough understanding of ultimate truth as it is in reality, thoroughly understand the eight conceptualizations, then by means of that thorough understanding, their causes and their focal objects, which are things conceptually projected, will not arise in the future. Since those are not produced and do not arise, the conceptualizations that perceive them will not arise in the future. Accordingly, it must be recognized that this cessation of conceptualization, along with real things, is the cessation of all projected elaborations. Such cessation of elaboration must be recognized to be the bodhisattva's [254] complete liberation according to the Mahāyāna.[443]

This presentation of the four kinds of searching is found also in Maitreya's *Ornament for the Mahāyāna Sūtras*, Asaṅga's *Compendium of Abhidharma* and *Compendium of the Mahāyāna*, and other treatises, where their presentations do not differ in meaning even slightly from those given in *Bodhisattva Levels* above. However, to make it easier to understand the meaning of those passages cited from *Bodhisattva Levels*, we now give a brief explanation of how it is presented in the *Compendium of Abhidharma*.

Searching for how a name does not apply to its referent through the force of how that referent exists is called "the thorough search for the name." This is differentiated in terms of three types of searches with regard to clusters of names, clusters of phrases, and clusters of letters. Thus the *Compendium of Abhidharma* states: "What is the thorough search for the name? It is to investigate how the particular characteristics of a cluster of names, a cluster of phrases, or a cluster of letters do not exist in an absolute sense."[444]

Searching for how a referent is not the basis of application of its name through the force of how that referent exists is called "the thorough search for the referent or thing." The *Compendium of Abhidharma* states: "What is the thorough search for the referent? It is to investigate how the characteristics of the aggregates, the elements, and the sense bases do not exist in an absolute sense."[445]

Searching for how a referent's mere entity is not the basis of application of its name through the force of how that referent's mere entity exists [255] is called "the thorough search for imputation as an entity." The *Compendium of Abhidharma* states: "What is the thorough search for imputation as an entity? It is to investigate how the relation between the expression and the expressed object is the cause of applying the convention that is the mere imputation as an entity."[446]

Searching for how a referent's attribute is not the basis of application of its name through the force of how that referent's attribute exists [255] is called "the thorough search for imputation as an attribute." The *Compendium of Abhidharma* states: "What is the thorough search for imputation as an attribute? It is to investigate how the relation between the expression and the expressed object is the cause of applying the convention that is the mere imputation as an attribute."[447]

Let us explain these further by illustrating them with some examples. In the case of a pot or suchlike, the thorough search for the name is to investigate how the term *pot* does not apply to a bulbous thing through the force of how it exists but is merely imputed by a thought wishing to express it. The thorough search for the referent is to investigate how something bulbous that is the basis of application of the term *pot* is not established as the basis of application of that term from the side of the bulbous thing, but is a mental expression or mere imputation by thought. The thorough search for imputation as an entity is to investigate how the entity expressed in the phrase "This bulbous thing is a pot" is not established by its own characteristics as the basis of designation of the name, but is merely imputed by thought. The thorough search for imputation as an attribute is to investigate how [256] the attribute expressed in the statement "This pot is produced" is not established by its own characteristics as the basis of designation of the name but is merely imputed by thought. Each of these four kinds of searching can consist of a correct assumption, a valid cognition, and a subsequent cognition.

The understanding known as "the thorough understanding of the name" refers to the mind that, having engaged in a thorough search for the name, realizes it is not established in the way it has been sought.[448] The same rationale applies to the rest. Because it is not established in the way it has been sought by the four kinds of searching, the realization that this name is merely imputed onto this referent and does not apply to it through the force of how the referent exists is "the thorough understanding of the name"; the realization that the referent is merely imputed as the basis of application of its name is "the thorough understanding of the referent"; the realization that the mere entity is nominally imputed on that referent without being established by the referent's characteristics or mode of existence is "the thorough understanding of imputation as an entity"; the realization that the attributes are nominally imputed on that referent without being established by the referent's characteristics or mode of existence is "the thorough understanding of imputation as an attribute." This is how these four kinds of thorough understanding arise.

In dependence on these four kinds of thorough searching and four kinds of thorough understanding, one realizes that the basis of application of names and thoughts do not exist as they appear to conceptual cognition. Once one has refuted a substantially different subject and object, or apprehender and apprehended, one enters into cognition only. When one knows the eight conceptualizations to be distorted cognition, then the delusion that is complete ignorance of cognition only as it is in reality, as well as things such as forms that are the focal objects congruent with those conceptualizations, do not arise. In this way, the conceptualizations, which are the cause, are removed by the opposing power of their antidotes, and one attains liberation from the mental afflictions as well as the subtle and coarse sufferings that are their result. [257]

Part 4

Emptiness according to the Madhyamaka Tradition

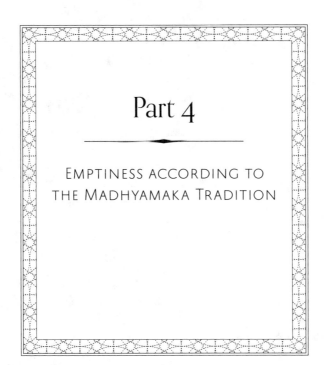

14

The Absence of Essential Nature according to Nāgārjuna

An Introduction to Nāgārjuna's Reasoning

Now we offer a somewhat extensive presentation of emptiness that is the final [or ultimate] nature of phenomena as understood in particular by Nāgārjuna and his Mādhyamika followers. As mentioned earlier, the great Indian master Nāgārjuna saw how the extensive teachings in the Mahāyāna's Perfection of Wisdom sūtras—which illustrate how all phenomena do not exist by virtue of essential nature—are conclusive and definitive in meaning. He refutes, with many rational arguments, the positions of those who claim that things truly exist—such as the Buddhist realists who say that phenomena such as the aggregates are established by way of their own characteristics, and the non-Buddhist realists who say that the self, time, and so on are truly existent things—and he establishes how all phenomena are empty of essential nature. He presents these arguments at great length in his renowned treatises on reasoning, such as the *Fundamental Treatise on the Middle Way* and *Sixty Stanzas of Reasoning*. [258]

So why does Nāgārjuna employ such extensive reasons in his Madhyamaka treatises to prove the profound emptiness that is the final mode of existence of phenomena? Various unwanted sufferings arise through the force of mental afflictions such as attachment and hatred, which are the internal motivations that are their karmic causes. Those mental afflictions arise from the conceptualizations of inappropriate attention. The conceptualizations of inappropriate attention arise from ignorance grasping at true existence that is confused about the actual mode of existence. The conceptualization of inappropriate attention is any of the four conceptualizations, such as holding the impure to be pure or holding that which is in the nature of suffering to be pleasurable. For example, when strong attachment arises upon seeing a certain person, the person who is the object of our attachment appears to be attractive in every way. Then one day, because of a disagreement, that person becomes our enemy. So the person who was previously an object of our attachment appears to be unpleasant in every way. That person who was our friend at one point and later our enemy did not undergo any change from his or her own side. That person appears to have good qualities and faults respectively because of the attachment and aversion that have arisen intensely within our own mindstreams, conditioned by superimpositions of good and bad in turn, due to the conceptualizations of inappropriate attention. Unwanted sufferings arise in this way through the force of the accumulation of various karmic actions. Familiarization with the mind that understands the meaning of emptiness counteracts how the mind grasping at true existence holds its object; and when such familiarization increases, the elaborations of grasping at true existence gradually cease. Thus the final root of the various sufferings [259] is understood to be how the delusion grasping at true existence apprehends its object in a distorted manner, and it is for the purpose of negating this grasping at true existence that the meaning of emptiness is taught so extensively in the sūtras and treatises.

This delusion of ignorance that is confused regarding its object is the root of all mental afflictions and suffering. And just as when the root of a tree is severed its boughs and leaves become withered, so when ignorance is extinguished all mental afflictions will cease. The *Sūtra Teaching the Tathāgata's Inconceivable Secret* says: "Śāntimati, it is like this. For example, if the root of a tree is cut away, all its parts—such as twigs, leaves, and branches—wither. Śāntimati, like that, if the identity view is completely pacified, all mental afflictions will be completely pacified."[449] Also, Nāgārjuna's *Fundamental Treatise on the Middle Way* states:

> Karma and afflictions arise from conceptualizations;
> these arise from the tendency to proliferate;
> the tendency to proliferate, however, ceases in emptiness.[450]

Nāgārjuna's *Praise of Dharmadhātu* says:

> The supremely mind-purifying
> Dharma is the absence of [inherent] nature.[451]

Also, Āryadeva's *Four Hundred Stanzas* says:

> Just as the tactile sense faculty pervades the whole body, [260]
> delusion abides in all [the mental afflictions].
> Therefore, by destroying delusion,
> all mental afflictions are destroyed.[452]

Here "delusion" must be understood to mean "ignorance grasping at a self." Now, when someone else praises us, for example, where we recognize this with the thought "They are praising me," the sense of "me" that appears to dwell deep in the mind is held to be an autonomous self. Due to having such a view of self, we create biased categories of self and other, where we are attached to those who support our side or share our opinions and we generate aversion or anger toward others who oppose our side or disagree with our opinions. In this way, all the defects and faults of the three doors [body, speech, and mind] arise. Candrakīrti's *Entering the Middle Way Autocommentary* explains this very clearly:

> Here "afflictions" refers to attachment and so on, while "faults" refers to birth, aging, sickness, death, misery, and so on. All these without exception arise from the identity view. It says in a sūtra that all mental afflictions "have the identity view as their root, have the identity view as their cause, and have the identity view as their source." Thus it is taught that they have the identity view as their very cause. So for those who have not abandoned the identity view, it follows that conditioning actions will ensue and that suffering such as birth and so on will arise. Therefore all of them without exception have the identity view [261] as their cause.[453]

Moreover, meditation such as that on foulness, which is taught to be the antidote to attachment, is not only incapable of removing hatred, it is even limited to just temporarily subduing attachment without being able to remove it from the root. Similarly, meditation such as that on loving-kindness is not only incapable of removing attachment, but it is also limited to just temporarily subduing hatred without being able to remove it from the root. The same rationale applies to pride and the rest. Thus the final root of mental afflictions such as attachment is the delusion grasping at true existence. And the final antidote that removes the delusion grasping at true existence is the wisdom realizing emptiness, which directly counteracts it and its way of grasping. Not only that, but when this root grasping at true existence is destroyed, mental afflictions such as attachment that depend on the delusion grasping at true existence will cease—just as when the root of a tree is severed its boughs will wither. This is explained explicitly in Candrakīrti's *Clear Words*:

> What is taught in order to clear away attachment will not exhaust hatred. What is taught in order to clear away hatred will not exhaust attachment. What is taught in order to exhaust pride will not destroy other stains. So these teachings are not pervasive [262] and do not have such great purpose. What is taught in order to exhaust delusion destroys all other mental afflictions. The conquerors have taught that all other afflictions are based on delusion.[454]

Establishing Phenomena to Be Devoid of Ultimate Arising through Refuting Arising from the Four Alternatives

Among all the texts composed by Nāgārjuna proving that phenomena have no essential nature, his *Fundamental Treatise on the Middle Way* is likened to the king. In the opening verse of salutation, in a manner consonant with the subject matter of the treatise, he pays homage to the Tathāgata for teaching suchness, the profound dependent arising, and he proves that dependently arisen causal phenomena are free from the eight alternatives of arising and ceasing and so forth. The main point here is as follows. The phenomena that usually benefit and harm us are the causally compounded type, upon which the presentations of cause and effect, agent and action, and so on are founded. Thus they are the most likely bases of error in thinking that things are truly established. The category of noncausal phenomena, which are incapable of producing results, are the less likely bases of error in thinking that things are truly established. The Buddhist and non-Buddhist Indian philosophers who accept things to be truly existent insist that causally compounded phenomena are proved to be truly established. For this reason, Nāgārjuna's *Fundamental Treatise on the Middle Way* says: [263]

> And without establishment of the causally compounded,
> how can the uncompounded be established?[455]

This prioritizes the refutation of the true establishment of causal phenomena. Moreover, Candrakīrti's *Clear Words* says: "Thinking that it is easier to refute cessation and so on after having refuted arising, the refutation of arising is presented first."[456] He is saying here that Nāgārjuna considers that once the inherent arising of things has been refuted, the refutation of inherent cessation will come easily. With this in mind, in his *Fundamental Treatise on the Middle Way* he first refutes intrinsic arising. So the text says:

> Not from self, not from others,
> not from both, not without a cause;
> any things, anywhere,
> do not arise at any time.[457]

This verse presents the refutation of inherent arising of dependently arisen causal phenomena by way of negating their arising from the four alternatives of self, other, both, and neither; and, having explicitly indicated the reason and the subject, it implicitly indicates the predicate of the thesis.[458]

In general, if something arises there are only two logically possible options: either it has a cause or it does not have a cause. If it has a cause, there are three ways in which this is logically possible: either both cause and effect are the same entity, or they are different entities, [264] or they are a combination of the same entity and different entities. If something were to inherently arise, then it would necessarily arise from one of the four alternatives. If arising from each of the four alternatives is refuted, then inherent arising will easily be refuted. According to both Buddhist and non-Buddhist realists, who claim that phenomena exist from their own side, if a result arises inherently, then it must arise from one of the four alternatives; if it doesn't arise from any of the four alternatives, then it cannot arise inherently. Since they accept this to be established by reasoning, they accept that things arise from one of the four alternatives. Therefore, if things are refuted to arise from any of the four alternatives, then it is easily established that they do not arise inherently. Because of this point, Nāgārjuna begins his *Fundamental Treatise on the Middle Way* by refuting the arising of things from the four alternatives. Nāgārjuna's presentation of this reasoning that refutes the arising from the four alternatives is a very famous and highly regarded refutation of the self of phenomena.

So as to easily understand this reasoning, consider the following argument: "The *subject*, external and internal things, do not inherently arise because they do not arise from any of the four alternatives—for example, like the reflection of a face in a mirror." This inference is called the *diamond slivers reasoning*. This is highlighted in Kamalaśīla's *Illumination of the Middle Way*, which states: "These four immutable diamond slivers are taught by the great masters; since they shatter all instances of things propounded by Buddhist and non-Buddhists without exception, [265] this path is by all means not to be contradicted."[459] Just as each shard or sliver of a diamond can pulverize ordinary jewels, so each corner of reasoning in this inference can refute each and every assertion of the opponents who accept true existence—thus it is called the *diamond slivers reasoning*.

The individual reasons that refute each of the four alternatives are presented as follows. (1) "The *subject*, external and internal things, do not arise at all from themselves at any time, in any place, or to any extent because arising again would be purposeless and endless." This reason refutes arising from self. (2) "The *subject*, external and internal things, do not arise from others at any time, in any place, or to any extent because it would follow that everything, whether its cause or not, would give rise to everything, whether its effect or not." This reason refutes arising from other. (3) "The *subject*, external and internal things, do not arise from both self and other at any time, in any place, or in any manner because arising from each of these, self and other, has been refuted separately." This reason refutes arising from both. (4) "The *subject*, external and internal things, do not arise causelessly at any time, in any place, or in any manner because every effort made for the sake of a result would be purposeless." This reason refutes arising without a cause. [266]

Now we turn to explaining each of the reasons that refute the arising from the four alternatives in more detail.

Refuting Arising from Self

The opponents who assert the arising from self belong to the non-Buddhist Sāṅkhya tradition. We can summarize how they posit the arising from self as follows. "A common effect exists in its mutually differing causes and conditions, because if it did not exist in those causes and conditions as one nature concomitant with the primal nature, it would be unfeasible. So that which is the nature of the barley grain, the cause, and that which is the nature of sprinkling water and so forth, the conditions, mutually contain the nature of the barley sprout and the nature of its causes and conditions, because such is the nature of all transformations."[460] Therefore, since they accept the seed and the sprout to be mutually different, they do not accept that a sprout arises from a sprout. However if they assert that the sprout arises from the seed and its nature, then since the two natures are one, it arises from its own nature, and its arising exists even when the cause has not yet manifested as a sprout. This is how they assert the arising from self. Kamalaśīla's *Commentary on the Difficult Points in the Compendium of Reality* quotes the following verse from a Sāṅkhya text:

> When [Rudrilla] asserted,
> "That which is curd is milk
> and that which is milk is curd,"
> he showed he was a native of the Vindhya hills.[461]

Refuting this position [of arising from self], Nāgārjuna's *Fundamental Treatise on the Middle Way* says:

> If the effect were to exist within
> the collection of its causes and conditions, [267]
> then it should be apprehended in the collection;
> but it is not apprehended in the collection at all.[462]

This is to say that the opponent's position can be refuted with a reason such as: "If you say that the effect, such as a sprout, exists within its causes and conditions, such as its seed and so on, then it must be apprehended; but since it is not, such an assertion is incorrect—just as a shawl, for example, is not apprehended within the composites of a pot."

Commenting on the above verse from *Fundamental Treatise on the Middle Way* that refutes the arising from self, *Buddhapālita's Commentary on the Fundamental Treatise* explains its meaning as follows:

> For instance, things do not arise from their own nature because their arising would be purposeless and endless. Things that exist in their own nature do not need to arise again. Indeed, if they were to exist and yet arise again, then since there would never be an occasion when they do not arise, this is unacceptable. Therefore things do not arise from themselves.[463]

If things were to arise from themselves, then arising would be purposeless and endless. It would be purposeless as follows. If sprouts and so on were to arise from themselves, then since they would exist at the time of their cause, it would be purposeless to arise again, for they would have already obtained their own being. If arising is for the purpose of obtaining one's own being, then it would be purposeless to arise again having already obtained it. Suppose someone suggests, "Even to have already obtained their own being does not contradict the need to arise again." But that would be endless, so it is refuted as follows. [268] In such a case, sprouts and so on would never not arise, because even though they already exist they would need to arise again. The Sāṅkhya say, "The effect exists in the form of a latent propensity that is not manifest at the time of the cause so it needs to manifestly arise, but it does not need to arise once it has already become manifest; thus there is no pervasion in the case of your earlier and later arguments." Nevertheless, they cannot escape that fault. For if what is manifest were to already exist, then there would be no need for it to arise. However, if it were to arise despite already existing, the fault of infinite regress would still remain. Furthermore, if what is manifest does not already exist, it is a contradiction to assert that only an already existent effect arises.

Consider the following syllogism: "For the *subject*, a sprout asserted to exist without actually manifesting at the time of its cause, arising again would be purposeless, because it exists; and for that same *subject*, arising again would be endless, because it exists; for example, a sprout that has already actually become manifest." Consider this argument rephrased as a consequence: "For the *subject*, external and internal things, arising again would be purposeless, because they already exist at the time of their cause."

Suppose the opponent says, "No pervasion." The response here is "For the *subject*, external and internal things, arising again would be endless, because arising again after having already arisen would be purposeful."[464] Candrakīrti's *Entering the Middle Way* says:

> If things arise from themselves, there is no benefit at all.
> Furthermore, something already born cannot repeat its birth.
> If you conceive that something already arisen does arise again,
> the production of sprouts and so on would not occur in this world,
> and seeds would reproduce themselves until the end of time.[465] [269]

Stating these two faults—effects of similar kind would not be produced and causes of similar kind would produce without stopping—shows that it contradicts reason, which is the same style of argument as that given in *Buddhapālita's Commentary on the Fundamental Treatise* cited above.[466]

There are some further faults as well. If it is accepted that effects arise from themselves, then the two—the effect that is produced and the cause that produces it—would be one. Also, an action and its agent would be identical. As for the first fault, Nāgārjuna's *Fundamental Treatise on the Middle Way* says:

> If cause and effect were identical then
> produced and producer would be the same.[467]

If cause and effect were the same entity, then a father and son or the eye and eye-consciousness would be identical, and many such faults would be incurred. As for the second fault, the *Fundamental Treatise on the Middle Way* says:

> If whatever is the fuel were the fire then
> agent and object would be identical.[468]

Although this opponent does not accept that father and son or agent and action are identical in general, he accepts them to be established by nature as the same entity. If he accepts them to be established by nature as the same entity, then they must be identical objectively. Since such faults are incurred, he cannot avoid this rational disproof. Candrakīrti's *Entering the Middle Way* says:

> If you accept arising from self, then produced and producer
> or action and agent would have to be identical. [270]
> But since they are not identical, arising from self is
> unacceptable,
> for it incurs faulty consequences, as explained at length
> elsewhere.[469]

Bhāviveka's *Blaze of Reasoning: Heart of the Middle Way Autocommentary* also presents several arguments to refute the arising from self:

> The Sāṅkhya posit the arising from self. To present these, the text says:
>
> > Here, arising from self
> > is incorrect even conventionally
> > for then its selfhood would exist [already],
> > just as curd does not arise from itself.
>
> Here "from self" means *from itself*. If it were correct that things arise from self, then they would be produced even without causes and conditions, but this is not seen even on the mundane level, let alone ultimately. In the phrase, "for then its selfhood would exist [already]," the term *selfhood* means "endowed with its own essential nature," in that the referent of the phrase "selfhood would exist" is the *self*. Its real nature (*dngos po*) is *selfhood* (*bdag nyid*). Thus, "for then its selfhood would exist" is interpreted to mean "for then it would exist in its own essential nature." If it were to arise, then since it exists, why should it arise again? For example, on a mundane level it is accepted that curd is produced from milk, but it is not accepted that curd is produced from curd itself. Things have their own self-nature but they do not arise from themselves, because this would incur the fault of contradicting their functionality according to their own nature.[470] [271]

At the time of arising, if something already exists having its own nature, there is no need for it to arise again. For example, it is said that curd is produced from milk but is not produced from the curd's own nature. *Blaze of Reasoning* goes on to say:

> If cause and effect are utterly different, then it is appropriate to posit the statements "This is the cause" and "That is the effect," but it is not appropriate to do so if they are not utterly different, because even a seed [in reality] would not be the cause of the sprout. Why not? Because since it would not be utterly different [from the effect], it would be in the nature of the effect itself.[471]

In this way, in the context where cause and effect are different in nature, it is correct to distinguish them by saying, "This is the cause of that." If you say that the nature of cause and effect are the same, then since it would not be correct to distinguish them, this would entail the fault that even a seed would not be the cause of the sprout, and so forth.

Refuting Arising from Other

As for the opponents who assert the arising from other, Prāsaṅgika Madhyamaka masters such as Candrakīrti maintain that these comprise all other Buddhist schools up to and including Svātantrika Madhyamaka. These schools posit the arising from other as follows. "Since arising from self is purposeless, the arising from self is untenable; and since that does not exist, the arising from both self and other is untenable. As for arising without a cause, since this is singularly the worst, its nonexistence is correct. [272] However it is incorrect to refute the arising from other. Since it is taught in the sūtras that things arise from four conditions established by their own nature, one must accept the arising from other even if one does not wish to." So they say that other effects established by their own characteristics arise in dependence on other causes established by their own characteristics. This is how they assert the arising from other.

To take an example of how this assertion is refuted, when commenting on the above-cited verse from *Fundamental Treatise on the Middle Way* that negates the arising from the four alternatives, *Buddhapālita's Commentary on the Fundamental Treatise* says: "There is no arising from other. Why not? Because it entails that everything would arise from everything."[472] If [a cause] were established by its own characteristics as something other [than its effect], then its dependent relationship can be refuted. If it is unrelatedly different, then when an effect arises from its cause, it would also arise from everything that is not its cause, and when a cause produces its effect, it would also produce every resultant thing that is not its own effect. So in this situation every effect and noneffect would arise from every cause and noncause. For example, if both seed and sprout were inherently different, then since a sprout could not depend on a seed, a sprout would not arise from a seed. Alternatively, just as a sprout arises from a seed, so a dense darkness that is to be cleared away would arise from a brightly burning flame that clears it. This is because if they were different by virtue of their own characteristics then they could not be dependently related, for they would be separate in the same manner as in the previous case.[473] To refute this, Candrakīrti's *Entering the Middle Way* says: [273]

> If one thing were to arise in dependence on some other,
> then dense darkness would arise from a burning flame.
> Indeed, everything would arise from everything, because
> not only would noncauses [be separate], but all else likewise.[474]

Also, just as a rice sprout would arise from a rice seed that is something other, so a rice sprout would arise from the embers of a fire or suchlike; and just as a rice sprout that is something other would arise from a rice seed, so pots, cloth, and so on would arise from a rice seed. Refutations such as these are employed. Furthermore Nāgārjuna's *Fundamental Treatise on the Middle Way* says:

> If cause and effect were separate,
> then cause and noncause would be alike.[475]

In response to such refutation of arising from other, Buddhist realists argue that the sūtras teach that things are produced from four conditions: the causal condition, which is present in the entity of the seed that establishes its own effect; the objective condition, which is the focal object that gives rise to the mind and concomitant mental factors observing it; the immediately preceding condition, which is the cause that has just ceased upon producing its effect; and the dominant condition, which gives rise to its effect according to its own faculty.[476] So, they argue, since things are taught to have four conditions, the refutation of arising from other contradicts the scriptures. In the context of countering this objection, Nāgārjuna's *Fundamental Treatise on the Middle Way* says: [274]

> An inherent nature of things
> does not exist in conditions and so on.
> If self-nature does not exist,
> then other-nature does not exist.[477]

Candrakīrti's *Clear Words* offers two ways of interpreting this verse. According to the first,[478] the conundrum is summarized as follows: "The nature of things that are effects does not exist as a different entity dependently within its conditions at a time prior to its own arising, just as, for example, the nature of a sprout does not exist as a different entity like fruit in a bowl within its condition, the seed. If it did so exist, then this must be perceived, but it is not perceived. Also, if it did exist at the time of its cause, then it would arise again without purpose. If the nature of things that are effects does not exist prior to its own arising, then it cannot inherently arise from other conditions, such as seeds." Now, someone might ask, "What is the ground on which you assert that if arising from other existed, then effects must exist prior to their own causes?" As long as one accepts arising in general, then the imminent cessation of the cause and the imminent arising of the effect must be simultaneous; this is not unfeasible if one accepts mere arising, or arising conventionally. But if one accepts ultimate arising, or arising by virtue of its own characteristics, then given that both the imminent activity of the cessation of the cause and the imminent activity of the arising of the effect must be simultaneous, this implies that cause and effect must be simultaneous. For this reason, too, the activity of the arising of the effect must depend on something such as a sprout as the agent of the activity of arising, to which "this arises" refers. [275] Therefore the sprout and the sprout's activity of arising are respectively the support and the supported. If the support and the supported were inherently established, then neither of them could change their natures into something else. If that were not so, then they would not satisfy the criterion of being inherently established as the support and the supported. This means that the sprout, for example, must exist at all times as the basis of activity of the sprout's arising. Therefore the sprout must exist as the basis of activity of its arising even when the sprout is about to arise. In that case, cause and effect would be simultaneous. This standpoint is also undermined by the two immediately preceding arguments that cause and noncause would be alike. According to the Madhyamaka tradition, which accepts mere conventional arising, if things are at one time the support and the supported, they need not be so all the time. So these cases are not similar.

According to the second way of interpreting the above verse,[479] the conundrum is summarized as follows: "Things that are effects, such as sprouts, do not exist when the causal conditions, such as seeds, are not yet transformed, because if they did exist at that time then they would be causeless. At the time of the cause, if things in the nature of the effect are nonexistent, there would be nothing in relation to which the conditions and so on could be posited as other, so to exist as inherently other than the seeds and so on would be untenable." According to the Madhyamaka tradition, which maintains phenomena do not exist inherently, if the causes and conditions that are different in relation to their effect were inherently established, then the effect on which they depend, since it must always be the basis of cause and condition, would have to exist at the time of the cause. It seems that the main point of this refutation [276] must be applied to the earlier and later arguments.

Given that Bhāviveka and the Svātantrika Madhyamaka masters accept arising from other to exist conventionally, when they engage in the refutation of arising from other, they apply the qualifier *ultimate* to the object of negation. Thus, when identifying the opponent in the context of the refutation of arising from other as it is presented in *Fundamental Treatise on the Middle Way*, Bhāviveka's *Blaze of Reasoning* says:

> Sautrāntika and the Vaibhāṣika say that external things such as sprouts and so on arise from other things, such as seeds, earth, water, fire, and wind, whereas the internal sense bases arise from other things, such as ignorance, craving, karmic action, and so on. Similarly, Vaiśeṣika say that substances such as earth are produced from other sets of subtle particles of earth—the second set of subtle particles, the third, and so on—sequentially.[480]

This presents the assertions of the opponents, both Buddhist and non-Buddhist, that external things such as seeds and internal things such as ignorance ultimately give rise to their own effects. Bhāviveka's *Blaze of Reasoning* refutes this position in the following manner:

> The root text says:
>
> > Other conditions such as the eye [sense faculty]
> > ultimately do not give rise to
> > the eye sense consciousness and so on
> > due to being other, like reeds. [277]
>
> If it has the ability to produce what is considered to be other, although similar in being other, the eye sense faculty and so on immediately causes the arising of eye consciousness but does not cause the establishment of such things as fences, pots, shawls, and so on. Conversely, reeds, woolen yarn, clay, and so on immediately cause the establishment of fences, shawls, pots, and so on but do not cause the arising of eye consciousness and so on. Thus, which particular reasons need to be stated in the case of each of those specific causes and conditions?[481]

Here it says that if the eye sense faculty and so on were to produce an eye consciousness and so on—that is, an effect ultimately different from itself—then cause and effect would be unrelatedly different. In that case, it would be difficult to explain any reason as to why, although similar, the eye faculty gives rise to eye consciousness but does not produce a fence or enclosure woven from fine saplings, whereas the individual reeds or fine saplings and so on produce such things as fences but do not give rise to eye consciousness and so on. That is to say, there would be the fault of not being able to state the reasons for specific causes and conditions. Except for the difference in applying or not applying the qualifier *ultimate* to the object of negation, this reasoning is similar to what was presented earlier in *Buddhapālita's Commentary on the Fundamental Treatise* and *Entering the Middle Way*—namely, that if there were *arising from other* then it follows that everything would arise from everything. [278]

Refuting Arising from Both Self and Other

Those who assert the arising from both are the Jaina and some members of the Sāṅkhya school. They posit the arising from both self and other as follows. Sāṅkhya theists who accept a creator god say: "Since the effect arises from Īśvara and the primal nature together, it arises from both." Jaina say: "Given that a pot is produced from a lump of clay, a rod, a wheel, some wire, some water, a potter, and so on, the earthenware pot arises from itself in that it arises from having the nature of clay, and it arises from other in that it arises from the activity of the potter, which is other. So although there is no arising from self or from other separately, there is definitely arising from both." Explaining how the opponent asserts the arising from both, Bhāviveka's *Blaze of Reasoning* states:

> Some Sāṅkhya consider that effects arise from producing causes that are defined, such as the earth, and those that are undefined, such as sprouts; thus they accept arising from self and other. Jaina consider that a gold finger ring arises from both self and other, from gold and from fire respectively, which they say exist before and exist after the effect—for that which arises immediately prior to the resultant "finger ring" exists before it, while that which does not have its nature exists after it.[482] [279]

Thus, as stated above, some Sāṅkhya maintain that since a sprout, for example, arises from a common cause or a defined cause such as the earth, it arises from other, and since it arises from its own seed, which is an uncommon cause or an undefined cause, it arises from self. Jaina say that since a ring, for example, arises from gold, it arises from self, and since it arises from fire, it arises from other.

To refute this, [Madhyamaka would argue that] to arise from a combination of both self and other is utterly illogical because the faults entailed by arising from each individually, as already stated, would also befall the position of arising from both. If it is accepted that in reliance on clay an earthenware pot arises from self, then this is refuted by the previously stated argument that arising would be purposeless; and if it is accepted that in reliance on a potter such a pot arises from other, then this is refuted by innumerable absurd consequences.[483] *Buddhapālita's Commentary on the*

Fundamental Treatise says: "There is no arising from both self and other because this would incur the faults of each together."[484] Candrakīrti's *Entering the Middle Way* also says:

> Arising from both is also essentially illogical because
> the faults already stated would befall this position.[485]

In Bhāviveka's *Heart of the Middle Way* and its autocommentary, [280] we also find the following presentation of the refutation of arising from both:

> We do not accept arising from self or other,
> nor having or lacking a nature.
> Both positions do not exist
> for the reasons already presented.

> Those who propound both are incorrect because there is the fault of contradiction. For if it arises from self, then how can it arise from other? And conversely, if it arises from other, how can it arise from self? They are contradictory! Also one should posit the refutations of each position, from self and from other, separately, as stated earlier.[486]

So, this states, if one accepts arising from self it would be a contradiction to assert arising from other; also, if one accepts arising from other this would contradict acceptance of arising from self. To accept arising from both self and other is also undermined by the faults incurred separately by each, as previously stated.

Refuting Arising without a Cause

Those who assert the arising without a cause are the Cārvāka. They posit arising without a cause as follows. "If arising were from a cause, then one must accept it to be either separately from self or from other, or from both together. Since these incur the above-mentioned faults, we do not accept arising from a cause; thus we do not have the faults of those three positions stated earlier. Just as someone who makes lotus stems hard and their petals soft [281] is never seen, so the creation of the various shapes and colors of its petals, its anthers, and its core is never seen. And just as in the case of external phenomena, such as peacocks and chickens, likewise in the case of those of an internal nature, someone who makes effort in designing their colors and shapes is never seen. So with regard to the production of things, they just arise naturally." These assertions are further explained when presenting the Cārvāka school's tenets in chapter 9 of volume 3 of *Science and Philosophy in the Indian Buddhist Classics*.

To refute this position, Bhāviveka's *Blaze of Reasoning* says:

> In response to these, it must be explained:
>
> > The eye, even conventionally,
> > is not asserted to arise adventitiously
> > because it has general and specific [characteristics]—
> > like a pot, for example.
>
> Any external or internal things for which a cause does not appear in the world does not exist at all. Even lotus flowers and so on have causes such as seeds, substance, and water. Similarly, to say that this world is designed through intention, the variegated adornments of the peacock and so on would be fashioned by means of intention, and the hardness of thorns, the softness of flowers, and so on would occur through the causal capacity of sentient beings' actions. Similarly, the eye [sense faculty], semen, blood, gestation, and so on, which have arisen due to the four great elements as their cause, are not said to arise adventitiously even as conventional truth, because they have general characteristics such as impermanence; and the eye [sense faculty] and so on are said to have a physical nature arisen from the elements [282] because they have particular characteristics—for example, like a pot. Also, because a pot has general characteristics, such as impermanence and so on, as well as particular characteristics, such as a broad belly, open mouth, and round shape, it is not said to arise adventitiously even conventionally.[487]

The above passage states that there are no external or internal things whatsoever that arise without a cause. External things such as lotus flowers are directly established to have causes such as seeds, water, and so on. To take a pot as an illustration, since it has general characteristics such as the nature of impermanence, it is established to have causes and conditions; and since it has particular characteristics such as a broad belly, it is dependent on its producing cause and comes into being accordingly. Thus to claim that it arises adventitiously without a cause even conventionally is proved to be incorrect. Bhāviveka's *Heart of the Middle Way* says:

> Because they are effects, because they arise sequentially,
> because they perish, because they transform,
> because their causes and conditions are specific,
> and because they arise, they should be known thus.[488]

As stated above, external and internal things are established as not arising adventitiously without any cause, because it is seen that they are effects, that they arise sequentially without arising all at once, that they have the nature of perishing in the end, that they transform from one state to another, that they do not arise from just any causes and conditions but [283] arise from their own specific causes and conditions, and that they arise newly. This is an illustration of the many reasons presented in Buddhist texts that refute arising without a cause.

Indeed, if things were to arise without a cause, then they would arise even from that which is not their cause, because everything would be similar in being a noncause; moreover, a crow could have the crest of a peacock, while a peacock could have the feathers of a parrot, because these would not depend on causes; also ordinary people would not need to struggle and work hard to produce crops for an autumn harvest and so on, because that would happen naturally. Such refutations as these are found in the Buddhist treatises. *Buddhapālita's Commentary on the Fundamental Treatise* says: "Also there is no arising without a cause because everything would arise from everything constantly and because every undertaking would be purposeless."[489] Candrakīrti's *Entering the Middle Way* says:

> If the belief in only causeless arising were the case,
> then everything would arise from everything constantly
> and sowing hundreds of thousands of seeds in this world
> for the sake of a crop would not produce a harvest.[490] [284]

Moreover, if things arose without a cause, this would entail the fault they would constantly arise or they would not arise at all, as explained in many Buddhist sources.

The Madhyamaka tradition's rejection of arising from the four alternatives—self, other, and so on—does not contradict the Buddha's teaching that things arise from four conditions, because that was taught in terms of the conventional and not the ultimate. Therefore one must posit the presentation of cause and effect conventionally by way of accepting the dependent arising of this mere conditionality.[491] Conversely, if one accepts arising from the four alternatives, then one must accept things to be established inherently; this is undermined by the reasons posited above. Candrakīrti's *Clear Words* says:

> *Qualm*: If there is no arising of things from self, from other, from both, or without a cause, then how can the Tathāgata have taught that due to ignorance as its condition, conditioning factors [arise]?
>
> *Response*: This is conventional, but it is not ultimate.
>
> *Qualm*: So what is the expressed object of the conventional presentation?
>
> *Response*: We accept this mere conditionality to be established as a convention, but it is not by way of accepting the four positions of arising because that would entail positing things as having inherent nature and that is untenable.[492]

This important point is also made in *Buddhapālita's Commentary on the Fundamental Treatise*, [285] which says: "Since it is unfeasible for things to arise in all these ways, they do not arise. Thus to say that they arise is a mere convention."[493]

In brief, this reasoning that refutes the arising from the four alternatives—as found in the tradition of those who maintain that things do not arise inherently, such as Nāgārjuna, Āryadeva, Candrakīrti, and so on—contradicts the arising from one of the four alternatives, as asserted by most Buddhist and non-Buddhist systems who are not satisfied with the arising of things to exist only nominally or as a mere imputation. This reasoning directly refutes such arising [i.e., from the four alternatives] and indirectly facilitates the ascertainment that things do not arise inherently.

Refuting Inherent Existence Based on the Triad of Cause, Effect, and Entity and on the Triad of Action, Agent, and Object of Action

In addition to the above-mentioned reasoning that refutes arising from the four alternatives, there are many varieties of reasoning set forth in Nāgārjuna's treatises, such as his *Fundamental Treatise on the Middle Way*, to establish that phenomena lack inherent existence. To illustrate these, we now present the analysis of two triads—one of cause, effect, and entity, and another of action, agent, and object of action—each being a reason that proves phenomena are not inherently established. The reasoning that refutes arising from the four alternatives outlined above involves inferential analysis of the *cause*. Also, the "Examination of Conditions" chapter in *Fundamental Treatise on the Middle Way* [286] examines the four types of *conditions* that give rise to external and internal things: causal condition, objective condition, immediately preceding condition, and dominant condition. Arguments are posited that refute their inherent existence collectively and that refute their inherent existence individually.

First let us consider the arguments that refute the inherent existence of conditions collectively. An opponent may argue that although the refutation of arising from the four alternatives disproves that effects inherently arise directly from their conditions, such a refutation of arising poses no problem for themselves. For instance, a visual consciousness is not *directly* produced by the three *conditions*,[494] such as the eye sense faculty and so on. A condition such as the eye sense faculty gives rise to a consciousness-producing *action*; and this *action* inherently produces the respective consciousness. To refute to this point, an argument is presented in *Fundamental Treatise on the Middle Way* as follows:

> Action does not have conditions,
> yet without conditions, there is no action.
> Conditions devoid of action do not [exist],
> nor do ones endowed with action.[495]

It is unfeasible for a condition, such as the eye sense faculty, to be endowed with inherently established action that gives rise to its resultant consciousness, because a consciousness that is not yet arisen does not have the inherently established action of arising and a consciousness that has already arisen does not have the action of arising again. Upon examining whether consciousness has the inherently established action of arising, consciousness already arisen does not need such an action because it cannot arise again having already arisen. Also, in the case of consciousness that has not yet arisen, the inherently established action of arising is untenable because if consciousness were to have the inherently established action of arising, [287] then when consciousness has the action of arising, the consciousness that is the agent of that action must [already] exist. Such faults as these are entailed. Now, suppose the opponent suggests, "Although consciousness does not have that action when it is either arisen or not arisen, consciousness about to arise does have that action." This is also incorrect because a consciousness about to arise that is neither arisen nor non-arisen does not exist. Then if they say, "When the action of arising has begun but arising has not been completed, it is not arisen, and when the action of arising has not yet begun, it is not non-arisen; so it is during the process of arising that it has that action." This too is incorrect. For if it were so, it must be accepted that some parts of that consciousness would have arisen while other parts of it would not have arisen, in which case it would be half arisen and half non-arisen; but there is nothing that is neither arisen nor non-arisen. Now, they may suggest, "Suppose the action of the process of arising exists in something both arisen and not arisen." In that case, since both the past and the future would be in the process of arising, this would incur the fault that all three times would be in the process of arising.

The opponent may then wonder, "Suppose that action without conditions were to give rise to consciousness." There is no action without conditions because if there were, then the fault of arising without a cause would necessarily follow. Again, they may say, "Suppose that conditions, such as the eye sense faculty, devoid of ultimately established action, were to give rise inherently to eye consciousness." However, the eye sense faculty is conventionally a condition of eye consciousness but cannot be an inherently established condition—so even in conventional terms, if the three conditions such as the eye sense faculty were devoid of the action of giving rise to eye consciousness, then this entails they would not be conditions of eye consciousness. Next, they may wonder, "Suppose only conditions with inherently established action were to give rise to eye consciousness."

Our response would be that conditions with inherently established action are just nonexistent. Such refutations as these are posited, but in brief, the argument "Since the eye sense faculty and so on have action that gives rise to their effects, [288] they are conditions ultimately" is refuted by the first and fourth lines of the above verse. The notion that, although action does not have conditions, action without conditions ultimately exists, is refuted by the second line. And the notion that, although devoid of action, they are posited as conditions ultimately is refuted by the third line. Therefore any condition whatsoever, whether with or without action, does not exist ultimately. The point of these kinds of reasoning is that conditions do not have an inherently established nature.

Next we present the arguments found in *Fundamental Treatise on the Middle Way* that individually refute the inherent existence of the four conditions that give rise to things. As an illustration of how to refute the inherent existence of the *causal condition*, consider the following. Realists argue that since the definition of *causal condition* is "that which establishes its effect," a causal condition exists by way of its own nature. The *Fundamental Treatise on the Middle Way* presents the fault with this as follows:

> When phenomena are not established
> as existent, nonexistent, or both,
> how can there be an "actualizing cause"?[496]
> If there were, it would be illogical.[497]

Upon analyzing whether a resultant phenomenon exists, does not exist, or both exists and does not exist at the time of its cause, an inherently existent cause is unfeasible. For that reason, it is incorrect to maintain that a causal condition is inherently established merely because the defining characteristics of a causal condition exist. The point of this reasoning is that if an effect produced by a cause were to exist at the time of the cause, then arising would be purposeless and endless. If an inherently existent sprout, which is nonexistent at the time of its cause, were produced by its cause, [289] then given that both are equally nonexistent at the time of the cause, the arising of the sprout would be no different from the non-arising of a rabbit's horns. This is because if an inherently existent thing is nonexistent at one time then it must be nonexistent at all times, so it would be impossible to differentiate "This is its cause, but that is not its cause." Whether existent, nonexistent, or even both at the time of its cause, it cannot be produced by its cause because being two mutually contradictory things does not exist, and because both faults cited above would be incurred.

To refute the inherent existence of the *objective condition*, Nāgārjuna's *Fundamental Treatise on the Middle Way* says:

> A phenomenon, being existent, just does not have
> an objective support, as you have emphatically indicated.
> If phenomena do not have objects,
> then why would they have objective conditions?[498]

Suppose someone says, "The objective condition is inherently established because it is a basis for the arising of consciousness." Now, is this saying, "For a consciousness that *exists* prior to perceiving the object there is an objective condition"? Or is it saying, "For a consciousness that *does not exist* prior to perceiving the object there is an objective condition"? If the former, then since that consciousness is established without depending on an objective condition, it would be unnecessary to posit an objective condition. For this reason, a consciousness that is an existent phenomenon simply does not have an objective condition, but as shown by your own assertions you admit that it would depend on an objective condition. If it is saying, "For a consciousness that does not exist prior to perceiving the object there is an objective condition," then such a consciousness would be unrelated to the objective condition because [290] when there is the perceived object there is no perceiving consciousness, and when there is the perceiving consciousness there is no perceived object. Although there is no need to refute the conventional existence of the relationship between the two—the perceived object and the perceiving consciousness—the point of this reasoning is to refute the inherent existence of the objective condition. So if the relationship between those two were inherently existent, then it would have to be established as the final nature of those two phenomena; and since that final nature would unerringly pervade any phenomena endowed with it, it would be present at all times and in all places. Thus the opponent's assertion is refuted.

To refute the inherent existence of the *immediately preceding condition*, Nāgārjuna's *Fundamental Treatise on the Middle Way* says:

Since phenomena are not arisen,
cessation is not tenable.
Thus an immediately preceding [condition] is not tenable.
If it has ceased, then what would be the condition?[499]

An opponent may argue, "The cause that has just ceased is inherently established as the immediately preceding condition of its effect." We may respond that resultant phenomena, such as sprouts, are not arisen because prior to having arisen it is unfeasible for the seed to have ceased; therefore it is unfeasible to assert that a seed that has just ceased is the immediately preceding condition of a sprout. Now, the opponent may argue, "If the seed has ceased prior to the sprout, then the seed's cessation would exist in between the seed that is supposedly the direct cause of the sprout and the sprout. In that case, the seed itself would not be the immediately preceding condition of the sprout that directly brings about its arising." Here we respond that, according to the Madhyamaka system, a consciousness about to cease is the immediately preceding condition of the later moment of consciousness, but a consciousness that has just ceased is not accepted to be its cause. Thus the opponent's assertion is refuted. [291]

To refute the inherent existence of the *dominant condition*, Nāgārjuna's *Fundamental Treatise on the Middle Way* says:

Since things without inherent nature
do not have real existence,
it is not tenable to state
"Because this exists, that occurs."[500]

Suppose someone says, "When such a cause exists, then such an effect occurs according to its own capacity. Since this is the dominant condition of that effect, it is inherently established." In response, the Madhyamaka tradition argues that it is incorrect to claim that the definition of the dominant condition is "When this cause exists by its own nature, then that effect occurs according to its own capacity," because the mode of existence of things is not by virtue of inherent nature. The reason for this is that inherent existence has been negated with regard to dependent arising. Thus the opponent's assertion is refuted.

Furthermore, Nāgārjuna's *Seventy Stanzas on Emptiness* explains that the reason why conditions, whether individually or collectively, do not have effects also refutes the inherent existence of conditions:

> All things are empty of [inherent] nature.
> Since all things in terms of that nature
> do not have causes and conditions
> either collectively or individually,
> they are therefore empty.[501]

As stated here, all external and internal things are empty of inherent nature. [292] Why is that so? It is because things do not have causes and conditions, whether collectively or individually, that can inherently produce them. Indeed, if causes and conditions individually were to inherently produce them, this would incur the fault that a rice sprout could be produced by a rice seed alone without relying on other things such as sprinkling water. If one accepts this, then a collection of causes and conditions has no purpose. Suppose someone asks, "Surely a collection of causes and conditions inherently produces things?" This is refuted on the grounds that since causes and conditions individually cannot inherently produce anything, it is unfeasible that their collection is able to do so. Thus the opponent's assertion is refuted. The point of this refutation is that if something were inherently established then its dependence on others would be unviable. Thus if each cause and condition were to give rise from its own side to the effect, it would not depend on other causes and conditions; and if each cause and condition is not inherently established, it would be unfeasible for their collection to be inherently established.

The refutation of inherent arising and ceasing through investigating the *effects* of phenomena is achieved by means of the inference that arising and ceasing are neither existent nor nonexistent. This will be easier to understand if we present it in the form of a syllogism as follows. "A sprout does not arise inherently or ultimately because if it exists at the time of its cause then it does not arise, and if it does not exist at the time of its cause then it does not arise ultimately." The point of this reasoning is as follows. If any effect that exists at the time of its cause were to be produced by its cause, then production would be purposeless and endless. Also, if an inherently existent sprout, for example, that does not exist at the time of its cause were to be produced by its cause, then the arising of a sprout and the non-arising of a rabbit's horns, being similarly nonexistent at the time of the cause, would be indistinguishable—but this is unfeasible. An effect established from its own side, being nonexistent at all times, could not be differentiated in terms of considering "This is its cause, [293] but that is not its cause." Also any effect that both exists and does not exist at the time of its cause cannot feasibly be produced by its cause because it is a mutual contradiction to both exist and not exist at the same time, and because it incurs the two faults mentioned above. Thus the opponent's assertion is refuted. As cited above, to this point Nāgārjuna's *Fundamental Treatise on the Middle Way* says:

> When phenomena are not established
> as existent, nonexistent, or both,
> how can there be an "actualizing cause"?
> If there were, it would be illogical.[502]

Likewise, Nāgārjuna's *Seventy Stanzas on Emptiness* says:

> What is existent does not arise for it [already] exists.
> What is nonexistent does not arise for it does not exist.
> Nor does what is both existent and nonexistent [arise] for these are incompatible.
> So since arising does not exist, neither does enduring nor cessation.[503]

So, because effects do not inherently arise, they do not inherently abide and they do not inherently cease. Many examples such as these are found in Madhyamaka texts.

The refutation of inherent arising and ceasing through investigating the *entity* is accomplished by means of the inference from being neither one nor many. This reasoning is presented in Śāntarakṣita's *Ornament for the Middle Way* root text and its autocommentary, which will be explained extensively later in chapter 15, so here we mention it only briefly. At many points in the *Fundamental Treatise on the Middle Way*, Nāgārjuna refutes an inherent relationship between two phenomena through investigating whether they are the same or different.[504] [294] This is especially clear in the proof of the selflessness of person found in chapter 18:

> If the self were the aggregates
> it would be endowed with arising and disintegrating.
> If it were different from the aggregates
> it would not have the characteristics of the aggregates.[505]

If the self and the aggregates were inherently the same, then like the aggregates, the self would have the characteristics of arising and disintegrating. Conversely, if the self were inherently different from the aggregates, then it would not have the characteristics of arising, abiding, and disintegrating that characterize the aggregates as causally compounded. This proves that the self does not exist inherently as either the same as the aggregates or as a different thing from them. To facilitate understanding, we present this in the form of a syllogism as follows. "The *subject*, a person, must be endowed with arising and disintegrating due to being inherently the same entity as the aggregates." And conversely, "The *subject*, a person, cannot have the characteristics of arising, abiding, and disintegrating, which characterize the aggregates as causally compounded, due to being inherently different from the aggregates." This reasoning, in expressing that it is contradictory for the self and the aggregates to be inherently either the same entity or different entities, directly undermines that [standpoint]. Additionally, it indirectly induces the ascertainment that the self is not established by virtue of its own nature even in the slightest. [295]

In brief, this reasoning demonstrates the following. If the self and the aggregates were inherently the same entity, then just as the aggregates arise and disintegrate, so the self would arise and disintegrate inherently each moment; and the self that is the basis on which the thought "I" arises would be the same as the aggregates of this lifetime without their identity being differentiated in any way. If the self were to inherently arise and disintegrate respectively each moment, then since the individual selves of earlier and later moments would be unrelated, this entails the fault that it would be impossible to think "I did this previously." If the self and the aggregates were the same in terms of conceptual identity (*ldog pa*), then this entails the fault that the self would have arisen newly in this life without having arisen in another and so would have a beginning; additionally, it entails the fault that just as the aggregates are many, so the self would be many. If the aggregates and the self were inherently different, then just as a horse does not have a hump and a dewlap that are the characteristics of a cow, so the self would not have the characteristics of arising, abiding, and disintegrating that characterize the aggregates as causally compounded. In that case, since it would be uncompounded, of the two kinds of objects of innate self-grasping—the focal object and the object as cognized—it could not be the focal object. Such faults as these would be incurred.

The *neither one nor many* reasoning is also found in Āryadeva's *Four Hundred Stanzas*:

> When whatsoever things are examined
> none of them exist as truly one. [296]
> Because there are none that are truly one,
> so there are none that are truly many.[506]

When any thing whatsoever, such as a pot or a woolen shawl, is examined as to whether it is truly established or not, it is found to be not truly established as one because it has parts. The reason why it is not truly established as one is the very reason that it is not truly established as many, because many comes from an aggregation of singular entities. In brief, external and internal things are not truly existent because they not truly established as either one or many, like a reflection.

As for proofs of the absence of an inherently established entity based on the triad of action, agent, and object of action, the second chapter of Nāgārjuna's *Fundamental Treatise on the Middle Way* refutes an inherently existent person by analyzing the action of going and coming, and the eighth chapter refutes it by analyzing the object of action and the agent. Here, the refutation of inherently existent action is first applied separately to the object of action and the agent and then is applied collectively to the object of action and the agent. An example of the examination of going and coming is as follows. When going over a path, there is the agent who goes over the path, the action of going over the path, and the path which is gone over. Among these, if we examine the path, there is the path already gone over, the path being gone over, and the path not yet gone over, where the action of going has not yet occurred. Among those three paths, when the *action of going* [297] is refuted by reasoning, in the case of *the path already gone over* the action of going has ceased and in the case of *the path not yet gone over* the action of going has not arisen, so these do not exist; but in the case of *the path being gone over* right now, the action of going must be posited. So while in the case of the path already gone over and the path not yet gone over, the conventional existence of the action of going is refuted, in the case of the path being gone over right now, the conventional existence of the action of going is not refuted; however, its inherent existence is refuted. Nāgārjuna's *Fundamental Treatise on the Middle Way* says:

> Firstly, where one has gone, one is not going;
> then, where one has not gone, one is not going;
> apart from having gone and not gone,
> going would not be known.[507]

The *action of going* is in the present, so there is no action of going in the case of the path over which the action of going has ceased nor the path over which the action of going has not arisen. Suppose someone suggests, "Surely, in the case of the path being gone over, the action of going exists inherently?" That is not correct because when one searches for an independent path being trodden or being gone over, it does not exist. Other than the part already trodden by foot where the action has ceased and the part not yet trodden by foot where the action has not arisen, when one searches for the imputed thing—the path in the process of being trodden—it is not known by valid cognition. This is because the foot has many parts, so when the foot is being placed down, the part trodden by the back of the heel is categorized as that gone over while the part trodden by the front of the toes is categorized as that not gone over. Now, our opponent may argue, "As for that path trodden by the heel and toes of the foot, surely it is an independent path being trodden where the heel and toes of one's foot depend on themselves?" [298] That too is not correct because when the front and back particles of the heel and toes are analyzed in the same way as we have analyzed the foot, an independent path being trodden is not found.

Having refuted by means of this reasoning an inherently existent path being gone over, which is neither that already gone over nor that not yet gone over, the action of going in that case is refuted, but the path being gone over in general is not refuted. Moreover, by means of the reasoning proving that the parts of the foot are not the foot and that the foot does not exist as something other than them, an inherently established foot is refuted, but the existence of the foot in general is not refuted.

Another way of refuting the inherent existence of the agent that goes and the action of going is presented in Nāgārjuna's *Fundamental Treatise on the Middle Way*:

> The going and the goer
> cannot be said to be the very same,
> and the going and the goer
> cannot be said to be utterly different.
>
> If the action of going
> were identical with the goer,
> then the doer and the deed done
> would have to be identical.
>
> If the going and the goer
> were thought to be utterly different,
> then there could be going without a goer
> and a goer without going.
>
> If they are not established
> either as the same thing
> or as different things,
> then how can those two exist at all?[508]

Thus, in response to an opponent's assertion that a person, such as Devadatta, is seen going for a walk and so is called a "goer," [299] and for this reason the goer and the action of going are inherently existent, the above stanzas present an argument as follows. If the two—the action of Devadatta going for a walk and the person that is Devadatta who is going for a walk—were inherently existent, then they must be established either as the same or as different inherently. If you say that the action of going and the goer are inherently the same, then this is untenable. For if those two were inherently the same, then the agent and the action would be identical, and this would incur the fault of there being no difference between saying "This is the action" and "This is the agent." If you say that the action of going and the goer are inherently different, then this would incur the fault of there being the apprehension of a completely separate action of going unrelated to the goer and a goer unrelated to the action of going. Thus if any agent and action whatsoever does not exist as inherently the same or as inherently different, how can those two exist as inherently established? In that case, they must be merely imputed. Thus the opponent's assertion is refuted. [300]

15

Other Madhyamaka Refutations of True Existence

Bhāviveka's Reasoning by Way of Drawing Parity

Up to this point we have given a rough presentation of the refutation of arising from the four alternatives and the refutation of inherent existence through investigating cause and effect, agent and action, and suchlike, as found in many great Madhyamaka texts, primarily Nāgārjuna's *Fundamental Treatise on the Middle Way*. Now we will present some other renowned reasonings establishing emptiness that are found in the texts of Madhyamaka masters who are followers of Nāgārjuna. In general these great masters, such as Bhāviveka, embrace as part of their own system the reasonings found in Nāgārjuna's Six Collections of Reasoning, such as the refutation of arising from the four alternatives. However, there does seem to be a difference between what each master takes to be their main reasoning. For example, Bhāviveka focuses on the reasoning by way of drawing parity. His *Heart of the Middle Way* says:

> Earth is not in the nature of solidity
> because it is an element, like wind.[509]

Likewise, this master states in the autocommentary for this treatise, *Blaze of Reasoning* [301]: "Therefore an argument in which the thesis and the predicate of the thesis are stated can be formulated as follows: 'Ultimately the eye sense faculty does not see forms because it does not see itself, like the ear.'"[510] So we can posit a syllogism: "The *subject*, earth, is not ultimately solid because it is an element, like water." And another: "The *subject*, the eye sense faculty, does not ultimately see forms because it does not see itself, like the ear sense faculty." Moreover, if all four elements such as earth were ultimately established, then there could be no difference between earth being solid and water not being solid and so on, because earth would be established essentially as solid without depending on anything else. So, since the other three elements would have to be solid by way of drawing parity, just as earth is solid, an ultimately established element is refuted. The reason for this is that if something ultimately exists, then it must exist through the force of the object's own mode of being without being posited through the causal capacity of the mind. In that case, since it would exist independently, it would not depend on anything else whatsoever. Likewise, for example, if smoke were to arise without depending on a cause, then this would imply that it must either depend on everything or not be dependent even on fire. Similarly, if the eye sense faculty were to see forms ultimately, then it must see without being dependent on anything else. In that case it must see itself, which is refuted by means of the reasoning by way of drawing parity, which entails that the ear sense faculty would have to see forms.

Some have raised objections against this argument as follows. [302] "Your proof that earth is not by nature solid is incorrect because it contradicts your own assertions, it contradicts direct perception, and it contradicts popular convention. The first objection holds because the Buddhist scriptures say, 'Brahmins, the term *everything* refers to the five aggregates, the twelve sense bases, and the eighteen elements,' and likewise, 'the definition of *form* is that which is suitable as form.' Although these scriptures teach about phenomena such as the five aggregates along with their definitions, you accept them as valid and yet refute those phenomena; thus you incur an internal contradiction. The second objection holds because to know an object's unique nature, there is no valid cognition that surpasses seeing with sensory cognition, yet while you yourself perform actions such as seeing with your eyes and apprehending the shapes and forms of the elements and so on, you refute those and undermine direct perception. The third objection holds because the earth and so on, as well as its nature of solidity and so on, are popular conventions commonly accepted in the world." That they present objections such as these due to their failure to recognize the difference between *nonexistent* and *not ultimately existent* is stated by Bhāviveka in *Blaze of Reasoning* as follows:

> Here, some argue: "Your teacher's scriptures say, 'Brahmins, the term *everything* refers to the five aggregates, the twelve sense bases, and the eighteen elements,' and likewise, 'the definition of *form* is that which is suitable as form.' You accept this teaching yet you refute its content, which contradicts your own assertions. Likewise, the direct perception of sensory consciousness is renowned for engaging in specific individual objects, [303] for there is no valid cognition that surpasses seeing. Indeed, you see with own your eyes the shapes and forms of the elements and so on and engage in the activity of apprehending and investigating their defining nature as solid and so forth, in keeping with what is accepted throughout the world, yet you refute those and undermine direct perception. Similarly, whatever forms, for example, and whatever their defining characteristics may be, such as solid, wet, hot, or moving, they are popularly accepted even among hermits and outcasts. Thus since it is made clear that the nature of things is renowned throughout the world, your position is contradicted by popular convention."[511]

Bhāviveka responds to these objections as follows. We do not succumb to any of these three faults because we do not refute the earth being merely solid, but we refute it being solid in an ultimate sense. Indeed, we do not succumb to the first fault you mention because the Tathāgata taught about the nature of phenomena in terms of conventional truth, while in terms of the ultimate he taught about its lack of nature. For example, the *Perfection of Wisdom Sūtra in One Thousand Stanzas* says: "Subhūti, thus all phenomena are empty of inherent nature because emptiness is desireless and in emptiness there is nobody who desires."[512] Also, we do not succumb to the second fault [304] because the sense consciousnesses are dull when it comes to seeking the mode of existence and they are just as incapable of seeing how things exist in reality as those with an eye disease who see the appearance of falling hairs, so the mere seeing by a sense consciousness cannot be taken as valid cognition.

Moreover, we do not succumb to the third fault because most ordinary people, being under the influence of confusion with regard to searching for how things exist, are incapable of seeking their mode of existence, and the context here concerns analyzing the ultimate nature. In repelling these objections, Bhāviveka's *Blaze of Reasoning* says: "It should be explained that because the qualification 'ultimately' is applied, our assertions, direct perception, and popular conventions are not undermined."[513]

So if things were ultimately existent, it would have to be accepted that they do not depend on causes and conditions and that they abide as separate entities without depending on a combination of many parts. However, the elements and the element derivatives do not abide as separate entities without depending on a combination of the eight substantial particles; also in the case of mind and mental factors it is mutually impossible for one to be absent while the other alone is present. All things arise from the gathering of their own causes and conditions, and if those are missing then they do not arise at all. Thus they are not ultimately established even to the slightest degree. This way of refuting the object of negation, ultimate existence, by means of proofs such as these can be found in many places throughout the treatises of this master, Bhāviveka. [305]

Śāntarakṣita's Reasoning of Being neither One nor Many

Regarding the investigation into the nature of phenomena presented in the Madhyamaka texts, as discussed briefly above, the analysis investigating being neither one nor many can be found in Nāgārjuna's *Fundamental Treatise on the Middle Way*, Āryadeva's texts,[514] and the texts of Bhāviveka and Candrakīrti. It also appears in the texts of Dharmakīrti, the master of Buddhist epistemology.[515] However, since it is presented with specific focus and at great length in Śāntarakṣita's *Ornament for the Middle Way* and its autocommentary and Kamalaśīla's *Illumination of the Middle Way*, here we will explain this style of reasoning on the basis of Śāntarakṣita's *Ornament for the Middle Way* and its autocommentary. Such reasoning also appears in the Mahāyāna sūtras. For example, the *Descent into Laṅkā Sūtra* says:

> Just as a visual form in a mirror
> is neither the same as it nor different,
> yet that appearance is not nonexistent,
> the characteristic of arising is like this.[516]

In general, this reasoning of being neither one nor many can be differentiated in terms of two forms. The first form of reasoning occurs in Madhyamaka texts in the context of examining the nature of the self, [306] which is refuted by analyzing the relationship between the person (the self) and the aggregates (its basis of imputation) in terms of whether they are the same entity or different. The second form is presented in Śāntarakṣita's *Ornament for the Middle Way* as follows:

> These things posited by our own and others' systems,
> since in reality they have neither
> a singular nor a manifold nature,
> have no inherent nature, like a reflection.[517]

Here, in the context of refuting permanent real things imputed by Buddhist and non-Buddhist traditions—such as the self, the cognizing knower, partless particles, and so on—the assertion that phenomena are truly singular in nature is refuted. And since a singular entity is not perceived, a group of them as truly many cannot be established either. Among the two forms of reasoning used in a refutation such as this, the first form will be explained later in the context of presenting Candrakīrti's analysis of the self by means of the sevenfold reasoning, since these are closely connected. The second form of reasoning is explained here in accordance with Śāntarakṣita's *Ornament for the Middle Way*. To facilitate an understanding of this, let us consider the following syllogism: "The *subject*, things posited by our own and others' systems, do not exist ultimately by virtue of inherent nature, because they do not exist as truly one or as truly many—for example, like a reflection." In a similar manner, Kamalaśīla's *Illumination of the Middle Way* says:

> If everything is established to be free of singularity, then it would be established to be free of plurality too, since the reason applied to singularity is applied to plurality and so on, [307] given that plurality is in nature a collection of single entities. Singularity and plurality pervade everything because they are characterized as mutually excluding.[518]

An inferential reason such as this is said to satisfy four essential points: (1) ascertainment of the object of negation, (2) ascertainment of the pervasion, (3) ascertainment of the lack of true singularity, and (4) ascertainment of the lack of true plurality.

As for the proof of the lack of true singularity, which is the first facet of the attribute of the subject in the above reasoning,[519] the argument is presented as follows: "The *subject*, things posited by our own and others' systems, do not exist as truly one, because they have parts." The pervasion is established as follows. In the case of causal phenomena, it is clear that physical things have directional parts while nonphysical things have temporal parts. In the case of noncausal phenomena, such as uncaused space, they also have parts, because the part that pervades the space inside a particular pot does not pervade the space inside a separate cup. Therefore, if something is an established thing, it necessarily has parts. It is not contradictory for a single phenomenon to have many parts in a conventional sense. However, in the case of being ultimately established, if the parts and the whole were different entities, then they would be totally unrelated; and conversely, if they were the same entity, then the parts would be one just as the whole is one, or the whole would be many just as the parts are many. Such faults as these would be incurred. That its *way of existing* is as singular in nature while its *way of appearing* is as manifold in nature cannot be denied. However, those two are not contradictory within the context of a mode of existence that is unreal—where the way of appearing does not accord with the way of existing. But in the context of being truly existent, it is absolutely impossible for the way of appearing to be discordant with the way of existing.

As for the proof of the lack of true plurality, which is the second facet of the attribute of the subject in the above reasoning,[520] the argument is presented as follows: "The *subject*, things posited by our own and others' systems, [308] do not exist as truly many, because their existence as truly one has been refuted." The pervasion is established because a plurality is in the nature of a collection of singular entities. Based on the reason of having parts, existing as either a truly established singularity or plurality is refuted. Then based on the reason of not being either a truly established singularity or plurality, being truly established is refuted. If something does not exist as either a truly established singularity or a truly established plurality, then it is necessarily not truly established. In general, this is proved by the reason that there cannot be a knowable object that is neither of those two, because the two—one and many—are directly contradictory in the sense of being mutually excluding. The refutation of truly established plurality will be presented in more detail below.

In order to refute the truly established singularity imputed by other systems, Śāntarakṣita's *Ornament for the Middle Way* outlines two types of argument: the refutation of *truly singular pervasive entities* and the refutation of *truly singular nonpervasive entities*. The first, the refutation of truly singular pervasive entities, is divided into two: the refutation of *truly singular permanent real things* and the refutation of *truly singular persons*. The second, the refutation of truly singular nonpervasive entities, is divided into two main categories: the refutation of *truly singular coarse and subtle external things* and the separate refutations of a *truly singular consciousness* as imputed by the two Buddhist realist systems, non-Buddhists, and the Cittamātra school. As for the proof of the *lack of true plurality*, which is the fourth point listed above, this is proved by positing the reason "True singularity is not perceived." The pervasion of the main reason is established by the fact that one and many are directly contradictory in the sense of being mutually excluding.

First, among the divisions of the refutation of truly singular pervasive entities, the reasoning that refutes truly singular permanent real things as imputed by non-Buddhist systems is stated in Śāntarakṣita's *Ornament for the Middle Way* as follows: [309]

> Being connected with successive effects,
> permanent things are not singular in nature.
> If each successive effect is different,
> then [the argument] supporting their permanence will
> degenerate.[521]

Here, a syllogism can be formulated as follows: "The *subject*—the primal nature, for example, asserted to be a permanent real thing—is not truly established as singular in nature because it is connected with its many successive effects that are induced in serial order." The opponent may respond by stating, "In the case of this reason, the pervasion is not ascertained, because there is no contradiction between being truly established as one and being connected with its successive effects induced in serial order." In this case, the question could be asked, "Does it have or does it not have propensities that give rise to its effects in serial order?" If the opponent replies that it does not, then one could argue, "The *subject*—the primal nature, for example, that is a permanent real thing—would give rise to all its effects at once, because according to you it gives rise to all its effects and it does not have propensities that give rise to them all in serial order." Conversely, if the opponent were to reply affirmatively that it does have propensities that give rise to its effects in serial order, then one could argue, "The *subject*—the primal nature, for example, that is a permanent real thing—is not truly established as permanent and one, because it has many different propensities that give rise to successive effects in serial order."

The reasoning that refutes truly singular, permanent, real analytical cessations imputed by certain Buddhist systems is presented in Śāntarakṣita's *Ornament for the Middle Way*:

> Even those uncompounded objects known
> by the wisdom arisen from meditation, [310]
> as propounded by this [Vaibhāṣika] system, are not singular
> because they are related with successive moments of
> consciousness.[522]

The Buddhist Vaibhāṣika school considers the uncompounded analytical cessations—which they accept to be objects of knowledge of the mental equanimity arisen from meditation—to be truly established as one. The Mādhyamika posit the following refutation to this view: "The *subject*, analytical cessations, are not truly established as one, because many moments of wisdom arise from meditation in succession and there is a corresponding relationship between subject and object."

As for the reasoning that refutes a truly singular person as it is imputed by the Buddhist Vātsīputrīya system, Śāntarakṣita counters the Vātsīputrīya assertion that the person is truly established as inexpressible in nature as either permanent or impermanent. His *Ornament for the Middle Way* says:

> Since the person cannot be shown
> to be either momentary or nonmomentary,
> it is clearly understood to lack
> a nature of being either one or many.[523]

Regarding this, a syllogism can be formulated as follows: "The *subject*, the person, is not truly established as one, because it is inexpressible as permanent." Also: "The *subject*, the person, is not truly established as many, because it is inexpressible as impermanent." The pervasion is established because [311] if something is momentary then it would have a cause separated into many parts that arise one from another sequentially in earlier and later moments, so it would be many in nature; and if something is not momentary then it would not have a cause separated into many parts that arise one from another in earlier and later moments, so it would be one in nature. Therefore, if it is inexpressible as either momentary or nonmomentary, it can easily be proved to lack truly established singularity or plurality.

As for the reasoning that refutes truly singular pervasive space and so on as it is imputed by non-Buddhist systems, Śāntarakṣita's *Ornament for the Middle Way* says:

> Because [it is] related with different directions,
> how can the pervasive be singular?[524]

Here, the following argument is posited: "The *subject*, pervasive space, time, and so on, cannot be truly established as singular because they are related commensurately and simultaneously with things such as trees that exist in directions having many different parts, such as the eastern direction."

Second, the refutation of truly singular nonpervasive entities is divided into two categories: the refutation of *truly singular external things* and the refutation of *truly singular consciousness*. Of these, the refutation of truly singular external things is divided into two. The first of these is the refutation of *truly singular coarse external things* as asserted by Vaibhāṣika. *Ornament for the Middle Way* says:

> Since real things are covered and uncovered [312]
> and so forth, coarse things are not singular.[525]

In the above passage, the following argument is posited: "The *subject*, coarse things such as pots, are not truly established as singular, because they have contradictory attributes in terms of substance, such as being covered and uncovered, contradictory attributes in terms of action, such as moving and not moving, and contradictory attributes in terms of qualities, such as changing and not changing color."

The second category of the refutation of truly singular external things is the refutation of *truly singular partless particles*. *Ornament for the Middle Way* says:

> What is the nature of the central particle
> that faces one of the partless particles
> that encircles it, conjoins with it,
> or dwells without space in between?
>
> If it is asserted that just this [one side]
> faces other partless particles,
> then in that case, accordingly, how could
> earth, water, and so on be extended?
>
> If it is asserted that different
> sides face other partless particles,
> then how could such a subtle particle as this
> be singular and partless?[526]

The followers of Kaṇāda, a non-Buddhist philosopher [and founder of the Vaiśeṣika school], maintain that the partless particles that constitute external objects conjoin each other. The Buddhist Vaibhāṣika say that partless particles are held by the force of substance and wind in a sphere with space in between each other and are unconjoined. [313] The Buddhist Sautrāntika say that partless particles dwell without space in between. In relation to the above, whatever the specifics of the opponents' view [of atomism] might be, the following argument is proposed: "The *subject*, a partless particle dwelling in the middle of particles in the ten directions, does not have a different location from the particles in the ten directions, because its side facing the east and its sides facing the particles in the other nine directions, such as the west, would be the same." If the opponent accepts this, then the proponent develops the argument further: "So it would be impossible to accumulate partless particles that gradually develop into coarse objects, such as earth or water, because of what you have accepted." Conversely, if the opponent says that its side facing the east and its side facing the particles in the other nine directions, such as the west, are different, then the proponent argues: "The *subject*, a partless particle dwelling in the middle of particles in the ten directions, would not be singular and partless, like the very subtle partless particles imputed by other Buddhist and non-Buddhist systems, because its side facing the east is different from its sides facing the particles in the other nine directions, such as the west."

The second category of the refutation of truly singular nonpervasive entities is the refutation of a truly singular consciousness. This has two subdivisions: refutation of a truly singular consciousness in the case of systems that accept external objects and refutation of a truly singular consciousness in the case of systems that do not accept external objects. The first of these has two subdivisions: refutation of the two Buddhist realist systems and refutation of the non-Buddhist systems. The first of these has two subdivisions: refutation of the Vaibhāṣika system that asserts consciousness to lack images and refutation of the Sautrāntika system that asserts consciousness to bear images.[527] As for the refutation of the Vaibhāṣika system that asserts consciousness to lack images, by first proving reflexive awareness, consciousness itself is proved to have two parts—the object-image (or objective aspect) and the subject-image (or subjective aspect). [314] In proving that, it is thereby refuted that consciousness lacks images and is truly singular. This is explained in Śāntarakṣita's *Ornament for the Middle Way*:

> Consciousness arises in the opposite way
> from anything in the nature of matter.
> That which is nonmaterial in nature
> is that which knows its own nature.[528]

In the above verse, the following argument is posited: "The *subject*, consciousness, is reflexive awareness because it arises in the nature of luminous awareness, opposite from the nature of matter—meaning that material things, such as chariots, are not illuminating so must be distinct from some other illuminator, whereas a thing such as an oil lamp, for example, is in the nature of illuminating itself, so it illuminates itself without depending on some other illuminator." The pervasion is established. "The nature of nonmaterial luminous awareness cognizes its own nature without depending on some other illuminator because it is the reflexive awareness of that very consciousness itself."

As for the refutation of the Sautrāntika system that asserts a truly singular consciousness bears images, Sautrāntika have three different views about how images appear to the consciousness. Among these, the refutation of first view, that of the Nonpluralists, is as follows. This view maintains that multiple images appear to a truly singular consciousness; regarding this, Śāntarakṣita's *Ornament for the Middle Way* says:

> Since they are not different from a singular consciousness,
> the images cannot be multiple.
> Therefore it cannot be established that
> objects are known via the causal capacity of those [images].
>
> Since it is not separate from such [multiple] images,
> a singular consciousness cannot occur. [315]
> If that were not so, then how could
> those two be called "singular"?[529]

The argument presented in the above lines is thus: "As for the *subject*, consciousness, when images such as blue, yellow, white, and red appear to a singular consciousness they cannot be asserted to be multiple, because those images are not a different entity from that truly singular consciousness." If the opponent accepts this, then the proponent develops the argument further: "In terms of appearing as images of the object, it is unfeasible to posit an object that is substantially different from the consciousness apprehending it, because when images such as blue, yellow, white, and red appear to a singular consciousness they cannot be asserted to be multiple." Also: "The *subject*, a sense consciousness apprehending a variegated array, is not truly established as singular because it is the same substance as its images of blue, yellow, white, and red." The opponent argues: "Even though it is the same substance as its images of blue, yellow, white, and red, this does not contradict its being truly established as singular." The proponent responds: "The *subject*, a sense consciousness apprehending a variegated array, cannot be accepted to be the same substance as the images of blue, yellow, white, and red because it is truly established to be a single substance, and the images of blue, yellow, white, and red are truly established to be different substances." Such reasons as these are used to refute the opponents. In brief, this system is shown to be illogical here by means of the reasoning that a singular consciousness having parts and the many images that are its parts cannot be included in a single basis that is truly established.

The second view, that of the Half-Eggists or the Successive Pluralists, is refuted as follows. The Half-Eggists say: "The faults posited in the case of the Nonpluralists above do not apply to us. The diverse images that appear to a consciousness, which are equal in number to the colors in a collection of various hues, such as white, [316] are not simultaneous but arise in succession. For example, when a burning torch is spun round very fast, although the earlier and later moments in perception arise successively, the observer makes the mistake of thinking that they arise simultaneously owing to the speed of the rotation. Just so, because these successive consciousnesses engage their objects so quickly, foolish people are mistaken in thinking that they arise simultaneously." Śāntarakṣita's *Ornament for the Middle Way* presents this view as follows:

> Regarding such things as white and so on,
> these consciousnesses arise successively.
> They arise so quickly that foolish people think
> these consciousness arise simultaneously.[530]

To refute this, an argument is presented to show how the reason that quickly engaging their objects is the cause of the mistaken appearance of simultaneity is inconclusive. Here, Śāntarakṣita's *Ornament for the Middle Way* says:

> When cognition of the sounds of words
> such as *latā* [and *tāla*] arise very quickly,
> why does it not arise in this case too
> as though it arises simultaneously?[531]

The argument proposed above is as follows: "In general, when the words *latā* (a slender branch) and *tāla* (a plamyra palm tree) are spoken very quickly, then the illusion may arise where the auditory consciousness hearing these two utterances mistakenly apprehends them to occur simultaneously, because the auditory consciousnesses that hear them would occur very quickly." If the opponent accepts this, then the proponent develops the argument further: "This means the distinct meanings of those words would not be understood. In that case, then this contradicts direct perception." Furthermore, even in the case of a conceptual consciousness, when it apprehends its objects very quickly [317] it would arise mistakenly apprehending them to be simultaneous, which again refutes that position.

The third view, that of the Proponents of an Equal Number of Subjects and Objects, is refuted as follows. This view maintains that even in the case of a variegated object where the eye consciousness apprehending it focuses on images equal in number to its objects, such as blue, yellow, and so on, the consciousness arises endowed with images of precisely that many objects. Śāntarakṣita's *Ornament for the Middle Way* says:

> If that were so, then even consciousness
> of a single type of image, such as white,
> would have a variety of focal objects
> since its beginning, middle, and end are different.[532]

Supposing they were of equal number, as the opponent suggests, consider the following argument: "The *subject*, a consciousness that perceives a single type of attribute or image such as white in a group of variegated colors, would be endowed with various images as focal objects, because even the single color white has many different parts, such as a beginning, middle, and end." If the opponent accepts this, then the proponent concludes: "So a consciousness apprehending a single image would be impossible."

The refutation of a truly singular consciousness as it is posited in non-Buddhist systems is illustrated as follows in *Ornament for the Middle Way*:

> Even according to non-Buddhist texts, a consciousness [318]
> endowed with a single appearance would not occur.[533]

In the above, the following argument is posited: "The *subject*, consciousness, even according to non-Buddhist traditions, would not have an appearance of only one object because all cognitions are endowed with many images."

In terms of refuting a truly singular consciousness within the Buddhist Cittamātra tradition, the Cittamātra are subdivided into Proponents of True Images and Proponents of False Images. The Proponents of True Images are subdivided into three categories, as in the Sautrāntika tradition. The only difference is that while Sautrāntika consider those images to be projected by external objects, Cittamātra do not accept external objects to be different in nature from the mind. The reasoning that refutes the Half-Eggist Proponents of True Images is stated in Śāntarakṣita's *Ornament for the Middle Way* as follows:

> Even if consciousness were truly
> manifold, it would be contradictory
> for those [images] to be singular,
> so undoubtedly they are separate.[534]

Here it is argued: "The *subject*, consciousness, would be manifold because it is truly established to be the same substance as its many images." And: "The *subject*, those images, would be singular because they are truly established to be the same substance as consciousness." If the opponent says there is no pervasion, it is further argued: "The *subject*, consciousness, must be a separate substance from its images [319] because consciousness is truly established to be singular while its images are truly established to be manifold."

The Proponents of an Equal Number of Subjects and Objects are refuted by the following reasoning from *Ornament for the Middle Way*:

> If you accept an equal number
> of consciousnesses and images,
> then it would hard to refute the way of analyzing
> partless particles when it is likewise applied here.[535]

In the above verse, the following argument is posited: "As for the *subject*, a knowable object, when looking at a variegated object it follows that corresponding consciousnesses equal in number to blue, yellow, and so on would not arise simultaneously, because this position is undermined in the same way that partless particles are undermined, as stated previously." The way in which this position is undermined by the reasoning that refutes partless particles is as follows. When a central subtle particle is surrounded by ten subtle particles, does that central particle have parts or not? If it does not have parts, then since the positions of the eleven particles—the central particle together with those of the ten directions—would converge, nothing but a single image would appear. So it would be impossible for a singular consciousness with images of a group of particles or even a coarse whole to arise, for in that case it would contradict the assertions of the Proponents of True Images. Conversely, if it does have parts, then just as the central particle would need to have ten sides facing the particles of the ten directions, so there would need to arise ten consciousnesses perceiving them. So it would be impossible for a singular consciousness to arise to which appears a coarse object with parts, for this would contradict the assertions of the Proponents of True Images.

As for refuting the Nonpluralist system, which argues that multiple images appear to a truly singular consciousness, [320] Śāntarakṣita's *Ornament for the Middle Way* says:

> To say that one [consciousness] has a variety [of images]
> is surely like the system of the Sky-Clad [Jaina]?
> A variety is not in the nature of singularity,
> just as a variety of precious gems [is not singular].
>
> If a variety is singular in nature
> then how can it appear as various entities?
> As for the obstructed, unobstructed, and so on,
> how could these be differentiated?[536]

If, as the traditions of Sky-Clad Jaina as well as Vedānta maintain, the consciousness to which many images appear were truly established as singular, then the following argument is posited in refutation: "The *subject*, consciousness, is not truly singular because a variety of images appear to it—for example, as in the case of a heap of various precious gems." Also: "If you accept such images to be truly singular, then the various appearances of blue, yellow, and so on, as well as images of the covered, uncovered, and so on, would not appear as different—which would be unfeasible, because those various images would be truly established as singular." However, a singular consciousness to which various images merely appear is not refuted; it is accepted even in the Madhyamaka tradition. What is refuted is the assertion that such a consciousness is truly established. [321]

As for the refutation of the Proponents of False Images within the Yogācāra tradition, those proponents claim: "The faults incurred by positing consciousness and its images to be ultimately either the same substance or different substances do not apply to us. Ultimately, or in reality, consciousness is primordially pure like a clear crystal. So images do not actually exist in the way they appear to that consciousness in terms of its natural capacity. Instead, images such as blue appear through the ripening of mistaken propensities of dualistic appearance that have continuously occurred since beginningless time. For example, it is like the mistaken appearance of falling hairs to one whose eyes are affected by a disease." To explain the opponents' assertions, *Ornament for the Middle Way* says:

> Some say that [consciousness] naturally
> does not have such images,
> for in reality, images do not exist
> but appear to consciousness due to error.[537]

To present an illustration of how to refute the assertions of the Proponents of False Images, the text goes on to say:

> If they do not exist, then how can it be
> that consciousness clearly experiences them?
> It is not similar to a consciousness
> that is different from its objects.[538]

If the image does not exist as a real thing other than as a mere appearance, then one may argue: "The *subject*, an image, cannot possibly be experienced or felt clearly by direct perception as one's own experience in the present moment, [322] because it does not exist as a real thing, just as the shape of a rabbit's horn cannot be experienced by a visual sense consciousness. The pervasion is established because there cannot be a consciousness that does not have real images." Such an argument refutes this position, and there are many other reasonings that refute it too.

As for the reasoning that proves the lack of true plurality, which is the second facet of the attribute of the subject in the above reason,[539] the argument is stated as follows: "The *subject*, things posited by our own and others' systems, do not exist as truly many, because their existence as truly one has been refuted." Śāntarakṣita's *Ornament for the Middle Way* says:

> Whatever things are analyzed,
> none of them has singularity.

> Whatever does not have singularity
> also does not have plurality.[540]

Here the following argument is posited: "The *subject*, a thing, is not established as truly many because it does not exist as truly one. The pervasion is established because to be many is to be a collection of single entities in nature."

The reasoning that establishes the pervasion in the main argument—the neither-one-nor-many argument—is stated in *Ornament for the Middle Way*:

> Apart from being one or many,
> it is not possible for a thing
> to be another alternative because
> those two are mutually excluding.[541]

In this verse the following argument is posited: "The *subject*, an object of knowledge, cannot be truly established if it is not truly established as one or many, because there is nothing that is neither one nor many. This follows because one and many are [323] directly contradictory in the sense of being mutually excluding."

In brief, the final point refuted by this reasoning as being neither one nor many is as follows. Having shown that it is impossible for the images of cognized objects to be partless in the sense of not having many parts—whether coarse or subtle, or earlier or later, as asserted in one or another of the Buddhist or non-Buddhist traditions—one shows that if they were truly established to have many parts, then this would entail certain contradictions. Although in a conventional sense it is not contradictory for there to be a single phenomenon having many parts, in the context of being truly established it is problematic, for if the parts and whole were different entities then they would be utterly different and unrelated, and if they were the same entity then the parts would be one like the whole or the whole would be many like the parts. By finally showing that a truly established plurality entails these inconsistencies, the notion that phenomena are truly established is refuted.

Tibetan commentators on the Madhyamaka tenets list five supremely important sets of reasoning to prove emptiness. Since these are renowned, we identify each of them here. The first is the inference of being neither one nor many based on an analysis of the entity. This has just been explained above. A syllogism can be formulated as follows: "The *subject*, a sprout, does not exist ultimately because it does not exist as ultimately one or many, for example, like a reflection in a mirror."

The second is the inference of the diamond slivers based on an analysis of the cause. This is the reasoning that refutes ultimate arising by way of refuting that phenomena arise from the four alternatives. A syllogism can be formulated as follows: "The *subject*, a sprout, does not arise ultimately because it does not arise ultimately from self, from other, [324] from both, or without a cause—for example, like a sky flower."

The third is the inference that refutes arising as either existent or nonexistent, based on an analysis of the effect. A syllogism can be formulated as follows: "The *subject*, a sprout, does not arise ultimately, because when existent at the time of its cause it does not arise again, and when nonexistent at the time of its cause it does not arise ultimately—like, for example, a sky lotus." Kamalaśīla's *Illumination of the Middle Way* says:

> As for refuting the arising of an existent effect, your claim "There is no inferential reason with an example that is commonly established for both parties" is also incorrect. We ask, "What is it that you call *existent*?" If you maintain that since it is impossible for something without constituents to be established in terms of its constituents, so by *existent* you mean an entity that is thoroughly established as an embodiment of all its constituents, [to this we say] whatever thoroughly established entity it may be, it does not exist as qualified by others to have been nonexistent previously. That which does not exist as qualified by others to have been nonexistent previously is not produced by anything in any way—like, for example, a sky lotus.[542]

If something existent at the time of its cause were to arise, then having already arisen, it would have to arise again. If something nonexistent at the time of its cause were to arise ultimately, then like a sky flower it could not be produced by a cause, because in the case of being truly established if it is nonexistent at one time then it must be nonexistent at all times. Since it is unfeasible for something truly established to rely on a cause, it is limited to being either permanently existent or completely nonexistent. [325]

The fourth is the inference that refutes arising from the four alternatives based on an analysis of both cause and effect. A syllogism can be formulated as follows: "The *subject*, a sprout, does not arise ultimately because many causes do not give rise to one effect alone, many causes do not give rise ultimately to many effects, one cause alone does not give rise to many effects, and one cause alone does not give rise to one effect alone—for example, like a reflection." Jñānagarbha's *Distinguishing the Two Truths* says:

> Many do not give rise to one effect,
> many do not give rise to many,
> one does not give rise to many effects,
> and one does not give rise to one.[543]

Here the qualification *ultimately* must be applied to the negation of "Many give rise to many." However, in the case of the other three [reasons stated], for "one cause alone" and "one effect alone," the application of the term *alone* is sufficient, so there is no need to apply the qualification *ultimately*. This is because there is no arising from one cause alone and there is no giving rise to one effect alone. The first is established because if something is causally compounded, then it must arise from many causes and conditions. The second is established because if one effect arises, then its directional parts and temporal parts must arise also. In a general sense, however, it is the case that one seed gives rise to one or many effects, and many causes and conditions give rise to one or many effects, because the kernel from a single seed gives rise to many effects such as a sprout, leaves, ears of corn, and so forth, [326] and several causes and conditions such as a seed, sprinkling water, and so on give rise to a single sprout as the effect. Although it is feasible for many causes to give rise to many effects *conventionally*, it is unfeasible for many causes to give rise to many effects *ultimately*. For example, when the three conditions give rise to a visual consciousness, this visual consciousness has three parts that are the imprints of the three conditions, so one phenomenon having many parts is not contradictory in a conventional sense, but it is unfeasible in the sense of being ultimately established.

The fifth inference is that of dependent arising, the king of reasons. A syllogism can be formulated as follows: "The *subject*, a sprout, does not ultimately arise, because it is dependently related—for example, like an illusion." Kamalaśīla's *Illumination of the Middle Way* says: "That which dependently arises is ultimately empty of an inherent nature—for example, like an illusion."[544] The reasoning of dependent arising will be explained in detail below.

Candrakīrti's Sevenfold Reasoning

As for the proofs of the selflessness of phenomena and the selflessness of persons that are found in the treatises of the great Indian Madhyamaka master Candrakīrti—particularly *Entering the Middle Way* and its autocommentary—the main argument that refutes the self of phenomena is the reasoning that refutes arising from the four alternatives, which he sources from Nāgārjuna's *Fundamental Treatise on the Middle Way*, [chapter 1 in particular], and the main argument that refutes the self of persons is the fivefold reasoning, which he sources from chapters 10 and 22 of *Fundamental Treatise on the Middle Way*. Nāgārjuna's text says: [327]

> The Tathāgata is not the aggregates, nor other than the
> aggregates;
> the aggregates are not within him; he is not within them;
> he does not possess the aggregates.
> What is the Tathāgata?[545]

In the above, [where the Tathāgata is taken as an example of the person or self], the relationship between the self and the aggregates is examined in terms of the following possible alternatives: (1) as the same, (2) as different, (3) as located in the aggregates, (4) as the locus of the aggregates, and (5) as possessing the aggregates, which are taken to be inherently established. In addition to these, Candrakīrti adds two more: (6) as the shape of the aggregates and (7) as the collection of aggregates. It is this sevenfold analysis that Candrakīrti uses with special emphasis. Candrakīrti speaks of this reasoning as being the main one for refuting the self of persons and as being an easy method for finding the profound view. His *Entering the Middle Way* says:

> How can what does not exist in the seven ways
> be said to exist? The yogin finds no such existence.
> By this means, he also enters into reality with ease;
> so its existence must be accepted as shown here.[546]

Here Candrakīrti is saying that when the thing that is imputed, such as a chariot, is sought by means of the sevenfold analysis, it is not to be found—which entails that the chariot does not exist inherently and that the yogin too is unable to find the chariot's existence. Using this method, the yogin, without damaging conventional presentations, also easily enters into suchness. [328] So one must accept that, in the context of Madhyamaka philosophy, the way in which a chariot is established is for it to be established without searching for the true referent of the term.

A syllogism using the sevenfold reasoning can be formulated as follows: "The *subject*, the person, is not inherently established, because it is not inherently established as the same entity as the aggregates nor as a different entity from them; also it is not established as located in the aggregates in an inherently existent manner, nor as the locus of the aggregates inherently, nor as possessing the aggregates in an inherently existent manner; also it is not the mere collection of the aggregates and it is not the shape of the collection. Just as, for example, when one searches for a chariot in the seven ways—as the same entity as its parts, as a different entity from them, as possessing them, as located in them, as the locus of them, as the mere collection of them, or as the shape of the collection—it is not found." When one negates the self to be the same entity as the aggregates, to be located in the aggregates, to be the locus of the aggregates, or in possession of the aggregates, one must apply a qualifier to the object of negation. However, when negating the self to be a different entity from the aggregates, or negating the mere collection of aggregates or the shape of the collection to be the self, there is no need to apply a qualifier to the object of negation since it is negated in a general sense.

Each of the seven points is refuted separately as follows. (1) If the self were inherently established to be the same entity as the aggregates, then this would incur the fault that just as the aggregates are five, so the self must be five, or just as I myself am one, so the five aggregates would have to be one. Indeed, if the self were inherently established to be the same entity as the mind, then because there are many consciousnesses—as when categorized into parts that include the six types of consciousness, such as the visual consciousness, [329] and many consciousnesses arising and ceasing in each moment—so the self would be many. Candrakīrti's *Entering the Middle Way Autocommentary* says:

> If it were so, in accordance with the position of those who say that the aggregates are the self, then since the aggregates are many, the self would be many. In the same way, if the mind were the self, then because it is divided into visual consciousness and so on and many consciousnesses arising and ceasing in each moment, the self too would be many.[547]

This consequence is directed not simply against an acceptance of them merely to be one entity or many; it is leveled against an acceptance of the self and the aggregates as utterly the same without any difference at all. That the person and the aggregates are utterly identical is not an assertion that the opponent has actually made at the start. The point is, however, that although being the same entity yet conceptually distinct is not a contradiction in the case of what is false [i.e., not truly existent], in the case of accepting the self and the aggregates to have true existence, if the two are the same entity then they would necessarily be inseparably one as well. So, it is through the force of drawing out this logical implication that the consequences of many selves or the five aggregates being one are demonstrated.

(2) As for refuting the self to be a different entity from the aggregates, if the self were established as a different entity from the aggregates, then it would be utterly different. In that case it must be established as independent. If established as independent, then it would necessarily follow that when the aggregates are hurt I would not be hurt, and when I am hurt the aggregates would not be hurt. However, since this is not the case, they are not established to be different. Another refutation has already been explained above in the context of refuting a permanent, unitary, and autonomous self. [330]

(3) The self does not exist by way of being inherently located in the aggregates and (4) the aggregates do not exist by way of being inherently located in the self. Although they are established as the locus and the located in terms of being merely nominally imputed, it would be inappropriate for the aggregates to be taken as the basis of imputation of the self in an absolute

sense, just as a water vase cannot be taken as a basis of imputation of water. Moreover, if the self and the aggregates were inherently established to be other, then since they would be completely different unrelated things, they could not be the locus and the located. For example, according to worldly perception a bowl and the yogurt inside it, being two different entities, are seen to be the locus and the located. But the self and the aggregates are not seen like this, so they are not inherently established as the locus and the located entity. Candrakīrti's *Entering the Middle Way Autocommentary* says:

> If they were absolutely different, then it would be correct for them to be the locus and the located in reality, like a bowl containing yogurt, for example. The bowl and the yogurt, being absolutely different, are seen according to worldly perception to be the locus and the located in reality. But the aggregates are not different from the self in this way, and the self also is not different from the aggregates. So, these two do not exist as the locus and the located in reality.[548]

(5) The self cannot possibly be inherently established to possess the aggregates—whether this applies to different entities, as in the statement "This man Devadatta has elephants," [331] or to entities that are not different, as in the statement "Devadatta has ears"—because the self does not exist as either inherently the same as or different from the aggregates such as form. Therefore the self is not inherently established to possess the aggregates. If the self were to possess the aggregates by way of being different entities, as in "Devadatta has elephants," then just as it is possible to place Devadatta somewhere apart from the elephants, so it must be possible to place the self somewhere apart from the aggregates—but that does not occur. Moreover, if the self were to possess the aggregates by virtue of being the same entity inherently, then they must be absolutely identical. In this case, the self and the aggregates would be indistinguishable, so the verbal conventions of *possessed* and *possessor* would be inadmissible. Candrakīrti's *Entering the Middle Way Autocommentary* says:

> Given that the self and the aggregates being the same or different has already been negated, if the possessive affix is applied either in the case of a perceived difference (e.g., Devadatta's cattle) or in

> the case of nondifference (e.g., Devadatta's body), it is untenable to say, "The self has a body," because the self and the body have neither sameness nor difference.[549]

(6) It is unfeasible for the collection of aggregates to be the self for the following reason. The person is imputed in dependence on the collection of aggregates, thus the collection of aggregates is the basis of imputation of the person, [332] but it is not the person; the basis of imputation and the imputed phenomenon are contradictory.[550] For example, with the elements having acted as a cause, blue and the eyes and so forth are imputed as element derivatives, so the causal elements [such as earth] and the element derivatives, such as blue, are contradictory.[551] This refutation of the collection of aggregates being the self, as taught in Nāgārjuna's *Precious Garland*, was presented above in the context of rebutting the opponents' objections to the refutation of the self. Candrakīrti's *Entering the Middle Way Autocommentary* says:

> Whatever is imputed in dependence upon something is not the mere collection of components that appropriate the imputation, because it is dependently imputed, like the element derivatives. Just as, with the elements having functioned as a cause, the element derivatives such as blue, the eyes, and so on are imputed, those two are not mere collections of elements. Likewise, the self, with the aggregates having functioned as a cause, has an imputed nature, but it cannot be the mere collection of aggregates.[552]

Also, it is unfeasible for the mere collection of aggregates to be the self for the following reason. If the mere collection of aggregates were the self, it would follow that the mere collection of parts of a chariot would be the chariot. This entails the fault that where the dismantled collection of parts of the chariot is piled up, the chariot would have to be there too. Candrakīrti's *Entering the Middle Way* says:

> If the mere collection [of parts] were the chariot, [333]
> then the chariot would exist where the dismantled pieces are placed.[553]

(7) It is unfeasible to posit a specific shape of the collection of aggregates to be the self because that specific shape exists only in the case of physical things. If a specific shape were asserted to be the self as one may suggest, then only phenomena having physical form would be the self; however, it would be illogical to posit a collection of mind and mental factors to be the self because collections of mind and mental factors do not have any shape. Thus this point is refuted. Candrakīrti's *Entering the Middle Way* says:

> If you say it is the shape then, since this exists only for physical things,
> just those would be the self according to you;
> the collections of mind and so on would not be the self
> because these do not have any shape.[554]

Also, it is unfeasible to posit the mere shape of the aggregates to be the person. This is because, for example, just as it is unfeasible for the mere shape of a chariot to be the chariot—whether posited in terms of the shape of individual parts of the chariot or the shape of the collection of parts—so it is unfeasible to posit the mere shape of the aggregates to be the person, whether posited as either of two categories—the shape of the individual aggregates or the shape of their collection. Candrakīrti's *Entering the Middle Way* says:

> If you say the shapes that the individual parts had before [assembly] [334]
> are the same as what is known as a chariot [when assembled],
> then just as in the case when they were separate
> so too now in this case there is no chariot.[555]

In brief, if the chariot were to exist not as merely nominally imputed but as something found from the side of its basis of imputation, then the chariot must exist within all the parts that are the chariot's basis of imputation. Not only that, but the chariot must be found even within the collection of individual particles of the chariot. If asserted to exist in that way, then the chariot would have to be observed within the particles of its parts by the visual consciousness; but since it is not observed, this assertion is incorrect. Also, if the individual parts are collected and the chariot is asserted to be the complete collection of individual parts, then the chariot must exist even when the collection of parts is dismantled because there is not even the slightest difference or dissimilarity between the entities of the parts when they are dismantled and when they are not dismantled.

Moreover, if the chariot exists as something found from the side of its basis of imputation, does one accept the chariot that is found in the locus of the chariot's wheels to be the same size as the wheels or bigger than the wheels? If an opponent accepts it to be the same size as the wheels, then they must accept that the *chariot endowed with parts* and the *wheels that are its parts* are no different in size, which is untenable. If they accept the chariot that is found in the locus of its wheels to be bigger than its wheels, [335] then to say that the chariot is found within the parts that are its basis of imputation would be mere words, [without meaning]. If they accept there to be an inherently existent chariot within the wheels that are its basis of imputation, this entails the fault that the visual consciousness apprehending the wheels in isolation would necessarily see the complete chariot. Also, since the chariot's parts and their collection are the chariot's appropriated objects, and the chariot itself is the appropriator, they would incur the fault of accepting the appropriated and the appropriator to be identical. Accordingly, if the self were to exist as something able to be found when it is sought among its bases of imputation, then just like the example of the chariot, these faults would be incurred. Therefore we may assert that it does not exist from its own side in the slightest.

The Logical Reason of Dependent Arising, the King of Reasonings

Owing to the reason that external and internal compounded things arise from their own respective causes and conditions, they are not produced by virtue of their own characteristics and they are not produced from the four alternatives; and owing to the reason that a person is imputed in dependence upon the aggregates that are her own basis of imputation, she is not found when sought in the seven ways. When the many reasonings that refute inherent existence taught in the Madhyamaka texts are boiled down, they finally come down to the reasoning of dependent arising, so this is called "the king of reasonings." It has the capacity to clear away both extremes simultaneously; the extreme of permanence or independent existence is directly eliminated by understanding the meaning of *dependent*, and the extreme of annihilation or total nonexistence is directly eliminated by understanding the meaning of *arising*. That is how this inference of *dependent arising* operates. [336] Candrakīrti's *Entering the Middle Way* says:

> Because things dependently arise,
> these [mistaken] conceptions cannot withstand analysis.
> So this reasoning of dependent arising
> rips to shreds the entire matrix of wrong views.[556]

A syllogism using the reason of dependent arising can be formulated as follows: "The *subject*, a sprout, does not exist inherently because it dependently arises—for example, like a reflection."

To be inherently existent is contradictory to being dependent on other causes and conditions. Candrakīrti's *Commentary on the Four Hundred Stanzas* says:

> If anything were to exist in terms of its own entity, its own nature, autonomously, or without depending on others, this would mean that it would exist in its own right, with the consequence that it would lack dependent arising. However, all causally compounded things do dependently arise. In that case, anything that dependently arises cannot be autonomous because it arises in dependence on causes and conditions. All these things are not autonomous; therefore nothing whatsoever has an inherent nature or self.[557]

Furthermore, *Questions of the Nāga King Anavatapta Sūtra* says:

> There is no phenomenon that has no causes and no conditions.
> Phenomena must be understood to have causes and conditions.
> [337]
> Whatever arises from conditions does not arise—
> it does not have the inherent nature of arising.
> Whatever depends on conditions is declared to be empty.
> Whoever understands emptiness in this way is diligent.[558]

The above passages explain how being *free from the extreme of existence*, owing to the absence of essential nature, and being *free from the extreme of nonexistence*, owing to being able to posit noninherently existent causation on that very basis, admits the interpretation of *dependent arising* to be commensurate with *not inherently existent*. This is the distinguishing feature of the Prāsaṅgika Madhyamaka tradition, according to masters such as Candrakīrti. As for the topic of dependent arising, this will be explained below when showing how *emptiness* and *dependent arising* are established to have the same meaning.[559]

16

The Object of Negation

HAVING EXPLAINED the various reasonings for establishing that phenomena do not exist ultimately, as presented in the Madhyamaka texts of Nāgārjuna such as *Fundamental Treatise on the Middle Way* and in the writings of the masters who follow him, let us now pose a few questions: What exactly do these varieties of reasoning negate? What is this essential nature that has no existence, of which phenomena are said to be devoid? What faults would ensue if such an essential nature were to exist? To know how to respond to these questions requires an understanding of what exactly is being negated in the context of establishing emptiness through reasoning—namely, the correct identification of the object of negation. [338] So first we must say a little about how the object of negation is identified. Let us consider an example. In order to understand that there is no water in a certain place, we need to know what water is, the absence (or presence) of which is the relevant issue. Likewise, to apprehend a thief, we need to identify what the thief looks like. So to ascertain the absence of inherent nature or the absence of self in phenomena, we need to clearly identify the self or nature that does not exist. If the object universal or image of the object to be negated does not appear clearly in one's mind, one will not know what its absence is like. Śāntideva's *Engaging in the Bodhisattva's Deeds* says:

> Without having identified the imputed thing
> you cannot apprehend its absence.[560]

In other words, if a generic image of the superimposed thing, which is the object to be negated, does not appear clearly to the mind, then the mind cannot correctly apprehend the absence of the object of negation. Although limitless objects of negation may be conceived, if one can identify their root and negate that in a generic way, then all other aspects of what is to be negated will naturally be eliminated as well. If one fails to do this in a way that refutes the object of negation in its entirety without leaving any residue, one will fall into the extreme of eternalism. Conversely, if an unrestricted object of negation is negated to excess without allowing for dependently related causation, then one would fall into the extreme of annihilation. Therefore it is extremely important to identify properly the parameters of the object of negation. For this reason, Nāgārjuna's *Fundamental Treatise on the Middle Way* says:

> Conceiving "it exists" is grasping at permanence.
> Conceiving "it does not exist" is the view of nihilism. [339]
> Therefore the wise do not take as their stance
> either "it exists" or "it does not exist."[561]

The above verse says that since to take as one's standpoint either the view of existence, which is the view of permanence, or the view of nonexistence, which is the view of nihilism, is the origin of many faults, the wise declare it is unsuitable to adhere to either of those positions.

One might ask, "In that case, what manner of apprehending things constitutes adhering to the view of eternalism or the view of nihilism?" In response to this, *Buddhapālita's Commentary on the Fundamental Treatise* says:

> Why does having the view of existence or nonexistence entail the fault of having the view of permanence or nihilism? The root text says:
>
> > Whatever exists essentially
> > is never nonexistent, so this is eternalism.
> > To say "It existed before but does not exist now"
> > thus entails nihilism. (15.11)
>
> So whatever exists by its own essential nature cannot be nonexistent later. Since its nature does not change this is therefore the view of existence, which entails the view of permanence. To say "The thing that existed before does not exist now" means an existent thing is viewed as annihilated, which is thus the nihilis-

> tic view. Since viewing things as existent or nonexistent engenders many faults, to say "Things do not exist essentially" is the middle way that sees suchness. That itself is established as the ultimate.[562]

The above passage states that if a thing is said to exist by its own nature, since there is no reversing of its nature, it would never become nonexistent. [340] So to claim that a thing exists by its own nature would be the view of permanence. If a thing is said to have arisen by its own nature in the previous moment and now this thing having subsequently disintegrated does not exist, this would be the view of nihilism. In the case of the Prāsaṅgika system, since things are not accepted to exist by their own nature, the views of permanence and nihilism based on an acceptance of essential nature do not occur. To accept that something inherently exists and then disintegrates later is considered to fall into the two extremes. However to accept that something exists earlier then disintegrates later is not considered to fall into the two extremes.

Those who do not understand the correct way to validly establish the presentations of action, agent, and so on take them to be nonexistent like a rabbit's horn, and merely to avoid verbal faults they simply declare them to be "neither existent nor nonexistent" in a manner that does not help them to avoid the two extremes of permanence and nihilism. *Buddhapālita's Commentary on the Fundamental Treatise* says: "Seeing that things simply do not exist, like a rabbit's horn, we do not declare that they are 'neither existent nor nonexistent' for the sake of avoiding verbal faults."[563] Thus to hold that phenomena are utterly nonexistent is the view of nihilism. Candrakīrti's *Clear Words* says: "It is like this. When they think, 'Everything is empty, so everything is nonexistent,' then it is a wrong view."[564] [341]

In general, "the object of negation" can refer to two things: one is when the *distorted grasping* is referred to as the object to be negated, and the other is when the *existence of inherent nature* held by it is referred to as the object to be negated. Of these, the first is the object of negation of the path, while the second is the object of negation of reasoning. Āryadeva's *Four Hundred Stanzas* says:

> Through seeing the absence of self in the object
> the seed of saṃsāric existence will completely cease.[565]

Here it says that through rationally refuting the conceived object of self-grasping, the seed of saṃsāric existence—the ignorance grasping at true existence—will entirely cease. To dispel the distorted subject that grasps at inherent existence, the object held by it—true existence—must first be refuted. So between the two—the object of negation of the path and the object of negation of reasoning—the primary object of negation is the latter. The latter also refers to inherent existence—the object to be negated in relation to the person and to phenomena—on the basis of dependent arising as the reasoning. Since something that exists cannot be refuted by reasoning, the object of negation must be something that has no existence at all.

One might ask, "If it does not exist, why is there a need to refute it?" Although something such as a form, for example, is not truly existent, the reifying conception holding it to be truly existent arises; therefore it needs to be refuted. The way to refute it, however, is not like smashing a pot with a hammer! One uses reasoning to generate a valid recognition that what has no existence indeed does not exist. When the recognition arises of that nonexistent thing as nonexistent, the distorted cognition holding it to exist is removed. In this way, proving by means of reasoning is not a case of newly proving something that did not exist before, like a seed produces a sprout. It is through reasoning [342] that one generates a valid recognition that a certain thing's way of being is indeed that way.

In general, the terms *truth* and *final nature* refer to emptiness, while the terms *truly existent* and *inherently established* indicate the object of negation to be refuted. Thus it is important to distinguish between the statement that *truth* and *nature* do exist and the statement that *truly existent* and *inherently established* do not exist. Now one might ask, "If the so-called nature or essential identity refuted here were to exist, then what must it be like?" Regarding the topic of *nature* or *own nature*,[566] Nāgārjuna's *Fundamental Treatise on the Middle Way* says:

> A nature is not fabricated
> and not dependent on others.[567]

Also:

> A nature changing into something else
> would be utterly implausible.[568]

This kind of nature is not created by something else such as causes and conditions. Similarly, what is posited as its own nature does not depend on anything else and it does not change into another state. It must have these three attributes, as Candrakīrti's *Clear Words* explains:

> What is that which is its own? That which is not made by anything. That which is made is not that which is its own—for example, like the heat of water. That which is not dependent on others is also that which is its own—for example, like one's wealth. [343] That which is dependent on others is not that which is its own—for example, like a borrower bereft of autonomy.[569]

In other words, that which is established as a something's own nature or mode of being must be unfabricated and not, like borrowers of goods, dependent on another. Nāgārjuna's *Fundamental Treatise on the Middle Way* says:

> It is implausible for a nature
> to arise from causes and conditions.
> If it did arise from causes and conditions
> then a nature would be something that is made.[570]

It is illogical for an inherently existent nature (*rang gi ngo bos grub pa'i rang bzhin*) to arise from causes and conditions. If it were to arise from causes and conditions, then that kind of nature would be fabricated. In that case, since it would be fabricated, it would not be an unfabricated nature. Moreover, given that fabricated and unfabricated are directly contradictory, it necessarily follows that when one is excluded the other is established. Also, since being *made* is encompassed by being *fabricated*, and a nature [of this type] is necessarily unfabricated, *being made* and *being a nature* or *established by nature* cannot be present within the same basis; thus they are just contradictory—that is, mutually excluding. *Questions of Lokadhara Sūtra* says:

> Since all phenomena are not real, they do not exist at all. Like an empty fist or a variety of attractive colors that beguile small

> children, [344] they only exist in reliance upon arising from imputation.[571]

The above passage states that all phenomena are not really established but exist as merely dependent and merely imputed by thought. So to be established from the object's own side without being merely imputed by thought, an internal cognition, is said to be *established as a self* or *established by its own nature*. The absence of this on the basis of a person is asserted to be the *selflessness of persons*, while the absence of this on the basis of any phenomenon that is not a person, such as the eyes or ears, is asserted to be the *selflessness of phenomena*. Candrakīrti's *Commentary on the Four Hundred Stanzas* says:

> Here, the term *self* refers to an inherent nature of things that does not depend upon something else. Since that does not exist, the self does not exist. Understanding this in terms of the twofold division of persons and phenomena, there is the selflessness of persons and the selflessness of phenomena.[572]

The same text says, as quoted above:

> If anything were to exist in terms of its own entity, its own nature, autonomously, or without depending on others, this would mean that it would exist in its own right, with the consequence that it would lack dependent arising. However, all causally compounded things do dependently arise. In that case, anything that dependently arises cannot be autonomous because it arises in dependence on causes and conditions. All these things are not autonomous; therefore nothing whatsoever has any inherent nature or self."[573]

To be established by its own entity, established by its own nature, established autonomously, and established without depending on others are synonymous.

Furthermore, to be established as merely imputed by thought or to be established as merely posited by the mind is what it means to be *conventionally established*. [345] Conversely, to be established as not merely imputed by thought, or to be established as not merely posited by the mind, or to exist as something found when sought in terms of whether it exists from the side of its basis of imputation is what it means to be *truly established, ultimately established, really established, established essentially, established by way of its own characteristics, established by way of its own nature*, and so on, which constitute the hypothetical criteria of the object of negation according to this tradition. The term *own characteristics* (Skt. *svalakṣaṇa*)[574] in the context of a Mādhyamika philosopher identifying what is to be negated is very different from the other two senses of the term: the first as defined in the epistemological texts, where *svalakṣaṇa* refers only to something that possesses causal capacity, and the second as employed in the Abhidharma texts, where *svalakṣaṇa* refers to unique characteristics such as the heat of fire. So this statement regarding the crucial differences in the meaning of the term is of great significance.[575]

As for how phenomena are posited by thought, *Questions of Upāli Sūtra* says:

> Flowers with open petals that delight so many minds,
> supreme golden mansions resplendent and attractive—
> none of these has a creator at all;
> they are posited through the power of conception.
> Through conceptualization the world is imputed.[576] [346]

Similarly, Candrakīrti's *Commentary on the Four Hundred Stanzas* says: "Therefore whatever things that exist only if there is the concept and do not exist if there is no such concept are definitely not inherently existent, like a snake imputed on a coiled rope."[577] This is to say that since an object found to exist as an entity in itself only exists as a conceptual imputation and an object not found to exist as an entity in itself does not exist as a conceptual imputation, all phenomena are established through the force of conception. Because of this reason, all phenomena such as attachment are not established by way of their own essential nature. In this context, *conception* is an ordinary cognition that arises naturally through the capacity of previous habituation, such as a mind conceiving "This is blue" or "This is yellow." It imputes in the following manner. When on the basis of a chariot's parts there arises a cognition thinking "chariot," the chariot that is the object of that cognition is only a mere appearance based on the chariot's parts or is merely imputed in dependence on the chariot's parts. But other than that, none of the chariot's parts, whether individually or as a collection, is the chariot. And since it does not exist separately from those even in the slightest, all phenomena are merely imputed by conception, like a rope taken to be a snake.

Although the way in which phenomena are established by means of conception is like imputing a snake onto a rope, these two are utterly dissimilar in terms of whether they actually exist and whether they can function. For they are indeed unalike in certain respects; the cognitions positing them are dissimilar in terms of whether they are factually concordant. According to worldly convention there is a difference regarding whether the basis in this case actually is the basis on which the thing is imputed. [347] And there is a difference regarding whether the application of the label is refuted by another valid cognition. In the statement "All phenomena are mere names, mere labels, mere imputations," the "mere" does not exclude there being phenomena other than just names or labels, nor does it indicate that things exist but are not established by valid cognition. What it does exclude is the existence of things by virtue of their essential nature.

17

Do the Mādhyamika Have Assertions?

THE VARIOUS ARGUMENTS discussed above as presented by Nāgārjuna, such as the reasoning that refutes arising from the four alternatives, and by Candrakīrti, such as the sevenfold analysis, emphatically refute that internal and external phenomena exist as something found among their bases of imputation when the imputed thing is sought. The question might now be raised, "In that case, apart from refuting another's position, do the Mādhyamika engage in establishing their own standpoint? Or do they make no assertions at all?" This doubt pertains to a point that is of great significance. In response to the objection raised by other fellow Buddhist schools against the establishment of all phenomena as empty of inherent existence—namely, that presentations such as the four noble truths, the three objects of refuge, and so on would become untenable—arguments are also presented in *Fundamental Treatise on the Middle Way* to show that such conventions are indeed tenable from the standpoint that asserts the emptiness of inherent existence. Nevertheless, as the verse from Nāgārjuna's *Fundamental Treatise on the Middle Way* cited in the previous chapter says, "Conceiving 'it exists' is grasping at permanence." Similarly, he states in *Sixty Stanzas of Reasoning*:

> These great and noble beings
> have no position and no dispute. [348]
> For those who have no position
> how can there be an opposing position?[578]

Nāgārjuna's *Refutation of Objections* also says:

> If I had any kind of thesis,
> then that fault would apply to me.

But I do not have a thesis;
thus I am totally without fault.[579]

Likewise, Āryadeva's *Four Hundred Stanzas* states:

Even if you try for a very long time
you cannot posit a counter-response
to someone who has no position
regarding existence, nonexistence, or both.[580]

Also, Candrakīrti's *Entering the Middle Way* says:

Those [objections] will certainly apply to someone who has a thesis;
but since we have no such thesis, those consequences cannot apply to us.[581]

Thus there are indeed statements of great Madhyamaka masters whose words literally do state that their tradition has no theses or assertions at all. Based on a literal reading of these passages, even some later commentators say that the Mādhyamika not only *do not have any position* asserting things to be truly existent as stated by their opponents, but they also *do not have any theses* accepted as their own position at all. For if they had their own position, then the Mādhyamika would have views holding to the extremes. Those commentators also maintain that, according to the Madhyamaka standpoint, even an inference proving the meaning of the thesis is not accepted, and refutation of all the extreme views of existence or nonexistence is effected through consequential reasoning that merely reveals their internal contradictions. [349] Therefore they claim that in this tradition there is no proof statement or reasoning posited to prove any thesis.

This analysis of whether the Mādhyamika have their own position or assertions is discussed in Bhāviveka's texts too. He presents an opponent's argument in *Blaze of Reasoning* as follows: "Since you do not posit your own position, are you not engaged in refutation only, the mere refutation of others' positions?"[582] In response to this he says: "As for our own position, we speak of things as being empty of essential nature, and this is the nature of all phenomena. So we are not engaged in refutation only but present our own position to be free of faults."[583]

Regarding this point, those who accept that the Mādhyamika have assertions within their own tradition explain it as follows. Among the passages quoted above, the verse from Nāgārjuna's *Fundamental Treatise on the Middle Way* cited in the preceding section says that to hold things to be inherently existent is the view of permanence, and that to accept that things exist inherently but later disintegrate is the view of nihilism; but it does not say that to hold them to be merely existent or merely nonexistent is the view of permanence or nihilism. The above quotation from Nāgārjuna's *Sixty Stanzas of Reasoning* says that since the Mādhyamika do not have any thesis or position that accepts things to be inherently existent, they have no disputes with the positions of others based on an assumption of having accepted that [things exist inherently]—for how can those who have no position that accepts things to exist by virtue of intrinsic characteristics[584] adhere to an opposing position that exists by virtue of intrinsic characteristics? [350] This verse, however, does not indicate that the Mādhyamika do not have any assertions or position in general.

The verse from Nāgārjuna's *Refutation of Objections* quoted above also does not show that the Mādhyamika do not have any assertions in general. It is a response to those realists who challenge them by asking: "If phenomena do not exist inherently, then do your words exist inherently or not? If they do, then you cannot be a nonessentialist. If you claim that your words do not exist inherently, then they would lack the capacity to refute inherent nature." In response to this the Mādhyamika say: "If we had a thesis based on an assumption of inherent existence, then this fault would apply to us. But since we do not have a thesis based on an assumption of inherent existence, we do not have that fault." That is what this verse means, so it should be applied in all such contexts [where it is denied that the Mādhyamika have no thesis or position of their own].

The verse from Āryadeva's *Four Hundred Stanzas* quoted above indicates that it is utterly impossible to posit a counter-response to those who are free from the faults of accepting any of the extreme positions: that things exist inherently, that all functional things do not exist at all, and that things that disintegrate both inherently exist and do not exist. Similarly, the verse from Candrakīrti's *Entering the Middle Way* considers whether refutation occurs by way of the refutation and what is refuted being in contact with each other or not. In the case of those who have a position assuming ultimate inherent existence, this entails a fault. But in the case of the Mādhyamika who accept both the refutation and what is refuted to be not inherently existent, [351] when one searches for the referent of the designation in terms such as whether there is contact between them, those faults do not occur.[585]

Candrakīrti's *Commentary on the Sixty Stanzas of Reasoning* says: "Since dependent arising is deceptive, it is not true. When one realizes it to be untrue, one's attachment to things is reverted."[586] It also goes on to say:

> If one has absolutely no position, then it would be as stated [in the root text]:
>
> > For those who have no position
> > how can there be an opposing position?
>
> Since there are no such real things, there is no position for oneself or others; thus the mental afflictions of those who see it in this way will definitely cease.[587]

When these quotations are put together, it is clear that in his *Sixty Stanzas of Reasoning* Nāgārjuna does not mean that, for the Mādhyamika, their own position and the opponents' position are totally nonexistent. Rather, he means that the Mādhyamika do not have inherently established assertions, or indeed, according to the tradition itself, the two positions are not truly existent.

Likewise, Nāgārjuna's *Refutation of Objections Autocommentary* says: "Moreover, we do not explain, without accepting and depending on conventional truth, [352] that 'all phenomena are empty.' One cannot teach about phenomena without accepting conventional truth."[588] This text continues on to say:

> If I had any thesis, then it would be as you have stated. If I were to accept the characteristics of a thesis it would incur those previously stated faults, so I do not have any thesis at all. Therefore how could I have any thesis regarding all things being empty, completely peaceful, and devoid of inherent nature? How could

> I have [accepted] the characteristics of a thesis? How could I have the faults that arise from the characteristics of a thesis? Here, I do not even state, "You have these faults because you have assumed the characteristics of a thesis."[589]

When we put this together with earlier quotations from the text, it is clear that Nāgārjuna's *Refutation of Objections* does not mean that the Mādhyamika do not have any assertions at all. Rather, these passages explain that the Mādhyamika do not have any inherently established assertions. Candrakīrti's *Clear Words* says:

> Some criticize, saying, "The Mādhyamika are no different from the nihilists." This is not right. The Mādhyamika speak of things as dependent arising; it is because they dependently arise that they say this life, the next life, and so on are all [353] without inherent nature.[590]

Also, this text says:

> And they say, "Even so, because nihilists consider the lack of inherent nature of things to mean nonexistence, they are similar regarding this view." No, they are not similar, because the Mādhyamika accept things to be conventionally existent, whereas nihilists do not accept that.[591]

Here the opponent argues: "For the Mādhyamika to say that things do not exist inherently is no different from the nihilistic view." In response to this criticism, the Madhyamaka proponents say: "The nihilists make such claims, thus they have those faults, but the Mādhyamika do not make such claims; therefore they do not succumb to those faults." If this response is not accepted, they continue: "The nihilists say things are 'nonexistent,' whereas we Mādhyamika do not say things are 'nonexistent' but instead are 'not existent,' therefore we do not succumb to those faults." And if this is not accepted, they continue: "We Mādhyamika say that although things are not inherently existent they are conventionally existent, and it is because they dependently arise that they do not exist inherently. So since we do not accept them to be nonexistent, this is not the same as the nihilistic view." Thus the scriptures clearly explain that the Mādhyamika have assertions according to their own tradition. Moreover, they indicate that to say all phenomena are not conventionally existent—or that they conventionally exist but this does not mean they exist—is no different from the nihilistic view.

Therefore Madhyamaka masters such as Nāgārjuna use many arguments to refute that phenomena are established from their own side. [354] Within their own tradition they accept such things as an effect to arise from its cause, in accordance with common understanding that does not search for the referent of the designation. Nāgārjuna's *Seventy Stanzas on Emptiness* says:

> "This arises in dependence on that"—
> such ways of the world are not refuted.[592]

Moreover, realist systems, whether Buddhist or non-Buddhist, which do not differentiate between *existent* and *inherently existent*, argue as expressed in the following verse from Nāgārjuna's *Fundamental Treatise on the Middle Way*:

> If all these things are empty,
> there can be no arising and no destruction.
> According to you it must follow
> that the four noble truths do not exist.[593]

Here the realists posit the following accusation: "If you Mādhyamika assert that all external and internal things are empty of existing by virtue of inherent nature, then you must accept that things are totally nonexistent, whereby they would have no arising or disintegrating and so on whatsoever." In response to this criticism, Nāgārjuna's *Fundamental Treatise on the Middle Way* says:

> In saying this, you do not understand
> the purpose of emptiness, nor emptiness itself,
> nor the meaning of emptiness.
> Therefore in this way you are thus frustrated.[594]

This response can be restated and explained as follows: "You realists [355] think that *empty of inherent nature* means *nonexistent*. You do not understand the purpose of teaching emptiness, which is to pacify all proliferating tendencies, such as attachment, without exception; nor do you understand the essential nature of emptiness, which has the nature of reversing all proliferating tendencies from a mind directly realizing suchness; nor do you understand that the term *dependent arising* means the *emptiness* of a nature bearing its own identity. Therefore in not being able to posit with ease the arising and disintegrating of compounded things, you are frustrated." This response establishes the fact that within the Madhyamaka system there are assertions of an affirmative position, such as the statement that all external and internal things are conventionally existent, and assertions of a negative position, such as the statement that all these things are empty of inherent existence. The response also demonstrates the need to differentiate between *conventionally existent* and *inherently existent* and between *nonexistent* and *not inherently existent*.

Nāgārjuna's *Fundamental Treatise on the Middle Way* says:

> If you view that all things
> exist from the side of their own nature,
> then you are viewing that things
> do not have any causes and conditions.[595]

If a pot, for example, were inherently existent, then it must follow that it would not have any causes and conditions, such as clay or a potter, or it would exist eternally or would never exist at all. If someone asserts it never exists at all, then the reasoning that there would be no agent or potter that makes the pot and so on [356] proves that the Prāsaṅgika Madhyamaka system has assertions that phenomena do not exist inherently and assertions that they are not utterly nonexistent but exist merely conventionally.

Further to this point, one may ask whether the Mādhyamika accept valid cognition or not? If they do accept valid cognition, then they must posit a knowable object that is the realized object of that valid cognition—thus it follows that they have assertions. If they do not accept valid cognition, then due to the lack of any determinate cognition that refutes the opponents' position and proves their own position, the Mādhyamika would not have any refutation of the opponents' position at all.

If someone says, "Although the Mādhyamika have no assertions of their own they refute others' assertions by way of revealing their internal contradictions, at which time, in dependence on realizing the incorrectness of the others' position, they dispel all wrong views; beyond this they have no other purpose at all," this too is incorrect. For if this were true then the Mādhyamika would be engaging in the mere refutation of other's positions, without having any positions of their own or accepting those of others, which means they would be engaging in refutation only.[596] As Candrakīrti's *Entering the Middle Way* says:

> Since you do not have any position of your own, it is also refutation only.[597]

This line presents an opponent's criticism: "If an argument engages merely in refuting another's position without positing one's own position, it is said to be 'refutation only.' Therefore in your case, Mādhyamika, your refutation would also be refutation only." The response that they do not incur this fault is explained at length and should be understood accordingly. [In his root text and commentary, Candrakīrti states why the Mādhyamika are not faulted: it is because things do not inherently exist, not because they "have no assertions" as some earlier Mādhyamika claim, for that is not an effective reason.] [357]

Moreover, just as some Buddhist schools accept all phenomena to be inherently existent out of fear that being not inherently existent is to be totally nonexistent, if the Mādhyamika too did not accept dependent arising to be devoid of inherent arising, then they would have to admit that dependent arising is inherently existent. This is because the two—inherently existent and not inherently existent—are directly contradictory, in the sense of being mutually excluding, since there is nothing that is neither of those two. [In other words, there is nothing that has both properties, and there is nothing that lacks both properties.] This is stated in Nāgārjuna's *Refutation of Objections*:

> If it negates *not inherently existent*,
> then it proves *inherently existent*.[598]

Also, according to the Madhyamaka tradition, although words do not inherently exist, they function to refute inherent existence. For example, this is similar to how one illusory person can prevent another illusory person's activity of coming or going. Nāgārjuna's *Refutation of Objections Autocommentary* says:

> It is like how, for whatever purpose, one emanated person hinders another emanated person from going forward; or, for whatever purpose, one illusory person conjured up by a magician hinders another illusory person from going forward. Here the emanated person that is hindered is empty and the activity of hindering is empty; or the illusory person that is hindered is empty and the activity of hindering is also empty. Likewise, it is correct for my words [358] that are empty to negate the inherent nature of all things, in that all things are merely empty. Thus it is not correct to say, "Since your words are merely empty, they cannot refute the inherent nature of all things."[599]

Similarly, if the Mādhyamika have no assertions, then the thesis that there is no arising from the four alternatives—as when *Fundamental Treatise on the Middle Way* says, "Not from self, not from others,"[600] and so on—would not be a thesis of the Mādhyamika and thus would not be a thesis of any proponent of Buddhist philosophy.

Some might assert that although the Mādhyamika have a negative thesis refuting inherent existence, they do not have an affirmative thesis proving the conventional existence of dependently related cause and effect. If it is indeed the case that the Mādhyamika do not have an affirmative thesis, then one would have to accept that the Mādhyamika do not have the thesis that effects arisen from causes exist. If so, then presentations of dependently related cause and effect would not be posited in the Madhyamaka tradition. In that case, one would have to accept that there are proponents of Buddhist philosophy who deny cause and effect.

In view of the above, the Mādhyamika do have both the theses of the *negating position that excludes* and the theses of the *affirming position that includes*. As an example of the first, consider the thesis that there is no arising from the four alternatives. Candrakīrti's *Clear Words* says: [359]

"Therefore these [terms] must be applied in this way: 'Any things, anywhere, do not arise at any time from self.' They must also be applied similarly to the other three theses."[601] As an example of the second, consider the thesis that things are merely conventionally existent—whether they are veridical in terms of worldly understanding, such as a pot, a pillar, a mountain, a house, and so on, or distorted in terms of worldly understanding, such as an illusion, an echo, the reflection of a face in a mirror, and so on. *Buddhapālita's Commentary on the Fundamental Treatise* says:

> Accordingly, the Tathāgata said, "What is accepted in the world to exist, I too agree that it exists; and what is accepted in the world to be nonexistent, I too agree that it does not exist."[602] Therefore, since it involves the operation of worldly convention, we can say, "What is accepted in the world to be veridical, the Tathāgata too considers to be veridical." Also, "What is accepted in the world to be nonveridical, the Tathāgata too considers to be nonveridical."[603]

Moreover, three kinds of theses are presented: a thesis for the other party only, a thesis shared by both one's own side and the other side, and a thesis that is unique to one's own tradition. Regarding the first, a thesis for the other party only, Candrakīrti's *Entering the Middle Way* says:

> Yet for the sake of the result, although nonexistent, I say "they
> exist." [360]
> From the worldly point of view, I speak of a self.[604]

For the purpose of realizing the emptiness of inherent existence that dispels the grasping at inherent existence, even though these things that are dependent natures do not exist inherently, from the perspective of worldly convention we say that "things exist inherently," so this is a provisional thesis.

Regarding the second, a thesis shared by both one's own side and the other side, Nāgārjuna's *Refutation of Objections* says:

> We do not explain anything
> without accepting conventional things.[605]

Our own and other traditions accept in common the conventions that something round bellied and flat bottomed that has the ability to hold water is called a *pot* and that something having the ability to support a beam is called a *pillar*, so these are shared theses.

Regarding the third, a thesis that is unique to one's own tradition, Candrakīrti's *Entering the Middle Way* says:

> Those who are wise have fully ascertained that
> this profound Dharma is not found in other [treatises]
> apart from this one [of Nāgārjuna], and likewise
> the tradition it gives rise to is not found elsewhere.[606] [361]

This profound emptiness is not taught correctly in other traditions or in other treatises apart from the *Fundamental Treatise on the Middle Way*, and this unique tradition of Madhyamaka that explains it with arguments and answers does not exist in non-Madhyamaka treatises, so this is a unique thesis.

18

The Svātantrika-Prāsaṅgika Distinction

Two Madhyamaka Interpretations of Nāgārjuna's Treatises

In his commentary on Nāgārjuna's *Fundamental Treatise on the Middle Way*, Buddhapālita uses consequential reasoning to refute each limb of arising from the four alternatives, and to explain Nāgārjuna's intent, he uses consequences as examples. Bhāviveka argues against Buddhapālita's use of consequences to refute arising from the four alternatives and so forth. Candrakīrti subsequently proves that Bhāviveka's criticisms of Buddhapālita do not apply to him and thereby refutes Bhāviveka's original explanations. Thus there arose, based on the differing explanations of Nāgārjuna's *Fundamental Treatise* proposed by Bhāviveka and other nonrealist masters, two great exegetical traditions of Madhyamaka commentary on Nāgārjuna's thought: the tradition of Bhāviveka and his followers and the tradition of Candrakīrti. Later masters came to call them the Svātantrika Madhyamaka system and Prāsaṅgika Madhyamaka system, respectively. This topic has already been discussed briefly in the presentation of Madhyamaka tenets in volume 3 of *Science and Philosophy in the Indian Buddhist Classics*. [362]

To illustrate how Bhāviveka criticizes Buddhapālita and how Candrakīrti later disproves that criticism, which together constitute the origin of the two Madhyamaka interpretations, let us begin with Bhāviveka's *Lamp of Wisdom*, which says:

> The other party [Buddhapālita] proposes, "Things do not arise from self in its own nature because their arising would be utterly purposeless and their arising would be endless." This is illogical because the inferential reasoning and the example are not stated,

> and because the fallacies in the opponents' statements are not dispelled.[607]

This states that Buddhapālita posits a consequential argument to refute the arising from self, which is taken to be the proponent's position. However, since a correct inferential reason able to prove that there is no arising from self, along with an example, are not stated, it presents only the thesis. Also, if the meaning of the Sāṅkhya statement "from self" were to be *from a self that is a manifest effect*, then that would prove what is already established; and if it were *from a self that is a potential unmanifest cause*, then everything endowed with arising would arise only from that, which is said to be a "contradictory pervasion." The [opponent's] criticisms must be dispelled by examining their theses, but [Buddhapālita] does not dispel them. In this way [Bhāviveka] posits several refutations. To present his own system, Bhāviveka's *Lamp of Wisdom* says: "Concerning this, the purpose of the chapter here is to provide answers to the refutations stated by the opponent and, by means of demonstrating faultless autonomous inferences, [363] to teach that conditioned things lack essential nature."[608] In response to the realists who try to prove that things are truly established, Bhāviveka explains that the chapters of Nāgārjuna's *Fundamental Treatise on the Middle Way* teach, by demonstrating with autonomous inferences, that causally compounded things do not have a truly established nature. This illustrates that not only does Bhāviveka accept autonomous inferences when explaining the meaning of *Fundamental Treatise on the Middle Way* but he also claims it is the intent of Nāgārjuna and his spiritual heirs to accept autonomous inferences.

In response to the above, Candrakīrti's *Clear Words* says: "We see that these criticisms are incorrect."[609] He proves that each of the criticisms Bhāviveka puts forward to Buddhapālita in turn do not apply. In *Clear Words*, many reasons are used to refute at length Bhāviveka's acceptance of autonomous inferences where the three modes are established from their own side. To understand this comprehensively one should study that text; here we will just briefly touch on an illustration of how Candrakīrti refutes autonomous inferences.

In this Prāsaṅgika tradition, since not even the tiniest particle is accepted to be established by virtue of intrinsic characteristics, there is no presentation of inferences where the three modes are established from their own side; and when some proponents of the Madhyamaka view accept autonomous inferences it is declared to be completely unsuitable. [364] Candrakīrti's *Clear Words* says: "If you are a Mādhyamika it is not correct to use autonomous inferences, because we do not accept others' positions."[610] Again, the same text says: "To express an autonomous syllogism after having accepted the Madhyamaka view is known to be grounds for accumulating many great faults."[611]

The definition of an *autonomous reason* or *evidence* is posited to be: that in which the basis of debate and the example, the positive and the negative pervasions of the evidence-predicate relationship, and the evidence being an attribute of the subject are, in the final analysis, qualified by the three modes established from their own side and not merely posited through the force of the opponent's thought. In brief, if there were evidence qualified by the three modes established from their own side and not merely posited through the force of convention, then it would be called "autonomous evidence." Here, *established from its own side*, *autonomous* (Skt. *svatantra*), *independent*, and *established by its intrinsic characteristics* come down to the same point—namely, the object to be negated.

As mentioned briefly above, in *Buddhapālita's Commentary on the Fundamental Treatise*, Buddhapālita states various reasonings to refute the Sāṅkhya assertion of arising from self. Bhāviveka claims that the reasonings Buddhapālita presents contain many fallacies and thus cannot by themselves refute arising from self. According to Bhāviveka's own tradition, [365] arising from self must be refuted by way of positing autonomous inferences, such as the following: "The *subject*, internal sense bases such as the eye faculty, do not arise from self ultimately, because they exist—for example, just as consciousness exists."[612] Candrakīrti outlines many faults in positing autonomous inferences to refute arising from self, for he says in *Clear Words*: "Moreover, this logician [Bhāviveka] wishes to demonstrate only his own consummate mastery in the science of debate."[613] Candrakīrti then poses some questions and answers in order to refute Bhāviveka's position, which can be summarized as follows. "When you prove that the eye faculty and so on do not arise from themselves, you apply the qualification 'ultimately.' So must it be applied to the predicate of the thesis? Or must it be applied to the subject sought to be known? If you say it must be applied to the predicate of the thesis, this is not correct. From the Madhyamaka point of view the qualification 'ultimately' does not need to be applied here because, according to the Madhyamaka tradition, it is not accepted even conventionally that the eye faculty and so on arise from themselves. Therefore, according to Madhyamaka, when refuting the arising from self, there is no need to apply the qualification 'ultimately.' When a sprout arises, it does not arise from any of the alternatives—self, other, or both. However, in a general sense, owing to the existence of the seed that is its cause, the resultant sprout exists. Moreover, the causal seed itself is not the same entity as its resultant sprout, and the resultant sprout itself is not inherently different from its causal seed, nor is that identical with the sprout. Since the causal seed itself is not the same entity as its resultant sprout, the seed and the sprout are not permanent. Also, since the causal seed itself is not inherently different from its resultant sprout [366] nor identical with that sprout, those two are not annihilated. That they have such a nature is taught in the [*Great Play*] sūtra. Also, since Nāgārjuna's *Fundamental Treatise on the Middle Way* teaches that the result is not the same entity as its cause and it is not ultimately different from it, likewise it teaches that both cause and effect are neither permanent nor annihilated." In his *Clear Words*, Candrakīrti refutes Bhāviveka's position as follows:

> This is not correct because arising from self is not accepted even conventionally. It is stated in the [*Rice Seedling*] sūtra:
>
> > When this sprout is generated from the seed that is its cause, it is not produced by itself; it is not produced by another; it is not produced by both; it is not produced by Īśvara; it does not proceed from time; it does not arise from subtle particles; it does not arise from primal nature; it does not arise from essential nature; and it is not produced without a cause.
>
> Also, similarly [it says in the *Great Play Sūtra*]:
>
> > When a sprout proceeds from an existent seed,
> > that which is the seed is not the entity of the sprout;
> > it is not different from it; and it is not identical with it.
> > Thus in nature it is not eternal and not annihilated.
>
> And the [*Fundamental Treatise*] root text says:

> Whatever arises in dependence on something
> is neither identical to it
> nor different from it,
> so it is not annihilated and not eternal. (18.10)

Thus it has been explained.[614]

Moreover, there is no need to apply the qualification "ultimate" in relation to the non-Buddhist opponent's position. For when refuting that the eye faculty and the rest arise from themselves, this must be refuted in terms of both truths since their non-Buddhist tradition deviates from an undistorted seeing of the two truths. [367] Thus it is not correct to apply the qualification of either of the two truths in response to the non-Buddhist opponent's treatises, so this suggestion is rejected. Candrakīrti's *Clear Words* says:

> Is a qualification made in relation to the opponent's doctrine? No, that is not appropriate, because their presentations are not accepted even conventionally. Insofar as non-Buddhists deviate from an undistorted seeing of the two truths, it is refuted in terms of both, and that is understood to be a good quality. Thus it is not correct to posit a qualification in relation to the opponent's doctrine.[615]

Suppose someone says, "The qualification 'ultimately' must be applied in relation to mundane convention." This too is inappropriate because there is no arising from self according to mundane convention. Ordinary people, when analyzing whether a sprout arises from a seed, for example, do not analyze whether it arises from self or from other; they merely apprehend that from a seed as the cause there arises a sprout as its result. So this suggestion is rejected. Candrakīrti's *Clear Words* says:

> As for whether in relation to that [mundane view] the qualification would be effective, ordinary people do not know about arising from self because ordinary people, without having entered into an investigation such as to whether it is from self or other, understand simply that an effect arises from its cause.[616] [368]

If the qualification is introduced with the intent to refute the arising of an *ultimate* eye faculty then there would be the fault that the subject is unestablished.[617] If it is said to be employed so that the ultimate arising of a *conventional* eye faculty could be refuted, then this too is incorrect because you do not state it as applied in that way;[618] and if you do state it then there would be the fault that the subject is not established for the opponent.[619] Thus Candrakīrti's *Clear Words* says:

> If this qualification is posited [by Bhāviveka] out of a wish to refute [an ultimate sense faculty] arising conventionally, then there would be the fault that the subject is unestablished or the reason is unestablished for oneself [as a Mādhyamika]; therefore we do not accept the eye faculty and so on in an ultimate sense.[620]

Furthermore, Candrakīrti refutes the need for applying the qualifier "ultimately" to the predicate of the thesis and so on—even according to Bhāviveka's own perspective—on the basis of examining the examples Bhāviveka cites. Bhāviveka says that in a proof, such as "Sound is impermanent because it is produced," a phenomenon in a merely general sense must be held as the predicate of the thesis and as the subject sought to be known, without being qualified in any way, such as "arisen from the elements" or "a quality of space," "produced" or "made manifest through previously existing conditions," "perishes having some other cause" or "perishes without having some other cause," and so on. [369] For if the predicate of the thesis and so on were held to be qualified as either "arisen from the elements" or "a quality of space" and so forth, then the inferential evidence and the predicate of the thesis to be inferred would not exist even conventionally. In such a case, when Buddhists prove to the non-Buddhist Vaiśeṣika that sound is impermanent, if the subject is held to be "sound arisen from the elements," then it would not be established for the Vaiśeṣika opponent; and if held to be "sound as a quality of space," then it would not be established for the Buddhists themselves. Similarly, if the Vaiśeṣika put to the Sāṅkhyas the thesis that "Sound is impermanent" or the thesis that "Produced sound is impermanent," then it would not be established for the Sāṅkhya opponent;[621] and if it were the thesis that "Sound made manifest through previously existing conditions is impermanent," then it would not be established for the Vaiśeṣika themselves. Likewise, among Buddhist philosophers, if the Sautrāntika put to the Vaibhāṣika the thesis that "It perishes having a cause" or the thesis that "It perishes having some other cause," then this would not be established for the Sautrāntika themselves; and if it were the thesis that "It perishes without having some other cause," then this would not be established for the Vaibhāṣika opponent. Therefore, in the context of proving that sound is impermanent, for example, it is sufficient for a phenomenon to be held in a merely general sense as the predicate of the thesis and as the subject sought to be known without being qualified in any way, such as either *arisen from the elements* or *a quality of space*, and so on. Similarly, in this context, it is sufficient for the eye faculty and so on to be held in a merely general sense as the subject without applying a qualification as either *ultimate* or *conventional*. Candrakīrti says, "Your earlier criticisms, [Bhāviveka], such as that the qualification 'ultimate,' do not need to be applied in relation to the Mādhyamika themselves, [370] and do not apply to me," thereby dispelling these criticisms. His *Clear Words* says:

> Just as how it is with the statement "Sound is impermanent," both the subject and the predicate are held in a general sense, not as qualified in a particular way. If they were held as qualified, there would be no accepted convention regarding the thing to be proved and the reason proving it. For if "sound that is arisen from the four great elements" is held to be the subject, then it is not established according to the [Mīmāṃsā] opponent.[622] But if "sound as a quality of space" is held to be the subject, then it is not established according to us Buddhists. Similarly, for the Vaiśeṣika, if "produced sound" is held to be the subject of the thesis "Sound is impermanent," it is not established according to their [Mīmāṃsā] opponents; but if "[sound] to be manifested" is held to be the subject, then it is not established according to [Vaiśeṣika] themselves. Likewise, in each respective case, if "perishes having another cause" is used, then it is not established according to us Buddhists; but if "perishes not having another cause" is used, then it is not established according to the [Mīmāṃsā] opponent. Therefore, just as previously the subject and attribute apprehended are merely general, so here a mere subject without a qualifier is to be apprehended.[623]

In the above manner, Bhāviveka's possible response to the objection is anticipated. On this view, Bhāviveka might assert that it is sufficient for the eye faculty and so on to be taken as the subject in a merely general sense without applying a qualification as either conventional or ultimate, even in the context of refuting arising from self. For, just as in the proof that sound is impermanent, it is sufficient for a phenomenon to be held in a merely general sense as the predicate of the thesis and as the subject sought to be known without being qualified in any way, such as either "arisen from the elements" or "a quality of space," and so on. [371] In response, Candrakīrti says that Bhāviveka's answer does not address the point. Consider the example "The *subject*, the eye faculty, does not arise from self ultimately, because it exists." In this refutation of arising from self, the predicate of the thesis of this argument, "does not arise from self ultimately," is accepted. Therefore the subject on which the predicate of the thesis is based—an internal sense base such as "the eye faculty," which is an entity found by a mere conventional consciousness—is accepted by Bhāviveka himself as not established ultimately or in reality. If he accepts this, then a sense base such as the eye faculty, although not an ultimate object, cannot possibly be an object of consciousness that is *unmistaken* with regard to the appearance of intrinsic character; in that case it would be an object of consciousness that is *mistaken* with regard to the appearance of intrinsic character. The two—distorted consciousness that is mistaken regarding the appearance of intrinsic character and undistorted consciousness that is unmistaken regarding the appearance of intrinsic character—are different minds that apprehend different objects, where the objects found by each are contradictory in the sense of being mutually excluding. For example, just as a sense consciousness with a diseased eye faculty has an appearance of falling hairs, likewise a consciousness that is mistaken with regard to the appearance of intrinsic character has an appearance of inherent existence even though there is no inherent existence; therefore that mistaken consciousness does not have even the slightest appearance of a noninherently existent true object that exists as it is in reality. And just as a sense consciousness without a diseased eye faculty does not have an appearance of falling hairs, likewise a consciousness that is unmistaken with regard to the appearance of intrinsic character [372] does not have an appearance of inherent existence, given that there is no inherent existence or false superimposition of that kind. Therefore how can that unmistaken consciousness have even the slightest appearance of a conventional nature, such as noninherently existent forms, sounds, and so on? It cannot.

Nāgārjuna too says, to summarize his position: "If an inherently established phenomenon were realized by one of the four types of valid cognition—valid direct perception, valid inferential cognition, valid comparative analogy, or valid testimony—then it would have to be proved to me that it is inherently established, or else I would have to refute the inherently established thing. But since the realization of something inherently established by means of the four types of valid cognition does not exist at any time, there is no need for the inherently established thing to be proved to me, and also no need for me to refute that thing. Also your valid direct perception and so on realizing inherently existent things would be nonexistent and the inherent things realized by them would be nonexistent." Nāgārjuna's *Refutation of Objections* explains that when these answers are investigated with skill, they do not fall back on him.

To take this point further, an argument typically sourced from Candrakīrti's position against Bhāviveka's standpoint proceeds as follows. "The distorted mistaken consciousness and undistorted unmistaken consciousness are very different in that the objects found by each are contradictory in the sense of being mutually excluding. Thus, since the object found by an undistorted unmistaken consciousness is not an object found by a distorted mistaken consciousness, the subject—a conventional thing such as the eye faculty—does not exist as an object found by a consciousness unmistaken regarding the appearance of intrinsic character. Therefore there is just no way of avoiding either the fallacy that the subject of the argument is nonexistent due to [373] lacking an essential nature or the fallacy that the reason is nonexistent due to the evidence not being based on a commonly accepted subject sought to be known. Thus given that in your own system, you accept that inherent existence exists conventionally and say that the subject of an autonomous syllogism and so on exists, your response that your argument contains a faultless subject and a faultless reason cannot in any way accord with reality."

Given the above, the example cited by Bhāviveka too remains inappropriate. When Buddhists prove to the Vaiśeṣika that sound is impermanent, it is sufficient for both parties—the Buddhist proponents and the Vaiśeṣika opponents—for a general notion of *sound* to be posited as the subject, without it being qualified in any way as arisen from the elements or as a quality of space. However in the case of a general notion of phenomena such as the eye faculty unqualified in any way as true or as false, neither Candrakīrti, who asserts the emptiness of inherent existence, nor Bhāviveka, who asserts the nonemptiness of inherent existence, accept that there can be anything that is neither of those two. Candrakīrti's refutation of Bhāviveka's rebuttal of the criticism is expressed as follows in *Clear Words*:

> That is not so. For in accepting the negation of arising as the predicate of the thesis, he accepts that the subject that is its basis—which is something found only by mistaken [consciousness]—is denied ultimately. Mistaken and unmistaken [minds] are very different. Therefore, as in the case of one with diseased eyes [seeing] falling hairs, [374] when the mistaken holds the nonexistent to exist, how can there be the slightest perception of an object that exists? But, as in the case of one without diseased eyes [not seeing] falling hairs, when the unmistaken does not reify the unreal, how can there be the slightest perception of an object that does not exist—[ordinarily perceived] by a conventional [mind]? For the master Nāgārjuna says:
>
> > If anything, owing to its nature, were known
> > by direct perception and so on,
> > then that would be proved or refuted.
> > But that does not exist; thus I am without fault.
>
> Because mistaken and unmistaken [minds] are very different with regard to that [appearance], the mistaken does not exist during the occurrence of the unmistaken—so how could any [such inference] have a conventional eye as the subject? For this reason, neither the fallacy of the non-establishment of the subject nor the fallacy of the non-establishment of the reason is avoided, so this is not an answer. Moreover, your example does not match [our situation]. Here what is established for both parties is "sound" in general and "impermanent" in general, without any qualification applied. But in our case neither the proponents of noninherent existence nor the proponents of inherent existence accept an eye in general either conventionally or ultimately. So your example does not match [our situation].[624]

To make this easier to understand, let us now summarize the above passage refuting Bhāviveka's rebuttal of the criticism. Candrakīrti's argument can be presented as follows.[625] In the proof that a visual form and so on does not arise from itself [375] and does not ultimately exist, if it were able to be found by an undistorted consciousness that is unmistaken with regard to intrinsic character, then in being the object of undistorted consciousness that is unmistaken with regard to intrinsic character, it must be ultimate.[626] In that case, a visual form qualified as true would be held as the subject [of the inference]. Thus it is not correct for you [Bhāviveka] to say that a general notion of form that is not qualified in any way as true or false is to be taken as the subject. Also, if it is the object of a consciousness unmistaken regarding undistorted nature, then it must be a true and undistorted object. An object that is false and distorted and one that is true and undistorted are directly contradictory in the sense of being mutually excluding. Visual forms and so on, which do not exist as they appear, are not true but false. So it is not correct to claim that they are established by a consciousness that is unmistaken with regard to intrinsic character. Therefore the valid cognition that establishes the subject, such as a visual form, is not correctly said to be a consciousness that is unmistaken with regard to its object's intrinsic character. The subject, a conventional visual form, established by a consciousness unmistaken with regard to intrinsic character does not exist at all. So your suggestion that a mere eye faculty or visual form, unqualified in terms of the two truths, is to be held as the subject is not appropriate. Also, this does not match your example of the Buddhists proving to the Vaiśeṣika that sound is impermanent, where sound, unqualified as arisen from the elements or as a quality of space, is taken as the subject. Thus Bhāviveka's position is refuted.

Bhāviveka and his followers say that although the subject, such as a visual form, is established by a visual consciousness that is unmistaken with regard to intrinsic character, there is no need to establish form that is qualified as either of the two truths merely on account of this. [376] When one takes form or the like as the basis of qualification and analyzes whether it exists ultimately, the subject is taken in a merely general sense without qualifying it as either of the two truths. They think this will avoid illogical fallacies.

According to the tradition of Candrakīrti and his followers, the notion that form *exists from its own side*, *exists by virtue of its intrinsic characteristics*, or *exists truly* comes down to the same thing. If form *were* to exist from its own side, then when one validly cognizes a form to exist, one would necessarily validly cognize a form to exist from its own side, to exist by virtue of its intrinsic characteristics, and to exist ultimately. In that case the subject, form, would have to exist by virtue of its intrinsic characteristics. Therefore, since there is no means of apprehending a form as the subject without it being qualified as either true or false, apprehending it as the subject in a general sense without it being qualified as true or false is refuted.[627]

The Prāsaṅgika tradition does not accept autonomous inferences because there is no agreed-upon method for establishing an object of knowledge as something that appears in common according to both the Prāsaṅgika proponents and the Svātantrika opponents. However, in a general sense, the Prāsaṅgika accept inferential cognition arisen in dependence on a reason qualified by the three modes. So one must differentiate between a type of reasoning that is accepted and a type of reasoning that is not accepted. A reason where the three modes are not established from their own side but merely accepted is an *inference acceptable for oneself* or an *inference acceptable for others*. In the context of positing an inference on the basis of an opponent's assertions, from the perspective of the opponent, since it is acceptable for himself [377] it is called an *inference acceptable for oneself*; but from the perspective of the Prāsaṅgika proponent, since it is acceptable for the opponent it is called an *inference acceptable for others*. Candrakīrti's *Clear Words* says: "For this very reason, to state the definitions pertaining to logic is pointless because the buddhas help disciples who do not understand reality by using what those individuals accept themselves."[628]

Some Tibetan commentators on Madhyamaka say that there is no difference between the Svātantrika Madhyamaka and the Prāsaṅgika Madhyamaka in terms of subtlety of the view [of emptiness].[629] They say that the difference between the two Madhyamaka systems concerns the method for determining suchness—namely, whether the thesis is proved on the basis of an autonomous inference or whether one demonstrates an internal contradiction within the opponents' system mainly through the use of consequential reasoning, without using autonomous inferences. Conversely, those masters who say that there is a difference between Svātantrika and Prāsaṅgika in terms of subtlety of the view generally base their thought on the following consideration. In terms of whether they accept autonomous inferences, the difference between these two traditions that follow Nāgārjuna clearly relates to whether they accept existence by virtue of intrinsic characteristics on the conventional level. Bhāviveka's texts, directly or indirectly, explain that what exists by virtue of intrinsic characteristics must exist conventionally. For example, [378] *Lamp of Wisdom* says:

> To say the imputed nature that is the mental and verbal expression "form" does not have any essential nature is to deny real things, because it denies mental expressions and verbal expressions.[630]

Here Bhāviveka is arguing that when Cittamātra say that the imputed nature does not have an intrinsically characterized essential nature, this entails the denial of the dependent nature; so clearly he is indicating that the imputed nature has an intrinsically characterized essential nature. Similarly in *Blaze of Reasoning*, when responding to the realists—who argue that if entities that are elements, such as earth, are asserted not to have any essential nature, such as solidity, wetness, and so on, then this would contradict both direct perception as well as common acceptance—Bhāviveka replies that because he accepts these not to have existence on the ultimate level, it does not contradict direct perception and common acceptance. This response indicates that Bhāviveka does accept that although earth, water, and so on do not exist ultimately, they are established by virtue of their own nature conventionally.

Moreover, this master explains the statement in the [*Rice Seedling*] sūtra that dependent natures do not arise [from any of the four alternatives] to mean that they do not arise *ultimately*. Thus for him, inherent arising is equivalent to arising by virtue of intrinsic characteristics, so when internal and external things are negated to exist by virtue of intrinsic characteristics he considers that the qualification "ultimately" must be applied. So this master admits that if things do not possess arising by virtue of intrinsic characteristics conventionally, [379] then they cannot be posited to be established by valid cognition in general.

Likewise, he says that the subtle particles that compose physical things are substantially existent, for *Blaze of Reasoning* states:

> If you argue that an aggregation of subtle particles of similar type after having gathered together [are not a cause of sense consciousness], positing as the reason "because they do not

> exist substantially," then such a reason would not be established. Why? This is because subtle particles of similar type assist one another in collecting together, and having formed parts of a coarse object, give rise to a mind that has the collection of subtle particles appearing to it. We accept things like pots, which are [formed] from an aggregation of subtle particles of similar type, to be conventional substances like the subtle particles. This is because even [aggregated] subtle particles are in the nature of a collection of the eight substances, and just as these are accepted to be substances, so the things that are collections of them, such as pots, are also substances.[631]

Moreover, Bhāviveka seems to say that what exists by virtue of intrinsic characteristics appears to a directly perceiving cognition and exists as it appears. *Blaze of Reasoning* states: "Since it is free of thought and of conceptual recollection, a directly perceiving consciousness sees a thing's intrinsic characteristics only."[632] In saying that a thing's intrinsic characteristics appear to direct perception, he accepts valid direct perception to be an unmistaken consciousness, as taught in Dignāga's *Compendium of Valid Cognition*, and that it is established by virtue of intrinsic characteristics conventionally. In the above presentation of the person[633] it was explained that Bhāviveka, when searching for the referent of the designation, posits the mental consciousness to be the person and says that it is established by virtue of intrinsic characteristics, or in other words, it exists from its own side.

Jñānagarbha too says the following in his *Distinguishing the Two Truths Autocommentary*:

> Because that which is a mere thing can function just as it appears, [380] that which arises in dependence on causes and conditions is known as "veridical conventional truth." Thus, in conformity with ordinary beings' cognition, manifold things that appear from causes are accepted to be veridical conventionality, because a thing exists in conformity with how it appears to consciousness. Ultimate arising, or such like, does not appear, for its acceptability as it appears is only imputed in dependence on philosophical tenets.[634]

In other words, things exist as they appear to direct perception and are able to function as they appear, but the object of negation, true existence, does not appear to a sense consciousness. Since he explains that things are not functional merely through the force of being posited by cognition but are able to function from their own side objectively, it is clear that this author accepts intrinsic characteristics conventionally.

Not only that, but also Śāntarakṣita and his spiritual heir Kamalaśīla, in *Compendium of Reality* and *Illumination of the Middle Way*, explain the Madhyamaka and the Cittamātra systems to be in agreement when presenting most of the reasonings of Dharmakīrti's seven treatises on valid cognition according to their own tradition, indicating that they too accept intrinsic characteristics conventionally.

According to the standpoint that considers there to be a difference between Svātantrika and Prāsaṅgika with respect to the view of emptiness, it is maintained that these two systems differ also with regard to the type of cognitions that establish phenomena. The Svātantrika consider the cognitions that establish phenomena to be faultless cognitions that are unmistaken with regard to the intrinsic characteristics of the appearing object or of the conceived object.[635] [381] The Prāsaṅgika do not accept such cognitions to be faultless, and furthermore they maintain that, even though they are mistaken with regard to the appearance of intrinsic character, they are able to establish their object. So the cognitions that establish phenomena are simply cognitions that impute conventions in general; they do not need to be unmistaken with regard to their appearing object or conceived object existing by virtue of intrinsic characteristics. Thus, although the Prāsaṅgika do not accept everything posited by convention-imputing cognition to be conventionally existent, they do not accept anything to be conventionally existent that is not posited by convention-imputing cognition.[636] Conversely, the Svātantrika consider that visual forms, sounds, and so on cannot be posited by a convention-imputing cognition, but can be posited to exist conventionally by appearing to a faultless sense consciousness and so on.[637]

In view of the above, when it comes to the reasoning analyzing suchness, the two Madhyamaka systems have different criteria for ultimate analysis. The Prāsaṅgika posit *ultimate analysis* to be a search for the referent of the designation, such as a "sprout," by searching for whether it arises from itself, from others, and so on—unsatisfied with it being a mere imputation. This is completely different from an analysis of mundane conventionalities, such as where something comes from, where it goes to, and what internal and external phenomena exist. The Svātantrika do not posit ultimate analysis in this way. Instead they posit *ultimate analysis* to be an analysis of whether the object is established by way of its own mode of existence without being posited by way of appearing to a faultless cognition. This also relates to the point that they identify the object of negation differently.

According to Svātantrika, there is no establishment from the side of the object without being posited by way of appearing to cognition, [382] yet there is establishment from the side of the object in general—and these are not considered to be contradictory. According to Prāsaṅgika, not only is there no establishment from the side of the object without being posited by way of appearing to cognition, but also there is no establishment from the side of the object in general. So there is a significant difference between the degrees of subtlety of the object of negation in the views of the two Madhyamaka systems, Svātantrika and Prāsaṅgika. Therefore, on the point of what is being rejected by the word "mere" in the statements found in the sūtras that phenomena are names, labels, and mere imputations, this too is interpreted differently by these two traditions. Svātantrika says that these words deny phenomena to be established from the side of their own unique mode of existence without being posited by way of appearing to a faultless cognition, whereas Prāsaṅgika, as noted earlier, says that these words deny them to be established from their own side (i.e., inherently).

Someone might argue, "If the object is not established from its own side apart from being merely posited by way of a convention-imputing cognition, then since in the same manner a cairn [a pile of stones that resembles a human at a distance] and an actual person would not be established as a person from their own side, those two could not be differentiated as to whether or not they are a person." Although both a cairn and an actual person are alike in being merely imputed by a conceptual cognition when the thought arises "that is a person," and are alike in not being established as a person from the side of the object that is the basis of imputation, they are different in terms of whether they are established as a person as follows. That the cairn is a person is refuted by conventional valid cognition and by popular agreement of others who say, "That is not a person." An actual person is not refuted to be a person by conventional valid cognition and so forth. [383]

19

Emptiness and Dependent Arising

How Emptiness and Dependent Arising Converge on the Same Meaning

NĀGĀRJUNA and his spiritual heirs delineate what it means to be empty of inherent existence on the basis of the presentation of cause and effect, where an effect arises in dependence upon its causes and conditions. They prove with many reasonings that in being empty of inherent existence, the presentations of cause and effect, agent and action, and so forth are feasible, whereas in the absence of that, any such presentations whatsoever would be unfeasible. Accordingly, since the Madhyamaka treatises teach that dependent arising is the meaning of emptiness, the most profound philosophical point of this tradition is the explanation that *empty* and *dependent arising* have the same meaning.

In a general sense, dependent arising is a topic explained by all proponents of Buddhist philosophy. The *Dependent Arising Sūtra* says:

> The Tathāgata proclaimed
> what phenomena are causally arisen,
> what are their causes, and what is their cessation.
> Just this was stated by the great Śramaṇa.[638]

This passage, cited in volume 1 of *Science and Philosophy in the Indian Buddhist Classics*,[639] [384] accords with the fundamental Buddhist teachings that the internal and external worldly environments and their inhabitants are not made by a creator god but arise through the operation of dependently arising cause and effect. However, Madhyamaka masters, who distinguish between coarse and subtle levels of meaning of dependent arising, prove that the final meaning of dependent arising means the absence of inherent existence. They posit *empty* and *dependent arising* to mean the same thing, in that they support one another and entail one another. Thus it is extremely important to understand the meaning of dependent arising. So we will explain its meaning here from the coarse level to the most subtle level, and we will analyze in detail how *empty* and *dependent arising* mean the same thing according to the Madhyamaka tradition.

The Etymology and Meaning of Dependent Arising

The phrase *dependent arising* is a translation of the compound Sanskrit word *pratītyasamutpāda*. The term *pratītya* has at least three meanings: meeting, relying, and dependently relating. Also the term *samutpāda* has at least three meanings: emerging, arising, and existing or established. This is stated in Candrakīrti's *Clear Words* where he writes: "The term *prati* has the meaning of meeting, and the term *iti* [verbal root *i*] has the meaning of going (*gati*). The term *pratītya* ending with the *lyab* suffix (in this context, *ya*) means meeting or relying." Then it says: "The term *pāda* preceded by *samut* has the meaning of emerging, so the term *samutpāda* means arising. Therefore *pratītyasamutpāda* means 'the arising of things in dependence on causes and conditions.'" Later the text goes on to say: "Someone else explains that *dependent* (Skt. *prati*) means meeting (Skt. *prāpti*) and *going* (Skt. [the verbal root] *i*) means relating, so taken together the term *dependently relating* (Skt. *pratītya*) means simply meeting (*phrad pa nyid*)."[640] [385]

The term *dependent* is explained to mean—with regard to things that have causes and conditions—"from causes and conditions," or "from a collection, meeting, or gathering of causes and conditions," or "from this basis of causes and conditions." And with regard to phenomena that do not result from causes, it is explained to mean "established in dependence on their own bases of imputation." Vasubandhu's *Explanation of the First Dependent Origination and Its Divisions* says:

> The term *dependent* indicates "from conditions," just as the expression "Fire arises in dependence on fuel" indicates "from that basis," the expression "Rain falls in dependence on clouds" indicates "from the gathering of clouds," and the expression

> "Medicinal herbs grow in dependence on the snowy mountains" indicates "from that ground."[641]

Additionally, Candrakīrti's *Clear Words* says: "To say, 'Meeting with *short*, depending on *short*, relying on *short*, there comes to be *long*,' is precisely what is accepted."[642]

The term *related* means meeting. So *meeting*—with regard to what is causally dependently related—is posited to be the manifestation of the ceasing of the seed simultaneous with the manifestation of the arising of the sprout, as well as the action of the seed about to cease simultaneous with the action of the sprout about to arise, where the action of arising of the effect and the action of ceasing of the cause are said to *meet*. With regard to what is noncausal, *meeting* is posited to be established through the meeting of something with its own basis of imputation. [386] Guṇamati's *Commentary on Explanation of the First Dependent Origination and Its Divisions* says: "*Relating with that condition* does not stop until the previous condition has disintegrated because the disintegration of the cause and the nature of the effect do not exist at two different times."[643] Also, Candrakīrti's *Clear Words* says: "Because the term *relating* (Skt. the verbal root *i*, which here means *going*) is synonymous with the term *meeting* (Skt. *prāpti*)."[644]

The term *arising* has two interpretations. The first is *to be produced*, which applies to causally compounded phenomena only and this is shared with the realists. The second is *to be established in dependence on such-and-such*, which is the meaning of *arising* that applies to all phenomena and is a unique teaching of the Madhyamaka tradition. Guṇamati's *Commentary on Explanation of the First Dependent Origination and Its Divisions* says: "The term *arising* means to be produced."[645] *Buddhapālita's Commentary on the Fundamental Treatise* says: "The agent is dependent on the object of action, it is based on the object of action, and it is the agent in relation to the object of action."[646] Although this says that the agent arises in dependence upon the object of action, the object of action is not the cause of the agent. When this reasoning is applied to other phenomena, such as a valid knower and the object known or a proof and that which is proved, they are said to arise in mutual dependence, but it is not the case that they are mutual causes.

As for dependent arising that is mutually established dependence, Nāgārjuna's *Fundamental Treatise on the Middle Way* [387] says:

The agent depends on the object of action,
and the object occurs in dependence on the agent.
Apart from this, we do not see
any other way of being established.

Appropriation is to be understood in the same way—
through the reasoning negating agent and object.
By means of [this analysis of] agent and object,
everything else is to be understood.[647]

The agent depends on the action, and the thing acted upon, the object, depends on the agent and the action. These are posited in reliance on each other. The same applies to cause and effect, where this cause is posited in reliance on generating its effect. If its effect did not exist, it could not be called the cause that produced it. And the effect is posited in reliance on having arisen from its cause. For example, fire is posited in reliance on the fuel that is its burned object, which is its product; it is not established in terms of its own autonomous nature. According to this tradition, since they are posited as mutually dependent not only as mere terms but also as objects, not only is the effect posited in reliance on the cause, but also the cause is posited in reliance on the effect. Also, although the cause is posited in reliance on the effect, the effect need not exist at the time of its cause; and since imputation as a cause occurs having considered the process of arising, it is posited in reliance on that. Candrakīrti's *Entering the Middle Way Autocommentary* says: "Not only are the limbs established in mutual dependence but also both cause and effect are mutually dependent."[648]

Furthermore, [388] there are many dependently arisen phenomena established in mutual dependence, such as limb and limb-possessor, quality and quality-possessor, definition and thing defined, valid knower and object known, and so forth. *Buddhapālita's Commentary on the Fundamental Treatise* says:

Just as the agent is imputed in dependence on the object of action while the object of action is imputed in dependence on the agent itself, likewise the effect is imputed in dependence on the cause while the cause is imputed in dependence on the effect itself; a limb-possessor is imputed in dependence on a limb

> while the limb is imputed in dependence on the limb-possessor; fire is imputed in dependence on fuel while fuel is imputed in dependence on fire; a quality-possessor is imputed in dependence on a quality while the quality is imputed in dependence on the quality-possessor; and the defined basis is imputed in dependence on the definition while the definition is imputed in dependence on the defined basis itself. There is no other way at all for them to be established apart from being imputed in relation in this way.[649]

Similarly, Candrakīrti's *Clear Words* says: "One should understand all things without exception to be negated as inherently existent by means of analyzing the agent and the object of action, such as limb and limb-possessor, quality and quality-possessor, valid knower and object known, and so forth, and thus to be established as mutually dependent."[650]

Most followers of the Buddhist Vaibhāṣika, Sautrāntika, and Cittamātra schools [389] consider the meaning of *dependent arising* to be meeting. Here, *meeting* refers to the meeting of the action of arising and ceasing in the case of cause and effect. Having taken *arising* to mean production, they say that *dependent arising* pervades all causally compounded phenomena. Vasubandhu's *Treasury of Knowledge Autocommentary* says: "What are the phenomena that arise through being dependently related? All causal phenomena."[651] And Asaṅga's *Compendium of Abhidharma* says: "Dependent arising is to be understood according to the forward direction and the reverse direction. This includes everything except for one facet: the dharma sphere (Skt. *dharmāyatana*) or the dharma expanse (Skt. *dharmadhātu*)."[652]

Dependent Arising in Terms of Cause and Effect

According to the first level of interpretation, *dependent arising* refers to the dependent arising of cause and effect, which is accepted by all schools of Buddhist philosophy. According to Buddhist tradition, since all compounded things arise depending on the causes and conditions that produce them, they do not arise causelessly. Although they have causes and conditions, the individual entities that are their effects do not exist at the time of their causes and conditions; therefore an effect is not the same entity as its cause. Since something permanent that does not have a cause producing it also cannot give rise to something in the nature of an effect, there is no arising from a permanent cause. Also, cause and effect must be of concordant type, in that all effects do not arise from all causes randomly. Particular effects arise from particular causes and conditions, [390] though it is impossible for one effect alone to arise from one singular cause. In brief, the phrase "this mere conditionality itself" (Skt. *idampratyayatāmātra*) that is found in the presentations of establishment from causes and conditions will now be explained in more detail.

In general, the phrase "this mere conditionality itself" is not a unique appellation of the Mādhyamika. The term *mere* according to general Buddhist theory excludes the presence of another agent (a creator), while according to the unique explanation of the Madhyamaka tradition, it excludes any arising from the four alternatives or any inherently established arising.[653] In general, the terms *itself* and *mere*, like the term *alone*, excludes not-having, having another, not-becoming, and so on; thus the term *itself* in the phrase "this conditionality itself" and the term *mere* in the phrase "this mere conditionality itself" must exclude having another [cause]. According to the Buddhist tradition in general, *dependent arising* is interpreted to refer to the dependent relationship of cause and effect because internal and external compounded things arise only through the operation of causes and conditions. However, that they do not, conversely, arise from the prior design of a creator and so forth has already been explained in detail in volume 1 of *Science and Philosophy in the Indian Buddhist Classics*. [391]

Dependent Arising in Terms of Dependent Imputation

According to a more subtle level of interpretation, dependent arising refers to dependent imputation. This is categorized into two types: dependent arising in terms of being established on the basis of its parts and dependent arising in terms of existing as merely nominally imputed. The first is to be understood in terms of how a whole and its parts are established as mutually dependent. This way in which a whole and its parts, or a limb-possessor and its limbs, and so forth, are dependently related—in the sense of being imputed in dependence on each other—is an explanation common to both Svātantrika and Prāsaṅgika systems. According to this interpretation dependent arising can be said to encompass all existent phenomena, not just causally conditioned things. In general, knowable objects fall into two distinct and mutually exhaustive categories according to whether they exist as functional things. Functional things are of two types: physical and nonphysical. Among these, physical things have directional parts such as east; in the case of nonphysical things, consciousness has temporal parts such as earlier and later, while unassociated conditioning factors have parts that are their respective states and bases of imputation. Thus functional things necessarily have parts. Even nonfunctional phenomena, such as uncaused space, must be accepted to have parts that encompass the eastern direction and parts that encompass the other directions. Since other uncaused phenomena are similar in this respect, anything whatsoever that is either a causal thing or an uncaused phenomenon is necessarily posited in such a manner that the whole depends on the parts and the parts depend on the whole. Indeed, as in the case of parts and part-possessor, collection and collection-possessor, limbs and limb-possessor, it is impossible for anything to be established as dependent on something but not mutually dependent.

As for the second, dependent arising in terms of existing as merely nominally imputed, to be merely posited by name or thought [392] allows for the correctness of each thing's functionality. Once inherent existence has been refuted, a faultless presentation of functionality can be posited on the basis of subtle dependent arising as merely named or merely labeled conventionally. This dependent arising is accepted only in the Prāsaṅgika Madhyamaka system. To understand the complete presentation of dependent arising, it is not enough just to understand dependent arising in terms of cause and effect and being established in relation to its parts; one must understand this dependent arising in terms of existing as merely nominally imputed. This means one must comprehend what it is to be "merely nominally imputed," and for "the referent of the designation not to be found when sought," and "how functionality is correct as merely labeled."

As for the analysis [of something in an ultimate sense] in which the referent of the designation is not found when sought, when considering the phrase "the referent of the designation that is sought," what is the referent of the designation, and in what way is it sought? The referent of the designation is the thing imputed by language and thought. Not being satisfied with mere nominal imputation, the referent of the designation is sought by way of analyzing whether it exists as something from its own mode of existence or mode of being. For example, in dependence on the aggregates that are its basis of imputation, this person is the object imputed by the term *person* and by the conceptual cognition thinking, "This is a person," thus it is known as the *referent of the designation*. As for searching for the referent of the designation, although it is this person, the way to search for the referent does not involve looking for whether it exists. Instead, not satisfied with this person as merely imputed by mind, one searches for how the person exists objectively. Searching in this way through the use of reasoning, one does not find the person to be any of the aggregates, whether individually or as a collection, and one does not find the person to be something apart from them. This kind of *not finding anything* [393] in the case of the person means that the person is not inherently existent but not that the person is totally nonexistent. If the person were inherently existent, then it would have to be found when sought in such a way, but if merely existent that is not necessary. For example, if a mirage were water, then when we come close to it we would have to see it, but this is not so in the case of a mirage itself [which is not water but merely appears to be water]. Nāgārjuna's *Precious Garland* says:

> A physical form seen from afar
> is seen clearly by those nearby.
> If a mirage were indeed water,
> why would those nearby not see it?[654]

Likewise, having calculated the years, months, days, minutes, seconds, and milliseconds, it is difficult to posit something as the "present" in the aftermath of delineating "Until now this is the past" and "From now this is the future." Thus the three times are each imputed by thought in dependence on their respective bases. Instead of being satisfied with this way of being merely posited, when one searches for the referent of the designation, it is not found. In contrast, if one is satisfied with the nominal imputation "This is a pot" based on a bulbous thing and does not analyze the referent of the designation, one can posit a pot. But if, unsatisfied with that, one searches for the pot that is the referent of the designation among any of its parts—spout, belly, neck, base, and so on—one does not find the pot, thus one cannot posit a pot [within the scope of ultimate analysis].

This way of establishing phenomena to exist as merely nominally imputed [394] is considered to be the essential point that encapsulates the refutation of inherent existence. Objects of knowledge are categorized into two types: causally compounded things and noncausal phenomena. In the first case, although causally compounded things include the five aggregates, these are condensed into three categories: physical form, consciousness, and unassociated conditioning factors. As for the first category, physical form, one begins by searching within one's own form aggregate itself. If this body in general, complete with five limbs, were established from its own side, then when one searches for it to be established as either the same as or different from its five limbs—the torso with a head, two arms, and two legs—nothing is found at all. Therefore, apart from being merely imputed on the basis of those five limbs, it does not exist as inherently established. In the case of the individual limbs, such as an arm, when one divides it into three portions and searches for it from the shoulder to the fingertips, the arm is not found. One searches for a hand among the five fingers, a finger among its three joints, a joint among it upper and lower parts and those of the four directions, such as the east. In the final analysis nothing can be found in the six directions. One's entire physical body, its limbs, their parts, and even its hair follicles do not exist as established from their own side.

This reasoning is to be applied to all physical phenomena, such as mountains, courtyards, houses, plants, forests, and so on. An example of how the object of negation appears is as follows. When the front or back of a house appears to a visual consciousness, it appears to be something established from its own side, not merely posited by imputation on the combination of bricks and mortar that are its parts, and it is held as such by conceptual cognition.[655] In general, one does not analyze whether the part-possessing house is established to be the same as or different from the individual bricks and mortar that are its parts. [395] However, if that house appearing as the object of negation above were to exist as something established from its own side, then when analyzed it would be established as either the same as or different from the individual bricks and mortar. Thus, as before, at the culmination of such an analysis there can arise a profound ascertainment thinking that the house does not exist as established from its own side but as based on a combination of bricks and mortar—though this is not an ascertainment thinking that the mere house does not exist.

Let us consider another illustration: a long wooden pole, which is taken to be a pillar. Now, if this wooden pole were established as a pillar from the side of the basis of imputation itself and not merely nominally imputed a "pillar," then even when this wooden pole (the basis of imputation) was standing in the courtyard at an earlier stage bearing branches and leaves, the cognition of a "pillar" would necessarily have arisen. But such a cognition did not arise at that time. For during the stage when it was bearing branches and leaves, the cognition of a "pillar" did not arise, only the thought "This is a tree trunk." Even after being cut and turned into a pole, the thought "pillar" arises only when a beam is hoisted onto it. But if one supposes that once it supports a beam it is thereafter posited as a *pillar*, this too is incorrect. For if that same pole is later modified and hoisted as a beam, the cognition of a "pillar" does not arise, only the thought "This is a beam." And if that same pole is used as a rafter, then the cognition of a "rafter" will arise, not that of a pillar or a beam.

As for the second category, consciousness, there are two kinds: sensory consciousness and mental consciousness. Let us consider an illustration, such as the mental consciousness based on a single day, which has three parts—morning, noon, and evening. The part that is the morning consciousness also has three parts—earlier, later, and intermediate. Even the intermediate consciousness is analyzed into three momentary parts—arising, abiding, and disintegrating. [396] At the culmination of analyzing whether the continuum of consciousness itself is inherently the same as or different from the earlier and later moments that belong to it, an understanding can arise that all these consciousnesses are not established to exist from their own side, apart from being merely nominally imputed on their earlier and later moments. Not only that, but also any consciousness at all, sensory or mental, cognizes by means of an appearance of an object. So apart from being posited as a consciousness in relation to an object that appears, consciousness cannot be posited at all if no object whatsoever appears. Therefore the cognizing subject, consciousness, is not established from its own side.

As for the third category, unassociated conditioning factors, let us consider an analysis of *time* as an illustration. If we analyze a long period such as an eon (Skt. *kalpa*) in terms of its parts—a continuous stream of a vast number of years, then years in terms of months, months in terms of days, days in terms of hours, hours in terms of minutes, minutes in terms of seconds, each in terms of its own parts—then nothing is found. Moreover, a *year* is not established from its own side but merely nominally imputed on a collection of months and days; for if it were established in such a way, then it would have to be either the same as them or different from them. If it were the same as them, then just as the bases of imputation are multiple, so the imputed phenomenon, a year, would also have to be multiple; or conversely, just as a year is singular, so those bases of imputation would also have to be singular. If it were different from them, then a year must be posited to exist after having eliminated each month and day; but it does not exist in such a way. In the case of unassociated conditioning factors, such as *impermanence* and *arising*, apart from "the arising of this" and "the disintegration of that" being merely nominally imputed in relation to things that arise and things that disintegrate, they are not established to exist from their own side.

Second, in the case of noncausal phenomena, such as space, apart from the term *space* being merely nominally imputed on the mere absence of physical obstructivity, [397] it is not established to exist from its own side. If it were established in such a way, then space would have to be posited without relating to the absence of obstructivity or physical contact, but that does not occur. As for space such as that inside a room, when one scrutinizes the parts of the room in the four directions, above, and below, it is not found. In this way, as when analyzing the selflessness of phenomena, one analyzes physical phenomena in relation to their directional parts and the eight substantial particles, consciousnesses in relation to their earlier and later moments, unassociated conditioning factors in relation to their individual bases of imputation and states, and noncausal phenomena in relation to their various conceptual identities. Phenomena that have no parts at all cannot possibly exist among objects of knowledge. Therefore if something is an established base (i.e., an existent) it must have parts. If it has parts, it must be merely imputed on its parts. Thus all phenomena are nothing other than merely imputed by language and thought, and any nominally imputed thing is not established to exist from its own side.

In brief, according to this Madhyamaka tradition that asserts "existing as merely nominally imputed," all phenomena can be posited from the perspective of a cognition that does not analyze their ultimate nature, though when investigated and sought in such a way [i.e., ultimately] they cannot be found. However, that *not finding* does not mean *not existing*. Existence must be accepted, but the manner of existence is through dependence or through a gathering of conditions—not through being established from the side of the object. Candrakīrti's *Entering the Middle Way* says: "So the conventional truth of the everyday world should not be submitted to thorough analysis."[656] [398]

As for the way in which phenomena are established as merely imputed by thought, all phenomena do not exist from the side of the *basis of imputation* but are merely posited by conception or established in dependence on thought that *imputes*. For example, on the basis of a rope that appears unclearly in the darkness, with its colored pattern and coiled form looking like that of a snake, the thought "It's a snake!" may arise. On that occasion, since there is no cause whatsoever for positing the parts of the rope or their collection to be the basis of identification of a snake, the snake in that instance is merely imputed by thought. Likewise, when the thought "I" arises on the basis of the aggregates, there is no cause for positing the collection that is a continuum of earlier and later moments based on the aggregates, or the collection at a single time, or its parts, to be the basis of identification of "I"; and there is no cause for positing a different entity from the whole or parts of the aggregates to be the basis of identification of "I." Therefore this "I" is merely posited by thought in dependence on the aggregates but is not established by its own essential nature, just like the snake based on a multicolored rope.

Furthermore, the expressions *conceptually imputed* and *nominally posited* have the same meaning. To give an example of being nominally posited, let us suppose that, after having built a house designed to have three rooms, one of the three rooms is designated as the meditation room, one as the bedroom, and one as the kitchen; however, although they are now established as the meditation room and so forth, they were not established as such prior to being nominally designated. To give another example, someone who wants to meet with Devadatta is told, "He is in the third room," and upon following these words he enters that room and is able to meet with Devadatta. However, not being satisfied with that alone, if he searches for whether the basis of imputation of the name Devadatta exists as the same nature as or different from his aggregates [399] and needs to meet with him after having found that "He exists in this way," then it would be impossible for him to meet with such a Devadatta. Likewise, any phenomenon whatsoever is merely posited by conceptual cognition and the name expressing it. As Nāgārjuna's *Precious Garland* says:

Things that are forms are mere nominal designations,
therefore space too is a mere nominal designation.
Without the elements, how can there be form?
Therefore it is also a mere nominal designation.[657]

The Mutual Entailment of Empty and Dependent Arising

As explained above, in the phrase "dependent arising," the term *dependent* means relying and *arising* means produced (in the case of causal things) or established (in the case of noncausal phenomena). According to the Madhyamaka interpretation, the phrase "dependent arising" means "established in dependence or reliance on language and thought, on parts, and on the basis of imputation." Thus to say, "This phenomenon is empty of being inherently established" means that it is dependently established. Therefore *empty* means dependent arising. Also, if something arises in dependence on causes and conditions, then it must be established in reliance on something else and not established inherently. Thus to say "This phenomenon is dependently established" means that it is empty of being inherently established. Therefore *dependent arising* means empty.

The cognition that realizes the lack of inherent nature of external and internal dependently related phenomena can induce, without relying on another cognition, [400] a correct ascertainment of all the presentations of cause and effect, action and agent, and so on as merely nominally imputed. At this point, *empty* appears to mean dependent arising. The cognition that ascertains external and internal things to be dependently related can induce, without needing to rely on another cognition, an ascertainment of them as empty of inherent existence. At this point, *dependent arising* appears to mean empty. Moreover, as long as one's ascertainment of a given phenomenon as empty due being dependently arisen has not faded, when at a later time one sees, hears, or remembers this phenomenon to be dependently arisen, one can gain an ascertainment indirectly that this phenomenon is empty of inherent existence. For such a person, *dependent arising* implies the meaning of empty, but it does not do so for another person. It is like when a person—as long as their ascertainment of a composite mass with a hump and horns and so on to be the attributes of a cow has not been forgotten—later sees something endowed with the attributes of a cow and is naturally able to generate the thought "This is a cow." The meaning of emptiness being the meaning of dependent arising is similar to this. *Buddhapālita's Commentary on the Fundamental Treatise* says: "Whatever dependent arising is, we explain it to be emptiness because it is dependent imputation, and that itself is the middle way."[658] In teaching that the meaning of *dependent arising* is identical to the meaning of *empty*, it also teaches that the meaning of *emptiness* too is identical to the meaning of *dependent arising*, and that this *emptiness* itself is the middle way. Candrakīrti's *Clear Words* says:

> That which is emptiness (*śūnyatāṃ*) is dependent imputation (*prajñaptirupādāya*) because emptiness itself is posited as "dependent imputation." In dependence on the chariot's parts, such as the wheels, [401] a chariot is imputed. That which is a thing's dependent imputation on its parts is the absence of inherent arising. Any absence of inherent arising is emptiness; the emptiness that has the characteristic of absence of inherent arising is itself the middle way. This is how it is explained.[659]

This dependent relationship—that is, the arising in dependence on its causes and conditions or on its basis of imputation—is what it means to be empty of inherent existence. To be empty of inherent existence is to be dependently related in the sense of dependent arising.

In brief, to be inherently established is necessarily to be established without depending on anything else. To be established in such a way is contradictory to dependent arising. So with the reason of dependent arising, inherent existence is refuted. Therefore to be empty of inherent existence does not mean that the presentations of action, agent, and so on cannot be posited; instead it proves their existence through many reasons that entail the meaning of dependent arising.

Those realists who claim that things are ultimately established owing to the reason of dependent arising incur the fault of falling to the extremes of eternalism and nihilism. Those who accept that, owing to the reason of dependent arising, things are not inherently established, like the reflection of the moon in water—yet the presentations of agent, action, and so on are correct conventionally—do not accept them to be truly established nor completely nonexistent. Thus they avoid the extremes of eternalism and nihilism. [402] Nāgārjuna's *Sixty Stanzas of Reasoning* says:

> In the case of those who accept
> dependent things to exist ultimately,
> how could false views of permanence
> and so on not arise?
>
> Those who accept dependent things
> to be neither real nor false,
> like a reflection of the moon on water,
> are not captivated by views.[660]

Also, Nāgārjuna's *Praise of the Transcendent One* says:

> Logicians assert that suffering
> is produced from itself, produced from others,
> produced from both, or produced without a cause.
> But you taught that it dependently arises.
>
> You taught that whatever
> dependently arises is itself empty.
> "Things have no independent existence"—
> this is your lion's roar, O Incomparable One.[661]

The realists assert that suffering arises from one of the four alternatives. The transcendent Buddha teaches that all phenomena dependently arise, and he explains that dependent arising means the emptiness of inherent existence, not total nonexistence. [403] This statement that things do not have even the slightest independent existence but are established relatively is said to be the declaration that, like a lion's roar, clears away all extremes of eternalism and nihilism. It is stated in the [*Bodhisattva's Scriptural Collection*] *Sūtra*: "Whoever sees dependent arising sees the Dharma. Whoever sees the Dharma sees the Tathāgata."[662] In other words, to see the suchness of dependent arising is to see the consummate Dharma, and to see the consummate Dharma is to see the Tathāgata.

Moreover, when the appearance of dependent arising dawns, the lack of inherent nature vividly emerges, so the extreme of existence is cleared away by *appearance*. Also, owing to the dawning of that phenomenon's emptiness of inherent existence itself, whatever appears manifests vividly as a mere conceptual imputation, whereby the extreme of nonexistence is cleared away by *emptiness*. While the lower philosophical systems [other than Prāsaṅgika] accept that the extreme of nonexistence is cleared away by appearance and the extreme of existence by emptiness, the converse of this—namely, that the extreme of existence is cleared away by appearance and the extreme of nonexistence by emptiness—is unique to the Prāsaṅgika system. Accordingly, to say "Emptiness and dependent arising appear as cause and effect" does not mean that emptiness acts as a cause from which external and internal phenomena arise. Rather, since emptiness that is the absence of inherent existence of phenomena is the final proof that the dependent arising of cause and effect is correct, emptiness must be understood to be the cause that proves dependent arising. Nāgārjuna's *Fundamental Treatise on the Middle Way* says:

> When emptiness is possible,
> everything is possible. [404]
> When emptiness is impossible,
> nothing is possible.[663]

This teaches that within the position of emptiness, all the conventions of action and agent are feasible.

In brief, although phenomena established by virtue of intrinsic characteristics do not exist even in the slightest, the Prāsaṅgika tradition, without needing to rely on another's perspective, is satisfied with accepting that all actions, agents, and so on of cause and effect are validly established. Not only that, but bringing forth an ascertainment of dependently arising phenomena induces an ascertainment of the absence of inherent nature—therefore empty and dependent arising accompany and support each other. Taking as a reason "It is empty," something established relatively is indubitably established. Since it is established relatively, it is not established by its own nature. Therefore, due to being empty, being mere appearance is established; and due to being mere appearance, being empty of inherent nature is established. So *appearing* and *empty* are not contradictory.

By accepting that phenomena are not established independently or inherently, the presentation of ultimate truth is correct; and even according to the traditions that establish them by valid cognition, by accepting that they are established merely in relation to something else, the presentation of conventional truth is also completely correct. Masters such as Candrakīrti do not accept inherent nature even conventionally, which is a crucial point unique to the great Madhyamaka tradition. [405]

Part 5

Buddhist Logic and Epistemology

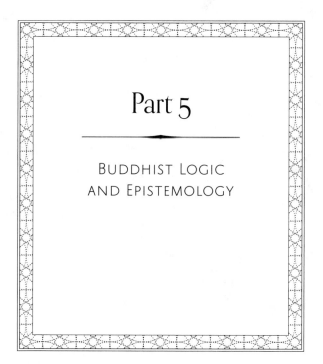

20

Indian Epistemology

WHAT IS KNOWN as the "science of reasoning" is included among the *five greater sciences* mentioned in early Buddhist sources. Within this branch of science, the main points that need to be understood are: the object known, the epistemic instruments that are the valid cognitions that know it, inference as a means of realizing it, and ways in which the mind knows its object. The logico-epistemological (*pramāṇa*) tradition is a discipline of knowledge that has flourished in India since ancient times. Many renowned thinkers in India, both Buddhist and non-Buddhist, engaged in extensive analyses and established their own positions on several of the key issues of epistemology: how valid cognition ascertaining its object arises on the basis of inferential reasoning; what specific qualifications are necessary for valid inference of this kind; what sort of relation obtains between the thesis proved and the evidence that proves it; presentations of the objects of knowledge; how the mind knows reality; how language and thought engage with reality; and what specific types of cognition exist among the categories of mind knowing reality.

According to some contemporary historians, among the first treatises on science in India was the medical text *Compendium of Caraka* (*Carakasaṃhitā*) compiled by Caraka (ca. 100 CE).[664] The third chapter of this text includes a presentation of twenty-four categories of logic, [406] within which are found the Vaiśeṣika system's six categories of logic. In general the most renowned non-Buddhist text about reasoning is the *Nyāya Sūtra*, the primary logical treatise composed by Akṣapāda Gautama—the definitive teacher of the Nyāya tradition. This text delineates sixteen categories of logic: valid means of knowing, objects of valid knowledge, doubt, purpose, example, tenet, components of inference, reasoning, ascertainment, debate, presentation, refutation only, fallacious inference, deceit, futile rejoinder, and defeat.[665] Since each of these sixteen categories of logic is refuted in Nāgārjuna's treatise *Finely Woven*, it is evident that these assertions of the Nyāya have been in existence from ancient times up to the present day. Based on the *Nyāya Sūtra*, the Naiyāyika posit four types of valid cognition—perception, inference, testimony, and comparative analogy—and they assert that a correct proof statement has five limbs.[666]

The non-Buddhist Sāṅkhya system is said to rely on such texts as the *Īśvarakṛṣṇa Tantra*, *Sixty Tantras*, *Seventy Golden Ones*, *Thirty Scriptural Traditions*, *Fifty Defining Characteristics*, and so on.[667] The *Īśvarakṛṣṇa Tantra*, also called the *Verses of Sāṅkhya*, says:

> Because perception, inference, and trustworthy testimony
> encompass all types of valid cognition, [407]
> three types of valid cognition are accepted.
> Objects known are established by means of valid knowing.[668]

Texts such as the one cited above give extensive presentations on the enumeration of valid cognition, its essential nature, the object of each type of valid cognition, how valid cognition establishes its object, and so on. The *Sāṅkhya Sūtra* explains: "The realization of the meaning of the pervasion through having realized earlier the relation between the evidence and the evidence-possessor is the *inference*, and the understanding of such a meaning by the person is the *consciousness that possesses the inference*."[669] This shows the way in which the evidential reason comes to be established, and how, on that basis, inferential cognition comes to arise.

The Vaiśeṣika system's main treatise is considered to be Kaṇāda's *Vaiśeṣika Sūtra*. It presents extensive proofs establishing sound to be a quality of space, using reasons of contradiction and of inherence, where cause, effect, and relation are synonymous. There are a variety of ideas as to when the *Nyāya Sūtra* and the *Vaiśeṣika Sūtra* were composed. However, since many of the treatises in an Indian language were written down during the second century, it seems that both of those treatises were written down around that time.

The Mīmāṃsā system's main treatise is considered to be Jaimini's *Mīmāṃsā Sūtra*, based on which a hugely important later thinker, Kumārila Bhaṭṭa (seventh century CE), composed his *Exposition of Verses on Mīmāṃsā*. [408] In this text he developed an extensive presentation of epistemology according to the Mīmāṃsā tradition. As for the Nirgrantha, now widely known as Jaina, epistemology is presented in the *Explanation of the Ten Auspicious Observances* (*Daśavaikālikaniryukti*) composed by Bhadrabāhu (fourth century BCE), and in later works such as *Entering into Reasoning* authored by the great master Siddhasena Divākara (seventh century CE).

As for the Buddhist systems, the logico-epistemological textual tradition is considered to have flourished since the time of the renowned master Dignāga in the fifth century CE. However, one may discern that that there were some earlier highly advanced logical analyses relating to epistemology from what is found in Nāgārjuna's *Refutation of Objections* and *Finely Woven* (second century CE). Moreover, many Mahāyāna sūtras contain presentations of the four forms of rationality, notably the four forms of rationality found in the *Unraveling the Intention Sūtra*, especially its presentation of the rationality of inferential proof.[670] In addition, the *Points of Discussion* (*Kathāvatthu*) attributed to Moggaliputta Tissa, which was compiled as part of the third Buddhist council during the period of Emperor Aśoka and included within the Abhidhamma Piṭaka of the Theravāda tradition, contains many detailed doctrinal debates. A paraphrase of this text is available in English these days as part of the translation of the Pali canon.[671] Included within the Abhidhamma Piṭaka of the Sarvāstivāda tradition, the *Compendium of Consciousness* (*Vijñānakāya*), attributed to Devakṣema/Devaśarman, contains many arguments that relate to proving the selflessness of the person. Similarly, Asaṅga presents various types of inference, along with examples illustrating them, in his monumental *Levels of Yogācāra*; within that work, his *Śrāvaka Levels* presents the four forms of rationality. Also, in the chapter "Examining the Dialectic" in his *Compendium of Abhidharma*, [409] he explains that a proof statement has five limbs and that valid cognition is categorized into three types: perception, inference, and testimony. In particular, Vasubandhu is said to have composed treatises expressly pertaining to the discipline of epistemology, such as *Practice of Debate*, *Heart of Debate*, and so on.[672]

Among the Buddhist thinkers, Dignāga carefully investigates the categories of logic presented in the *Nyāya Sūtra* and proposes eight categories within his own system of epistemology: (1) correct perception and (2) correct inference, both of which enable oneself to ascertain the object of knowledge; also (3) fallacious perception and (4) fallacious inference, which are for identifying distortions in each of the previous two; then (5) correct proof statement or inference for the sake of others and (6) correct refutation, both of which, after having ascertained the object of knowledge oneself, are for the sake of bringing others to that realization; also (7) fallacious proof statement and (8) fallacious refutation, which are for identifying distortions in the previous two. These eight categories of logic are delineated by Dignāga in the following treatises (some of which are no longer extant): *Investigation of the Universal* (*Sāmānyalakṣaṇaparikṣā*), *Investigation of the Nyāya System* (*Nyāyaparīkṣā*), *Investigation of the Vaiśeṣika System* (*Vaiśeṣikaparīkṣā*), *Investigation of the Sāṅkhya System* (*Sāṅkhyaparīkṣā*), *Investigation of the Object*, *Investigation of the Three Times*, *Entering into Valid Reasoning*, *Classification of the Winds*,[673] *Introduction to Logic* (*Hetumukha*), *Introduction to Entering into Valid Reasoning*, and *Drum of a Wheel of Reasons*.[674] In particular, he composed the six-chapter work *Compendium of Valid Cognition*, also known as the *Sūtra on Valid Cognition*, [410] in the form of both a root text in verse as well as an autocommentary; it is a foundational treatise for the entire discipline of Buddhist epistemology.

After Dignāga some highly skilled proponents of non-Buddhist epistemology appeared, in particular the Vaiśeṣika master Praśastapāda (sixth century CE), the Nyāya master Uddyotakara (sixth century), the Mīmāṃsā master Kumārila (seventh century), and the Jaina master Mallavādin (eighth century). These four composed treatises to refute many of the points stated by Dignāga concerning epistemology and logic and to prove that the presentations of their own *pramāṇa* traditions were correct. Thus the level of discourse in philosophy and epistemology in India was raised considerably.

Dignāga's immediate disciple Īśvarasena appears to have composed a commentary on *Compendium of Valid Cognition* that unfortunately is no longer extant. Īśvarasena's student was Dharmakīrti (seventh century), who is the most highly renowned master in the history of Indian epistemology. To provide detailed explanations of the meaning of Dignāga's *Compendium of Valid Cognition* and its autocommentary, this master composed seven treatises on valid cognition. He wrote three primary treatises, likened to the body, that present fully the eight categories of logic: *Exposition of Valid Cognition*, the lengthiest version; *Ascertainment of Valid Cognition*, the medium-length version; and *Drop of Reasoning*, the shortest version.

[411] He also wrote four secondary treatises, likened to the limbs of the body, that present only some portion of the eight categories, expanding upon them: *Drop of Reasons*, *Investigation of Relations*, *Proof of Other Mindstreams*, and *Reasoning for Debate*. Among these, *Drop of Reasons* presents in particular the defining characteristics of reasons for something hard to know, expanding upon the "Inference for Oneself" chapter of *Exposition of Valid Cognition*. The root text and commentary of *Investigation of Relations* expands on the demonstration of the thesis-evidence relation found in the "Inference for Oneself" chapter. This text in particular explains how the relation between thesis and evidence is posited conventionally and is not ultimately existent. *Proof of Other Mindstreams* gives a clear response to the question that arises in the "Perception" chapter when explaining forms and so on to be mere cognition only: "If what appears to the disputant is in the nature of their own mind, then how can it be feasible for the proof statement's locus of presentation, a person of a different continuum, to exist?" The text shows how there can be a person who is a different continuum from the disputant even though there are no forms and so on that are different substances from the consciousness that brings about the appearance. *Reasoning for Debate* expands upon the "Inference for Others" chapter and in particular explains: the proof statement, definitions of the proponent and the opponent showing how to train in the path of proof statements, how to engage in debate, refutation that is the essence of debate, the presentation of consequential reasoning, the categories of futile rejoinder (*jāti*)[675] that deviate from it, and so on.

Thus Dharmakīrti's seven treatises in general, and in particular his most renowned work *Exposition of Valid Cognition*, [412] present Dignāga's tradition of logic and epistemology in a systematic way. In particular, he elucidates the points that Dignāga did not state clearly, or, if stated, that he did not explain in detail. For example, although Dignāga sets forth the definition of *evidence* to be "that which is qualified by the three modes," he does not give much explanation about its instances—*effect* evidence, *nature* evidence, and evidence consisting in *nonperception*—nor does he explain in depth the rationale by which the presence of the three modes within correct evidence is ascertained.[676] Similarly, while Dignāga states that in any correct inferential reasoning there must be an invariable relation of unaccompanied nonoccurrence (*avinābhāvaniyama*)[677] between the evidence and the thesis, Dharmakīrti determines this type of relation to consist of two kinds—causal relation and intrinsic relation—so he gives lengthy explanations about how the categories of correct evidence have a definitive enumeration as three—effect, nature, and nonperception—and other such difficult points of epistemology. Moreover, he refutes the extensive criticisms of Dignāga's epistemological views in general, especially about his proof of the exclusion of other to be the linguistic referent (or word meaning), put forward by the non-Buddhist masters Praśastapāda, Uddyotakara, Kumārila, and Mallavādin. Thus he proves Dignāga's own system to be correct and further raises the level of Buddhist epistemology considerably.

Devendrabuddhi (seventh century) wrote a commentary on the final three chapters of *Exposition of Valid Cognition*. His disciple Śākyabuddhi (or Śākyamati; seventh century) wrote his *Commentary on the Exposition of Valid Cognition*. His other disciple Vinītadeva, as well as a lineage that followed, including Prajñākaragupta, [413] Dharmottara, Mahāmati, Jamāri, and Mokṣākaragupta, also wrote commentaries on the seven treatises of Dharmakīrti. Then in the eighth century Śāntarakṣita wrote his highly renowned text on valid cognition, *Compendium of Reality*, and his disciple Kamalaśīla wrote his *Commentary on the Difficult Points in the Compendium of Reality*. These two texts present responses to each of the criticisms leveled by certain non-Buddhist logicians against not only Dignāga's position but also certain points made by Dharmakīrti pertaining to epistemology, and they give detailed refutations of objections to their presentation of the exclusion of other in the "Investigating Word Meaning" chapter in particular. In addition [to the above masters], Śaṅkarānanda (eleventh century), also known as Mahāmati,[678] composed an explanation of the autocommentary on the first chapter of *Exposition of Valid Cognition*, as well as the treatises *Proof of Relation* and *Proof of Exclusion*. And Jitāri (eleventh century) wrote several treatises on epistemology, such as *A Beginner's Primer on Logic*, *Distinguishing the Systems of the Blessed One*, *Ascertainment of Dharma and Dharmin*, and *Presenting the Principles of Inferential Evidence*. From the fact that these texts are included in the Pramāṇa section of the Tengyur one can discern how so many works on logic and epistemology came to be composed [in India].

The purpose for giving such detailed explanations about epistemology, as presented by both Buddhist and non-Buddhist Indian masters from one generation to the next, is to demonstrate the following: how the attainment of human goals is dependent on valid cognition; how all the varieties of suffering, which people do not want, come from not knowing correctly the nature of reality; [414] and how once one has gained correct valid cognition, one will be able to accomplish one's aims in reliance on it. Seeing the importance of these understandings, [the masters] offered their extensive presentations on epistemology. Accordingly, Dharmakīrti's *Ascertainment of Valid Cognition* says: "Since correct understanding is a necessary precursor for obtaining what is beneficial and abandoning what is harmful, this text has been composed for the purpose of teaching those who lack this expertise."[679] Likewise, Dharmakīrti's *Drop of Reasoning* says: "Since the accomplishment of every being's goal is preceded by correct understanding, this text has been taught."[680]

21

Buddhist Notions of Valid Cognition

HAVING GIVEN a rough overview of Indian epistemology in general, we now address the presentations of Buddhist epistemology. The main texts of the two great masters of the Indo-Tibetan Buddhist epistemological tradition, Dignāga and Dharmakīrti, are respectively *Compendium of Valid Cognition* and *Exposition of Valid Cognition*. Commenting on the meaning of these texts, the primary approach of the Indian and Buddhist epistemological thinkers that followed has been to organize the subject matter [of these two seminal works] broadly into the following key topics: the refutation of misconceptions pertaining to the enumeration of valid cognition, its definition, the object to be known, and the resultant knowing. So here too we will adopt this method. This approach can be exemplified by the following passage from Vinītadeva's *Commentary on the Drop of Reasoning*: [415]

> Since correct understanding eliminates the four types of misconception, it is a faultless understanding. The four types of misconception are these: misconception pertaining to the number, misconception pertaining to the definition, misconception pertaining to the object of experience, and misconception pertaining to the result.[681]

This states the main points of epistemology from the perspective of eliminating the four types of misconception pertaining to the enumeration of valid cognition, its definition, its object of experience, and its resultant experience.

Of these, first we have the analysis of the enumeration of valid cognition as follows. In Mokṣākaragupta's *Language of Logic* it says that among Indian epistemologists of non-Buddhist traditions there are those who enumerate valid cognition as being of only one type and others who say there are three, or four, or five, or six, and so on. This text states:

> The words "two types of valid cognition" eliminate the misconception of it as being of one, or three, or four, or five, or six types. The Cārvāka accept only direct perception to be valid cognition. The Sāṅkhya accept direct perception, inferential cognition, and trustworthy testimony. The Naiyāyika accept direct perception, inferential cognition, trustworthy testimony, and comparative analogy. Those [Mīmāṃsaka] following Prabhākara accept direct perception, inferential cognition, trustworthy testimony, comparative analogy, and postulation. The Mīmāṃsaka [following Bhaṭṭa] accept direct perception, inferential cognition, trustworthy testimony, comparative analogy, postulation, and absence.[682] [416]

The Cārvāka accept only direct perception to be valid cognition. In fact, the key reason they give for their nonacceptance of such things as any future life is because they do not see it now. Therefore they say that valid cognition is wholly encompassed within direct perception and there is no need for any so-called valid cognition apart from that. This point is expressed in Kamalaśīla's *Commentary on the Difficult Points in the Compendium of Reality* as follows: "Apart from direct perception there is no other valid cognition by which future lives and so on would be established."[683] The Sāṅkhya accept both direct perception and inferential cognition with the addition of trustworthy testimony to be valid cognition. The Naiyāyika accept comparative analogy in addition to the above three. The Mīmāṃsaka following Prabhākara accept postulation in addition to the above four, while the Mīmāṃsaka following Bhaṭṭa accept absence in addition to the above five. Caraka accepts eleven types of valid cognition, for in addition to the above six he accepts rationality, nonperception, probability, tradition, and supposition. The definitions of each of these and the reasons they are posited as valid cognition should be understood from the presentation of tenets for each tradition in volume 3 of *Science and Philosophy in the Indian Buddhist Classics*.

Thus there exist diverse views regarding how many types of valid cognition there are. The founders of the Buddhist epistemological system, Dignāga and Dharmakīrti, declare that since there are definitively two types of object of knowledge—unique particulars and generic universals—there are also definitively two types of valid cognition that apprehend them—perceptual valid cognition (which takes as its observed object a unique particular) and inferential valid cognition (which takes as its observed object a generic universal). [417] Dignāga's *Compendium of Valid Cognition Autocommentary* says:

> Valid cognition is of two kinds: "perception and inference." They are only two because "The object to be known is of two kinds." Apart from the particular and the universal, there is no other object to be known. Perception has only the particular as its object, while inference has only the universal.[684]

The meaning of this is encapsulated in Dharmakīrti's *Exposition of Valid Cognition*:

> Because objects of knowledge are twofold, valid cognition is twofold.[685]

To expand upon this, it means that valid cognition has a definitive enumeration as two types: *perception* and *inference*. This is because objects known by valid cognition have a definitive enumeration as two types: *particulars* and *universals*. Thus, since objects known by valid cognition have a definitive enumeration that is mutually excluding, there is no third possibility or other valid cognition that knows them apart from perception and inference. That is what this master resolutely proves. The "Perception" chapter of Dharmakīrti's *Exposition of Valid Cognition* says:

> There is no object of knowledge apart from
> that which is manifest and that which is hidden.
> So since objects of knowledge are only twofold,
> valid cognition is explained to be twofold. [418]
> Because objects of knowledge are seen to be twofold,
> their enumeration as three or one is excluded.[686]

This presents Dignāga's intent. Since the object of knowledge of a valid cognition is either perceived in a manifest manner or inferred via a hidden manner, objects of knowledge are of two kinds; therefore the valid cognition that knows them has a definitive enumeration of two kinds also. As for types of objects of knowledge, since no third alternative is seen apart from particulars and universals, so in the case of valid cognition also, the existence of a third possibility apart from perception and inference is excluded by valid cognition. This refutes the account of valid cognition posited in non-Buddhist systems such as Cārvāka that accept valid cognition to be only direct perception, and others that accept further alternatives such as trustworthy testimony, comparative analogy, postulation, and so on.

Dharmakīrti's *Exposition of Valid Cognition* provides four reasons to prove that valid cognition's object of knowledge is definitely of two kinds:

> Because some can perform a function and others cannot
> function.
> [...]
> Because some bear a resemblance and others a non-resemblance,
> because some are objects of words and others are not,
> because when other causes [apart from the object] are present,
> there is cognition of some but not of others.[687]

A unique *particular* can function to produce its own effects, whereas a *universal* cannot function. When an object is known by valid cognition, [419] [that object] is a commonly appearing *universal* in the case of a cognition having a resemblance (or likeness) as its appearing object, whereas it is a uniquely appearing *particular* in the case of a cognition having a non-resemblance as its appearing object. One that is the object of language just as it appears to a cognition having it as its appearing object is a *universal*, whereas one that is not so is a *particular*. In the case of a *universal*, a cognition apprehending it exists due to the mere presence of other contributing causes, such as a linguistic convention, effort, and so on; whereas in the case of a *particular*, if it is not established by way of its own essential nature then a cognition apprehending it does not exist, for it does not rely merely on other contributing causes. The main point here is to prove that the types of valid cognition are definitely enumerated as two. In brief, this is summed up in Prajñākaragupta's *Ornament of Exposition of Valid Cognition* as follows: "Only the objects of direct perception and inferential cognition are the epistemic objects of correct realization, not of anything else, because there is no other means of realizing something that is a universal or a particular individual."[688] Not only that, Prajñākaragupta also maintains that the objects of valid cognition being of only two types is established by perceptual reflexive awareness. His *Ornament of Exposition of Valid Cognition* says: "Here it is explained that the objects being of two types is established only by direct perception because the realization of resemblance or nonresemblance is an attribute of cognition itself, and that is established by perceptual reflexive awareness."[689]

What is the essential nature or definition of valid cognition? The Sanskrit word for valid cognition is *pramāṇa*, which is composed of two parts, *pra* and *māṇa*. Although the prefix *pra* can have many meanings, according to the treatises on valid cognition it means first, while the second part, *māṇa*, means to measure, comprehend, realize, or know. [420] Therefore valid cognition is that which first, or newly, comprehends something that was not realized before. This explanation accords with that found in Dharmakīrti's *Exposition of Valid Cognition*: "It also reveals an object not known before." Alternatively, the syllable *pra* may indicate "excellent" or "supreme," which in Sanskrit is *paramārtha*. Here too, the syllable *māṇa* means to measure, comprehend, or know. So valid cognition is that which is nondeceptive and supremely knows its object. This explanation accords with that found in *Exposition of Valid Cognition*: "Valid cognition is nondeceptive cognition."[690] Thus the definition of *valid cognition* is: a newly acquired and nondeceptive cognition. As the treatises on epistemology explain, the part of this definition that says "newly" excludes subsequent cognition from being valid cognition; the part that says "nondeceptive" excludes correct assumption, doubt, and distorted cognition from being valid cognition; and the part that says "cognition" excludes the physical eye sense faculty and so on from being valid cognition. In brief, Prajñākaragupta's *Ornament of Exposition of Valid Cognition* says: "As a general indication of the definition of *valid cognition*: valid cognition is nondeceptive consciousness. Valid cognition is nondeceptive because when it is present, the object of knowledge is established; also because if cognition were deceptive, the opposite would be the case."[691]

As for identifying the meaning of "nondeceptive" in the context of the above definition of valid cognition found in *Exposition of Valid Cognition*,

Devendrabuddhi, a direct disciple of Dharmakīrti, makes the important point that it applies to both the object and the subject of cognition. He explains that the subject is nondeceptive and its respective object is nondeceptive. His *Commentary on Difficult Points in the Exposition of Valid Cognition* says [421]:

> The line "Valid cognition is nondeceptive cognition" is stated because if it operates regarding what is deceptive, it is deceptive. Any cognition that has that [kind of object] is deceptive, and any that does not have a deceptive [object, in terms of its functionality,] is nondeceptive. This is the meaning of "that which is nondeceptive." When *nondeceptive* refers to the object that has been determined, then since the object's ability to perform its function is established, the said object is nondeceptive in terms of its nature as that [i.e., being able to perform its function]; so here it is an attribute of the object. The understanding of it [i.e., the object] to be such a way [i.e., able to perform its function] is nondeceptive cognition; so here it is an attribute of the subject. Any cognition that has that [kind of object] is nondeceptive cognition.[692]

An object established in accordance with how it is determined by a nondeceptive cognition is that cognition's nondeceptive object. Dharmakīrti's *Exposition of Valid Cognition* says:

> [Regarding its object's] ability to perform a function,
> it is nondeceptive.[693]

For example, just as valid direct perception sees fire as being able to perform the function of burning, so in accordance with how the object actually exists fire is able to perform the function of burning. As for *nondeceptive* in the case of the determined object of a nondeceptive subject, Dharmakīrti's *Exposition of Valid Cognition* says:

> It also reveals an object not known before.[694]

Through revealing the mode of existence of a previously unknown object, a valid cognition by its own accord determines its object. In general, a *non-*

deceptive subject can refer to nondeceptive cognition, nondeceptive words, nondeceptive person, [422] and nondeceptive sense faculty.

When commenting on the meaning of *nondeceptive* (Skt. *avisaṃvādaka*) as a facet of the definition of valid cognition, Dharmottara explicitly distinguishes between two types of objects of valid cognition: the observed object and the engaged object. He claims that in saying "Valid cognition is nondeceptive regarding its object," Dharmakīrti's *Drop of Reasons* primarily states that valid cognition has *ascertainment* as a result. Here valid cognition *obtains* the identified thing that is its object, so this cognition is posited to cause obtainment of that thing just as it is indicated. In that case, although an inferential cognition realizing the presence of fire through the evidence of smoke, for example, is a cognition that is mistaken with regard to its observed object, it is nondeceptive in that it obtains its conceived object, fire.[695] Since this cognition obtains that thing just as it is indicated, it must be posited as valid. Conversely, in the case of a cognition apprehending a mirage to be water, since it cannot possibly obtain that thing just as it is indicated, it is only mistaken and thus unviable as valid cognition. This is considered to be a very important distinction. Dharmottara takes Dharmakīrti's intended meaning to be that which is described immediately above when he explains the defining characteristic of valid cognition to be *nondeceptive*. The long and short versions of Dharmottara's *Investigation of Valid Cognition* provide extensive analyses of some important points that amount to new explanations. It will be easier to notice these if we quote at length some passages from the short *Investigation of Valid Cognition*, so this is what we will do now. It says:

> *Valid cognition* is nondeceptive cognition. *Nondeceptive* means causing one to obtain the indicated thing that is capable of producing an effect (or fulfilling a purpose). *Causing to obtain* [423] operates through indicating the engaged object [or object of activity]. Therefore the *activity of valid cognition* is causing to indicate, which is a phase of causing to obtain. The object may be indicated either by means of direct perception that specially determines it or merely sees it, or by means of nonperceptual inferential cognition that ascertains it with unmistaken rational evidence.[696]

The meaning of "nondeceptive" in the definition of valid cognition is explained here as: causing to obtain the indicated thing that is capable of producing an effect. The meaning of *causing to obtain* is explained as: causing to indicate its engaged object [or object of activity]. The *way of indicating the engaged object* is explained as twofold: to indicate by means of perceptual cognition that directly perceives, or to indicate by means of inferential cognition that is nonperceptual. This explains the general meaning of *nondeceptive*. In the context of a more extensive explanation of the meaning of the text, the object of valid cognition is categorized into two types: the observed object and the engaged object or the ascertained object [i.e., the object of activity]. Thus valid cognition is understood by way of examining how its object is nondeceptive. Dharmottara's short *Investigation of Valid Cognition* says:

> To be understood is to be determined, not simply observed.
>
> As for the intention: since it is nondeceptive
> it is valid cognition even though mistaken.
>
> The intention expresses that the desired object is determined. In that case, obtainment of the determined is also nondeceptive. Since determining itself is the very activity of valid cognition, it is a necessary (Skt. *niyata*) activity. Given that a cognition is valid cognition by virtue of what it does, it is a necessary activity. [424] That which is its necessary activity is also expressed as its result. Therefore valid cognition has determining as a result. In the phrase "Valid cognition has ascertaining as a result," the term *ascertaining* signifies understanding or determining. Here [*Exposition of Valid Cognition*] says, "Determining signifies a phase of obtaining" and "has engaging as a result," which is explained to mean: "Since it is a phase of engaging, determining that is a phase of obtaining is valid cognition." So, since it is a cause of engaging, it is determining that is a phase of engaging. Therefore valid cognition is a cognizing subject of an object not previously realized. Now, one may ask, if the cause of *obtaining* is different from the cause of *realizing*, then another cognition would be the cause of obtaining any real thing that is realized, so even a cognizing subject that had already realized its object would be a valid cognition. Since determining is the cause of obtainment, the realization of any thing with which a person

> engages causes obtainment of the object. Therefore, since there is no cause of obtainment for others, such as the second or third moment, not already obtained before, it does not constitute valid cognition.[697]

Now, someone may consider, "If valid cognition in the sense of being nondeceptive is posited to obtain the identified thing that is its engaged object, then since valid perception exists only for a single moment, one cannot posit the engaged object to be that which is obtained. Since inferential cognition is similar in this respect, neither perception nor inferential cognition can be posited to be valid cognition." This doubt is examined in Dharmottara's short *Investigation of Valid Cognition*: [425]

> *Qualm*: If determining, which is a phase of obtaining, is the activity of valid cognition, then direct perception would not be valid cognition because it lacks the activity of valid cognition. If one maintains that the arising of conceptual cognition, whether affirmative or negative, from direct perception is its activity, this would mean that the activity of valid cognition would be something different from the cognition, which cannot be correct [for you]. Furthermore, given that activity is an effect, there would be the consequence for you that you do not uphold the view that an effect is different [from its cause]. In that case it would scarcely be called "direct perception," and inferential cognition too would not be valid cognition. Given that the activity of valid cognition is a kind of determining that is a phase of obtaining, if inferential cognition being that kind of determining ceases, since it does not remain for more than a moment, how could inferential cognition possibly be determining that is a phase of obtaining? Indeed, if another conceptual cognition apart from inferential cognition were to arise, by means of what would it obtain?
>
> *Response*: In that case, either the entire assembly of inferential cognitions and so on preceding the final moment of obtainment would be valid cognition, or just the conceptual cognition immediately preceding the obtainment would be valid cognition, but not the inferential cognition itself. By means of this, *conceptual direct perception* is demonstrated.

Therefore the situation here is as follows. When the pervaded is known based on the subject, then the pervader is necessarily ascertained, for this is the activity of inferential cognition, whereas the activity of other conceptual cognitions is merely to experience. Accordingly, [426] at the time of engaging in analysis when all the sense consciousnesses have ceased, seeing the function of analysis or seeing the pervaded object based on the subject is not a realization that ascertains another phenomenon related to the subject; rather, from experience, the activity of thinking is ascertained to be "mere analyzing" (Skt. *vicāramātra*). So apart from their own functioning, whatever is an appearance to a special cognition must be viewed as the activity of another cognition, owing to positive and negative concomitance. Although "I see that" is just a perceptual ascertainment, it is a special cognition within conceptual cognition. Conceptual cognition does not see that thing, but it analyzes it. Therefore conceptual cognition, having abandoned its own activity of analyzing, adopts the function of seeing that is the activity of perception. Thus, as long as the seeing that is the activity of perception is present, it is direct perception itself that establishes the object. And as long as there is conceptual cognition of the one bearing a relationship based upon seeing the other to which it is related, it is inferential cognition that does so [i.e., establish the object]. In this case, inferential cognition itself is the cause of indication. For the cause of indicating the engaged object based on seeing something else that is related cannot be the activity of another conceptual cognition. Therefore all those kinds of conceptual cognition *having the activity of perception* are valid cognitions and indicate seeing that still retains its force, whereas those kinds *having the activity of inferential cognition* are not valid inferential cognitions that still retain its force. [427] Thus the cause of obtainment is direct perception and inferential cognition only. In that case, for example, inferential cognition obtains its own object, and just as other conceptual cognitions similarly ascertain and engage in other things, so also should direct perception be understood. This too is totally correct because, since that which is the cause of indicating the engaged object is valid cognition,

> that which is the *cause of indicating* the engaged object is the very cognition that *indicates* the engaged object. Accordingly, that which is indicated is the engaged object, while the indicating is the cognition that indicates it.[698]

In brief, Dharmottara distinguishes between two types of objects of valid cognition: the observed object and the engaged object. This is because the activity of valid cognition is not posited in terms of the object that appears but must be posited in terms of the object that is ascertained; it establishes the truth of Dharmakīrti's statement that valid cognition possesses the result of ascertainment. For example, in his long *Investigation of Valid Cognition*, Dharmottara states the following:

> What then is the engaged object of a positing cognition? It is the conceived object determined by cognition, for if it is that which is sought, then a person engages with it. Thus even when an object is not [directly] observed by the cognition, in being the engaged object of an inferential cognition, it is expressed as the engaged object of that cognition. So that which is determined [428] is its engaged object, which is its cause of obtainment, for if it is not ascertained then there will be no engagement. Such a cognition does not cause obtainment [of the object] through producing the means of functioning; rather, it is through enabling engagement with it. This is not like a person who cannot walk by himself being enabled to do so by holding his hand; rather, where the engaged object is not cognized and thus cannot be engaged, it functions to indicate the object. To indicate the object is to fully determine it. Therefore only the object that is engaged is ascertained by the cognition. Causing ascertainment is causing its engagement itself, because it is engaged by means of that [ascertainment]. Thus valid cognition is expressed as having the result of ascertainment.
>
> Because it has been indicated that "its activity of causing engagement causes ascertainment itself," a subject that takes on an object not realized before is thereby shown to be a valid cognition. This being so, if the activity of causing engagement were to be different from ascertainment, where the object realized

> by one of them is obtained indirectly by the other, then since the cause of obtaining engagement itself is valid cognition, it would be a cognizing subject that realizes something that has already been cognized before. If the mere cause of realization is the cause of engagement, then whatever causes this thing to be realized is the valid cognition that obtains it, since that engaged object would be engaged by just that person. Thus, with respect to other types of cognition, since there is no cause of obtainment that did not exist previously, it is not valid cognition. If there is no ascertainment, then since there is no other method, it does not cause engagement, thus it is not the engaged object; also it does not cause obtainment, because there is no other means to do so. Therefore, [429] given that perception and inferential cognition obtain the object of engagement by way of ascertainment, they are both, without difference, stated to be valid cognition with reality as their object. If a cognition does not ascertain, then even if such a direct perception were to observe the object through bearing its appearance, it is not posited to be valid direct perception. This is because without ascertainment it cannot be an engaged object, so it cannot be obtained. Therefore it is not in relation to apprehending its object that a cognition is determined to be valid, because that alone is not a feature of the obtainment of the object. The activity of obtaining the engaged object of valid cognition is the very meaning of ascertainment; it is not simply observing it.[699]

The above passages from Dharmottara's *Investigation of Valid Cognition* have been quoted at length here because they explain how very important it is to understand precisely what is meant by saying that valid cognition is nondeceptive. Now, in both Dharmakīrti's *Exposition of Valid Cognition* and *Ascertainment of Valid Cognition* it is stated that direct perception is nonascertaining in nature.[700] Dharmottara, however, interprets the meaning of this nondeceptiveness of valid cognition to mean that *it ascertains its engaged object*. Therefore there is evidently a need to further investigate how Dharmottara's account does not contradict these two texts by Dharmakīrti. [430]

22

Direct Perception

HAVING INVESTIGATED the enumeration and definition of valid cognition in general, we will now explain the two types of valid cognition separately. First, there is direct perception, which we present in two sections: the definition of direct perception and its categories. We will do this on the basis of Dignāga's *Compendium of Valid Cognition Autocommentary*, which explicitly lists the views of earlier Indian thinkers on perception. He writes:

> The followers of Kapila (the Sāṅkhya) assert that the engagement of auditory and other senses is perception. They say that when the auditory, tactual, visual, gustatory, and olfactory senses, controlled by the mind, engage their objects—sounds, tangibles, forms, tastes, and smells—and apprehend them respectively, this is perceptual valid cognition.[701]

Thus the Sāṅkhya consider valid perception to be the engagement of the physical sense faculties, such as the eye, with regard to their respective objects, such as form. The Vaiśeṣika posit direct perception regarding a substance to involve a relation between a sense faculty and its object: "The Vaiśeṣika say that, as mentioned in the sūtra, perception regarding a substance is established only from a relation."[702] As for the Naiyāyika, [431] the same text [by Dignāga] explains: "The Naiyāyika say that a cognition that arises from contact between a sense faculty and its object, and is inexpressible, unmistaken, and determinate in nature, is perception."[703] In other words, when contact between a sense faculty and its object gives rise to a cognition, which is a mind that conceptually cognizes and determines its object, it is valid direct perception. The Mīmāṃsaka say that when contact between a sense faculty and an existent object gives rise to a cognition, it is direct perception. On this, Dignāga's *Compendium of Valid Cognition Autocommentary* states: "The Mīmāṃsaka say that when a cognition arises from an appropriate meeting of a person's sense faculties with something existent, it is perception."[704] In particular the Mīmāṃsaka maintain that only the first moment of cognition directed toward its object is nonconceptual, while all other perceptions are just conceptual. As for the proponents of *śabdabrahma* (word-sound as Brahman), Kamalaśīla's *Commentary on the Difficult Points in the Compendium of Reality* reports:

> There is no cognition in the world except for
> those that operate in connection with word-sounds;
> it is simply the case that all cognitions
> are always associated with word-sounds.[705]

Since they assert that any type of cognition whatsoever operates in connection with word-sound, then even perception operates in such a manner and thus is conceptual. As for Dignāga's own standpoint, *Compendium of Valid Cognition* says:

> Direct perception is free from conceptualization
> that attaches a name, a type, and so on.[706] [432]

Hence Dignāga posits *cognition that is free from conceptuality* that differentiates in terms of name, type, quality, activity, substance, and so on to be direct perception. Dharmakīrti adds *nondeceptive* to this, so according to his system the definition of *direct perception* is: a cognition that is unmistaken and free from conceptuality. His *Ascertainment of Valid Cognition* says: "Direct perception is unmistaken and free from conceptuality; a cognition that is nonconceptual and does not arise erroneously owing to an eye disorder, fast spinning, boat travel, disturbance, and so on is direct perception."[707]

In Dignāga's *Compendium of Valid Cognition* and its autocommentary, although the term *nondeceptive* is not directly applied as a facet of the definition of direct perception, it is explained that direct perception must be unmistaken with regard to its appearing object. For instance, Dignāga's *Compendium of Valid Cognition Autocommentary* says: "As for mistaken cognition, because it conceives a mirage to be water, and so forth, it is fallacious perception."[708] By stating that nonconceptual mistaken cognition, such as a cognition mistaking a mirage for water, is fallacious perception, this passage indirectly indicates that correct perception must be unmistaken.

In general, if cognition is unmistaken, it must be free from conceptuality. So why is there a need to mention both *unmistaken* and *free from conceptuality* in the definition of direct perception? Dharmottara's *Commentary on the Drop of Reasoning* says: "*Qualm*: Why are both of those attributes stated? [433] *Response*: 'Unmistaken' is mentioned in order to exclude mistaken cognition endowed with a diseased eye faculty. 'Free from conceptuality' is mentioned in order to exclude inferential cognition."[709] If merely being *free from conceptuality* were direct perception, then a sensory cognition to which falling hairs appear and so on would be direct perception; so to exclude this, *unmistaken* is stated. Also, if merely being *unmistaken regarding its object* were accepted to be direct perception, then an inferential cognition would be direct perception; so to exclude this, *free from conceptuality* is stated.

Proving that Perception Is Free from Conceptuality and Unmistaken

The "Perception" chapter of Dharmakīrti's *Exposition of Valid Cognition* provides extensive logical arguments as to why direct perception is free from conceptuality. First it shows that it is proved by perception itself that direct perception is free from conceptuality, then it is proved by inferential cognition based on reasoning. In particular, it is refuted at great length in each case that sense direct perception, for example, is *conceptual cognition associating a referent* or *conceptual cognition associating a word*, which proves the point that sense consciousness is free from conceptuality.[710] Next, in response to someone else's claim that sense consciousness is conceptual, it argues: in that case all cognitions would necessarily be conceptual, so there would be no factor experiencing the cognition apprehending a form; and since experience necessarily precedes recollection, recollection of the past would be impossible; moreover, a mind seeing unique particulars would be impossible. [434] Thus by positing a great number of criticisms in this way, it is thoroughly refuted. Such detailed points as these can be understood from the explanations given in Dharmakīrti's *Exposition of Valid Cognition* and its commentaries. Now, by way of brief introduction, we will present Dharmakīrti's statement that the fact of direct perception being free from conceptuality is established by both direct perception and inferential cognition.

First, with regard to being proved by direct perception, Dharmakīrti's *Exposition of Valid Cognition* says:

> Perception is free from conceptuality
> as is proved by direct perception itself.
> All conceptualizations are language dependent,
> as is known by each individual's reflexive awareness.[711]

In general, the way things appear to perception within one's own experience proves that the direct perceptions apprehending forms and so on are free from conceptuality. All the conceptual cognitions of every living being are dependent on names or linguistic conventions, so they must have a linguistic referent (or word meaning) as their appearing object, whereas all direct perceptions, such as sensory cognitions, must apprehend a unique particular as their appearing object because the perceptual reflexive awareness within each individual's own experience must know that those conceptual cognitions and direct perceptions have those objects and appearances. Thus it is proved [that direct perception is free from conceptuality]. The above verse also says that one's own experience proves that perceptual cognitions, such as sense consciousness, within one's own continuum are free from conceptuality. Dharmakīrti's *Exposition of Valid Cognition* continues on to say:

> Even when resting in the stillness of our inner nature,
> having withdrawn the mind from everything else, [435]
> the cognition that sees forms with visual consciousness
> is nevertheless produced by the sensory faculties.
>
> When thoughts gradually arise again
> we know "our thoughts are like this,"
> which was not present in the state of
> sensory realization mentioned earlier.[712]

The above stanzas state that even when, having withdrawn the conceptual mind from scattering toward external things, one rests in the stillness of one's inner nature free from disturbances caused by thought, the visual cognition that sees various forms with the eye consciousness is still present. Such cognition establishes something nonconceptual based only on a sense consciousness arisen from the physical sense faculty that is its own uncommon dominant condition. Someone may wonder, "At the time of having withdrawn the mind from scattering toward all objects, is conceptual thought present?" If it were, then after having arisen from the state of mental withdrawal, when a slight thought occurs, pondering, "What were those earlier thoughts like during the state of mental withdrawal?" one would have to know by means of recollection that "Thoughts of mine like this occurred during the state of mental withdrawal earlier"—but the remembering cognition that arises later has no such knowledge.

Second, with regard to being proved by inferential cognition that direct perception is free from conceptuality, Dharmakīrti's *Exposition of Valid Cognition* says:

> A unique particular seen at one time
> is not seen on another occasion. [436]
> Yet there is no universal different from that
> because something different is not cognized.[713]

Also it says:

> It does not have the activity of a sensory cognition
> because it lacks an appearance due to mere speech.
> It does not [operate] without having relationships
> because this would entail that it cognizes itself.[714]

In stanzas such as those above, Dharmakīrti says that if sense consciousness were conceptual, then sensory cognition and conceptual cognition associating a label would similarly have a resemblance as the appearing object, but that is unfeasible. Sense consciousnesses are cognizing subjects that take unique particulars as their observed objects because language cannot directly engage with unique particulars by way of denotation. Dharmakīrti states that through reasonings such as these, cognitions that arise from the sensory faculties are established to be free from conceptuality.

Now, someone might ask, "If this is how direct perception is free from conceptuality, then how is it unmistaken?" In general, a mistaken consciousness is posited to be *a cognition that is mistaken with regard to its appearing object*. As for how it is mistaken, in the case of an inferential cognition realizing *sound is impermanent*, it is mistaken with regard to its *appearing object* in that its appearing object is engaged in a distorted manner, or does not exist as it appears. However, in the case of an inferential cognition apprehending *sound is permanent*, not only is it mistaken with regard to its appearing object, but it is also mistaken with regard to its *engaged object* in that its engaged object is engaged in a distorted manner, or does not exist as it is held; thus it is a *distorted cognition*. Therefore [437] cognition that is mistaken with regard to its appearing object is of two types: cognition that conforms with reality and cognition that does not conform with reality.

Mistaken cognitions have two kinds of causes of error regarding their respective objects: deep causes of error and temporary causes of error. A cognition that is distorted with regard to its cognized object's mode of existence and the latent propensities of that cognition are deep causes of error. These act as causes of error for conceptual mental cognitions to be distorted regarding their appearing object, which does not exist as it appears. As for how temporary causes of error, such as an eye disorder and so on, act as causes of error for sensory cognitions and nonconceptual mental cognitions, Vinītadeva's *Commentary on the Drop of Reasoning* says:

> Where [Dharmakīrti] says, "No error produced by such things as eye disorder, fast spinning, boat travel, elemental disturbance, and so on," the phrase *eye disorder* refers to eye disease; *fast spinning* refers to the spinning of a firebrand, or the like; *boat travel* refers to traveling by boat; and *elemental disturbance* refers to a disturbance of wind or bile, which is an imbalance of the elements.[715]

Thus temporary causes of error may exist in the basis (namely, the sense organ), in the object, in the location, or in the immediately preceding condition. Those causes of error influence the primary sensory consciousnesses to arise as mistaken regarding their appearing objects. The text goes on to say: "An eye disorder induces double vision, such as seeing a double moon. Fast spinning causes one to cognize a firebrand as a ring of fire. Traveling in a boat, [438] one sees the trees on the river bank passing by. Disturbed by wind, bile, and so on, one sees things glowing and so on."[716]

From the perspective of a standpoint shared by the Sautrāntika and Cittamātra systems, it is on the basis of being free from these four temporary causes of error that perception is posited as obtaining its object in an unmistaken manner, as stated in Vinītadeva's *Commentary on the Drop of Reasoning*: "The treatise [*Drop of Reasoning*] intends to represent the views of [both] Sautrāntika and Yogācāra, and both systems posit the definition of *nondeceptive* to be that which obtains its object; thus they both say it is unmistaken."[717] Sensory cognitions are posited to be either mistaken or unmistaken primarily in virtue of whether there are or are not temporary causes of error present. To this end the *Commentary on the Drop of Reasoning* says:

> Where there is a cause of error present, the cognition arises as mistaken. Where there is no cause of error present, it does not arise as mistaken. Where there is no cause of error present owing to an eye disorder, fast spinning, boat travel, elemental disturbance, and so forth, it does not arise as mistaken owing to an eye disorder, fast spinning, boat travel, elemental disturbance, and so on.[718]

In this context, any and all direct perceptions, since they necessarily do not arise as mistaken owing to the above-mentioned temporary and deep causes of error, [439] are asserted to be unmistaken cognitions—where the object actually exists as it appears to the cognition. Dharmakīrti's *Drop of Reasoning* says: "Here, direct perception is free from conceptuality and unmistaken. Conceptuality is cognition to which a signifying term and object appear suitable to be associated; so it is free from that. Direct perception is cognition in which no error has been induced by an eye disorder, fast spinning, boat travel, elemental disturbance, and so on."[719] The way in which mistakes arise in cognition owing to those causes of error has been explained at length in volume 2 of *Science and Philosophy in the Indian Buddhist Classics*.[720]

In the case of direct perception, since all the qualities of its observed object—in terms of place, time, and nature—clearly appear without being mixed up, the object actually exists as it appears. Jitāri's *A Beginner's Primer on Logic* says: "A cognition that directly perceives its object is direct perception. Conceptual thought and mistaken cognition do not directly perceive the essential nature of their object."[721] Because it directly perceives its object, it is nonconceptual and unmistaken.

In brief, these passages illustrate that a cognition that is free from a construing awareness that apprehends word and referent as suitable to be associated, and that is not influenced by deep causes of error such as grasping at permanence nor by temporary causes of error that exist in the basis, the object, [440] the location, or the immediately preceding condition, is posited as a *direct perception* or as an *unmistaken cognition* that directly perceives its engaged object.

As presented in these Buddhist epistemological texts, all direct perceptions are necessarily *unmistaken* in general, though each of the four types of direct perception, such as sense perception and so on, are not necessarily established separately as unmistaken. Having proved direct perceptions to be *free from conceptuality* in general, these are indirectly proved not to be mistaken cognitions that are conceptual. All mistaken nonconceptual cognitions are fallacious perceptions, as is proved in the context of explaining fallacious perception. When the definitions of each of the four types of direct perception are presented, these are rationally proved to be *free from conceptuality*, though apart from this they are not rationally proved to be *unmistaken*.

Categories of Perception

When categorized, there are four kinds of direct perception: (1) sense perception, (2) mental perception, (3) reflexive awareness, and (4) yogic perception. The significance of Dignāga and Dharmakīrti categorizing perception into these four types is stated in Dharmottara's *Commentary on the Drop of Reasoning*:

> "This is fourfold" relates to what is referred to as perception. It should be understood that these four kinds are: cognition induced by a sense faculty, mental perception, reflexive awareness, and yogic perception. These divisions are presented so as

> to exclude wrong notions. [441] Some philosophers say that the sense faculties themselves are perceivers, so in order to exclude that, the first category is stated; cognition induced by a sense faculty is direct perception but it is not a sense faculty. Some philosophers raise objections against mental direct perception, so in order to dispel such objections, the second category is stated. Some philosophers do not accept mind and mental factors to be reflexively aware, so in order to exclude that, the third category is stated. Some philosophers do not accept perception by yogic means, so in order to dispel that, the fourth category of direct perception is stated.[722]

This fourfold categorization of perception is based on the Sautrāntika and Yogācāra traditions.

Sense Direct Perception

As for the first category, the definition of *sense direct perception* is: a cognition that is unmistaken and free from conceptuality and that arises in dependence on its uncommon dominant condition, a physical sense faculty, and on its objective condition, a visual form. Moreover, although an eye consciousness apprehending a visual form, for example, arises from a combination of three conditions—its objective condition (a visual form), its dominant condition (the eye sense faculty), and its immediately preceding condition (the moment of consciousness that arose immediately preceding it)—it is named in accordance with the sense faculty that is its dominant condition. Dignāga's *Compendium of Valid Cognition* says:

> It is named based on the sense faculty
> because this is its uncommon cause.[723]

Since the physical sense faculty is its uncommon cause, [442] this enables one to identify it in particular, just as a seed that comes from barley is called a "barley seed" and a sound that comes from a drum is called a "drum sound."

There are five kinds of sense perception, which range from sense perceptions apprehending visual forms to sense perceptions apprehending tangible objects.

Mental Direct Perception

As for the second category, the definition of *mental direct perception* is: a cognition that is unmistaken and free from conceptuality and that arises in dependence on its own uncommon dominant condition, a mental sense faculty. Regarding its kinds, a sūtra passage states: "O monks, the cognition of visual form is of two types: one based on the eye [sense faculty] and the other on the mental [faculty]."[724] There are two types of mental direct perception: mental perception that is presented in the above quotation [which is based on a prior sensory cognition], and mental perception that is not mentioned there. An example of the first is a mental perception apprehending a visual form, which arises within an ordinary being's mindstream. An example of the second is a clairvoyant mental perception that cognizes another person's mind. Suppose someone asks whether there is valid mental direct perception. Although there is mental perception that is valid cognition, since reflexive awareness and yogic perception are both mental direct perception, Dharmakīrti's *Exposition of Valid Cognition* explains that there is no valid cognition that is a mental perception within the continuum of an ordinary being such as that taught in the above sūtra quotation. [443] However, one must understand that this differs from the Prāsaṅgika Madhyamaka view that even among the mental perceptions within an ordinary being's mindstream there is valid cognition.

With respect to mental direct perception apprehending a visual form, its three conditions are posited as follows. The final moment of the sense perception that arises immediately before the mental perception is both the dominant condition and the immediately preceding condition of that mental perception. It is posited as the dominant condition from the perspective of the sense faculty that gives rise to that mental perception, and as the immediately preceding condition from the perspective of giving rise to its experiential nature. These two are the same entity but are conceptually distinct.[725] The visual form concurrent with the final moment of that sense perception is posited as the objective condition of that mental perception. These three conditions imprint three distinct traces on the basis of the mental perception—the factor of the object's appearance, the factor of experience, and the factor of the ability to apprehend the object—which are deposited respectively by the objective condition, the immediately preceding condition, and the dominant condition. Dharmottara's *Commentary on Ascertainment of Valid Cognition* says:

> As for the term "mental," since all cognitions are mental in nature, this must refer to dependence on just the mental [sense faculty]. The term "also" indicates it is subsumed within direct perception itself. Sense consciousness itself is immediately preceding and is a condition, for it is that from which it arises. This specifically indicates the cause. The object of the sense consciousness that immediately precedes it is what causes it to apprehend without obstruction. This specifically indicates the object. Such type of mental [cognition] is asserted to be direct perception.[726] [444]

In this context, the term "cause" refers to the dominant condition and the immediately preceding condition, while the term "object" refers to the objective condition.

Now someone might wonder, "When five sense perceptions have ceased simultaneously, do five mental perceptions arise at the same time, or does only one arise? If the former, then there would be many mindstreams within a single person. If the latter, then the waxing and waning of the result would not follow upon the waxing and waning of the cause." The first scenario is not accepted. As for the second, there is no problem. Since there is none other than a single mental consciousness directing the mind toward the second moment of the sense perception's observed object, many mental perceptions do not arise at the same time. How to dispel misconceptions about the definition of mental perception, its manner of arising and so on, as well as more extensive explanations about how mental perception arises and so on, have already been discussed in the section on the Sautrāntika tenets in chapter 12 in volume 3 of *Science and Philosophy in the Indian Buddhist Classics.*

Reflexive Awareness

Now we explain the third category, reflexive awareness, which is synonymous with perceptual reflexive awareness. Buddhist tenet systems in general include both those that accept reflexive awareness and those that do not accept it. The schools that do *not* accept reflexive awareness are Vaibhāṣika, Sautrāntika-Svātantrika Madhyamaka, and Prāsaṅgika Madhyamaka. Those that *do* accept reflexive awareness are Sautrāntika, Cittamātra, and Yogācāra-Svātantrika Madhyamaka. Although the Vaibhāṣika accept clear and aware experience as a factor of consciousness, they accept sense consciousness to be without images, thus they do not posit a subject-image or reflexive awareness. Apart from the object, form, and the visual consciousness to which it appears, they do not accept [445] that any intermediary—that is, an object-image (Skt. *grāhyākāra*) or a subject-image (Skt. *grāhakākāra*)—appears to the mind. Therefore they do not accept reflexive awareness.

Moreover, the Vaibhāṣika maintain, although cognitions demarcate other objects, they do not demarcate themselves; for example, there is nothing that is in the nature of both the cutter and the cut. Śubhagupta's *Proof of External Objects* says:

> In that we define cognition
> simply in terms of demarcating its object,
> it is irrelevant to ask us,
> "How does cognition know its object?"
>
> This consciousness is not the agent,
> nor is it the ultimate object acted upon.
> One can say it is cognition only, but
> to say it is the agent is a fabrication.[727]

Similarly, Kamalaśīla's *Summary of the Proponents' Positions in the Drop of Reasoning* says: "The Vaibhāṣika and so on claim that perceptual reflexive awareness is unfeasible because to act upon itself is contradictory."[728]

The Sautrāntika-Svātantrika Madhyamaka master Bhāviveka argues against the position that reflexive awareness appears by itself alone—separately from the appearance of an object to the mind—in such a way that while the mental cognition is directed toward it, a dualistic appearance of cognizer and cognized does not arise. [446] To prove that reflexive awareness as posited by the Sautrāntika and so on is incorrect, Bhāviveka's *Heart of the Middle Way* says:

> If the object-appearance itself
> is accepted to be mind's focal object,
> then apart from the object-appearance
> what else has the nature of mind?[729]

Commenting on the above text, Bhāviveka's *Blaze of Reasoning* says:

> According to us, the dawning of an object-appearance of a form, or suchlike, is seen to be just the nature of consciousness, but apart from the object-appearance no other self-appearance is seen. If there were a second entity in the nature of consciousness apart from the object-appearance itself, then what it is must be shown.[730]

In a similar manner, Jñānagarbha's *Distinguishing the Two Truths* says:

> Because reflexive awareness is untenable.[731]

Prāsaṅgika Madhyamaka does not accept reflexive awareness for the following reason. The apprehension of blue or the like, merely by means of establishing the object, blue, thereby establishes that blue is cognized. Since there is no need to establish that blue is cognized apart from establishing blue itself, this system does not accept reflexive awareness. Candrakīrti's *Clear Words* says: "[This is] because the number of valid cognitions [447] that occur is dependent upon the objects cognized, and because it is established that individual valid cognitions are found to have their own nature merely in conformity with the aspects of their [respective] cognized objects."[732] In other words, that there are two types of valid cognition is determined by there being two types of objects cognized; and in dependence on the cognized object's image appearing to valid cognition, the individual nature of the valid cognition cognizing it is established. For apart from establishing the cognized object, there is no need to establish valid cognition in some other way as in both the Sautrāntika and Cittamātra systems, because it is established merely by establishing the cognized object. Nāgārjuna's *Refutation of Objections* says:

> If valid cognitions were self-established,
> then cognized objects would be independent
> of the establishment of valid cognitions for you,
> for self-establishment is not dependent on anything else.[733]

In the above verse it says that if it were as others declare—namely, that it is not enough for valid cognition to be established merely by establishing the cognized object, but that valid cognition is established by valid cognition—then there must be a valid cognition that does not depend on the object cognized. In that case, there must be a functional thing that does not depend on causes and conditions. For this reason, any and all valid cognitions are established by the cognized object itself. As for the textual sources that do not accept reflexive awareness, the *Descent into Laṅkā Sūtra* says:

> Just as a blade cannot cut itself
> nor a finger point to itself,
> so too is the case of
> mind looking at itself.[734] [448]

Just as a knife is unable to cut itself, the tip of a finger is unable to touch itself, a man cannot carry himself on his own shoulders no matter how much effort he makes, a fire is unable to burn itself, and an eye is unable to look at itself, so too, as these textual sources say, consciousness cannot apprehend consciousness itself.

Those who accept reflexive awareness categorize experience into a bipartite[735] format: self-experiencing and other-experiencing. They say that when other-experiencing is refuted on the basis of one's own mental continuum then self-experiencing is proved. But since this division of cognizing consciousness is not exhaustive, consciousness not being self-experiencing does not exclude it from being merely experiencing—just as an oil lamp not being self-illuminating does not exclude it from being merely illuminating. Suppose someone objects, "An oil lamp *is* illuminated by itself." We reply, "In that case, darkness would be obscured by itself." If they accept this, then we reply, "So darkness would not be seen, just as a pot [is not seen] in the dark." Nāgārjuna's *Fundamental Treatise on the Middle Way* says:

> If the oil lamp were to illuminate
> itself and other things,
> then darkness would have to conceal
> itself and other things for sure.[736]

Someone might wonder, "If there were no reflexive awareness, then how could it be possible for an earlier experience to be remembered at a later time?" In the case of something such as blue, a recollection thinking "This was seen" is a recollection of the object, and a recollection thinking "I saw this" is a recollection of the subject. While the cognition that experienced the object earlier [449] had the experience and the cognition that remembers it later did not have the experience, both the experience and the recollection are produced through the causal capacity of one object. Even though the cognition that experienced the object earlier did not experience itself, it allowed the arising of a recollection later that remembered the subject. Although there is no reflexive awareness, other ways of generating memories are explained. For example, Śāntideva's *Engaging in the Bodhisattva's Deeds* says:

> "If reflexive awareness did not exist
> then how could consciousness remember?"
> Recollection arises from being related to an experience
> of the other [object], just as with a rodent's poisonous bite.[737]

Here, addressing the question, "If there were no reflexive awareness, then how could recollection occur?" Śāntideva responds by stating that when a recollection of the subject arises from an experience of the object, it is not a recollection deprived of consciousness because the recollection arises from a connection between the subject and object, as in "I saw this thing earlier." This is illustrated with the following example. Suppose a hibernating creature was bitten by a rat during the winter. At that time, although the rat transmitted an infection, the creature experienced the bite but did not experience the infection. Then some time later, upon hearing the sound of a thunderclap, he wakes up, at which point the potency of the infection has become manifest and the creature remembers, "When that rat bit me earlier, it transmitted an infection," even though he did not experience the infection at the time. In this scenario, the rat's bite is like the experience of the object apprehended earlier. The infection transmitted at the time of the bite is like the experience of the subject that was present consecutively with the apprehension of the object. At that time, the subject did not experience itself, just as the infection was not experienced at the time of the bite. The recollection of the bite is like the recollection of having experienced the object. The recollection of having experienced the object remembers the earlier subject, even though that subject did not experience itself. Thus even though the transmission of the infection earlier is not experienced via the recollection of the bite, [450] it is said to be like a recollection.

Also, reflexive awareness is not accepted because this would entail that action, agent, and object would be one. For example, since a woodcutter, the wood that is chopped, and the chopping of the wood are *not* one, it is declared unfeasible for a cognition to apprehend itself. This is because, according to the Prāsaṅgika Madhyamaka system, a cognition is imputed in dependence on its cognized object and therefore is not established by virtue of its intrinsic characteristics, and a cognized object is established in dependence on its cognition; thus not only are their terms mutually dependent but their referents also are merely imputed in mutual dependence. For this reason, reflexive awareness is not accepted.

Someone may wonder, "According to this Prāsaṅgika tradition, all cognitions such as the apprehension of blue and so on must be accepted to exist. If an apprehension of blue itself knows that it exists, then one must accept reflexive awareness. Conversely, if such a consciousness is cognized by another one, then this would lead to an infinite regress." This is a very difficult point indeed, so we will illustrate how the object and the subject are remembered. Since the recollection of the object itself also remembers the subject, there is no need for a separate recollection of the subject. Accordingly, since an eye consciousness apprehending blue and so on establishes the object, blue, it also establishes the knower of blue; indeed, apart from establishing blue, there is no need for some other way of establishing the knower of blue. The eye consciousness apprehending blue, by virtue of knowing blue, does not require some other intermediary valid cognition. Instead, the eye consciousness apprehending blue directly elicits a cognition that remembers the perception of blue. That very cognition itself, which remembers the perception of blue by the eye consciousness apprehending blue, realizes the eye consciousness apprehending blue. When that recollecting cognition remembers blue, it does not remember its cognized object by way of relinquishing *the eye consciousness apprehending blue* from within its sphere of cognition. [451] Rather, it is a recollection that, having discerned the apprehension of blue, thinks, "I saw blue." That recollecting cognition itself is a recollection of both the blue and the eye consciousness apprehending blue. Therefore, although the eye consciousness apprehending blue does not realize the eye consciousness apprehending blue, it is nevertheless considered to "establish itself" because the eye consciousness apprehending blue elicits the subsequent recollecting cognition.

With respect to the second, those who accept reflexive awareness, one might ask, "How is its existence established?" In general, Sautrāntika and so on present valid cognition and the object cognized as follows. The establishment of the object cognized is dependent on the establishment of the valid cognizer, and the establishment of the valid cognizer is dependent on a singularly unmistaken reflexive awareness or subjective aspect.[738] Such a subjective aspect establishes itself and does not need any other mind to establish it, thus it does not succumb to the fault of infinite regress. Moreover, insofar as something is an existent phenomenon, it must be established by valid cognition. Now, someone might ask, "If an object such as blue is established by an apprehension of blue, by what valid cognition is that apprehension of blue established?" The apprehension of blue is not established by the apprehension of blue itself, and it is not established by another valid cognition that is a completely different entity from it. Therefore, as proved by irreproachable reasoning, it must be established by a "perceptual reflexive awareness" that experiences the apprehension of blue. That reflexive awareness is said to be nothing other than the subjective aspect [of cognition] that is free from dualistic appearance and that is oriented exclusively inward.[739] In the case of every cognition, the factor that is clear awareness experiencing its own nature is the experiencing subject, while the objective aspect of that cognition is the experienced object. Here, the self-experiencing factor is known as *reflexive awareness*.

To illustrate this, when an eye consciousness apprehending blue arises, there arises both the factor that is an appearance of blue as external [452] and the factor that is clear awareness experiencing itself. The former is said to be the objective aspect and the latter the subjective aspect or reflexive awareness. For example, when a clear crystal ball is placed on a blue cloth, there is one factor that is the color change [in the crystal] affected by the blue [cloth] and one factor that is the clear nature of the crystal itself, both of which occur simultaneously. Accordingly, Dignāga's *Compendium of Valid Cognition Autocommentary* says: "In the case of cognition, two appearances arise: the appearance of itself and the appearance of the object."[740]

There is no difference between *the objective aspect of an eye consciousness apprehending blue*, *the eye consciousness apprehending blue*, and *the blue image appearing to an eye consciousness apprehending blue*; thus the objective aspect of an eye consciousness is the eye consciousness itself.[741] As for the meaning of "the image appearing to an eye consciousness," this refers to the eye consciousness itself arising and, due to its causes, assuming the image of its object, though there is nothing apart from itself that arises as that image. There is no difference between *the clarity and awareness experiencing the eye consciousness*, *the subjective aspect of the eye consciousness*, and *the perceptual reflexive awareness experiencing the eye consciousness*. Although both the Sautrāntika and Cittamātra systems agree on this meaning of *appearing image*, they differ in the following way. Sautrāntika asserts that an eye consciousness endowed with a blue image arises from a visual form that is external to the perceiver's own mental continuum, whereas Cittamātra says that the image arises owing to the causal capacity of internal latent propensities.

Buddhist masters who accept reflexive awareness [453] mainly use the following reasons to prove the existence of reflexive awareness: (1) the rational proof of the bipartite manner of cognition, (2) the proof of that from recollection, (3) the reason distinguishing between perception and experience, and (4) the reason of being in the nature of luminous clarity.

1) The rational proof of the bipartite manner of cognition goes as follows. Owing to the difference between the two distinct appearing images of the object and of consciousness—the object-image and the subject-image—the bipartite manner of cognition is established, which in turn proves the existence of reflexive awareness. The main argument proving the existence of reflexive awareness is as follows: "The *subject*, cognition, experiences itself because it arises as an image of its object, as in the case of affective states such as happiness and so on." In general, when cognition arises, the part that is the appearance of an external object and the part that is clear awareness experiencing its own nature both arise. The former is said to be the object-image and the latter the subject-image. A famous example is: "When a lamp is lit, it does not illuminate itself and other things such as pots consecutively; instead it illuminates them simultaneously." The property of the subject and the pervasion of this reason are established by the reasoning that proves these two modes. When any cognition engages an object, the *object-image* must definitely be present, which consists in the appearing image of the object and the experience of it. It has already been

refuted that it can be experienced by something substantially different from it. So when the *object-image* is established to be experienced by the *subject-image*, which is the factor of clear awareness experiencing its own nature, given that the existence of the *object-image* entails the existence of an experience of it, the pervasion is established. Dignāga's *Compendium of Valid Cognition Autocommentary* says:

> Owing to the distinction between cognition of the object and
> cognition of that [cognition], cognition itself is bipartite.
>
> The cognition of an *object*, such as a form, has an appearance of the object and of itself. [454] The cognition of an *object-cognition* has an appearance of the cognition that resembles the object and an appearance of itself. Otherwise, if the cognition of the object were to have only the appearance of the object, or only the appearance of itself, then the cognition of the object-cognition would not be different from the cognition of the object.[742] Furthermore, an object [of cognition] of the distant past would not appear to a cognition that arises later. Why not? Because it is not its object. Therefore it is established that cognition has two aspects.[743]

Thus here, the bipartite manner of cognition is proved because there are two distinct aspects—that which knows the object, such as visual form, and that which knows the subject cognizing it. Jinendrabuddhi's *Spacious and Stainless: Commentary on the Compendium of Valid Cognition* says:

> Why inquire about a bipartite division when a tripartite one is the object of inquiry?[744] The intent here is that when a bipartite division is established, then reflexive awareness is also established. For if a bipartite division is established, then a likeness to the object, which is in the nature of it [i.e., cognition], is the object correctly cognized by that consciousness. So by definition, reflexive awareness is established.[745]

Furthermore, Dharmakīrti's *Exposition of Valid Cognition* says:

> Due to establishing the bipartite [manner of cognition],
> reflexive awareness is also amply established.[746]

That is to say, the reasoning that proves the bipartite manner of a single cognition—the objective aspect and the subjective aspect—also [455] amply establishes reflexive awareness. One can understand this more fully by referring to *Exposition of Valid Cognition* and its commentaries.

2) The proof of the bipartite manner of cognition and the existence of reflexive awareness by the reason of recollection is as follows. "The *subject*, an apprehension of blue, has experience, because it is remembered at a later time." When one remembers, "I saw blue earlier," that recollection apprehends in a manner that includes both a part that remembers the object, as in the thought "Blue was seen," and a part that remembers the subject, as in the thought "I saw it." Where a cognition seeing blue did not arise earlier, a cognition recollecting seeing blue will not arise later. Likewise, where a cognition experiencing an apprehension of blue did not arise earlier, a cognition remembering that apprehension of blue itself—the cognizing subject—will not arise later. Therefore, since at the time of remembering the object its cognizing subject is also remembered, this proves that at the time of experiencing the object earlier, its cognizing subject was also experienced. This means that experience was present in the earlier apprehension of blue by the reason that it was remembered later. As for proving the presence of reflexive awareness experiencing itself in the earlier apprehension of blue, since an example that is established according to the opponent[747] cannot be found, it is not proved. In proving the presence of experience in the apprehension of blue, the experience of that is necessarily one of two mutually exclusive alternatives—either by itself or by another cognition. The first is not acceptable to the opponent. As for the second, when [Dharmakīrti's] own tradition refutes this they argue, "If that which pervades experience is refuted, then mere experience becomes untenable." This is accepted to be the best argument for proving reflexive awareness.

There are two objections to the apprehension of blue being experienced by a cognition other than itself. The first is that it would lead to an infinite regress. If the cognition that determines blue were determined by another cognition, then there would be no end to arising. [456] If the later cognition does not need another cognition to know it, then the earlier cognition also would not need another one. But if the later one needs another cognition, then that cognition too would also need another one, thereby incurring the fault of an infinite regress. The second criticism is that other objects would not be determined. If the earlier cognition were determined by the later one, then it would not realize other objects such as forms, and it would not transfer its focus to them. This is because if a much earlier cognition were determined by a much later cognition, then since the earlier cognition would be its observed object, the later one would need to arise. For in the absence of an epistemically proximate *internal* observed object, it could not engage an epistemically remote *external* one much earlier in the series of cognitions. Dignāga's *Compendium of Valid Cognition* says:

> The recollection at a later time also establishes
> the bipartite manner [of cognition] and reflexive awareness.[748]

The meaning of this is explained in Dignāga's *Compendium of Valid Cognition Autocommentary*:

> > The recollection at a later time also establishes
> > the bipartite manner [of cognition] . . .
>
> Since in the case of cognition, just as of its object, there arises recollection of the experience at a later time, the bipartite manner of cognition is established,
>
> > . . . and reflexive awareness.
>
> Why is this so?
>
> > Because it is not ever without experience.
>
> There is no recollection of seeing something that is not experienced, as in the case of remembering visual form and so on. Suppose someone asks: "Is this [cognition]—just like visual form and so on—experienced by another cognition?" This too is incorrect, because:
>
> > If it were experienced by another cognition
> > there would be an infinite regress.

> Here "there would be an infinite regress" [457] if it were experienced by another cognition. How so?
>
> > Because there is memory regarding that too.
>
> Regarding that cognition experienced by another cognition also, there would have to be another memory of it observed later. So, then, if that [memory] were experienced by another cognition, there would be an infinite regress.

> Thus there would be no transference [of focus]
> to another object, yet that is observed.
> Therefore undoubtedly reflexive awareness must be accepted.[749]

3) The reason distinguishing between perception and experience may be stated as follows. "The *subject*, a sense consciousness apprehending a visual form, is endowed with perception and experience that are different, because although it does not arise in the nature of the object perceived it does perceive a likeness of that object, and without arising in the nature of experiencing itself, it cannot serve to illuminate." Regarding this, Dharmakīrti's *Exposition of Valid Cognition* says:

> Thus in the case of all cognitions
> perception and experience are different:
> perceiving the likeness of the object
> and illuminating itself, it is self-experiencing.[750]

This states that in the case of all cognitions, perception and experience are different. Although it does not arise in the nature of the perceived object, it directly perceives the object through a resemblance to the thing that is perceived. It also experiences itself through arising as illumination in the nature of the experienced object, thus it experiences itself as the experienced object, which is posited as the reason. [458]

4) The reason proving the existence of reflexive awareness due to being in the nature of luminous clarity can be argued as follows. "The *subject*, a clear sense consciousness, is said to clearly illuminate itself, because it is the very nature of the object-image that is the experienced object of reflexive awareness." Just as an oil lamp illuminates both itself and other things without

requiring anything else to illuminate them and does not illuminate them consecutively, so too consciousness simultaneously illuminates both itself and other things without requiring anything else to illuminate them. Also, just as when a clear crystal ball is placed on a blue object, there is no contradiction between its being in the nature of blue and being in the nature of its own clarity, so too in the case of consciousness, there is no contradiction between it bearing the image of blue and being in the nature of its own clarity. The main point of this reasoning is that if consciousness is in the nature of its own luminous clarity, one must accept that consciousness illuminates itself; and if consciousness is *not* in the nature of its own luminous clarity, one must accept that it does not illuminate objects. Accordingly, Dharmakīrti's *Exposition of Valid Cognition* says:

> Because it illuminates itself, the object
> is illuminated by the nature of that.[751] [459]

Yogic Direct Perception

As for the fourth category, in Buddhist epistemological literature the existence of yogic direct perception is proved by means of reasoning based on empirical fact, such as the following. "The *subject*, loving-kindness and wisdom realizing impermanence—for example, within the mindstream of an ordinary person—is in the nature of a cognition that has the potential to realize its meditation object unmixed with an object universal if it has been cultivated without separation from the branches of meditative practice,[752] because it is a stable basis and is a quality that arises only in the nature of mind without depending on renewed effort in meditation." Dharmakīrti's *Exposition of Valid Cognition* says:

> Therefore, whatever one intensively meditates upon,
> whether it be something real or unreal,
> once that meditation has been perfectly completed
> it will result in a clear, nonconceptual cognition.[753]

Whatever the object may be, whether something real or unreal, when one meditates upon it intensively to the most powerful extent and perfectly completes it, this results in the arising of a nonconceptual cognition to which there appears an image, unmixed with an object universal, that is the object of meditation.

As for proof of [love, wisdom, and so on] being a stable basis, since love, wisdom, and so on are qualities that arise in the nature of mind only, and their basis consists in limitless moments of mere mental clarity and awareness, it is proved that they have a stable basis. Dharmakīrti's *Exposition of Valid Cognition* says:

> Your claim [that they are limited] being made, if it were
> dependent on renewed effort [460]
> or merely on an unstable basis,
> then those qualities would not increase,
> but their nature is not like that.[754]

Moreover, that same text says:

> Therefore, in arising from those [stable bases],
> they are qualities that naturally arise.[755]

As for [love, wisdom, and so on] not being dependent on renewed effort in meditation, Dharmakīrti's *Exposition of Valid Cognition* says:

> Love and so forth arise in the mind through habituation
> and naturally develop further,
> just as, owing to fire and so on, effects naturally develop further
> in wood, mercury, gold, and so on.[756]

When one meditates for a long time on love, wisdom, and so on, they naturally develop further in the mind. This is because they are qualities of the mind that, once they have become habitual, give rise to a continuum of many instances of similar type by means of effort exerted even on a single occasion without requiring effort every single time. Just as firewood naturally feeds the fire until it becomes ash or mercury naturally purifies stains on a piece of gold, when one has trained well in these qualities, further instances of similar type arise naturally without blemish. [461]

Thus due to satisfying these two attributes—being a stable basis and not being dependent on renewed effort once habituated—it is proved that love and so on can increase limitlessly, as follows. "The *subject*, mental states such as love and so on, are limitless when cultivated with both intense and continuous application, because they are qualities in the nature of the mind that grow from previously sown seeds of similar type." Dharmakīrti's *Exposition of Valid Cognition* says:

And since the mental states of love and so on
grow from earlier seeds of a similar type,
how could they be limited
if they are being cultivated?[757]

These are some illustrations of the extensive teachings on how to prove the existence of yogic direct perception.

To offer another example, just as the illumination of a light completely dispels the darkness, so a mind strongly habituated to good qualities will through their capacity bring to cessation the sets of faults. Insofar as love and so on are qualities that depend on a stable mental basis, they will increase owing to stability and powerful habituation. When meditation is maintained without separating from conducive conditions that increase owing to that habituation, then habituation will increase without limit; and since the sets of faults have no valid support, their propensities will gradually [462] become reduced until they are finally extinguished. The way to accomplish this is set out in detail in the path of reasoning in the Buddhist treatises.

Fallacious Perception

Having discussed the four kinds of direct perception, it is also important to understand another type of perception—that which is fallacious. Given that correct perception is established as unmistaken with regard to its appearing object, fallacious perception is explained to be the opposite or converse of that. Dignāga's *Compendium of Valid Cognition* says:

Mistaken cognition, conventional consciousness,
inference, that which arises from inference,

recollection, and desire, along with [perceptions distorted by
an] eye disorder
and so forth, are fallacious perceptions.[758]

This verse lists six types of fallacious perception that are conceptual cognitions and one type of fallacious perception that is nonconceptual. The first six are: conceptual cognition that is mistaken with regard to its engaged object, such as a distorted conceptual cognition apprehending a mirage to be water; conventional conceptual cognition, such as a conceptual cognition apprehending a coarse composite object or a continuum; inferential cognition, which is a mind apprehending a reason or evidence; inferential cognition realizing the thesis, which arises from a mind apprehending the reason; conceptual cognition remembering a past thing; and conceptual cognition wishing to actualize something in the future. The type of fallacious perception that is nonconceptual is: distorted nonconceptual cognition, such as a sense consciousness under the influence of an impaired sense faculty that is its basis, as in the case of an eye disorder or the like.

Dharmakīrti's *Exposition of Valid Cognition* presents what he calls "four types of fallacious perception."[759] Here the above seven types of fallacious perception are subsumed into four kinds as follows. A conventional conceptual cognition apprehending a coarse composite object or a continuum and so on is subsumed into: (1) conceptual cognition that is based on a linguistic convention. A conceptual cognition apprehending a mirage to be water and so on is subsumed into: (2) conceptual cognition that superimposes something else onto its object. [463] The remaining four conceptual cognitions listed above—inferential cognition through conceptual cognition wishing to actualize something in the future—are subsumed into: (3) a mind that has a hidden object. The type of fallacious perception that is nonconceptual is subsumed into: (4) a nonconceptual cognition that arises from a temporary cause of error where an impaired sense faculty is its dominant condition. The first three of these fallacious perceptions are conceptual, whereas the fourth is nonconceptual. Texts such as Dignāga's *Compendium of Valid Cognition Autocommentary* explain that both mistaken cognition and conventional [conceptual] cognition are taught for the purpose of establishing that they are not cognitions that arise from the sense faculties. Dharmakīrti's *Exposition of Valid Cognition* says:

> In order to establish that they do not arise from the sense faculties,
> two types are explained on account of the perception of errors.[760]

Suppose someone asks, "Why do those philosophers consider these two to be causes of error in sensory cognition?" Conceptual cognition based on a linguistic convention, such as a thought apprehending a pot, and conceptual cognition that superimposes something else onto its object, such as a thought apprehending a mirage to be water, are causes of error in sensory cognition when a person is in a specific spatiotemporal location; this is because they immediately follow, respectively, a visual consciousness seeing a pot and a visual consciousness seeing the color of a mirage in that spatiotemporal location. Dharmakīrti's *Exposition of Valid Cognition* says:

> Conceptual cognition that is based on a linguistic convention
> and that which superimposes something else onto its object [464]
> are both a cause of error on specific occasions
> because they immediately follow a direct perception.[761]

Again, someone might ask, "For what purpose does [Dharmakīrti] present the remaining four—those subsumed into conceptual cognition that has a hidden object?" Although it was already established by means of the rational arguments outlined above that those four conceptual cognitions are not sensory cognitions, nevertheless they are categorized as fallacious perception. This is because they are seen to be homologous examples of the reason proving that conceptual cognition that is based on a linguistic convention and conceptual cognition that superimposes something else onto its object are not sensory cognitions. Dharmakīrti's *Exposition of Valid Cognition* says:

> Inference and so on, established [as conceptual], are stated
> for the purpose of proving that the first two are just that.[762]

The purpose of presenting the type of fallacious perception that is nonconceptual is explained as follows. In Dignāga's verse quoted above, the phrase "along with [perceptions distorted by an] eye disorder" applies not only to an eye disorder, such as jaundiced eyes and so on, but is stated to indicate that all cognitions arisen from impaired sense faculties are fallacious perception, because it is not only an eye disorder that is identified as a source of fallacious perception. Dharmakīrti's *Exposition of Valid Cognition*, having subsumed the six fallacious perceptions such as mistaken conceptual cognition into three categories, offers the following argument, summarized as follows. "The *subject*, the proof that they are not sense consciousnesses, has the purpose of subsuming the homologous examples into two categories, because it indicates the basis of debate in the proof that the first two items are not sense consciousnesses, [465] and that the remaining four items, since their homologous examples are of the same kind, are subsumed into two categories." The purpose of presenting the type of fallacious perception that is nonconceptual is as stated above.

Nonconceptual fallacious perceptions—indicated by the words "along with [perceptions distorted by an] eye disorder" in the verse above—can be interpreted in different ways, but Jinendrabuddhi specifically explains this in terms of the object regarding which it is mistaken or unmistaken. His *Spacious and Stainless Commentary on the Compendium of Valid Cognition* says:

> Thus a cognition with an eye disorder and so on having an appearance of falling hairs is not nondeceptive with regard to what is desired, such as real falling hairs, and is simply not a valid cognition regarding that. [It is similar for] one with eyes impaired by jaundice causing a white conch to appear as a yellow conch and so on, one having an image of an unclear blue patch instead of a clear blue patch due to the eyes being covered for a long time by cataracts or due to being far away, or one that is mistaken owing to traveling in a boat where even the trees stationed on the riverbank appear to have the action of moving. Although these ways and others are mistaken due to apprehending what is not so to be so, since they are related to the real thing and thereby nondeceptive regarding their desired objective, some must be counted as valid in relation to some [aspects of their object]. Thus, operating from that basis and provided there is no obstacle, one accomplishes the desired objective, which has the

> capacity to function through simply being a real thing, such as a conch. [466] Otherwise, if these are not accepted to be valid cognition owing to a distorted appearance only, even though they are nondeceptive, then inferential cognition too must not be accepted [as valid cognition] for the very same reason. But it is not the case that inferential cognition is not accepted. Therefore there is no contradiction regarding such cognitions being valid with respect to the thing—that is, the conch that has causal capacity—in relation to which they are nondeceptive. The following can also be said: any cognition in which a person fully engages that necessarily accomplishes the desired objective, provided there is no obstacle, is a valid cognition of that [person] regarding that [objective]. Perception and inference are examples, as already asserted.[763]

The main points of this passage can be expressed as follows. First, nonconceptual cognition that is nondeceptive and engages its object is posited to be valid direct perception. Next, a sensory cognition having an appearance of falling hairs does not fulfill the criterion of being nondeceptive, so it is not a valid direct perception. Nevertheless, sensory cognitions such as those impaired by jaundiced eyes having an appearance of a yellow conch or affected by boat travel having an appearance of moving trees are valid direct perceptions. This is because, on the one hand, they are nonconceptual and thus not inferential cognitions, and on the other hand, they are nondeceptive regarding their desired objectives—the conch and the trees. Otherwise, if merely being mistaken necessarily entailed not being valid cognition, then the same would apply to inferential cognition.

Now, someone may wonder, "If Dignāga's words 'along with [perceptions distorted by an] eye disorder' indicate that all cognitions having defective sense faculties are fallacious perceptions, then this contradicts the teachings." That fault does not apply here. Since that which is deceptive owing to the sense faculty being impaired by an eye disorder [467] is taught to be fallacious, those two sensory cognitions of a yellow conch and moving trees are taught to be fallacious perception. However, sensory cognitions of a conch and trees in general are not taught to be fallacious perception; thus it is only those nonconceptual cognitions endowed with any deceptive factors that are illustrations of fallacious perception.

Dharmottara's explanation differs from the above in certain respects. His *Commentary on Ascertainment of Valid Cognition* says:

> Since the appearance of this affected image does not accord with the real thing, the appearance does not rely on the real thing; thus it is fallacious perception, like conceptual cognition.
>
> *Qualm*: Although the appearance of falling hairs is not an appearance that accords with the real thing, aren't some affected cognitions that arise from a sense faculty accepted to arise from something existent, such as the moon? Or are all appearances said not to accord with reality?
>
> *Response*: The phrase "because it is deceptive" is explained as follows. Because things do not exist externally as they appear to [they are deceptive]—like a cognition to which falling hairs appear where no object at all exists—so it is in the case of the appearance of something such as a double moon, where no object exists, because a double moon and moving trees do not exist externally as they appear to. Since the affected appearance is deceptive and misleading, it does not accord with reality, thus it is fallacious perception.[764] [468]

This master explains that any sensory cognitions having an affected basis, in that they are mistaken in every respect regarding place, time, and manner, are not suitable to be direct perception. Because a sense consciousness apprehending a yellow conch is not unmistaken regarding some factor of the conch, it is not a valid cognition. Indeed, that cognition cannot implicitly realize its object without explicitly realizing it, because no factor of the conch appears as an image [within the mind] apart from the yellow appearance. Suppose someone suggests, "Although the white color does not appear, the shape of the conch appears." The shape of the conch and its white color must appear as the same entity, but its color does not appear since it is unrelated to yellow—so to say its shape appears to direct perception is totally beyond reasoning. Although the conch is obtained and apprehended by valid perception that apprehends the conch as a tangible object [i.e., by tactile perception], the earlier claim has no meaning. Other cases, such as the appearance of moving trees, are to be understood in the same way.

Further points concerning fallacious perception, taught as part of eliminating sources of error with regard to developing correct perception, can be found in chapter 4 in volume 2 of *Science and Philosophy in the Indian Buddhist Classics.*

23

Valid Inferential Cognition

ALTHOUGH MOST Indian philosophers accept inferential cognition, there are some subtle differences between the ways they posit its definition, support, evidence, and so forth. In terms of the Buddhist logico-epistemological tradition, Dignāga is the first to make a terminological division of inference into two types—for one's own purpose and for the purpose of others. Dignāga's *Compendium of Valid Cognition* says [469]:

> Of the two types of inference, for one's own sake is this:
> perceiving the object via a trimodal reason.[765]

In accordance with the above verse, the definition of an inference for one's own purpose is: a construing awareness that perceives its object of comprehension, which is something hidden, in dependence on a reason qualified by the three modes. This type of construing awareness is called an *inference for one's own purpose*. It is called *for one's own purpose* because it functions to eliminate superimpositions within the mindstream of the person possessing it, and it is called an *inference* because it is a cognition that perceives the trimodal reason and infers the thesis upon recollecting the relation between the reason and the predicate. When—through the force of repeated analysis by means of valid cognition, subsequent cognition, and so on, which are minds apprehending the reason definitively qualified by the three modes, as explained below—a determinate cognition regarding the hidden phenomenon that is the object of comprehension, or a valid cognition arisen from thinking which realizes that, initially arises, it is called *valid inferential cognition*. This kind of valid inferential cognition is said to be traceable back to an initial direct perception that determines the subject (the basis of debate) and to culminate in a yogic direct perception that directly realizes its hidden object of comprehension unmixed with a universal. Thus on occasions when the object cannot be taken as an object of direct perception, but must be known by means of reasoning as a hidden object of comprehension based on a correct reason or correct evidence as its support, such as a newly nondeceptive construing awareness, it is called a *valid inferential cognition for one's own purpose*. [470]

Inferential valid cognition has different kinds of reasons as its support. Categorized according to the object's mode of existence, or the mind's ability to realize it, there are three types: inferential cognition based on empirical fact, inferential cognition based on popular convention, and inferential cognition based on trustworthy testimony.

As for the first, the definition of *valid inferential cognition based on empirical fact* is: a construing awareness that is newly nondeceptive regarding its object of comprehension, a slightly hidden object, in reliance on correct evidence based on empirical fact. An example is a valid inferential cognition realizing that sound (the basis of debate here) is impermanent and changeable in nature through the evidence that it is produced by causes and conditions. Dharmottara's *Commentary on the Drop of Reasoning* says:

> It is because its three modes are established by valid cognition that evidence based on empirical fact engages its object. One does not seek for some additional evidence in a scriptural source. Thus, since it does not rely on scripture, anything established by that means is thoroughly established even if it contradicts scripture, because that does not undermine it.[766]

When it comes to proving the thesis and realizing the object to be comprehended, the two respectively—inferential evidence based on empirical fact and valid inferential cognition based on that—do not need to rely on scriptural refutation or proof. Thus they are said to operate only by way of concurring with their object's mode of existence.

As for the second, the definition of *valid inferential cognition based on popular convention* is: a construing awareness that is newly nondeceptive regarding its object of comprehension, a language-based popular convention, in reliance on correct evidence based on popular convention. [471] An example is a valid inferential cognition realizing that the word *tree* can be used to refer to that which has boughs and foliage. Śākyabuddhi's *Commentary on Exposition of Valid Cognition* says:

> As for "an inference known as '[that based on] popular convention,'" a popular convention that conforms with mere acceptance is posited to be that which is signified by an arbitrary word in conformity with what is merely accepted. Thus, through nature-evidence, it can be inferred that what is signified by an arbitrary word can be applied to an existent phenomenon. It is the cognizing subject of such a convention that is being inferred here. Since such a cognition would have been created through successive stages by popular convention, this type of inference is referred to as *inference based on popular convention*.[767]

Thus it is explained that because the thesis of such an inference consists of merely a language-based popular convention, the two—the evidence that proves the thesis and the inferential cognition that realizes the thesis in dependence on it—are respectively called *correct evidence based on popular convention* and *inferential cognition based on popular convention*.

As for the third, the definition of *valid inferential cognition based on trustworthy testimony* is: a construing awareness that is newly nondeceptive regarding its object of comprehension, a very hidden object, in reliance on correct evidence based on trustworthy testimony that has passed the threefold analysis.[768] [472] An example is a valid inferential cognition that realizes its object of comprehension, a very hidden object—which is not an object of a person's direct perception nor inferential cognition based on empirical fact—in dependence on its reason, a scriptural statement that has passed the threefold analysis. Śākyabuddhi's *Commentary on Exposition of Valid Cognition* says:

> As for trustworthy testimony, its status as nondeceptive is inferred from a general situation where the words of those who are free of faults are nondeceptive—for example, "All causally compounded things are momentary." So the statements [of those] free of faults regarding very hidden objects are also [nondeceptive].[769]

This is saying that based on having ascertained that the meanings of statements of those who teach how objects of knowledge in general exist are nondeceptive, such as "Causally compounded things are impermanent," one can then generate valid inferential cognition based on this trustworthy testimony that realizes its very hidden subject matter. This occurs in reliance on a correct reason that has passed the threefold analysis, with regard to statements of those who speak about very hidden objects of knowledge in particular.

Next, an inference for the purpose of others is not a cognition but is in the nature of a meaningful statement. Therefore these two—inference for one's own purpose and inference for the purpose of others—cannot be characterized by a single definition. Dharmottara's *Commentary on Ascertainment of Valid Cognition* says: "As for the two types of inference, they do not have a single definition because they have very different natures. One of them is a cognition, while the other is a statement."[770]

The definition of an *inference for the purpose of others* is: [473] a statement that clearly demonstrates by means of the three modes, without omission or duplication, the thesis to be ascertained in order to produce ascertainment of it in others. As for the etymology, since it causes a person—who is other than the one positing the proof statement—to realize the thesis, it is said to be *for the purpose of others*. It is called an *inference* because it is imputed in dependence on a reason and purpose. As for the reason designated, since it is the cause of the inference that is its result, the name of the result is given to the cause. As for the purpose designated, this proof statement is to bring about realization that has the ability to generate its resultant inference. The actual refutation is a meaningful expression. Dignāga's *Compendium of Valid Cognition Autocommentary* says:

> Just as an understanding endowed with the evidence is produced within oneself from evidence qualified by the three modes, likewise out of a wish to produce an understanding endowed with the evidence in the other party, one states the evidence qualified by the three modes. This is an inference for the purpose of others because it is designated on the basis of the effect arisen from the cause.[771]

Furthermore, Dharmakīrti's *Drop of Reasoning* says: "An inference for the purpose of others is the expression of evidence qualified by the three modes because it is designated on the basis of the effect arisen from the cause. Specific arguments are of two kinds: one that has a homologous predicate and one that has a heterogeneous predicate."[772]

A more extensive presentation of inference for one's own purpose and inference for the purpose of others, along with their definitions and divisions, as well as the correct reasons that are the basis of inference, can be found in volume 2 of *Science and Philosophy in the Indian Buddhist Classics*.[773] [474]

24

The Result of Valid Cognition

Now that we have given a rough presentation of the enumeration, definitions, and divisions of valid cognition (Skt. *pramāṇa*) so as to dispel distorted notions about them, we will explain the result of valid cognition (Skt. *pramāṇaphala*) according to [Dignāga and Dharmakīrti's] own system in order to dispel distorted notions about that too. Indian epistemologists in general agree that the accomplishment of a person's wishes depends on valid cognition. They are also united in explaining that it must depend on a cognition that is nondeceptive regarding its object and that has the function of showing actual reality. However, they disagree about how to explain the three facets of the functioning of valid cognition: action, agent, and object.[774] The object of action (Skt. *prameya*) is the object known by valid cognition, the agent (Skt. *pramātṛ*) is the knower, and the action of knowing (Skt. *pramiti* or *pramā*) is the result. The most significant difference between the traditions concerns whether *pramāṇa*[775] and its result are considered to be the same entity or different entities. Non-Buddhist philosophers posit *pramāṇa* and its result to be different entities, whereas Buddhist philosophers who uphold the tradition of Dignāga, Dharmakīrti, and their followers posit *pramāṇa* and its result to be the same entity.[776] The main point of those who explain *pramāṇa* and its result to be different entities seems to be that they interpret *pramāṇa* to be the instrument or cause of realizing the epistemic object (or object of comprehension). So, since realization of the epistemic object arises in dependence on that instrumental *pramāṇa*, it is the result of that *pramāṇa*.

Among non-Buddhist philosophical traditions, Nyāya claims that cognition is without images (Skt. *ākāra*)[777] and that *pramāṇa* is a meeting of the sense faculty with its object, which results in the realization of the object. [475] The *Nyāya Sūtra* says: "That which is produced from the commensurate meeting of a sense faculty and its object is the result of *pramāṇa*."[778] This explains *pramāṇa* and its result to be, respectively, a prior cause followed by its subsequent effect. The Vaiśeṣika, who posit six categories of objects of knowledge, such as quality and so on, explain the apprehension of attributes to be *pramāṇa* and the realization of substances endowed with attributes to be the result. So they accept *pramāṇa* and its result to be different entities that are cause and effect, similar to the Naiyāyika. The Mīmāṃsaka present a variety of options along the following lines. The initial perception of an object, or the earlier nonconceptual consciousness to which it appears, is *pramāṇa*, and the determinate cognition that subsequently arises from that mind, which conceives it to be a universal, an attribute, and so on, is the result. Or, the conceptually determinate mind is *pramāṇa*, then based on that the engagement in the object is the result. Similarly, the engagement in the object is *pramāṇa*, and the obtainment of the object is the result. Alternatively, the obtainment of the object is *pramāṇa*, and the accomplishment of the desired goal is the result. Indeed, as it is commonly accepted in the world, the act of accomplishing is different from the object that is accomplished, so *pramāṇa* and the result of *pramāṇa* must be posited to be different entities only. The tradition's commentarial text [Kumārila's *Exposition of Verses on Mīmāṃsā*] says:

> First there is the perceiver of existents
> endowed with nonconceptual cognition,
> like the mind of a child or a fool,
> which is produced from simple things.
> Then for things that are other than that, [476]
> such as which class things belong to and so on,
> the mind operates with conceptual cognition,
> which is also asserted to be perception.[779]

Likewise, Kamalaśīla's *Summary of the Proponents' Positions in the Drop of Reasoning* identifies the Mīmāṃsā master Jaimini's way of positing *pramāṇa* and its result:

> According to Jaimini and so on, since it is widely known in the world that the object to be proved and that which proves it are mutually different natures, it is indeed correct that the result

> is only something different from its *pramāṇa*, just as an axe itself is not its [resultant] cut. Accordingly, this state of affairs is composed of the following four factors: the one who knows, that which is known, the instrument of valid knowing, and the realization. Here, the one who knows is a person, that which is known is an object such as a visual form, the instrument of valid knowing is a sense consciousness or suchlike, and the realization is the act of having discerned.[780]

Among the Buddhist systems, as already noted elsewhere, the Vaibhāṣika explain sense consciousness to be without images. Vasubandhu's *Treasury of Knowledge* says:

> As a basis conjoined [with consciousness], the eye faculty sees
> forms. [477]
> It is not the consciousness based on it that does so.[781]

When it is a basis conjoined with consciousness, a sense faculty is *pramāṇa*, whereas the sense consciousness that arises from it is the result. So Vaibhāṣika seems to agree with the non-Buddhist traditions mentioned above that posit *pramāṇa* to be a prior cause and its result to be its subsequent effect, thus being different things.

In general, the Buddhist epistemologists follow the explanation found in Dignāga's *Compendium of Valid Cognition* that *pramāṇa* and its result are the same entity. According to this approach, there are three distinct presentations of the result of *pramāṇa*, which can be understood on the basis of certain later presentations known as "the first, second, and third notion of the result."

In general, regarding the result of *pramāṇa*, two such results are explained: the meditated result and the unmediated result. The purpose of developing presentations on *pramāṇa* is to help one obtain these two types of results. The mediated result of *pramāṇa* refers to how when one has correctly realized what is to be adopted and discarded and then engages in or avoids them respectively, one attains one's provisional or final desired goals.[782] Such results arise through the causal capacity of *pramāṇa*; and since other phenomena are required in between the *pramāṇa* and its result, this is called a *mediated result of pramāṇa*. Those mediated results of *pramāṇa* must be established primarily in dependence on *pramāṇa*, as Dharmakīrti's *Exposition of Valid Cognition* says [478]:

> Because it is the main factor based on which
> one engages in things to be adopted or discarded.[783]

For example, when we enter into commerce, we consider what kinds of commodities to trade in before engaging in that activity and analyze whether this may yield a profit. Once we have reached a definite conclusion through weighing those considerations and understanding how to gain good results and avoid bad results of such trade, we enter into it and come to experience its good results, such as profit. In this way, establishing the mediated result of *pramāṇa*, such as happiness, depends on a mind continuously trained in *pramāṇa* that is an unmediated result, which in turn depends on realizing the object of comprehension that is the result of *pramāṇa*.

As for the unmediated result of *pramāṇa*, there are two types: one that is a different entity from the *pramāṇa* itself and one that is the same entity as it. The first is ascertainment directly induced by *pramāṇa*. An example is the ascertainment thinking "This is a flower," where that is a conceptual cognition immediately preceded by a visual cognition seeing a flower. Since it is a result directly produced by *pramāṇa*, it is called an *unmediated result of pramāṇa*. The second is the *pramāṇa* itself from the perspective of it having cognized its object. For example, [in the context of a visual cognition of blue] the blue is the *object*, while *pramāṇa* refers to the cognition that, on the basis of bearing the image of the blue, is nondeceptive regarding the blue, and the cognition of blue is explained to be the *result*. Here, although this [resultant act of having cognized] is not separate in nature from the cognition, from the perspective of the relationship of defining each other the two are termed *cause and effect*. [479] The reason for calling it an *unmediated result of pramāṇa* is that it is the resultant object established by *pramāṇa* and there is no other phenomenon acting as an intermediary.

In this context, that which *establishes* is called the "cause" and that which *is established* is called the "result," but since these are mere nominal imputations, they are not actually results arisen from *pramāṇa*. How *establishing* and *being established* have come to be considered cause and effect is as follows. Various *pramāṇa* such as knowing yellow and knowing blue must be established to have different facets cognizing their epistemic objects because the objects that appear to them have different aspects. In the context of the phrase "result of *pramāṇa*," the act of being characterized is the *result* and that which characterizes is the *pramāṇa*, while the *object known* is the object regarding which superimpositions are eliminated by both *pramāṇa* and its result. These three are respectively called the *action*, *agent*, and *object*.

Buddhist epistemologists, having analyzed the assertions of the Vaibhāṣika and so on, refute them as follows. In the context of presenting the result of *pramāṇa* (or the instrumental effect) according to their own tradition, they say it must be a cognition in which an image of its object appears as an unmediated result of *pramāṇa*. Regarding this, three different presentations are explained: (1) the result of *pramāṇa* that is based on assuming the epistemic object to be established as an external thing; (2) the result of *pramāṇa* that is based on assuming the epistemic object, such as a visual form and so on, to be in the nature of consciousness, as established in the Vijñaptimātra[784] system, having refuted the epistemic object, such as form and so on, to be an external thing; (3) the result of *pramāṇa* that is based on the realists' assumption of an external thing, such as a visual form, to be the epistemic object, while nevertheless establishing that visual forms in the nature of consciousness, and such like, must necessarily be accepted to be the result of cognition. [480] As mentioned above, these are known as "the first, second, and third notions of the result."

1) The first notion of the result of *pramāṇa* is taught as follows in Dignāga's *Compendium of Valid Cognition*:

> Because it is known to include the act,
> although primarily considered to be the result,
> it is labeled simply *pramāṇa*,
> for it is also not devoid of the act.[785]

Regarding this verse, Dignāga's *Compendium of Valid Cognition Autocommentary* says:

> "Because it is known to include the act," although considered "to be the result" of *pramāṇa*. Here, we do not accept the result to be something different from an instrumental *pramāṇa*, as the

> non-Buddhists maintain. Rather the resultant cognition arises bearing an image of the object, thus "it is known to include the act" of cognition. Therefore it is called *pramāṇa*, "for it is also not devoid of the act." For example, an effect that arises in conformity with a cause is said to take on the form of the cause, "for it is also not devoid of the act." It is just so in this case here.[786] [481]

An object-cognizing consciousness is posited metaphorically to be [both] a *pramāṇa* [i.e., the instrumental cognition] and its result [i.e., the resultant cognition]. For example, a resultant cognition that arises in conformity with its cause is commonly said to "take on the form of its cause." The two—*pramāṇa* and its result—are posited as cause and effect metaphorically, though not in the sense of being different entities. According to [Dignāga and Dharmakīrti's] own tradition, a resultant cognition that arises bearing an image of the object is posited to be a valid cognition comprehending that object. The meaning of this presentation is delineated at length in the "Perception" chapter of Dharmakīrti's *Exposition of Valid Cognition*, beginning:

> Here, consciousness has a similar nature
> in being mere experience.

And concluding:

> Because it applies by way of imputation
> to things considered to be different.[787]

These verses explicate the topic through the threefold approach of refuting non-Buddhist notions, presenting one's own system, and dispelling objections to that.

Moreover, an example is given as follows: blue is the *epistemic object*; its being known clearly and nondeceptively via the appearance of blue's image is *pramāṇa* (i.e., the instrumental cognition); and the realization of blue is the *result* (i.e., the resultant cognition). Thus the engaged object of this *pramāṇa*'s activity is *blue*, the way in which it is acted upon by *pramāṇa* is *clearly and nondeceptively* via an appearance of that blue's image, and its result is the *realization of the object, blue*.

This first notion of the result of *pramāṇa* is taken primarily in accordance with the Sautrāntika notion of the result, though it is accepted by Cittamātra too. The notion of the result of *pramāṇa* that is unique to the Sautrāntika tradition is as follows: an external form is the *epistemic object*; its being known clearly and nondeceptively as an external form via the appearance of its object's image is *pramāṇa* (i.e., the instrumental cognition); [482] and the *pramāṇa* realizing the external form is the *result* (i.e., the resultant cognition).

2) The second notion of the result of *pramāṇa* is taught as follows in both the root text and autocommentary of Dignāga's *Compendium of Valid Cognition*:

> Alternatively, reflexive awareness is the result,
> because from its nature the object is ascertained.
> *Pramāṇa* is simply the image of the object,
> for it is known by means of this.[788]

The meaning of this presentation is explained in Dharmakīrti's *Exposition of Valid Cognition*, beginning:

> What [mind] knows the object? That which knows
> individually.[789]

And concluding:

> It would not be that which knows the object.[790]

These verses explain the topic in great detail and offer critical analysis and points of debate.

This second notion of the result of *pramāṇa* has two aspects: the result of *pramāṇa* in the case of an awareness of something other and the result of *pramāṇa* in the case of an awareness of itself (i.e., reflexive awareness).[791] As for the result of *pramāṇa* in the case of an awareness of something other, where blue in the nature of consciousness is the cognized object, the *pramāṇa* that newly and nondeceptively cognizes blue in the nature of consciousness once its object's image appears is the result of *pramāṇa* realizing blue in the nature of consciousness. [483] This cognition that newly and nondeceptively cognizes a visual form, once its object's image appears, is established to be a *pramāṇa* realizing form because it satisfies the three roles that are established in the case of realizing of an object. These three roles can be illustrated by means of an example, such as an axe cutting down a tree. Here, the agent (the axe) operates through the causal capacity of something else, in that it relies on a person wielding it in his hand; it is endowed with its own action, in that it rises and falls; and it meets with its main objective goal, in that the tree is cut into logs. Thus the three roles are satisfied. *Pramāṇa* is similar to this. Here, the agent (*pramāṇa* realizing form) operates through the causal capacity of something else, in that the subjective aspect experiencing itself relies on reflexive experience; it is endowed with its own action, in that it realizes its object once its image appears; and it meets with its main objective goal, in that it eliminates superimpositions involved in apprehending its object to be not as it is. Thus the three points are satisfied.

The second aspect of the second notion is the result of *pramāṇa* in the case of an awareness of itself (i.e., reflexive awareness). Here, regarding a realization of blue in the nature of consciousness, the objective aspect is the cognized object, the subjective aspect is the instrumental *pramāṇa* capable of inducing a new ascertainment, and the valid perceptual reflexive awareness determining it is the result. In keeping with this, the object, agent, and action are respectively termed *apprehended*, *apprehender*, and *experience*, because the apprehended is the cognized object, the apprehender is the instrumental *pramāṇa*, and the experience is the resultant reflexive awareness. Accordingly, Dignāga's *Compendium of Valid Cognition Autocommentary* says:

> Reflexive awareness here is also the result. Cognition arises with two appearances: the appearance of itself and the appearance of the object. From among these two appearances, that which is reflexive awareness [484] is the result. Why?
>
> From its nature the object is ascertained.
>
> When cognition is endowed with [an image of] the object-field, then in accordance with the reflexive awareness that conforms to it, it realizes the object—as desirable or undesirable.[792]

3) The third notion of the result of *pramāṇa* is presented as follows in Dignāga's *Compendium of Valid Cognition*:

> At that time, that appearance is the cognized *object*,
> while the [instrumental] *pramāṇa* and its result
> are the *apprehender* [of the appearance] and the *cognition* [of itself].
> Thus those three are not considered to be different.[793]

This is presented in both the root text and the autocommentary. Its meaning is indicated in a long passage in Dharmakīrti's *Exposition of Valid Cognition* beginning:

> Even if an external object were to exist . . .[794]

And concluding:

> It is called *reflexive awareness*, as explained.[795]

These verses present the topic in great detail and provide critical analysis and points of debate.

An example is given as follows: the *epistemic object* is the visual form that is considered an external object according to the Sautrāntika; *pramāṇa* is the new and nondeceptive cognition of form when its object's image appears; and the *result of pramāṇa* is the realization of form that is in the nature of consciousness.

Given that cognition of the object is dependent upon the instrumental *pramāṇa*, [485] it is a viewpoint shared by all proponents of reason that the result of *pramāṇa* is cognition of its object. However, there are differences of opinion concerning what *pramāṇa* is to be identified with and whether the result of *pramāṇa*—namely cognition of the object—is something different in substance from the *pramāṇa* itself. Thus when Dharmakīrti's *Exposition of Valid Cognition* and other such texts posit the author's own system on the basis of refuting at great length other philosophers' notions of the result of *pramāṇa*, the first notion of the result of *pramāṇa* is taught in accordance with the commonly accepted belief in external things as posited by the Sautrāntika system. The second notion of the result of *pramāṇa* accords with the assertions of the Cittamātra system, particularly the nonexistence of external things, where by delineating the three aspects—*pramāṇa*, its result, and its object—of reflexive awareness and awareness of something other, it very clearly teaches the Vijñaptimātra view that refutes external things. The third notion of the result of *pramāṇa* does not in itself teach that an external thing is refuted to be the epistemic object. Instead, it presents the result of *pramāṇa* based on the Sautrāntika's assumption of an external thing, such as a visual form, to be the epistemic object, while nevertheless establishing that visual forms and so on in the nature of consciousness must necessarily be accepted to be the result of cognition. Thus it teaches the Vijñaptimātra explanation of the result of *pramāṇa* to be correct.

In brief, according to the traditions of both Dignāga and Dharmakīrti, *pramāṇa* and its result are not posited to be different things but are the same entity, and must be posited on the basis of a single cognition only. *Pramāṇa* does not refer to the cause or the method of realizing the epistemic object. Rather, the very mind itself that realizes the object is the instrumental *pramāṇa*, and the realization of the object by that mind is posited to be its result. Therefore it is called the *result of pramāṇa*. Since it is the object based on which *pramāṇa* itself is posited, it is unfeasible for them to be different things. In particular, [486] according to the Vijñaptimātra tradition, which does not accept external things, not only are the two—*pramāṇa* and its result—a single entity, but also *pramāṇa* and the epistemic object must be established to be a single entity. For, if the epistemic object of *pramāṇa* is established in accordance with either the second or third interpretation of the result of *pramāṇa*, something in its own nature (i.e., of valid cognition) must be the epistemic object, which proves that other things that are not in the nature of *pramāṇa* itself could not be the epistemic object. This means that, in the final analysis, all three—*pramāṇa*, its result, and its object—are the same entity.

25

Valid Reasoning

A Brief Overview of Correct Inferential Reasoning

We turn now to valid reasoning and provide an overview of correct inferential reasoning, which is the basis on which one ascertains certain objects of knowledge among their three states [manifest, hidden, and very hidden]. To develop an understanding of slightly hidden phenomena, such as the impermanence of sound, one relies on inferential reasoning, while to develop an understanding of very hidden phenomena, one relies on scriptural proof (i.e., trustworthy testimony). This is how subtle phenomena are ascertained. We already gave a rough presentation of the definition and categories of correct evidence in chapter 20 in volume 2 of *Science and Philosophy in the Indian Buddhist Classics*. Now we will explain further about how to establish the definition of *correct evidence* to be "that which satisfies the three modes."

In his *Compendium of Valid Cognition*, Dignāga first refutes the non-Buddhist claims that correct evidence is defined as that which satisfies one mode, two modes, six modes, and so on; then he presents his own system defining correct evidence as that which satisfies the three modes. [487] According to Dharmakīrti's *Exposition of Valid Cognition* and so forth, the positive pervasion and the negative pervasion of a stated syllogism are not established by appearing only in the set of homologous cases and by only not appearing in the set of heterogeneous cases, respectively, but rather are established by being *ascertained as present only* within the set of homologous cases and *ascertained as necessarily absent* in the set of heterogeneous cases. When a correct proof statement expressed in terms of a homologous case and a correct proof statement expressed in terms of a heterogeneous case signify both the positive pervasion and the negative pervasion respectively, there is no need for each of the two proof statements to signify directly each of the two pervasions because through signifying one of them directly, the other can be signified indirectly. Also when the two pervasions are ascertained by valid cognition, there is no need for each of the two to be realized directly because through realizing one of them directly, the other can be realized indirectly. Also, in the end, this depends on a causal relation, such as the relation between fire and smoke, or an intrinsic relation, such as the relation between [the characteristics of] being produced and being impermanent. On account of this point, it is established by many reasons that correct evidence is of three kinds—correct effect-evidence, correct nature-evidence, and correct evidence consisting in nonperception.

Establishing the Definition of *Correct Evidence* to Be "That Which Satisfies the Three Modes"

Dignāga's *Compendium of Valid Cognition* says:

> To be present in the object of inference and in the homologous class,
> and to be absent in the case of their absence.[796]

This states the definition of *correct evidence* to be: that which satisfies the three modes. Examples of what these two lines of verse exclude—such as having only the attribute of the subject and so on—and the purpose of excluding each [as being incorrect evidence] are stated in Dignāga's *Compendium of Valid Cognition*: [488]

> Evidence that has only one mode or two modes
> functions without fulfilling the purpose.
> [For example] sound is permanent because it is produced,
> because it is physical, because it is not an object of knowledge,
> because it is not physical, because it is an object of hearing, and
> sound is impermanent because it is an object of vision.[797]

Here, the examples are posited as follows. "The *subject*, sound, is permanent, because it is produced."[798] This has only the attribute of the subject. Then, in relation to the Vaiśeṣika claim that subtle particles are permanent, "The *subject*, sound, is permanent, because it is physical." This has only the positive pervasion. Then, on the basis of what the Vaiśeṣika wish to assert, "The *subject*, sound, is permanent, because it is not an object of knowledge." This has only the negative pervasion. Then, in relation to the Vaiśeṣika response, "The *subject*, sound, is permanent, because it is not physical." This has both the attribute of the subject and the forward pervasion. Then, "The *subject*, sound, is permanent, because it is an object of hearing." This has both the attribute of the subject and the negative pervasion of only not appearing in the set of heterogeneous cases. Then, "The *subject*, sound, is impermanent, because it is an object of visual consciousness." This inference has both the positive and the negative pervasions, but the attribute of the subject is not established.

Dharmakīrti's *Drop of Reasons* says: "Non-Buddhists claim that an inferential reason is defined as satisfying six [modes]: those three [commonly accepted] as well as a further three, which are it is not refuted, it is asserted uniquely, and it is known."[799] In other words, some non-Buddhist philosophers claim that on the basis of the three modes—the attribute of the subject, [489] the positive pervasion, and the negative pervasion—there are an additional three modes: the thesis is not refuted by valid cognition, the contrary position is not proved by valid cognition, and the proof is known as an object appearing to cognition. This amounts to six modes, which these non-Buddhist philosophers claim to be the definition of correct evidence.[800] In opposition to this, Dignāga's *Compendium of Valid Cognition*, as cited above, has the purpose of refuting that the six modes constitute the definition of correct evidence and proving that satisfying the three modes is the definition of correct evidence.

As for those who assert the six modes, they state [the fourth mode to be]: "Cognition of the thesis not to be refuted by valid cognition." Now, if they claim this refers to the disputant having ascertained that the thesis is not refuted by valid cognition, then they will have to admit that within the mindstream of the person to whom the proof statement "Sound is impermanent because it is produced" is posited, the ascertainment has already arisen that the thesis, "Sound is impermanent," is not refuted by valid cognition; so they do not wish to realize the thesis "Sound is impermanent." In that case, there is the fault that from the perspective of the correct disputant for that proof, the application of "produced" would not be correct evidence in that argument. On the other hand, if they claim this [cognition of the thesis not to be refuted by valid cognition] refers to a cognition within the disputant of simply not seeing that the thesis is refuted by valid cognition, then, for example, in the proof that "Sound is impermanent because it is produced," this would mean that the disputant simply has a doubt about whether sound is permanent or impermanent. Here, however, the disputant does not see the thesis, "Sound is impermanent," to be free of being refuted by valid cognition. Therefore, when that disputant establishes the attribute of the subject in that argument, he just does not see that the thesis in that argument, "Sound is impermanent," is refuted by valid cognition; but once that cognition too has arisen in the mental continuum of that disputant, [490] there is the fault that it is incorrectly stated in a way that is opposite to the attribute of the subject. Dharmakīrti's *Drop of Reasons* says:

> If it is the case that there is the ascertainment that valid cognition will engage the opposite of the thesis, then an inference proving the thesis would be purposeless; even if the thesis were to be open to refutation, the person simply would not have the capacity to do so. Now if there is no ascertainment, then there would also be no valid refutation. This would mean that the opposite of the thesis could possibly exist, so this "absence of valid refutation" would be devoid of any capacity [to refute].[801]

As for the [fifth] mode, "The contrary position is not proved by valid cognition," the disputant is posited to have a single instance of just not seeing the absence of valid proof of the contrary position. For example, in the case of a correct disputant for the proof that "Sound is impermanent because it is produced," who has only established the attribute of the subject of that argument, since he simply does not see the absence of valid proof of the contrary position, "Sound is not impermanent," it is hard for him to admit it. Moreover, if such a single instance is posited to be a single instance of the disputant's ascertainment of the absence of valid proof of the contrary position, then a single instance of ascertainment of the absence of valid proof of the contrary position, "Sound is not impermanent," must be accepted to have arisen within the mindstream of the correct disputant in the proof that "Sound is impermanent due to being produced." In that case, since he would realize the thesis "Sound is impermanent," then from the perspective of the correct disputant for that proof, it would be impossible to avoid the fault that "produced" in that argument would not be correct evidence. Dharmakīrti's *Drop of Reasons* says: "Due to this, even having a single instance [491] of a desire to express something is excluded."[802] Regarding this passage, Vinītadeva's *Commentary on the Drop of Reasons* says:

> By excluding a cognizing subject who does not consider it to have a valid refutation, other characteristics are excluded. It is also said to exclude having a desire to express something else. For it must be understood that only by excluding a cognizing subject who does not consider it to have a refutation can the wish to express something else be excluded.[803]

As for the [sixth] mode, "The proof is known as an object appearing to cognition," if this refers to the proof being known as an object appearing to cognition within the mindstream of the disputant, then [it would already be known due to having cognized the first three modes]. For example, in the case of the correct disputant for the proof that "Sound is impermanent because it is produced," the moment the disputant has established the [commonly accepted] three modes of this argument by valid cognition, what you refer to as this specific single mode in relation to the cognizance of the three modes of the proof of the thesis, "Sound is impermanent," has already arisen. [Thus enumerating it as a separate mode is redundant.] In general too, the three modes are defined from the point of view of the evidence that brings about an understanding of something hidden—not from the point of view of their roles as causes. Therefore, in this context of demonstrating that satisfying the three modes is the definition of correct evidence, ascertaining or cognizing these three modes is already implied and understood; thus there is no need to specify explicitly "the mode that it is known." Dignāga's *Compendium of Valid Cognition* says:

> Knowledge or obtainment [of the evidence] is implied here
> because it is that which produces understanding.[804]

Also, [492] Dharmakīrti's *Drop of Reasons* says: "Since understanding here is not different from the three modes that constitute the defining characteristics [of correct evidence] that bring about another understanding in this way, it is not some other defining characteristics."[805] Thus, apart from the three modes, it is incorrect to posit another three in addition [as part of the definition of correct evidence]: the thesis is not refuted by valid cognition, the contrary position is not proved by valid cognition, and the proof is known as an object appearing to cognition.

How the Positive and Negative Pervasions of the Evidence Depend on Its Relation to the Predicate of the Probandum or Negandum

As mentioned above, establishing the second and third modes—the positive and negative pervasions of correct evidence—relies on ascertaining the relation between the evidence and the predicate [of the probandum and the negandum, respectively]. Let us now explain this in a little more detail. To ascertain the correct evidence's negative pervasion, it is insufficient simply to not see the evidence in the set of heterogeneous cases without having to rely on ascertaining the invariable relation (of unaccompanied nonoccurrence) between the evidence and the predicate. For, as stated in Dignāga's *Compendium of Valid Cognition*: "A similarity in taste is not ascertained merely through a similarity in appearance."[806] For example, based on the reason that this sweet-tasting fruit one has already eaten is similar in appearance to a fruit that grows on the same tree, one would have to realize that all the remaining fruit not yet eaten [493] are sweet tasting, but such a realization is impossible even though they are similar in growing on the same tree. Another example involves the amla berry. When one sees an amla berry with its many different qualities of potency and flavor, such as being ripe, sweet, sour, and so on, then having realized that the amla berry one sees is like others in simply being an amla berry, one would have to realize that the many other unseen amla berries also have those qualities. But since its qualities depend on whether other features—the collection of conducive conditions such as earth and water—are present or absent, and since the various potencies, flavors, and states of ripening of any individual amla berries are established by direct experience, there is no ascertainment that all amla berries have those same qualities; thus a realization of them having those qualities is not obtained. Dharmakīrti's *Exposition of Valid Cognition* says:

An individual substance appears to have different potencies
based on specific features such as the earthen land.
But is not possible to ascertain that these are present
in other cases merely by seeing them in the case of one.[807]

Thus the negative pervasion is not established simply by not seeing the evidence in the set of heterogeneous cases; rather, one must ascertain that the evidence is *only nonexistent* in the set of heterogeneous cases. For example, since an ascertainment of the absence of smoke in all places without fire can be established through having ascertained that it is impossible for there to be a shared location in which smoke is present but fire is absent, there is no need to ascertain it in each and every place lacking fire. The reason for this [494] is that one can ascertain in a general way that the evidence, such as smoke, is absent in all places where there is no fire. That is the main point here.

In the context of discussing effect-evidence, Dharmakīrti's *Exposition of Valid Cognition Autocommentary* says: "That which is qualified in a particular way is accepted to be taken as evidence of something in general; but if something in general without qualification is stated, it is not accepted because it is mistaken."[808] In other words, by setting as evidence a particular kind of smoke qualified as gray or blue, mere fire in general can be inferred; but by setting as evidence a mere universal, then a particular kind of fire, such as a fire burning sandalwood or juniper, cannot be inferred. This process of reasoning is extremely important. Also, positive and negative inference between a nature and what has this nature is unmistaken, and positive and negative inference between a cause and its effect is unmistaken. Therefore, in an argument employing evidence such as [the characteristic of] being *produced*, through excluding the nature of something with which it is invariably related, such as being *impermanent*, the nature of *produced* itself, the evidence, is thereby excluded. Also, through excluding the cause, such as *fire*, the effect, such as *smoke*, is thereby excluded. Dharmakīrti's *Exposition of Valid Cognition* says:

Therefore, [by excluding] that to which a nature
is related, that nature too would be excluded;
and by [excluding] a cause, so too its effect,
because [this inference] is not mistaken.[809]

In brief, this shows that merely not seeing the evidence in the set of heterogeneous cases does not establish the negative pervasion; and since there is an unmistaken inference between the cause and effect and between a nature and what has this nature, [495] an invariable relation (of unaccompanied nonoccurrence) is established between the evidence and the predicate (of the probandum and of the negandum) in the case of both effect-evidence and nature-evidence.

If an invariable relation (of unaccompanied nonoccurrence) were *not* established between the evidence and the predicate, but instead (in the case of both effect-evidence and nature-evidence) they were totally different unrelated things, then there would be no reason for the evidence, such as produced or smoke, to be excluded due to the predicate, such as impermanent or fire, being excluded. For example, just because someone else does not have any horses it does not follow that they do not have cattle, such as cows and yaks. Similarly, the existence of the evidence, such as produced or smoke, would not entail the existence of the predicate (of the probandum), such as impermanent or fire. Again, just because another person has cattle, such as cows and yaks, it does not follow that they also have horses. Śākyabuddhi's *Commentary on Exposition of Valid Cognition* says:

> Here it states that if one does not accept this, then to claim, "If the proven does not exist, then the proof does not exist," is unestablished. The root text adds, "If that were not so." If one does *not* accept the intrinsic relation, then just as [it would not apply in the case of] the thesis to be proved, "by excluding one thing," so too [in the case of] the proof, "Why would there be the exclusion of another?" In that case, if a brahmin boy's ownership of horses is excluded, his ownership of cattle would be excluded, for if having horses is excluded, then since they would not differ from each other, having cattle would also be excluded. If the absence of relation is excluded, then the converse is accepted; so someone may ask, "Why so? It is not accepted." In reply to this, the root text says, "That person has no horses." [496] By teaching that being unrelated in that way is not excluded, it also expresses the absence of entailment; thus the root text says, "Likewise, how could the presence of one thing

> [follow from the presence of another]?" It is not ascertained that being related to one entails being related to the other, for otherwise if [a person] had horses then he would have cows. Suppose someone says, "Since the subject is either one or many, what applies to one would also apply to the other." But here too there is no ascertainment.[810]

To summarize, Śākyabuddhi's commentary, along with Dharmakīrti's root text and autocommentary, proves that examples establishing the positive and negative pervasions of effect-evidence and nature-evidence are dependent on the invariable relation (of unaccompanied nonoccurrence) between the evidence and the predicate of the thesis.

Furthermore, because the positive and negative pervasions of effect-evidence and nature-evidence are dependent on the invariable relation between the evidence and the predicate, when one posits as evidence the absence of the cause, *fire*, and the absence of the nature that pervades it, *fuel*, then evidence for a negation and so on proves the absence of *smoke* and the absence of *wood* in specific cases. This constitutes inferential evidence that the positive and negative pervasions of effect-evidence and nature-evidence are dependent on the invariable relation between the evidence and the predicate, as explained in Dharmakīrti's *Exposition of Valid Cognition Autocommentary*:

> Since in the absence of this, that is impossible, when one exists the other must be established. For example, only the intrinsic relation is demonstrated:
>
> Therefore the absence of cause and nature
> proves [the absence of their instances] in specific cases, [497]
> and this is inferential evidence.
>
> When only those are excluded, what is related to them is excluded. Therefore, since it is accepted that some other things are refuted and proved, it is said to be inferential evidence that negates the cause and the pervasive nature. If not related, then how can excluding one prove the negation of the other?[811]

In brief, this is to say that in the case of the two different [characteristics]—produced and impermanent—if being impermanent is negated, then being produced is negated; this is the definition of the relation between produced and impermanent. As for [the characteristics] produced and impermanent being different, the universal images of produced and impermanent that appear separately to conceptual cognition are established by the perceptual reflexive awareness experiencing them. As for produced being negated, if impermanent is negated, this is ascertained by inferential cognition in dependence on the refuting evidence that proves being permanent to be empty of being produced. In dependence on such ascertainment, the negative pervasion—an ascertainment that being produced is only nonexistent within [the category of] being permanent—is established. Therefore the positive and negative pervasions of correct evidence are reliant on the relation.

How Correct Evidence Is Limited to Three Kinds: Effect, Nature, and Nonperception

When classified in terms of its nature, correct evidence qualified by the three modes is ascertained to be only of three types: effect, nature, and nonperception. These are: (1) correct evidence consisting in nonperception, such as proving the absence of a pot in a certain place by means of evidence that is the nonperception of a pot by valid cognition; (2) correct nature-evidence, such as proving that the ashoka tree on the eastern side is indeed a tree [498] by means of evidence that it is an ashoka tree; (3) correct effect-evidence, such as proving that fire is present on a smoky mountain pass by means of evidence that smoke is present. Dharmakīrti's *Ascertainment of Valid Cognition* says:

> Inferential reasoning defined in such a way is of three kinds—*nonperception*, *nature*, and *effect*—and only these. The evidence is of three kinds: nonperception, nature, and effect. For example, there is no pot in a certain place because its visible characteristics are not seen; for indeed, if it existed, then it would be seen, otherwise it would not. Also, because this is an ashoka tree, it is a tree. And from [the evidence of] smoke, there is fire in this [place].[812]

Similarly Dharmakīrti's *Drop of Reasons* says:

> That defined in such a way is of three kinds. Inferential evidence is of three kinds only: nature, effect, and nonperception. For example, *existent* [as a real thing] is used to prove something to be impermanent; *smoke* is used to prove that in a certain place there is fire; and *nonperception of what is an object of perception* is used to prove that it does not exist."[813]

Correct evidence is established to have a definitive enumeration as three—effect, nature, and nonperception—in the following manner. For example, smoke and fire are different, and since by negating fire smoke is necessarily negated, smoke and fire are established to be related. Although it is established by direct perception that the absence of fire necessarily entails the absence of smoke in general, in a specific case, [499] such as when a doubt has arisen regarding whether smoke is present or absent on a lake without fire at night, one may need to prove it with rational evidence—in this case one must posit *correct evidence consisting in nonperception of the cause.* Also, although the positive and negative pervasions between fire and smoke can be ascertained by direct perception in general, in a specific case, such as when a doubt has arisen regarding whether fire is present or absent on a smoky mountain pass, one may need to prove it with rational evidence—in this case one must posit *correct effect-evidence.* Then, for example, an ashoka and a tree are different, but because by negating a tree the ashoka is necessarily negated, ashoka and tree are established to be related. And in a specific case, such as when a doubt has arisen regarding whether an ashoka is present or absent on a rocky cliff bereft of trees, one may need to prove it with rational evidence—in this case one must posit *correct evidence consisting in nonperception of a pervader.* Also, in a specific case, such as when a doubt has arisen regarding whether a tree is present or absent in a place endowed with ashokas, one may need to prove it with rational evidence—in this case one must posit *correct nature-evidence.* Therefore, among these types of evidence, since nonperception of the cause and nonperception of a pervader are included within *evidence for a negation,* correct evidence is ascertained to be of three kinds—effect, nature, and nonperception—as illustrated by the above.

Dharmakīrti's *Drop of Reasons* says:

> It is of three kinds only because an invariable relation of unaccompanied nonoccurrence (Skt. *avinābhāvaniyama*) is ascertained. That is, the pervasion between the reason and the predicate is explained to be an invariable relation of unaccompanied nonoccurrence. Since there are none other than three types of inferential evidence, just this is ascertained.[814]

In such a case as where the evidence, smoke, proves that there is fire on a smoky mountain pass, the relation between the evidence and predicate is *directly* shown to be a *causal relation*—so evidence of this kind is *correct effect-evidence*. In such a case where the evidence, being produced, [500] proves that sound is a functional thing, the relation between the evidence and the predicate is *directly* shown to be a naturally occurring *intrinsic relation*. Here, the evidence posited in such-and-such a proof is related to the predicate of the thesis posited in such-and-such a proof on account of its mere presence—so evidence of this kind is *correct nature-evidence*. In such a case where the evidence, being completely pervaded by billowing smoke, proves that in a place in the east completely pervaded in such a way there is an absence of persistently bristling hair that is an effect of the cold, the relation between the evidence and the predicate is *indirectly* shown to be a *causal relation*. Here, both the cause (the continuous presence of tangible cold) and the effect that is the inverse of the predicate (the presence of persistently bristling hair as an effect of the cold) are established on the basis of being ascertained as cause and effect—so evidence of this kind is *correct evidence for a negation*. In such a case where the evidence, an absence of trees, proves that ashokas are absent on a rocky cliff bereft of trees, the relation between the evidence and the predicate is *indirectly* shown to be a naturally occurring *intrinsic relation*. Here, the evidence posited in such-and-such a proof is related to the predicate of the thesis posited in such-and-such a proof on account of its mere presence being concomitant with it, and the inverse of the evidence (in this case, trees) and the inverse of the predicate (in this case, ashokas) are established on the basis of being ascertained by valid cognition—so evidence of this kind is *correct evidence for a negation*. Thus correct evidence is definitively established as being of three kinds—effect, nature, and nonperception.

In general, correct evidence in a specific argument is posited on account of there being a relation between the evidence and the predicate. In particular, the relation between the evidence and the predicate is either a causal relation or an intrinsic relation; and based on whether these are direct or indirect, three kinds of correct evidence—effect, nature, and nonperception—are definitively identified. [501] Regarding this crucial point, Dharmakīrti says that in general if there is no relation between the evidence and the predicate in a specific argument, then an understanding of what is to be understood will not occur. In order to generate an understanding of what is to be understood, the evidence and the predicate must be related. There are two kinds of evidence-predicate relations: causal relation and intrinsic relation. It has been *explicitly* taught that by depending *directly* on these two relations, correct effect-evidence and correct nature-evidence are posited respectively; thus it is *implicitly* taught that by depending on them *indirectly*, correct evidence for a negation is posited. Dharmakīrti's *Ascertainment of Valid Cognition* says: "Not all instances of nonperception involve perception of nonexistence. Therefore to infer the absence of one based on the absence of the another, it is necessary to admit an intrinsic relationship between the two. Otherwise, logical proof would not constitute a means to producing understanding."[815] Dharmakīrti's *Drop of Reasoning* explains further:

> If they have an intrinsic relation, then one thing brings about an understanding of the other thing, because if they were not related, there would be no such unmistaken ascertainment. The evidence is related to the object to be proved; and it is so [related] directly, because it is the nature of the object to be proved or because it arises from the object to be proved. That which is not its nature, or which does not arise from it, is because it is something unrelated to it. So those two alone, intrinsic and causal relations, are nature-evidence and effect-evidence. Only from those two are functional things established.[816] [502]

In general, correct evidence can be categorized in various ways, such as in terms of the predicate of the probandum. All these subdivisions, such as correct effect-evidence and so on, have been explained in some detail, together with supporting quotations from authentic scriptures, in volume 2 of *Science and Philosophy in the Indian Buddhist Classics*.[817]

26

Valid Cognition in the Prāsaṅgika Tradition

In general, both Buddhist and non-Buddhist philosophers offer presentations of valid cognition and its cognized object. They all seem to agree in saying that if an object cognized by a mind accepted to be valid cognition were negated by another valid cognition, then the assertion that the previous one was valid cognition would turn out to be incorrect. This point is made in Dharmakīrti's *Exposition of Valid Cognition*:

> Whenever there is valid cognition about something,
> it will counteract other [nonvalid cognitions].[818]

Also, Jñānagarbha's *Distinguishing the Two Truths* says [503]:

> If a valid cognition could be refuted by another valid cognition,
> then the very criterion of valid cognition would lose
> credibility.[819]

Given that Candrakīrti does not accept anything to exist by virtue of intrinsic characteristics—not even a mere particle—in his *Clear Words*, he presents extensive criticisms of the views of the lower philosophical schools on many points concerning their way of positing both the object of knowledge and valid cognition. In *Entering the Middle Way* too he states: "Because ordinary knowing is always invalid."[820] Owing to these, some commentators say that the Prāsaṅgika Madhyamaka system does not posit its own presentation of valid cognition apart from commonly accepted convention. Conversely, some masters such as Jé Tsongkhapa say that not only do the Prāsaṅgika Mādhyamika posit a presentation of valid cognition, they have a unique way of presenting valid cognition owing to the fact that they do not accept intrinsic characteristics even conventionally. So here, in accordance with this later viewpoint, we will explain briefly the unique way in which the Prāsaṅgika Madhyamaka tradition posits valid cognition.

Candrakīrti's *Clear Words* says: "Because the number of valid cognitions is posited in dependence on the objects known," and continues:

> Therefore, in this way, it is established that ordinary things are known by means of the four types of valid cognition. Moreover, these are established by way of mutual dependence as follows: if there are valid cognitions, then there are things known, and if there are things known, then there are valid cognitions. However, there are no valid cognitions and objects known that are established through their essential nature.[821] [504]

Here it says that both a valid cognition and the object known must be posited as established in mutual dependence, like long and short. If there are valid cognitions, then the objects known must be accepted, and if there are known objects, then the valid cognitions must be accepted. Given that the compound Sanskrit word *pramāṇa*, which means "valid cognition," includes the term *māṇa*, which means "to measure, comprehend, realize, or know," if there is a knower then an object known must be accepted. As for the meaning of *valid cognition*, something is posited to be valid cognition merely on account of being nondeceptive with regard to its principal object, in accordance with how *nondeceptive understanding* is commonly accepted as a convention in the world. However, according to this tradition, valid cognition does not need to newly realize its object, and it is not accepted to be nondeceptive with regard to the inherent nature or intrinsic character of its object.

Similarly, in conformity with ordinary conventions, the term *manifest* (*mngon sum*; Skt. *pratyakṣa*) actually refers to the object [rather than to *perception* as stated in other traditions]; and because of this, the term *manifest* nominally refers to the subject (i.e., direct perception). In that an unmistaken cognizing subject is needed for establishing a true object, a mistaken subject can establish a false object. Also, although a subject's recollection arises later, this is not due to a mind cognizing the subject—the *subjective aspect* oriented exclusively inward—being present earlier at the time of cognizing the object. Memory arises through the later recollection of the object itself, which induces a recollection of the subject, too. In a similar fashion, subsequent cognition is also posited to be valid cognition. Mental direct perception too is posited in a manner quite unlike that of the epistemologists [such as Dignāga and Dharmakīrti, who follow other Buddhist systems]. Indeed, since the main tenet of the Prāsaṅgika tradition is the nonacceptance of intrinsic character, its proponents have many unique ways of presenting valid cognition. [505]

The Definition and Divisions of Valid Cognition

The Prāsaṅgika tradition posits the definition of *valid cognition* to be: cognition that is nondeceptive regarding its principal object. The phrase "its principal object" excludes distorted cognition from being valid cognition, such as a conceptual cognition apprehending a rabbit's horn or a sensory cognition to which a snow mountain appears as blue. For, although they realize their appearing object and thus are nondeceptive regarding their epistemic object, they are not nondeceptive regarding their principal object since they do not realize their main object of engagement. Therefore, in agreement with the realists, correct assumption, doubt, and distorted cognition are not valid cognitions. Nāgārjuna's *Refutation of Objections* says:

> [You say] there would be no direct perception.
> [Likewise there would be no] inference, testimony, and
> analogy,
> object established by inference or by testimony,
> or object established by analogy, whatever it may be.[822]

As explicitly stated in Nāgārjuna's *Refutation of Objections Autocommentary*,[823] valid cognition is categorized into four types: valid direct perception, which realizes objects that are manifest; inferential cognition based on empirical fact, which realizes objects that are slightly hidden; inferential cognition based on trustworthy testimony, which realizes objects that are very hidden; and valid comparative analogy, which, in dependence on an example already realized, realizes the similarity between the example and that which is hidden to it. The last two types of valid cognition [506] are included within inferential cognition. Therefore this enumeration of valid cognition into four does not mean that Nāgārjuna does not accept the two-fold division of valid cognition—perception and inference—to be inclusive. The definition of direct perception is: cognition that is nondeceptive regarding its principal object and that does not rely on a correct reason. When direct perception is categorized by way of its dominant condition there are two types: valid sense direct perception and valid mental direct perception. The definition of *sense direct perception* is: a cognition that is nondeceptive regarding its principal object, unaffected by temporary causes of error, free from conceptuality, and arisen from its uncommon dominant condition, a physical sense faculty. When categorized there are five types: valid sense direct perceptions apprehending forms, sounds, smells, tastes, and tangible objects. The definition of *mental direct perception* is: a mental cognition that is nondeceptive regarding its principal object and that does not rely on a reason. Unlike Buddhist epistemologists in general, this tradition posits both conceptual and nonconceptual types of valid mental direct perception.

The definition of *valid inferential cognition* is: cognition that is nondeceptive regarding its principal object in reliance on a correct reason. When categorized there are two types: inferential cognition based on empirical fact and inferential cognition based on trustworthy testimony. Inferential cognition based on trustworthy testimony must be synonymous with what Candrakīrti's *Clear Words* explains to be valid scriptural testimony. Also that which is known as *valid comparative analogy* is included within inferential cognition based on empirical fact and inferential cognition based on trustworthy testimony. Candrakīrti's *Clear Words* says:

> That [which] is present for ordinary [cognition] is not something hidden, because everything is an object directly perceived; therefore its corresponding cognizing subject is posited to be direct. A double moon, for example, is not direct in relation to unobstructed cognition; [507] it is only direct based on that which has obstruction. Cognition that arises from evidence unmistakenly proving the probandum, which has a hidden object, is inferential cognition. That which is based on a statement of those who are trustworthy, where something beyond the ordinary senses is directly cognized, is scriptural testimony.

> Realization through a resemblance of something [not] experienced is valid comparative analogy, as in thinking, "A gayal is like a gaur ox." Therefore we posit ordinary things to be known through four types of valid cognition.[824]

This tradition does not accept reflexive awareness, for reasons explained above in this chapter.[825]

Mental Direct Perception

The Prāsaṅgika system accepts that mental direct perception apprehending form occurs within the mental continuum of an ordinary being, but does not accept it to be a final moment as the epistemologists of other schools do, because a subsequent conceptual cognition apprehending form is necessarily a mental direct perception apprehending form. There are different kinds of mental direct perception: mental direct perception having the aspect of an object of the five sense consciousnesses; mental direct perception having the aspect of an inner experience such as happiness; mental direct perception of a subjective sense basis of phenomena; and mental direct perception such as recollection of the distant past. Examples of these are given as follows. The first includes cases such as a conceptual cognition apprehending form that has been induced by a sense perception apprehending form, which is found in Candrakīrti's *Commentary on the Four Hundred Stanzas*: [508]

> A cognition generated from a physical sense faculty arises determining an aspect of the present object, though since the object and the consciousness are impermanent both will have ceased; and the mental cognition that arises afterward arises in the same manner—namely, generated through the capacity of its cause, such as a visual cognition and so on. Thus, when a conceptual cognition generated from a sensory cognition arises, it arises having its aspect.[826]

As for the second, a mental direct perception having the aspect of an experience such as happiness and so on, there are cases of mental direct perception that take as their object feelings that are pleasant, unpleasant, or neutral. Candrakīrti's *Commentary on the Four Hundred Stanzas* says: "It does not experience [its object] along the lines of feeling and so on; and it does not positively determine form, sound, and so on by means of the senses."[827]

As for the third, a mental direct perception of a subjective sense basis of phenomena, this includes cases such as mental direct perception that remembers upon awakening an object experienced during the dream state. Candrakīrti's *Commentary on the Four Hundred Stanzas* says: "This is like remembering an object experienced during a dream once one has awakened."[828]

As for the fourth, a mental direct perception such as recollection of the distant past, one may consider the case of [509] a mental direct perception that through the capacity of latent propensities in the mind remembers something that happened in the distant past that, since it has ceased, does not exist at the time of its recollection. An example would be having a recollection of a wound inflicted on one's body, as if it happened yesterday, though many eons have passed since one's death on that occasion. Candrakīrti's *Commentary on the Four Hundred Stanzas* says:

> They have bodies bearing birthmarks arisen from wounds inflicted through being stabbed with weapons in former lives, which have not disappeared; and only from having bodies bearing such birthmarks do they remember their former lives, such that they see the events that occurred in their former lives just as they were experienced. Therefore there is recollection of former lives.[829]

The Difference between Prāsaṅgika and Svātantrika on What It Means for a Cognition to Be Valid with Respect to Its Object

The two Madhyamaka traditions—Prāsaṅgika and Svātantrika—have different criteria of validity regarding the object. In general, the Svātantrika maintain that phenomena are established by virtue of their intrinsic characteristics. They are not satisfied with anything being merely conventionally imputed, but instead claim that when one searches for the referent as it is imputed, it is found. In particular, when valid cognitions are valid regarding their object, they must be valid regarding their object's intrinsic character, which is not merely imputed by language and thought. This, they claim, is the final criterion of being established by valid cognition. [510] Moreover, they maintain that a conceptual valid cognition must be unmistaken regarding the intrinsic character of its *conceived object* and a nonconceptual valid cognition must be unmistaken regarding the intrinsic character of its *appearing object*. Not only that, but if the latter is mistaken regarding the intrinsic character of its appearing object, then its epistemic object cannot be said to have been found. Jñānagarbha's *Distinguishing the Two Truths Autocommentary* says: "Because it exists as a real thing just as it appears to cognition."[830] In other words, there is no doubt that its intrinsic character appears to sensory cognition because it exists objectively.

The Prāsaṅgika do not accept even in a conventional sense that there is anything established by its own essential nature or by its intrinsic characteristics. They say that to be valid cognition regarding an object is to accord with customary classificatory convention, where valid cognition concerns something merely conventionally imputed, such as "This is a pot" or "This is a pillar." They utterly repudiate the possibility of valid cognition regarding something that is found when one has sought for a referent as conventionally imputed, or valid cognition regarding blue and so on established by virtue of intrinsic characteristics. A longer passage in Candrakīrti's *Commentary on the Four Hundred Stanzas* says: "Because this logician is completely unaccustomed to the conventions of the world," and continues on to refute the logician, "That which is erroneous, deceptive, and illusion-like is not nondeceptive because the thing exists in one way yet appears in another. It is incorrect to consider something like this to be valid cognition because it would absurdly imply that every cognition would also be valid cognition."[831] [511] In other words, a subject that is deceptive regarding its principal object cannot establish as true any object whose existence accords with its way of appearing, which would be to exist through its intrinsic characteristics. For if it could, it would be deceptive regarding its principal object and yet valid regarding it also, which absurdly implies that all cognitions would be valid. The realists say that if forms, sounds, and so on lacked a nature established by virtue of intrinsic characteristics, then they would be unreal and empty of all ability to function. So in the absence of valid cognition regarding the five sensory objects' intrinsic characteristics, there would be no valid cognition regarding those five objects at all; and any valid cognition regarding those five objects must be valid regarding those five objects' intrinsic characteristics.

Also, as partially cited above, Candrakīrti's *Clear Words* says: "So that which is characterized—as well as a characteristic, whether particular or universal—that is present for ordinary [cognition] is not something hidden, because everything is an object directly perceived; therefore its corresponding cognizing subject is posited to be direct."[832] Thus, according to the Prāsaṅgika tradition, when any phenomenon whatsoever, whether particular or universal, is taken as the direct object of a dualistic consciousness, then the appearance of that phenomenon must definitely manifest. Since any image that appears is a direct or manifest object, the term "direct" explicitly refers to the object, [512] while the term "direct" nominally refers to the subject. For example, the color *white* is "actually direct" for a visual consciousness apprehending white, while the visual consciousness *apprehending white* is "nominally direct" in relation to white and is actually a directly perceiving valid cognition.

Therefore, given that any object directly perceived must be direct, any cognition that is nondeceptive with regard to its direct principal object is a valid direct perception. In the case of a dualistic cognition, its appearance-image must be realized through experience without relying on inferential evidence, so it must be valid direct perception regarding that appearance. The two types of self-grasping cognition, in terms of taking the appearances of the two types of self as their direct objects, induce through their own causal capacity a valid determinate cognition ascertaining this appearance-image without relying on inferential evidence. A sensory cognition bearing an appearance of a double moon, in terms of taking the appearance of a double moon as its direct object, induces through its own causal capacity a valid determinate cognition ascertaining this appearance-image without depending on inferential evidence. Both of these are also valid direct perceptions regarding their respective appearance-images.

Although a distorted cognition, such as the two types of self-grasping and the sensory cognition having an appearance of a double moon, is valid cognition regarding its appearance-image, it is not valid cognition in general. For example, according to the Sautrāntika tradition, distorted cognition is not posited merely on account of being a consciousness that is mistaken regarding its *appearing object*; rather, distorted cognition is posited on account of being a consciousness that is mistaken regarding its *object as cognized*. [513]

The principal object of a nonconceptual cognition is taken to be its *principal appearing object*, but its mere appearance-image is not its principal appearing object. Its principal appearing object is just the appearing object that is the causal basis of the appearance of that appearance-image within it. For example, the mere white-appearance is not the principal appearing object of a visual cognition apprehending white; rather, the white that is the causal basis of that white-appearance is the principal appearing object of a visual cognition apprehending white. Now, if valid cognition were posited by way of being valid regarding the mere appearance-image within it, then this would entail the fault that even a sensory cognition bearing an appearance of falling hairs would be valid cognition because it would be valid regarding the mere appearance-image of falling hairs. So one must understand the difference between the validity and nonvalidity of a sensory cognition bearing an appearance of blue and a sensory cognition bearing an appearance of falling hairs in relation to how these two—its mere appearance-image and its principal appearing object—are distinguished, and with regard to what they are valid.

In brief, in this [Prāsaṅgika] system, valid cognition is posited merely by way of being nondeceptive cognition regarding its *object as cognized*. There is no assertion that valid cognition must be newly realizing, as the epistemologists of other schools claim. For if one says that valid cognition must be newly realizing, then the criterion of being valid regarding that thing would become the criterion of being valid regarding that thing found upon searching for the referent of its designation.

Furthermore, Candrakīrti's *Clear Words* says:

> Moreover, because the term *direct* signifies an object that is not hidden, an object toward which the sense is directly oriented is direct. In describing [the etymology of *pratyakṣa*] as "toward which the sense is directly oriented," it becomes established that what is not hidden, such as a pot or blue, [514] is direct. And because the cognition that determines it has a cause that is direct [i.e., the manifest object], thus it is said to be direct, just as a grass fire and a straw fire [are named after their respective causes].[833]

For example, just as according to mundane convention a fire that is causally dependent on grass or straw is respectively called a "grass fire" or a "straw fire," so according to this [Prāsaṅgika] system a recollection of white that arises from having seen white is dependent on the manifest white that is its object as cognized; and since it is a nondeceptive experiential cognition, it is said to be a valid direct perception. Moreover, there is a common locus between subsequent cognition and valid cognition (i.e., something that is both), and a common locus between valid direct perception and conceptual cognition.

Again Candrakīrti's *Clear Words* says: "Because you maintain that only cognition that is free from conceptuality is direct perception, and because for that reason it is not used as a customary convention—yet you wish to explain the customary conventions of valid cognition and cognized object—your notion of valid direct perception turns out to be pointless."[834] And it continues on to say: "And according to the scriptures too, since it is not [stated] that only cognition that is free from conceptuality is direct perception, it is incorrect."[835] Although epistemologists of other schools in general say that direct perception must be free from conceptuality, according to this Prāsaṅgika system ordinary people in the world [515] do not have a notion of direct perception being free from conceptuality. As long as these epistemologists maintain that direct perception must be free from conceptuality, they explain direct perception to be established through seeking the referent of the designation. So the Prāsaṅgika maintain that there is no need to state *free from conceptuality* as a separate part of the definition of direct perception. They quote a well-known passage from a scripture, [as yet unfound but identified as] the *Abhidharma Sūtra*, which says: "With visual consciousness one knows blue but does not think 'This is blue.'" Even this sūtra passage does not demonstrate a need to mention *free from conceptuality* separately as a defining characteristic of direct perception. Thus he [Candrakīrti] speaks of this insistence on direct perception being free from conceptuality to be incorrect.

Presenting an opponent's argument, Āryadeva's *Four Hundred Stanzas* says:

> How can your body be impermanent
> when you see a scar formed previously?[836]

In response to this standpoint, the Prāsaṅgika explain the following type of direct perception to be possible. If a birthmark similar to a wound inflicted on one's body in a former life, having been a cause of death on that occasion, were to appear on one's body in the present life, then conditioned by seeing that birthmark on one's body in the present life, there arises a direct mental perception recollecting one's former life as if it were yesterday through the causal capacity of the ripening of previously sown propensities. In this system, it is established that direct perception need not be free from conceptuality. Thus according to the Prāsaṅgika, although a cognition remembering white, for example, is a realization of white that is direct or manifest, it is not a valid cognition that directly realizes white. So a difference between these must be posited. If it is valid direct perception, there is no certainty that its object must be directly realized. There is also a difference between the two—a visual cognition apprehending white, and a cognition remembering white induced by it—in terms of [516] whether white is seen clearly.

To illustrate briefly how Candrakīrti's *Clear Words* refutes valid cognition as asserted by the Svātantrika and other schools, let us consider the following argument. According to Dharmakīrti's *Exposition of Valid Cognition*, two types of valid cognition—valid direct perception and valid inferential cognition—are posited because there are two types of objects (*yul*)—unique particulars and universals. In this way, Svātantrika and other traditions posit particulars and universals to be established by way of seeking the referent of their designations. According to the Prāsaṅgika system, however, this kind of approach is untenable and if one were to proceed along such lines, it would lead to the following problems.[837] If, on the one hand, there is the object characterized as the locus of the two types of characteristics, particular and universal, then there would be a third epistemic object [in addition to those two], which would entail that the definitive twofold enumeration of valid cognition is incorrect. But if, on the other hand, the object characterized as the locus of those two does not exist, then those two types of characteristics (particular and the universal) would not exist, which would [again] entail the fault that the twofold enumeration of valid cognition is incorrect. Furthermore, the defining characteristics and valid cognition as asserted by the logicians do not exist even conventionally, let alone as being established ultimately. In such a manner, the logicians' standpoint is refuted. For more detail regarding this, Candrakīrti's *Clear Words* presents a lengthy discussion that begins, "Moreover, if in conformity with the pair of characteristics—the particular and the universal—two types of valid cognition are posited," and concludes with, "But if it is in an ultimate sense, then since there is no objective basis of identity, the pair of characteristics also would not exist; so how could there be two types of valid cognition?"[838]

Moreover, even according to commonly accepted convention, two types of valid cognition cannot be posited separately in terms of the unique particular and the universal. For according to this system, conceptual mental direct perception is accepted in the manner explained above; and given that those mental direct perceptions take a universal as their observed object, inferential cognitions are valid direct perceptions in relation to their appearance-image as explained above. Therefore, in this tradition, although they are subsumed within the two types of valid cognition, direct perception and inferential cognition, [517] these two are posited in terms of their *object as cognized* being either a direct or a hidden epistemic object.

Furthermore, since it is incorrect to accept the epistemic object of valid cognition in accordance with the lower tenet systems as twofold—the unique particular and the universal—so too the way in which the lower tenet systems divide valid cognition into only the two—direct perception and inferential cognition—is incorrect. Objects of comprehension, or epistemic objects, include the three—the direct, the slightly hidden, and the very hidden—as well as the hidden that is an object associated with an example [similar to it]. Thus because there are four types of cognized objects, there are four types of valid cognition: valid direct perception, valid inferential cognition, valid trustworthy testimony, and valid comparative analogy. To this end, Candrakīrti's *Clear Words* says: "When in this way the twofold categorization of epistemic objects is unfounded, then trustworthy testimony and the rest will not be excluded from being additional valid cognitions simply on account of not being a cognizing subject of either the particular or the universal."[839]

In brief, regardless of whichever of the two standpoints one adheres to—that the Prāsaṅgika Madhyamaka masters accept a presentation of valid cognition within their own system or that they do not—it is clear that this system not only does not endorse the epistemological system of Buddhist logicians such as Dignāga and Dharmakīrti, but it also refutes their epistemological views. This can be understood from passages in Candrakīrti's *Clear Words* that present critiques of [foundationalist] epistemology. Nevertheless, Indian Madhyamaka masters such as Śāntarakṣita and Kamalaśīla, while wholeheartedly presenting their fundamental view of reality in accordance with Nāgārjuna's tradition—that phenomena lack true existence—when it comes to issues of epistemology, [518] they take Dignāga's and Dharmakīrti's presentation as their own standpoint. This is clearly evidenced in Śāntarakṣita's *Compendium of Reality*, which shows that there are Madhyamaka Buddhist masters who uphold and propagate the *pramāṇa* tradition pioneered by Dignāga and his heirs. [519]

Part 6

Denotation and the Exclusion Theory of Meaning

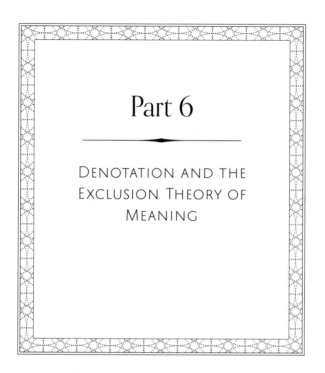

27

Indian Theories of Language

AN EXTREMELY IMPORTANT topic within Indian Buddhist epistemology is the presentation of what is called the *exclusion of other* (Skt. *anyāpoha*) theory of meaning. This is a topic of relevance within Indian philosophers' inquiry into what exactly is the referent of signifying terms. There seem to be two main reasons for this. First, the proponents of six philosophical traditions—Sāṅkhya, Yoga, Vaiśeṣika, Nyāya, Mīmāṃsā, and Vedānta—consider the Vedas to be a valid authority and since ancient times have analytically investigated how the Vedic scriptures indicate their expressed meaning. Second, there is a long lineage of explanations about grammar and linguistics disseminated over many generations, such as Pāṇini's treatises on Sanskrit grammar, which focus on sentences and parts of expressions—names, words, and letters—and how particles, cases, affixes, and so forth operate and how application of these to a word and so on indicate the meaning. Pāṇini is the most famous author of texts on Sanskrit grammar and is broadly considered to have flourished in around the fourth century BCE. When commenting on Pāṇini's main treatise, another ancient grammarian, Vyādi, explains that a class word, such as *cow*, refers to particular cows or individuals that instantiate the universal type *cow*. [520] In contrast to this another grammarian, Vajapyāyana, explains that the class word *cow* does not refer to a particular cow but refers to the universal type *cow*, which pervades all individual cows. So various explanations such as these are presented and explored.[840]

Another grammarian, Bhartṛhari (fifth century CE), gives the following account of how to understand the meaning of a signifying term. To illustrate how a signifying term indicates its meaning, consider the sentence "The white cow is drinking water." Although the individual words as parts of the sentence are able to indicate their distinct meanings separately, the meaning of the expression is directly indicated in a flash by the expression taken as a whole; it cannot be indicated by the individual parts taken separately.[841] This way of understanding in a flash on the basis of the sentence's expressed meaning is called an *intuition* (*spobs pa*; Skt. *pratibhā*).[842] Dignāga seems to give a similar explanation regarding this point in his *Compendium of Valid Cognition*:

> The meaning of a sentence is called
> an *intuition*, and because that arises first,
> the meaning of a word is assigned [521]
> after having extracted it from the sentence.[843]

Additionally, Dignāga's *Compendium of Valid Cognition Autocommentary* says: "A word has no meaning [by itself] but is assigned one through analyzing it in accordance with the scriptures after having extracted it from the sentence. For, as in the case of a phenome such as a base or an affix, it does not function alone." Also: "The sentence itself along with its meaning are the *linguistic referent* in the primary sense because they are not different. The assumption of another interpretation of *language* and *meaning* in that [treatise] is to be closely scrutinized because it is unwarranted."[844]

Another account of the meaning [of a signifying term] is provided by the Nyāya tradition and the Mīmāṃsā tradition, according to Kumārila Bhaṭṭa, as follows. They say that the locus of meaning of a signifying term is not posited on the basis of the expression but must be posited on the basis of relations among the words along with their configuration. According to these philosophers, when someone says, for example, "Devadatta! Bring the cow," although the separate parts of the sentence—Devadatta, bring, and cow—can through their own causal capacity indicate their distinct meanings, it is through the causal capacity of the unique configuration of the words and their relations to each other that a particular sentence is able to indicate the external state of affairs that is its signified objective: Devadatta bringing the cow.[845] [522]

Then another account is given by Prabhākara (a different interpreter of the Mīmāṃsā tradition), who rejects the first two systems outlined above. According to his tradition, the meaning of particular words that occur within an expression must be posited in relation to other words within that same expression. As for the locus of meaning of a signifying term, this is posited on the basis of mutual relationships among words within the expression. Then, according to this tradition, the meaning of a sentence must be posited on the basis of the arrangement of meanings of individual words taken together, so that the individual words arranged in a particular way indicate the meaning located in the parts of the expression, though they do not indicate the meaning by themselves.[846]

As for the investigation of Sanskrit grammar in general, the linguistic analysis that has taken place in India over many centuries from ancient times to the present is considered extremely important. The most influential master throughout this time is Pāṇini, the author of a highly sophisticated grammatical treatise the *Aṣṭādhyāyī* ("Eight Chapters"). Then there was another early grammarian, Vyādi. After him came Kātyāyana, the author of the *Annotations* (*Vārttika*), a commentary on Pāṇini's *Aṣṭādhyāyī*, [and Patañjali (second century BCE),[847] author of the *Great Commentary on Grammatical Analysis* (*Vyākaraṇamahābhāṣya*)]. Several centuries later there arose the unsurpassable master Dignāga and his senior contemporary, Bhartṛhari, composer of the renowned *Treatise on Grammar* (*Vākyapadīya*). Other illuminators (Skt. *candra*) of language include the Buddhist master Candragomin, the Jaina grammarian Pūjyapāda, Abhinava Śakatāyana, and more, who composed treatises on linguistics and greatly enriched Sanskrit grammar. [523]

Since we are presenting an investigation into word meaning here, where it is essential to understand the background of such an investigation, we have provided here a brief introduction to grammar and linguistics.

Presenting the View that Language Denotes Meaning via Affirmation

Although the various groups of Indian philosophers who accept the authority of the Vedas have different ways of identifying the linguistic referent (or word meaning) as presented above, in general they all agree in maintaining that signifying terms that engage via affirmation must engage their object by way of its being established through the capacity of a real thing. To present what it means to "engage via affirmation" in a manner that is easy to understand, the "Examination of Word Meaning" chapter in Kamalaśīla's *Commentary on the Difficult Points in the Compendium of Reality* says: "According to those who propound the meaning of a word to be affirmative, the referent of a word is an ultimately real thing because what words indicate through affirmation and negation is the nature of reality. Thus it must be understood that the linguistic referent is affirmative."[848] All the philosophers who uphold the authority of the Vedas unanimously posit *valid testimony* to be genuine valid cognition, quite apart from direct perception and inferential cognition. Their main points are as follows: first, they claim the Vedas to be valid; second, they claim that a signifying term engages its object through the capacity of reality.

Furthermore, the Sāṅkhya claim that the principal (Skt. *pradhāna*) or primal nature (Skt. *prakṛti*) is the linguistic referent. [524] A word such as *cow* engages its object through the capacity of the real thing, so everything that is the same entity as the cow must be signified by that word; thus the real eternal universal principal of *cow* must be signified by it also. Having first taken something such as a white cow to be the basis for affixing the name, when one affixes the label "This is a cow," it is the real eternal cow universal to which the name *cow* applies. Since that partless universal principal is the object of the linguistic convention—where the principal or primal nature of a white cow is the principal or primal nature of a black one, and the principal or primal nature of a black cow is the principal or primal nature of a white one—it pervades every type of cow. So later when one sees a black cow, one can understand "This is a cow too" without needing to newly affix the label *cow*.

The Mīmāṃsā school accepts a separate class or universal to be the linguistic referent. Not only signifying terms but also their component parts—names, letters, and so on—are stable and permanent in their own nature. So they say that a signifying term and its meaning have a stable relationship ultimately or in reality. Moreover, this Mīmāṃsā tradition accepts as valid that the Vedic injunctions are not composed by human beings, so they say that signifying terms are not necessarily dependent on human endeavor.

The Vaiśeṣika and Naiyāyika are in general agreement regarding their views, and they both accept the six categories of objects of knowledge—substance, quality, activity, universal, particular, and inherence—to be the linguistic referent, as can be understood from their use of the expression *category*, or literally "referent of the word" (*tshig gi don*; Skt. *padārtha*). [525] Moreover, in reliance on Akṣapāda Gotama's *Nyāya Sūtra*, the Naiyāyika declare that the individual, the configuration [of limbs] (Skt. *ākṛti*), and the universal constitute the meaning of the word. Among these, the term *individual* signifies "substances," "particular qualities," and "actions." Kamalaśīla's *Commentary on the Difficult Points in the Compendium of Reality* quotes the *Nyāya Sūtra*, saying: "The sūtra states, 'The individual has a physical body that is the substratum of particular qualities.'"[849]

The general meaning of the term *universal* is explained in this sūtra, which the *Commentary on the Difficult Points in the Compendium of Reality* quotes as saying: "The sūtra also states, 'The universal has the nature of giving rise to [a cognition of] similarity.'"[850] This explains that the universal is the cause of generating a cognition of similarity or resemblance, and this is the meaning of the word *universal*. For example, they say that having taken a white cow as the basis for fixing the label, when one employs the label *cow*, it applies to the individuals—white cows, black cows, and so on—and to the separate universal *cow*, which is substantially different. The separate universal *cow* that exists in the white cow also exists in the black cow; and the separate universal *cow* that exists in the black cow also exists in the white cow. Those two separate *cow* universals [526] are not in the slightest bit different from each other. So these philosophers say that in the case of employing the convention *cow*, having taken a white one as the basis for fixing the label earlier, when one later sees another of the same kind, such as a black cow, one understands it to be a cow without needing to fix the label *cow* anew. This tradition maintains that a *universal*, as stated in the *Nyāya Sūtra* cited above, is the cause of applying common concept terms to any phenomena that accord with it.

There are two types of universals: an unrestricted universal and a restricted universal. In the case of unrestricted universals, *existence*, for example, is said to be the cause of applying the concept term *exists* to its individual instances, existents. In the case of restricted universals, *cow* and *tree*, for example, are said to be, respectively, the cause of applying the concept term *cow* to its individual instances, cows, and the cause of applying the concept term *tree* to its individual instances, trees. Given that *cow* is the universal of only cows, and *tree* is the universal of only trees, they are said to be restricted universals. Also, since *cow*, the restricted universal of cows, is substantially different from cows, it is not a cow. It is the cause of applying the concept term "This is a cow," and it pervades all individual cows, white ones and the rest. Although it is substantially different from its individual instances, in being a universal that pervades one individual instance, it also pervades the others. These assertions are no different from the Sāṅkhya system.

The "configuration" expressed above is explained to be the mark of the universal. Kamalaśīla's *Commentary on the Difficult Points in the Compendium of Reality* quotes the *Nyāya Sūtra*, saying: "The sūtra states, 'Configuration is expressed to be the mark of the universal.'"[851] Kamalaśīla's *Commentary* then explains what this means:

> Here the "mark of the universal" includes the limbs of living beings, such as the head, legs, and so forth, because it is by these that the universal, cowhood and so forth, is indicated. The "configuration" in some cases directly makes cognizant the *universal*, as when cowhood is made cognizant from seeing the head, legs, and so on *appearing together*, while in other cases it is the *mark of the universal*, as when cowhood is made cognizant from the individual limbs, such as the horns and so forth, *appearing individually*. Thus the configuration makes cognizant the universal and its marks.[852]

According to the Naiyāyika, if signifying terms were not expressed through the capacity of real things that are the six linguistic referents—substance, quality, and so on—then it would be difficult to posit the conventional presentations of daily events and activities in the world. For example, the phrase "staff-holder" signifies its meaning in terms of the basis *substance*, "white" and "black" in terms of the basis *quality* or *color*, "circumambulating" in terms of the basis *action*, [528] "exists" in terms of the basis *existence*, "cow," "horse," and "elephant" in terms of the bases *universal* and *particular*, and "cloth based on these yarns" in terms of the basis *inherence*. Indeed, if substance and the rest did not exist, then there would be no objects of concept terms pertaining to the same category such as a staff-holder, horn-bearer, and so on.[853] As for the reasoning on which this Nyāya assertion is based, Kamalaśīla's *Commentary on the Difficult Points in the Compendium of Reality* presents their argument as follows:

> This is [an argument using] nature-evidence: "Anything that appears mutually distinct from something has a basis, like auditory consciousness and so on. The concept term *staff-holder*

> and the rest appear distinct." So if they have no basis, then they would appear everywhere without distinction. This argument demonstrates the fault.[854]

In brief, since the Naiyāyika accept (1) the individual and (2) the configuration to be meaning of the word or the linguistic referent, they maintain that (3) unique particular external things, (4) the universal, (5) being related to the universal, and (6) inherence are also the linguistic referent, thus they accept (7) belonging to the universal to be the linguistic referent. [529]

28

Dignāga's Exclusion Theory of Meaning

Refutation of Other Schools' Notions of the Linguistic Referent

The great Indian epistemologist Dignāga refutes the theory of meaning posited by non-Buddhist traditions where words denote their referents via affirmation, and he disproves one by one their claims that the linguistic referent is the particular individual, the real eternal class or universal, the relationship to such a universal or inherence, the particular instantiation of such a universal, and so on. He pioneered the tradition that posits signifying terms to have exclusions as their object, in that they denote their referents via negation. It seems that this master composed an important treatise, *Investigation of the Universal* (*Sāmānyalakṣaṇaparikṣā*), that proved how a term indicates its referent through negating or excluding whatever is not it, but unfortunately this text disappeared a long time ago and, apart from a couple of verses quoted in later epistemological treatises, is not encountered these days. This text explicitly presents the theory of the exclusion of other, which Kamalaśīla's *Commentary on the Difficult Points in the Compendium of Reality* quotes as follows:

> Distinct individual referents and words
> are not accepted to be the signified and the signifier
> because they have not been perceived before.
> It is taught to be the universal only.[855]

As it is, Dignāga's *Compendium of Valid Cognition* and its autocommentary are his most important treatises extant these days; [530] even besides the "Exclusion of Other" chapter, these two treatises clearly show how Dignāga proves that the exclusion of other is the linguistic referent.

As for the investigation into the exclusion of other in the *Compendium of Valid Cognition*, it is helpful to consider some background to Dignāga's definitive enumeration of valid cognition as twofold: direct perception and inferential cognition. Other traditions posit language-based valid cognition to be a specific type of valid cognition that is different from direct perception and inferential cognition. Dignāga refutes this. He proves that language-based valid cognition is included within inferential cognition, and from this his presentation of exclusion of other emerges, as stated in his *Compendium of Valid Cognition*:

> Like [the reason of] being produced, its referent
> is signified through the exclusion of other.[856]

Just as in the proof "Sound is impermanent because of being produced," the evidence "produced" is ascertained in a general way to be nonexistent as "permanent"—which is the *excluded other* that is opposite to the predicate of the thesis "impermanent"—likewise a signifying term also indicates its referent in a general way by excluding the converse thing that is not itself. The way of ascertaining that the evidence is absent in the set of heterogeneous cases when establishing the negative pervasion is similar to how a term makes its meaning clear in a general way by excluding what is not itself, which proves that language-based valid cognition does not exist separately from inferential cognition. In this way, Dignāga initiated within his own system a unique philosophical view—the exclusion of other—demonstrating that signifying terms indicate their referents via the exclusion of other. A concise identification of the view of *exclusion* (Skt. *apoha*) or the *exclusion of other* (Skt. *anyāpoha*) that is the system initiated by Dignāga [531] is given at the beginning of the chapter "Examination of Word Meaning" in Kamalaśīla's *Commentary on the Difficult Points in the Compendium of Reality*:

> The view of the proponents of exclusion is as follows: "Ultimately that which a term signifies does not have a real nature of its own even in the slightest because it engages by way of conceiving as different those things that are not different; thus all language-based cognition is just mistaken. However, where it is connected indirectly with a real thing it is not deceptive regarding that thing even though it is mistaken." That is what they

> maintain. The nature that conceptual cognition superimposes onto things that are not different is called "exclusion of other" because it comes from the experience of a real thing as excluded from others, and because that itself also appears to be excluded from others, and because it is ascertained as being one with the contemporaneous mistaken expression that is excluding, and because it has the result of realizing the thing excluded from others. Thus they establish that "an exclusion of other is the linguistic referent."[857]

The line from Dignāga's *Compendium of Valid Cognition* quoted earlier, "Like [the reason of] being produced, its referent," appears near the beginning of the "Exclusion of Other" chapter, the main body of which has fifty-one verses. Although the root text and commentary on these verses are rather hard to comprehend—compounded by the fact that there are two sets of Tibetan translations that sometimes disagree and the Sanskrit original is no longer available except for short citations in other texts—and the analyses relating to Sanskrit grammar are difficult to understand—especially when found in Tibetan only—this is a very important chapter that requires some careful consideration. The root text and commentary on this chapter include the following topics [532]: the refutation of the linguistic referent propounded by other systems that claim words engage via affirmation (presented in verses 2–11c) and the establishment that words engage via exclusion in accordance with Dignāga's own system (demonstrated in verses 11d–13 and 33–37). To facilitate an understanding of the most significant points in Dignāga's proof that the exclusion of other is the linguistic referent, a concise explanation of the meaning of these verses will be provided here accordingly.

When Dignāga refutes the notions of word meaning propounded by other systems, which claim that words engage via affirmation, he presents logical arguments refuting each of their candidates for the linguistic referent in turn: (1) the particular individual, (2) the universal alone, (3) the commensurate relation between the universal and the individual, and (4) the individual belonging to (or instantiating) the universal.[858]

1) Dignāga argues that it is incorrect for the *particular individual* to be the linguistic referent, as demonstrated in the *Compendium of Valid Cognition*:

> A class word does not [signify] particulars
> because they are limitless and because it is mistaken.[859]

Two reasons are presented here. The first reason is: particular individuals cannot be the object of a term signifying a separate universal because particular individuals are limitless in number—therefore they cannot be related with the signifying term, and a signifying term that is not related with its object cannot signify that object. [533] The second reason is: because a class word, such as *existent*, is accepted by the Nyāya-Vaiśeṣika school[860] to apply to *qualities* and *actions* in the same way that it applies to *substances*, it follows that this term becomes a basis of uncertainty or error as to whether it applies to a substance in any given case. Dharmakīrti also presents other reasons based on these two arguments, as stated in his *Exposition of Valid Cognition*:

> Terms indicate [their referent] when applied as a *label*
> for the sake of creating a classificatory *convention*—
> at which time [when the convention is used] the individual no longer exists.
> So the label is not based on that [individual].[861]

Signifying terms indicate their referent when applied as a label to that which is signified. If such a label were applied based upon the individual, then at the later time of using the convention it would be impossible to know the referent of the earlier labeling, because the individual at the earlier time of labeling would not exist. Since it would have ceased by the time of using the convention later, it cannot be the same as the referent of the later convention.

2) Dignāga refutes that a class word signifies the *universal alone*, as demonstrated in the *Compendium of Valid Cognition*:

> And it does not signify the connection, nor the universal,
> because it is heard without a difference regarding different referents.[862]

It is incorrect for a class word to signify the universal alone because [534] in ordinary usage there are phrases such as "existent substance" that are in grammatical agreement by having a shared locus of reference. To be in grammatical agreement (i.e., with the same case inflection), both parts of the phrase must apply to a single basis. Accordingly, the term *existent*, which is part of that co-designative phrase, must be accepted to apply to a particular pot, for example. In this case, that class-word *existent* cannot signify a universal alone. This is the fault demonstrated here. Dignāga's *Compendium of Valid Cognition Autocommentary* says: "If so, then 'existent substance,' 'existent quality,' and 'existent action,' which have different meanings, would not be co-designative with the terms *substance*, *quality*, and *action*; however, it is seen that they are."[863] Someone may argue, "There is no fault here, for the phrase 'existent substance,' which is an instance of the class word *existent*, simply signifies that it exists; and in the case of such an existent, since the basis instantiates the substance, the phrase 'existent substance' means it is a co-designative expression." That also is not correct. For if it were, then that phrase would signify *existent* and *substance* as the predication of an attribute upon a basis, in which case those two would be different substances. Thus it is refuted. Concerning this, Dignāga's *Compendium of Valid Cognition* says: [535]

> Because [terms] that signify a quality and a bearer of that
> quality
> are ascertained to have different grammatical case endings,
> it is established that terms signifying
> the same substance and basis are in agreement.[864]

According to the Sanskrit grammatical tradition, whenever terms are employed predicatively, such as "the existence of the substance," different endings must be applied to the two words signifying the attribute and the bearer of the attribute. The word for "substance," *dravya*, has the possessive particle or third case ending applied to it, thus becoming "of substance," *dravyasya*, while the word for "existence" has the first case ending applied to it. Conversely, since phrases such as "blue lotus" and "white cloth" are terms signifying a common locus, where the two words in each instance are co-designative, they must agree in having the same first case ending. That is what the above verse demonstrates. Dharmakīrti expresses further criticisms of the assertion that the universal alone is the linguistic referent. *Exposition of Valid Cognition* says:

Because a person knows how he or she
can function to accomplish a goal,
he or she applies signifying terms
to things that can accomplish them.[865]

A person employs ordinary words such as *cow* [536] for the sake of accomplishing his or her own desired goal. Because a separate universal or class cannot function to accomplish the desired goal, such as riding or milking, there is no point in applying an ordinary word such as *cow* to a universal that is an entirely different thing.

3) Dignāga refutes that a class word signifies the *commensurate relation between the universal and the individual*, as demonstrated in the *Compendium of Valid Cognition*:

A relation is signified by means of
the attributes of the relation-bearer,
just as a real thing is signified by its functionality,
and those are related with other things too.[866]

Suppose someone asks, "Does a general or class word signify autonomously the commensurate relation between the universal and the individual?" The relation must be signified by means of being related with the attributes of the relation-bearer, but it cannot be signified autonomously because the attributes of the relation-bearer are limitless given they are related with other things too. Thus a class word cannot signify the commensurate relation between the universal and the individual. Dignāga's *Compendium of Valid Cognition Autocommentary* says: "A relation, since it relates, relates with other things such as attachment. Therefore, since the relation is signified through the attributes of the relation-bearer, and since there are no terms that signify the relation through its own attributes, [537] it also cannot be signified by a class word."[867]

4) Dignāga argues that the *individual instantiating the universal* is not the referent of a class word. Some non-Buddhists say that a class word, such as *existent*, signifies only an individual that is qualified by that universal or is an instantiation of the universal for a few reasons: because both the class word *existent* and the individual term *pot* are co-designative, because that class word is easily related to the item instantiating the universal, and

because it is not mistaken regarding the item instantiating the universal. So the class word signifies the item instantiating the universal. This seems to be the meaning here. To refute that, Dignāga's *Compendium of Valid Cognition* says:

> It is not the instantiation because it is not independent,
> because it is figuratively imputed, and because there does not
> exist [a resemblance].[868]

The meaning of the first of these three reasons, "because it is not independent," is explained in the *Compendium of Valid Cognition Autocommentary*: "If so, then the term *existent* indicates a substance such that the universal and [the term's] own form are subordinate, but it does not do so directly."[869] The meaning of this is as follows. It is not feasible for a class word, such as *existent*, to signify an individual that instantiates the universal [538] because that term *existent* directly signifies its referent—the universal *existent*. But if it is applied to an individual instantiation of the universal existent, then it does not do so independently but must be understood in dependence on or in relation to another term, such as *pot* (that is, the word *existent* cannot by itself designate an existent individual, only when it is accompanied by another term, such as *pot*). The reason for this is that upon hearing the term *existent* in general, a particular existent, such as an existent pot, does not appear to the hearer's mind.

The second reason, "because it is figuratively imputed," is explained in Dignāga's *Compendium of Valid Cognition Autocommentary*: "The term *existent* signifies its own word form or the universal as its proper referent. Since it is applied to those, it is figuratively imputed upon its instantiation. That upon which something is figuratively imputed does not indicate its proper referent."[870] The meaning of this is as follows. Suppose someone suggests: "The refutation 'because it is not independent' does not apply here. For, the term *existent*, which is part of the phrase 'existent pot,' signifies *existent* as its primary referent and indirectly signifies an individual existent, such as a *pot*." If that were so, then the term *existent* would be applied to a pot as a figurative imputation [and not as a genuine expression of it].

The third reason, "because there does not exist [a resemblance]," is explained in Dignāga's *Compendium of Valid Cognition Autocommentary*: "A resemblance also does not exist. Even in the case of [a class word applying to] an instantiation, qualitative resemblance does not exist as a resemblance through transference of a notion, [539] and it also does not exist as a resemblance influenced by other qualities."[871] The meaning of this is as follows. Suppose someone suggests, "If the term *existent* were applied by way of figurative imputation to an existent individual pot, then just as a senior servant is figuratively imputed as 'king,' the term *existent* must apply by way of figurative imputation to an instantiation of *existent* such as a pot because there is a resemblance. But would such a resemblance be a resemblance through transference of a notion, or a resemblance influenced by other qualities—since it is not possible to be both?" The first of these, that it is a resemblance through transference of a notion, is incorrect. This is because, for example, when a lily and a conch are stated to be "white," that cognition of white color must be transferred to the lily and to the conch in turn, but such transference of a notion to both *existent* and *pot* does not occur (in that they are simultaneous). Then one may ask, "So is it a resemblance influenced by other qualities? For example, when a red crystal that has changed color is cognized, even though the color stain that caused the change in hue of that crystal did not previously appear to cognition, that red crystal was nevertheless able to appear to the mind." That too is incorrect. According to your view, merely from hearing the term *existent* that is part of the phrase "existent pot," one must be able to understand "existent pot" even without previously knowing the meaning of *existent*. But this is inconsistent with your view because since the primary meaning of the term that is heard, "existent," must refer to *existent*, when one hears the phrase "existent pot," having understood *existent* previously, one would have to understand subsequently the pot that is an instantiation of it.[872]

Another refutation of the assertion that the term *existent* applies by way of figurative imputation to existent individuals such as a pot [540] is presented in Dignāga's *Compendium of Valid Cognition*:

> Because their essential natures would be mixed
> the cognition of all of them would be distorted.[873]

If a class word were applicable by way of figurative imputation to individuals, then all cognitions that arise in dependence on [hearing] such expressions as "existent pot" would only be understood by way of figurative imputation upon their objects or through the mediation of another object.

If so, then, just as a mind thinking "It is blue" regarding the hue of a crystal affected by a colored object, the things cognized would not accord with how they are in reality. This is how it is refuted. Thus, in the "Exclusion of Other" chapter in his *Compendium of Valid Cognition*, Dignāga refutes the claims that the linguistic referent is the particular individual, or the universal alone, or the commensurate relation between the universal and the individual, or the individual instantiating the universal, for he teaches that a signifying term has an exclusion as its object.

Establishing that Signifying Terms Have the Exclusion of Other as Their Object

According to Dignāga's own tradition, the exclusion of other [or what is differentiated via negating its opposite] is established to be the linguistic referent. The *Compendium of Valid Cognition* says:

> Thus a term is an exclusion of other. [541]

The verses following this line summarize what it means:

> Although that which is signified has many [attributes],
> they are not all understood from the term.
> However, in conformity with its relation to that,
> a term functions to differentiate its referent.
> A term too has many attributes.
> Its referent is made known
> by just that which is exclusive,
> but not by the qualities of the term.[874]

The meaning of this is as follows. In general, although a single signified object, such as an ashoka tree, has many particular attributes, such as flowers, fruit, and so on, those cannot all be known from the single term *ashoka*. That term makes its referent, an ashoka tree, known via an exclusion in conformity with the relation of unaccompanied nonoccurrence (both positive and negative) that they are established to have—such as the exclusion of what is not an ashoka. Moreover, only an ashoka in general is understood here, not every particular ashoka. The meaning of the second verse is explained in Jinendrabuddhi's *Spacious and Stainless: Commentary on the Compendium of Valid Cognition*:

> If someone asks, "What portion does the term make known?" it is explained thus. "A term too has many attributes" means it has many attributes that include particular and universal attributes. "Its referent [is made known by just that which] is exclusive" refers to that by which the universal attribute *tree*, and the term itself, and so on are made known and not mistaken. [542] "By just that" means it is "made known" by that attribute alone. "Just" shows what is excluded. "But not by the qualities of the term" refers to the term (*qua* sound) that is itself an object known and so on. Those [qualities of the term] do not make known [the referent] because it is just mistaken regarding those. Thus, although those [qualities of the term] are not the meaning of the term *tree*, they are observed in the case of [individuals] such as taste and so on but not in the case of universals such as the word for tree itself.[875]

In brief, according to the tradition of the proponents of exclusion, signifying terms differentiate their object via negation. When the phrase "This is a tree" is applied to an ashoka, for example, from among the many qualities, such as substance, product, and so on, which the ashoka that is an instance of *tree* possesses, that term excludes only *non-tree*. It signifies only *tree* to be an attribute of that ashoka but does not signify any other attributes. The direct object of signifying terms and conceptual cognitions is only the attribute differentiated by the mind, and from within that, a particular attribute is apprehended or taken as the object. Regarding this, Dharmakīrti's *Exposition of Valid Cognition* says:

> The ascertainments and signifying terms
> that serve to remove [false superimpositions]
> are as numerous as those superimpositions of [false] attributes.
> Hence they all have distinct referents.[876]

Both these lines of the root text and their commentary clearly make the same point here. [543]

Suppose someone asks, "If according to your own tradition the exclusion of other is the linguistic referent, then what does the 'other' that is excluded refer to? How does a term exclude an *other* such as this?" Dignāga's *Compendium of Valid Cognition* responds:

> Tree, earthen, substance, real thing,
> and object of knowledge, then in reverse order,
> these four, three, two, and one are the reasons
> for uncertainty and conversely for certainty.[877]

This very important stanza is an intermediate verse that occurs in both the root text and the autocommentary. Although Dignāga does not comment further on it, Jinendrabuddhi's *Spacious and Stainless: Commentary on the Compendium of Valid Cognition* says:

> This intermediate verse is taught for the purpose of penetrating the textual passage: "It is only by way of exclusion [of their opposite] that they make known [their meaning]." The term "object of knowledge" is a cause of *uncertainty* regarding the four—real thing, substance, earthen, and tree—because although it does not exist in them [uniquely], it is seen. The same is to be expressed in the later cases. The term "real thing" is likewise [a cause of uncertainty] regarding the three—substance, earthen, and tree. The term "substance" is likewise [a cause of uncertainty] regarding the two—earthen and tree. The term "earthen" is likewise [a cause of uncertainty] regarding the one—tree. Then "the reason" for *earthen* is posited "conversely," where "conversely" [544] refers to the concordant direction as follows. The term "tree" is a cause of *certainty* regarding the four—earthen, substance, existent, and tree—because although it is seen in them, it is not seen in their heterologous classes. The same is to be expressed in the later cases. The term "earthen" and so on is likewise [a cause of certainty] regarding each of the sets reduced in stages, thus known as a cause of certainty regarding *substance* and so on. Indeed, if they are made known through being established as seen, the referents of four, three, two and one respectively are ascertained. As for the reverse direction, the

> term "object of knowledge" and so on, since it is seen in a *real thing* and so on, is a cause of uncertainty because although it does not exist in that [uniquely], it is only ever seen. Therefore: "It is only by way of exclusion [of their opposite] that they make known [their meaning]."[878]

This says that according to Dignāga, signifying terms indicate their referent only by means of an exclusion that excludes what is not it. An exclusion that "excludes what is not it" accords with the order of the extension range (or scope) of class words where the wider pervades the narrower, as in the case of sets and subsets. For example, in the following order, where the scope of the former term is greater than that of the latter, each of the terms "object of knowledge" (or "existent"), "real thing," "substance," "earthen," and "tree" are in turn causes of *uncertainty* regarding the four objects—real thing, substance, earthen, and tree; then respectively regarding the three objects—substance, earthen, and tree; then respectively regarding the two objects—earthen and tree; then respectively regarding the one object—tree. When those terms are taken in the reverse order, where the scope of the former term is narrower than that of the latter, the term *tree* is the cause of *certainty* regarding the four objects—object of knowledge, real thing, substance, and earthen; [545] then *earthen* likewise regarding the three objects; then *substance* likewise regarding the two objects; then *real thing* likewise is the cause of certainty regarding the one object, *object of knowledge.*

In brief, according to Dignāga's understanding, signifying terms do not express or take as their direct object external things that are unique particulars. He explains that terms engage their objects in a universal manner. They differentiate their objects via negation and indicate their meaning only through excluding something other that is not it. The *other* that is excluded with the term *exclusion of other* is just as explained in the root verse quoted from Dignāga's *Compendium* and the passage from Jinendrabuddhi's *Commentary* above. There is a difference between a wider and a narrower range of excluded objects in accordance with the ordered sets of class words having wider or narrower scope given the context in which they occur. In the case of a narrower class word such as *tree*, for example, not only does it not exclude those objects referred to by the terms *object of knowledge*, *real thing*, and *substance*, but because the term *tree* has an invariable relation (of unaccompanied nonoccurrence) with the objects signified by those terms—object of knowledge, real thing, and so on—those objects can be ascertained in dependence on the term *tree*. Conversely, in the case of a wider class word such as *real thing*, for example, while it also does not exclude the objects of class words narrower than it—substance, tree, and such like—those objects cannot be ascertained in dependence on the term *real thing*.

Accordingly, the way in which terms differentiate their object via negation [546] is explained as quoted above from the "Exclusion of Other" chapter: "Like [the reason of] being produced, its object is signified through the exclusion of other."[879] It is also stated in Dignāga's *Compendium of Valid Cognition Autocommentary*: "Just as *produced*, since it excludes *not produced*, makes known *impermanent* and so forth, likewise a term that differentiates another term signifies a universal, and by means of that it makes its referent known."[880]

Suppose someone inquires, "According to you proponents of exclusion, term and meaning are not established to have an autonomous relationship that really exists. Also you explain that signifying terms differentiate their objects via negation. In that case, when a speaker utters a signifying term on a certain occasion motivated by a desire to express something, how can such a term unmistakenly indicate its unique meaning?" This doubt seems to be cleared away by Dignāga's root text and commentary. The *Compendium of Valid Cognition* says:

> Because it is not seen to apply to the referents of other terms,
> and because it is seen to apply to those of its own [class of]
>   referents,
> it is easy to connect the term [to its referent]
> and without any error at all.[881]

Regarding these points, Dignāga's *Compendium of Valid Cognition Autocommentary* says:

> The meaning of a term is signified by way of positive and negative concomitance, [547] where it respectively applies to homologous cases and does not apply to heterogeneous cases. As for the homologous cases, its application to all of them certainly

> cannot be stated, but only to some, because it is impossible to state all the limitless referents. As for the heterogeneous cases, although these too are limitless, it can be shown not to apply to them because it is just not seen there [among those cases]. Therefore, since it is not seen to apply to cases other than what it is related to, its way of signifying its referent is said to be an inference based on its exclusion of those [other cases]. If it were an inference by means of positive concomitance then the term *tree* would not lead to any doubts about whether the same individual is an ashoka tree or so forth. But as in the case of that doubt, there would also be doubts about whether it is earthen or a substance and so on. But since the word *tree* is not seen to apply to what is not earthen and so on, it is an inference through negative concomitance only.[882]

On a later occasion Dignāga's *Compendium of Valid Cognition Autocommentary* explains a similar point: "Neither terms nor reasons are able to signify their referents except through a relationship [of negative concomitance], because it is impossible to realize all the many attributes of its object. And since they do not signify diverse individuals, they are not mistaken regarding their referents."[883] [548]

Let us summarize briefly the meaning of these passages from the root text and autocommentary. How a signifying term signifies its meaning generally relies on positive and negative concomitance, which is similar to how an inference proves its thesis. Such negative and positive concomitance is ascertained by way of the two classes—similar and dissimilar, or in other words, homologous and heterogeneous. Of these, a term not only does not signify the dissimilar or heterogeneous class, it also does not signify *all* the subsets of the similar or homologous class, because it is impossible for a term to signify all the limitless existents in the homologous class. Conversely, in the case of negative concomitance or the heterogeneous class, although this is limitless like the homologous class, there is a difference in that the term, being absent from all dissimilar or heterogeneous cases, can be ascertained in a general way not to apply to those. Therefore, although the two—term and referent—do not have a relationship that is established through the causal capacity of a real thing, a term such as *tree* does not apply to phenomena that are not related to it as signifier and signified. So the referent *tree* can be understood to be absent in its heterogeneous class, *non-tree*. Thus it is established that a term signifies its referent, in this case *tree*, by way of excluding *non-tree*. Therefore, on the basis of a signifying term, one can unmistakenly understand its meaning.

The upshot of what Dignāga states in his *Compendium of Valid Cognition* and autocommentary is that it is far better to accept his own tradition of exclusion—as a universal—to be the linguistic referent, because this view does not succumb to the faults pointed out against maintaining any of the following to be the linguistic referent: (1) the particular individual, (2) the separate universal, (3) the relation between the universal and the individual, or (4) the individual that belongs to (or instantiates) the universal. Moreover, in maintaining the exclusion of other to be the linguistic referent, the attributes of a universal are satisfied as well: being unitary, being permanent, [549] and pervading all its instances. Dignāga's *Compendium of Valid Cognition Autocommentary* says:

> The attributes of a universal are established.
>
> The attributes of a universal—unity, permanence, and presence in every individual [member of the class]—are established only in this [philosophical account], where these characteristics are fulfilled respectively because it is not diverse, because its substratum is not interrupted, and because it is realized in all members [of the class]. Thus, since it is without fault and since it enhances good qualities, one should say that it is only through the exclusion of other things that terms signify their referents.[884]

The last line of the above passage from Dignāga's autocommentary is quoted in Jinendrabuddhi's *Spacious and Stainless: Commentary on the Compendium of Valid Cognition* and translated slightly differently there into Tibetan: "Terms signify their referents only through their being qualified as the converse of other things."[885] According to Dignāga's tradition, a term such as *pot* signifies its object in such a way that the thing qualified as the converse of a non-pot must be the signified object, pot. Commenting on this point, Jinendrabuddhi says:

> As for making its referent understood, it is the positive concomitance, [550] and this is impossible without the exclusion [of the contrary]. This preclusion of contrary referents, which is the exclusion, cannot be applied without the positive concomitance. For this reason, the term does not have two separate functions—one of exclusion and the other of expressing the referent. Furthermore, since its referent is by its very nature differentiated, the very act of expressing it entails understanding it in terms of the exclusion of other.[886]

To illustrate this with an example, consider a pair of twins. If somebody points to one of them and says, "This is that one's twin," the other can be understood indirectly to be the twin. It is not a case of having to understand separately that each of the two is a twin.[887]

According to Dignāga, signifying terms differentiate their object via negation only, as explained in his *Compendium of Valid Cognition Autocommentary*: "Although there are no external objects, various conceptual cognitions realizing the object arise in dependence on latent propensities of habituation to objects, like notions that arise from speech in conformity with its conditions."[888] The fact that various cognitions arise in dependence on speech is established by reflexive awareness within each person's direct perception. Dignāga's *Compendium of Valid Cognition* says: [551]

> That which is understood from speech
> gives rise to various realizations.
> This is self-cognized, and such [reflexive awareness]
> is nothing beyond direct perception.[889]

In brief, according to Dignāga's tradition, having taken a white cow as a basis for assigning a label and having applied the label *cow* to that assembled conglomeration of a hump and so on, then when one later sees a black cow it will give rise to the thought "This too is a cow." But it does not occur through the capacity of an objectively distinct universal *cowhood* that pervades both white and black individuals and exists as a separate entity from both, as the Vaiśeṣika and Naiyāyika maintain; and it does not occur by way of the two—a cow and the term *cow*—being related through the force of reality [in an intrinsic manner], as the Mīmāṃsaka maintain. Dignāga explains that when the label applied earlier is later used as a classificatory convention, it is through understanding the black individual to be qualified by the exclusion of the converse, *non-cow*. Furthermore, although the thing at the time of assigning the label based on the white individual earlier is completely absent at the time one employs the classificatory convention later, in terms of what appears to a conceptual mind, the referent and the term [i.e., the particular individual cow that appears and the imputation *cow*] appear mixed together as a single item; and the referent of the word (the exclusion), which does not exist as an external object even having been conceived as such, is applied to an external object.[890] [552] In that case, upon first assigning the label *cow* to a white individual, a relationship is made between the term and the referent by a combination of the term *cow* and the convention of pointing it out, based on which one ascertains the object *cow* from the term; but one does not realize that object from the term alone. Concerning such a relationship, Dignāga's *Compendium of Valid Cognition* says: "Because it is a conceptualization, it is not [really] related."[891] This explains that it is merely imputed by thought or conceptualization but is not established through the causal capacity of real things.

The reason why Dignāga's theory of the exclusion of other has been presented here in some detail, based on his *Compendium of Valid Cognition* and its autocommentary, is the following. First, since the root text and autocommentary are not extant in Sanskrit these days (apart from short excerpts) but are found only in Tibetan translation, one must rely on the Tibetan texts alone if one wants to understand precisely the difficult points of this master's logico-epistemological theory. Second, since most authors on epistemology who expound Dignāga's views do so primarily on the basis of Dharmakīrti's interpretation, it seems that Dignāga's own unique and important views remain unappreciated by later commentators. Finally, when we present Dignāga's most significant views on the basis of citing his own texts, we can understand in broad terms the history of the development of successive Buddhist epistemologists' contributions toward the rational establishment of the theory of exclusion [553] and the referent of words. In view of these, we have endeavored to offer here an explanation of the theory of exclusion based on Dignāga's own words.

29

Dharmakīrti's Exclusion Theory of Meaning

Dharmakīrti's Arguments Demonstrating How Language and Thought Operate by Way of the Exclusion of Other

The thinker that has made the most significant contribution to this novel theory of exclusion, following its innovation by Dignāga, is Dharmakīrti, who appeared in the first half of the seventh century CE. This is a fact well known in both Buddhist and non-Buddhist circles in India. In his *Exposition of Valid Cognition* and its autocommentary, the presentation of the exclusion of other emerges as follows. In the case of correct nature-evidence, such as the proof that sound is impermanent because it is produced, Dharmakīrti explains that the evidence and the thesis are established as intrinsically related. Other traditions argue that if that were so, then there would be no difference between produced and impermanent, in which case that nature-evidence, being no different from the predicate, would be fallacious inferential evidence that is unestablished. So it is in the course of responding to this objection that the theory of the exclusion of other is presented. In contrast, as explained earlier, in Dignāga's *Compendium of Valid Cognition* the theory emerges as a further exploration of the definitive twofold division of valid cognition into direct perception and inferential cognition, where the language-based valid cognition asserted previously by other systems is here subsumed within the class of inferential valid cognition.

In any case, the most detailed presentation of the exclusion of other that Dharmakīrti sets forth can be found in the first chapter of his *Exposition of Valid Cognition* and its autocommentary, [554] which remain extant in Sanskrit editions along with a great many of their Indian and Tibetan commentaries. Since this master's presentation of the exclusion of other is very well known, we do not address it here in detail. According to Dharmakīrti, a signifying term and its meaning do not have an intrinsic relationship that is established through the causal capacity of real things; also, a term does not engage its object through a denotative capacity grounded in reality but signifies its object through excluding what is not it. Additionally, he posits that a class word not only operates by way of excluding among its instances what is not it, but it also does not engage via a real universal that is different from its instances; and a class word cannot directly signify its particular instances without being related to an exclusion of other and so on. Thus it is well known that he embraces as his own standpoint the view that, as stated by Dignāga, an exclusion of other is established to be the linguistic referent. However, it seems to be the case that when Dignāga sets forth his presentation of the exclusion of other, he does so primarily from the perspective of signifying terms. Dharmakīrti, on the other hand, presents it from the perspective of both language and thought, and in particular he analyzes how thought engages its object. So there seems to be a subtle difference between their approaches. In view of this, we will address here a few of the unique aspects of Dharmakīrti's presentation of the theory of the exclusion of other.

The first chapter of Dharmakīrti's *Exposition of Valid Cognition* contains three verses that present in a succinct manner the exclusion of other according to his own tradition. Since these verses are so important, we cite them here: [555]

> Because all real things exist
> as individual entities by their own nature,
> they support the exclusion from
> homologous things and heterogeneous things.
>
> Therefore, through that by which
> something is excluded from others,
> diverse types are differentiated;
> through such differentiation, realizations occur.
>
> Therefore certain differentiations
> are known by way of some attributes

but cannot be [known] by way of others;
thus they remain distinct.[892]

The first verse explains that functional things such as sounds are not established by mere conceptual imputation, but as real things that are distinct and exist by virtue of their own nature; thus they support the exclusion from homologous things and heterogeneous things. Moreover a basis, such as sound and so on, is not mixed with the homologous class related to being produced, such as a pot, nor with the heterogeneous class, such as permanent and unproduced, but arises from its own cause as excluded from them. This shows that something such as sound, as a basis, has many attributes such as produced (excluded from *unproduced*) and impermanent (excluded from *permanent*). The second verse explains that for this reason, one can correctly posit it to be realized by cognition that sound as a basis is excluded from other bases of exclusion by means of differentiating the diverse excluded attributes, as in the case of sound being impermanent because it is produced. The third verse explains that excluded attributes posited in relation to different bases of exclusion [556] can be known by way of different terms that make it understood. But since by understanding the term, such as *produced*, one is not able to understand something else, such as *impermanent*, produced and impermanent remain different from the perspective of conceptual cognition.[893]

To present in greater detail the content of these three verses summarizing the theory of the exclusion of other, there follow 143 verses in Dharmakīrti's *Exposition of Valid Cognition*, together with their autocommentary. Broadly speaking, these verses, 43–185, cover the following topics. The first sixteen verses[894] refute that language and thought engage via affirmation. Then the following fifty-four verses and two lines[895] prove that language and thought have the exclusion of other as their object. Then the next seventy-one verses and two lines,[896] together with their explanations, demonstrate the rebuttal of arguments against the exclusion of other. Finally, the last verse[897] [557] shows that language and thought involved in negation are effortlessly established to have the exclusion of other as their object. This contains in a nutshell all the sections of the first chapter of this treatise covering the theory of the exclusion of other.[898]

In opening his detailed explanation about the exclusion of other, Dharmakīrti's *Exposition of Valid Cognition Autocommentary* states the following: "*Qualm*: How should it be understood that 'terms and reasons bring about realization through exclusion and not by way of affirmation through the capacity of the essential nature of real things'? *Response*: It is because other valid cognitions and other terms operate [as well]."[899] This is Dharmakīrti's main argument proving that language and thought have exclusions as their objects. That is to say, all the attributes in the pot's nature are neither indicated by the phrase "impermanent pot" nor realized by the thought apprehending it, because with regard to a pot, the valid cognition realizing it to be impermanent and the statement "It is impermanent" operate later. Thus in indicating that other valid cognitions and other phrases operate in relation to the pot, Dharmakīrti implies that direct perception and inferential cognition have utterly different ways of operating. He states that if a thought apprehending *sound* were to engage its object by way of affirmation in the manner of a direct perception, then—just as a direct perception apprehending *sound* always perceives the attributes that are the same nature as sound in the sense of being inseparable and necessarily coexistent—there would be nothing realized by another valid cognition that is not apprehended by the thought apprehending *sound*. So one might ask, "In that case, would this problem equally apply to direct perception?" [558] No, it is not similar because direct perception is *nondeterminate* in nature, while conceptual cognition is a mind having a *determinate* nature (in other words, perception does not ascertain its object, while conceptual cognition ascertains its object).[900] So if conceptual cognition were to apprehend all the attributes based on sound, then it would necessarily ascertain them, whereas such necessity does not apply in the case of direct perception. Thus they must be differentiated. A direct perception seeing an object is a condition that *induces* a determinate cognition of it, for by inducing a determinate cognition that arises after the direct perception, it is said to be able to realize it. These two—the direct perception to which an object clearly appears and its induced conceptual cognition—are established to have a special relationship. Dharmakīrti's *Exposition of Valid Cognition Autocommentary* says:

> Direct perception does not ascertain anything at all because it does not ascertain that which it apprehends. Why not? Because that object simply appears to it. Therefore it is not by way of ascertaining or not ascertaining that direct perception appre-

hends or does not apprehend. Those that ascertain are not like that, for since some ascertain and others do not ascertain, they operate differently, thereby either apprehending or not apprehending.[901]

As for satisfying the conditions for ascertaining an object, the following is an example of a determinate cognition induced by a direct perception in the case of something familiar. Although a brahmin's father is his procreator and taught him to read, owing to familiarity he thinks "My father is coming" when he sees him approaching, not "My teacher is coming."[902] [559]

Now one might ask, "How is an exclusion from other posited to be a universal in Dharmakīrti's tradition?" It is because it appears as such to a mind apprehending a universal. A "universal" is not established as a real thing; however, under the influence of latent propensities of language-based cognition since time without beginning, a cognition apprehending a universal arises that apprehends discrete and separate phenomena to be of a single type.[903] A cognition apprehending a universal is explained by means of the following example. Although separate individual trees, such as an ashoka and a juniper, are substantially different from each other, those two do not appear substantially different to the thought apprehending them as trees, and so they are merged into a single appearance. That appearance as the *converse of non-tree* based on the ashoka and the juniper is posited by conceptual cognition to be a universal. However, the universal that pervades both the ashoka and the juniper is not a separate entity.

To present some of the unique features of Dharmakīrti's views on the exclusion of other, let us consider the following example. When a conceptual cognition apprehending a tree arises, as in thinking "This is a tree, and that too is a tree," the mind differentiates between *tree* and *non-tree*, and ascertains an ashoka or a juniper and so on to be excluded from being a non-tree. The various differences between an ashoka and a juniper are not seen at that time due to the force of obscuration in the mind, and instead those two are ascertained similarly as *trees*. That appearance, fabricated by the mind apprehending individual trees to be the same or similar, as *trees*, is posited to be an ashoka universal or a juniper universal in accordance with conventional thinking.

The point that needs to be understood here is as follows. A cognition apprehending different individual trees similarly as trees arises because they are the same type. [560] What it means to be the same type must refer to a resultant cognition of resemblance generated in accordance with reality. All individual trees are the same in performing the function of a tree; and in particular, all of them are similarly able to produce a direct perception apprehending a tree and a conceptual cognition apprehending a tree, as in thinking, "This is a tree." For example, the dominant condition (a visual sense faculty), the objective condition (an external object and sufficient light), and the immediately preceding condition (mental attention) all produce a shared result—a visual cognition apprehending a form as the perceived thing—even though there is no separate universal (called "the cause of visual cognition") that pervades them all. Regarding this, Dharmakīrti's *Exposition of Valid Cognition* says:

> Some accomplish the same purpose,
> such as inducing the same cognition,
> for even though they are different owing to their nature
> they are ascertained [as the same], like the sense faculties and
> so on.[904]

Dharmakīrti explains this further in his *Exposition of Valid Cognition Autocommentary*:

> Different individual trees, such as the ashoka, are cognized as a single image due to their [shared] nature alone, even though they are not mutually distributed one over another. In addition, they function to produce other things, such as fire and houses, with their wood acting as the condition for accomplishing those purposes. But water and so on, which is not so different as to be separate from them, [561] does not [function in that way], just as the ear and so on [does not give rise to] a cognition apprehending a form.[905]

Moreover, many causes, although not mutually concomitant, can produce the same result. For example, certain medicines of different types taken together or separately are able to cure fever, even though there is no separate universal that commonly pervades them.[906] Accordingly, in presenting his own system, Dharmakīrti's *Exposition of Valid Cognition Autocommentary* says: "If such cognition arises from only the differentiation from others, what need is there for a universal here?"[907] Also: "That is to say, a cognition bearing mixed images is just mistaken; it is produced naturally by the series of different things that cause the conceptual cognition."[908] Even though there is no separate universal, a cognition apprehending a universal apprehends, for example, different individual trees to be the same kind, *tree*, based indirectly on individual trees that are different substances; and it is a cognition that is mistaken regarding an appearance of the exclusion of non-tree to be an external tree.

A conceptual cognition apprehending a tree that arises in the wake of a direct perception apprehending a tree is a cognition that is mistaken with regard to its image appearing to be an external tree; [562] yet there is no contradiction in explaining the notions of universal, concomitance, and so on on the basis of it. Those conceptual cognitions are not like cognitions that mistake a mirage to be water. For, a conceptual cognition apprehending a tree, although considered mistaken as to its appearing object, nevertheless obtains its object because it is induced by a direct perception apprehending a tree. Dharmakīrti's *Exposition of Valid Cognition Autocommentary* says: "*Obtainment* [by valid cognition] is due to the invariable relationship (of unaccompanied nonoccurrence) with the object, but it is not on the basis of the appearance [of the object alone]."[909]

Cognitions apprehending universals must in the end link back to a particular individual phenomenon. A conceptual cognition apprehending a tree, for example, is related to the direct perception apprehending a tree that induced it; and, since this arises through having taken the tree as its observed object, the direct perception apprehending a tree is related to that tree. This is how the relationship between direct perception and conceptual cognition can be understood, which is very clearly presented in the "Perception" chapter of Dharmakīrti's *Exposition of Valid Cognition*:

> If it is said, "So [universals] would be undermined as attributes
> of real things,"
> this fault does not arise, because the cognition of that [universal]
> was preceded by an apprehension of the real thing.[910]

Here, the following doubt is presented: "In the case of a cognition apprehending a universal based on a real thing, if there is no need for it to be concomitant with the presence or absence of a real thing, then this would undermine such a universal being a universal based on a real thing." Dharmakīrti responds by arguing that [563] although a thought apprehending a pot, for example, is not concomitant with the presence or absence of the real thing that is the basis of its appearing object, since it is preceded by a direct perception apprehending a pot, it does not have this fault. Regarding this point, Devendrabuddhi's *Commentary on Difficult Points in the Exposition of Valid Cognition* says:

> If it is said, "So [universals] would be undermined as attributes of real things . . ."
>
> *Qualm*: When a consciousness apprehends a universal in the absence of the actual thing, this would surely undermine it being an attribute of the thing.
>
> *Response*: The above-mentioned fault would not occur.
>
> *Qualm*: Why not?
>
> *Response*:
>
> . . . that was preceded by an apprehension of the real thing.
>
> This is saying that because it would be a cognition of the universal, or universal-cognition, and because a universal, such as *form* and so on, is an object of cognition due to the nature of the thing itself, it is not accepted to be an attribute of the thing.
>
> *Qualm*: So what is it?
>
> *Response*: When a thought arises in dependence upon propensities that are deposited due to having seen forms and so on, an object-image of its own is conceived to be the image of form and so on and is engaged thus. Since it arises through the efficacy of having seen forms and so on, and since it conceives it to be that, the convention "It is an attribute of the thing" is employed. That is the meaning of this verse.[911]

Here, Devendrabuddhi posits two reasons why the universal that is the exclusion of other, which is the object of a conceptual cognition apprehending a form and so on, is called the "attribute of the thing" such as form and so on: (1) such a cognition apprehending a universal arises from the propensities deposited by a direct perception apprehending form, and (2) such a cognition [564] conceives its own observed object or appearance fabricated by the cognition itself to be the aspect of an external form and so on. Accordingly, Dharmakīrti's *Exposition of Valid Cognition* says:

> A reflection in conceptual cognition
> is related to that [real thing] in the end.
> So, since it relates to an exclusion of other finally,
> a term signifies an exclusion of other.
>
> A reflection of other [things], like an exclusion,
> appears in cognition born from terms,
> but that is not the real nature of the thing
> for it arises from mistaken propensities.[912]

As explicitly stated in Dharmakīrti's *Exposition of Valid Cognition* and its autocommentary, the "universal" that is the object of cognition apprehending a universal is posited only as a conceptual appearance, so it is from the perspective of mistaken conceptual cognition only that such a universal is concomitant with its instances; there is no separate phenomenon concomitant with its different instances at all. As for the exclusion of other that is generally accepted by Dharmakīrti's tradition, (1) it is concomitant with real things, (2) it is not contradictory as the cause of cognition of a universal, [565] and (3) the conventions of signifying terms also appear to have the exclusion of other as their objects.[913] When presenting the three reasons why the exclusion of other is the basis of the cognition of a universal, Dharmakīrti states that the exclusion of other does pervade the different instances. This suggests the need to differentiate between explanations from ultimate and conventional standpoints. As for the universal that appears to conception in general, there are said to be three types: (1) a universal that is based on a real thing, such as the referent of the term *pot*, (2) a universal that is based on a non-thing, such as the referent of the term *nonexistent rabbit's horn*, and (3) a universal that is based on both, such as the referent of the term *object of knowledge*. These are said to appear to conceptual cognition through the force of propensities generated by (1) seeing a real thing, (2) conceptualizing an unreal thing, and (3) conceptualizing both of those.[914]

As for how terms signify their referents, Dharmakīrti generally agrees with Dignāga's explanation that the relation between term and referent operates according to the ordinary conventions of the world even though this is not a relation that is established in reality. A term such as *pot* signifies its referent through being qualified as excluding what is other than itself in being a *non-pot*, but it cannot signify its referent through the capacity of a real thing or in an affirmative manner. Therefore, according to Dharmakīrti's tradition, signifying terms do not apply ultimately to particular individual phenomena. Indeed, the purpose of linguistic conventions in the world is to accomplish the desired aims of living beings and to avoid those that are not desired. [566] Moreover, if we consider the word *cow*, for example, although the word does not take a particular cow that exists externally as its direct object, the thought apprehending a cow, to which an image resembling an external cow appears, indirectly obtains a real cow—for it can accomplish one's desired aims, such as extracting milk and so on. Dharmakīrti's *Exposition of Valid Cognition Autocommentary* says:

> In the world, people do not suffer miserably due to words not being used or the terms used somehow not corresponding to their referents. So how do they relate to words? They do so by taking the terms as always leading to fruitful activity, for that which is fruitless activity is to be utterly shunned. Thus, by this application of the term to certain things only, certain results are seen. In all these cases, however, the applications of terms have the characteristic of helping to obtain what is desired and to shun what is not desired. So having understood their roles in accomplishing or not accomplishing what is desired and what is not desired, one sincerely acts to adopt or avoid, make others do the same, and apply the terms that accord with such tasks. As for those [terms] that do not, these are to be utterly shunned.[915]

This same text says later:

> We take as our object the thing that appears differentiated to conceptual cognition, which has arisen from propensities that exist since beginningless time. As for the speaker and the lis-

> tener, on the basis of that conceptual cognition, the speaker wishes to communicate that thing exactly as it appears to him, and a conceptual cognition bearing the form of that thing is produced [in the listener].[916] [567]

In brief, in dependence on hearing the word *cow*, a cognition is subsequently induced that differentiates between *cow* and *non-cow* and is able to understand the assembled mass—a hump and so on—that exists right there to be the opposite of non-cow. In keeping with the motivation of a person wishing to express it, a relation between term and referent is made between the two—the mundane convention (the word *cow*) and the assembled mass (the hump and so on). Although external individual cows are separate things that are mutually unrelated, they are all similar in performing the function of a cow and in being able to produce similar identifying cognitions of "This is a cow" in the minds of people looking at a cow. Since Dharmakīrti, unlike Dignāga, explains that this cognition apprehends what exists right there as qualified by the negation of its dissimilar type, *non-cow*, the way in which he explains how language and thought operate through the exclusion of other (i.e., what is not it) is drawn mainly from an account of cause and effect. Thus there seems to be a difference between these two masters as to what explanation is emphasized.

Thus, when presenting the exclusion of other, Dharmakīrti explains that since different individuals can produce the same result, a conceptual cognition qualified by excluding what is not it engages its object through combining those different phenomena into a single thing. This way of explaining the exclusion of other seems to have been adopted by most of the Buddhist logicians who came after Dharmakīrti. For example, [568] Śubhagupta, who flourished around the eighth century, says in his *Investigation of the Exclusion of Other*:

> Therefore, in the case of different natures,
> because similar results and so on are seen,
> cognition imputes them to be unitary
> and employs conventions accordingly.[917]

Similarly, Dharmottara's *Explanation of Exclusion* says: "Different particular individuals are seen as different. That seeing immediately precedes an ascertainment that conceives them to be not different. Therefore the individuals of a single perception are realized as being of a similar nature differentiated from those that do not bring about the expected result."[918] Also, Śaṅkarānanda's *Proof of Exclusion* says:

> In dependence on realizing that,
> they bring about the same result;
> such cognition is firm ascertainment,
> for in experience they are not nondifferent.[919] [569]

30

Repelling Objections to the Exclusion Theory

Objections Cited in Śāntarakṣita's *Compendium of Reality*

As outlined above, during the late fifth or early sixth century, Dignāga propagated the theory of the exclusion of other—namely, that a signifying term expresses its object by way of an exclusion of other that precludes what is not it, without the need for a separate universal, as asserted by the Vaiśeṣika and the Naiyāyika. On this basis, an account can be offered that explains how class words and cognitions of universals are feasible. This clearly raises problems for the assertion of six categories of objects of knowledge, which is the main tenet of the Vaiśeṣika and the Nyāya schools. Similarly, this exclusion theory states that words and referents do not have an absolute intrinsic relationship, but instead, the relation between a term and its referent is one that operates by way of ordinary linguistic conventions in the world. Even so, given that signifying terms have exclusions as their objects, a word such as *pot* does not signify all the attributes of the pot, yet it is proved to be able to signify its meaning unmistakenly. These statements challenge the Mīmāṃsaka who believe the words of the Vedas to be a valid authority not composed by human beings and that, in general, words and their referents possess ultimate intrinsic connection. Given these, there appeared among non-Buddhist Indian philosophical traditions in the sixth and seventh centuries some thinkers who engaged in extensive refutations of Dignāga's view of the exclusion of other. The most famous of these [570] are the Nyāya master Uddyotakara (sixth century) and the Mīmāṃsā master Kumārila Bhaṭṭa (seventh century). Here we will provide a brief synopsis of the main criticisms of Dignāga's view of the exclusion of other posited by these two non-Buddhist masters and show how the Buddhist epistemologists Dharmakīrti and Śāntarakṣita responded to these objections, respectively, in the *Exposition of Valid Cognition* with its autocommentary and in the "Examination of Word Meaning" chapter of the *Compendium of Reality*.

First let us review the main arguments posited in Uddyotakara's *Exposition of Nyāya Reasoning* to refute Dignāga's exclusion of other, as reported in Śāntarakṣita's *Compendium of Reality* as follows.

1) If a term signifies its referent by way of excluding what is not it, then in the case of a word such as *cow*, one could grant that this term can be posited to exclude non-cow, since *cow* and *non-cow* are directly contradictory in the sense of being mutually excluding. But in the case of a term such as *all*, it is not possible to posit something that is its opposite in the sense of being mutually excluding. This entails the fault that the claim that a term has an exclusion as its object remains inconclusive. This same objection can be raised against terms that signify collections, such as "two" or "three," because in refuting the referent of *one*, for example, the referent of a group of *two* [571] is thereby refuted.[920]

This objection is refuted as follows. It is not correct that the term *all* does not have an exclusion as its object. Indeed, in the sentence "All phenomena lack self-existence," the term "all" is not uttered in isolation but is expressed in relation to something, a given subject that is the basis [such as a vase]. This is because there is the possibility of entertaining the mistaken thought "Only external things, such as pots, lack self-existence, but everything else possesses self-existence," and it is to dispel such a thought [that the statement "All phenomena lack self-existence" is made]. Thus these criticisms raised by the other party do not apply to us. This rebuttal is presented in Śāntarakṣita's *Compendium of Reality*, together with its commentary [by Kamalaśīla], beginning with "In the case of the term *all* also" up to "Out of ignorance it is declared to follow."[921]

2) Again, in the case of the exclusion of other said to be signified by the term *cow*, is it *real* like a cow, or is it *unreal*? If real, then it is either the cow itself or something different from the cow. If it is the cow, then the proponents of exclusion are merely arguing about semantics. If it is not the cow, then the term *cow* would have the character of signifying *non-cow*. Alternatively, if it is unreal, then this would contradict experience because according to the experience of ordinary people, something totally *unreal* does not arise in one's mind based on an understanding of the term *cow*.[922]

This objection is refuted as follows. The universal *cow* that is the exclusion of other is conceptually conceived to be an external cow, but since it does not exist as a cow, it is unreal. [572] Nevertheless, having conceived the universal *cow* or exclusion of other that is the meaning of the term *cow*, a cow is ascertained; and since the universal *cow* is like a reflection of the cow conjoined with thought, it is not an unreal mere negation. The rebuttal of these objections is presented in two verses of the *Compendium of Reality*, together with its commentary, beginning with "It is neither real nor unreal."[923]

3) Again, with respect to the exclusion that is the exclusion of non-cow, is it the same as the cow, or different from it? If *different*, then either it subsists in a cow, or does not subsist in it. If it *subsists* in the cow, then that exclusion would be an attribute of the cow. In that case, the phrase "This cow exists" would not signify an existent cow because one part of that phrase, the word "cow," signifies the exclusion that is an attribute of the cow, so it does not signify the cow that is the basis. Alternatively, if that exclusion does *not subsist* in the cow, then it would be incorrect to apply the sixth-case genitive particle in the phrase "exclusion of cow." Moreover, if that exclusion is *not different* from the cow, then Dignāga's presentation of exclusion would be pointless.[924]

This objection is refuted as follows. If the word *cow* were to primarily indicate the exclusion of non-cow directly, then those faults posited above could arise. However, the signifying term *cow directly* signifies a reflection of the thing, cow, or the meaning of the word *cow*, while it *indirectly* signifies the exclusion of non-cow. [573] The hearer too, through the meaning of the word *cow* directly appearing, indirectly realizes the exclusion of non-cow. It is explained that these objections are stated out of ignorance of the main points of this philosophical system. These points are made clear in two verses of the *Compendium of Reality* together with its commentary, beginning with "The direct object of the term."[925]

4) Again, with respect to the exclusion that is the exclusion of non-cow, is it the same in the case of all cows or is it different in each individual case? If the same, then that kind of exclusion would be related to cows of all times and places, so it would exist in all of them. In this case, that exclusion would be no different from the universal *cowhood*. Alternatively, if the exclusion of cow exists in each individual instance of cow, then like the instances of cow, the exclusion of cow would be innumerable. Therefore Dignāga's statement

"A class word does not signify particular individuals because individuals are innumerable," found in his *Compendium of Valid Cognition* and autocommentary, would not be correct.[926]

This objection is refuted as follows. Those exclusions of cow are phenomena conjoined with thought on the basis of a cow therefore they are not established as the same or different in an ultimate sense. So the objection stated above does not apply. This is explained in *Compendium of Reality*, together with its commentary, in the verse beginning with "Difference, nondifference, and all."[927] [574]

5) Again, if the exclusion of other is the object signified by terms, is it signified by way of affirmation or is it signified by way of negation? If it is an object signified by way of affirmation, then it would be meaningless to say "An exclusion of other is the referent of a term." Alternatively, if it is the object signified by way of a negation, then that exclusion of other must also be signified by an exclusion of other, in which case exclusion would become endless.[928]

This objection is refuted as follows. Terms signifying a pot and so on give rise to a reflection or an appearance of the linguistic referent in a thought through which it is directly ascertained, while the exclusion of what it is not is realized indirectly. Since the exclusion of other is not signified directly, the fault of its being endless does not occur, and likewise the fault of terms not having exclusions as their object does not occur. Thus the objections stated above do not apply here. This is shown in *Compendium of Reality*, together with its commentary, in four verses beginning with "Is the referent of a term an exclusion of other?"[929]

That the most extensive objections to Dignāga's theory of the exclusion of other appear in a text of the Mīmāṃsā master Kumārila Bhaṭṭa is something well known in both Buddhist and non-Buddhist circles. He composed a text called *Exposition of Verses on Mīmāṃsā* [575] that contains a chapter specifically about the exclusion of other. Based on the very important arguments it contains, in his *Exposition of Valid Cognition* Dharmakīrti presents in depth critical responses to Kumārila Bhaṭṭa's objections, such as: there is the consequence that understanding [of cow and non-cow] would be mutually dependent; since in the case of the term *object of knowledge* there is nothing to be excluded, the statement that terms have exclusions as their objects remains inconclusive; furthermore, if all terms were to have exclusions as their objects, then they would all be synonymous.

Śāntarakṣita's *Compendium of Reality* in particular provides detailed refutations of these objections, where he cites many quotations directly from Kumārila's *Exposition of Verses on Mīmāṃsā* pertaining to his refutation of the exclusion of other.[930] We will now present briefly Kumārila's main objections to the exclusion of other theory as cited in *Compendium of Reality* and how one might respond to those arguments.

Objections Based on Examining Whether the Exclusion of Other Is an Implicative or a Nonimplicative Negation

In response to the proponents of exclusion who claim that a term such as *cow* signifies an exclusion of non-cow, Kumārila Bhaṭṭa poses the following question: "Is this type of exclusion an implicative negation or a nonimplicative negation?" First, suppose you accept it to be an *implicative* negation. Given that we assert the referent of the term *cow* to be the universal that is *cowhood* and you assert the referent of the term *cow* to be the universal that is the *exclusion of non-cow*, [576] there is no difference between the referents [in that they are both universals], so it becomes merely a debate about semantics. Furthermore, you accept this universal to be an unreal phenomenon, and the fact is that unreal phenomena must be posited on the basis of a real thing. So what is the basis of the exclusion that is the exclusion of non-cow? If you accept this universal to be the nature of a particular individual, such as a cow, then it cannot be the experienced object of a cognition apprehending a universal because according to you, unique particular phenomena are not the experienced objects of thought apprehending a universal. Also, it is incorrect to accept this universal *cow* itself to be the nature of a mottled cow, or suchlike, because if it were, then it could not be the universal concomitant with a black cow and so on. Having incurred many faults such as these, your claim "The universal *cow* is an exclusion of other" is merely a case of using different terms, because the referent is the universal itself, the *cowhood* that pervades all cows. Thus you succumb to the fault of proving what has already been proved. Now, suppose you accept the universal that is the linguistic referent to be a *nonimplicative* negation. This entails the fault that a term signifying a mere negation, *non-cow*, would not enable one to understand a cow that is an external thing.[931]

This objection is refuted as follows. Even though a real universal based on an external thing, which you assert to be the linguistic referent, does not exist, an external thing such as an elephant is realized by way of a mistaken cognition conceiving the linguistic referent—the exclusion of other itself—to be an external thing. Although that cognition is mistaken, [577] since it relates indirectly to an external thing such as an elephant, it obtains the external thing. It is like, for example, a mind that is mistaken in apprehending the glimmer of a jewel to be a jewel, yet this does not contradict obtainment of the jewel. As demonstrated by many logical reasonings, the universal that is the *exclusion of other* is not like the real universal *cowhood* you have imagined; therefore the fault of proving what has already been proved does not occur. Moreover, since we do not posit this universal to be a nonimplicative negation, we do not succumb to the faults incurred by accepting it to be a nonimplicative negation. These refutations of the above objections are presented in the *Compendium of Reality*, together with its commentary, beginning with "That universal is asserted to be *cowhood*."[932]

The Argument That All Signifying Terms Would Be Synonymous

The question of what follows from the assertion that all signifying terms have exclusions as their object, as the proponents of exclusion maintain, is addressed in Kamalaśīla's *Commentary on the Difficult Points in the Compendium of Reality* as follows:

> *Qualm*: Any terms that signify different universals such as *cow*, *horse*, and so on, as well as any terms that signify particular attributes such as mottled and so on, would all be synonymous according to your view because the referents would not be different, just as in the case of terms such as *tree* (Skt. *vṛkṣa*) and *root drinker* (Skt. *pādapa*).[933]

This is because when it comes to exclusion or negation, apart from the negation of some other thing, there is no entity with a nature of its own that can be posited. This would mean that terms cannot be differentiated with respect to their meaning, and from this it follows that all terms would be synonymous. As for the main grounds for this line of thinking, this is explained in Kamalaśīla's *Commentary on the Difficult Points in the Compendium of Reality* as follows: [578] "The argument is thus: 'Those that are different from each other must be real things, such as particular individuals. Exclusions too are different from one another.' This is [an argument using] nature-evidence."[934] In that case, only real things, which are affirmative, can be the meaning of a term. Those who claim that terms engage via affirmation do not incur this fault that terms are synonymous, because in their system they are able to maintain that terms signify different meanings.[935]

Citing the line "From diverse excluded objects, different [meanings]"[936] from Dignāga's *Compendium of Valid Cognition*, Kumārila anticipates a Buddhist rejoinder that in the case of the compound "blue lotus," since the individual elements of the compound exclude different things, the elements "blue" and "lotus" are not synonymous. But, he argues, such a rejoinder remains untenable.

Kumārila's response is refuted as follows. According to you, given that a term or thought applies ultimately to an object, it would be pointless for any other evidence or inferential reason to operate. Furthermore, terms that express *sound*, *produced*, *impermanent*, and so on and the cognitions that ascertain them do not have different objects and purposes, so it is just the terms and cognitions that are different, which entails the fault that they would be synonymous. According to our own tradition, since the terms expressing "A pot is impermanent," or the evidence establishing it, and so on are employed only to clear away fabrications such as apprehending a pot to be permanent, [579] the fault that innumerable factors, such as pot's production and so on, would be the signified object or the established object does not arise. For this reason, terms and subsequent thoughts expressing a pot's production and so on are needed to eliminate individual fabrications. Therefore they are not pointless; the fault that terms and cognitions would be synonymous does not arise for us.

In addition to this explanation, some counter-objections have been raised against those who claim that terms engage via affirmation, as to how co-denoting terms would be unfeasible, in Dharmakīrti's *Exposition of Valid Cognition*, beginning with "If a referent of a compound is precluded" up to "It is established as signifying an exclusion,"[937] and in sixteen verses of Śāntarakṣita's *Compendium of Reality* together with its commentary [by Kamalaśīla], beginning with "As in the case of not being existent."[938]

Objections Based on Examining Gender, Number, Verbs, Injunction, and Modification

Further, the opponent argues: It is incorrect to maintain that terms necessarily have exclusions as their object, for terms with parts that are affixes of gender (such as "masculine," "feminine," and "neuter") or number ("one," "two," and so on) cannot be related to an exclusion of other, because an exclusion of other is unreal and thus is devoid of gender and so on, [580] therefore it cannot be signified by a term.[939] Sanskrit verbs ending with the particle *-ti*, as in *paccati* ("cooks") and *gaccati* ("goes"), are terms that primarily indicate an activity, in which case there is no exclusion of other. Why not? It is difficult enough in the case of nouns such as *pot* to posit an excluded object of its contrary term (i.e., *non-pot*), but in the case of verbs, such as *cooking*, an excluded object of its contrary term, *not cooking*, cannot be posited as an implicative negation. And if posited as a nonimplicative negation, as in saying "not not," then since the double negation indicates the original, the object signified would be an affirmative thing, "cooking." Furthermore, regarding an activity such as *cooking*, differences between earlier and later parts must be posited, as in lightly cooking or thoroughly cooking. But such temporal attributes cannot be posited on the basis of unreal nonimplicative negations, since these are of one taste (i.e., undifferentiated). By this reasoning, particles of injunction, conjunction, and so on, as well as modifying words—such as utterly, completely, thoroughly, and so on—likewise cannot be posited to have exclusions as their object.[940]

This objection is refuted as follows. Signifying terms with affixes that indicate gender (such as "masculine," "feminine," and "neuter"), number ("one," "two," and so on), verbs, and so on are merely affixed according to the speaker's desire but do not operate through the capacity of the real object. Indeed, if they were to operate through the causal capacity of a real thing, [581] then it would be possible for a single thing to be engaged by a term having three genders, which would absurdly entail a single thing having three distinct natures. Likewise, numerals are also employed out of a desire, but do not operate through the capacity of a real thing. For if they were to denote their objects through the capacity of a real thing then, as in the case of "many queens in one woman," a single thing would be engaged by a numeral indicating many, so the one would absurdly be many; or conversely, as in the case of "one ring of trees in many forests," although there are many distinct things they would be engaged by a numeral indicating one, so the many would absurdly be one. Furthermore, it is not incorrect for the word *cooking* to have an exclusion of others as its object because this term excludes other activities such as eating and sitting quietly not doing anything. In this way, these criticisms are refuted at length in Śāntarakṣita's *Compendium of Reality*, from "As for the connection of gender, number, and so on" up to "The exclusion of what is not intended is established."[941]

The Term *Exclusion* Itself Does Not Necessarily Engage via Exclusion

Additionally, the opponent argues: Since the term *exclusion* itself does not have an exclusion as its object, then it is not the case that all terms necessarily engage via exclusion. Indeed, if the term *exclusion* were to have an exclusion as its object, then it must exclude *nonexclusion*. If it excludes nonexclusion, then it would indicate its original form (owing to the double negation), so that exclusion would be something objectively established.[942] [582]

This objection is refuted as follows. Even in relation to exclusion, when a term is applied, it is done so on the basis of eliminating what is not it—and not by way of applying the term to a real separate universal. And when a term is applied to an exclusion of other by way of eliminating what is not it, there is no danger of an infinite regress. For when a term is applied to an exclusion, it must be applied on the basis of eliminating what is not an exclusion of other. When so applied, if it requires another separate term that eliminates what is not it and so on, then clearly there will be an infinite regress. However, there is no such need to apply separate terms. The term that eliminates what is not an exclusion of other is capable of indicating the exclusion of the other. Also, the term *exclusion of other* itself has the capacity to indicate the elimination of what is not an exclusion of other. This is because exclusion and its negation are both absent in each other; and as they are directly contradictory in the sense of being mutually excluding, a term directly signifying one of them can bring about an understanding of the other's negation. Thus the suggested faults do not apply here. This way of refuting the above objection is presented in five verses of Dharmakīrti's *Exposition of Valid Cognition*, beginning with "That which is different from something" up to "Because it is expressed as 'different.'"[943] And it is presented similarly in thirty-two verses of Śāntarakṣita's *Compendium of Reality* together with its commentary, from "Terms that are not an exclusion of other" up to "They are just like [the terms] *pot* and so on."[944]

As an aside to his rebuttal of the above objection in his *Exposition of Valid Cognition Autocommentary*, Dharmakīrti makes the following points. [583] When a signifying term expresses its meaning, it expresses it through being qualified by an exclusion of other. The two activities of *exclusion of other* and *expressing its meaning* are not separate. Since they are a single activity, the function of those two is the same. These points he makes have great significance.[945] Based on statements such as this, Śāntarakṣita's *Compendium of Reality* says that the term *pot* directly expresses its meaning *pot*, while it indirectly indicates the nonimplicative negation based on a pot that is the *converse of non-pot*.[946]

The Term "Object of Knowledge" Has Nothing to Exclude, so Terms Do Not Necessarily Have Exclusions as Their Object

The opponent argues further: Signifying terms do not necessarily have exclusions as their object, as in the case of terms such as *object of knowledge*, *epistemic object*, and *comprehended object*, because those terms do not have an excluded object—since it is not possible to posit an "unknown object" or an "uncomprehended object," so it is unfeasible for them to have exclusions as their object—and because what is not an object of knowledge cannot be excluded. Moreover, if those terms were assumed to have excluded objects, then those identified as excluded objects would themselves be known objects. Such faults as these would occur. Therefore, the opponent claims, in accordance with mundane conventions, the linguistic referent is just affirmative.[947] [584]

This objection is refuted as follows. In general, the purpose of applying terms to things such as pots is for the sake of dispelling doubts and producing correct ascertainment in the minds of listeners. Indeed, if the listeners had no doubts about anything, then they would not rely on the instruction of others. Therefore, since the qualms of the listeners are cleared away, it is not correct to say that signifying terms such as *object of knowledge* do not have an excluded object. This above objection is refuted in two verses of Dharmakīrti's *Exposition of Valid Cognition*, together with its autocommentary, beginning with "Having removed some points [of doubt] in their minds."[948] A detailed refutation of the same objection is presented in fifteen verses of Śāntarakṣita's *Compendium of Reality*, together with its commentary by Kamalaśīla, from "As for words like *epistemic object*, *knowable object*, and so on" up to "All things are not meant to be spoken of."[949]

The Fallacy of Mutually Dependent Understanding

Again, the opponent argues: According to the proponents of exclusion, upon hearing the term *cow* the listener understands *cow* through having excluded *non-cow*. In that case, they must understand the excluded object, non-cow. Since *non-cow* is by nature the negation of *cow*, to understand this they must have already understood *cow*, because without having identified *cow* that is to be negated, it is not possible to ascertain the negation that is its absence. For without knowing its nature, one cannot negate it. Therefore this entails the fallacy that the two understandings of *cow* and *non-cow* are mutually dependent. [585] Thus there would be no possible opportunity to understand *cow* on the basis of the term *cow*. So if individual phenomena are not accepted to be the referent of a term such as *cow*, then it will be impossible to avoid the fallacy of mutually dependent understanding explained above.[950] This same fallacy of mutually dependent understanding is widely known to have been raised by the Nyāya master Uddyotakara; and according to Śāntarakṣita's *Compendium of Reality*, the same argument has also been made by the non-Buddhist master Bhāmaha, who was active in the seventh century.[951]

This objection is refuted by means of a reason by way of drawing parity as follows.[952] When the label *tree* is imputed onto that which is endowed with branches and foliage, does it or does it not exclude *non-tree*? If you say it does exclude it, then *tree* cannot be apprehended without apprehending *non-tree*, and *non-tree* cannot be cognized without apprehending *tree*. So even according to your tradition, the fallacy is also entailed that an understanding of the two—tree and non-tree—is mutually dependent. Conversely, if you say that the label *tree* does not exclude *non-tree*, then this would incur the fallacy that, just as the term *tree* is not applied to a juniper alone without including sandalwood and the rest, likewise, when the label *tree* is applied, it would not be applied to trees without including non-trees. Having rebutted the criticism by means of a reason by way of drawing parity, the actual refutation of the objection is as follows. Prior to applying the label *tree*, a direct perception distinguishes between something possessing and not possessing branches and foliage, which then induces a conceptual cognition [586] to which there appears—by way of appearing as an external entity having branches and foliage—an appearance as a class type different from something not having branches and foliage. Having distinguished between the different class-types that possess and do not possess branches and foliage, the exclusion of other that appears as different from something not having branches and foliage is taken to be the linguistic referent, and based on this the label *tree* is applied. This label induces a conceptual cognition to which an appearance of an external tree arises, and through the force of mistakenly imputing the appearance and the external tree to be the same, one can obtain the particular individual tree. In that case, a label applied to an exclusion of other does not entail the fallacy of mutually dependent understanding. This way of rebutting the above objection [of circularity] is presented in eight verses of Dharmakīrti's *Exposition of Valid Cognition*, together with its autocommentary, beginning with "By the exclusion of non-tree" up to "Being mistaken, how can it realize a real thing?"[953] It is also presented in five verses of Śāntarakṣita's *Compendium of Reality*, beginning with "Also the combination of those like that" up to "Nor is any object denoted as qualified by the exclusion of other."[954]

Following his refutation of the theory of the exclusion from other, Kumārila writes the following verse as part of his conclusion, which is cited in Śāntarakṣita's *Compendium of Reality*:

> Therefore only words conjoined with a negating term
> can have the factor of exclusion of other;
> in all other cases, understanding
> is brought about by [expressing] the thing itself.[955]

Here he says that signifying terms in which negating terms are explicitly present are suitable to have exclusions as their object, but others in which negating terms are not explicitly present [587] bring about an understanding of their referent through affirmation.

The Emergence of Indian Epistemological Literature

Now let us briefly review the emergence of the above epistemological literature [pertaining to this debate on the theory of *apoha*, "exclusion of other"] authored by Indian masters of logic and epistemology—both Buddhist and non-Buddhist. In the fifth century, the Buddhist master Dignāga established his theory of the exclusion of other as the linguistic referent in his treatise *Compendium of Valid Cognition*, together with its autocommentary, as well as in his now-lost treatise *Investigation of the Universal.* Then in the sixth century, the Nyāya master Uddyotakara composed his treatise *Exposition of Nyāya Reasoning*, in which he refuted Dignāga's argument. After that, in the seventh century, the Mīmāṃsā master Kumārila Bhaṭṭa composed *Exposition of Verses on Mīmāṃsā*, which also presented extensive refutations of Dignāga's position. Later in the seventh century, the Buddhist master Dharmakīrti not only refuted the objections raised by both Uddyotakara and Kumārila, but he also developed numerous further arguments supporting the theory of the exclusion of other. In doing so, he engaged in extensive refutation of the Nyāya-Vaiśeṣika assertion of real universals that are distinct from the particulars that instantiate them, and helped establish the system of the proponents of exclusion to be sound. After that, during the late seventh century and early eighth century, the Vaiśeṣika master Bhāmaha presented some criticisms of the exclusion theory. Then in the eighth century, the Buddhist master Śāntarakṣita composed his great *Compendium of Reality.*[956] [588] In the "Examination of Word Meaning" chapter he addressed the views of the three earlier non-Buddhist masters who criticized the position of the proponents of exclusion, and directly citing their texts he examined each of their points in detail and refuted them.

Dharmakīrti composed *Exposition of Valid Cognition* and its autocommentary in which, as noted above, he rebutted the objections raised by both Uddyotakara and Kumārila in general. In particular he presented detailed refutations of the Mīmāṃsā view that accepts real universals and claims that term and meaning are inherently related through the force of reality. Furthermore, as stated in the later part of "Inference for Oneself," the first chapter of *Exposition of Valid Cognition*, Dharmakīrti provided extensive refutations of the view asserting the Vedas to be a valid authority that is uncreated and eternal. Responding to these arguments [of Dharmakīrti], in the ninth century, Jayanta Bhaṭṭa composed *Sprigs of Reasoning* (*Nyāyamañjarī*), in which he examined both Uddyotakara's and Kumārila's arguments against Dignāga's exclusion theory, as well as the Buddhist epistemologists' rebuttal of those objections, especially the main features of Dharmottara's explanation of the exclusion of other. [589] After this, in the tenth century, the Nyāya master Trilocana composed a subcommentary on the *Commentary on the Nyāya Sūtra* by Vātsyāyana, an earlier Nyāya master, and became widely known for defending the Nyāya tradition as well as for answering Dignāga's critical arguments. Finally, his disciple Vācaspatimiśra once again refuted the proponents of exclusion and defended the Nyāya tradition against their criticisms. The assertions of these two later Nyāya masters were then refuted by the Buddhist epistemologist Jñānaśrīmitra.[957] Then the Buddhist epistemologist Ratnakīrti propagated the assertions of Jñānaśrīmitra, whereupon the Nyāya master Udayana refuted both of these Buddhist masters.[958] In the tenth century the Mīmāṃsā masters Parthasārathi Miśra and Bhāṭṭaputra Jayamiśra both defended the validity of Kumārila's tradition and argued against the proponents of exclusion. In addition to these, the Jaina master Mallavādin (eighth century) was widely known for criticizing the proponents of exclusion. So, beginning with the arrival of Dignāga and for the next six hundred years that followed, there arose an astonishing tradition in India in which both Buddhist and non-Buddhist philosophers [590] engaged in detailed analyses of epistemology in general and of the question of word meaning in particular, each aiming criticisms at the other and defending against them in turn.

31

Later Proponents of Exclusion

We have by now explained how Dharmakīrti refuted the objections of those who criticized Dignāga's exclusion of other theory and expanded upon the main points of the reasonings that establish the view of the exclusion of other. We also gave a brief presentation of how Śāntarakṣita's *Compendium of Reality* established the tradition of the proponents of exclusion to be free from error. Now, let us identify a few of the most important Buddhist epistemologists who, following Dignāga and Dharmakīrti, elaborated further their arguments establishing the theory of the exclusion of other and offered new explanations. First there is Śākyabuddhi, a disciple of Devendrabuddhi, who in turn is a direct disciple of Dharmakīrti. He upholds the intent of Dharmakīrti's *Exposition of Valid Cognition* and identifies three main types of the exclusion of other. Śākyabuddhi's *Commentary on Exposition of Valid Cognition* says:

> There are three facets of the exclusion of other, as follows. First, a particular individual is a unique exclusion because it is from this that others from which it is differentiated are excluded. Hence the text says:
>
> > They support the exclusion from
> > homologous things and heterogeneous things. [591]
>
> Here too [a particular individual] is posited to be the basis of conventions that depend on terms or evidence, but it is not the object signified by terms. Second, since it excludes others, it is the mere exclusion of other; and it is presented by earlier masters to be no different in all cases because mere negation is no

> different in every case. Third, because it appears to conceptual cognition, since it functions to exclude others, the author of the treatise explains it to be the signified object.[959]

This passage presents three facets of the exclusion of other: (1) the *basis* of the exclusion of other, which is a particular individual thing, such as a pot; (2) the *factor* of the exclusion of other, which is a nonimplicative negation that is the mere exclusion of what is not it, such as the absence of non-pot in the case of a pot; and (3) the *agent* of the exclusion of other, such as the image that appears to a conceptual cognition of a pot. As for the first, even though it is posited to be the basis of classificatory conventions that depend on terms or reasons, it is not the direct referent of the term but is said to be a particular real thing. The second is a nonimplicative negation, since it is a mere negation or exclusion of what is not it. The third is posited in terms of an appearance within conceptual cognition, which Dharmakīrti explains in the root text is the direct referent of a term. Accordingly, these three types of exclusion are widely known by the terms *objective* exclusion, *nonimplicative* exclusion, and *mental* exclusion, [960] [592] though Śākyabuddhi's *Commentary on Exposition of Valid Cognition* does not explicitly use these labels.

Second there is Dharmottara (eighth century), indisputably one of the most important Buddhist epistemologists after Dignāga and Dharmakīrti, who analyzed in detail the arguments establishing the exclusion of other. This master not only wrote extensive commentaries on Dharmakīrti's *Ascertainment of Valid Cognition* and his *Drop of Reasoning*, but he also composed his own famous treatise, *Explanation of Exclusion*, in which he gives a detailed analysis of many difficult points about the theory of the exclusion of other. The opening homage verse of this text praises the proponents of exclusion most highly by summarizing the meaning of the exclusion of other as follows:

> Teaching the nature of conceptual cognition to be the exclusion of other
> and explaining it to be neither cognition, nor something external, nor reality itself, but mere fabrication,
> the Victorious Subduer, free from all faults, spoke thus to migrating beings.

> Now with my head bowed down to the teacher, I offer my
> explanation of the exclusion of other.[961]

The main body of the text begins with the question "What is the meaning of a word?" It answers as follows: "The appearance within conceptual cognition is the signified object associated with a word. Conceptual cognition arises in the aspect of the signified object perceived. Therefore, because of both its effect and what it appropriates, the appearance [within conceptual cognition] is the meaning of the word (Skt. *śabdārtha*)."[962] [593] Then it continues: "You say that its appearance, which is not an object, is engaged by way of conceiving it as an object. What is the meaning of this? It means that it is a fabricated nature, nothing apart from a particular object-image."[963] According to Dharmottara's tradition, as explained above in the homage verse, the "meaning of a word" is posited based on the observed object of conceptual cognition. It is neither in the nature of an external thing nor an internal attribute of consciousness, for it is only a superimposition. Moreover, the particular individual thing that is the basis of the superimposed appearance in conceptual cognition is not differentiated from the exclusion, but it must be posited as combined into one with that appearance in cognition. This is only a fabrication. Although some consider the object-image of conceptual cognition to be the linguistic referent, he understands this to be rejected, as it is stated in the following lines from Dharmakīrti's *Exposition of Valid Cognition*:

> How can that which is not different from
> the cognition instantiate another thing?[964]

According to Dharmottara's own tradition, the fabrication that is the *observed object* of conceptual cognition as outlined above is identified as the signified object. That a nonexistent thing does appear to conceptual cognition is established by experience, and this is because conceptual cognitions [594] are in their nature tainted by ignorance. Thus Dharmottara's *Explanation of Exclusion* says: "Although ascertained through the nature of experience, a nonexistent is apprehended owing to the latent propensities of ignorance."[965] In connection with this, Dharmottara identifies four kinds of conceptualization, and goes on to state: "Thus one conceives existent things such as pots, nonexistent things such as Īśvara, existent attributes such as blue, and nonexistent attributes such as permanent [in the case of sound]."[966] Since these four kinds of conceptualization have different ways of superimposing upon their respective objects, there is conceptualization regarding existent things and attributes, and conceptualization regarding unreal things and attributes, though all four kinds of conceptualization are alike in having been preceded by seeing similar real things. Furthermore, his *Explanation of Exclusion* says:

> When conceptual cognition superimposes an exclusion of other that brings about an understanding of an exclusion of its converse, then since the mere negation of the converse itself reaches back to a real thing, a real thing is known. A term or conceptual cognition has a nonimplicative negation as its object; it does not engage by way of implicative negation. Therefore, when a superimposed nonimplicative negation is realized, since it is conceived to be not different, it is an ascertainment of the mere negation of something external. Thus, given that the absence of the converse that is something external [595] is ascertained by conceptual cognition, the absence of the converse that is a superimposition is the observed object. For this reason, it is without doubt that Dharmakīrti also understood it to be nonimplicative negation only.[967]

Thus, in the context of the exclusion of other, according to Dharmottara, Dharmakīrti's intended point is that the negation involving the exclusion of other must be taken to be a nonimplicative negation only.

In the concluding part of his treatise *Explanation of Exclusion*, Dharmottara summarizes the main points of his views on the theory of the exclusion of other, citing Dharmakīrti's *Exposition of Valid Cognition* to support his statements as follows:

> What is the object of conceptual cognition? It is the linguistic referent. Thus the linguistic referent does not exist ultimately. As Dharmakīrti says:
>
> > Although the linguistic referent and
> > its coreferents do not exist,

> they are expressed as commonly accepted,
> but they cannot exist as real things. (PV 1.84)

When that superimposition is cognized, the external thing that it resembles is realized. Thus even though external, it is imputed to be the linguistic referent. As Dharmakīrti says:

> Because an exclusion of other is realized
> through realizing its nature as a superimposition,
> there is no contradiction in expressing
> it to be the "linguistic referent." (PV 3.169)

At the time of applying the term, the exclusion of other itself that is the object of conceptual cognition or in the nature of ascertainment is taken to be the signified object itself. If that were not so, then how could a single exclusion of other itself be the signified object? Thus the object of conceptual cognition, which is the exclusion of other, is associated with the signified object apart from other things. As it is said, owing to a certain similarity, a pot and cupped hands perform a similar function and so on. [596] Therefore it must be stated that exclusions are twofold: that which is in the nature of ascertainment and that which is the object of conceptual cognition. As Dharmakīrti says:

> Terms signify by means of "engaging
> through having excluded the other."
> So since this comes from those,
> how could it not be an exclusion? (PV 1.96)[968]

Among the notable Buddhist epistemologists after Dharmottara there was Śāntarakṣita (eighth century), who engaged in a detailed analysis of the theory of the exclusion of other. His treatise *Compendium of Reality* agrees with Śākyabuddhi in presenting three types of exclusion of other:

> Exclusion of other is of two kinds,
> implicative negation and nonimplicative negation.
> Implicative negation also is of two kinds,
> owing to a difference between mental and objective.[969]

The above lines appear in the context where Śāntarakṣita states that the objections against the theory raised by Kumārila and others stem from their lack of familiarity with the presentation of exclusion and the need to distinguish between the types of exclusion of other. [597] He then proceeds to explain that in his own system [Yogācāra-Svātantrika Madhyamaka] the exclusion of other in general is of two types—implicative negation and nonimplicative negation—and the first of these, implicative negation, also is subdivided into two types—mental exclusion and objective exclusion. In commenting on the verse cited above, Kamalaśīla's *Commentary on the Difficult Points in the Compendium of Reality* says:

> "Owing to a difference between mental and objective" means that it is due to a difference in nature of the mental and due to a difference in nature of the objective. As for the nature of the mental, the things that appear to cognition are ascertained as a single homologous form. As for the nature of the objective, in nature the object is a specific individual distinguished from things in the heterogeneous class.[970]

This presents, in explicit terms, the difference between a mental exclusion of other and an objective exclusion of other that is a specific individual.

Śāntarakṣita's *Compendium of Reality* presents four reasons for applying a label such as "exclusion of the converse of *tree*" [i.e., the exclusion of *non-tree*] to a mental exclusion of the converse of *tree* as follows. (1) The mental exclusion of the converse of *tree*, such as a thought apprehending a tree, appears unmixed with appearances in thought apprehending other things. (2) In dependence on that exclusion of the converse of *tree*, one obtains [cognizance of] a particular individual tree. (3) Through the causal capacity of experiencing different individual trees, there arises in thought an appearance of a mental exclusion of the converse of *tree*. (4) Those who experience the mental exclusion of the converse of *tree* [598] mistakenly conceive it to be a tree.[971]

Of the three types of exclusion from other, the mental exclusion is the actual signified object, while the other two—the exclusion that is a nonimplicative negation and the exclusion that is a particular individual thing—are suitably called the "linguistic referent" by means of postulation (Skt. *arthāpatti*) based on the signifying term.[972] Moreover, although in the case of a term such as *pot* there is no ultimately signified object whatsoever, upon such a term having directly signified its object, *pot*, the exclusion of its converse, *non-pot*, is indirectly understood owing to the force of convention. Those two are said to occur in serial order. Kamalaśīla's *Commentary on the Difficult Points in the Compendium of Reality* says:

> Therefore, because words give rise to cognition that ascertains the object, a conventionally established entity is accepted to be the linguistic referent. Also, because terms do not have any referent ultimately, an affirmative entity is negated ultimately, but since an affirmative entity is accepted to be the linguistic referent, it is not [negated] conventionally. When the object signified is an affirmative entity, an exclusion of other is understood indirectly; therefore it is appropriate for the affirmation to precede the exclusion.[973] [599]

The way in which these three exclusions of other are realized by the mind is explained in Kamalaśīla's *Commentary on the Difficult Points in the Compendium of Reality*:

> An exclusion that is a particular individual is something ascertained by sensory [cognition] only. As for an exclusion in the nature of a reflection, since it is ultimately in the nature of cognition, it is established by perceptual reflexive awareness. The word "also" [in the root text] includes things that are not explicitly stated, for an exclusion in the nature of a nonimplicative negation is also understood indirectly, as indicated by the phrase "The nature of this is not the nature of the other."[974]

Furthermore, Kamalaśīla explains how signifying terms such as "This is a pot," which is free of the five circumstances [as follows]—episodes of madness, sleep, meditation, recitation, and error—relate to the final referent, a particular individual, as stated in his *Commentary on the Difficult Points in the Compendium of Reality*:

> The relationship here, where the term relates indirectly to the thing, has the characteristics of cause and effect. In the first

> place, the thing is experienced as it exists. From this there is the desire to express it. Then there is movement of the palate and so on. From this there is utterance of the term. Thus when there is this kind of indirect relation between a term and an actual thing such as an external fire, there occurs a cognition through postulation of the thing as excluded from those of dissimilar type. Therefore both types of exclusion—nonimplicative negation and exclusion from other in the nature of a real thing—are called the *linguistic referent*.[975] [600]

In the concluding part of the text connected with the passage cited above, Kamalaśīla comments on a key phrase found in Dignāga's *Compendium of Valid Cognition Autocommentary*: "A term is said to signify its meaning when it excludes the meanings of other terms."[976] In interpreting this statement, Kamalaśīla's *Commentary on the Difficult Points in the Compendium of Reality* says:

> This is what the master means. A term does not denote a referent that is a separate external thing apart from a reflection generated in thought that conceives the thing to be external, because all phenomena are devoid of activity. Therefore, through generating a reflection in thought that engages by way of conceiving it as an external object, it is said that "a term signifies its referent."[977]

Thus it seems that Śāntarakṣita's *Compendium of Reality* and Kamalaśīla's *Commentary on the Difficult Points in the Compendium of Reality* do not merely refute non-Buddhist masters' criticisms of the exclusion of other and the linguistic referent but also present many new explanations of their own views.

Among the texts composed by Indian Buddhist epistemologists after Śāntarakṣita and Kamalaśīla, [601] specifically examining the exclusion of other, those that remain extant today include the following. In the early part of the tenth century, the great brahmin Śaṅkarānanda composed a treatise called *Proof of Exclusion*, which was followed in the latter part of the tenth century by Jñānaśrīmitra's *Explanation of Exclusion* and his student Ratnakīrti's *Proof of Exclusion*. The explanations of the exclusion of other found in Śaṅkarānanda's *Proof of Exclusion* seem mainly to present

Dharmakīrti's thought in accordance with Dharmottara's explanations. On some occasions, for example, he directly quotes the statement "Because the appearance within it, which does not exist as an external thing, is engaged through conceiving it to be an external thing,"[978] which is found in both Dharmottara's *Commentary on Ascertainment of Valid Cognition* and his *Explanation of Exclusion*. As for the two texts on the theory of exclusion by Jñānaśrīmitra and Ratnakīrti respectively, although they were not translated into Tibetan, the Sanskrit versions of these works remain extant, providing an opportunity for scholars to critically engage with them. While the overall framework of Jñānaśrīmitra's explanation of the exclusion of other appears to follow Dharmottara, he interprets the theory of exclusion in accordance with his Vijñaptimātra standpoint that rejects the reality of external objects; thus he differs from Dharmottara when it comes to positing the nature of the object of both perception and inference. Furthermore, he explicitly refutes Dharmottara's assertion that Dharmakīrti considers the exclusion of other to be primarily a nonimplicative negation, and he maintains [602] that at the time of excluding the converse [depending on the form of negation involved in that context], the exclusion could be either a nonimplicative negation or an implicative negation.[979] Ratnakīrti's *Proof of Exclusion*, which is based on his teacher Jñānaśrīmitra's *Explanation of Exclusion*, mentions by name the earlier and later non-Buddhist masters who criticize the proponents of exclusion and explicitly refutes their assertions. According to this master's own tradition of the exclusion of other, what is referred to as "the exclusion of other" is posited to be external objects qualified by the exclusion of other, and he states that this is the linguistic referent. He distinguishes between what he calls the primary and ordinary, or direct and indirect, meaning; and he states that when something is understood from, say, the phrase "This is a cow," then *cow* can be understood on the basis of such words. This too, he says, is in terms of being a *cow* as qualified by the exclusion of non-cow, which means that the *exclusion of non-cow* is understood indirectly. This view seems somewhat different from that of Śāntarakṣita. For according to Śāntarakṣita, the referent, an *appearance of cow*, is understood directly from the word *cow*, while the *exclusion of non-cow* is understood indirectly, thus involving a temporal sequence. In contrast, Ratnakīrti says that both the principal and the ordinary referents are understood simultaneously, so there is no temporal sequence involved.[980]

In general, the views of the Buddhist epistemologists on the theory of the exclusion of other in the tenth century might be discerned from Mokṣākaragupta's *Language of Logic*. [603] Here we quote a large section of this text dealing with the exclusion of other, as follows:

> *Qualm*: What is this *exclusion*?
>
> *Response*: An external thing such as a pot as it is conceived is called an *exclusion*, to be understood in the sense that other dissimilar kinds are excluded from it. Also, the mental image as it appears is an exclusion, because the dissimilar are excluded or differentiated in this mental image. Further, a mere negation as it is, which is a nonimplicative negation, is also an exclusion, because exclusion itself is called an *exclusion*.
>
> *Qualm*: If it is only an affirmation, as it is conceived, then to be called an *exclusion* comes to be [without meaning].
>
> *Response*: That is not so. What is meant here is an affirmation qualified by exclusion. The proponents who emphasize affirmation say that when we understand *cow*, we subsequently ascertain indirectly the exclusion, *not non-cow*. The proponents who emphasize exclusion say that when we understand the exclusion, we subsequently understand indirectly the differentiated thing, *cow*. These are both incorrect, because at the time of employing an agreed-upon convention, we do not observe a series [of ascertainments] to follow an initial occurrence of either one. It is not as some people claim that upon having understood an affirmation by means of postulation, one subsequently understands the exclusion, and upon having understood the exclusion, one subsequently understands the excluded. Therefore it must be said that *an understanding of cow* itself is posited to be *an understanding of the exclusion of non-cow*.
>
> Although it is pointed out that uttering the word *cow* does not connect with the phrase "exclusion of other," it is not that we do not understand the exclusion that is the qualifier [of *cow*], [604] because the word *cow* is applied as a label to the thing that is excluded from *non-cow*. For example, when we understand *blue lotus* from the term *indīvara* ("blue lotus") applied as a label

> to a blue lotus, at that time precisely the quality *blue* is obviously not excluded. Likewise, when we understand *cow* upon hearing the word *cow* applied as a label to the exclusion of *non-cow*, at that time precisely, since it is its qualifying exclusion, the exclusion itself is obviously not excluded.
>
> A direct perception apprehending nonexistence that is a nonimplicative negation is only able to produce a conceptual cognition of nonexistence. But given that such conceptual cognitions of affirmations can only draw forth later affirmations that conform with them, they too must be called "apprehension of nonexistence." Otherwise, if the exclusion of other is not understood when the object is understood from hearing the word *cow*, then how does a thinker alight upon *cow* having excluded what is other? In such a case, when he is ordered to "tether the cow" he would end up tethering the horse and so on. Therefore it is settled that the external object is established as the linguistic referent only out of exaggerated conceptualizing but not by way of an excluded particular, because, as in the case of direct perception, there is no excluded particular that operates in a definitive context of space, time, and aspect. As Dharmakīrti, the supreme master of logic and epistemology, has stated: "Because without the activation of a sense faculty there is no appearance in the mind, as in the case of seeing the linguistic referent" (PV 1.15a–c). [605]
>
> Moreover, if a real thing in the nature of a particular individual were the signified object, then since its entire nature would be known, affirmation and negation would be unfeasible. For when it is present, it would be meaningless to say "It exists" and impossible to say "It does not exist," and when it is absent, it would be meaningless to say "It does not exist" and impossible to say "It exists." Yet there is the common practice of employing words such as *exist* and so on. Therefore the main point here is that particular individuals are not the objects signified by words ultimately.[981]

When we examine the words of this passage quoted here, it is evident that a number of Buddhist epistemologists adopt Śākyabuddhi's explanation of *Exposition of Valid Cognition* as presenting three facets of the exclusion of other—the basis of exclusion, the agent of exclusion, and the factor of exclusion—and accept it as correct within their own traditions. One also learns that the proponents of exclusion are divided into two camps: the proponents who emphasize affirmation, who say that first one understands the basis, *cow*, after which one indirectly understands *exclusion of non-cow*; and the proponents who emphasize negation, who say that first one understands the basis, *exclusion of non-cow*, after which one indirectly understands *cow*. According to Mokṣākaragupta himself, when *cow* is understood in dependence on the words "This is a cow," it is understood by way of the *exclusion of non-cow*. Therefore, as he explains above, both positions are incorrect, for "an understanding of cow" itself is posited to be "an understanding of the exclusion of non-cow."

Furthermore, in the "Perception" chapter of *Language of Logic*, Mokṣākaragupta posits an *observed object* and an *ascertained object* in the case of both direct perception and conceptual cognition, similar to Dharmottara. [606] While the observed object of direct perception is a momentary real thing, its ascertained object must be posited in terms of a continuum. It is also clear that he defines a universal in terms of engendering a cognition of resemblance. Furthermore, in the course of his explanation of the object of direct perception, he explains how, in texts such as Dharmakīrti's *Exposition of Valid Cognition*, the statement that only a particular is the experienced object of direct perception should be understood in an inclusive sense and not in terms of a phrase that excludes. He states that a universal must also be accepted as an object of direct perception. Moreover, in the case of direct perception apprehending a pot, for example, the particular momentary real thing that it perceives is posited to be its observed object, and the class-universal *pot* that has a continuum of moments is posited to be that perception's ascertained object and engaged object. Conversely, the observed object of a conceptual cognition or an inferential cognition is a universal only, while its ascertained object or conceived object is a unique particular only. If one maintains that the object of direct perception is necessarily a particular, then it would be unfeasible for the pervasion in a proof—for example, that there is fire on a mountain pass because smoke is present—to be established by direct perception. Mokṣākaragupta's *Language of Logic* says:

> *Qualm*: If unique particulars only are the object of direct perception, but not universals, then how can the pervasion between the universals—smoke and fire—be apprehended by direct perception?
>
> *Response*: There is no problem here because the statement that *unique particulars only* are the object [of perception] is meant in the sense of an inclusion; it is not saying that *only unique particulars* are the object [of perception], which is meant in the sense of an exclusion.[982]
>
> *Qualm*: So what is it saying?
>
> *Response*: A universal can also be its object. Accordingly, there are two kinds of objects of valid cognition: the observed object and the conceived object. The observed object of a direct perception is a single moment as it appears. The conceived object of a conceptual cognition that arises immediately following the direct perception is a universal only. [607] There are also two kinds of such a universal: that of a particular (the vertical universal) and that of a class (the horizontal universal). Of these, a collection universal—an individual, such as a pot, consisting of many moments of the same kind, or different kinds, taken as a unit only—is the object of a direct perception that establishes it. A class universal—the different kinds and so on of many individuals—is the object of direct perception that apprehends a pervasion. The observed object of inferential cognition is a universal, while the conceived object is a particular individual only.[983]

Here, universals are distinguished into two types: a vertical universal, which has the nature of a combination of earlier and later moments of a single phenomenon, and a horizontal universal or class universal, which pervades different, mutually unconnected individuals. The first is the ascertained object or engaged object of sensory direct perception. The second is posited as the object of direct perception that apprehends in the context of a logical pervasion. Here, what are called the vertical universal and the horizontal universal seem to be what are respectively called the collection universal (Skt.

**samudāyasāmānya*) and the class universal (Skt. *jātisāmānya*) by Dignāga and his spiritual heir, Dharmakīrti.

To give a rough explanation of [the contribution of] Tibetan Buddhist epistemologists, three traditions can be identified by their time period: earlier, intermediate, and later. The earlier tradition is that of Ngok Lotsāwa Loden Sherab and Chapa Chökyi Sengé along with their followers. The intermediate tradition is that of [608] Jamgön Sakya Paṇḍita Kunga Gyaltsen, as evidenced by his *Treasury of the Science of Valid Cognition*.[984] The later one is that of the Ganden tradition of Jé Tsongkhapa, Gyaltsab Jé, and Khedrup Jé. While the explanations of the theory of exclusion among these traditions differ somewhat, the context for this volume is primarily a presentation of the views of the Indian Buddhist masters. So if one wishes to learn about the explanations given by the Tibetan masters on these subjects, one should consult the great treatises on epistemology authored by these specific masters.

To summarize, in this section we have presented: (1) the assertions of the Indian masters Dignāga and Dharmakīrti, along with their followers, who represent the proponents of exclusion; (2) the objections to the theory of exclusion made by those who claim that terms engage via affirmation; (3) how these objections have been refuted subsequently by the proponents of exclusion; and (4) how, in the course of doing this, they further sharpened the arguments for the theory of exclusion and deepened the explanations of it based on these arguments. Among the important topics discussed by Indian philosophers over the centuries the following are included: how language and thought engage their object; how to understand the signified object or linguistic referent; the relationship between term and referent; how a meaning is understood from a signifying term; what the basis of engagement of a cognition of a universal is; the function of a cognition of a universal; how a mind of recognition is generated; the difference between an object of sense consciousness and an object of conceptual cognition; the difference between how sense consciousness and conceptual cognition engage their objects; how sense consciousness and conceptual cognition, though significantly dissimilar, [609] are both firmly related; and how a signifying term is indirectly related in the end to a functional particular. Through an exchange of views over a period of many centuries, the most distinguished philosophers of both Buddhist and non-Buddhist schools were able to attain a very high level of refinement and sophistication in their logical and epistemological views. That this is so can be inferred from reading the treatises of the great Indian epistemologists.

In the present work we have assembled within a single collection many important subjects sourced from the word of the Buddha and especially from the treatises of the great early Indian Buddhist thinkers extant in Tibetan translations that pertain to accounts of reality and profound philosophical views. Included here are detailed presentations of important philosophical arguments set forth by both Buddhist and non-Buddhist masters. We have organized these presentations into a specific format and have provided accompanying commentarial explanations.

This completes the final volume presenting philosophical topics from the *Science and Philosophy in the Indian Buddhist Classics* series.

Notes

Abbreviations

Toh The Tohoku Catalogue. *A Complete Catalogue of the Tibetan Buddhist Canons*. Sendai, Japan: Tohoku Imperial University, 1934.

Pd Pedurma. The comparative editions of the Tibetan canons, the Kangyur and Tengyur, referred to in Tibetan as *Dpe bsdur ma*, published between 2006 and 2009 in Beijing by the Tibetan Tripiṭaka Collation Bureau (Bka' bstan dpe sdur khang) of the China Tibetology Research Center (Krung go'i bod rig pa zhib 'jug ste gnas).

1. A different excerpt of this same introduction appeared in volume 3.
2. His Holiness the Dalai Lama has coined the expression "seventeen Nālandā masters" to refer to a number of great Indian masters who composed treatises on Buddhist philosophy and practice between 200 and 1200 CE and whose depth and breadth of study is epitomized by the tradition of Nālandā Monastic University and similar institutions—a tradition that began prior to the founding of such institutions.
3. Under the entry "philosophy and analysis," Alan Lacey (2005, 253) states: "An embarrassment for the professional philosopher is that he cannot produce any succinct, or even agreed, definition of his profession. 'What is philosophy?' is itself a philosophical question."
4. Such thinkers are often known as the pre-Socratics, though some later ones were contemporary with Socrates; here, the appellation indicates that they predate the influence of Socrates.
5. As presented in the poem by Hesiod (seventh century BCE) *Theogony* (genealogy of the gods).
6. Regarding Daniélou's suggestion that Orphism is derived from the influence of Jainism, introduced into Greece by wandering Jain missionaries or brought back by visitors to Persia, see McEvilley 2002, 197–224.
7. Burnet 1930, 136, fragments 41, 42.
8. Burnet 1930, 133n1.
9. Curd 2020 "Xenophanes of Colophon and Heraclitus of Ephesus."
10. Both of the premises and the conclusion are *assertions*—independent clauses, having both a subject and a predicate. The subject and the predicate are known

as the *terms* of the assertion. Subjects may be either individual or universal, but predicates can only be universals. An assertion can be either affirmative or negative.

11. Aristotle also introduced the use of variables—where the terms or phrases in the argument are represented by individual letters, thus clarifying the logical form of the argument: "All A is B; some B is C; therefore some A is C." The types of premises Aristotle considered are: "All A is B," "Some A is B," "No A is B," and "Some A is not B." The use of variables and quantification, such as "all" and "some," developed into crucial components of formal logic devised by modern philosophers beginning with Gottlob Frege (1848–1925). Up until that point, Aristotle's logic reigned supreme.
12. This resembles the style of debate used in Buddhist institutions as presented in volume 1 of *Science and Philosophy in the Indian Buddhist Classics*, 64–69.
13. Aristotle, *Posterior Analytics*, Bk. 1, chap. 2.
14. Aristotle, *Posterior Analytics*, Bk. 2, chap. 19.
15. An infinite regress is entailed if each demonstration must be grounded in another demonstration. However, Aristotle also introduces *intuition* as that which apprehends the primary premises, though he does not explain what it is.
16. McEvilley 2002, chap. 1.
17. The Vedas, transmitted by "seers" (*mantradraṣṭā*), are the oldest scriptures of Hinduism and were classified initially into three categories: the Saṃhitā (hymns and formulas), the Brāhmaṇa (commentaries on rituals and sacrifices), the Āranyaka (texts on symbolic sacrifices). Later a fourth category, the Upaniṣads, a.k.a. the Vedānta (texts on meditation and philosophy) also came to be accepted as authoritative. The first category, the Saṃhitā, contains the *Ṛg Veda*, *Yajur Veda*, *Sāma Veda*, and *Atharva Veda*. The oldest, the *Ṛg Veda* Saṃhitā texts, were composed orally circa 1500–1000 BCE. The Vedas were written down after many centuries.
18. Dasgupta 1922, 16–17.
19. Barua 1921, 410.
20. Barua 1921, 5.
21. Dasgupta 1922, 17–19.
22. Sastri 1951, vi.
23. Matilal 1998, 2.
24. See chapter 20 below. For a fairly detailed summary of the Nyāya system, see also chapter 5 in volume 3 of *Science and Philosophy in the Indian Buddhist Classics*.
25. Gethin 2023, 161.
26. Gethin 2023, 165. Gethin notes that this suggestion comes from a 1933 work of Stanislaw Schayer, who says that the *definition of implication* is the equivalence of the statements "if p is true, then so is q" ($p \supset q$) and "the assertion that p is true but q is not true is false" ($\sim [p \,\&\, \sim q]$). The *law of transposition* is the equivalence of the statements "if p then q" ($p \supset q$) and "if not q, then not p" ($\sim q \supset \sim p$).

27. Matilal 1998, 88.
28. Kapstein 2001, 59.
29. Sastri 1951, iii–iv.
30. Sastri 1951, xvii.
31. See Sastri 1951, xvi–xx.
32. Balcerowicz 2012, 189.
33. The sixteen categories according to the Nyāya system are listed in chapter 20 of the present volume. Doubt is the third item in that list.
34. Matilal 1998, 14.
35. Dasgupta 1922, 226.
36. Dasgupta 1922, 227.
37. Bronkhorst 1999, 16.
38. Krishna 1991, 29.
39. Krishna 1991, 30.
40. *Darśana* here is in the sense of a philosophical view, as discussed in the introductory essay to volume 3 of *Science and Philosophy in the Indian Buddhist Classics.*
41. Loux 1998, 25.
42. See for example Duerlinger 2003, 3, Ganeri 2007, 204, and Arnold 2005, 119.
43. That is, the yoga uniting calm abiding (*śamatha*) and special insight (*vipaśyanā*). For a detailed description of how to develop calm abiding, see chapter 24 in volume 2 of *Science and Philosophy in the Indian Buddhist Classics.*
44. See volume 2 in *Science and Philosophy in the Indian Buddhist Classics*, 25.
45. Such an established conclusion is known as *siddhānta* (*grub mtha'*), often translated as "tenet." See volume 3 in *Science and Philosophy in the Indian Buddhist Classics*, 12 and 73–74.
46. See page 244 below.
47. See also volume 2, *Science and Philosophy in the Indian Buddhist Classics*, 116 and 378.
48. Nāgārjuna, *Vigrahavyāvartanī*, verse 26. Toh 3828, 27b. Pd 57:76.
49. See page 330 below.
50. Nāgārjuna, *Mūlamadhyamakakārikā*, 1.1. Toh 3824, 1a. Pd 57:3.
51. See pages 245–46 below.
52. The seven points are that a chariot is not different from its parts, it is not identical to them, it does not possess them, it is not in them, they are not in it, it is not the mere collection of them, and it is not the shape of the collection. Strictly speaking, the analysis of the self is a fivefold one, where the last two points are omitted since the self is not something physical. But it is often spoken of as a sevenfold analysis in the texts, presumably to match the chariot example.
53. *Kaṭha Upaniṣad* 3.3–4: "Know the self as a rider in a chariot and the body as simply the chariot. Know the intellect as the charioteer, and the mind as simply the reins. The senses, they say, are the horses, and sense objects are the paths around them." Olivelle 1998, 389: *ātmānaṃ rathinaṃ viddhi śarīraṃ ratham*

eva tu | buddhiṃ tu sārathiṃ viddhi manaḥ pragraham eva ca || indriyāṇi hayān āhūr viśayāṃs teṣū gocaran |.

54. This is one of three verses attributed to the arhat nun Śailā in chapter 9 of Vasubandhu's *Treasury of Knowledge Autocommentary*. A version of this teaching is also attributed to the nun Vajirā in *Saṃyuttanikāya* I:552–44. As stated by Kapstein 2001, 78–79: "These verses attributed to the nun Vajirā are among the canonical passages most frequently cited in the whole of later Buddhist philosophy; for we find condensed here as nowhere else the fundamental themes that are interwoven throughout the Buddhist inquiry into the reality of the self and the nature of persons."
55. *Milindapañha*, 2.1.1. Translated in Rhys Davids 1890, 45.
56. Garfield 2015, 106–9.
57. Candrakīrti, *Madhyamakāvatāra*, 6.120. Toh 3861, 212a. Pd 60:537.
58. *Madhyamakāvatārabhāṣya*, 281: *shing rta yan lag can mes tshig na de'i yan lag kyang nges par tshig par 'gyur ba de bzhin du rnam par dpyod pa'i gtsubs shing gtsubs pa las byung ba blo'i me mi dmigs pa'i sreg par byed pa can gyis shing rta lus med par bsregs pa na shes rab kyi me'i bud shing du gyur pa yan lag dag gis kyang bdag nyid zug tshugs par mi byed de nges par bsregs pa'i phyir ro /.*
59. Oral History of Tibetan Studies: oralhistory.iats.info/interviews/peter-verhagen (see video at minute 58).
60. Dasgupta 1922, 1.
61. Kollmar-Paulenz 2007, 325. The received story of this debate is considered apocryphal by most modern scholars, but it nonetheless highlights actual trends in the Tibetan assimilation of Buddhism.
62. In Buddhism's division of existences into three realms (*dhātu*), most beings abide in the desire (*kāma*) realm, which encompasses not only humans and animals but also beings in the hells up through six heavenly states. The two higher realms, also heavenly states, are the form (*rūpa*) and formless (*arūpa*) realms. The form realm is said to consist of four *dhyāna*s, or meditative absorptions, and the formless realm has four levels of even greater refinement of mental stability. The attainment of calm abiding occurs after the ninth stage of mental stabilization upon entering the first *dhyāna* of the form realm. See also pages 301–2 of volume 1 and chapter 24 in volume 2 of *Science and Philosophy in the Indian Buddhist Classics*.
63. Gethin 2001, 13.
64. Gethin 2001, 20.
65. Of course, in the broadest way of categorizing what is knowable, knowing subjects are also included among known things. But for the purpose of identifying and examining each group precisely, they are categorized separately.
66. Bronkhorst 1985.
67. This account accords with the Geluk interpretation, which is the predominant one employed throughout the present series.
68. This means that it must be nondeceptive regarding its object as cognized (*'dzin*

stangs kyi yul). For further explanation of the *object as cognized*, see chapter 17 in volume 2 of *Science and Philosophy in the Indian Buddhist Classics*.

69. When considering the notion of *meaning*, classical Indian philosophers did not distinguish between *sense* and *reference* in the way that modern Western philosophers have done. Reference seems to be the primary interpretation, and the term translated here as "word meaning" (*śabdārtha*) is also translated elsewhere as the "linguistic referent." It can be argued, however, that certain classical Indian philosophers did indeed posit theories that are tantamount to drawing such a distinction; see Siderits 1991, 77.
70. The notion of nonduality (*advaita*) here is that everything is in reality Brahman, the pure and eternal self. Other notions of duality or nonduality are presented in other systems.
71. The term *object of knowledge* or *epistemic object* (*shes bya*) is equivalent to *existent* (*yod pa*). Stated in an unrestricted plural form, it includes all phenomena and encompasses the entire scope of reality.
72. *Pitāputrasamāgamanasūtra*. Toh 60, 60b. Pd 42:147.
73. *Pitāputrasamāgamanasūtra*. Toh 60, 61b. Pd 42:150.
74. The Sanskrit term *tathatā* (Tib. *de bzhin nyid*), here translated as "suchness," is one of the many terms that refer to the way things are: the final nature of reality. According to the major Buddhist traditions, this is the absence of true existence.
75. *Akṣayamatinirdeśasūtra*. Toh 175, 123b. Pd 60:311.
76. *Nairātmyaparipṛcchāsūtra*. Toh 173, 6b. Pd 60:17.
77. Nāgārjuna, *Mūlamadhyamakakārikā*, 24.8–10. Toh 3824, 14b. Pd 57:36.
78. The "collections" here refers to the two collections of merit and wisdom, which when fully accumulated will result in the attainment of a buddha's body and mind, respectively.
79. Jñānagarbha, *Satyadvayavibhaṅga*, verse 2. Toh 3881, 1a. Pd 62:755.
80. Candrakīrti, *Madhyamakāvatāra*, 6.80. Toh 3861, 208a. Pd 60:528.
81. Vasubandhu, *Abhidharmakośa*, 6.4. Toh 4089, 18b. Pd 69:43.
82. Yaśomitra, *Abhidharmakośavyākhyāsphuṭārthā*. Toh 4092, 6.160b. Pd 80:1224.
83. "Particles" here refers to the eight substantial particles posited in Buddhist Abhidharma that constitute coarse material things or larger portions of matter. See part 3 in volume 1 of *Science and Philosophy in the Indian Buddhist Classics*.
84. Pūrṇavardhana, *Lakṣaṇānusāriṇī*. Toh 4093, 6.155a. Pd 81:1307.
85. Pūrṇavardhana, *Lakṣaṇānusāriṇī*. Toh 4093, 6.155a. Pd 81:1307.
86. Yaśomitra, *Abhidharmakośavyākhyāsphuṭārthā*. Toh 4092, 6.160b. Pd 80:1223.
87. Pūrṇavardhana, *Lakṣaṇānusāriṇī*. Toh 4093, 6.155a. Pd 81:1307.
88. According to the Vaibhāṣika system, *ultimately existent* and *ultimate truth* coincide, but according to other Buddhist traditions these two have quite different meanings.
89. Vasubandhu, *Abhidharmakośabhāṣya*. Toh 4090, 6.7b. Pd 79:695.
90. Pūrṇavardhana, *Lakṣaṇānusāriṇī*. Toh 4093, 6.155a. Pd 81:1308.
91. Yaśomitra, *Abhidharmakośavyākhyāsphuṭārthā*. Toh 4092, 6.160b. Pd 80:1224.

92. Dharmakīrti, *Pramāṇavārttika*, 3.3. Toh 4210, 118b. Pd 97:526.
93. Dharmakīrti, *Pramāṇavārttika*, 1.70. Toh 4210, 97a. Pd 97:476.
94. Dharmakīrti, *Pramāṇavārttika*, 1.68. Toh 4210, 97a. Pd 97:475.
95. Dharmakīrti, *Pramāṇavārttika*, 3.4. Toh 4210, 118b. Pd 97:526.
96. Vasubandhu, *Abhidharmakośabhāṣya*. Toh 4090, 2.94a. Pd 79:233.
97. Vasubandhu, *Abhidharmakośabhāṣya*. Toh 4090, 4.167b. Pd 79:413.
98. Maitreya, *Madhyāntavibhāga*, 1.2–3. Toh 4021, 40b. Pd 70:902.
99. Maitreya, *Dharmadharmatāvibhāga*, verse 2. Toh 4023, 50b. Pd 70:926.
100. Vasubandhu, *Vyākhyāyukti*, chap. 3. Toh 4061, 95a. Pd 77:234.
101. Vasubandhu, *Vyākhyāyukti*, chap. 4. Toh 4061, 109b. Pd 77:272.
102. Vasubandhu, *Vyākhyāyukti*, chap. 3. Toh 4061, 95a. Pd 77:235.
103. The term "final" here refers to what is perceived at the culmination of ultimate analysis, the final nature, which is the ultimate truth. The term "pure path" refers to a mind of meditative equipoise perceiving the ultimate truth. This mind of wisdom is completely free from any dualistic appearance, and when it arises it functions to gradually purify the mindstream of all defilements and obscurations. Thus it is called the *pure path*.
104. *Saṃdhinirmocanasūtra*, chap. 4. Toh 106, 11a. Pd 49:24.
105. Maitreya, *Madhyāntavibhāga*, 1.15. Toh 4021, 4b. Pd 71:10.
106. Vasubandhu, *Madhyāntavibhāgaṭīkā*, on chap. 1. Toh 4027, 5b. Pd 71:10.
107. An ārya being is a male or female Buddhist practitioner who has, on the basis of specific training, developed a mind of meditative equipoise directly perceiving the ultimate nature of reality.
108. Vasubandhu, *Vyākhyāyukti*, chap. 3. Toh 4061, 95a. Pd 77:233.
109. See chapter 4 on the two truths according to Madhyamaka below.
110. Maitreya, *Mahāyānasūtrālaṃkāra*, 7.1. Toh 4020, 6a. Pd 70:815.
111. Although everything is free of the natural stain from the very beginning, temporary stains arise from causes and conditions. These are the obstructions within a sentient being's mental continuum, of which there are two types: (afflictive) obstructions to liberation and (nonafflictive) obstructions to omniscience. Both types of obstructions can be removed eventually, so they are called temporary, or adventitious, stains. They need to be purified or removed by cultivating virtue and understanding reality.
112. Vasubandhu, *Sūtrālaṅkāravyākhyā*. Ultimate Reality chapter (*de kho na nyid*). Toh 4026, 145a. Pd 70:1171.
113. Asaṅga, *Viniścayasaṅgraha*. Toh 4038, 44a. Pd 74:849.
114. Bhāviveka, *Tarkajvālā*, chap. 5, on verse 10 of his *Madhyamakahṛdaya*. Toh 3856, 203a. Pd 58:494. A sky flower, or a flower in the sky, is a traditional example of something that does not exist.
115. Vasubandhu, *Triṃśikā*, verse 21. Toh 4055, 2b. Pd 77:5.
116. Bhāviveka, *Tarkajvālā*, chap. 5, on verse 11. Toh 3856, 203a. Pd 58:495.
117. The phrase "self of phenomena" is the usual translation of the Tibetan term *chos*

kyi bdag. The word "self" here does not refer to a personal self but to an ontological status that is a type of independent existence. The same principle applies in the case of the phrase "self of person," *gang zag gi bdag*. In both these contexts, the term "selfhood" (*bdag nyid*) also occurs.

118. The phrase "dualistic appearance" usually refers either to the dualistic appearance of subject and object or to the object appearing as truly existent. In the context of Madhyamaka the latter is the primary meaning. This erroneous appearance arises specifically through the activity of propensities deposited in the mindstream by the arising of ignorance. This appearance of true existence blocks the perception of ultimate reality, the emptiness of true existence. The direct perception of emptiness (Skt. *śūnyatā*) is the antidote to the mind of ignorance grasping at true existence, which is the root cause of all mental afflictions and their resultant sufferings. Meditation on emptiness gradually purifies the mindstream of the root cause of suffering.
119. *Pitāputrasamāgamanasūtra*. Toh 60, 60b. Pd 42:147.
120. *Pitāputrasamāgamanasūtra*. Toh 60, 61a. Pd 42:147.
121. *Akṣayamatinirdeśasūtra*. Toh 175, 123b. Pd 60:311.
122. Nāgārjuna, *Mūlamadhyamakakārikā*, 18.9. Toh 3824, 11a. Pd 57:26.
123. There are several types of elaboration, including the superimposition of true existence (which is conceptual and arises owing to afflictive ignorance) and the appearance of true existence (which is perceptual and arises owing to the imprints of afflictive ignorance, also known as nonafflictive ignorance).
124. Bhāviveka, *Tarkajvālā*, chap. 3. Toh 3856, 56a. Pd 58:114.
125. Śāntideva, *Bodhisattvacaryāvatāra*, 9.2. Toh 3871, 31a. Pd 61:1017.
126. Bhāviveka, *Tarkajvālā*, chap. 3. Toh 3856, 59a. Pd 58:149.
127. Candrakīrti, *Prasannapadā*, chap. 24. Toh 3860, 163b. Pd 60:397.
128. The Tibetan words *kun rdzob* (Skt. *saṃvṛti*) and *tha snyad* (Skt. *vyavahāra*) are often used interchangeably in the context of the two truths. According to Tsongkhapa's interpretation of the Prāsaṅgika Madhyamaka account, the term *kun rdzob* in the context of conventional truth (*kun rdzob bden pa*) refers to the two types of so-called ignorance—afflictive and nonafflictive. The former refers to actual ignorance, which is a specific type of afflictive mind that grasps things to be truly existent. The latter refers to certain propensities left in the mindstream by the arising of ignorance, which then give rise to the appearance of things as truly existent. Both forms of so-called ignorance obstruct the direct perception of ultimate reality. The first syllable, *kun*, means "all" and in this context refers to the ultimate nature of all phenomena; *rdzob* means "obscure" or "conceal," which refers to the obstruction that conceals the ultimate nature. Thus, owing to the power of afflictive and nonafflictive ignorance, conventional things are respectively grasped and appear to exist in a way that they do not exist. The term *tha snyad* refers to the various conceptual and linguistic conven-

tions as well as the manifold things expressed by them, which corresponds to the third meaning of *kun rdzob* listed below.

129. *Pitāputrasamāgamanasūtra*. Toh 60, 60b. Pd 42:147.
130. *Akṣayamatinirdeśasūtra*. Toh 175, 123b. Pd 60:311.
131. Jñānagarbha, *Satyadvayavibhaṅga*, verse 3. Toh 3881, 1a. Pd 62:755.
132. Jñānagarbha, *Satyadvayavibhaṅga*, verse 15. Toh 3881, 2b. Pd 62:756.
133. *Laṅkāvatārasūtra*, chap. 8. Toh 107, 174b. Pd 49:429.
134. Candrakīrti, *Prasannapadā*, on 24.8. Toh 3860, 163a. Pd 60:396.
135. The notions of "linguistic conventions" (labels initially applied) and "classificatory conventions" (terminology subsequently employed) are introduced in volume 2 of *Science and Philosophy in the Indian Buddhist Classics* (see chapter 3, especially page 70).
136. In general there are several ways of positing the basis that is divided into the two truths. Some say that *the nature of phenomena* is the basis of division, some say it is just *truth itself*, some say it is *objects that are not imaginary*, some say it is *unanalyzed objects*, and so on. However, many masters explain that objects of knowledge—that is, all that exists—are the basis of division into the two truths because this assertion is supported by authentic scriptural sources and their commentaries, as well as by correct reasoning. (The term *object of knowledge* is synonymous with *existent*. So anything that exists is included within the two truths.)
137. The phrase "distorted conceiving," or simply "conceiving," is a technical term that refers to a type of grasping, apprehending, or viewing that is identified with the mind of ignorance posited to be the root of saṃsāra, the fundamental cause of all mental afflictions and suffering. Different traditions provide different accounts of what this ignorance, or conceiving, actually consists of.
138. Candrakīrti, *Madhyamakāvatārabhāṣya*, chap. 5. Toh 3862, 243b. Pd 60:656.
139. Kamalaśīla, *Madhyamakāloka*. Toh 3887, 219a. Pd 62:1323. The meaning of this passage is that if *P* is not established by the exclusion of ~*P*, and ~*P* is not established by the exclusion of *P*, then neither *P* nor ~*P* exist as mutually exclusive.
140. *Prajñāpāramitāhṛdaya*. Toh 21, 145a. Pd 34:403.
141. *Kāśyapaparivartasūtra*, chap. 43. Toh 87, 130b. Pd 43:363.
142. Nāgārjuna, *Bodhicittavivaraṇa*, 67c–68. Toh 1800, 41b. Pd 18:115.
143. Candrakīrti, *Madhyamakāvatāra*, 6.23. Toh 3861, 205b. Pd 60:564.
144. Candrakīrti, *Madhyamakāvatārabhāṣya*, on 6.23. Toh 3862, 253b. Pd 60:680.
145. *Saṃdhinirmocanasūtra*, chap. 3. Toh 106, 7b. Pd 49:16.
146. *Saṃdhinirmocanasūtra*, chap. 3. Toh 106, 8a. Pd 49:18.
147. *Saṃdhinirmocanasūtra*, chap. 3. Toh 106, 8b. Pd 49:19.
148. *Saṃdhinirmocanasūtra*, chap. 3. Toh 106, 8b. Pd 49:19.
149. *Saṃdhinirmocanasūtra*, chap. 3. Toh 106, 7a. Pd 49:16.
150. An "ordinary being" is someone who has not yet generated a mind of meditative equipoise directly perceiving emptiness (*śūnyatā*) within his or her mindstream. It is this mind of wisdom that gradually purifies the meditator's mindstream of

mental afflictions and obscurations that block the attainment of liberation (and of obscurations that block the attainment of omniscience eventually).

151. *Saṃdhinirmocanasūtra*, chap. 3. Toh 106, 8a. Pd 49:18.
152. *Saṃdhinirmocanasūtra*, chap. 3. Toh 106, 8a. Pd 49:19.
153. *Saṃdhinirmocanasūtra*, chap. 3. Toh 106, 8a. Pd 49:18.
154. Nāgārjuna, *Śūnyatāsaptati*, verse 68. Toh 3827, 16b. Pd 57:71.
155. Nāgārjuna, *Yuktiṣaṣṭikā*, verse 36. Toh 3825, 21b. Pd 57:54.
156. Bhāviveka, *Tarkajvālā*, chap. 3. Toh 3856, 60b. Pd 58:152.
157. Bhāviveka, *Mādhyamakārthasaṅgraha*, verses 2–6. Toh 3855, 329b. Pd 58:851–52.
158. Jñānagarbha, *Satyadvayavibhaṅga*, verses 9–11. Toh 3881, 2a. Pd 62:756.
159. Śāntarakṣita, *Madhyamakālaṃkāra*, verses 69–70. Toh 3884, 55b. Pd 62:901.
160. Śāntarakṣita, *Madhyamakālaṃkāravṛtti*. Toh 3885, 73a. Pd 122:947.
161. For a detailed discussion about reflexive awareness and the Buddhist traditions that accept or reject it, see chapter 21 below.
162. Tsongkhapa, *Short Treatise on the Stages of the Path to Enlightenment*. Collected Works, *pha*, 205b. Also Ngawang Palden of Mongolia, *Presentation of the Two Truths: A Melodious Song of Glorious Springtime*. Collected Works, *ka*, 79a.
163. Bhāviveka, *Mādhyamakārthasaṅgraha*, verses 2–6. Toh 3855, 329b. Pd 58:852.
164. *Vimalakīrtinirdeśasūtra*, chap. 8. Toh 176, 220b. Pd 60:569.
165. Nāgārjuna, *Yuktiṣaṣṭikā*, verse 36. Toh 3825, 21b. Pd 57:54.
166. *Kauśikaprajñāpāramitā*. Toh 19, 143a. Pd 89:77.
167. Haribhadra, *Abhisamayālaṃkāravṛtti*, chap. 1. Toh 3793, 91b. Pd 52:236.
168. Candrakīrti, *Madhyamakāvatāra*, 6.179. Toh 3861, 213b. Pd 60:539.
169. The "inner supports of the sense faculties" refers to physical bases of the sense faculties. For example, the eyeball is the physical basis of the subtle visual sense faculty located inside it. The physical supports of the subtle sense faculties are each pervaded by consciousness.
170. Candrakīrti, *Madhyamakāvatāra*, 6.183–218. For an explanation of the term *non-thing* in this context, see Tsongkhapa 2021, 507: "Since they, things, originate from their causes and conditions, they lack intrinsic existence as composites. This fact about them is referred to as 'non-thing,' and the composite is itself empty of composite's own essence."
171. Candrakīrti, *Madhyamakāvatārabhāṣya*, on 6.179–80. Toh 3862, 313a. Pd 60:825.
172. "Other-entity" here can also be said to have three meanings: the supreme emptiness of phenomena, the superior wisdom directly realizing emptiness, and nirvāṇa.
173. Candrakīrti, *Madhyamakāvatārabhāṣya*, chap. 6. Toh 3862, 313b. Pd 60:826.
174. Bhāviveka, *Madhyamakahṛdaya*, 23.12–13. Toh 3855, 4a. Pd 58:9. See below in section e.
175. Bhāviveka, *Tarkajvālā*, chap. 3. Toh 3856, 56b. Pd 58:142.
176. Jñānagarbha, *Satyadvayavibhaṅga*, verse 3. Toh 3881, 1a. Pd 62:755.
177. Jñānagarbha, *Satyadvayavibhaṅga*, verse 12. Toh 3881, 2a. Pd 62:756.

178. Jñānagarbha, *Satyadvayavibhaṅgavṛtti*, verse 12. Toh 3882, 6b. Pd 62:769.
179. Jñānagarbha, *Satyadvayavibhaṅga*, verse 21. Toh 3881, 2b. Pd 62:757.
180. Jñānagarbha, *Satyadvayavibhaṅgavṛtti*, on verse 8. Toh 3882, 5b. Pd 62:766.
181. Śāntarakṣita. *Madhyamakālaṃkāra*, verse 64. Toh 3884, 55b. Pd 62:901.
182. The only unmistaken cognition within the mindstream of a sentient being is the direct realization of emptiness. An "ordinary being" is someone who has not yet generated that realization.
183. Candrakīrti, *Madhyamakāvatāra*, 6.24. Toh 3861, 205a. Pd 60:564.
184. Candrakīrti, *Madhyamakāvatārabhāṣya*, chap. 6. Toh 3862, 253b. Pd 60:681.
185. Candrakīrti, *Madhyamakāvatārabhāṣya*, chap. 6. Toh 3862, 254a. Pd 60:682.
186. Candrakīrti, *Madhyamakāvatārabhāṣya*, chap. 6. Toh 3862, 253b. Pd 60:681.
187. Candrakīrti, *Madhyamakāvatārabhāṣya*, chap. 6. Toh 3862, 254a. Pd 60:682.
188. Buddhapālita, *Buddhapālitamūlamadhyamakavṛtti*, chap. 18. Toh 3842, 255. Pd 57:653.
189. Here the Tibetan term *rang mtshan* (Skt. *svalakṣaṇa*) is translated as "intrinsic characteristics" to indicate that it refers to the subtle object of negation within the Prāsaṅgika system.
190. Nāgārjuna, *Mūlamadhyamakakārikā*, 24.10. Toh 3824, 14b. Pd 57:36.
191. Bhāviveka, *Madhyamakahṛdaya*, 23.12–13. Toh 3855, 4a. Pd 58:9.
192. Candrakīrti, *Madhyamakāvatāra*, 6.80. Toh 3861, 208a. Pd 60:528.
193. Tibetan, *'jig tshogs lta ba* (Skt. *satkāyadṛṣṭi*); literally, "view of the perishable aggregates." See glossary.
194. Candrakīrti, *Catuḥśatakaṭīkā*, chap. 10. Toh 3865, 161b. Pd 60:1315.
195. The Sanskrit term here, *pūrvapakṣa*, literally means the "former position." For further explanation about its use see note 408 in volume 2 of *Science and Philosophy in the Indian Buddhist Classics*.
196. Bhāviveka, *Prajñāpradīpamūlamadhyamakavṛtti*, chap. 1. Toh 3853, 134b. Pd 57:922.
197. In the context of Indian philosophy, Devadatta and Yajñadatta are placeholder names of people, like John Doe in English.
198. Candrakīrti, *Catuḥśatakaṭīkā*, chap. 10. Toh 3865, 160b. Pd 60:1313.
199. See also volume 2 of *Science and Philosophy in the Indian Buddhist Classics*, 463.
200. For more detail, readers may refer to the outline of Sāṅkhya tenets in volume 3 of *Science and Philosophy in the Indian Buddhist Classics*.
201. These three qualities can also be translated as "mobility," "darkness," and "lightness," respectively.
202. Bhāviveka, *Tarkajvālā*, chap. 6. Toh 3856, 229b. Pd 58:558.
203. Bhāviveka, *Prajñāpradīpamūlamadhyamakavṛtti*, chap. 18. Toh 3855, 179b. Pd 57:1249.
204. Candrakīrti, *Madhyamakāvatāra*, 6.121ab. Toh 3861, 210a. Pd 60:532.
205. Īśvarakṛṣṇa, *Sāṅkhyakārikā*, verse 17: *saṃghātparārthatvāt triguṇādiviparyayādaghiṣṭānāt / puruṣostibhoktṛbhāvāt kaivalyārtham pravṛtteśca //*. Phukan 1960.

206. Kamalaśīla, *Tattvasaṅgrahapañjikā*, chap. 1. Toh 4267, 150b. Pd 107:553. A nature-inference uses nature-evidence as its reason. The three types of correct evidence—effect-evidence, nature-evidence, and evidence consisting in non-perception—have been introduced in chapter 20 in volume 2 of *Science and Philosophy in the Indian Buddhist Classics*. They are also revisited in chapter 23 of the present volume.
207. Īśvarakṛṣṇa, *Sāṅkhyakārikā*, verse 18: *janmamaraṇakaraṇānām pratiniyamād ayugapatpravṛtteśca / puruṣabahutvaṃ siddhaṃ traiguṇyaviparyayāccaiva //*. Phukan 1960.
208. Āryadeva, *Jñānasārasamuccaya*. Toh 3850, 34b. Pd 57:872.
209. Kaṇāda, *Vaiśeṣikasūtra*, 3.2.2: *tasya dravyatva nityatve vāyunā vyākhyāte //*.
210. Bhāviveka, *Prajñāpradīpamūlamadhyamakavṛtti*, chap. 18. Toh 3852, 179b. Pd 57:1248.
211. Bhāviveka, *Tarkajvālā*, chap. 7. Toh 3856, 252b. Pd 58:590.
212. Definite goodness and high status refer, respectively, to liberation and higher rebirth.
213. Candrakīrti, *Madhyamakāvatārabhāṣya*, chap. 6. Toh 3862, 295b. Pd 60:779.
214. Śāntarakṣita, *Tattvasaṅgraha*, 7.4–9 [Jha 7.171–76]. Toh 4266, 8a. Pd 107:19.
215. Kaṇāda, *Vaiśeṣikasūtra*, 3.2.4: *prāṇa apāna nimeṣa unmeṣa jīvana manogati indriyāntaravikāraḥ sukha duḥkha ichchhā dveṣa prayatnā //*
216. Śāntarakṣita, *Tattvasaṅgraha*, 7.7 [Jha 7.177]. Toh 4266, 8a. Pd 107:19.
217. Śāntarakṣita, *Tattvasaṅgraha*, 7.8–9 [Jha 7.178–9]. Toh 4266, 8a. Pd 107:19.
218. Śāntarakṣita, *Tattvasaṅgraha*, 7.10 [Jha 7.180–81]. Toh 4266, 8a. Pd 107:19.
219. Śāntarakṣita, *Tattvasaṅgraha*, 7.15–16 [Jha 7.185–86]. Toh 4266, 8b. Pd 107:20.
220. Kamalśīla, *Tattvasaṅgrahapañjikā*, chap. 7. Toh 4266, 195b. Pd 107:508. In this section Kamalaśīla is commenting on arguments set forth by various Nyāya masters, especially Uddyotakara.
221. Praśastapāda, *Padārthadharmasaṅgraha*, 4.9.
222. Kaṇāda, *Vaiśeṣikasūtra*, 3.1.19: *pravṛttinivṛttī ca pratyagātmani dṛṣṭe paratra liṅgam //*.
223. Candrakīrti, *Catuḥśatakaṭīkā*, chap. 10. Toh 3865, 158. Pd 60:1308.
224. Śāntarakṣita, *Tattvasaṅgraha*, 7.16 [Jha 7.187]. Toh 4266, 8b. Pd 107:20.
225. Śāntarakṣita, *Tattvasaṅgraha*, 8.1–3 [Jha 7.222–24]. Toh 4266, 10a. Pd 107:23.
226. Kumārila, *Mīmāṃsā Ślokavārttika*, chapter on *ātmavāda*, 28. Cited in Kamalśīla, *Tattvasaṅgrahapañjikā*. Pd 107:530.
227. Śāntarakṣita, *Tattvasaṅgraha*, 8.7 [Jha 7.228]. Toh 4266, 10a. Pd 107:24.
228. Śāntarakṣita, *Tattvasaṅgraha*, 8.8 [Jha 7.229–30]. Toh 4266, 10a. Pd 107:24.
229. Śāntarakṣita, *Tattvasaṅgraha*, 8.22–24 [Jha 7.243–45]. Toh 4266, 10b. Pd 107:25.
230. Śāntarakṣita, *Tattvasaṅgraha*, 11.1 [Jha 7.328]. Toh 4266, 13b. Pd 107:25.
231. Kamalaśīla, *Tattvasaṅgrahapañjikā*, chap. 11. Toh 4266, 219b. Pd 107:571.
232. Bhāviveka, *Tarkajvālā*, chap. 8. Toh 3856, 252a. Pd 58:614.
233. This is a characteristic of the Sanskrit alphabet, where *a* occurs first among the

vowels, which are listed before the consonants, and where each unmodified consonant includes the sound "a" when spoken.

234. Bhāviveka, *Tarkajvālā*, chap. 8. Toh 3856, 254a. Pd 58:619.
235. Bhāviveka, *Tarkajvālā*, chap. 8. Toh 3856, 251a. Pd 58:612. Here Bhāviveka is glossing the epithet of the self: "great puruṣa."
236. Bhāviveka, *Tarkajvālā*, chap. 8. Toh 3856, 254b. Pd 58:620.
237. Bhāviveka, *Madhyamakahṛdaya*, 8.23. Toh 3855, 28b. Pd 58:67.
238. Bhāviveka, *Madhyamakahṛdaya*, 8.12. Toh 3855, 28a. Pd 58:66.
239. Gauḍapāda, *Māṇḍūkyakārikā*, book 3, verse 8; also book 2, verses 17–18. Cited in Śāntarakṣita, *Madhyamakālaṃkāravṛtti*. Toh 3885, 80b. Pd 62:967.
240. Śāntarakṣita, *Tattvasaṅgraha*, 10.1 [Jha 7.311]. Toh 4266, 13a. Pd 107:33.
241. Kamalaśīla, *Tattvasaṅgrahapañjikā*, chap. 10. Toh 4266, 216b. Pd 107:563.
242. Prajñāvarman, *Viśeṣastavaṭīkā*. Toh 1110, 28a. Pd 1:68.
243. Nemicandra, *Dravya Saṅgraha*, 1.2: *jivaḥ upayogamayaḥ amurtiḥ kartā svadehaparināmaḥ / bhoktā saṃsārasthaḥ siddhaḥ saha visrasā urdhvagatiḥ //*.
244. Umāsvāmi, *Tattvārthādhigamasūtra*, 5.23.
245. Umāsvāmi, *Tattvārthādhigamasūtra*, 5.24.
246. Prajñāvarman, *Viśeṣastavaṭīkā*. Toh 1110, 28a. Pd 1:69. Here the author is glossing the key words of the root text, *Viśeṣastava*.
247. Devendra Muni 1983, 63.
248. *Questions of the Nāga King Sāgara Sūtra* (*Sāgaranāgarājaparipṛcchāsūtra*). Toh 155, 205b. Pd 58:539.
249. Dharmakīrti, *Pramāṇavārttika*, 2.268. Toh 4210, 117b. Pd 97:524.
250. Kamalaśīla, *Tattvasaṅgrahapañjikā*, chap. 7 [Jha 7, on verse 220]. Toh 4267, 202a. Pd 107:525. This argument functions by way of inferring the absence of something based on the nonobservation of something that is its pervader. For example, if there are no animals present in the room now, this implies that there is no dog in the room now. Here, "animal" is the pervader (the broader category), and "dog" is the pervaded (the narrower category)—all dogs are animals, but not all animals are dogs.
251. Kamalaśīla, *Tattvasaṅgrahapañjikā*, chap. 7 [Jha 7, on verse 220]. Toh 4267, 202a. Pd 107:526.
252. Kamalaśīla, *Tattvasaṅgrahapañjikā*, chap. 14 [Jha 9, on verse 502]. Toh 4267, 259b. Pd 107:659.
253. This is referring to Śāntarakṣita, *Tattvasaṅgraha*, 8.2 [Jha 7.223]. Toh 4266, 10a. Pd 107:23.
254. Kamalaśīla, *Tattvasaṅgrahapañjikā*, chap. 8 [Jha 7, on verse 274]. Toh 4267, 211a. Pd 107:549.
255. Bhāviveka, *Tarkajvālā*, chap. 6, on verse 22. Toh 3856, 233a. Pd 58:567.
256. Kamalaśīla, *Tattvasaṅgrahapañjikā*, chap. 8 [Jha 7, on verse 226]. Toh 4267, 203b. Pd 107:530.
257. Nāgārjuna, *Mūlamadhyamakakārikā*, 27.7. Toh 3824, 18a. Pd 57:43.

258. Candrakīrti, *Madhyamakāvatārabhāṣya*, chap. 6, on verses 122–23. Toh 3862, 294b. Pd 60:780.
259. Candrakīrti, *Madhyamakāvatārabhāṣya*, on 6.146. Toh 3862, 302b. Pd 60:799.
260. Śāntarakṣita, *Tattvasaṅgraha*, 12.2 [Jha 7.337].Toh 4266, 14a. Pd 107:35.
261. Vasubandhu, *Abhidharmakośabhāṣya*, chap. 9. Toh 4090, 82a. Pd 79:877.
262. Vasubandhu, *Abhidharmakośabhāṣya*, chap. 9. Toh 4090, 82b. Pd 79:878.
263. The "six primary consciousnesses" are the five sense consciousnesses and the mental consciousness, which arise in dependence upon their respective sense faculties and objects. They are identified as "primary" in that they discern the presence of an appropriate object, while their accompanying mental factors, which are identified as "secondary," discern the attributes of such objects. For further explanation about the various types of mind and mental factors, see volume 2 of *Science and Philosophy in the Indian Buddhist Classics*.
264. Vasubandhu, *Abhidharmakośabhāṣya*, chap. 9. Toh 4090, 83b. Pd 79:880.
265. The notion of a *dharma* has evolved over time. As mentioned in the translator's introduction, the earliest list of dharmas is identified as a set of beneficial psychic characteristics, known as the thirty-seven dharmas that contribute to awakening. Later the notion of *dharma* came to encompass all the mental and physical aggregates within the continuum of a person. Eventually its meaning expanded to include all phenomena.
266. Vasubandhu, *Abhidharmakośabhāṣya*, chap. 9. Toh 4090, 86b. Pd 79:888.
267. Vasubandhu, *Abhidharmakośabhāṣya*, chap. 9. Toh 4090, 87a. Pd 79:888.
268. Vasubandhu, *Abhidharmakośabhāṣya*, chap. 9. Toh 4090, 87a. Pd 79:890.
269. Vasubandhu, *Abhidharmakośabhāṣya*, chap. 9. Toh 4090, 82a. Pd 79:877.
270. Candrakīrti, *Madhyamakāvatāra*, 6.147–49. Toh 3861, 211b. Pd 60:578.
271. Kamalaśīla, *Tattvasaṅgrahapañjikā*, chap. 12 [Jha 7, on verse 339]. Toh 4267, 222a. Pd 107:577.
272. An argument of this form is composed of a subject, a predicate, a reason, and an example. Here the *subject* is "an autonomous self" (as explicitly stated), the *predicate of the probandum* is "does not exist by its own nature—as imagined by some philosophers," the *logical reason* is "because it is not established either as the same nature or as a different nature from the aggregates," and the *homologous example* is "a rabbit's horn" (as explicitly stated).
273. In a formally structured argument, there is the positive pervasion (where the predicate pervades the reason) and the negative pervasion (where the negation of reason pervades the negation of the predicate). These two types of pervasion are logically equivalent. The pervasion is what enables the logical entailment to follow.
274. Devendrabuddhi, *Pramāṇavārttikapañjikā*, chap. 2. Toh 4217, 108b. Pd 98:258
275. Candrakīrti, *Prasannapadā*, chap. 18. Toh 3860, 111b. Pd 60:273.
276. The "linguistic referent" is the meaning of the word. This is a universal image that appears to a conceptual cognition. Here, a universal image of a self-

sufficient person appears to the mind, in relation to which the evidence for this argument is established as valid.

277. In the context of refuting something, such as the non-Buddhist notion of the self, even if a nonexistent is taken as the subject this does not entail the fault that the evidence is not established as an attribute of the subject. This is proved with extensive reasoning in Gyaltsab Jé's *Illuminating the Path to Liberation* and Khedrup Jé's *Ocean of Reasoning: A Commentary on Exposition of Valid Cognition*. The above two, however, seem to be based on Jé Tsongkhapa's treatment of the question in the opening part of his commentary on the *Ornament for the Middle Way*, where he explains how what he has stated represents the intent of Kamalaśīla's *Illumination of the Middle Way*.

278. Asvabhāva, *Mahāyānasūtrālaṅkāraṭīkā*. Toh 4029, 59a. Pd 71:158.

279. The "conceived object" is one of four types of objects of mind: the appearing object (*snang yul*), the observed object (*gzung yul*), the conceived object (*zhen yul*), and the engaged object (*'jug yul*)—also known as the object of application. This typology is used in several major systems of Buddhist epistemology. In this context, the *conceived object* is an object of conceptual cognition only, not of direct perception. It is the same as the *engaged object* of a conceptual cognition. For a more detailed presentation of these four types of objects see chapter 17 in volume 2 of *Science and Philosophy in the Indian Buddhist Classics*.

280. The Tibetan term *sbyor ba* (Skt. *prayoga*) is often translated as "syllogism." This type of argument takes the following form: the *subject* is the *predicate* (*of the probandum*) because of the *evidence* (or *reason*), as in the case of the stated *example*. In Western logic, however, a "syllogism" is a totally different form of argument in which a conclusion is drawn from two premises—e.g., "All men are mortal; Socrates is a man; therefore Socrates is mortal." We avoided translating the term *sbyor ba* as "syllogism" in volume 2 of *Science and Philosophy of the Indian Buddhist Classics* in order not to cause confusion, for in that context it rarely occurs. But it has proved impossible to find an acceptable alternative in the present context. So, since volume 3 translates *sbyor ba* as "syllogism," volume 4 will follow suit.

281. Haribhadra, *Abhisamayālaṃkāravṛtti*, chap. 5, on verse 20. Toh 3793, 125b. Pd 52:316.

282. Asaṅga, *Abhidharmasamuccaya*, part 2 (*Viniścayasamuccaya*). Toh 4049, 77a. Pd 76:194.

283. Asaṅga, *Śrāvakabhūmi*, vol. 19. Toh 4036, 187a. Pd 73:465.

284. Vinītadeva, *Triṃśikāṭīkā*. Toh 4070, 9b. Pd 78:22.

285. Vasubandhu, *Abhidharmakośabhāṣya*, chap. 9. Toh 4090, 90b. Pd 79:898.

286. Madhyamakasiṃha, *Saṅkṣiptanānādṛṣṭivibhājana*. Toh 3898, 3a. Pd 63:870.

287. Candrakīrti, *Catuḥśatakaṭīkā*, chap. 12. Toh 3865, 190b. Pd 60:1381.

288. Here we should note that Buddhist schools in general negate a "truly existent self" (*bden par grub pa'i bdag*), whereas only the Prāsaṅgika Madhyamaka negate an "inherently existent self" (*rang bzhin gyis grub pa'i bdag*). Other Bud-

dhist schools say that a basis of identity (*mtshan gzhi*) of the person is found at the culmination of ultimate analysis seeking the person among the aggregates that are its basis of imputation, whereas the Prāsaṅgika Madhyamaka say that only the mere absence of the person is found (i.e., emptiness, or *śūnyatā* in Sanskrit). According to the Prāsaṅgika Madhyamaka tradition, to accept or reject that a basis of identity is found through ultimate analysis is what constitutes accepting or rejecting an inherently existent self.

289. The traditional order in which the non-Buddhist and Buddhist tenet systems are presented is demonstrated in volume 3 of *Science and Philosophy in the Indian Buddhist Classics*. The non-Buddhist schools of tenets are: Sāṅkhya, Vaiśeṣika, Nyāya, Mīmāṃsā, Vedānta, Jaina, and Lokāyata. The Buddhist schools of tenets are: Vaibhāṣika, Sautrāntika, Cittamātra, and Madhyamaka—where the latter is subdivided into Svātantrika Madhyamaka and Prāsaṅgika Madhyamaka. The order in which the Buddhist schools appear represents a development in their views, moving from lower to higher in terms of sophistication and status.
290. Candrakīrti, *Madhyamakāvatārabhāṣya*, on 6.150. Toh 3862, 303b. Pd 60:802.
291. Candrakīrti, *Madhyamakāvatārabhāṣya*, on 6.162. Toh 3862, 307a. Pd 60:809.
292. Nāgārjuna, *Mūlamadhyamakakārikā*, 17.33. Toh 3824, 10b. Pd 57:25.
293. Saṅghabhadra, *Abhidharmakośaśāstrakārikābhāṣya*, chap. 4. Toh 4091, 163a. Pd 79:1102.
294. *Akṣayamatinirdeśasūtra*. Toh 175, 150b. Pd 60:375.
295. Candrakīrti, *Madhyamakāvatārabhāṣya*, chap. 6. Toh 3862, 296b. Pd 60:792. Vasubandhu too cites this stanza in his *Abhidharmakośabhāṣya*. Although this stanza is not found in any of the sūtras in the Tibetan Kangyur, an equivalent is found in the *Vajirā Sutta* of the Pali canon in the *Connected Discourses* (*Saṃyutta Nikāya*), I.5 (*Bhikkhunī Saṃyutta*), Bodhi 2000, 230.
296. A *nonerroneous cognition* (*blo gnod med*) is one that is free from temporary causes of error.
297. Candrakīrti, *Madhyamakāvatāra*, 6.150b–151. Toh 3861, 211b. Pd 60:579.
298. Candrakīrti, *Madhyamakāvatārabhāṣya*, on 6.126. Toh 3862, 296a. Pd 60:783.
299. Candrakīrti, *Madhyamakāvatārabhāṣya*, on 6.126. Toh 3862, 295b. Pd 60:782.
300. Vasubandhu, *Abhidharmakośabhāṣya*, chap. 9. Toh 4090, 82a. Pd 79:876.
301. Dharmakīrti, *Pramāṇavārttika*, 2.45. Toh 4210, 109a. Pd 101:1660.
302. Bhāviveka, *Tarkajvālā*, chap. 3. Toh 3856, 80b. Pd 58:200.
303. Haribhadra, *Aṣṭasāhasrikāprajñāpāramitā-vyākhyābhisamayālaṅkārāloka*, chap. 1. Toh 3791, 9a. Pd 51:910.
304. The six collections of consciousness are the eye consciousness, ear consciousness, nose consciousness, tongue consciousness, body consciousness, and mental consciousness. In the Cittamātra school these are also known as the six types of operative consciousness; see chapter 13 in volume 3 of *Science and Philosophy in the Indian Buddhist Classics*.
305. *Laṅkāvatārasūtra*, vol. 9. Toh 107, 182a. Pd 58:558.
306. *Saṃdhinirmocanasūtra*, chap. 5. Toh 106, 12b. Pd 59:28.

307. *Mahāparinirvāṇasūtra*, vol. 55. Toh 119, 202b. Pd 53:471.
308. *Mahāparinirvāṇasūtra*, vol. 55. Toh 119, 203a. Pd 53:471.
309. Nāgārjuna, *Ratnāvalī*, 1.80–81. Toh 4158, 109b. Pd 96:295.
310. This is probably a reference to the Judeo-Christian standpoint that does not accept the existence of former lifetimes but does accept an afterlife.
311. *Āyuṣpattiyathākāraparipṛcchāsūtra*. Toh 308, 152b. Pd 72:424.
312. Āryadeva, *Catuḥśataka*, 7.10. Toh 3846, 8b. Pd 57:798.
313. Dharmakīrti, *Pramāṇavārttika*, 2.165 [2.164cd]. Toh 4210, 113b. Pd 97:515.
314. Bhāviveka, *Madhyamakahṛdaya*, 3.205. Toh 3855, 11a. Pd 58:28.
315. Śāntarakṣita, *Tattvasaṅgraha*, 26.40. Toh 4266, 69b. Pd 107:171.
316. *Surataparipṛcchāsūtra*. Toh 71, 181b. Pd 43:513.
317. Dharmakīrti, *Pramāṇavārttika*, 2.35. Toh 4210, 108b. Pd 97:503.
318. Dharmakīrti, *Pramāṇavārttika*, 2.38. Toh 4210, 109a. Pd 97:503.
319. Dharmakīrti, *Pramāṇavārttika*, 2.146 [147bc]. Toh 4210, 113a. Pd 97:513.
320. Āryaśūra, *Jātakamālā*, chap. 29. Toh 4150, 110b. Pd 94:265.
321. Bhāviveka, *Tarkajvālā*, chap. 3. Toh 3856, 106a. Pd 58:260.
322. Dharmottara, *Paralokasiddhi*. Toh 4251, 246b. Pd 106:669.
323. Dharmottara, *Paralokasiddhi*. Toh 4251, 246b. Pd 106:670.
324. Dharmottara, *Paralokasiddhi*. Toh 4251, 246b. Pd 106:670.
325. Dharmottara, *Paralokasiddhi*. Toh 4251, 247a. Pd 106:671.
326. Dharmottara, *Paralokasiddhi*. Toh 4251, 248b. Pd 106:674.
327. Dharmakīrti, *Pramāṇavārttika*, 2.45. Toh 4210, 112a. Pd 97:510.
328. Kamalaśīla, *Tattvasaṅgrahapañjikā*, chap. 29. Toh 4267, 101b. Pd 107:1235.
329. Though this often refers to the first part of the five works that together bear the name *Yogācārabhūmi*, here it refers to all five: the *Multiple Levels* (Toh 4035), *Śrāvaka Levels* (4036), and *Bodhisattva Levels* (4037), which together count as one text often called the *Chapters on the Levels* (*Sa'i dngos gzhi*), plus the *Compendium of Ascertainments* (Toh 4038), the *Compendium of Bases* (Toh 4039, encompassing also the *Compendium of Vinaya Bases*, Toh 4040), the *Compendium of Enumerations* (Toh 4041), and the *Compendium of Explanation* (Toh 4042).
330. Asaṅga, *Mahāyānasaṅgraha*, chap. 1. Toh 4048, 2b. Pd 76:5.
331. There are two non-Mahāyāna vehicles: that of the śrāvaka ("hearer") and that of the pratyekabuddha ("solitary realizer"). These are often considered together. In order to attain complete liberation from saṃsāra (a lower attainment than buddhahood), śrāvakas and pratyekabuddhas only need to realize the selflessness of the person, defined as: "the emptiness of a self-sufficient, substantially existent person." This definition is common to the Vaibhāṣika, Sautrāntika, Yogācāra, and Svātantrika Madhyamaka schools. When they say "selflessness of the person," they are not referring to the emptiness of an inherently existent self as taught by the Prāsaṅgika school. In their view, in order to attain nirvāṇa, one must understand emptiness and selflessness in the context of the sixteen attri-

butes of the four noble truths. For further information, see volume 3 of *Science and Philosophy in the Indian Buddhist Classics*.

332. The term "nature" is used here to translate *mtshan nyid* (Skt. *lakṣaṇa*), not *rang bzhin* (Skt. *svabhāva*), though in certain other contexts the latter term is found to refer to the three natures (Skt. *trisvabhāva*).
333. The term *rnam rig* (Skt. *vijñapti*) is ambiguous and can be understood as (1) a cognition or (2) the content of that cognition. How this term is translated into English depends on the context, which is determined by how each Indian author interprets it in his texts. For example, Vasubandhu's *Twenty Stanzas* states that *cognition* is synonymous with "mind," "mentality," and "consciousness," whereas in the context of Asaṅga's *Compendium of the Mahāyāna* this term is interpreted (by the authors of the present commentary) to mean the content of cognition, or percept, here translated as "cognizance" in accordance with volume 3 of *Science and Philosophy in the Indian Buddhist Classics* (see chapter 13 below).
334. Asaṅga, *Mahāyānasaṅgraha*, chap. 1. Toh 4048, 3a. Pd 76:5.
335. Asaṅga, *Viniścayasaṅgraha*. Toh 4038, zi:55b. Pd 74:875–77.
336. Asaṅga, *Viniścayasaṅgraha*. Toh 4038, zhi:195a. Pd 74:470.
337. Asaṅga, *Viniścayasaṅgraha*. Toh 4038, zi:18b. Pd 74:787.
338. The basis of designation (*gdags gzhi*) is a real thing in the world (e.g., an individual cow). It is not the shared feature of similar kinds of things (e.g., cowhood). The basis on which a name is introduced (a particular individual) is not the direct object of the term (a universal).
339. Asaṅga, *Mahāyānasaṅgraha*, chap. 2. Toh 4048, 16b. Pd 76:39.
340. Asaṅga, *Mahāyānasaṅgraha*, chap. 2. Toh 4048, 16b. Pd 76:39.
341. Chapter 6 in volume 2 of *Science and Philosophy in the Indian Buddhist Classics* introduces the four classificatory conventions mentioned above and discusses how discernment apprehends the object's signs or distinguishing marks.
342. Asaṅga, *Mahāyānasaṅgraha*, chap. 2. Toh 4048, 13b. Pd 76:31.
343. Maitreya, *Madhyāntavibhāga*, 1.2. Toh 4021, 40b. Pd 70:902.
344. Maitreya, *Madhyāntavibhāga*, 1.3. Toh 4021, 40b. Pd 70:902.
345. Asaṅga, *Mahāyānasaṅgraha*, chap. 2. Toh 4048, 18b. Pd 76:44.
346. People do not usually remark on the sky's clear nature in a general sense but only when there are no clouds to be seen.
347. Asaṅga, *Mahāyānasaṅgraha*, chap. 2. Toh 4048, 19a. Pd 76:56.
348. Sthiramati, *Triṃśikābhāṣya*. Toh 4046, 167b. Pd 77:550.
349. Asaṅga, *Mahāyānasaṅgraha*, chap. 2. Toh 4048, 16b. Pd 76:39.
350. Asvabhāva, *Mahāyānasaṅgrahopanibandhana*, chap. 3. Toh 4051, 227a. Pd 76:593.
351. Asaṅga, *Mahāyānasaṅgraha*, chap. 2. Toh 4048, 18b. Pd 76:44.
352. Asvabhāva, *Mahāyānasaṅgrahopanibandhana*, chap. 3. Toh 4051, 227a. Pd 76:593.

353. The "perfectly pure" class of phenomena includes the "naturally pure," which refers only to emptiness.
354. Asaṅga, *Mahāyānasaṅgraha*, chap. 2. Toh 4048, 19b. Pd 76:47.
355. Maitreya, *Madhyāntavibhāga*, 1.7. Toh 4021, 40b. Pd 70:903.
356. Vasubandhu, *Madhyāntavibhāgaṭīkā*, chap. 1. Toh 4027, 3a. Pd 71:6
357. Maitreya, *Madhyāntavibhāga*, 1.15. Toh 4021, 41a. Pd 70:903.
358. Maitreya, *Madhyāntavibhāga*, 1.12. Toh 4021, 40b. Pd 70:903.
359. Maitreya, *Madhyāntavibhāga*, 1.12. Toh 4021, 41a. Pd 70:903.
360. Maitreya, *Madhyāntavibhāga*, 1.15. Toh 4021, 41a. Pd 70:903.
361. Maitreya, *Madhyāntavibhāga*, 1.17. Toh 4021, 41a. Pd 70:904.
362. See pages 74–75, which list the sixteen types of emptiness.
363. Vasubandhu, *Madhyāntavibhāgaṭīkā*, chap. 1. Toh 4027, 211b. Pd 71:550.
364. Asaṅga, *Mahāyānasaṅgraha*, chap. 2. Toh 4048, 19a. Pd 76:46.
365. Vasubandhu, *Mahāyānasaṅgrahabhāṣya*, chap. 4. Toh 4050, 151a. Pd 76:389.
366. Dignāga, *Prajñāpāramitāsaṅgraha*, verse 26. Toh 3809, 293b. Pd 55:1379.
367. Asaṅga, *Mahāyānasaṅgraha*, chap. 2. Toh 4048, 21b. Pd 76:51.
368. Asaṅga, *Bodhisattvabhūmi*, chap. 4. Toh 4037, 24b. Pd 73:582.
369. The phrase "basis of conception" (*zhen gzhi*) here means much the same as *basis of application* (*'jug gzhi*) except that the former is used in the case of conceptual cognition only.
370. Asaṅga, *Bodhisattvabhūmi*, chap. 4. Toh 4037, 25b. Pd 73:584.
371. Asaṅga, *Viniścayasaṅgraha*. Toh 4038, zhi:194b. Pd 74:470.
372. Asaṅga, *Viniścayasaṅgraha*. Toh 4038, zhi:279b. Pd 74:675.
373. Asaṅga, *Viniścayasaṅgraha*. Toh 4038, zi:21a. Pd 74:793.
374. The notion of a "construing awareness" is introduced in volume 2 of *Science and Philosophy in the Indian Buddhist Classics*, page 69: "The definition of a conceptual cognition is: a construing awareness (*zhen rig*) that apprehends *word* and *referent* as suitable to be associated."
375. Asaṅga, *Viniścayasaṅgraha*. Toh 4038, zi:21a. Pd 74:793.
376. Asaṅga, *Viniścayasaṅgraha*. Toh 4038, zi:21a. Pd 74:794.
377. Asaṅga, *Viniścayasaṅgraha*. Toh 4038, zi:21a. Pd 74:794.
378. Asaṅga, *Viniścayasaṅgraha*. Toh 4038, zi:21a. Pd 74:794.
379. Asaṅga, *Viniścayasaṅgraha*. Toh 4038, zi:21b. Pd 74:795.
380. Asaṅga, *Bodhisattvabhūmi*, chap. 4. Toh 4037, zhi:28b. Pd 73:590.
381. Asaṅga, *Bodhisattvabhūmi*, chap. 4. Toh 4037, zhi:25b. Pd 73:584.
382. The *direct object of the term* (*rjod byed kyi dngos yul*) is the linguistic referent (*sgra don*), which is not an object in the real world but the object universal (*don spyi*), a mental image. It is the appearing object of the conceptual cognition apprehending it, or that which such a conceptual cognition directly relates to.
383. The *conceived object of the term* (*rjod byed kyi zhen yul*) is the object in the real world. It is that which such a conceptual cognition relates to indirectly via the object universal.
384. Asaṅga, *Mahāyānasaṅgraha*, chap. 2. Toh 4048, 18b. Pd 76:44.

385. Asaṅga, *Bodhisattvabhūmi*, chap. 4. Toh 4037, 25a. Pd 73:582.
386. Asaṅga, *Bodhisattvabhūmi*, chap. 4. Toh 4037, 25a. Pd 73:583.
387. Asaṅga, *Bodhisattvabhūmi*, chap. 4. Toh 4037, 25a. Pd 73:583.
388. Sāgaramegha, *Bodhisattvabhūmivyākhyā*, chap. 4. Toh 4047, 68b. Pd 75:771.
389. Asaṅga, *Viniścayasaṅgraha*. Toh 4038, zhi:12a. Pd 74:771.
390. Vasubandhu, *Viṃśatikā*, verse 1. Toh 4056, 3a. Pd 77:8.
391. The "three realms" are the desire realm, the form realm, and the formless realm, which together comprise the realms of cyclic existence. For further explanation see chapter 21 in volume 1 of *Science and Philosophy in the Indian Buddhist Classics*.
392. This refers to the Vaibhāṣika and Sautrāntika traditions (depicted in part 1 above).
393. This relates to the sixth reasoning that refutes the object of negation listed in the subsequent paragraphs: the necessary simultaneity of perception and the perceived.
394. Dharmakīrti, *Pramāṇaviniścaya*, chap. 1. Toh 4211, 166a. Pd 97:645.
395. Dharmakīrti, *Pramāṇaviniścaya*, chap. 1. Toh 4211, 167a. Pd 97:648.
396. Asaṅga, *Mahāyānasaṅgraha*, chap. 2. Toh 4048, 15b. Pd 76:36.
397. Asaṅga, *Mahāyānasaṅgraha*, chap. 2. Toh 4048, 16a. Pd 76:37.
398. Vinītadeva, *Ālambanaparīkṣāṭīkā*. Toh 4265, 180a. Pd 106:479.
399. Dignāga, *Ālambanaparīkṣā*, verses 1–2. Toh 4205, 86a. Pd 97:430.
400. Vasubandhu, *Viṃśatikā*, verse 12. Toh 4056, 3b. Pd 77:9.
401. Vasubandhu, *Viṃśatikāvṛtti*, on verses 11–15. Toh 4057, 6b. Pd 77:19.
402. The point here is that this realist definition is too wide to apply to an external object alone, which adds support to the Cittamātra claim that there are no external objects.
403. Dharmakīrti, *Pramāṇavārttika*, 3.320. Toh 4210, 130b. Pd 97:554.
404. Dharmakīrti, *Pramāṇavārttika*, 3.322–23. Toh 4210, 130b. Pd 97:554.
405. Prajñākaragupta, *Sahāvalambanirṇaya*. Toh 4255, 275a. Pd 106:752.
406. Dharmakīrti, *Pramāṇavārttika*, 3.387. Toh 4210, 133a. Pd 97:560.
407. There are "three modes" that constitute the criteria of a correct logical reason or evidence: (1) the evidence is an attribute of the thesis's subject, (2) it is ascertained to be present only in the set of homologous cases, and (3) it is ascertained to be only absent in the set of heterogeneous cases. The three modes are expressed more briefly as: (1) the attribute of the subject, (2) the positive pervasion, and (3) the negative pervasion. In the passage above they are condensed into two: the pervasion and the attribute of the subject. For a detailed presentation of the three modes and the structure of inferential reasoning in general, see part 5 in volume 2 of *Science and Philosophy in the Indian Buddhist Classics*.
408. Dharmakīrti, *Pramāṇavārttika*, 3.388ab. Toh 4210, 133a. Pd 97:560.
409. Dharmakīrti, *Pramāṇavārttika*, 3.388cd. Toh 4210, 133a. Pd 97:560.
410. Dharmakīrti, *Pramāṇavārttika*, 3.389. Toh 4210, 133a. Pd 97:560.
411. Dharmakīrti, *Pramāṇavārttika*, 3.390abc. Toh 4210, 133a. Pd 97:560.

412. Asaṅga, *Mahāyānasaṅgraha*, chap. 2. Toh 4048, 15b. Pd 76:37.
413. For a description of how to develop the refined state of meditative concentration known as *calm abiding*, see chapter 24 in volume 2 of *Science and Philosophy in the Indian Buddhist Classics*.
414. Dignāga, *Ālambanaparīkṣāvṛtti*. Toh 4206, 86b. Pd 97:433.
415. Dharmakīrti, *Pramāṇavārttika*, 3.326. Toh 4210, 131a. Pd 97:555.
416. Vasubandhu, *Viṃśatikāvṛtti*. Toh 4057, 4a. Pd 77:13.
417. Dharmakīrti, *Saṃtānāntarasiddhi*. Toh 4219, 355b. Pd 98:941.
418. Asaṅga, *Mahāyānasaṅgraha*, chap. 2. Toh 4048, 15a. Pd 76:35.
419. The Tibetan editors of our present volume are commenting here on how to understand *rnam rig tsam* (Skt. *vijñaptimātra*), rendered here as "cognizance only," particularly the second syllable *rig*, which can also mean "awareness."
420. Asaṅga, *Mahāyānasaṅgraha*, chap. 2. Toh 4048, 13b. Pd 76:32.
421. Vinītadeva, *Prakaraṇaviṃśakaṭīkā*. Toh 4065, 183a. Pd 77:485.
422. To a direct perception perceiving a pot, the object appears along with all its attributes that are the same as it with respect to nature, time, and object—in being the same substance, duration, and establishment. But this direct perception only realizes the pot, not its attributes. A sense consciousness does not know everything that appears to it. It only knows its main object, which is its object as cognized. Therefore, its appearing object and its object as cognized are different. While its appearing object is not necessarily its object as cognized, the latter is necessarily one of its appearing objects—indeed, its principal appearing object.
423. Asaṅga, *Mahāyānasaṅgraha*, chap. 1. Toh 4048, 3b. Pd 76:8.
424. Vasubandhu, *Pratītyasamutpādādivibhaṅganirdeśa*. Toh 3995, 116b. See Guṇamati's *Commentary on Explanation of the First Dependent Origination and Its Divisions* (*Pratītyasamutpādādivibhaṅganirdeśaṭīkā*). Toh 3996. Pd 66:1020.
425. The following series of five arguments can be seen to support the *possibility* of experience arising in the absence of external objects rather than the *necessity* of it doing so. In terms of their general format, Vasubandhu first presents the realists' objections to that possibility followed by the Cittamātra defense of it. The first response of the Cittamātra also highlights a problem with the Sautrāntika position regarding a time lag between the objective condition's existence and the subject's experience of it. In general, the Cittamātra arguments here seem to be focused on rebutting objections to their own position and presenting problems with their opponent's position, rather than positing affirmative arguments to establish the impossibility of external objects existing outside the realm of cognition (which can be said to characterize idealism). Indeed, there are differences of opinion among scholars as to whether Vasubandhu's text presents an idealist position; see Kellner and Taber 2014.
426. The point here is that given Sautrāntika assert external objects to be the objective condition of perception, when a perception has arisen, the object would already have ceased and would no longer be existent.
427. Vasubandhu, *Viṃśatikāvṛtti*, on verse 16. Toh 4057, 8a. Pd 77:22.

428. In ancient Indian religious traditions, gandharvas are celestial beings especially associated with singing and playing beautiful music; they are said to subsist on scents and odors.
429. Vasubandhu, *Viṃśatikāvṛtti*. Toh 4057, 4a. Pd 77:12.
430. Vasubandhu, *Viṃśatikāvṛtti*. Toh 4057, 4b. Pd 77:13.
431. Vasubandhu, *Viṃśatikāvṛtti*. Toh 4057, 9b. Pd 77:25.
432. Vasubandhu, *Viṃśatikāvṛtti*. Toh 4057, 8b. Pd 77:23.
433. Vasubandhu, *Viṃśatikāvṛtti*, on verse 18cd. Toh 4057, 9a. Pd 77:24.
434. Asaṅga, *Bodhisattvabhūmi*, chap. 4. Toh 4037, 28a. Pd 73:590.
435. The conceptualizations thinking "I" and "mine" constitute the identity view, as does the pride thinking "I," so they are not presented as cause and effect here.
436. The "three bases" here refers to: the conceptualization that projects real things; the identity view and the pride thinking "I"; and the three root mental afflictions, which are attachment, hatred, and delusion.
437. Asaṅga, *Bodhisattvabhūmi*, chap 4. Toh 4037, 28b. Pd 73:591.
438. Sāgaramegha, *Bodhisattvabhūmivyākhyā*, chap. 4. Toh 4047, 74b. Pd 75:785.
439. Sāgaramegha, *Bodhisattvabhūmivyākhyā*, chap. 4. Toh 4047, 73b. Pd 75:783.
440. Asaṅga, *Bodhisattvabhūmi*, chap 4. Toh 4037, 29a. Pd 73:592.
441. Ignorance of the true nature of reality pervades the mindstreams of all ordinary beings, whether one is intellectually gifted or not. Without an ability to use language and concepts it is impossible to learn how to uproot it or to employ the type of analysis needed for such a task.
442. Asaṅga, *Bodhisattvabhūmi*, chap. 4. Toh 4037, 29b. Pd 73:594.
443. Asaṅga, *Bodhisattvabhūmi*, chap. 4. Toh 4037, 31a. Pd 73:597.
444. Asaṅga, *Abhidharmasamuccaya*. Toh 4049, 103a. Pd 76:258.
445. Asaṅga, *Abhidharmasamuccaya*. Toh 4049, 103a. Pd 76:258.
446. Asaṅga, *Abhidharmasamuccaya*. Toh 4049, 103a. Pd 76:258.
447. Asaṅga, *Abhidharmasamuccaya*. Toh 4049, 103b. Pd 76:259.
448. Here, "the way it has been sought" refers to the four kinds of searching, utilized as ultimate analysis, during which one searches for the object of scrutiny to exist as that very thing from its own side independently of being imputed by language and thought. Since nothing exists in such a manner, such an object cannot be found, and instead one finds its absence, or emptiness.
449. *Tathāgatācintyaguhyanirdeśasūtra*, chap. 15. Toh 47, 161b. Pd 39:439.
450. Nāgārjuna, *Mūlamadhyamakakārikā*, 18.5. Toh 3824, 11a. Pd 57:26.
451. Nāgārjuna, *Dharmadhātustava*, verse 26. Toh 1118, 65b. Pd 1:180.
452. Āryadeva, *Catuḥśataka*, 6.10. Toh 3846, 7b. Pd 57:796.
453. Candrakīrti, *Madhyamakāvatārabhāṣya*, chap. 6. Toh 3862, 292b. Pd 60:774.
454. Candrakīrti, *Prasannapadā*, colophon. Toh 3860, 198b. Pd 60:480.
455. Nāgārjuna, *Mūlamadhyamakakārikā*, 7.33. Toh 3824, 5b. Pd 57:13.
456. Candrakīrti, *Prasannapadā*, chap. 1. Toh 3860, 5a. Pd 60:10.
457. Nāgārjuna, *Mūlamadhyamakakārikā*, 1.1. Toh 3824, 1a. Pd 57:3.
458. There are different ways of parsing Nāgārjuna's famous verse here, either in

accordance with Bhāviveka or with Candrakīrti. (1) Bhāviveka presents the argument in the form of a syllogism—as a thesis with a fourfold reason. The subject of the argument is "any things." The predicate is "anywhere, do not arise at any time." So the thesis is "any things, anywhere, do not arise at any time." Bhāviveka says that this is proved by the fourfold reason "because they do not arise from self, from others, from both, or without a cause." He further argues that the qualifier "ultimately" must be applied to the predicate: "anywhere, do not arise 'ultimately' at any time." He uses this argument to refute ultimate arising. If a thing arises ultimately, then it must arise either from self, or from others, or from both, or without a cause. But nothing arises in any of those ways; therefore nothing arises ultimately. (2) Candrakīrti does not interpret this stanza as a syllogism in which the reason "Not from self, not from others, not from both, and not without a cause" proves the thesis "any things, anywhere, do not arise at any time." Instead we must apply the phrase "do not arise" from the fourth line to all four positions stated in the first two lines: from self, from others, from both, or without a cause. By negating the four ways of arising, we indirectly negate true existence. In short, we should understand this stanza to propose four theses:

1. Any things, anywhere, do not arise at any time from self.
2. Any things, anywhere, do not arise at any time from others.
3. Any things, anywhere, do not arise at any time from both.
4. Any things, anywhere, do not arise at any time without a cause.

Nāgārjuna proves these four theses one by one later in the text. They can then be used as reasons to demonstrate that there is no ultimate arising. For further discussion see Sopa and Rochard 2017, 356.

459. Kamalaśīla, *Madhyamakāloka*. Toh 3887, 202a. Pd 62:1282.

460. The summary provided here seems to be based on Īśvarakṛṣṇa, *Sāṅkhyakārikā*, verse 9, which contains five brief arguments supporting the conclusion: "The effect is something that exists." While this verse has been interpreted in several different ways by both classical and modern scholars, the gist of it can be presented as follows. (1) Because of the nonproduction of the nonexistent, (2) because a material cause is taken, (3) because of the nonexistence of the possibility of anything, (4) because that which is capable can produce only what it is capable of, and (5) because of being the same nature as the cause, the effect is therefore something that exists. Skt. *asad-akaraṇād upādāna-grahaṇāt sarva-saṃbhavābhāvāt / śaktasya śakya-karaṇat kāraṇabhāvāc-ca satkāryam //*. Sanskrit in Phukan 1960.

461. Kamalaśīla, *Tattvasaṅgrahapañjikā*, chap. 1. Toh 4267, 152a. Pd 107:401. The reference to the Vindhya hills appears to be a pun on the name Vindhyavāsin, the author of the verse cited here.

462. Nāgārjuna, *Mūlamadhyamakakārikā*, 20.3. Toh 3824, 11b. Pd 57:27.

463. Buddhapālita, *Buddhapālitamūlamadhyamakavṛtti*. Toh 3842, 161b. Pd 57:451.

464. The pervasion between the reason and the predicate here can be expressed as: if it is purposeful to arise again after having already arisen, then arising again would be endless.

465. Candrakīrti, *Madhyamakāvatāra*, 6.8–9. Toh 3861, 204a. Pd 60:562.
466. See the previous page: Buddhapālita, *Buddhapālitamūlamadhyamakavṛtti*. Toh 3842, 161b. Pd 57:451.
467. Nāgārjuna. *Mūlamadhyamakakārikā*, 20.20. Toh 3824, 12a. Pd 57:29.
468. Nāgārjuna, *Mūlamadhyamakakārikā*, 10.1. Toh 3824, 12a. Pd 57:15.
469. Candrakīrti, *Madhyamakāvatāra*, 6.13. Toh 3861, 204b. Pd 60:562.
470. Bhāviveka, *Tarkajvālā*, chap. 3. Toh 3856, 91a. Pd 58:226.
471. Bhāviveka, *Tarkajvālā*, chap. 3. Toh 3856, 92a. Pd 58:229.
472. Buddhapālita, *Buddhapālitamūlamadhyamakavṛtti*. Toh 3842, 161b. Pd 57:451.
473. For an explanation of this point, see Tsongkhapa 2021, 208: "Just as, according to the opponent, a rice seed that produces the rice sprout is, by virtue of its intrinsic characteristic, 'other' than its effect, the rice sprout, in the same way, those things that do not produce rice sprouts—fire, charcoal, barley seeds, and so on—are also, by virtue of their intrinsic characters, 'other' than the rice sprout. This is the way in which those who propound other-arising assert their position. Now, if these two cases of being 'other' are admitted as equal, then just as from a rice seed—which is 'other'—a rice sprout grows, then by extension, a rice sprout should arise from fire, charcoal, and so on as well. Similarly, just as a rice sprout—which is 'other'—grows from a rice seed, things like a vase, cloth, and so on too must also come from a rice seed. Like this, parallels are drawn [between the two types of 'other']."
474. Candrakīrti, *Madhyamakāvatāra*, 6.14. Toh 3861, 204b. Pd 60:563.
475. Nāgārjuna, *Mūlamadhyamakakārikā*, 20.20. Toh 3824, 12a. Pd 57:29.
476. These four conditions are introduced in chapter 2 in volume 2 of *Science and Philosophy in the Indian Buddhist Classics* in the context of how sense consciousness arises.
477. Nāgārjuna, *Mūlamadhyamakakārikā*, 1.3. Toh 3824, 1a. Pd 57:3.
478. Candrakīrti, *Prasannapadā*, chap. 1. Toh 3860, 26a. [Pd 60:61.]
479. Candrakīrti, *Prasannapadā*, chap. 1. Toh 3860, 26b. [Pd 60: 62.]
480. Bhāviveka, *Tarkajvālā*, chap. 3. Toh 3856, 93b. Pd 58:231.
481. Bhāviveka, *Tarkajvālā*, chap. 3. Toh 3856, 94a. Pd 58:232.
482. Bhāviveka, *Tarkajvālā*, chap. 3. Toh 3856, 103a. Pd 58:252.
483. The notion of "other" here, as in the previous section, is an "inherently existent other," which for many reasons has been proved untenable. There would be no problem if it were "merely other" in a conventional sense. But in the context of ultimate analysis—such as this refutation of arising from the four alternatives—the practitioner is searching for something that exists by its own nature or bears an identity from its own side independently of being cognized. To perceive the mere absence of such an object is a realization that gradually purifies the mindstream of the root of suffering—ignorance that grasps its object in a distorted manner.
484. Buddhapālita, *Buddhapālitamūlamadhyamakavṛtti*, chap. 1. Toh 3842, 161b. Pd 57:451.
485. Candrakīrti, *Madhyamakāvatāra*, 6.98. Toh 3861, 209. Pd 60:571.

486. Bhāviveka, *Tarkajvālā*, chap. 3. Toh 3856, 103a. Pd 58:253.
487. Bhāviveka, *Tarkajvālā*, chap. 3. Toh 3856, 103b. Pd 58:254.
488. Bhāviveka, *Madhyamakahṛdaya*, 3.192. Toh 3855, 10b. Pd 58:24.
489. Buddhapālita, *Buddhapālitamūlamadhyamakavṛtti*, chap. 2. Toh 3842, 161b. Pd 57:451.
490. Candrakīrti, *Madhyamakāvatāra*, 6.99. Toh 3861, 209a. Pd 60:572.
491. Here, to accept "the dependent arising of this mere conditionality" indicates that dependent arising is denied to exist ultimately but is accepted to exist conventionally. Since each of the four alternative ways of arising is based on the assumption that things exist inherently, all four of them are rejected by the Prāsaṅgika Madhyamaka school.
492. Candrakīrti, *Prasannapadā*, chap. 1. Toh 3860, 18b. Pd 60:42.
493. Buddhapālita, *Buddhapālitamūlamadhyamakavṛtti*, chap. 2. Toh 3842, 161b. Pd 57:451.
494. The three conditions of a sense consciousness are the objective condition, the immediately preceding condition, and the dominant condition. The fourth condition, the causal condition, is a general category that includes all the other causes of a sense consciousness apart from the three specific conditions already mentioned. There are so many other causes of visual consciousness, such as karma, the body, the eyeball that houses the eye sense faculty, light, and so on. For a presentation of the three conditions of a sense consciousness see chapter 2 in volume 2 of *Science and Philosophy in the Indian Buddhist Classics*.
495. Nāgārjuna, *Mūlamadhyamakakārikā*, 1.4. Toh 3824, 1b. Pd 57:4.
496. Within the context of the twelve links of dependent arising, the "actualizing cause" refers to *attachment*, *grasping*, and *existence*, depicted respectively as the eighth, ninth, and tenth links of dependent arising. These together constitute the condition that enables the "projecting cause" to ripen. The actualizing cause is also known as the "completing cause." Attachment and grasping are mental afflictions, while existence is a type of karma. The "projecting cause" refers to the mental affliction ignorance, which precedes and accompanies *conditioning action*, a type of karma. Ignorance is the first of the twelve links and is the root cause of cyclic existence, or *saṃsāra*.
497. Nāgārjuna, *Mūlamadhyamakakārikā*, 1.7. Toh 3824, 2a. Pd 57:4.
498. Nāgārjuna, *Mūlamadhyamakakārikā*, 1.8. Toh 3824, 2a. Pd 57:4.
499. Nāgārjuna, *Mūlamadhyamakakārikā*, 1.9. Toh 3824, 2a. Pd 57:4.
500. Nāgārjuna, *Mūlamadhyamakakārikā*, 1.10. Toh 3824, 2a. Pd 57:4.
501. Nāgārjuna, *Śūnyatāsaptati*, verse 3. Toh 3827, 24b. Pd 57:65.
502. Nāgārjuna, *Mūlamadhyamakakārikā*, 1.7. Toh 3824, 2a. Pd 57:4.
503. Nāgārjuna, *Śūnyatāsaptati*, verse 4. Toh 3827, 24b. Pd 57:65.
504. See for example Nāgārjuna, *Mūlamadhyamakakārikā*, 2.18, 6.4, 10.1–2, 21.10, 22.2, 27.15–16.
505. Nāgārjuna, *Mūlamadhyamakakārikā*, 18.1. Toh 3824, 10b. Pd 57:26.
506. Āryadeva, *Catuḥśataka*, 14.19. Toh 3846, 16a. Pd 57:815.

507. Nāgārjuna, *Mūlamadhyamakakārikā*, 2.1. Toh 3824, 2b. Pd 57:5.
508. Nāgārjuna, *Mūlamadhyamakakārikā*, 2.18–21. Toh 3824, 3a. Pd 57:6.
509. Bhāviveka, *Madhyamakahṛdayakārikā*, 3.27. Toh 3855, 4b. Pd 58:10.
510. Bhāviveka, *Tarkajvālā*, chap. 3. Toh 3856, 76a. Pd 57:998.
511. Bhāviveka, *Tarkajvālā*, chap. 3. Toh 3856, 60a. Pd 58:150.
512. *Daśasāhasrikāprajñāpāramitāsūtra*, chap. 32. Toh 11, 377a. Pd 32:676.
513. Bhāviveka, *Tarkajvālā*, chap. 3. Toh 3856, 60a. Pd 58:151.
514. See for example Āryadeva, *Catuḥśataka*, 14.19. Toh 3846, 16a. Pd 57:815: "When different things are scrutinized none of them have singularity. Since they have no singularity, they have no plurality either."
515. See for example Dharmakīrti, *Pramāṇavārttika*, 3.359. Toh 4210, 132a. Pd 97:558: "When things are analyzed they have no real nature ultimately, since they do not have either a singular or a manifold nature."
516. *Laṅkāvatārasūtra*, chap. 8. Toh 107, 184b. Pd 49:453.
517. Śāntarakṣita, *Madhyamakālaṃkāra*, verse 1. Toh 3884, 53a. Pd 62:895.
518. Kamalaśīla, *Madhyamakāloka*. Toh 3887, 218b. Pd 62:1323.
519. The above-mentioned inferential reason under consideration is: "The *subject*, things posited by our own and others' systems, do not exist ultimately by virtue of inherent nature, because they do not exist as truly one or as truly many—for example, like a reflection."
520. See the previous note for the reason under consideration here.
521. Śāntarakṣita, *Madhyamakālaṃkāra*, verse 2. Toh 3884, 53a. Pd 62:895.
522. Śāntarakṣita, *Madhyamakālaṃkāra*, verse 3. Toh 3884, 53a. Pd 62:895.
523. Śāntarakṣita, *Madhyamakālaṃkāra*, verse 9. Toh 3884, 53a. Pd 62:896.
524. Śāntarakṣita, *Madhyamakālaṃkāra*, verse 10ab. Toh 3884, 53a. Pd 62:896.
525. Śāntarakṣita, *Madhyamakālaṃkāra*, verse 10cd. Toh 3884, 53a. Pd 62:896.
526. Śāntarakṣita, *Madhyamakālaṃkāra*, verses 11–13. Toh 3884, 53a. Pd 62:896.
527. The term *rnam pa* (Skt. *ākāra*) is translated as "image" here in the context of perceptual cognition, where under the influence of its objective condition, the cognition bears an image in the likeness of its observed object.
528. Śāntarakṣita, *Madhyamakālaṃkāra*, verse 16. Toh 3884, 53a. Pd 62:896.
529. Śāntarakṣita, *Madhyamakālaṃkāra*, verses 22–23. Toh 3884, 53b. Pd 62:897.
530. Śāntarakṣita, *Madhyamakālaṃkāra*, verse 24. Toh 3884, 53b. Pd 62:897.
531. Śāntarakṣita, *Madhyamakālaṃkāra*, verse 25. Toh 3884, 53b. Pd 62:897.
532. Śāntarakṣita, *Madhyamakālaṃkāra*, verse 32. Toh 3884, 54a. Pd 62:898.
533. Śāntarakṣita, *Madhyamakālaṃkāra*, verse 35. Toh 3884, 54a. Pd 62:898.
534. Śāntarakṣita, *Madhyamakālaṃkāra*, verse 46. Toh 3884, 54a. Pd 62:899.
535. Śāntarakṣita, *Madhyamakālaṃkāra*, verse 49. Toh 3884, 54b. Pd 62:899.
536. Śāntarakṣita, *Madhyamakālaṃkāra*, verses 50–51. Toh 3884, 54b. Pd 62:899.
537. Śāntarakṣita, *Madhyamakālaṃkāra*, verse 52. Toh 3884, 54b. Pd 62:900.
538. Śāntarakṣita, *Madhyamakālaṃkāra*, verse 53. Toh 3884, 54b. Pd 62:900.
539. The inferential reason under consideration was presented in the early part of this section: "The *subject*, things posited by our own and others' systems, do not

exist ultimately by virtue of inherent nature, because they do not exist as truly one or as truly many—for example, like a reflection." The reason ascertained to be the attribute of the subject has two facets, which are the last two of the four points highlighted in that context: ascertainment of the lack of true singularity and ascertainment of the lack of true plurality. The former has been dealt with above and we are now addressing the latter.

540. Śāntarakṣita, *Madhyamakālaṃkāra*, verse 61. Toh 3884, 55a. Pd 62:900.
541. Śāntarakṣita, *Madhyamakālaṃkāra*, verse 62. Toh 3884, 55a. Pd 62:900.
542. Kamalaśīla, *Madhyamakāloka*. Toh 3887, 202b. Pd 62:1283.
543. Jñānagarbha, *Satyadvayavibhaṅga*, verse 14. Toh 3881, 2a. Pd 62:756.
544. Kamalaśīla, *Madhyamakāloka*. Toh 3887, 205a. Pd 62:1290.
545. Nāgārjuna, *Mūlamadhyamakakārikā*, 22.1. Toh 3824, 3a. Pd 57:31.
546. Candrakīrti, *Madhyamakāvatāra*, 6.120. Toh 3861, 212a. Pd 60:537.
547. Candrakīrti, *Madhyamakāvatārabhāṣya*, on 6.126. Toh 3862, 296a. Pd 60:783.
548. Candrakīrti, *Madhyamakāvatārabhāṣya*, on 6.142. Toh 3862, 302a. Pd 60:797.
549. Candrakīrti, *Madhyamakāvatārabhāṣya*, on 6.143. Toh 3862, 302a. Pd 60:798.
550. The notion of "contradictory" in Buddhist philosophy means that there is nothing that instantiates both items. It does not concern language per se. Here, it is impossible for something to be both *that which is imputed on the basis "B"* and *the basis "B" on which it is imputed.*
551. For an account of the four primary elements (earth, water, wind, and fire) and the derivative forms that arise from their accumulation (the five sensory objects and the five sense faculties), see chapter 9 in volume 1 of *Science and Philosophy in the Indian Buddhist Classics*.
552. Candrakīrti, *Madhyamakāvatārabhāṣya*, on 6.135. Toh 3862, 300a. Pd 60:792.
553. Candrakīrti, *Madhyamakāvatāra*, 6.152. Toh 3861, 211b. Pd 60:536.
554. Candrakīrti, *Madhyamakāvatāra*, 6.136. Toh 3861, 211a. Pd 60:577. This is not the version in the Pedurma root text but matches what appears in the autocommentary.
555. Candrakīrti, *Madhyamakāvatāra*, 6.153. Toh 3861, 211b. Pd 60:579 (as above).
556. Candrakīrti, *Madhyamakāvatāra*, 6.115. Toh 3861, 209b. Pd 60:532.
557. Candrakīrti, *Catuḥśatakaṭīkā*, chap. 14. Toh 3865, 220b. Pd 60:1452.
558. *Anavataptanāgarājaparipṛcchāsūtra*. Toh 156, 230b. Pd 58:598.
559. See part 6 below, page 455.
560. Śāntideva, *Bodhisattvacaryāvatāra*, 9.138. Toh 3871, 36a. Pd 61:1029.
561. Nāgārjuna, *Mūlamadhyamakakārikā*, 15.10. Toh 3824, 9a. Pd 57:21.
562. Buddhapālita, *Buddhapālitamūlamadhyamakavṛtti*, chap. 15. Toh 3842, 226b. Pd 57:588.
563. Buddhapālita, *Buddhapālitamūlamadhyamakavṛtti*, chap. 18. Toh 3842, 244a. Pd 57:652.
564. Candrakīrti, *Prasannapadā*, on 24.11. Toh 3860, 164. Pd 60:399.
565. Āryadeva, *Catuḥśataka*, 14.25. Toh 3846, 16b. Pd 57:815.
566. The term we translate into English as *nature* (*rang bzhin*, Skt. *svabhāva*) has at

least three meanings: conventional nature, which mainly refers to a thing's conventional characteristics; ultimate nature, which refers to a thing's emptiness of inherent existence; and inherent nature, which is not an attribute of anything at all because it does not exist—nevertheless, everything appears to exist by its own inherent nature to sentient beings' conventional consciousness and is grasped to exist inherently by an innate mind of ignorance apprehending it. Inherent nature is the object of negation of reasoning that is being discussed in the present context. Neither ultimate nature nor inherent nature can possess any of the three attributes: being fabricated, dependent on others, or able to change from one state to another. Nāgārjuna's verses cited here are interpreted in Tsongkhapa's *Steps on the Path to Enlightenment* as referring to the ultimate nature. Therefore the Sanskrit term *svabhāva* is translated here simply as "nature." For further details, see Sopa and Rochard 2017, 244–45.

567. Nāgārjuna, *Mūlamadhyamakakārikā*, 15.2cd. Toh 3824, 8b. Pd 57:21.
568. Nāgārjuna, *Mūlamadhyamakakārikā*, 15.8. Toh 3824, 9a. Pd 57:21.
569. Candrakīrti, *Prasannapadā*, on 15.2. Toh 3860, 89a. Pd 60:216.
570. Nāgārjuna, *Mūlamadhyamakakārikā*, 15.1. Toh 3824, 8b. Pd 57:20.
571. *Lokadharaparipṛcchāsūtra*, chap. 7. Toh 174, 59a. Pd 60:143.
572. Candrakīrti, *Catuḥśatakaṭīkā*, chap. 12. Toh 3865, 190b. Pd 60:1381.
573. Candrakīrti, *Catuḥśatakaṭīkā*, chap. 14. Toh 3865, 220b. Pd 60:1452.
574. The term *svalakṣaṇa* will mostly be translated as "intrinsic characteristics" or "intrinsic character" in the context of referring to the subtle object of negation in the Prāsaṅgika Madhyamaka system.
575. For further discussion see chapter 15 of Tsongkhapa 2006.
576. *Upāliparipṛcchāsūtra*. Toh 68, 129b. Pd 43:358.
577. Candrakīrti, *Catuḥśatakaṭīkā*, chap. 8. Toh 3865, 133a. Pd 60:1249.
578. Nāgārjuna, *Yuktiṣaṣṭikā*, verse 50. Toh 3825, 22a. Pd 60:995 (as cited in Candrakīrti's commentary).
579. Nāgārjuna, *Vigrahavyāvartanī*, verse 29. Toh 3828, 28a. Pd 57:77.
580. Āryadeva, *Catuḥśataka*, 16.25. Toh 3846, 18a. Pd 57:820.
581. Candrakīrti, *Madhyamakāvatāra*, 6.173. Toh 3861, 212b. Pd 60.582.
582. Bhāviveka, *Tarkajvālā*, chap. 3. Toh 3856, 60b. Pd 58:152.
583. Bhāviveka, *Tarkajvālā*, chap. 3. Toh 3856, 60b. Pd 58:152.
584. In this context, *rang gi mtshan nyid* is translated as "intrinsic characteristics" or "intrinsic character" to indicate that it refers to the subtle object of negation within the Prāsaṅgika Madhyamaka system.
585. The special technique employed by Nāgārjuna and his followers is to focus on the relationship between things, such as: the destroyer, the act of destroying, and the object destroyed; the fire, the burning, and the object burned; the producer, the act of producing, and the object produced. If these are inherently existent, then they either really contact each other or do not make any contact at all. When we analyze whether a refutation comes in contact or lacks contact with what it refutes, we find that it does not exist in either way—because this

analysis is searching for inherent contact or the lack of it. So a refutation does not exist ultimately. However, this analysis does not negate the existence of a refutation in general.

It is well known that the tradition of Jé Tsongkhapa and his followers explains that the Mādhyamika have their own assertions. An earlier Tibetan Madhyamaka master, Mabja Jangchup Tsöndrü, also said it was incorrect to maintain that the Mādhyamika only refute their opponents' positions, for he says in *Ornament of Correct Explanations of Fundamental Treatise on the Middle Way*, in Collected Works of the Kadam, 36.13b: "Moreover, since by accepting others' positions to be refuted entails accepting the three—the refuted object, the refuting agent, and the act of refuting—how could we not have our own assertions? Therefore it is utterly senseless to say, 'We refute the position of others but do not have any position of our own,' which is also described many times in the scriptures as a 'refutation only.'"

586. Candrakīrti, *Yuktiṣaṣṭikāvṛtti*. Toh 3864, 27b. Pd 60:995.
587. Candrakīrti, *Yuktiṣaṣṭikāvṛtti*. Toh 3864, 27b. Pd 60:995.
588. Nāgārjuna, *Vigrahavyāvartanīvṛtti*. Toh 3832, 128a. Pd 57:348.
589. Nāgārjuna, *Vigrahavyāvartanīvṛtti*. Toh 3832, 128b. Pd 57:349.
590. Candrakīrti, *Prasannapadā*, chap. 18. Toh 3860, 117b. Pd 60:287.
591. Candrakīrti, *Prasannapadā*, chap. 18. Toh 3860, 118a. Pd 60:288.
592. Nāgārjuna, *Śūnyatāsaptati*, verse 70. Toh 3827, 26b. Pd 57:71.
593. Nāgārjuna, *Mūlamadhyamakakārikā*, 24.1. Toh 3824, 15b. Pd 57.35.
594. Nāgārjuna, *Mūlamadhyamakakārikā*, 24.7. Toh 3824, 14b. Pd 57:36.
595. Nāgārjuna, *Mūlamadhyamakakārikā*, 24.16. Toh 3824, 15a. Pd 57:36.
596. Here, "refutation only" (*sun ci phyin du rgol ba*, Skt. *vitaṇḍā*) is a form of sophistry. It is listed as the twelfth among the sixteen categories of logic presented in the *Nyāyasūtra*—see page 154 in volume 3 of the present series (where it is translated as "cavil"). These sixteen categories of logic are also identified by Nāgārjuna in his *Vaidalyasūtra*—see page 298 in volume 2 of the present series (where it is translated as "refutation").
597. Candrakīrti, *Madhyamakāvatāra*, 6.172. Toh 3861, 212b. Pd 60.581.
598. Nāgārjuna, *Vigrahavyāvartanī*, verse 26. Toh 3828, 27b. Pd 57:76.
599. Nāgārjuna, *Vigrahavyāvartanīvṛtti*, on verse 23. Toh 3832, 127a. Pd 57:345.
600. Nāgārjuna, *Mūlamadhyamakakārikā*, 1.1. Toh 3824, 1a. Pd 57:3.
601. Candrakīrti, *Prasannapadā*, chap. 1. Toh 3860, 5a. Pd 60:11. See also note 458.
602. *Trisaṃvaranirdeśasūtra*, Toh 45 Kangyur, dkon brtsegs, *ka*, 94b, as identified in Tillemans 2016, 58. A similar passage is found in the Pali canon in Saṃyutta Nikāya III 22.94, where an important qualifier "the wise in the world," is found, making the text read: "A proponent of the Dhamma does not dispute with anyone in the world. Of that which the wise in the world agree upon as not existing, I too say it does not exist. And of that which the wise in the world agree upon as existing, I too say that it exists" (Bodhi 2000, 949).

603. Buddhapālita *Buddhapālitamūlamadhyamakavṛtti*, chap. 18. Toh 3842, 255b. Pd 57:653.
604. Candrakīrti, *Madhyamakāvatāra*, 6.81. Toh 3861, 208a. Pd 60:528.
605. Nāgārjuna, *Vigrahavyāvartanī*, verse 28. Toh 3828, 28a. Pd 57:77.
606. Candrakīrti, *Madhyamakāvatāra*, 11.53. Toh 3861, 218b. Pd 60:595.
607. Bhāviveka, *Prajñāpradīpamūlamadhyamakavṛtti*, chap. 1. Toh 3853, 59a. Pd 57:915.
608. Bhāviveka, *Prajñāpradīpamūlamadhyamakavṛtti*, chap. 13. Toh 3853, 153a. Pd 57:1180.
609. Candrakīrti, *Prasannapadā*, chap. 1. Toh 3860, 5b. Pd 60:12.
610. Candrakīrti, *Prasannapadā*, chap. 1. Toh 3860, 6a. Pd 60:13.
611. Candrakīrti, *Prasannapadā*, chap. 1. Toh 3860, 8b. Pd 60:19.
612. This is the example of an autonomous inference used explicitly or implicitly throughout this section discussing the debates between Bhāviveka and Candrakīrti. It sometimes appears in an abbreviated form, such as: "The eye faculty does not arise from self, because it exists."
613. Candrakīrti, *Prasannapadā*, chap. 1. Toh 3860, 8b. Pd 60:19.
614. Candrakīrti, *Prasannapadā*, chap. 1. Toh 3860, 8b. Pd 60:19.
615. Candrakīrti, *Prasannapadā*, chap. 1. Toh 3860, 8b. Pd 60:19.
616. Candrakīrti, *Prasannapadā*, chap. 1. Toh 3860, 9a. Pd 60:20.
617. If one of the two parties simply does not know the subject or does not know that the reason is an attribute of the subject, the syllogism cannot function to prove its thesis. One of the basic elements of understanding that is required is absent so the further understanding cannot be generated. This is called "the fault of not establishing the reason as a property of the subject," or more briefly, "the fault that the subject is unestablished." A syllogism also succumbs to this fault when the subject is not established in common by both the proponent and the opponent. Prāsaṅgika and the lower schools do not agree about what it means for a subject to be held in common. According to the lower schools, both the proponent and the opponent must similarly establish the subject by valid knowledge that is unmistaken with regard to its inherent nature. However, Prāsaṅgika do not accept that anything has an inherent nature—so do not agree with the lower schools about what constitutes valid knowledge.
618. Bhāviveka does not state the inference with the applied qualification to be: "The conventional eye faculty does not arise ultimately." Rather, he states it to be: "The eye faculty do not arise ultimately."
619. The Sāṅkhya opponent does not accept the eye faculty to be conventional—i.e., merely imputed by convention—but rather to be substantially existent.
620. Candrakīrti, *Prasannapadā*, chap. 1. Toh 3860, 9a. Pd 60:20.
621. With regard to the opponent in this debate, see note 622 below.
622. Modern scholarship suggests that the opponent here is the Mīmāṃsā school rather than the Sāṅkhya school as stated in the above commentary. Accord-

ingly, these two debates concern the Buddhists versus the Mīmāṃsaka and the Vaiśeṣika versus the Mīmāṃsaka. See MacDonald 2015, 106nn218–19.

623. Candrakīrti, *Prasannapadā*, chap. 1. Toh 3860, 9a. Pd 60:21.

624. Candrakīrti, *Prasannapadā*, chap. 1. Toh 3860, 9b. Pd 60:21.

625. Candrakīrti is setting out to prove that Bhāviveka's view is self-contradictory. He argues that because Bhāviveka accepts the negation of arising as the predicate of the thesis, he implicitly accepts that the subject does not ultimately exist. Any subject such as an eye sense faculty or a visible form is established only by a conventional consciousness, such as a visual consciousness, so it is something found only by a mistaken consciousness influenced by ignorance. Bhāviveka must admit this because he accepts "does not ultimately arise" as the predicate of the thesis based on such a subject. If those subjects were ultimately existent, it would be contradictory to use them as the basis of a proof that such things do not ultimately arise. It is impossible to prove the predicate "does not ultimately arise" as an attribute of a subject that ultimately exists.

626. The main issue here in this debate between Svātantrika and Prāsaṅgika concerns the appearance of the object as inherently existent to the mind perceiving it. Is the mind perceiving its object as inherently existent mistaken or unmistaken regarding that appearance? More crucially, can a mind be valid regarding its object even if it is mistaken regarding its object appearing as inherently existent? Bhāviveka considers that a valid sense consciousness is unmistaken regarding its object and its object's inherent nature, for he accepts that its object does exist inherently, just as it appears. But according to Candrakīrti, forms and colors that appear to a visual consciousness do not exist inherently as they appear, so these consciousnesses are false perceivers. Although a visual consciousness that sees a color or a shape may be valid, what appears to such a consciousness is false because it appears to be inherently existent—yet it is not so in reality. The only unmistaken consciousness within the continuum of a sentient being is the direct realization of *śūnyatā*. So the only object found by an unmistaken consciousness is the ultimate truth itself.

627. Here, being qualified as "true" means being found by an unmistaken cognition and being qualified as "false" means being found by a mistaken cognition. In a debate between the Prāsaṅgika and their opponents, both parties agree that there is nothing—forms, eyes, and so on—validly established in general that is not established either by an unmistaken or mistaken cognition. The Prāsaṅgika consider it is established by a mistaken cognition, which is not acceptable to their opponents; their opponents consider it is established by an unmistaken cognition, which is not acceptable to the Prāsaṅgika. Neither party accepts the other's notion of validity, and neither party accepts that there is any third alternative—a general notion of validity that is neither mistaken nor unmistaken. For further discussion about Candrakīrti's critique of Bhāviveka's notion of valid cognition, see Sopa and Rochard 2017, 359–404.

628. Candrakīrti, *Prasannapadā*, chap. 1. Toh 3860, 11b. Pd 60:20.

629. The Tibetan master Taktsang Lotsāwa seems to say that there is a difference between Svātantrika and Prāsaṅgika in terms of the view. In contrast, two Sakya masters, Gorampa and Shākya Chokden, as well as later masters of the Nyingma or Early Translation school, such as Ju Mipham, do not say there is a difference between Svātantrika and Prāsaṅgika in terms of subtlety of the view. However, they do say that they differ in terms of whether they accept autonomous inferences, whether they accept valid cognition, and whether they have assertions within their own tradition.
630. Bhāviveka, *Prajñāpradīpamūlamadhyamakavṛtti*, chap. 15. Toh 3853, 242a. Pd 57:1410.
631. Bhāviveka, *Tarkajvālā*, chap. 5. Toh 3856, 209b. Pd 58:510.
632. Bhāviveka, *Tarkajvālā*, chap. 5. Toh 3856, 207a. Pd 58:504.
633. See chapter 8 of the present volume.
634. Jñānagarbha, *Satyadvayavibhaṅgavṛtti*. Toh 3882, 5b. Pd 62:767.
635. In each case it is the main object that is being referred to. The main object of a perceptual cognition is its appearing object, whereas the main object of a conceptual cognition is its object as cognized, or "conceived object." In the case of a conceptual cognition, the appearing object is a universal image, not the object itself, so its main object can never be its appearing object. However, in the case of a perceptual cognition, there is some debate about whether its appearing object may also be its object as cognized (not conceived object, which only belongs to the realm of conceptual cognition).
636. In other words, everything existent is necessarily conventionally imputed, but not everything conventionally imputed is necessarily existent. See Tsongkhapa, *Essence of True Eloquence: Distinguishing the Provisional and the Definitive Meaning*, 73b. For an English translation, see Thurman 1984, 296.
637. This means that the two Madhyamaka systems have adopted different criteria of existence.
638. *Pratītyasamutpādasūtra*. Toh 212, 125b. Pd 62:343.
639. This citation is presented in volume 1, 440n54.
640. Candrakīrti, *Prasannapadā*, chap. 1. Toh 3860, 2b–3b. Pd 60:5–7. For a full explanation of the exact Sanskrit derivation of the term *pratītyasamutpāda* refer to MacDonald 2015, 18–39.
641. Vasubandhu, *Pratītyasamutpādādivibhaṅganirdeśa*, chap. 1. Toh 3995, 2b. Pd 66:719.
642. Candrakīrti, *Prasannapadā*, chap. 1. Toh 3860, 4a. Pd 60:8.
643. Guṇamati, *Pratītyasamutpādādivibhaṅganirdeśaṭīkā*, chap. 1. Toh 3996, 72a. Pd 66:906.
644. Candrakīrti, *Prasannapadā*, chap. 1. Toh 3860, 3a. Pd 60:6. For a discussion about the Tibetan translation of Candrakīrti's quotes of Bhāviveka's words such as this, see MacDonald 2015, 27. In the analysis that appears in footnotes to this discussion, the symbol √ stands for the root of the Sanskrit verb.

645. Guṇamati, *Pratītyasamutpādādivibhaṅganirdeśaṭīkā*, chap. 1. Toh 3996, 72a. Pd 66:906.
646. Buddhapālita, *Buddhapālitamūlamadhyamakavṛtti*, chap. 8. Toh 3842, 201a. Pd 57:547.
647. Nāgārjuna, *Mūlamadhyamakakārikā*, 8.12–13. Toh 3824, 6a. Pd 57:14.
648. Candrakīrti, *Madhyamakāvatārabhāṣya*, chap. 6. Toh 3862, 309a. Pd 60:815.
649. Buddhapālita, *Buddhapālitamūlamadhyamakavṛtti*, chap. 8. Toh 3842, 202a. Pd 57:550.
650. Candrakīrti, *Prasannapadā*, chap. 8. Toh 3860, 65b. Pd 60:155.
651. Vasubandhu, *Abhidharmakośabhāṣya*, chap. 3. Toh 4090, 125b. Pd 79:310.
652. Asaṅga, *Abhidharmasamuccaya*, chap. 1. Toh 4049, 65a. Pd 76:167. The twelve links of dependent arising involves a forward direction and a reverse direction, each of which may be contemplated in terms of the process of defilement (based on the functioning of ignorance, the first link) and the process of purification (based on the cessation of ignorance). The third link, consciousness, is divided into two parts: causal consciousness and resultant consciousness. The terms *dharma sphere* and *dharma expanse* seem to be synonymous and may be defined differently in different traditions. No explanation has been provided here.
653. The expression "this mere conditionality itself," or "this mere conditionality," not only appears in Prāsaṅgika Madhyamaka treatises such as Candrakīrti's *Prasannapadā* and *Madhyamakāvatārabhāṣya* but also in the treatises of the lower schools, such as Haribhadra's *Abhisamayālaṃkāravṛtti*, Dharmapāla Suvarṇadvīpa's *Commentary Illuminating the Difficult Points of the Ornament for Clear Knowledge* (*Abhisamayālaṅkāravṛttiduravabodhālokaṭīkā*), Devendrabuddhi's *Pramāṇavārttikapañjikā*, Kamalaśīla's *Tattvasaṅgrahapañjikā*, and so forth.
654. Nāgārjuna, *Ratnāvalī*, 1.52. Toh 4158, 108b. Pd 96:293.
655. It is held as such by a specific type of conceptual cognition rooted in the identity view (Skt. *satkāyadṛṣṭi*).
656. Candrakīrti, *Madhyamakāvatāra*, 6.35. Toh 3861, 205a. Pd 60:527.
657. Nāgārjuna, *Ratnāvalī*, 1.99. Toh 4158, 110b. Pd 96:297. The first lines of the Sanskrit text in translation read: "Since it is the mere absence of form, space is merely a designation" (*rūpasyābhāvamātratvād ākāśaṃ nāmamātrakam*). See Dunne and McClintock 1997, 24n30.
658. Buddhapālita, *Buddhapālitamūlamadhyamakavṛtti*, chap. 24. Toh 3842, 271a. Pd 57:720–21.
659. Candrakīrti, *Prasannapadā*, chap. 24, on verse 18. Toh 3860, 167. Pd 60:406.
660. Nāgārjuna, *Yuktiṣaṣṭikā*, verse 44. Toh 3825, 22a. Pd 57:55.
661. Nāgārjuna, *Lokātītastava*, verses 21–22. Toh 1120, 22a. Pd 57:55.
662. *Bodhisattvapiṭakasūtra*, chap. 4. Toh 56, 38a. Pd 41:96.
663. Nāgārjuna, *Mūlamadhyamakakārikā*, 24.14. Toh 3824, 15a. Pd 57:36.
664. Though composed by the rishi Agniveśa; see chapter 6 in volume 3 of *Science and Philosophy in the Indian Buddhist Classics.*

665. These sixteen categories, stated in *Nyāya Sūtra* 1.1.1, are clearly explained in the presentation of Nyāya philosophy in volume 3 of *Science and Philosophy in the Indian Buddhist Classics*. They are classified in terms of their function by Ganeri 2003, 416: "The first two items are the various methods of knowing and the domain of knowables. They constitute the Nyāya epistemology and metaphysics. The next seven are the theoretical components in the process of critical inquiry . . . The final seven are terms of art in the theory of debate."
666. The five limbs or steps in a proof statement (or syllogism) are as follows: (1) proposition (*pratijñā*): the preliminary statement of the thesis to be proved; (2) reason (*hetu*): the statement of the reason or evidence; (3) exemplification (*udāharaṇa*): the citation of a familiar example to illustrate the universal relation between the reason and the predicate; (4) application (*upanaya*): the application of the universal case to the present case; and (5) conclusion (*nigamana*): the assertion of the thesis again as proven or established. These five limbs are presented in the Nyāya tradition but may also be found in other traditions, such as the Caraka as mentioned earlier.
667. Jamyang Shepa, *Great Exposition of Tenets*, 76. Sanskrit titles not provided in that work.
668. Īśvarakṛṣṇa, *Sāṅkhyakārikā*, verse 4.
669. Kapila, *Sāṅkhyasūtra*, 1.100.
670. The four forms of rationality are presented in volume 2 of *Science and Philosophy in the Indian Buddhist Classics*, pp. 293–97.
671. See pages 12–13 of the translator's introduction above for further discussion on this text.
672. Hajime Nakamura writes: "Vasubandhu is said to have written four *logical works*: (1) *Vādavidhi*, (2) *Vādavidhāna*, (3) *Vādakauśala* and (4) *Tarkaśāstra*. . . . The *Rtsod-pa sgrub-pa* which is refuted in the *Pramāṇasamuccaya* must be the same as the *Vādavidhi*" (Nakamura 1987, 273). However, these texts are no longer extant in either Sanskrit or Tibetan.
673. No record of such a text has been found in any other source.
674. Among Dignāga's texts listed here, those no longer extant are provided with their Sanskrit titles but do not appear in the bibliography.
675. This is the fifteenth among the sixteen categories of logic listed in the *Nyāyasūtra*. It is sometimes translated as "self-defeating objection" or "self-confuting reply."
676. The "trimodal definition" refers to the three modes that constitute the criteria of a correct reason or evidence, where the evidence is (1) an attribute of the subject, (2) the positive pervasion, and (3) the negative pervasion. For a detailed presentation of the three modes and the structure of inferential reasoning in general, see volume 2, part 5 of *Science and Philosophy in the Indian Buddhist Classics*.
677. See volume 2 of the present series (pp. 286–87): "If the evidence is not 'accompanied' by the predicate, then the evidence simply cannot occur."
678. Several individuals named Mahāmati appear in Buddhist literature. There is

no reason to suppose that the individual mentioned here is the same as the one mentioned above.

679. Dharmakīrti, *Pramāṇaviniścaya*, chap. 1. Toh 4211, 152b. Pd 97:614.
680. Dharmakīrti, *Nyāyabindu*, chap. 1. Toh 4212, 231a. Pd 97:812.
681. Vinītadeva, *Nyāyabinduṭīkā*, chap. 1. Toh 4230, 3b. Pd 105:7.
682. Mokṣākaragupta, *Tarkabhāṣā*, chap. 1. Toh 4264, 338a. Pd 106:937.
683. Kamalaśīla, *Tattvasaṅgrahapañjikā*, chap. 27. [Jha, 22]. Toh 4267, 90b. Pd 107:1209.
684. Dignāga, *Pramāṇasamuccayavṛtti*, on 1.2. Toh 4204, 14b. Pd 97:58.
685. Dharmakīrti, *Pramāṇavārttika*, 3.1. Toh 4210, 118b. Pd 97:526.
686. Dharmakīrti, *Pramāṇavārttika*, 3.63–64ab. Toh 4210, 121a. Pd 97:513.
687. Dharmakīrti, *Pramāṇavārttika*, 3.1b, 3.2. Toh 4210, 118b. Pd 97:530.
688. Prajñākaragupta, *Pramāṇavārttikālaṅkāra*, chap. 2. Toh 4221, 155b. Pd 99:1155.
689. Prajñākaragupta, *Pramāṇavārttikālaṅkāra*, chap. 2. Toh 4221, 157a. Pd 99:1158.
690. Dharmakīrti, *Pramāṇavārttika*, 2.1. Toh 4210, 107b. Pd 97:500.
691. Prajñākaragupta, *Pramāṇavārttikālaṅkāra*, chap. 2. Toh 4221, 2a. Pd 99:770.
692. Devendrabuddhi, *Pramāṇavārttikapañjikā*, chap. 2. Toh 4217, 1b. Pd 98:3.
693. Dharmakīrti, *Pramāṇavārttika*, 2.1. Toh 4210, 107b. Pd 97:500.
694. Dharmakīrti, *Pramāṇavārttika*, 2.5. Toh 4210, 107b. Pd 97:500.
695. The observed object of a conceptual cognition is a universal, a generic mental image, whereas the conceived object is the actual thing itself, the engaged object or object of application.
696. Dharmottara, *Pramāṇaparīkṣā*. Toh 4249, 221b. Pd 106:600.
697. Dharmottara, *Pramāṇaparīkṣā*. Toh 4249, 224a. Pd 106:606–07. Citing Dharmakīrti, *Pramāṇavārttika*, 3.56ab.
698. Dharmottara, *Pramāṇaparīkṣā*. Toh 4249, 224b. Pd 106:607–09.
699. Dharmottara, *Pramāṇaparīkṣā*. Toh 4248, 205b. Pd 106:556.
700. For example, *Pramāṇavārttika* says, "Direct perception does not ascertain anything," and *Pramāṇaviniścaya* says, "How could perception be classified other than as nonascertaining in nature?"
701. Dignāga, *Pramāṇasamuccayavṛtti*, chap. 1. Toh 4204, 21b. Pd 97:75.
702. Dignāga, *Pramāṇasamuccayavṛtti*, chap. 1. Toh 4204, 19a. Pd 97:69. This definition of perception is the one found in the *Vaiśeṣikasūtra*; see Hattori 1968, 134n4.1.
703. Dignāga, *Pramāṇasamuccayavṛtti*, chap. 1. Toh 4204, 2b. Pd 97:33.
704. Dignāga, *Pramāṇasamuccayavṛtti*, chap. 1. Toh 4204, 25a. Pd 97:83.
705. Kamalaśīla, *Tattvasaṅgrahapañjikā*, chap. 5. Toh 4267, 185a. Pd 107:583.
706. Dignāga, *Pramāṇasamuccaya*, 1.3cd. Toh 4203, 1b. Pd 97:3.
707. Dharmakīrti, *Pramāṇaviniścaya*, chap. 1. Toh 4211, 154a. Pd 97:618.
708. Dignāga, *Pramāṇasamuccayavṛtti*, chap. 1. Toh 4204, 16a. Pd 97:256.
709. Dharmottara, *Nyāyabinduṭīkā*. Toh 4231, 5b. Pd 105:256.
710. This twofold categorization of conceptual cognition according to purpose—conceptual cognition associating a word and conceptual cognition associating

a referent—is presented in volume 2 of *Science and Philosophy in the Indian Buddhist Classics*, p. 70.

711. Dharmakīrti, *Pramāṇavārttika,* 3.123. Toh 4210, 123a. Pd 97:10.
712. Dharmakīrti, *Pramāṇavārttika,* 3.124–25. Toh 4210, 123a. Pd 97:537.
713. Dharmakīrti, *Pramāṇavārttika,* 3.126. Toh 4210, 123a. Pd 97:537.
714. Dharmakīrti, *Pramāṇavārttika,* 3.132. Toh 4210, 123b. Pd 97:537.
715. Vinītadeva, *Nyāyabinduṭīkā.* Toh 4230, 5a. Pd 104:11.
716. Vinītadeva, *Nyāyabinduṭīkā.* Toh 4230, 5b. Pd 105:12.
717. Vinītadeva, *Nyāyabinduṭīkā.* Toh 4230, 4b. Pd 105:10.
718. Vinītadeva, *Nyāyabinduṭīkā.* Toh 4230, 4b. Pd 105:12.
719. Dharmakīrti, *Nyāyabindu*, chap. 1. Toh 4212, 231a. Pd 97:812.
720. Refer to volume 2, part 1, pp. 78–82.
721. Jitāri, *Bālāvatāratarka*, chap. 1. Toh 4263, 326a. Pd 106:902.
722. Dharmottara, *Nyāyabinduṭīkā.* Toh 4231, 5b. Pd 104:13.
723. Dignāga, *Pramāṇasamuccaya*, 1.4. Toh 4203, 1a. Pd 97:3.
724. Although this sūtra passage is very famous, it does not appear to be identified in any of the treatises on valid cognition. A text considered to be a source for categorizing direct perception is Jñānavajra's *Heart Ornament of the Tathāgata: Commentary on the Descent into Laṅkā Sūtra*, which states: "Thus the Tathāgata spoke: 'O bhikṣus, the consciousness that cognizes visual form is of two kinds—the visual and the mental that arises following it.'" Jñānavajra, *Laṅkāvatārasūtravṛtti-tathāgatahṛdayālaṅkāra*, chap. 2. Toh 4019, 65a. Pd 70:155.
725. What it means to be the "same entity but conceptually distinct" (*ngo bo gcig dang ldog pa tha dad*) can be understood easily as follows. For example, one speaks of "an atom's impermanence," where the quality impermanence is conceptually distinct from the atom, but the atom and its impermanence are actually the same individual entity.
726. Dharmottara, *Pramāṇaviniścayaṭīkā*, chap. 1. Toh 4229, 86a. Pd 104:963.
727. Śubhagupta, *Bāhyārthasiddhi*, verse 94. Toh 4244, 192b. Pd 106:517.
728. Kamalaśīla, *Nyāyabindupūrvapakṣasaṃkṣipta.* Toh 4232, 92b. Pd 105:260.
729. Bhāviveka, *Madhyamakahṛdaya*, verse 19. Toh 3855, 20b. Pd 58:48.
730. Bhāviveka, *Tarkajvālā*, chap. 5. Toh 3856, 205a. Pd 58:500.
731. Jñānagarbha, *Satyadvayavibhaṅga*, verse 6. Toh 3881, 1a. Pd 62:756.
732. Candrakīrti, *Prasannapadā*, chap. 1. Toh 3860, 25a. Pd 60:58.
733. Nāgārjuna, *Vigrahavyāvartanī*, verse 40. Toh 3828, 28a. Pd 58:78.
734. *Laṅkāvatārasūtra*, chap. 9. Toh 107, 179b. Pd 49:441.
735. The term "bipartite" is used here because "consciousness itself is proved to have two parts" (*cha gnyis dang ldan pa*), as stated in the above section on Śāntarakṣita's reasoning of being neither one nor many (see page 283).
736. Nāgārjuna, *Mūlamadhyamakakārikā*, 7.12. Toh 3824, 5a. Pd 57:11.
737. Śāntideva, *Bodhisattvacaryāvatāra*, 9.23. Toh 3871, 31b. Pd 61:1019.
738. The "subjective aspect" or "subject-image" (*'dzin rnam*) is an appearance of the "objective aspect" or "object-image" (*gzung rnam*) within a cognition. The

"objective aspect" is considered by some systems to be an internal representation of the object, thus in the nature of cognition, and by other systems to be a transparent revealing of the external object itself, thus not in the nature of cognition. In the latter context, the term *image* may be deemed inappropriate, depending on whether it is taken to be transparent or opaque.

739. To say that reflexive awareness is "oriented exclusively inward" seems preferable to saying that it is "directed exclusively inward." This is because, although both are accurate translations of the Tibetan (*kha nang kho na la phyogs*), the latter implies that reflexive awareness is a subject apprehending an object (namely, itself), which does not allow for other possible interpretations of its nature and function. Consider, for example, the standpoint of Sakya Paṇḍita, expressed as follows by Georges Dreyfus: "Consciousness does not take itself as an object, but merely self-cognizes while being aware of other objects" (Dreyfus 1997, 403). So according to this view, the explanations of reflexive awareness as having an object are "metaphorical."

740. Dignāga, *Pramāṇasamuccayavṛtti*, chap. 1. Toh 4204, 16a. Pd 97:62.

741. This equivalence of the objective aspect of a sensory cognition and the sensory cognition itself is specifically a view of the Geluk school of Tibetan Buddhism. Some other schools consider that the direct object of perception is an appearance that is a representation of the object within awareness—what they call the "objective aspect." According to them, perception consists in a three-way relationship between the object, the objective aspect, and the subjective aspect, where the object causes the objective aspect to appear within the awareness, and this appearance is apprehended by the subjective aspect. But according to the Geluk system, the appearance of an object to perception is not a representation; it is the transparent revealing of the external object itself. Perception consists in just a two-way relationship between the object and the cognition of it, where the "objective aspect" is the cognition *qua* awareness of the object, and the "subjective aspect" is the cognition *qua* awareness of the subject. See Dreyfus 1997, 407–8.

742. Detailed analyses of this argument and its background can be found in Hattori 1968, 108n1.69, and Kellner 2010, 210–12. See also Yiannopoulos 2020, 500–501.

743. Dignāga, *Pramāṇasamuccayavṛtti*, chap. 1, on verse 11ab. Toh 4204, 16b. Pd 97:62.

744. The inquiry into a tripartite division, mentioned in the preceding verse 10 that is not quoted here, concerns the object of valid cognition (Skt. *prameya*), which is the appearance or object-image; the causal valid cognition (Skt. *pramāṇa*), which is the apprehending aspect or subject-image; and the resultant valid cognition (Skt. *phāla*), which is the awareness itself. These three are inseparable.

745. Jinendrabuddhi, *Viśālāmalavatīnāmapramāṇasamuccayaṭīkā*, chap. 1. Toh 4268, 35b. Pd 108:86.

746. Dharmakīrti, *Pramāṇavārttika*, 3.425. Toh 4210, 135b. Pd 97:563.

747. The "opponent" here includes the Vaibhāṣika, the Sautrāntika-Svātantrika Mādhyamika, and the Prāsaṅgika Mādhyamika.
748. Dignāga, *Pramāṇasamuccaya*, 1.11cd. Toh 4203, 2a. Pd 97:4.
749. Dignāga, *Pramāṇasamuccayavṛtti*, chap. 1. Toh 4204, 16b. Pd 97:63.
750. Dharmakīrti, *Pramāṇavārttika*, 3.459. Toh 4210, 136b. Pd 97:566.
751. Dharmakīrti, *Pramāṇavārttika*, 3.482. Toh 4210, 136. Pd 97:569.
752. This refers to the stages of meditation that result in the union of calm abiding and special insight. See also chapter 18 in volume 2 of *Science and Philosophy in the Indian Buddhist Classics*.
753. Dharmakīrti, *Pramāṇavārttika*, 3.285. Toh 4210, 129a. Pd 97:551.
754. Dharmakīrti, *Pramāṇavārttika*, 2.120–21. Toh 4210, 112a. Pd 97:511.
755. Dharmakīrti, *Pramāṇavārttika*, 2.125. Toh 4210, 112a. Pd 97:511.
756. Dharmakīrti, *Pramāṇavārttika*, 2.124. Toh 4210, 112a. Pd 97:511.
757. Dharmakīrti, *Pramāṇavārttika*, 2.126. Toh 4210, 112a. Pd 97:511.
758. Dignāga, *Pramāṇasamuccaya*, 1.7. Toh 4203, 2a. Pd 97:4.
759. Dharmakīrti, *Pramāṇavārttika*, 3.288. Toh 4210, 129b. Pd 97:551.
760. Dharmakīrti, *Pramāṇavārttika*, 3.289. Toh 4210, 129b. Pd 97:551.
761. Dharmakīrti, *Pramāṇavārttika*, 3.290. Toh 4210, 129b. Pd 97:552.
762. Dharmakīrti, *Pramāṇavārttika*, 3.289. Toh 4210, 129b. Pd 97:552.
763. Jinendrabuddhi, *Viśālāmalavatīnāmapramāṇasamuccayaṭīkā*, chap. 1. Toh 4268, 29b. Pd 108:71.
764. Dharmottara, *Pramāṇaviniścayaṭīkā*, chap. 1. Toh 4229, 125a. Pd 104:1057.
765. Dignāga, *Pramāṇasamuccaya*, 2.1. Toh 4203, 4a. Pd 97:553 (as translated in the commentary).
766. Dharmottara, *Nyāyabinduṭīkā*, chap. 4. Toh 4231, 29b. Pd 104:67.
767. Śākyabuddhi, *Pramāṇavārttikaṭīkā*, chap. 4. Toh 4220, 267b. Pd 99:674.
768. To qualify as trustworthy testimony, a scriptural passage must satisfy three criteria, or pass the *threefold analysis*: (1) it is not refuted by valid direct perception with regard to teaching about directly perceptible things; (2) it is not refuted by valid inference based on empirical fact with regard to teaching about slightly hidden things that are not directly perceptible; and (3) it is not invalidated by contradictions between earlier and later assertions in the scripture, direct and indirect contradictions, and so forth, with regard to teaching about very hidden, imperceptible things. For further discussion, see chapter 20 in volume 2 of *Science and Philosophy in the Indian Buddhist Classics*.
769. Śākyabuddhi, *Pramāṇavārttikaṭīkā*, chap. 1. Toh 4220, 267b. Pd 98:1533.
770. Dharmottara, *Nyāyabinduṭīkā*, chap. 2. Toh 4231, 168a. Pd 104:1166.
771. Dignāga, *Pramāṇasamuccayavṛtti*, chap. 3. Toh 4204, 40b. Pd 97:121.
772. Dharmakīrti, *Nyāyabindu*, chap. 2. Toh 4212, 233a. Pd 97:816.
773. An "inference for one's own sake" or "for one's own purpose" is discussed in part 4 of volume 2 in the section on inferential cognition beginning on page 270. An "inference for the purpose of others" is discussed in part 5 in the section on proof statements beginning on page 304.

774. The analysis of cognition in terms of the three components—action, agent, and object—is based on the *kāraka* tradition long established within Sanskrit grammar. These are three of the six syntactic-semantic categories presented in Pāṇini's *Aṣṭādhyāyī—apādāna, sampradāna, karaṇa, adhikaraṇa, karman*, and *kartṛ* (and its subset *hetu*)—later elaborated upon by Patañjali and others. For a translation and explanation of these six syntactic-semantic categories, see Cardona 1997, 137–38.
775. Given that non-Buddhist philosophers employ the term *pramāṇa* in the sense of an "instrument of knowing," whereas Buddhist philosophers such as Dignāga and Dharmakīrti employ it in the sense of an "act of knowing," the Sanskrit term *pramāṇa* will mainly be retained without translation in the context of this discussion concerning *pramāṇaphāla*.
776. Here, valid cognition and its result are both *awareness*—respectively the objective aspect and the subjective aspect.
777. The term often translated as *aspect* (*rnam pa*; *ākāra*) has several meanings. It can refer to an image, feature, or way of apprehending. In the case of a sense consciousness, it refers to the image that is transferred onto that consciousness by its objective condition. And in the case of any conceptual or nonconceptual consciousness, it refers to that consciousness's way of holding its object (i.e., its object as cognized). It can also refer to any feature of an object or subject of awareness. In the present context it refers to an image within perceptual awareness.
778. This passage is cited in Sakya Paṇḍita's *Treasury of Valid Cognition and Reasoning Autocommentary*. It seems to be a rendering of *Nyāyasūtra* 1.1.4., which from the Sanskrit reads: "Cognition that is produced from the commensurate meeting of a sense faculty and its object is *perception* (Skt. *pratyakṣa*)."
779. Kumārila Bhaṭṭa, *Mīmāṃsā Ślokavārttika*. Cited in Jñānaśrībhadra, *Pramāṇaviniścayaṭīkā*, chap. 2. Toh 4228, 184. Pd 104:464.
780. Kamalaśīla, *Nyāyabindupūrvapakṣasaṃkṣipta*. Toh 4232, 92b. Pd 105:260.
781. Vasubandhu, *Abhidharmakośa*, 1.42. Toh 4089, 3b. Pd 79:7.
782. The Tibetan term *don* (Skt. *artha*), translated here as "goal," is highly ambiguous and Dharmakīrti uses it in at least four senses: (1) aim, goal, or purpose; (2) object or thing; (3) meaning; and (4) referent. In some contexts these senses may overlap.
783. Dharmakīrti, *Pramāṇavārttika*, 2.3cd. Toh 4210, 107. Pd 97:500.
784. The Vijñaptimātra (Cognition Only) school is another name for the Cittamātra (Mind Only) school.
785. Dignāga, *Pramāṇasamuccaya*, 1.8. Toh 4203, 2a. Pd 97:4.
786. Dignāga, *Pramāṇasamuccayavṛtti*, chap. 1. Toh 4204, 16a. Pd 97:61.
787. Dharmakīrti, *Pramāṇavārttika*, 3.302–19. Toh 4210, 130a. Pd 97:553.
788. Dignāga, *Pramāṇasamuccaya*, 1.9. Toh 4203, 2a. Pd 97:4.
789. Dharmakīrti, *Pramāṇavārttika*, 3.320. Toh 4210, 130b. Pd 97:554.
790. Dharmakīrti, *Pramāṇavārttika*, 3.340. Toh 4210, 131b. Pd 97:556.

791. In general there is divergence of opinions in the commentaries about how to posit the second and third analyses of the result of valid cognition. However, here the second analysis of the result of valid cognition is posited on the basis of Khedrup Jé's *Ocean of Reasoning: A Commentary on Exposition of Valid Cognition*, where according to the Vijñaptimātra system it is categorized into two kinds: the result of valid cognition in the case of an awareness of something else and the result of valid cognition in the case of a reflexive awareness.

792. Dignāga, *Pramāṇasamuccayavṛtti*, chap. 1. Toh 4204, 16a. Pd 97:62.

793. Dignāga, *Pramāṇasamuccaya*, 1.10. Toh 4203, 2a. Pd 97:4.

794. Dharmakīrti, *Pramāṇavārttika*, 3.341. Toh 4210, 131b. Pd 97:556.

795. Dharmakīrti, *Pramāṇavārttika*, 3.366. Toh 4210, 132b. Pd 97:558.

796. Dignāga, *Pramāṇasamuccaya*, 2.5. Toh 4203, 4a. Pd 97:8.

797. Dignāga, *Pramāṇasamuccaya*, 2.6–7. Toh 4203, 4a. Pd 97:8.

798. The Vaiśeṣika school asserts that sound is permanent because it is an attribute of space. In their system, space is a permanent, unitary, and all-pervading substance. See the presentation of the Vaiśeṣika system in volume 3 of *Science and Philosophy in the Indian Buddhist Classics*.

799. Dharmakīrti, *Hetubindu*. Toh 4213, 251b. Pd 97:822.

800. It can be argued that while the first three modes are necessary and sufficient conditions for inferential knowledge, they are not sufficient to produce certainty. There is much debate in both Eastern and Western philosophical circles about whether certainty is a necessary component of knowledge.

801. Dharmakīrti, *Hetubindu*. Toh 4213, 252a. Pd 97:866.

802. Dharmakīrti, *Hetubindu*. Toh 4213, 253a. Pd 97:868.

803. Vinītadeva, *Hetubinduṭīkā*. Toh 4234, 173b. Pd 105:468.

804. Dignāga, *Pramāṇasamuccaya*, 2.6ab. Toh 4203, 4a. Pd 97:8.

805. Dharmakīrti, *Hetubindu*. Toh 4213, 254b. Pd 97:873.

806. Dignāga, *Pramāṇasamuccayavṛtti*, chap. 2. Toh 4204, 33a. Pd 97:103.

807. Dharmakīrti, *Pramāṇavārttika*, 1.21. Toh 4210, 95b. Pd 97:471.

808. Dharmakīrti, *Pramāṇavārttikavṛtti*. Toh 4216, 181b. Pd 97:903. Dharmakīrti's autocommentary only covers the first chapter of his *Pramāṇavārttika*.

809. Dharmakīrti, *Pramāṇavārttika*, 1.23. Toh 4210, 95b. Pd 97:471.

810. Śākyabuddhi, *Pramāṇavārttikaṭīkā*. Toh 4220, 106a. Pd 101:1087. Commenting on Dharmakīrti, *Pramāṇavārttika*, 1.24–25. Pd 97:471–72.

811. Dharmakīrti, *Pramāṇavārttikavṛtti*. Toh 4216, 271b. Pd 97:924. Commenting on Dharmakīrti, *Pramāṇavārttika*, 1.29. Pd 97:472.

812. Dharmakīrti, *Pramāṇaviniścaya*, chap. 2. Toh 4211, 170b. Pd 97:656.

813. Dharmakīrti, *Hetubindu*. Toh 4213, 240a. Pd 97:837.

814. Dharmakīrti, *Hetubindu*. Toh 4213, 240a. Pd 97:837.

815. Dharmakīrti, *Pramāṇaviniścaya*, chap. 2. Toh 4211, 183. Pd 97:687.

816. Dharmakīrti, *Nyāyabindu*, chap. 2. Toh 4212, 232a. Pd 104:28.

817. See pages 319–36.

818. Dharmakīrti, *Pramāṇavārttika*, 4.99. Toh 4210, 143. Pd 97:583.
819. Jñānagarbha, *Satyadvayavibhaṅga*, verse 28. Toh 3881, 2b. Pd 62:757.
820. Candrakīrti, *Madhyamakāvatāra*, 6.31a. Toh 3861, 206a. Pd 60:565.
821. Candrakīrti, *Prasannapadā*, chap. 1. Toh 3860, 25a. Pd 60:58 and 60:60.
822. Nāgārjuna, *Vigrahavyāvartanī*, verses 5d–6c. Toh 3828, 27a. Pd 57:74.
823. Nāgārjuna, *Vigrahavyāvartanīvṛtti*. Toh 3832, 128b. Pd 57:349.
824. Candrakīrti, *Prasannapadā*, chap. 1. Toh 3860, 25b. Pd 60:60. The negating particle inserted here appears in the Sanskrit, *ananubhūtārthādhigama*, though not in the Tibetan, *nyams su myong ba'i don rtogs pa*. However, the presence or absence of the negating particle may not affect the main point, which seems to concern a resemblance of something experienced to something not experienced. For a discussion about this point, see Seyfort Ruegg 2002, 133n257.
825. See page 389.
826. Candrakīrti, *Catuḥśatakaṭīkā*, chap. 11. Toh 3865, 180b. Pd 60:1358.
827. Candrakīrti, *Catuḥśatakaṭīkā*, chap. 11. Toh 3865, 171b. Pd 60:1338.
828. Candrakīrti, *Catuḥśatakaṭīkā*, chap. 11. Toh 3865, 183a. Pd 60:1364.
829. Candrakīrti, *Catuḥśatakaṭīkā*, chap. 10. Toh 3865, 162a. Pd 60:1316.
830. Jñānagarbha, *Satyadvayavibhaṅgavṛtti*. Toh 3882, 5b. Pd 62:767.
831. Candrakīrti, *Catuḥśatakaṭīkā*, chap. 13. Toh 3865, 196b. Pd 60:1395.
832. Candrakīrti, *Prasannapadā*, chap. 1. Toh 3860, 25b. Pd 60:60.
833. Candrakīrti, *Prasannapadā*, chap. 1. Toh 3860, 24b. Pd 60:57. For further discussion of this passage see MacDonald 2015, 274, and Seyfort Ruegg 2002, 124.
834. Candrakīrti, *Prasannapadā*, chap. 1. Toh 3860, 25a. Pd 60:59.
835. Candrakīrti, *Prasannapadā*, chap. 1. Toh 3860, 25b. Pd 60:59.
836. Āryadeva, *Catuḥśataka*, 10.7. Toh 3846, 11b. Pd 57:805.
837. The following argument operates as an example of ultimate analysis, here examining the relationship between the object characterized and its characteristics, where one searches for the basis of identity (*mtshan gzhi*) of the former in terms of the latter and vice versa, but does not find it because such an objective basis of identity does not exist. However, it also operates on a conventional level, as any child can attest—for it is clear that the Cheshire Cat's grin cannot exist independently of the Cheshire Cat.
838. Candrakīrti, *Prasannapadā*, chap. 1. Toh 3860, 20a–23b. Pd 60:47–55. For full translations of this passage from Sanskrit and Tibetan sources, see Seyfort Ruegg 2002, 104–21, and MacDonald 2015, 224–62. The terms *rang mtshan* (*svalakṣaṇa*) and *spyi mtshan* (*sāmānyalakṣaṇa*) are ambiguous between "particular characteristics" and "unique particulars" in the first case, and "universal characteristics" and "universals" in the second case. The translations by Ruegg and MacDonald prioritize the interpretation as particular and universal *characteristics* in this passage, while the Tibetan commentary above prioritizes the interpretation as particular and universal *objects*. For a discussion about the translation of these terms in this context of Candrakīrti's argument, see MacDonald 2015, 225n445. For a discussion about the meaning of these terms in

the context of Vasubandhu's texts and those of Dignāga and Dharmakīrti, see Dunne 2004, 79–83.

839. Candrakīrti, *Prasannapadā*, chap. 1. Toh 3860, 23b. Pd 60:55. For an explanation of this passage that also notes the absence of *sva-* (i.e., *svalakṣaṇa*, the particular) in the extant Sanskrit texts, which affects the argument slightly, see MacDonald 2015, 263–64n502.

840. Potter 2015, 5:6.

841. This summary of Bhartṛhari's assertions is taken from Potter 2015, 5:123, based on Bhartṛhari, *Vākyapadīya*, 1.13.

842. Mark Siderits outlines three basic positions on the comprehension of sentences, and this one he calls "the pure sentence theory." According to this theory, a word is not an independent semantic unit; rather, the sentence is the basic indivisible unit. This exemplifies the *context principle* (i.e., a word has a meaning only in the context of a sentence). See Siderits 1991, 35.

843. Dignāga, *Pramāṇasamuccaya*, 5.46. Narthang Tengyur, 11b. Pd 97:51. This translation differs slightly from the translation by Sudhanarakṣita/Vasudharakṣita and Shama Sengyal cited elsewhere in this volume. The Sanskrit reads: *apoddhāre padasyāyaṃ vākyād artho vivecitaḥ / vākyārthaḥ pratibhākhyo 'yaṃ tenādāv upajāyate.*

844. Dignāga, *Pramāṇasamuccayavṛtti*, chap. 5. Narthang Tengyur, 170a. Pd 97:404. Literally, it says that the assumption is "not held by a hook" or is "unanchored" (*lcags kyu med pa*, Skt. *niraṅkuśa*).

845. See Siderits 1991, 35. Siderits calls this position the "words-plus-relation theory" (Skt. *abhihitānvayavāda*)—i.e., the relation of that which is (already) designated. According to this theory, the word is the basic semantic unit, not the sentence. This exemplifies the *composition principle* (i.e., the meaning of a sentence is determined by the meanings of its component words).

846. See Siderits 1991, 35. Siderits calls this position the "related designation theory" (Skt. *anvitābhidāna*)—i.e., the designation of that which is (already) related. According to this theory, although the meaning of a word is its referent, its meaning can fulfill its function only in relation to the meanings of other words in the sentence. So this theory combines the *context principle* and the *composition principle.*

847. According to modern scholarship, this is not the Patañjali who authored the *Yoga Sūtra.* For references to that supposedly later author, see volume 3 of the present series.

848. Kamalaśīla, *Tattvasaṅgrahapañjikā*, chap. 16 [Jha 11]. Toh 4267, 311b. Pd 107: 808.

849. Kamalaśīla, *Tattvasaṅgrahapañjikā*, chap. 16 [Jha 11]. Toh 4267, 316a. Pd 107: 820. (*Nyāyasūtra*, 2.2.64.)

850. Kamalaśīla, *Tattvasaṅgrahapañjikā*, chap. 16 [Jha 11]. Toh 4267, 316a. Pd 107: 820. (*Nyāyasūtra*, 2.2.66.)

851. Kamalaśīla, *Tattvasaṅgrahapañjikā*, chap. 16 [Jha 11]. Toh 4267, 316b. Pd 107: 821. (*Nyāyasūtra*, 2.2.65.)
852. Kamalaśīla, *Tattvasaṅgrahapañjikā*, chap. 16 [Jha 11]. Toh 4267, 316b. Pd 107: 821.
853. See Kamalaśīla, *Tattvasaṅgrahapañjikā*, chap. 16 [Jha 11]. Toh 4267, 312a. Pd 107: 809.
854. Kamalaśīla, *Tattvasaṅgrahapañjikā*, chap. 16 [Jha 11]. Toh 4267, 312a. Pd 107: 810.
855. Kamalaśīla, *Tattvasaṅgrahapañjikā*, chap. 21 [Jha 16]. Toh 4267, 331a. Pd 107: 858. (Dignāga's verse is cited in Kamalaśīla's commentary on Śāntarakṣita's verses, Jha 961–63.) The point here is that an individual occurs only for a moment. An individual sound or word comes into existence at the time of applying a label, not before, and in the next moment it has disappeared. Reference needs to be based on something more enduring than this in order to function.
856. Dignāga, *Pramāṇasamuccaya*, 5.1. Translated by Kanakavarman and Dad pa'i Sherab. Narthang, Pramāṇa, ce, 9a. Pd 97:47. Sanskrit: *kṛtakatvādivat svārtham anyāpohena bhāṣate*.
857. Kamalaśīla, *Tattvasaṅgrahapañjikā*, chap. 21 [Jha 16, on verse 1]. Toh 4267, 311b. Pd 107:808.
858. Kamalaśīla's *Tattvasaṅgrahapañjikā* starts to address these points at Jha 16, verse 871.
859. Dignāga, *Pramāṇasamuccaya*, 5.2ab. Narthang Tengyur, 9b. Pd 97:47. Sanskrit: *na jātiśabdo bhedānām ānantyavyabhicārataḥ*. For further comment, see Hayes 1988, 255–57.
860. The Nyāya and Vaiśeṣika philosophical views are so deeply connected and similar that these schools are often bunched together in traditional Tibetan sources.
861. Dharmakīrti, *Pramāṇavārttika*, 1.92. Toh 4210, 98a. Pd 97:478.
862. Dignāga, *Pramāṇasamuccaya*, 5.2cd. Narthang Tengyur, 9b. Pd 97:47. Sanskrit: *[na] vācako yogajātyor vā bhedārthair apṛthakśruteḥ*.
863. Dignāga, *Pramāṇasamuccayavṛtti*, chap. 5. Narthang Tengyur, 157b. Pd 97:379. There are some significant differences between the translations of this text by Shama Sengyal (in Dergé Tengyur) and Depai Sherab (in Narthang and Peking Tengyur). The main point of the argument here concerns topics outlined in the traditional texts and commentaries on Sanskrit grammar, which are perhaps difficult to understand. When *exists* and *substance* operate as co-designative expressions—although this is rendered in Tibetan as "substance that exists" or "existent substance" (*yod pa'i rdzas*), where the possessive particle *'i* is applied to the term *exists*—in the Sanskrit phrase, *sad dravyam*, the terms *exists* and *substance* both have the same first case ending and are thus in agreement. Conversely, when these two terms operate attributively or predicatively—rendered in Tibetan as "the existence of substance" (*rdzas kyi yod pa*)—in the Sanskrit phrase, *dravyasya sattā*, the third case ending or possessive particle is applied to

substance and the first case ending is applied to *exists*. So one must understand that there is this difference.

864. Dignāga, *Pramāṇasamuccaya*, 5.3. Toh 4203, 9b. Pd 97:21. Sanskrit not available (see note 866 below). This verse seems to follow the words of Bhartṛhari, *Vākyapadīya*, 3.14.8: *vibhaktibhedo niyamād guṇaguṇyabhidhāyinoḥ / sāmānādhikaraṇyasa prasiddhir dravyaśabdayoḥ //*.

865. Dharmakīrti, *Pramāṇavārttika*, 1.93. Toh 4210, 98a. Pd 97:478.

866. Dignāga, *Pramāṇasamuccaya*, 5.3. Narthang Tengyur, 9b. Pd 97:47. Sanskrit: Not available. Given that it appears in different forms in different commentaries, the wording of this verse seems somewhat unfixed. For further discussion see Hayes 1988, 259–61.

867. Dignāga, *Pramāṇasamuccayavṛtti*, chap. 5. Narthang Tengyur, 157b. Pd 97:379. This paraphrases a point stated in Bhartṛhari, *Vākyapadīya*, chap. 3, that a relation must be signified in connection with the relation-bearer's attributes, but there is no signifying term that intrinsically expresses the relation. For further discussion see Hayes 1988, 260.

868. Dignāga, *Pramāṇasamuccaya*, 5.4. Narthang Tengyur, 9b. Pd 97:47. Sanskrit: Not available.

869. Dignāga, *Pramāṇasamuccayavṛtti*, chap. 5. Narthang Tengyur, 158a. Pd 97:379.

870. Dignāga, *Pramāṇasamuccayavṛtti*, chap. 5. Narthang Tengyur, 158a. Pd 97:379.

871. Dignāga, *Pramāṇasamuccayavṛtti*, chap. 5. Toh 4204, 67a. Pd 97:187.

872. For further explanation of Dignāga's arguments against these four candidates for the linguistic referent accepted by certain non-Buddhist systems, see Sen 2011, 173–78.

873. Dignāga, *Pramāṇasamuccaya*, 5.6. Translated by Kanakavarman and Dad pa'i Sherab. Narthang, Pramāṇa, ce, 10a. Pd 97:47. Sanskrit: Not available.

874. Dignāga, *Pramāṇasamuccaya*, 5.11d–13d. Narthang Tengyur, 10a. Pd 97:48. The order of the lines differs somewhat in Sanskrit, as cited and reconstructed by Frauwallner 1959, 102, verses 12–13, in Hayes 1988, 306: *bahudhāpy abhidheyasya na śabdāt sarvathā gatiḥ / svasambandhānurūpyeṇa vyavacchedārthakāry asau // anekadharmā śabdo 'pi yenārtham nātivartate / pratyāyati tenaiva na śabdaguṇatvādibhiḥ //*. The last verse here, beginning with "A term too has many attributes," is the root verse quoted in Jinendrabuddhi's commentary below.

875. Jinendrabuddhi, *Viśālāmalavatīnāmapramāṇasamuccayaṭīkā*, chap. 5. Toh 4268, 255b. Pd 108:628. Here a contrast is being drawn between the attribute that is the referent of the term *tree* (which is a universal) and the attributes of the term *tree* itself (which is a sound known by direct auditory perception, thus an individual).

876. Dharmakīrti, *Pramāṇavārttika*, 1.50. Toh 4210, 96b. Pd 97:474.

877. Dignāga, *Pramāṇasamuccaya*, 5.35. Narthang Tengyur, 11a. Pd 97:50. Sanskrit: *vṛkṣatvapārthivadravyasajjñeyāḥ prātilomyataḥ / catustridvyekasaṃdehe nimittaṃ niścaye 'nyathā //*.

878. Jinendrabuddhi, *Viśālāmalavatīnāmapramāṇasamuccayaṭīkā*, chap. 5. Toh 4268, 276a. Pd 108:678.

879. Dignāga, *Pramāṇasamuccaya*, 5.1. Narthang Tengyur, 9a. Pd 97:47. Sanskrit: *kṛtakatvādivat svārtham anyāpohena bhāṣate.*

880. Dignāga, *Pramāṇasamuccayavṛtti*, chap. 5, on verse 33. Narthang Tengyur, 166b. Pd 97:397.

881. Dignāga. *Pramāṇasamuccaya*, 5.34. Narthang Tengyur, 11a. Pd 97:50. This differs slightly from Shama Sengyal's translation. Sanskrit: *adṛṣṭer anyaśabdārthe svārthasyāṃśe 'pi darśanāt / śruteḥ sambandhasaukaryaṃ na cāsti vyabhicāritā //.*

882. Dignāga, *Pramāṇasamuccayavṛtti*, chap. 5, on verse 34. Narthang Tengyur, 166b. Pd 97:397. This way of establishing a connection between the word and its referent is through a process of induction, primarily by way of the word simply not being observed to apply to anything in the dissimilar class.

883. Dignāga, *Pramāṇasamuccayavṛtti*, chap. 5, on verse 35. Narthang Tengyur, 167a. Pd 97:398.

884. Dignāga, *Pramāṇasamuccayavṛtti*, chap. 5, on verse 36. Narthang Tengyur, 167b. Pd 97:399. The last line of this quotation appears in Dharmakīrti, *Exposition of Valid Cognition*. See Hattori 1975, 71n4, for the Sanskrit: *śabdo 'rthāntaranivṛttiviśiṣṭān eva bhāvān āha //.*

885. Jinendrabuddhi, *Viśālāmalavatīnāmapramāṇasamuccayaṭīkā*, chap. 5. Toh 4268, 253a. Pd 108:621.

886. Jinendrabuddhi, *Viśālāmalavatīnāmapramāṇasamuccayaṭīkā*, chap. 5. Toh 4268, 253a. Pd 108:621–22.

887. Jinendrabuddhi, *Viśālāmalavatīnāmapramāṇasamuccayaṭīkā*, chap. 5. Toh 4268, 253a. Pd 108:621.

888. Dignāga, *Pramāṇasamuccayavṛtti*, chap. 5, on verse 36. Narthang Tengyur, 170a. Pd 97:405.

889. Dignāga, *Pramāṇasamuccaya*, 5.49. Narthang Tengyur, 11b. Pd 97:51. Sanskrit: Not available.

890. As reported in Jinendrabuddhi, *Viśālāmalavatīnāmapramāṇasamuccayaṭīkā*, chap. 5. Toh 4268, 254a. Pd 108:624.

891. Dignāga, *Pramāṇasamuccaya*, 5.52. Narthang Tengyur, 11b. Pd 97:52. Sanskrit: Not available.

892. Dharmakīrti, *Pramāṇavārttika*, 1.40–42. Toh 4210, 96a. Pd 97:473.

893. This synopsis of the three verses from the root text is based on Khedrup Jé's *Ocean of Reasoning: A Commentary on Exposition of Valid Cognition*, 117–19.

894. Dharmakīrti, *Pramāṇavārttika*, 1.43–58. Toh 4210, 96a. Pd 97:473.

895. Dharmakīrti, *Pramāṇavārttika*, 1.59–113b. Toh 4210, 97a. Pd 97:475.

896. Dharmakīrti, *Pramāṇavārttika*, 1.113c–184. Toh 4210, 99a. Pd 97:479.

897. Dharmakīrti, *Pramāṇavārttika*, 1.185. Toh 4210, 106b. Pd 97:486.

898. The presentation of these subdivisions of the root text discussing the exclusion of other is based on Gyaltsab Jé's *Illuminating the Path to Liberation: A Commentary on Exposition of Valid Cognition.*

899. Dharmakīrti, *Pramāṇavārttikavṛtti*. Toh 4216, 275a. Pd 97:932.
900. This point is debated by later commentators such as Dharmottara, as indicated in chapter 21 above.
901. Dharmakīrti, *Pramāṇavārttikavṛtti*. Toh 4216, 278a. Pd 97:940.
902. Dharmakīrti, *Pramāṇavārttikavṛtti*. Toh 4216, 278b. Pd 97:941.
903. Dharmakīrti, *Pramāṇavārttikavṛtti*. Toh 4216, 280a. Pd 97:944.
904. Dharmakīrti, *Pramāṇavārttika*, 1.73. Toh 4210, 97b. Pd 97:476.
905. Dharmakīrti, *Pramāṇavārttikavṛtti*. Toh 4216, 284a. Pd 97:953.
906. This is based on Dharmakīrti, *Pramāṇavārttikavṛtti*. Toh 4216, 284a. Pd 97:953.
907. Dharmakīrti, *Pramāṇavārttikavṛtti*. Toh 4216, 289b. Pd 97:967.
908. Dharmakīrti, *Pramāṇavārttikavṛtti*. Toh 4216, 292b. Pd 97:974.
909. Dharmakīrti, *Pramāṇavārttikavṛtti*. Toh 4216, 289a. Pd 97:965.
910. Dharmakīrti, *Pramāṇavārttika*, 3.53. Toh 4210, 120b. Pd 97:530.
911. Devendrabuddhi, *Pramāṇavārttikapañjikā*, chap. 3. Toh 4268, 144a. Pd 98:342.
912. Dharmakīrti, *Pramāṇavārttika*, 3.164–65. Toh 4210, 124b. Pd 97:540.
913. This is based on Jinendrabuddhi, *Viśālāmalavatīnāmapramāṇasamuccayaṭīkā*, chap. 1. Toh 4268, 283a. Pd 97:951.
914. Dharmakīrti, *Pramāṇavārttika*, 1.205. Toh 4210, 102b. Pd 97:487. This point is also explained in the "Exclusion of Other" chapter in Dharmakīrti's *Pramāṇaviniścaya*.
915. Dharmakīrti, *Pramāṇavārttikavṛtti*. Toh 4216, 287a. Pd 97:960.
916. Dharmakīrti, *Pramāṇavārttikavṛtti*. Toh 4216, 208b. Pd 97:1042.
917. Śubhagupta, *Anyāpohavicāra*, verse 1. Toh 4246, 197a. Pd 107:532.
918. Dharmottara, *Apohaprakaraṇa*. Toh 4250, 242b. Pd 106:657.
919. Śaṅkarānanda, *Apohasiddhi*. Toh 4256, 298b. Pd 106:811.
920. Śāntarakṣita, *Tattvasaṅgraha*, 20.117–20 [Jha 16.982–85]. Toh 4266, 37a. Pd 107:91. Citing Uddyotakara, *Nyāyavārttika*, on 2.2.63.
921. Śāntarakṣita, *Tattvasaṅgraha*, 20.319–22 [Jha 16.1185–88]. Toh 4266, 44a. Pd 107:108.
922. Śāntarakṣita, *Tattvasaṅgraha*, 20.121 [Jha 16.986]. Toh 4266, 37a. Pd 107:91. Commenting on Uddyotakara, *Nyāyavārttika*, on 2.2.63.
923. Śāntarakṣita, *Tattvasaṅgraha*, 20.323–24 [Jha 16.1189–91]. Toh 4266, 44a. Pd 107:108.
924. Śāntarakṣita, *Tattvasaṅgraha*, 20.128 [Jha 16.990–94]. Toh 4266, 37a. Pd 107:92. Continuing to comment on Uddyotakara, *Nyāyavārttika*, on 2.2.63.
925. Śāntarakṣita, *Tattvasaṅgraha*, 20.325–26 [Jha 16.1192–93]. Toh 4266, 44a. Pd 107:109.
926. Śāntarakṣita, *Tattvasaṅgraha*, 20.130–31 [Jha 16.995–96]. Toh 4266, 37b. Pd 107:92. Continuing to comment on Uddyotakara, *Nyāyavārttika*, on 2.2.63.
927. Śāntarakṣita. *Tattvasaṅgraha*, 20.327 [Jha 16.1194]. Toh 4266, 44a. Pd 107:109.
928. Śāntarakṣita, *Tattvasaṅgraha*, 20.132–35 [Jha 16.997–1000]. Toh 4266, 37b. Pd 107:92. Continuing to comment on Uddyotakara, *Nyāyavārttika*, 2.2.63.

929. Śāntarakṣita, *Tattvasaṅgraha*, 20.330–33 [Jha 16.1196–99]. Toh 4266, 44a. Pd 107:109.
930. Śāntarakṣita, *Tattvasaṅgraha*, 20.49–110 [Jha 16.915–75]. Toh 4266, 34b–42b. Pd 107:85–90. Citing Kumārila Bhaṭṭa, *Mīmāṃsā Ślokavārttika*, "Apoha" chapter.
931. Śāntarakṣita, *Tattvasaṅgraha*, 20.49–56 [Jha 16.915–24]. Toh 4266, 34b. Pd 107:85. Citing Kumārila Bhaṭṭa, *Mīmāṃsā Ślokavārttika*, "Apoha" chapter, 1–10.
932. Śāntarakṣita, *Tattvasaṅgraha*, 20.156 [Jha 16.1022]. Toh 4266, 38a. Pd 107:94.
933. Kamalaśīla, *Tattvasaṅgrahapañjikā*, chap. 21 [Jha 16.925]. Toh 4267, 324b. Pd 107:842.
934. Kamalaśīla, *Tattvasaṅgrahapañjikā*, chap. 21 [Jha 16, on verse 927]. Toh 4267, 324b. Pd 107:842.
935. Śāntarakṣita, *Tattvasaṅgraha*, 20.59–63 [Jha 16.925–29]. Toh 4266, 35a. Pd 107:86. Citing Kumārila Bhaṭṭa, *Mīmāṃsā Ślokavārttika*, "Apoha" chapter, 42–46.
936. Dignāga, *Pramāṇasamuccaya*, 5.14. Narthang Tengyur, 10a. Pd 97:48. Sanskrit: Not available.
937. Dharmakīrti, *Pramāṇavārttika*, 1.129–84. Toh 4210, 99b. Pd 97:481.
938. Śāntarakṣita, *Tattvasaṅgraha*, 20.164–79 [Jha 16.1030–45]. Toh 4266, 38b. Pd 107:95.
939. Śāntarakṣita, *Tattvasaṅgraha*, 20.108 [Jha 16.973]. Toh 4266, 41b. Pd 107:103. Citing Kumārila Bhaṭṭa, *Mīmāṃsā Ślokavārttika*, "Apoha" chapter, 135.
940. Śāntarakṣita, *Tattvasaṅgraha*, 20.107–12 [Jha 16.974–78]. Toh 4266, 43a. Pd 107:105. Citing Kumārila Bhaṭṭa, *Mīmāṃsā Ślokavārttika*, "Apoha" chapter, 139–43.
941. Śāntarakṣita, *Tattvasaṅgraha*, 20.256–78 [Jha 16.1122–44]. Toh 4266, 41b. Pd 107:103–05.
942. Śāntarakṣita, *Tattvasaṅgraha*, 20.114 [Jha 16.979]. Toh 4266, 36b. Pd 107:90. Citing Kumārila Bhaṭṭa, *Mīmāṃsā Ślokavārttika*, "Apoha" chapter, 144.
943. Dharmakīrti, *Pramāṇavārttika*, 1.124–28. Toh 4210, 99a. Pd 97:480.
944. Śāntarakṣita, *Tattvasaṅgraha*, 20.197–229 [Jha 16.1166–98]. Toh 4266, 43a. Pd 107:90.
945. Dharmakīrti, *Pramāṇavārttikavṛtti*. Toh 4216, 290a. Pd 97:969.
946. Śāntarakṣita, *Tattvasaṅgraha*, 20.156 [Jha 16.1022]. Toh 4266, 38b. Pd 107:94.
947. Śāntarakṣita, *Tattvasaṅgraha*, 20.114–16 [Jha 16.979–81]. Toh 4266, 36b. Pd 107:90. Citing Kumārila Bhaṭṭa, *Mīmāṃsā Ślokavārttika*, "Apoha" chapter, 144.
948. Dharmakīrti, *Pramāṇavārttika*, 1.122–23. Toh 4210, 99a. Pd 97:480.
949. Śāntarakṣita, *Tattvasaṅgraha*, 20.300–314. The Tibetan original of this volume erroneously provides 20.291–315 here. [Jha 16.1156–80]. Toh 4266, 43a. Pd 107:106.
950. Śāntarakṣita, *Tattvasaṅgraha*, 20.77–79 [Jha 16.944–46]. Toh 4266, 35b. Pd

107:87. Citing Kumārila Bhaṭṭa, *Mīmāṃsā Ślokavārttika*, "Apoha" chapter, 83–86.

951. Śāntarakṣita, *Tattvasaṅgraha*, 20.46 [Jha 16.914]. Toh 4266, 34b. Pd 107:85.
952. A reason by way of drawing parity is a type of reasoning introduced by Bhāviveka and was presented in chapter 15 above.
953. Dharmakīrti, *Pramāṇavārttika*, 1.113c–121d Toh 4210, 99a. Pd 97:479.
954. Śāntarakṣita, *Tattvasaṅgraha*, 20.197–201 [Jha 16.1060–67]. Toh 4266, 39b. Pd 107:97–98.
955. Śāntarakṣita, *Tattvasaṅgraha*, 20.136 [Jha 16.1002]. Toh 4266, 37b. Pd 107:92. Citing Kumārila Bhaṭṭa, *Mīmāṃsā Ślokavārttika*, "Apoha" chapter, 164.
956. Both Śāntarakṣita's *Tattvasaṅgraha* and Kamalaśīla's *Tattvasaṅgrahapañjikā* meticulously present various arguments criticizing proponents of exclusion. However, since the names Jayanta Bhaṭṭa, Trilocana, Vācaspatimiśra, and so on do not appear in them, one can infer that their texts were written after Śāntarakṣita's treatise. Kamalaśīla's *Tattvasaṅgrahapañjikā* mentions the names of the non-Buddhist masters Uddyotakara, Kumārila, Śaṅkarasvāmin, Aviddhakarṇa, Bhāmaha, Prabhākara, and the Jaina master Sumati, as well as authors of the root texts of certain major philosophical sects.
957. Jñānaśrīmitra's *Apohaprakaraṇa* explicitly mentions the names of the two non-Buddhist masters, Trilocana and Vācaspatimiśra, and refutes them.
958. Although the treatises on exclusion composed by the Buddhist epistemologists Jñānaśrīmitra and Ratnakīrti were not translated into Tibetan, the Sanskrit texts are currently available.
959. Śākyabuddhi, *Pramāṇavārttikaṭīkā*. Toh 4220, 200b. Pd 98:1425. Citing Dharmakīrti, *Pramāṇavārttika*, 1.40cd.
960. In Tibetan, respectively, *don gyi gzhan sel*, *med dgag gi gzhan sel*, and *blo'i gzhan sel*.
961. Dharmottara, *Apohaprakaraṇa*. Toh 4250, 236b. Pd 106:640.
962. Dharmottara, *Apohaprakaraṇa*. Toh 4250, 236b. Pd 106:640.
963. Dharmottara, *Apohaprakaraṇa*. Toh 4250, 236b. Pd 106:640.
964. Dharmakīrti, *Pramāṇavārttika*, 1.71cd. Toh 4210, 97b. Pd 97:467.
965. Dharmottara, *Apohaprakaraṇa*. Toh 4250, 244b. Pd 106:661.
966. Dharmottara, *Apohaprakaraṇa*. Toh 4250, 244b. Pd 106:662.
967. Dharmottara, *Apohaprakaraṇa*. Toh 4250, 244b. Pd 106:661.
968. Dharmottara, *Apohaprakaraṇa*. Toh 4250, 246a. Pd 106:665. The abbreviation PV refers to citations of Dharmakīrti's *Pramāṇavārttika*. Gorampa's treatise *The Explanation of the Difficult Points of [Sapaṇ's] Treasury of Valid Cognition and Reasoning That Completely Clarifies the Seven Texts* (57b6 and 59b3) illuminates Dharmottara's comments on the above words: "Therefore two types of exclusion must be posited: that which is in the nature of ascertainment and that which is the object of conceptual cognition." Gorampa explains the two types of exclusion according to Dharmottara's tradition to be: an exclusion of other that is a nonimplicative negation, and a mental exclusion of other. Dharmottara's

text itself seems to be saying that at the time of applying the term, the object of conceptual cognition, or the mental exclusion of other, functions to exclude the other [heterogeneous objects]; and this functions as the signified object that is free from other things that are not it. These two exclusions—that which is in the nature of ascertainment, which is a nonimplicative negation, and that which is the object of conceptual cognition, which is a mental exclusion of other—are the signified object. However, this does not contradict external things being imputed as the linguistic referent.

969. Śāntarakṣita, *Tattvasaṅgraha*, 20.139 [Jha 16.1004]. Toh 4266, 37b. Pd 107:95.

970. Kamalaśīla, *Tattvasaṅgrahapañjikā*, chap. 21 [Jha 16, on verse 1004]. Toh 4267, 337a. Pd 107:874.

971. Kamalaśīla, *Tattvasaṅgrahapañjikā*, chap. 21 [Jha 16, on verses 1007–09]. Toh 4267, 311b. Pd 107:808. Also, chap. 21 [Jha 16, on verses 1007–08]. Toh 4267, 337b. Pd 107:875.

972. Kamalaśīla, *Tattvasaṅgrahapañjikā*, chap. 21 [Jha 16, on verses 1009–11]. Toh 4267, 338b. Pd 107:877.

973. Kamalaśīla, *Tattvasaṅgrahapañjikā*, chap. 21 [Jha 16, on verses 1095–96]. Toh 4267, 345a. Pd 107:904.

974. Kamalaśīla, *Tattvasaṅgrahapañjikā*, chap. 21 [Jha 16, on verses 1061–62]. Toh 4267, 349a. Pd 107:893. The line cited at the end of this quotation [Jha 16, verse 1014] is explained to mean that the nature of this thing (for example, the reflection of a cow) is not the nature of the other thing (the reflection of a horse).

975. Kamalaśīla, *Tattvasaṅgrahapañjikā*, chap. 21 [Jha 16, on verses 1013–15]. Toh 4267, 339a. Pd 107:878.

976. These words are quoted in Kamalaśīla's *Tattvasaṅgrahapañjikā*, chap. 21 [Jha 16, on verse 1015]. Toh 4267, 339a. Pd 107:878. This translation of Dignāga's *Pramāṇasamuccayavṛtti* differs slightly from Shama Sengyal's translation. Toh 4204, 268. Pd 97:207.

977. Kamalaśīla, *Tattvasaṅgrahapañjikā*, chap. 21 [Jha 16, on verses 1017–18]. Toh 4267, 339a. Pd 107:879.

978. This is found in Dharmottara, *Pramāṇaviniścayaṭīkā*, Pd 104:1233, and in Śaṅkarānanda, *Apohasiddhi*, Pd 106:801.

979. Jñānaśrīmitra, *Apohaprakaraṇa*. Not found in the Tengyur. Sanskrit text, p. 205, line 16. A separate epistemological text by this master, entitled *Establishing the Nature of Cause and Effect* (*Kāryakāraṇabhāvasiddhi*), is found in the Tengyur, Toh 4258.

980. Ratnakīrti, *Apohasiddhi*. Sanskrit text, verses 8–9. The Sanskrit text of this work, together with an English translation, can be found in McAllister 2020.

981. Mokṣākaragupta, *Tarkabhāṣā*. Toh 4264, 360a. Pd 106:991–93. See also Kajiyama 1966, 122. The abbreviation PV refers to a citation of Dharmakīrti's *Pramāṇavārttika*.

982. The main point here concerns a difference in the position, and thus the scope, of the term "only" (*kho na*; Skt. *eva*). For a description of the theory of the two

or the three types of exclusion (Skt. *vyavaccheda*) in this context, see Kajiyama 1966, 57n132.

983. Mokṣākaragupta, *Tarkabhāṣā*. Toh 4264, 345b. Pd 106:955–56. See Kajiyama 1966, 56–59.

984. The presentation of the exclusion of other according to Sakya Paṇḍita's tradition can be understood from the fourth chapter, "Examining Affirmation and Exclusion"; the fifth chapter, "Examining Signified and Signifier"; and the third chapter, "Examining Universal and Particular," in his *Treasury of Valid Cognition and Reasoning*. This text explains that of the three types of exclusion of other, only mental exclusion is a genuine exclusion of other; also the direct referent of a word is not a real thing since it is only a superimposition; and the conceived object expressed is the conceived object of thought. The *Treasury*'s own tradition often agrees with the words of *Exposition of Valid Cognition* and its autocommentary, though it seems not to state many of the explanations given by Dharmakīrti's followers—Dharmottara, Śāntarakṣita, and especially Jñānaśrīmitra, Mokṣākaragupta, and so forth.

Glossary

absence (*dngos po med pa*; *abhāva*). Nonexistence, negation.

afflictions (*nyon mongs*; *kleśa*; Pali: *kilesa*). *Also* mental afflictions. Nonvirtuous mental states, such as attachment, hatred, and ignorance, which motivate contaminated actions that cause one to continue to be born in cyclic existence.

afflictive mental consciousness (*nyon yid*; *kliṣṭamanas*). According to the Cittamātra system, which posits eight types of primary consciousness, when a thought grasping at "I" arises, it is the afflictive mental consciousness that conceives the foundation consciousness to be the *self* and conceives the collection of six consciousnesses to be *mine*.

aggregates of appropriation (*nyer len gyi phung po*; *upādānaskandha*). The five appropriated aggregates are the psychophysical constituents that function as the basis of imputation of a conventionally existent person or self. They include the body, the primary consciousness, various mental factors, and all the other causal factors within the continuum of a person, traditionally listed as five: form, feeling, discernment, conditioning factors, and consciousness. They are what is grasped or appropriated in the continual round of rebirth, which occurs as a result of contaminated actions motivated by mental afflictions, especially grasping. Therefore the aggregates themselves, as well as the rebirth taken, are in the nature of suffering.

analysis (*dpyod pa*; *vicāra*; Pali: *vicāra*, lit. "sustained thought"). This is a mind of analytical wisdom that mentally dissects its object of meditation, which may be either conventional or ultimate reality, in a subtle and precise way. It is more refined than investigation.

analytical cessation (*so sor brtags 'gog*; *pratisaṃkhyānirodha*). This is the mere absence of an obstruction that has been removed from the mindstream by means of the wisdom of meditative equipoise analyzing the ultimate, which uproots its cause and ensures that this particular obstruction can never arise again. This is a true cessation, of which there are many—each at different stages of the path—finally culminating in nirvana or omniscience.

appearing object (*snang yul*; *pratibhāsaviṣaya*). This refers to what appears to a consciousness apprehending an object. In general, to a directly perceiving awareness, the object manifestly appears; to a conceptual awareness, a mental image of the object appears mixed with an appearance of the object itself.

appropriation (*nye bar len pa*; *upādāna*). *Also* grasping. As one of a pair, in conjunction with the appropriator, *appropriation* refers to the appropriated object. As one of a triad, in conjunction with the appropriator and the appropriated, *appropriation* refers to the act of appropriating.

aspect (*rnam pa*; *ākāra*). *Also* image, feature, way of apprehending. In the case of a sense consciousness, this refers to the image that is transferred onto that consciousness by its objective condition. And in the case of any conceptual or nonconceptual consciousness, it refers to that consciousness's way of holding its object (i.e., its object as cognized). It may also refer to any feature of an object or subject of awareness.

attribute of the subject (*phyogs chos*; *pakṣadharmatā*). This is the first element of the trimodal criterion of a valid argument, where the evidence is an attribute of the subject that is the basis of debate. More precisely, it refers to the ascertainment by valid cognition that the evidence is present in the subject of the thesis sought to be proven. *See* syllogism; three modes.

autonomous inference (*rang rgyud kyi rjes dpag*; *svatantrānumāna*). Proponents of autonomous inference assert that an inference is valid if, and only if, both the proponent and the opponent establish the three modes by means of valid knowledge that is unmistaken with regard to their intrinsic characteristics. This differs from an inference acceptable for others.

awareness (*rig pa*; *saṃvitti*). *Also* intelligence, knowledge. Awareness is stated to be the nature of cognition and the function of consciousness. It is treated as synonymous with cognition and consciousness.

base (*skye mched*; *āyatana*). *See* sense base.

basis of identity (*mtshan gzhi*; *lakṣya*). *Also* locus of characteristics, identity-bearer. A conventional basis of identity of a person includes the individual person as well as their characteristics, which are used to identify that person in daily life. As for an ultimate basis of identity of a person, other Buddhist schools say that a basis of identity of the person is found at the culmination of ultimate analysis seeking the person among the aggregates that are its basis of imputation, whereas the Prāsaṅgika say that only the mere absence of the person is found (i.e., *śūnyatā*), because nothing can be found to exist as the person from its own side.

basis of imputation (*gdags gzhi*, *gdags pa'i gzhi*; *prajñaptivastu*). *Also* basis of designation. Any permanent or impermanent thing is imputed upon its basis of imputation. The basis of imputation of a thing may include its attributes, its parts, or any of its other characteristics.

bodhisattva (*byang chub sems pa*). A person who has entered the Mahāyāna path. Such a being (*sattva*) has a continuous, spontaneous wish to attain enlightenment (*bodhi*) in order to bring other sentient beings to the state of enlightenment.

calm abiding (*zhi gnas*; *śamatha*). A special type of single-pointed meditative concentration. Calm abiding arises as a result of having progressively developed nine specific levels of concentration. It is accompanied by bodily and mental pliancy and their concurrent forms of bliss. It is united with special insight so as to subdue or remove the mental afflictions.

causal relation (*de byung 'brel*; *tadutpattisaṃbandha*). *Also* cause-and-effect relation. This is a relation that involves impermanent things only: any cause and its effect. It is a one-way relation, not mutual. An effect is related to its cause—not the other way around: smoke is causally dependent upon fire, but the reverse is not true. *See also* intrinsic relation; relation.

cause of error (*'khrul pa'i rgyu*; *bhrāntihetu*). In terms of location, there are two types: external and internal causes of error. In terms of subtlety, there are two types: temporary and deep causes of error. A deep cause of error is only ever internal.

classificatory convention (*tha snyad*; *vyavahāra*). This refers to a term as it continues to be used after its initial establishment as a linguistic convention. *See also* linguistic convention.

cognition (*blo*; *buddhi*). *Also* mind, intellect. The nature of cognition is awareness. It is treated as synonymous with awareness and consciousness.

cognition only (*rnam rig tsam*; *vijñaptimātra*). *Also* consciousness only, awareness only. This is the cognizing subject.

cognizance only (*rnam rig tsam*; *vijñaptimātra*). *Also* appearance only, percept only. This is the cognized object.

common acceptance (*'jig rten la grags pa*; *lokaprasiddha*). Mundane awareness or ordinary understanding that accepts what occurs without engaging in ultimate analysis.

common locus (*gzhi mthun*; *samānādhikaraṇa*). *Also* shared basis. This is where two particular attributes or classes of object are instantiated in one thing, which means that they are not contradictory.

compassion (*snying rje*; *karuṇā*). A mind wishing beings to be free from suffering.

conceived object (*zhen yul*). A conceived object is an object of thought only. Thought conceives something, and the object that it holds is the conceived object. A thought's conceived object is a mental image that represents its focal object held in a certain way—rightly or wrongly, depending on whether that thought is correct or incorrect.

concentration (*ting nge 'dzin*; *samādhi*). *See* meditative concentration.

conceptual cognition (*rtog pa'i shes pa*; *savikalpakajñāna*). *Also* conceptual mind, conceptual consciousness, thought. A conceptual cognition does not arise due to the causal capacity of an observed object nearby. Instead, it arises due to previous habituation and to latent potencies of language-based thought processes. *See also* construing awareness.

conceptual identity (*ldog pa*; *vyāvṛtti*). *Also* distinguisher, abstract entity. The term *ldog pa* indicates something isolated from other things or features. It may be used in combination with another word to refer, for example, to a thing itself (*rang ldog*), to an instantiation (*gzhi ldog*), or to a definition (*don ldog*).

conceptualization of inappropriate attention (*tshul bzhin ma yin pa'i rnam rtog*).

There are four fundamental conceptualizations of inappropriate attention: holding impure things as pure, holding things in the nature of suffering as pleasurable, holding impermanent things as unchanging, and holding selfless things as a self or as belonging to a self.

conceptually distinct (*ldog pa tha dad*). Conceptually distinguishable. For example, a product and an impermanent thing are inseparable in reality and therefore one individual entity, yet they are conceptually distinct because for a conceptual consciousness the one term does not evoke the other. *See also* different conceptual identities.

condition (*rkyen*; *pratyaya*). Conditions are impermanent factors that function as causes or assist causes in producing their effects. There are four types of conditions listed as giving rise to a sense consciousness: objective condition—what is perceived; dominant condition—a sense faculty; immediately preceding condition—a previous moment of consciousness; and causal condition—any other conditions required, such as a body, karma, or proximity.

conditioned thing (*'dus byas*; *saṃskṛta*). *Also* conditioned phenomena. Whatever is produced by causes and conditions. Also, an object perceived by a sense consciousness.

conditioning action (*'du byed*; *saṃskāra*). The second of the twelve links of dependent arising.

conditioning factors (*'du byed*; *saṃskāra*). *Also* formative factors. The fourth of the five aggregates constituting the basis of imputation of a person. There are conditioning factors concomitant with the mind, such as volition, and conditioning factors not concomitant with the mind, referring to those factors not included in either form or mental phenomena.

confusion (*rmongs pa*, *mgo rmongs*; *moha*). *See* ignorance.

consciousness (*shes pa*, *rnam par shes pa*; *jñāna*, *vijñāna*). Consciousness is that which knows its object, or that which knows differentiated aspects of its object. The nature of consciousness is said to be clear (or luminous) and aware. It is treated as synonymous with awareness and cognition. It is also treated as synonymous with mind and mentality.

consequence (*thal 'gyur*; *prasaṅga*). *Also* logical consequence, consequential reasoning. A logical consequence is a formally structured argument designed to uproot a wrong view. It usually has the form "If *A* then *B*," and correspondingly, "If ~*B* then ~*A*." A logical consequence can be valid without the two parties in a debate having a commonly accepted valid knowledge of its components. There are two types of consequences: affirming consequences and refuting consequences.

construing awareness (*zhen rig*). This is a cognition that apprehends word and referent as suitable to be associated. As such, it defines conceptual cognition.

consummate nature (*yongs grub*; *pariniṣpannalakṣaṇa*). *Also* thoroughly established, perfect nature. This is the emptiness that is the dependent nature being empty of the imputed nature. It is one of the three natures featured in the Cittamātra system. *See* three natures.

contradictory (*'gal ba*; *viruddha*). *Also* mutual exclusion. Two things are contradictory if nothing instantiates both; in other words, there is no common locus or shared basis. *See also* contradictory in the sense of being contrary; contradictory in the sense of being mutually excluding; directly contradictory.

contradictory in the sense of being contrary (*lan cig mi gnas 'gal*; *sahabhāvavirodha*). This is a less strict way of being *indirectly* contradictory. In such a case, there are no instances that are both, yet there are instances that are neither. An example of this is *red* and *yellow*. Whatever is red cannot be yellow, and whatever is yellow cannot be red. There is no positive common ground: something that is both. But there is a common ground of their negations: something that is neither red nor yellow, such as *blue*. Therefore red and yellow are not strictly contradictory. In Western philosophy, they are called *contrary*.

contradictory in the sense of being mutually excluding (*phan tshun spangs te gnas pa'i 'gal ba*; *parasparaparihārasthitivirodha*). This includes cases that are *directly* contradictory as well those that are *indirectly* contradictory in a strict sense. In each case, being both things is impossible, and being neither is impossible. There is no third ground or possibility at all, whether positive or negative. The difference between them is as follows. *Directly* contradictory in the sense of being mutually excluding requires that the two are contradictory in terms of reality and that the terminology itself shows this, such as *permanent* and *impermanent*. However, *indirectly* contradictory in the sense of being mutually excluding requires only that the two are contradictory in terms of reality, but not in terms of terminology or understanding, such as *permanent* and *produced*. Here, if one mentally or verbally cuts out *permanent*, this does not mean one will naturally understand *produced*; or if one cuts out *produced*, then one does not necessarily understand *permanent*. Therefore they are not directly contradictory according to Buddhist logic. *See also* directly contradictory.

cooperative condition (*lhan cig byed rkyen*; *sahakāripratyaya*). Although not the primary producer of the object, it functions as a complementary condition to help the substantial cause produce its effects.

conventional analysis (*tha snyad dpyod pa'i rigs pa*). This kind of analysis is commonly used in daily life; we identify things in terms of their conventional characteristics. *See also* ultimate analysis.

conventional truth (*kun rdzob bden pa*; *saṃvṛtisatya*). Various notions of conventional truth are presented in the different traditions. However, in general we can say that this term here refers to whatever is true from the perspective of cognition that conceals ultimate reality. *See also* ultimate truth.

conventional truth (*tha snyad kyi bden pa*; *vyavahārasatya*). As above, various notions of conventional truth are presented in the different traditions. However, in general we can say that this term here refers to whatever is true from the perspective of mundane cognition. *See also* ultimate truth.

correct (*yang dag pa*; *samyag*). True, real, actual, veridical (*versus* distorted).

correct assumption (*yid dpyod*; *manaḥparikṣā*). This is defined as construing awareness that with conviction conceives the main thing that is its engaged object, but does not obtain a realization of its object of scrutiny.

correct effect-evidence (*'bras rtags yang dag*; *saṃyakkāryahetu*). This is evidence based on a causal relationship; it proves the existence of the cause based on the existence of its effect. For example, "On a smoky mountain pass there is fire, because there is smoke."

correct evidence consisting in nonperception (*ma dmigs pa'i rtags yang dag*; *saṃyaganupalabdhihetu*). This is simply the negative form of the other two types of evidence—correct effect-evidence and correct nature-evidence; it proves the nonexistence or negation of one thing based upon the nonexistence or negation of another, which are related either causally or in terms of being the same nature.

correct nature-evidence (*rang bzhin gyi rtags yang dag*; *saṃyaksvabhāvahetu*). This is evidence based on an intrinsic relationship; it proves one thing on the basis of another that is of the same nature as it. For example, "Sound is impermanent because it is produced."

defined thing (*mtshon bya*; *lakṣya*). *Also* definiendum. This is a *dharma*, a thing, or a quality that is identified in terms of the characteristics encapsulated in its definition.

definition (*mtshan nyid*, *ngo bo*; *lakṣaṇa*, *bhāva*). *Also* characteristics. A definition encapsulates the particular characteristics of a *dharma*, a thing, or a quality in terms of which it is identified. A definition and its definiendum are coreferential or coextensive.

delusion (*gti mug*; *moha*). *See* ignorance.

denial (*skur 'debs*; *apavāda*). *Also* over-negation, denigration, repudiation. This refers to the implicit or explicit denial of the existence of something that actually exists. It is the opposite of *reification*.

dependent arising (*rten 'brel*; *pratītyasamutpāda*). According to varying degrees of subtlety, the term *dependent* may mean: dependent on causes, dependent on parts, or dependent upon imputation. A prime example of causal dependence would be the twelve links of dependent arising.

dependent nature (*gzhan dbang*; *paratantralakṣaṇa*). This is the causally conditioned nature of a thing. It is one of the three natures featured in the Cittamātra system. *See* three natures.

different (*tha dad*; *nānā*, *bhinna*). *Also* distinct, separate, diverse. Things that are distinct from each other in every respect.

different conceptual identities (*ldog pa tha dad*). Things that are conceptually and verbally distinct, though they do not necessarily exist apart from each other.

different entities (*ngo bo tha dad*). Things that exist apart from each other, though they may be causally related.

direct perception (*mngon sum*; *pratyakṣa*). A mind that perceives its object directly, or free of conceptuality. Free of any temporary causes of error, it is valid. *See also* valid cognition.

directly (*mngon sum du*; *sākṣāt*, *pratyaṣaṃ*). *Also* manifestly. An object appears directly, or nakedly, to the direct perception apprehending it, without the medium of a mental image.

directly contradictory (*dngos 'gal*; *sākṣādvirodha*). This is synonymous with *directly contradictory in the sense of being mutually excluding*. Two things are directly contradictory if the terminology itself shows that it is impossible to be both and impossible to be neither. This means that by eliminating or negating one side, you prove the other. This kind of proof gives rise to an immediate understanding. So if two things are contradictory in terms of reality but not in terms of terminology or understanding, then they are not directly contradictory. *See also* contradictory in the sense of being mutually excluding.

distinguishing mark (*mtshan ma*; *nimitta*). *Also* sign. This refers to the distinguishing characteristic of an object that serves as a basis for applying a label or linguistic convention.

distorted (*log pa, phyin ci log pa*; *viparyāsa*). Inverse, contrary, erroneous, wrong.

distorted cognition (*log shes*; *viparītajñāna*). *Also* distorted consciousness. A distorted cognition is mistaken with regard to how it holds its principal object, in addition to how that object appears. Whether perceptual or conceptual, it is not any kind of valid knowledge.

distorted conventionality (*kun rdzob log pa*; *mithyāsaṃvṛti*). That which is commonly accepted to be a distorted object just as it appears to the conventional cognition clearly perceiving it.

dominant condition (*bdag rkyen*; *adhipatipratyaya*). Generally this refers to the sense organ or faculty that empowers its respective sense consciousness when in contact with an appropriate object.

dualistic appearance (*gnyis snang*; *dvayapratibhāsa*). There are several types of dualistic appearance, each of which is considered mistaken in some way: the mind, or subject, and its object appearing as separate entities; the object appearing mixed with an image of it; the object appearing together with its attribute; and the object appearing as truly existent. The Cittamātra are more concerned with the first and the Mādhyamika with the last. A direct realization of *śūnyatā* lacks any of these mistaken elaborations.

elaboration (*spros pa*; *prapañca*). *Also* proliferating tendencies. There are several types of elaboration, including afflictive ignorance that propagates cyclic existence, the superimposition of true existence, and the appearance of true existence.

elements (*khams*; *dhātu*). When classified as six, these are earth, water, fire, wind, space, and consciousness. When classified as eighteen, these are the six internal bases of sense consciousness (the sense faculties), the six external bases of sense consciousness (their objects), and the six sense consciousnesses themselves, which arise in dependence upon the sense faculties and their objects. The same term is translated as "realm" when referring to the desire, form, and formless realms. *See also* sense base.

emptiness (*stong pa nyid*; *śūnyatā*). Emptiness is the final nature of all phenomena according to the Yogācāra and Madhyamaka schools of philosophy. There are different interpretations of emptiness ranging from coarse to subtle as follows: emptiness of a permanent, partless, and independent person; emptiness of a self-sufficient, substantially existent person; emptiness of a substantial difference between the apprehender and the apprehended; emptiness of true existence; and emptiness of inherent existence.

engage via affirmation (*sgrub 'jug*). The notion that a signifying term denotes its referent by being established through the capacity of the real thing.

engage via exclusion (*sel 'jug*). The notion that a signifying term denotes its referent by excluding what is not it. While Dignāga emphasizes language here, Dharmakīrti presents this theory from the perspective of both language and thought.

engaged object (*'jug yul*; *pravṛttiviṣaya*). *Also* object of activity, object of application. This is generally considered to be the main object of awareness to which cognition applies.

entity (*ngo bo*; *bhāva*, *rūpa*, *vastu*). An individual thing. *Also* essential nature, definition.

essential nature (*rang gi ngo bo nyid*; *svabhāva*, *svarūpa*). All phenomena lack an essential nature. The Prāsaṅgika interpret this to mean that all phenomena lack inherent nature. The Cittamātra interpret this in three ways, corresponding to the three natures. *See also* three natures.

established by valid cognition (*tshad mas grub pa*; *pramāṇasiddha*). This defines what it means to exist. *See also* valid cognition.

evidence (*rtags*; *liṅga*, *hetu*). *Also* reason, sign, mark. This is the evidence or reason posited in a formal argument to show that the predicate applies to the subject. Evidence may be either correct or fallacious. Correct evidence must satisfy the three modes. *See* three modes.

exclusion (*sel ba*; *apoha*). *See* engage via exclusion.

exclusion of other (*gzhan sel*; *anyāpoha*). *See* engage via exclusion.

exist (*yod pa*; *bhāva*, *sat*). To exist, existent. To be established by valid cognition.

explicitly (*dngos su*; *vastutaḥ*). *Also* directly. To explicitly understand something means that the object appears to the mind knowing it.

five aggregates (*phung po lnga*; *pañcaskandhā*). *See* aggregates of appropriation.

focal object (*dmigs pa*, *dmigs yul*, *dmigs rten*; *ālambanaviṣaya*). *Also* objective support. This refers to any main object of perception or thought. When a mind apprehending it holds the focal object to possess certain attributes, then that is the *object as cognized*. Thus the focal object and the object as cognized are different.

foundation consciousness (*kun gzhi rnam shes*; *ālayavijñāna*). Cittamātra/Yogācāra followers posit eight primary minds: the six sense consciousnesses, the afflictive mental consciousness, and the foundation consciousness. They consider the foundation consciousness to be the receptacle of the karmic seeds and imprints as well as being the basis of identity of the self.

general characteristics (*spyi mtshan*; *sāmānyalakṣaṇa*). *Also* universal characteristics. Characteristics shared by things of the same kind or belonging to the same category.

homologous example (*mthun dpe, udāharaṇa*). The homologous example is provided when setting forth a formally structured argument to help the opponent recognize the relation between the evidence and the predicate in his or her own experience.

identity view (*'jig tshogs la lta ba*; *satkāyadṛṣṭi*). *Also* view of the perishable collection. This is a self-grasping mind, of which there are two types: acquired identity view and innate identity view. The latter is a subtle form of afflictive ignorance considered to be the root of cyclic existence.

ignorance (*ma rig pa*; *avidya*). *Also* delusion, confusion. This usually refers to afflictive ignorance, which is a distorted awareness. It is a mental factor rather than a primary mind. Ignorance is not simply not knowing the truth; it is the opposite of knowing the truth, a radical misunderstanding of reality. There are many types of ignorance, often categorized into two: ignorance of cause and effect and ignorance of ultimate reality.

image (*rnam pa*; *ākāra*). *See* aspect.

immediately preceding condition (*de ma thag rkyen*; *samanantarapratyaya*). The immediately preceding condition of any consciousness is a prior moment of consciousness.

implicative negation (*ma yin dgag*; *paryudāsapratiṣedha*). Here, the object of negation is directly negated and the words expressing that negation also state or infer some other positive phenomenon, whether directly or indirectly. For example, the stout Devadatta does not eat during the daytime.

implicitly (*shugs la*). The terms *explicitly* and *implicitly* may be applied to words, teachings, and understanding. To implicitly understand something means that the object is realized without actually appearing to the mind knowing it.

imprints (*bag chags*; *vāsanā*). *See* propensities.

imputed nature (*kun btags*; *parikalpitalakṣaṇa*). This is the merely nominally or conceptually constructed nature of a thing. It is one of the three natures featured in the Cittamātra system. *See* three natures.

imputedly existent (*btags yod*; *prajñaptisat*). Something that does not exist substantially but instead exists through being imputed in dependence upon its basis of imputation.

inappropriate attention (*tshul min yid byed*; *ayoniśomanasikāra*). *See* conceptualization of inappropriate attention.

indirectly (*rgyud nas*). An object appears indirectly to the mind apprehending it when it appears through the medium of a mental image. However, since the object appears to it, that mind explicitly understands its object.

inference (*rjes dpag*; *anumāna*). The term *inference* may refer to an inferential understanding or to a formally structured argument designed to engender that understanding through the use of valid reasoning.

inference acceptable for others (*gzhan grags kyi gtan tshigs*; *parasiddhānumāna*). This kind of inference is not an autonomous inference. It is used merely to refute an opponent's thesis. Here the opponent already accepts the subject, the reason, and the pervasion of the inference, and may even consider that these are established by valid knowledge. However, the proponent need not accept the reason, the pervasion, or that any elements of the inference are established by a shared notion of valid knowledge. This kind of inference, when viewed from the opponent's perspective, is also called an inference acceptable for oneself (*rang grags kyi gtan tshigs*; *svasiddhānumāna*).

inherent nature (*rang bzhin*; *svabhāva*). A nature of things posited to exist from its own side independently of being labeled, which is interpreted slightly differently in the various traditions and generally proved to be nonexistent. *See* nature.

inherently existent (*rang bzhin gyis grub pa*; *svabhāvasiddhi*). Inherently established or existing from its own side independently of being labeled, which is interpreted slightly differently in the various traditions and generally proved to be nonexistent.

innate (*lhan skyes*; *sahaja*). *Also* natural, spontaneous, simultaneously arisen. This usually refers to a mind that arises naturally through the ripening of potentialities imprinted in the mindstream by actions done in a former life.

intrinsic characteristics (*rang mtshan*; *svalakṣaṇa*).These are particular characteristics in terms of which something is posited to exist from its own side independently of being labeled, which is interpreted slightly differently in the various traditions and generally proved to be nonexistent.

intrinsic relation (*bdag gcig 'brel*; *tādātmyasaṃbandha*). *Also* nature-relation. This is a relation whose components do not exist separately and yet are not identical in that they can be distinguished conceptually. Consider, for example, a universal and its instances or an object and its attributes; there is no universal separate from its instances, and there is no object separate from its attributes. An intrinsic relation is one-way, not mutual. An instance is related to its universal, not the other way around: an oak tree is dependent upon being a tree in terms of its nature, but the reverse is not implied. Nevertheless, if two components of an intrinsic relation are coextensive, then a two-way relationship ensues, because each is an instance of the other: an impermanent thing is a product and vice versa. This two-way relationship is very different from the Madhyamaka relation of mutual dependence. *See also* causal relation; relation.

invariable relation. *See* unaccompanied nonoccurrence.

investigation (*rtog pa*; *vitarka*; Pali: *vitakka*, lit. "applied thought"). *Also* examination, inquiry. This is a conceptual, analytical wisdom-mind that mentally dissects the characteristics of its object of meditation in a general way. It is coarser than analysis.

label (*brda*; *saṃketa*). *See* linguistic convention.

latent propensity (*bag chags*; *vāsanā*). *Also* imprint, potency, tendency. These are causally effective predispositions or propensities imprinted on the mindstream by any virtuous, nonvirtuous, or neutral activity of body, speech, or mind. Of greatest concern are those imprinted through the functioning of mental afflictions and their seeds.

linguistic convention (*brda*; *saṃketa*). *Also* label. This refers to a term as it is initially applied to an object. *See also* classificatory convention.

linguistic referent (*sgra don*, *sgra'i don*; *śabdārtha*). *Also* word meaning, referent of a term. The linguistic referent is the meaning of the word. This is a universal image that appears to a conceptual cognition.

manifest (*mngon 'gyur*; *pratyakṣa*). This can mean one of three things: activated, more gross, or clearly evident.

manifold (*ji snyed pa*). The varying phenomena included within conventional reality.

meaning of a term (*sgra don*, *sgra'i don*; *śabdārtha*). *See* linguistic referent.

meditative concentration (*ting nge 'dzin*; *samādhi*). There are many levels of concentration, which may accompany different types of mind. When gradually developed in conjunction with a virtuous mind, concentration (*samādhi*) eventually gives rise to calm abiding (*śamatha*).

mental afflictions (*nyon mongs*; *kleśa*). *See* afflictions.

mental consciousness (*yid shes*, *yid kyi rnam shes*; *manojñāna*, *manovijñāna*). This is one of the six primary consciousnesses. However, unlike the five sense consciousnesses, it does not arise in dependence on a physical sense organ. It arises in dependence on its object and its dominant condition, a previous moment of consciousness, which functions as the mental sense faculty. *See also* sense consciousness.

mental factor (*sems 'byung*; *caitta*; Pali: *cetasika*). These are secondary consciousnesses that accompany a primary consciousness. Where the main mind cognizes an object, its concomitant mental factors cognize the object's attributes.

mere negation (*med dgag*; *prasajyapratiṣedha*). *See* nonimplicative negation.

mind (*sems*; *citta*). The nature of mind is luminous clarity and awareness. In this regard it is the same as consciousness. However, when differentiated from mental factors, which are also types of consciousness, mind refers to any of the six types of primary consciousness within the continuum of a living being.

mistaken cognition (*'khrul shes*; *bhrāntajñāna*). *Also* mistaken consciousness. A mistaken cognition is mistaken with regard to how its object appears, not to how it is held. A mistaken cognition, whether it is a perception or a thought, need not be distorted. It is valid if it holds its principal object correctly.

mode of existence (*gnas lugs*). Mode of being, way of existing. This is how the object actually exists, which may be different to how it appears or how it is held by a mind apprehending it.

mutually dependent relation (*phan tshun bltos pa'i 'brel ba*; *parasparasāpekṣasaṃbandha*). This is a relationship of terminological dependence, which has much wider application than the more strict relations: causal relation and intrinsic relation. It is presented within the Prāsaṅgika Madhyamaka system only as the most profound meaning of dependent arising. It applies to all phenomena, because everything is established as mutually dependent upon its basis of imputation. This is what it means to lack inherent existence.

nature (*rang bzhin*; *svabhāva*). The term *nature* has at least three meanings: conventional nature, which mainly refers to a thing's conventional characteristics; ultimate nature, which refers to a thing's emptiness of true existence; and inherent nature, or self-nature, which some Buddhist schools argue is not an attribute of anything at all because it does not exist.

negative pervasion (*ldog khyab*; *vyatirekavyāpti*). This is the third element of the trimodal criterion of a valid syllogism, where the absence of the predicate entails the absence of the evidence. More precisely, it refers to the ascertainment by valid cognition that the evidence is *only* absent in the set of heterogeneous cases owing to its relation to the predicate of the thesis to be proven. *See also* pervasion; syllogism.

nirvāṇa (*mya ngan las 'das pa*). The term *nirvāṇa* indicates a state beyond suffering and its causes. The Mahāyāna texts present a fourfold terminological division of nirvāṇa: natural nirvāṇa, nirvāṇa with remainder, nirvāṇa without remainder, and nonabiding nirvāṇa. Only the last three are genuinely types of nirvāṇa.

nonimplicative negation (*med dgag*; *prasajyapratiṣedha*). *Also* mere negation. This is when the object of negation is directly negated, and the words expressing that negation do not state or infer some other positive phenomenon, directly or indirectly.

object as cognized (*'dzin stangs kyi yul*; *muṣṭibandhaviṣaya*). *Also* held object. This may be an object of thought or of direct perception. It is that mind's main object held in a certain way—rightly or wrongly, depending on whether that mind is correct or incorrect.

object universal (*don spyi*; *arthasāmānya*). This is a technical term referring to the appearing object of a conceptual consciousness.

object-image (*gzung rnam*; *grāhyākāra*). *Also* objective aspect. A cognition may be considered to have two parts—an externally oriented objective aspect (or object-image), and an internally oriented subjective aspect (or subject-image). The object-image is considered by some systems to be an internal representation of the object, thus in the nature of cognition, and by other systems to be a transparent revealing of the external object itself, thus not in the nature of cognition and not actually an image.

objective aspect (*gzung rnam*; *grāhyākāra*). *See* object-image.

objective condition (*dmigs rkyen*; *ālambanapratyaya*). This is the main object of focus.

observed object (*gzung yul*; *grāhyaviṣaya*). This is the same as the appearing object; in the case of direct perception, it is a real thing, and in the case of thought, it is a universal.

one (*gcig*; *ekatva*). *Also* same, single, unitary. Absolute identity, including conceptual and terminological identity.

opponent (*rgol ba*, *phyi rgol*; *uttaravādin*). The defender within a formally structured argument; the one who speaks later and to whom the proponent is trying to prove something. The term *opponent* may apply to a school of thought or to a person representing it.

ordinary being (*so so'i skye bu*; *pṛthagjana*). Any living being who has not realized directly the ultimate nature of persons or phenomena.

own characteristics (*rang mtshan*, *svalakṣaṇa*). This term is interpreted in several ways and can be used to mean: the *particular characteristics* of a phenomenon in terms of which it is defined; the *unique particulars* that are causally effective real things found in Dignāga's and Dharmakīrti's epistemology; and the *intrinsic characteristics* in terms of which something is posited to exist from its own side independently of being labeled, which is interpreted slightly differently in the various traditions. *See also* intrinsic characteristics; particular characteristics; unique particular.

particular (*bye brag*; *viśeṣa*). An instance of a general category or universal.

particular characteristics (*rang mtshan*; *svalakṣaṇa*). These are characteristics that are unique to a phenomenon in terms of which it is defined. *See* own characteristics.

person (*gang zag*; *pudgala* / *skyes bu*; *puruṣa*). The term *pudgala* is used in the Indian schools to refer to the agent of actions in the ordinary sense. In Jainism, *pudgala* does not mean "person" but instead "matter." The term *puruṣa* refers to the conscious self and thus can also be translated as "self." In Sāṅkhya, it is an entity that is completely devoid of change, the only one of the twenty-five principles that is not matter. It is unborn, permanent, and unitary but is not the creator of transformations. When *puruṣa* is used to refer to the deity or the eternal self, it is often translated as "supreme person."

pervaded object (*khyab bya*; *vyāpya*). That which is encompassed by another. An instance is pervaded by any of its universals. For example, impermanent things are encompassed by existent things; they are included within the domain of existent things. In this case, impermanent things are the pervaded.

pervader (*khyab byed*; *vyāpaka*). That which encompasses another. A universal encompasses all its instances. For example, existent things encompass or include impermanent things as well as permanent things. In this case, existent things are the pervader.

pervasion (*khyab pa*; *vyāpti*). To encompass or include; to extend over a domain. Pervasion is an expression of relationship. There are two types of relation—causal relation and intrinsic relation—therefore there are two types of pervasion. As an example of the latter type, a universal pervades all its instances. For example, the universal, horse, encompasses all kinds of horse and all individual horses. Pervasion in the context of logic requires that, in a formally structured argument, the predicate must pervade the evidence.

positive pervasion (*rjes khyab*; *anvayavyāpti*). This is the second element of the trimodal criterion of a valid argument, where the presence of the evidence entails the presence of the predicate. More precisely, it refers to the ascertainment by valid cognition that the evidence is present in *only* the set of homologous cases owing to its relation to the predicate of the thesis to be proven. *See also* pervasion; syllogism.

predicate of the thesis (*bsgrub bya'i chos*; *sādyadharma*). Property or attribute of the probandum.

primal nature (*prakṛti, rang bzhin*). In the Sāṅkhya school, this is the eternal and unitary cause of the world and its various transformations. It is unconscious matter that is only a cause and is never an effect or transformation. It is unmanifest and pervades all the objects of knowledge. Its three qualities (*sattva, rajas,* and *tamas*), which are in equilibrium when unmanifest, pervade all its manifest transformations.

principal (*pradhāna, spyi gtso bo*). This is another name for the primal nature in the Sāṅkhya school.

probandum (*bsgrub bya*; *sādhya*). *Also* thesis. Combination of the subject and the predicate of a formally structured argument, which is to be proved by the evidence posited.

proliferating tendency (*spros pa*; *prapañca*). *See* elaboration.

proof (*sgrub byed*; *sādhana*). The evidence, or reason, that proves the thesis, or probandum, in a formally structured argument.

proof statement (*sgrub ngag*; *sādhanavākya*). A type of argument to clear away doubt that oscillates between two standpoints.

propensities (*bag chags*; *vāsanā*). *Also* imprints. These are causally effective latent predispositions imprinted on the mindstream by any virtuous, nonvirtuous, or neutral activity of body, speech, or mind. Of greatest concern are those imprinted through the functioning of mental afflictions and their seeds.

proponent (*snga rgol*; *pūravādin*). The person who speaks first and is trying to prove something to an opponent within the context of a formally structured argument. The term *proponent* may apply to a school of thought or to a person who represents it.

quality (*yon tan*; *guṇa*). Attribute or property; good, neutral, or bad qualities (but most commonly good qualities).

reality as it is (*ji lta ba*; *tathatā*). The unvarying nature that is ultimate reality.

real thing (*dngos po*; *vastu, bhāva*). *Also* thing, causal thing, impermanent thing. The word *dngos po* has at least two meanings: a thing that arises and ceases in dependence on causes and functions to produce a result or a truly existent thing.

reflexive awareness (*rang rig*; *svasaṃvedana*). *Also* self-cognizing consciousness. This is a directly perceiving, inwardly focused mind that observes an outwardly focused, other-cognizing mind. These aspects of mind are substantially identical. The Prāsaṅgika do not posit any reflexive awareness.

refutation (*sun 'byin*; *dūṣaṇa, niṣedha*). This is a form of consequential reasoning employed to destroy a distorted conviction or a distorted conception that holds on to one standpoint.

reification (*sgro btags*; *samāropa*). *Also* superimposition, exaggeration. This refers to the implicit or explicit acceptance of the existence of something that does not actually exist. It is the opposite of *denial.*

relation (*'brel ba*; *saṃbandha*). According to earlier Buddhist systems, there are just two ways of being related: causal relation and intrinsic relation (or related as being of the same nature). A relation holds between two things or attributes and is characterized as follows: if this does not exist, then definitely that does not occur. This definition is known as *unaccompanied nonoccurrence.* It applies to both types of relation and in one direction only, not mutually (unless both components within an intrinsic relation are coextensive). A third type of relation is presented in the Madhyamaka system: mutually dependent relation. *See also* causal relation; intrinsic relation; unaccompanied nonoccurrence.

same (*gcig*; *ekatva*). *See* one.

same entity (*ngo bo gcig*; *ekarūpatā*, *ekavastu*). This applies where the things concerned do not exist apart from each other yet may be differentiated conceptually and terminologically. For example, a thing and its attributes.

same meaning (*don gcig*; *ekārtha*). *Also* synonymous. This applies where the referent or extension of two different terms is the same. There is a formal eightfold criterion provided: whatever is *a* is *b*, whatever is *b* is *a*, whatever is not *a* is not *b*, whatever is not *b* is not *a*, if *a* exists then *b* exists, if *b* exists then *a* exists, if *a* does not exist then *b* does not exist, if *b* does not exist then *a* does not exist.

self (*bdag*; *ātman*). In the context of Buddhist philosophy, this either refers to the self as apprehended in an ordinary sense, or it refers to the object of negation—a person or any other phenomenon grasped in an unrealistic manner. It is the self-grasping mind's *object as cognized* to exist from its own side independently of being labeled.

self-grasping (*bdag 'dzin*; *ātmagrāha*, *ahaṃkāra*). This generally refers to a mind grasping at true existence, whether of the person or of phenomena.

sense base (*skye mched*; *āyatana*). These are the twelve sources of sense consciousness: internally, the six sense faculties, and externally, the objects of the six sense consciousnesses. *See also* elements.

sense consciousness (*dbang shes*; *indriyajñāna*). *Also* sensory cognition. The six sense consciousnesses include the mental sense consciousness, which is often treated separately. The five sense consciousnesses refer to those of the eye, ear, nose, tongue, and body. Each arises in dependence on its respective object together with its own uncommon dominant condition, the subtle sense organ located in its fleshly counterpart. The mental consciousness does not depend on a subtle sense organ as its dominant condition but on a previous moment of mind. *See also* mental consciousness.

sense faculty (*dbang po*; *indriya*). These are the subtle sense organs located in their fleshly counterparts, such as the eyeball, which function as the internal sources of their respective sensory cognitions. However, the mental sense faculty is not an organ, it is a previous moment of mind.

subject (*chos can*; *dharmin*). Literally, something that has attributes. This term also refers to the subject of a formally structured argument.

subject (*yul can*; *viṣayin*). Literally, something that takes an object. This term refers to persons, minds, and words.

subject-image (*'dzin rnam*; *grāhakākāra*). *Also* subjective aspect. This is an appearance of the object-image, or the objective aspect, within a cognition.

subsequent cognition (*bcad shes*; *pṛṣṭhalabdhajñāna*). This is a cognition that follows upon a perception, and it often takes the form of a conceptual judgment that interprets the content of the perception. It is not a newly realizing cognition because its object has already been apprehended by the perception.

substantial cause (*nyer len gyi rgyu*; *upādānakāraṇa*). The substantial cause of something must be a continuum of what is of a similar type as itself. It is the primary cause of that thing, whether it is something material, something in the nature of consciousness, or a conditioning factor that is neither of those two.

substantial particle (*rdzas kyi rdul phra rab*; *dravyaparamāṇu*). This is the smallest discrete unit of matter, of which there are eight types: the four primary elements (earth, water, fire, and wind) and the four element derivatives (form, smell, taste, and tactility). According to Vasubandhu's Abhidharma system, even one aggregated atom in the desire realm must consist of all eight types of substantial particles.

substantially existent (*rdzas su yod pa*; *dravyasat*). Vasubandhu's Abhidharma system posits substantially existent things, such as indivisible atomic particles and moments of consciousness, to be the bases of imputation upon which coarse objects must be imputed. A substantially existent thing supposedly bears its identity from its own side and can be found by ultimate analysis. The Prāsaṅgika do not accept anything to be substantially existent.

suchness (*de nyid*, *de bzhin nyid*; *tathatā*). The way things are, the ultimate nature of reality.

superimposition (*sgro btags*; *samāropa*). *See* reification.

syllogism (*rtags sbyor*, *sbyor ba*; *prayoga*). This is a positively stated argument that has the following form: the *subject* is the *predicate* because it is the *evidence*, as in the *homologous example*. For a syllogism to be correct it must be characterized by the three modes. However, it need not be an autonomous inference, where the three modes must be known by both parties using a commonly accepted notion of validity.

thesis (*bsgrub bya*; *sādhya*). *See* probandum.

thing (*dngos po*; *vastu*, *bhāva*). *See* real thing.

three modes (*tshul gsum*; *trirūpa*). This is the trimodal criterion of a valid syllogism, which requires that (1) the evidence is an attribute of the subject, (2) the presence of the evidence entails the presence of the predicate, and (3) the absence of the predicate entails the absence of the evidence. The latter two modes are called the *positive pervasion* and the *negative pervasion*, respectively. *See also* attribute of the subject; negative pervasion; positive pervasion.

three natures (*mtshan nyid gsum*; *trilakṣana*). As presented in the *Unraveling the Intention Sūtra* as well as in other sūtras such as *Descent into Laṅkā Sūtra*, the three natures are: the dependent nature, the imputed nature, and the consummate nature. These are a fundamental feature of the Cittamātra system.

tīrthika (*mu stegs pa*). A term used in Buddhist texts to describe adherents of non-Buddhist schools of Indian philosophy and practice.

ultimate analysis (*don dam dpyod pa'i rigs pa*; Sanskrit not provided). This is a type of analysis utilized to develop an understanding of ultimate truth. According to the Prāsaṅgika Madhyamaka tradition, it is an analytical search for an object existing from its own side—i.e., ultimately. The object analyzed cannot be found to exist in that way. What is found is a mere lack of its existing ultimately. This is the ultimate or final nature of the object analyzed—the ultimate truth, *śūnyatā*. *See also* conventional analysis.

ultimate truth (*don dam bden pa*; *paramārthasatya*). Various notions of ultimate truth are presented in the different traditions. According to the Prāsaṅgika Madhyamaka tradition, it is *śūnyatā*, the emptiness of inherent existence. *See also* conventional truth.

unaccompanied nonoccurrence (*med na mi 'byung*; *avinābhāvaniyama*). *Also* invariable relation. This is a criterion that encapsulates both types of relation: the causal relation and the intrinsic relation. Most notably, it is crucial in the context of a correct inference because it is the kind of relation that must hold between the evidence and the predicate to be inferred. This means that when the *pervaded* is present the *pervader* too is necessarily present, and when the *pervader* is absent the *pervaded* too is necessarily absent.

unassociated conditioning factors (*ldan min 'du byed*; *viprayuktasaṃskāra*). *Also* dissociated formative factors. These encompass all impermanent phenomena not included in the class of material form or the class of mental phenomena.

unique particular (*rang mtshan*, *rang gi mtshan nyid*; *svalakṣaṇa*). A unique particular is a real thing that is causally effective. *See* own characteristics.

universal (*spyi*; *sāmānya*). A universal is an abstract object of thought that encompasses all its instances. Although a universal is not causally effective and is therefore unreal, its instances may be real things. There are different types of universal: an *object universal* (*don spyi*) is a universal that encompasses its specific instances; a *word universal* (*sgra spyi*) is the universal type of a word that is expressed through the specific utterances that are its tokens. *See also* word universal.

unmistaken cognition (*ma 'khrul ba'i shes pa*; *abhrāntajñāna*). A cognition that is not mistaken with regard to its appearing object.

unreal (*dngos med*; *avastu*, *abhāva*). There are at least two senses of unreal: an *unreal thing*, which exists but does not arise or cease in dependence upon causes and does not function to produce any result, and a *non-thing*, which does not exist at all. A non-thing is unreal, but it is not an unreal thing. An unreal thing is a permanent phenomenon. Additionally, in some contexts *unreal* can mean "not really existent" or "not truly existent."

valid cognition (*tshad ma*; *pramāṇa*). *Also* valid knowing, valid instrument of knowing. Some sources say it is newly acquired and nondeceptive cognition. Others say it is cognition that correctly knows its principal object. Most agree that there are two types of valid cognition: direct perception and inferential understanding.

veridical conventionality (*yang dag kun rdzob*; *samyaksaṃvṛti*). That which is commonly accepted to be a veridical object just as it appears to the conventional cognition clearly perceiving it. This is necessarily a conventional truth.

view (*lta ba*; *dṛṣṭi*). *Also* viewing. This mainly refers to a type of mind that grasps its object in a certain way, often in a mistaken or distorted manner. It can also refer to a shared belief or philosophical tenet.

view of the perishable collection (*'jig lta*, *'jig tshogs la lta ba*; *satkāyadṛṣṭi*). *See* identity view.

wisdom (*shes rab*; *prajñā*). *Also* intelligence. One of the five mental factors with a determinate object, it accompanies every instance of cognition. Its main function is to investigate the characteristics of its object. There is innate wisdom and wisdom acquired through learning and mental cultivation.

word meaning (*sgra don*, *sgra'i don*; *śabdārtha*). *See* linguistic referent.

word universal (*sgra spyi*; *śabdasāmānya*). *See* universal.

wrong view (*log lta*; *mithyādṛṣṭi*). *Also* distorted view. This an afflictive intelligence that, upon considering something that exists, such as karmic cause and effect, views it to be nonexistent. It is a distorted apprehension that causes one to behave perversely regarding what to accept or reject, whereby one abandons virtue and engages in nonvirtue. The root wrong view is a distorted cognition holding its object to be truly existent.

Bibliography

Buddhist Sūtras and Tantras

Bodhisattva's Scriptural Collection Sūtra. Bodhisattvapiṭakasūtra. Byang chub sems dpa'i sde snod mdo. Toh 56, Sūtra, kha.

Dependent Arising Sūtra. Pratītyasamutpādasūtra. Rten cing 'brel bar 'byung ba'i mdo. Toh 212, Sūtra, tsha.

Descent into Laṅkā Sūtra. Laṅkāvatārasūtra. Lang kar gshegs pa'i mdo. Toh 107, Sūtra, ca.

Great Final Nirvāṇa Sūtra. Mahāparinirvāṇasūtra. Yongs su mya ngan las 'das pa chen po'i mdo. Toh 119, Sūtra, ta.

Great Play Sūtra. Lalitavistarasūtra. Rgya cher rol pa'i mdo. Toh 95, Sūtra, kha.

Heart Sūtra. Prajñāpāramitāhṛdaya: Bhagavatīprajñāpāramitāhṛdaya. Shes rab snying po: Bcom ldan 'das ma shes rab kyi pha rol tu phyin pa'i snying po. Toh 21 (also 531), Prajñāpāramitā, ka.

Instructions of Vimalakīrti Sūtra. Vimalakīrtinirdeśasūtra. 'Dri ma med par grags pas bstan pa'i mdo. Toh 176, Sūtra, ma.

Kāśyapa Chapter Sūtra. Kāśyapaparivartasūtra. 'Od srung gi le'u gyi mdo. Toh 87, Ratnakūṭa, cha.

Kauśika Perfection of Wisdom. Kauśikaprajñāpāramitā. 'Shes rab kyi pha rol tu phyin pa kau shi ka. Toh 19 (also 554), Prajñāpāramitā, ka.

Meeting of the Father and Son Sūtra. Pitāputrasamāgamanasūtra. Yab sras mjal ba'i mdo. Toh 60, Ratnakūṭa, nga.

Perfection of Wisdom Sūtra in One Thousand Stanzas. Daśasāhasrikāprajñāpāramitāsūtra. Shes rab kyi pha rol tu phyin pa khri pa'i mdo. Toh 11, Prajñāpāramitā, ga, nga.

Pile of Precious Things Collection. Ratnakūṭa. Dkon mchog brtsegs pa chen po'i chos kyi rnam grangs le'u stong phrag brgya pa. Toh 45–93, Ratnakūṭa, ka, kha.

Questions of Lokadhara Sūtra. Lokadharaparipṛcchāsūtra. 'Jig rten 'dzin gyis yongs su dris pa'i mdo. Toh 174, Sūtra, ma.

Questions of Surata Sūtra. Surataparipṛcchāsūtra. Des pas zhus pa'i mdo. Toh 71, Ratnakūṭa ca.

Questions of the Nāga King Anavatapta Sūtra. Anavataptanāgarājaparipṛcchāsūtra. Klu'i rgyal po ma dros pas zhus pa'i mdo. Toh 156, Sūtra, pha.

Questions of the Nāga King Sāgara Sūtra. Sāgaranāgarājaparipṛcchāsūtra. Klu'i rgyal po rgya mtshos gyi mdo. Toh 153–55, Sūtra, pha.

Questions of Upāli Sūtra. Upāliparipṛcchāsūtra. Vinayaviniścayopāliparipṛcchāsūtra. 'Dul ba rnam par gtan la dbab pa nye bar 'khor gyis mdo. Toh 68, Ratnakūṭa, ca.

Questions regarding Selflessness Sūtra. Nairātmyaparipṛcchāsūtra. Bdag med pa dris pa'i mdo. Toh 173, Sūtra, ma.

Questions regarding Transference of Life Sūtra. Āyuṣpattiyathākāraparipṛcchāsūtra. Tshe 'pho ba ji ltar 'gyur ba zhus pa'i mdo. Toh 308, Sūtra, sa.

Rice Seedling Sūtra. Śālistambasūtra. Sa lu ljang pa'i mdo. Toh 210, Sūtra, tsha.

Sūtra Teaching the Tathāgata's Inconceivable Secret. Tathāgatācintyaguhyanirdeśasūtra. De bzhin gshegs pa'i gsang ba bsam gyis mi khyab pa bstan pa'i mdo. Toh 47, Ratnakūṭa, ka.

Teachings of Akṣayamati Sūtra. Akṣayamatinirdeśasūtra. Blo gros mi zad pas bstan pa'i mdo. Toh 175, Sūtra, ma.

Teachings on the Three Vows Sūtra. Trisaṃvaranirdeśasūtra. Sdom pa gsum bstan pa'i le'u gyi mdo. Toh 45, Ratnakūṭa, ka.

Ten Levels Sūtra. Daśabhūmikasūtra. Sa bcu pa'i mdo. Toh 44, Avataṃsaka, kha. This sūtra is chapter 31 of the *Flower Garland Sūtra* collection.

Unraveling the Intention Sūtra. Saṃdhinirmocanasūtra. Mdo sde dgongs 'grel. Toh 106, Sūtra, ca.

Buddhist Canonical Treatises

Āryadeva (ca. second century). *Compendium of the Essence of Wisdom. Jñānasārasamuccaya. Ye shes snying po kun las btus pa.* Toh 3850, Madhyamaka, tsha.

———. *Four Hundred Stanzas on the Practice of Bodhisattvas. Catuḥśataka. Bstan bcos bzhi brgya pa.* Toh 3846, Madhyamaka, tsha.

Āryaśūra (n.d.). *Garland of Birth Stories. Jātakamālā. Skyes pa'i rabs kyi rgyud.* Toh 4150, Jātaka, hu.

Asaṅga (fourth century). *Bodhisattva Levels. Bodhisattvabhūmi. Byang chub sems dpa'i sa.* Toh 4037, Cittamātra, wi.

———. *Compendium of Abhidharma. Abhidharmasamuccaya. Chos mngon pa kun las btus pa.* Toh 4049, Cittamātra, ri.

———. *Compendium of Ascertainments. Viniścayasaṅgraha. Rnam par gtan la dbab pa bsdu ba.* Toh 4038, Cittamātra, zhi, zi.

———. *Compendium of Bases. Vastusaṅgraha. Gzhi bsdu ba.* Toh 4039, Cittamātra, zi.

———. *Compendium of Enumerations. Paryāyasaṅgraha. Rnam grang bsdu ba.* Toh 4041, Cittamātra, 'i.

———. *Compendium of Explanation. Vivaraṇasaṅgraha. Rnam par bshad pa bsdu ba.* Toh 4042. Cittamātra, 'i.

———. *Compendium of the Mahāyāna. Mahāyānasaṅgraha. Theg pa chen po bsdus pa.* Toh 4048, Cittamātra, ri.

———. *Śrāvaka Levels. Śrāvakabhūmi. Nyan thos kyi sa.* Toh 4036, Cittamātra, dzi.

———. *Yogācāra Levels. Yogācārabhūmi. Rnal 'byor spyod pa'i sa.* Toh 4035, Cittamātra, tshi.

Asvabhāva (n.d.). *Commentary on the Ornament for the Mahāyāna Sūtras. Mahāyānasūtrālaṅkāraṭīkā. Theg pa chen po'i mdo sde'i rgyan gyi rgya cher bshad pa.* Toh 4029, Cittamātra, bi.

———. *Explanation of the Compendium of the Mahāyāna. Mahāyānasaṅgrahopanibandhana. Theg pa chen po bsdus pa'i bshad sbyar.* Toh 4051, Cittamātra, ri.

Bhāviveka (sixth century). *Blaze of Reasoning: Heart of the Middle Way Autocommentary. Tarkajvālā: Madhyamakahṛdayavṛttitarkajvālā. Dbu ma'i snying po'i grel pa rtog ge 'bar ba.* Toh 3856, Madhyamaka, dza.

———. *Heart of the Middle Way. Madhyamakahṛdaya. Dbu ma'i snying po.* Toh 3855, Madhyamaka, dza.

———. *Lamp of Wisdom: Commentary on Fundamental Treatise on the Middle Way. Prajñāpradīpamūlamadhyamakavṛtti. Dbu ma'i rtsa ba'i 'grel pa shes rab sgron ma.* Toh 3853, Madhyamaka, tsha.

———. *Summary of the Meaning of the Middle Way. Mādhyamakārthasaṅgraha. Dbu ma'i don bsdus pa.* Toh 3857, Madhyamaka, dza.

Buddhapālita (late fifth to early sixth century). *Buddhapālita's Commentary on the Fundamental Treatise. Buddhapālitamūlamadhyamakavṛtti. Dbu ma rtsa ba'i 'grel pa buddha pā li ta.* Toh 3842, Madhyamaka, tsa.

Candrakīrti (seventh century). *Clear Words. Prasannapadā. Tshig gsal ba.* Toh 3860, Madhyamaka, 'a.

———. *Commentary on the Four Hundred Stanzas. Catuḥśatakaṭīkā. Bzhi brgya pa'i rgya cher 'grel pa.* Toh 3865, Madhyamaka, ya.

———. *Commentary on the Sixty Stanzas of Reasoning. Yuktiṣaṣṭikāvṛtti. Rigs pa drug cu pa'i 'grel pa.* Toh 3864, Madhyamaka, ya.

———. *Entering the Middle Way. Madhyamakāvatāra. Dbu ma la 'jug pa.* Toh 3861, Madhyamaka, 'a.

———. *Entering the Middle Way Autocommentary. Madhyamakāvatārabhāṣya. Dbu ma la 'jug pa'i bshad pa.* Toh 3862, Madhyamaka, 'a.

Devendrabuddhi/Devendramati (seventh century). *Commentary on Difficult Points in the Exposition of Valid Cognition. Pramāṇavārttikapañjikā. Tshad ma rnam 'grel gyi dka' 'grel.* Toh 4217, Pramāṇa, che.

Dharmakīrti (seventh century). *Ascertainment of Valid Cognition. Pramāṇaviniścaya. Tshad ma rnam nges.* Toh 4211, Pramāṇa, ce.

———. *Drop of Reasoning. Nyāyabindu. Rigs pa'i thigs pa.* Toh 4212, Pramāṇa, ce.

———. *Drop of Reasons. Hetubindu. Gtan tshigs thigs pa.* Toh 4213, Pramāṇa, ce.

———. *Exposition of Valid Cognition. Pramāṇavārttika. Tshad ma rnam 'grel.* Toh 4210, Pramāṇa, ce.

———. *Exposition of Valid Cognition Autocommentary. Pramāṇavārttikavṛtti. Tshad ma rnam 'grel gyi 'grel pa.* Toh 4216, Pramāṇa, ce.

———. *Investigation of Relations. Sambandhaparīkṣā. 'Brel pa brtag pa.* Toh 4214, Pramāṇa, ce.

———. *Proof of Other Mindstreams. Saṃtānāntarasiddhi. Rgyud gzhan grub pa.* Toh 4219, Pramāṇa, che.

———. *Reasoning for Debate. Vādanyāya. Rtsod pa'i rigs pa.* Toh 4218, Pramāṇa, che.

Dharmapāla Suvarṇadvīpa (a.k.a. Gser gling pa). *Commentary Illuminating the Difficult Points of the Ornament for Clear Knowledge. Abhisamayālaṅkāravṛttiduravabodhālokaṭīkā. Mngon par rtogs pa'i rgyan zhes bya ba'i 'grel pa rtogs par dka' ba'i snang ba'i 'grel bshad.* Toh 3794. Prajñāpāramitā, ja.

Dharmottara (ca. eighth century). *Commentary on Ascertainment of Valid Cognition. Pramāṇaviniścayaṭīkā. Tshad ma rnam par nges pa'i 'grel bshad.* Toh 4229, Pramāṇa, dze.

———. *Commentary on the Drop of Reasoning. Nyāyabinduṭīkā. Rigs pa'i thigs pa'i rgya cher 'grel pa.* Toh 4231, Pramāṇa, we.

———. *Explanation of Exclusion. Apohaprakaraṇa. Gzhan sel ba'i rab tu byed pa.* Toh 4250, Pramāṇa, zhe.

———. *Investigation of Valid Cognition: Long. Pramāṇaparīkṣā. Tshad ma brtag pa.* Toh 4248, Pramāṇa, zhe.

———. *Investigation of Valid Cognition: Short. Pramāṇaparīkṣā. Tshad ma brtag pa.* Toh 4249, Pramāṇa, zhe.

———. *Proof of the Afterlife. Paralokasiddhi. 'Jig rten pha rol grub pa.* Toh 4251, Pramāṇa, zhe.

Dignāga (fifth century). *Compendium of Valid Cognition. Pramāṇasamuccaya. Tshad ma kun las btus pa.* Toh 4203, Pramāṇa, ce. Also translated by Kanakavarman and Depai Sherab (Dad pa'i shes rab) in Narthang Tengyur 4467, Pramāṇa, ce.

———. *Compendium of Valid Cognition Autocommentary. Pramāṇasamuccayavṛtti. Tshad ma kun las btus rang 'grel.* Toh 4204, Pramāṇa, ce. Also translated by Kanakavarman and Depai Sherab (Dad pa'i shes rab) in Narthang Tengyur 4469, Pramāṇa, ce.

———. *Drum of a Wheel of Reasons. Hetucakraḍamaru. Gtan tshigs 'khor lo.* Toh 4209, Pramāṇa, ce.

———. *Entering into Valid Reasoning. Nyāyapraveśa. Tshad ma rigs par 'jug pa.* Toh 4208, Pramāṇa, ce.

———. *Introduction to Entering into Valid Reasoning. Nyāyapraveśaprakaraṇa. Tshad ma rigs par 'jug pa'i sgo.* (Not in Derge.) Peking Tengyur 5706, Pramāṇa, ce; Narthang Tengyur, Pramāṇa, ce.

———. *Investigation of the Object. Ālambanaparīkṣā. Dmigs brtag.* Toh 4205, Pramāṇa, ce.

———. *Investigation of the Object Autocommentary. Ālambanaparīkṣāvṛtti. Dmigs brtag rang 'grel.* Toh 4206, Pramāṇa, ce.

———. *Investigation of the Three Times. Trikālaparīkṣā. Dus gsum brtag pa.* Toh 4207, Pramāṇa, ce.

———. *Stanzas Summarizing the Perfection of Wisdom. Prajñāpāramitāsaṅgrahakārikā. Shes rab kyi pha rol tu phyin ma bsdus pa'i tshig le'ur byas pa.* Toh 3809, Pramāṇa, pha.

Guṇamati (n.d.). *Commentary on Explanation of the First Dependent Origination and Its Divisions. Pratītyasamutpādādivibhaṅganirdeśaṭīkā. Rten cing 'brel bar 'byung ba dang po dang rnam par dbye ba bstan pa'i rgya cher bshad pa.* Toh 3996, Sūtra Commentary, chi.

Haribhadra (eighth century). *Commentary on the Perfection of Wisdom in Eight Thousand Stanzas: Explanation of the Ornament for Clear Knowledge. Aṣṭasāhasrikāprajñāpāramitāvyākhyābhisamayālaṅkārāloka. Shes rab kyi pha rol tu phyin pa brgyad stong pa'i bshad pa, Mngon par rtogs pa'i rgyan gyi snang ba.* Toh 3791, Prajñāpāramitā, cha.

———. *Short Commentary on the Ornament for Clear Knowledge. Abhisamayālaṃkāravṛtti. Mngon par rtogs pa'i rgyan gyi 'grel pa.* Toh 3793, Prajñāpāramitā, ja.

Jinendrabuddhi (n.d.). *Spacious and Stainless: Commentary on the Compendium of Valid Cognition. Viśālāmalavatīnāmapramāṇasamuccayaṭīkā. Yangs pa dang dri ma med pa ldan pa zhes bya ba tshad ma kun las btus pa'i 'grel bshad.* Toh 4268, Pramāṇa, ye.

Jitāri (eleventh century). *Ascertainment of Dharma and Dharmin. Dharmadharminviniścaya. Chos dang chos can gtan la dbab pa.* Toh 4262, Pramāṇa, zhe.

———. *A Beginner's Primer on Logic. Bālāvatāratarka. Byis pa 'jug pa'i rtog ge.* Toh 4263, Pramāṇa, zhe.

———. *Distinguishing the Systems of the Blessed One. Sugatamatavibhaṅgakārikā. Bde bar gshegs pa gzhung rnam par 'byed pa'i tshig le'ur byas pa.* Toh 3899 (also 4547), Madhyamaka, a.

———. *Presenting the Principles of Inferential Evidence. Hetutattvopadeśa. Gtan tshigs kyi de kho na nyid bstan pa.* Toh 4261, Pramāṇa, zhe.

Jñānagarbha (ca. eighth century). *Distinguishing the Two Truths. Satyadvayavibhaṅga. Bden pa gnyis rnam par 'byed pa.* Toh 3881, Madhyamaka, sa.

———. *Distinguishing the Two Truths Autocommentary. Satyadvayavibhaṅgavṛtti. Bden pa gnyis rnam par 'byed pa'i 'grel pa.* Toh 3882, Madhyamaka, sa.

Jñānaśrībhadra (eleventh century). *Commentary on Ascertainment of Valid Cognition. Pramāṇaviniścayaṭīkā. Tshad ma rnam par nges pa'i 'grel bshad.* Toh 4228, Pramāṇa, tshe.

Jñānaśrīmitra (tenth century). *Establishing the Nature of Cause and Effect. Kāryakāraṇabhāvasiddhi. Rgyu dang 'bras bu'i ngo bo grub pa.* Toh 4258, Pramāṇa, zhe.

———. *Explanation of Exclusion. Apohaprakaraṇa. Gzhan sel gyi rab tu byed pa.* Not in Tibetan Tengyur.

Jñānavajra (twelfth century). *Heart Ornament of the Tathāgata: Commentary on the Descent into Laṅkā Sūtra. Laṅkāvatārasūtravṛtti. Lang kar gshegs pa'i mdo'i 'grel pa.* Toh 4019, Sūtra Commentary, pi.

Kamalaśīla (eighth century). *Commentary on Compendium of Reality. Tattvasaṅgrahapañjikā. Tshad ma'i de kho na nyid bsdus pa'i dka' 'grel.* Toh 4267, Pramāṇa, ze.

———. *Illumination of the Middle Way. Madhyamakāloka. Dbu ma snang ba.* Toh 3887, Madhyamaka, sa.

———. *Summary of the Proponents' Positions in the Drop of Reasoning. Nyāyabindupūrvapakṣasaṃkṣipta. Rigs pa'i thigs pa'i phyogs snga ma mdor bsdus pa.* Toh 4232, Pramāṇa, we.

Madhyamakasiṃha (n.d.). *Compendium of Distinctions among Views. Saṅkṣiptanānādṛṣṭivibhājana. Lta ba tha dad pa rnam par phye ba mdor bsdus.* Toh 3898, Madhyamaka, a.

Maitreya (fourth century). *Distinguishing Phenomena from Ultimate Reality. Dharmadharmatāvibhāga. Chos dang chos nyid rnam par 'byed pa'i tshig le'ur byas pa.* Toh. 4023, Cittamātra, phi.

———. *Distinguishing the Middle from the Extremes. Madhyāntavibhāga. Dbus dang mtha' rnam par 'byed pa.* Toh 4021, Cittamātra, phi.

———. *Ornament for the Mahāyāna Sūtras. Mahāyānasūtrālaṅkāra. Theg pa chen po'i mdo sde'i rgyan.* Toh 4020, Cittamātra, phi.

Mokṣākaragupta (seventh century). *Language of Logic. Tarkabhāṣā. Rtog ge'i skad.* Toh 4264, Pramāṇa, zhe.

Nāgārjuna (second century). *Commentary on Bodhicitta. Bodhicittavivaraṇa. Byang chub sems 'grel.* Toh 1800, Tantra Commentary, ngi (also 4556, Madhyamaka, gi).

———. *Finely Woven. Vaidalyasūtra. Zhib mo rnam 'thag.* Toh 3826, Madhyamaka, tsa.

———. *Fundamental Treatise on the Middle Way. Mūlamadhyamakakārikā. Dbu ma rtsa ba'i tshig le'ur byas pa.* Toh 3824, Madhyamaka, tsa.

———. *Praise of Dharmadhātu. Dharmadhātustava. Chos dbyings bstod pa.* Toh 1118, Stotra, ka.

———. *Praise of the Transcendent One. Lokātītastava. 'Jig rten las 'das par bstod pa.* Toh 1120, Stotra, ka.

———. *Precious Garland. Ratnāvalī. Rin po che'i phreng ba.* Toh 4158, Jātaka, ge.

———. *Refutation of Objections. Vigrahavyāvartanī. Rtsod pa bzlog pa.* Toh 3828, Madhyamaka, tsa.

———. *Refutation of Objections Autocommentary. Vigrahavyāvartanīvṛtti. Rtsod pa bzlog pa'i 'grel pa.* Toh 3832, Madhyamaka, tsa.

———. *Seventy Stanzas on Emptiness. Śūnyatāsaptati. Stong pa nyid bdun bcu pa.* Toh 3827, Madhyamaka, tsa.

———. *Sixty Stanzas of Reasoning. Yuktiṣaṣṭikā. Rigs pa drug cu pa.* Toh 3825, Madhyamaka, tsa.

Prajñākaragupta (tenth century). *The Necessary Simultaneity of Perception and the Perceived. Sahāvalambanirṇaya. Lhan cig dmigs par nges pa.* Toh 4255, Pramāṇa, zhe.

———. *Ornament of Exposition of Valid Cognition. Pramāṇavārttikālaṅkāra. Tshad ma rnam 'grel gyi rgyan.* Toh 4221, Pramāṇa, te, the.

Prajñāvarman (ca. eighth century). *Commentary on Praise of the Exalted. Viśeṣastavaṭīkā. Khyad par du 'phags pa'i bstod pa'i rgya cher bshad pa.* Toh 1110, Stotra, ka.

Pūrṇavardhana (ca. eighth century). *Investigating Characteristics: Commentary on the Treasury of Knowledge. Abhidharmakośaṭīkālakṣaṇānusāriṇī. Mdzod kyi 'grel bshad mtshan nyid rjes 'brang.* Toh 4093, Abhidharma, cu.

Ratnakīrti (tenth century). *Proof of Exclusion. Apohasiddhi. Sel ba grub pa.* Not in the Tibetan Tengyur. The Sanskrit text with an English translation are found in McAllister 2020.

Sāgaramegha (n.d.). *Commentary on Bodhisattva Levels. Bodhisattvabhūmivyākhyā. Rnal 'byor spyod pa'i sa las byang chub sems dpa'i sa'i rnam par bshad pa.* Toh 4047, Cittamātra, yi.

Śākyabuddhi (Śākyamati) (seventh century). *Commentary on Exposition of Valid Cognition. Pramāṇavārttikaṭīkā. Tshad ma rnam 'grel gyi 'grel bshad.* Toh 4220, Pramāṇa, je, nye.

Saṅghabhadra (fifth century). *Commentary on the Treasury of Knowledge. Abhidharmakośaśāstrakārikābhāṣya. Chos mngon pa mdzod kyi bstan bcos kyi tshig le'ur byas pa'i rnam par bshad pa.* Toh 4091, Abhidharma, khu.

Śaṅkarānanda (eleventh century). *Proof of Exclusion. Apohasiddhi. Sel ba grub pa.* Toh 4256, Pramāṇa, zhe.

———. *Proof of Relation. Pratibandhasiddhi. 'Brel ba grub pa.* Toh 4257, Pramāṇa, zhe.

Śāntarakṣita (eighth century). *Compendium of Reality. Tattvasaṅgraha. De kho na nyid bsdus pa.* Toh 4266, Pramāṇa, ze.

———. *Ornament for the Middle Way. Madhyamakālaṅkāra. Dbus ma rgyan.* Toh 3884, Madhyamaka, sa.

———. *Ornament for the Middle Way Autocommentary. Madhyamakālaṃkāravṛtti. Bdu ma rgyan gyi 'grel pa.* Toh 3885, Madhyamaka, sa.

Śāntideva (eighth century). *Engaging in the Bodhisattva's Deeds. Bodhisattvacaryāvatāra. Byang chub sems dpa'i spyod pa la 'jug pa.* Toh 3871, Madhyamaka, la.

Sthiramati (ca. sixth century). *Commentary on the Thirty Stanzas. Triṃśikābhāṣya. Sum cu pa'i bshad pa.* Toh 4046, Cittamātra, shi.

Śubhagupta (ca. eighth century). *Investigation of the Exclusion of Other. Anyāpohavicāra. Gzhan sel brtag pa.* Toh 4246, Pramāṇa, zhe.

———. *Proof of External Objects. Bāhyārthasiddhi. Phyi rol gyi don grub pa.* Toh 4244, Pramāṇa, zhe.

Vasubandhu (fourth century). *Commentary on Distinguishing the Middle from the Extremes. Madhyāntavibhāgabhāṣya. Dbus dang mtha' rnam par 'byed pa'i 'grel pa.* Toh 4027, Cittamātra, bi.

———. *Commentary on the Compendium of the Mahāyāna. Mahāyānasaṅgrahabhāṣya. Theg pa chen po bsdus pa'i 'grel pa.* Toh 4050, Cittamātra, ri.

———. *Commentary on Ornament for the Mahāyāna Sūtras. Sūtrālaṅkāravyākhyā. Mdo sde'i rgyan gyi bshad pa.* Toh 4026, Cittamātra, phi.

———. *Explanation of the First Dependent Origination and Its Divisions. Pratītyasamutpādādivibhaṅganirdeśa. Rten cing 'brel par 'byung ba dang po'i rnam par dbye ba bshad pa.* Toh 3995, Sūtra Commentary, chi.

———. *Principles of Exegesis. Vyākhyāyukti. Rnam par bshad pa'i rigs pa.* Toh 4061, Cittamātra, shi.
———. *Thirty Stanzas. Triṃśikā. Sum cu pa.* Toh 4055, Cittamātra, shi.
———. *Treasury of Knowledge. Abhidharmakośa. Chos mngon pa'i mdzod.* Toh 4089, Abhidharma, ku.
———. *Treasury of Knowledge Autocommentary. Abhidharmakośabhāṣya. Chos mngon pa'i mdzod kyi bshad pa.* Toh 4090, Abhidharma, ku–khu.
———. *Twenty Stanzas. Viṃśatika. Nyi shu pa.* Toh 4056, Cittamātra, shi.
———. *Twenty Stanzas Autocommentary. Viṃśatikāvṛtti. Nyi shu pa'i rang 'grel.* Toh 4057, Cittamātra, shi.
Vinītadeva (early eighth century). *Commentary on Investigation of the Object. Alambanaparīkṣāṭīkā. Dmigs brtag 'grel bshad.* Toh 4265, Pramāṇa, zhe.
———. *Commentary on the Drop of Reasoning. Nyāyabinduṭīkā. Rigs pa'i thigs pa'i rgya cher 'grel pa.* Toh 4230, Pramāṇa, we.
———. *Commentary on the Drop of Reasons. Hetubinduṭīkā. Gtan tshigs kyi thigs pa rgya cher 'grel pa.* Toh 4234, Pramāṇa, we.
———. *Commentary on the Thirty Stanzas. Triṃśikāṭīkā. Sum cu pa'i 'grel bshad.* Toh 4070, Cittamātra.
———. *Commentary on the Twenty Stanzas. Prakaraṇaviṃśakaṭīkā. Rab tu byed pa nyi shu pa'i 'grel bshad.* Toh 4065, Cittamātra, shi.
Yaśomitra (a.k.a. Jinaputra) (ca. eighth century). *Clarifying the Meaning of the Treasury of Knowledge. Abhidharmakośavyākhyāsphuṭārthā. Chos mngon pa mdzod kyi 'grel bshad don gsal.* Toh 4092, Abhidharma, gu, ngu.

Other Sources Cited

Agniveśa. *Compendium of Caraka. Carakasaṃhitā.* Compiled by Caraka during the second century. Translated into Tibetan by Lobsang Tenzin and Shastri Lobsang Norbu. Varanasi: Institute of Higher Tibetan Studies, 2006.
Akṣapāda Gautama (second century, Nyāya). *Nyāya Sūtra.*
Arnold, Dan. 2005. *Buddhists, Brahmins, and Belief: Epistemology in South Asian Philosophy of Religion.* New York: Columbia University Press.
Balcerowicz, Piotr. 2012. "When Yoga Is Not Yoga: The Nyāya-Vaiśeṣika Tradition and the *Artha-śāstra.*" In *World-View and Theory in Indian Philosophy*, edited by Piotr Balcerowicz, 173–249. New Delhi: Manohar.
Barua, Benimadhab. 1921. *A History of Pre-Buddhist Indian Philosophy.* Calcutta: University of Calcutta.
Bhadrabāhu (fourth century BCE). *Explanation of the Ten Auspicious Observances. Daśavaikālikaniryukti.*
Bhartṛhari (fifth century, Grammarian). *Treatise on Grammar. Vākyapadīya.*
Bodhi, Bhikkhu, trans. 2000. *The Connected Discourses of the Buddha: A New Translation of the Saṃyutta Nikāya.* Boston: Wisdom Publications.
Bronkhorst, Johannes. 1985. "Dharma and Abhidharma." *Bulletin of the School of Oriental and African Studies* 48.2: 305–20.

———. 1999. *Why Is There Philosophy in India?* Amsterdam: Royal Netherlands Academy of Arts and Sciences.

Burnet, John. 1930. *Early Greek Philosophy*. London: Adam & Charles Black.

Cardona, George. 1997. *Pāṇini: His Work and Its Traditions*, vol. 1. Delhi: Motilal Banarsidass.

Curd, Patricia. 2020. "Presocratic Philosophy." *Stanford Encyclopedia of Philosophy* (Fall 2020 edition), edited by Edward N. Zalta. https://plato.stanford.edu/archives/fall2020/entries/presocratics.

Dasgupta, Surendranath. 1922. *A History of Indian Philosophy*, vol. 1. Cambridge: Cambridge University Press.

Devendra Muni Shastri (1931–99). 1983. *A Source-Book in Jaina Philosophy*. Translated by T. G. Kalghatgi from the Hindi *Jain Darshan Swaroop aur Vishleshan*. Udaipur, Rajasthan: Sri Tarak Guru Jain Granthalaya.

Dreyfus, Georges B. J. 1997. *Recognizing Reality: Dharmakīrti's Philosophy and Its Tibetan Interpretations*. Albany: State University of New York Press.

Duerlinger, James. 2003. *Indian Buddhist Theories of Persons: Vasubandhu's "Refutation of the Theory of a Self."* London: RoutledgeCurzon.

Dunne, John. 2004. *Foundations of Dharmakīrti's Philosophy*. Boston: Wisdom Publications.

Dunne, John, and Sara McClintock, trans. 1997. *The Precious Garland: An Epistle to a King*, by Ācārya Nāgārjuna. Boston: Wisdom Publications. Revised edition forthcoming 2024.

Frauwallner, Erich. 1959. "Dignāga: Sein Werk und Seine Entwicklung." *Wiener Zeitschrift für die Kunde Süd- und Ostasiens* 3: 83–163.

Ganeri, Jonardon. 2007. *The Concealed Art of the Soul*. Oxford: Oxford University Press.

Garfield, Jay. 2015. *Engaging Buddhism: Why It Matters to Philosophy*. New York: Oxford University Press.

Gauḍapāda (sixth century, Vedānta). *Māṇḍūkyakārikā*, a.k.a. *Gauḍapādakārikā*.

Gethin, Rupert. 2001. *The Buddhist Path to Awakening*. Oxford: Oneworld Publications.

———. 2023. "Moggaliputta Tissa's *Points of Discussion* (*Kathāvatthu*): Reasoning and Debate in Early Buddhist Thought." In *The Routledge Handbook of Indian Buddhist Philosophy*, edited by William Edelglass, Pierre-Julien Harter, and Sara McClintock, 160–71. London: Routledge.

Gorampa Sonam Sengé. (Go rams pa Bsod nams seng ge, 1429–89). *The Explanation of the Difficult Points of [Sapaṇ's] Treasury of Valid Cognition and Reasoning That Completely Clarifies the Seven Texts. Tshad ma'i rigs gter gyi dka' gnas rnam par bshad pa sde bdun rab gsal*. In *The Complete Works of the Great Masters of the Sa sKya Sect*, vol. 12. Tokyo: Toyo Bunko, 1978.

Gowans, Christopher. 2010. "Medical Analogies in Buddhist and Hellenistic Thought: Tranquillity and Anger." In *Philosophy as Therapeia*, edited by Clare Carlisle and Jonardon Ganeri, 11–34. Cambridge: Cambridge University Press.

Gyaltsab Jé (Rgyal tshab Dar ma rin chen, 1364–1432). *Illuminating the Path to Liberation: A Commentary on Dharmakīrti's Exposition of Valid Cognition. Tshad ma rnam 'grel gyi tshig le'ur byas pa'i rnam bshad thar lam phyin ci ma log par gsal bar byed pa.* Collected Works, vol. cha.

Hattori, Masaaki, trans. 1968. *Dignāga, On Perception: Being the Pratyakṣapariccheda of Dignāga's Pramāṇasamuccaya.* Harvard Oriental Series 47. Cambridge, MA: Harvard University Press.

Hayes, Richard P. 1988. *Dignaga on the Interpretation of Signs.* Studies of Classical India 9. Dordrecht: Kluwer Academic Publishers.

Heirman, Ann, and Stephan Peter Bumbacher, eds. 2007. *The Spread of Buddhism.* Leiden: Brill.

Īśvarakṛṣṇa (fourth–fifth century, Sāṅkhya). *Verses of Sāṅkhya. Sāṅkhyakārikā.* a.k.a. *Īśvarakṛṣṇa Tantra.* Sanskrit edition in Phukan 1960. Translated into Tibetan in 1974 by Thupten Chokdrup (Thub bstan mchog grub).

Jaimini (n.d., Mīmāṃsā). *Mīmāṃsā Sūtra.*

Jamyang Shepai Dorjé ('Jam dbyang Bzhad pa'i rdo rje, 1648–1721). *Great Exposition of Tenets. Grub mtha' chen mo.* In Collected Works, vol. pha.

Jayanta Bhaṭṭa (ninth century, Nyāya). *Sprigs of Reasoning. Nyāyamañjarī.*

Jha, Ganganatha, trans. 1937, 1939. *The Tattvasaṅgraha of Śāntarakṣita with the Commentary of Kamalaśīla*, 2 vols. Baroda: Oriental Institute. (Reprint, Delhi: Motilal Banarsidass, 1986). Volume 1: https://archive.org/details/TattvasangrahaVol1. Volume 2: https://archive.org/details/tattvasangrahaof015823mbp.

Kajiyama, Yuichi. 1966. *An Introduction to Buddhist Philosophy: An Annotated Translation of the Tarkabhāṣā of Mokṣākaragupta.* Kyoto: Kyoto University.

Kaṇāda, a.k.a. Ulūka (first-second century, Vaiśeṣika). *Vaiśeṣika Sūtra. Bye brag pa'i mdo.*

Kapila (n.d., Sāṅkhya). *Sāṅkhya Sūtra.*

Kapstein, Matthew. 2001. *Reason's Traces: Identity and Interpretation in Indian and Tibetan Buddhist Thought.* Studies in Indian and Tibetan Buddhism. Boston: Wisdom Publications.

Kātyāyana (n.d., Grammarian). *Annotations [on the Aphorisms of Pāṇini's Aṣṭādhyāyī]. Vārttika.*

Kauṭilya (ca. second century BCE). *Treatise on Gains. Arthaśāstra.*

Kellner, Birgit. 2010. "Self-Awareness (*svasaṃvedana*) in Dignāga's Pramāṇasamuccaya and -Vṛtti: A Close Reading." *Journal of Indian Philosophy* 38.3: 203–31. https://doi.org/10.1007/s10781-010-9091-y.

Kellner, Birgit, and John Taber. 2014. "Studies in Yogācāra-Vijñānavāda Idealism 1: The Interpretation of Vasubandhu's *Viṃśikā*." *Asiatische Studien/Études Asiatiques* 68.3: 709–56.

Khedrup Jé Gelek Palsang (Mkhas grub rje Dge legs dpal bzang po, 1385–1438). *Ocean of Reasoning: A Commentary on Exposition of Valid Cognition. Tshad ma rnam 'grel gyi rgya cher bshad pa rigs pa'i rgya mtsho.* In Collected Works, vols. nga and cha.

Kollmar-Paulenz, Karénina. 2007. "The Buddhist Way into Tibet." In *The Spread of Buddhism*, edited by Ann Heirman and Stephan Peter Bumbacher, 303–40. Leiden: Brill.

Krishna, Daya. 1991. *Indian Philosophy: A Counter Perspective*. Delhi: Oxford University Press.

Kumārila Bhaṭṭa (seventh century, Mīmāṃsā). *Exposition of Verses on Mīmāṃsā. Mīmāṃsā Ślokavārttika. Dpyod pa ba'i shig su bcad pa'i rnam 'grel.*

Lacey, Alan. 2005. *A Dictionary of Philosophy*. Taylor and Francis e-Library.

Loux, Michael J. 1998. *Metaphysics: A Contemporary Introduction*. London: Routledge.

Mabja Jangchub Tsöndrü (Rma bya Byang chub brtson 'grus, eleventh century). *Ornament of Correct Explanations of Fundamental Treatise on the Middle Way. Dbu ma rtsa ba'i 'grel ba 'thad pa'i rgyan*. In Collected Works of the Kadam, vol. 36.

MacDonald, Anne. 2015. *In Clear Words: The Prasannapadā, Chapter One*, vol. 2: *Annotated Translation, Tibetan Text*. Vienna: Österreichische Akademie der Wissenschaften.

Matilal, Bimal Krishna. 1998. *The Character of Logic in India*. Albany: State University of New York Press.

McAllister, Patrick. 2020. *Ratnakīrti's Proof of Exclusion*. Vienna: Osterreichische Akademie der Wissenschaften.

McEvilley, Thomas. 2002. *The Shape of Ancient Thought: Comparative Studies in Greek and Indian Philosophies*. New York: Allworth Press.

Nemicandra (twelfth century, Jaina). *Compendium of Substances. Dravya Saṅgraha. Rdzas bsdus pa.*

Ngawang Palden of Mongolia (Sog po chos rje Ngag dbang dpal ldan, 1797–1864). *Presentation of the Two Truths: A Melodious Song of Glorious Springtime*. In Collected Works, vol. ka.

Pāṇini (ca. fourth century BCE, Grammarian). *Eight Chapters. Aṣṭādhyāyī.*

Patañjali (second century BCE, Grammarian). *Great Commentary on Grammatical Analysis. Vyākaraṇamahābhāṣya.*

Phukan, R., ed. 1960. *The Sāṃkhya Kārikā of Īṣvarakṛṣṇa: Being a Treatise on Psycho-Physics for Self-Realisation*. Calcutta: K. L. Mukhopadhyay.

Points of Discussion. Kathāvatthu. Gtam gyi gzhi. Pali canon, Abhidhamma Piṭaka. Cf. Gethin 2023.

Potter, Karl H., ed., with Harold G. Coward and K. Kunjunni Raja. 2015. *Encyclopedia of Indian Philosophies*, vol. 5: *The Philosophy of the Grammarians*. Delhi: Motilal Banarsidass.

Praśastapāda (sixth century, Vaiśeṣika). *Compendium of the Attributes of the Categories. Padārthadharmasaṅgraha. Bye brag pa'i mdo 'grel tshig don chos bsdus pa.*

Rhys Davids, T. W., trans. 1890. *The Questions of King Milinda*. Oxford: Clarendon Press.

Sakya Paṇḍita Kunga Gyaltsen (Sa skya paṇḍita Kun dga' rgyal mtshan, 1182–1251). *Treasury of Valid Cognition and Reasoning. Pramāṇayuktinidhi. Tshad ma rigs pa'i gter*. In Collected Works of Sakya, Pd 17.

———. *Treasury of Valid Cognition and Reasoning Autocommentary. Pramāṇayuktinidhivṛtti. Tshad ma rigs gter rang 'grel*. In Collected Works of Sakya, Pd 17.

Samten, Geshe Ngawang, and Jay Garfield, trans. 2006. *Ocean of Reasoning: A Great Commentary on Nāgārjuna's Mūlamadhyamakakārikā* [by Tsongkhapa]. New York: Oxford University Press.

Sastri, Kuppuswami. 1951. *A Primer of Indian Logic, According to Annambhaṭṭa's Tarkasaṃgraha*. Madras: Kuppuswami Sastri Research Institute.

Sen, Prabal Kumar. 2011. "The Apoha Theory of Meaning: A Critical Account." In *Apoha: Buddhist Nominalism and Human Cognition*, edited by Mark Siderits, Tom Tillemans, and Arindam Chakrabarti, 170–206. New York: Columbia University Press.

Seyfort Ruegg, David. 2002. *Studies in Indian and Tibetan Madhyamaka Thought, Part 2: Two Prolegomena to Madhyamaka Philosophy*. Vienna: Arbeitskreis für Tibetische und Buddhistische Studien, Universität Wien.

Siddhasena Divākara (seventh century, Jaina). *Entering into Reasoning. Nyāyāvatāra.*

Siderits, Mark. 1991. *Indian Philosophy of Language: Studies in Selected Issues*. Dordrecht: Kluwer Academic Publishers.

Sopa, Geshe Lhundub, with Dechen Rochard. 2017. *Steps on the Path to Enlightenment: A Commentary on Tsongkhapa's Lamrim Chenmo*, vol. 5: *Insight*. Somerville, MA: Wisdom Publications.

Thurman, Robert A. F., trans. 1984. *Tsong Khapa's Speech of Gold in the Essence of True Eloquence: Reason and Enlightenment in the Central Philosophy of Tibet*. Princeton, NJ: Princeton University Press.

Tillemans, Tom J. F. 2016. *How Do Mādhyamikas Think? And Other Essays on the Buddhist Philosophy of the Middle*. Studies in Indian and Tibetan Buddhism. Somerville, MA: Wisdom Publications.

Tsongkhapa (Tsong kha pa, 1357–1419). *Essence of True Eloquence: Distinguishing the Provisional and the Definitive Meaning. Drang ba dang nges pa'i don rnam par phye ba'i bstan bcos legs bshad snying po*. Collected Works, vol. pha. English translation in Thurman 1984.

———. 2021. *Illuminating the Intent: An Exposition of Candrakīrti's Entering the Middle Way*. Translated by Thupten Jinpa. The Library of Tibetan Classics 19. Somerville, MA: Wisdom Publications.

———. *Ocean of Reasoning: Commentary on Fundamental Treatise on the Middle Way. Dbu ma rtsa ba'i tshig le'ur byas pa shes rab ces bya ba'i rnam bshad rigs pa'i rgya mtsho*. Collected Works, vol. ba. English translation in Tsongkhapa 2006.

———. 2006. *Ocean of Reasoning: A Great Commentary on Nāgārjuna's Mūlamadhyamakakārikā*. Translated by Geshe Ngawang Samten and Jay L. Garfield. Oxford: Oxford University Press.

———. *Short Treatise on the Stages of the Path to Enlightenment. Lam rim chung ngu.* Collected Works, vol. pha.

Uddyotakara (sixth century, Nyāya). *Exposition of Nyāya Reasoning. Nyāyavārttika. Rigs pa'i rnam 'grel.*

Umāsvāmi/Umāsvāti (ca. third century, Jaina). *Clear Realization of the Nature of Reality Sūtra. Tattvārthādhigama Sūtra. De kho na nyid mngon par rtogs pa'i mdo.*

Vātsyāyana (ca. fourth–fifth century, Nyāya). *Commentary on the Nyāya Sūtra. Nyāyasūtrabhāṣya. Rigs pa'i mdo'i bshad pa.*

Yiannopoulos, Alexander. 2020. "The Structure of Dharmakīrti's Philosophy: A Study of Object-Cognition in the Perception Chapter (*pratyakṣapariccheda*) of the *Pranāṇasamuccaya*, the *Pramāṇavārttika*, and Their Earliest Commentaries." PhD dissertation, Emory University.

Index

M

N

O

P

Q

About the Authors

HIS HOLINESS THE DALAI LAMA is the spiritual leader of the Tibetan people, a Nobel Peace Prize recipient, and a beacon of inspiration for Buddhists and non-Buddhists alike. He is admired also for his more than four decades of systematic dialogues with scientists exploring ways to developing new evidence-based approaches to alleviation of suffering and promoting human flourishing. He is the co-founder of the Mind and Life Institute and has helped to revolutionize traditional Tibetan monastic curriculum by incorporating the teaching of modern science. He is a great champion of the great Indian Nalanda tradition of science, philosophy, and wisdom practices.

THUPTEN JINPA is a well-known Buddhist scholar and has been the principal English-language translator for His Holiness the Dalai Lama for more than three decades. A former monk and a Geshe Lharampa, he also holds a BA in philosophy and a PhD in religious studies, both from Cambridge University. He is the author and translator of many books and teaches at McGill University in Montreal.

DECHEN ROCHARD has a BA in philosophy from the University of London and a PhD in Buddhist philosophy from the University of Cambridge. She also completed the first ten years of the geshe degree program at the Institute of Buddhist Dialectics in Dharamsala, India, including the study of Madhyamaka. She is currently translating texts for The Gaden Phodrang Foundation and is a fellow of the Dalai Lama Centre for Compassion (Oxford) and an honorary fellow of the University of Bristol.

What to Read Next from the Dalai Lama

Buddhism
One Teacher, Many Traditions

The Compassionate Life

Ecology, Ethics, and Interdependence
The Dalai Lama in Conversation with Leading Thinkers on Climate Change

Essence of the Heart Sutra
The Dalai Lama's Heart of Wisdom Teachings

The Essence of Tsongkhapa's Teachings
The Dalai Lama on the Three Principal Aspects of the Path

The Good Heart
A Buddhist Perspective on the Teachings of Jesus

Imagine All the People
A Conversation with the Dalai Lama on Money, Politics, and Life as It Could Be

Kalachakra Tantra
Rite of Initiation

The Library of Wisdom and Compassion series:
1. Approaching the Buddhist Path
2. The Foundation of Buddhist Practice
3. Saṃsāra, Nirvāṇa, and Buddha Nature
4. Following in the Buddha's Footsteps
5. In Praise of Great Compassion
6. Courageous Compassion
7. Searching for the Self
8. Realizing the Profound View
9. Appearing and Empty

The Life of My Teacher
A Biography of Kyabjé Ling Rinpoché

Meditation on the Nature of Mind

The Middle Way
Faith Grounded in Reason

Mind in Comfort and Ease
The Vision of Enlightenment in the Great Perfection

MindScience
An East-West Dialogue

Opening the Eye of New Awareness

Practicing Wisdom
The Perfection of Shantideva's Bodhisattva Way

Science and Philosophy in the Indian Buddhist Classics
Volume 1: The Physical World

Science and Philosophy in the Indian Buddhist Classics
Volume 2: The Mind

Science and Philosophy in the Indian Buddhist Classics
Volume 3: Philosophical Schools

Sleeping, Dreaming, and Dying
An Exploration of Consciousness

The Wheel of Life
Buddhist Perspectives on Cause and Effect

The World of Tibetan Buddhism
An Overview of Its Philosophy and Practice

About Wisdom Publications

Wisdom Publications is the leading publisher of classic and contemporary Buddhist books and practical works on mindfulness. To learn more about us or to explore our other books, please visit our website at wisdomexperience.org or contact us at the address below.

Wisdom Publications
132 Perry Street
New York, NY 10014 USA

We are a 501(c)(3) organization, and donations in support of our mission are tax deductible.

Wisdom Publications is affiliated with the Foundation for the Preservation of the Mahayana Tradition (FPMT).